The Self in the Family

WILEY SERIES IN COUPLES AND FAMILY DYNAMICS AND TREATMENT

Florence W. Kaslow, Series Editor

Treating the Changing Family: Handling Normative and Unusual Events
Michele Harway, Editor

In-Laws: A Guide to Extended-Family Therapy
by Gloria Call Horsley

Handbook of Relational Diagnosis and Dysfunctional Family Patterns
Florence W. Kaslow, Editor

Child-Centered Family Therapy
by Lucille L. Andreozzi

Strange Attractors: Chaos, Complexity and the Art of Family Therapy
by Michael Butz, William G. McCown, and Linda Chamberlain

Infertility: Psychological Issues and Counseling Strategies
by Sandra Leiblum

The Self in the Family: A Classification of Personality, Criminality, and Psychopathology
by Luciano L'Abate (with the collaboration of Margaret S. Baggett)

The Self in the Family

A Classification of Personality, Criminality, and Psychopathology

Luciano L'Abate

with the collaboration of Margaret S. Baggett

JOHN WILEY & SONS, INC.

New York • Chichester • Brisbane • Toronto • Singapore • Weinheim

To the United States of America and to its people, who have given the author and his collaborator so much.

This text is printed on acid-free paper.

Though this book is nonfiction, the names and distinguishing traits of all clients and individuals mentioned in this book have been changed.

Library of Congress Cataloging-in-Publication Data:
L'Abate, Luciano, 1928–
The self in the family : a classification of personality, criminality, and psychopathology / by Luciano L'Abate, with the collaboration of Margaret Baggett.
p. cm. — (Wiley series in couples and family dynamics and treatment)
Includes bibliographical references.
ISBN 0-471-12247-5 (cloth : alk. paper)
1. Family—Psychological aspects. 2. Personality development. 3. Mental illness—Etiology. 4. Criminal behavior. 5. Self psychology. 6. Socialization. I. Baggett, Margaret. II. Title. III. Series.
RC455.4.F3L333 1997
616.89—dc20 96-19639

ISBN #0-471-12247-5

10 9 8 7 6 5 4 3 2 1

Series Preface

Our ability to form strong interpersonal bonds with romantic partners, children, parents, siblings, and other relations is one of the key qualities that defines our humanity. These relationships shape who we are, and what we become—they can be a source of great gratification or tremendous pain. Yet, only in the mid-20th century did behavioral and social scientists really begin focusing on couples and family dynamics, and only in the past several decades have the theory and findings that emerged from those studies been used to develop effective therapeutic interventions for troubled couples and families.

We have made great progress in understanding the structure, function, and interactional patterns of couples and families—and have made tremendous strides in treatment. However, as we stand poised on the beginning of a new millennium, it seems quite clear that both intimate partnerships and family relationships are in a period of tremendous flux. Economic factors are changing work patterns, parenting responsibilities, and relational dynamics. Modern medicine has helped lengthen the life span, giving rise to the need for transgenerational caretaking. Cohabitation, divorce, and remarriage are quite commonplace, and these social changes make it necessary for us to rethink and broaden our definition of what constitutes a family.

Thus, it is no longer enough simply to embrace the concept of the family as a system. In order to understand and effectively treat the evolving family, our theoretical formulations and clinical interventions must be informed by an understanding of ethnicity, culture, religion, gender, sexual preference, family life cycle, socioeconomic status, education, physical and mental health, values, and belief systems.

The purpose of the *Wiley Series in Couples and Family Dynamics and Treatment* is to provide a forum for cutting-edge relational and family theory, practice, and research. Its scope is intended to be broad, diverse, and international, but all books published in this series share a common mission—to reflect on the past, offer state-of-the-art information on the present, and speculate on, as well as attempt to shape, the future of the field.

FLORENCE W. KASLOW

Florida Couples and Family Institute

Preface

> . . . one's own theory—in the service of coherence, belief, and beauty—necessarily distorts, as well as organizes, a viewpoint about human nature. (Emde, 1995, p. 1041)

The purpose of this work is to elaborate, update, and expand on a developmental theory of interpersonal competence and socialization (L'Abate, 1994b) by adding parts that were not included in the original work because of space constraints but that are integral components of the theory as a whole. This theory of the self in the family stresses that the family is the major setting in which personality development and socialization take place. From this setting develop functional as well as dysfunctional personality propensities. The latter, up to the present time, were considered separate from the former, and psychopathology was viewed as being separate from criminality. This theory and the *selfhood model*—a specific model of personality propensities derived from the theory—link together all three domains: functional/dysfunctional, psychopathological, and criminal. This work aims, therefore, to show how the existing evidence converges toward the family as the setting from which these personality propensities and their deviations develop and are socialized.

This theory developed from some general ideas about behavior in a *vacuum* (L'Abate, 1964) to very specific ideas about the individual in the family (L'Abate, 1976), family functioning (L'Abate, 1985a, 1985b, 1986), and, finally, personality socialization within a relational context (L'Abate, 1994a, 1994b, 1994c). Everything written here is a sequel to previous works. To avoid repetitious self-reference, no citations of previous works (and their accompanying references) will be repeated unless absolutely necessary. In an early version (L'Abate, 1994b), descriptions of the theory borrowed the metaphors of a compass, a map, and a straitjacket. Here, the metaphor of a coathanger is useful. The theory forms a framework on which can hang a vast variety of constructs from diverse theories, theorettes (small theories), models, and empirical sources.

Examples of how the theory can function as a coathanger can be found throughout this work. For instance, in Chapter 4, there are many formulations of feelings and emotions. However, most of them, as will be shown, involve *lists* without any framework that would allow for a systematic understanding of how feelings and emotions relate to each other and how they reflect individual differences and personality propensities. A more egregious example, found in later chapters, pertains to psychiatric nosology, which consists of *lists* of symptoms and syndromes that have no relation to each other, much less to personality socialization and criminality.

The metaphor of the theory as a coathanger will become evident in how personality, criminality, and psychopathology can be put together within the same framework. Up to the present time, these domains of experience and knowledge were considered separately; that is, most personality theories avoided references to both psychopathology and criminality. Theories of criminality made only sparse reference to personality or psychopathology, except to mention the possible overlap among these domains. Theories of psychopathology made few references to either personality or criminality. Linking the three domains requires integrating what, until now, have seemed disparate and diverse fields of knowledge.

A theory is different from a paradigm and a model. A paradigm is a very general, abstract worldview—for example, the family as a unit of interdependent personalities that influences personality socialization throughout the life span. A theory has a more specific and concrete function: to develop models that can be tested empirically as well as clinically. Previous paradigms viewed personality in a *vacuum,* or, at best, as a vague and unspecified personality–situation interaction. The theory specifies that the family paradigm is the major determinant of personality socialization throughout the life span. The school/work setting can be very important in the rewards or stresses that it poses for and imposes on growing individuals. Without the support of a secure home setting, many individuals would not be able to cope with either school or work. Leisure activities contribute to enjoyment. Other necessary tasks are performed for survival. We all depend on a grocery store to survive, and most of us need to visit a beauty salon or barbershop to look better. Leisure time can be used to link the physical and recreational activities that mediate home and occupational stresses.

The major characteristic of this work is its reliance on external, observable resources. In many personality textbooks, inferred, internal/intrapsychic, or hypothetical traits or states have reached the level of reification. The traditional *trait approach* to personality theory, the prevailing paradigm in the present day, is reviewed and critiqued. Because it stresses visible relationship patterns rather than internal variables, the present theory is quite different from existing intrapsychic approaches to personality.

Part One introduces and gives evidential support for the theory. Chapter 1 focuses on the basic tenets of the original theory. Chapter 2 reviews: (a) existing theories or concepts that are epistemologically or empirically *independent* of this theory but have constructs that are similar and, possibly, in agreement, and (b) evidence that is *indirectly* related to and supportive of the validity of the theory. Chapter 3 summarizes evidence that is *directly* supportive because it was derived specifically from the theory itself. Chapter 4 argues that hurt is the fundamental but neglected feeling that determines a great deal of our behavior in interpersonal relationships, intimate and otherwise. Feelings and emotions are considered from the viewpoint of a selfhood model summarized in previous chapters. Chapter 5 includes most of the available evidence to support the validity of a likeness continuum in personality differentiation and intimate relationships (mate selection, marriage, parent–child relationships, and friendships). Chapter 6 reviews seven theoretical models that relate individual behavior to family behavior (or vice versa). Two psychoanalytic models are included—one on relationship styles and one on family defenses—as are Olson's circumplex model, Constantine's theorizing, and McCubbin's empirical work with families. All seven models are integrated, admittedly tentatively, with the theory or with the selfhood model.

Part Two emphasizes particularly how the prototypical selfhood model of personality socialization—derived from the theory—is applied to the classification of personality, criminality, and psychopathology. In linking personality with criminality and psychopathology, Chapter 7 offers a critique of past classifications from the perspective of the present theory and models. A new classification of personality, criminality, and psychopathology according to the relational and contextual selfhood model is described. Chapter 8 presents the selfhood model as a cornerstone for a classification of criminalities. Chapters 9 and 10 expand the theory and selfhood model to affective disorders and psychopathologies, respectively. Chapter 11 advocates that addictions and psychosomatic illnesses be classified separately from criminalities, personalities, and psychopathologies because there is not, as yet, a one-to-one relationship between personalities and addictions nor between psychosomatic illnesses and psychopathologies.

Part Three expands on the implications of the theory and prototypical model for psychological interventions: Chapter 12 relates the theory to preventive approaches, and Chapter 13 shows its potential for crisis interventions and psychotherapies. Chapter 14, in Part Four, demonstrates how a simple arithmetical model can describe and evaluate the theory and the prototypical models elaborated from it.

This work aspires to fulfill Berscheid's (1995) request for a "grand theorist." The author is neither a sociologist nor an anthropologist, as Berscheid would have liked, but, years ago, a graduate course in the sociology of the family brought to his attention the nonexistence of a field of family psychology. If there is a sociology of the family *qua* family, why should there not be a psychology of the family? How is the individual related to his or her family?

The aim of the theory described herein is to correct inadequacies in past classifications by introducing a selfhood model that includes, links, and relates the fields of personality functioning, criminality, and psychopathology. The intended outcome is a possible integration of these three fields, which have developed, until now, in separate and relatively independent fashion.

Scholars of personality—teachers, researchers, graduate students, and advanced undergraduates—will profit or benefit from reading this work and implementing the selfhood model. Clinicians interested in applying an integrative, contextual, and relational theory to their practice may find it helpful to use the methods and techniques developed in parallel with the theory to test and evaluate it.

This work is different from other texts on personality theory in that it does not repeat shopworn concepts and theories. It integrates social psychological theories (i.e., social comparison, resource exchange, environmental psychology, and ecology) into a competence–setting interaction. Additionally, developmental, therapeutic, normative, and psychopathological viewpoints are blended in a way that is unique in textbooks on personality. The integration of past and current viewpoints is planned as a refreshing respite from the endless repetition of theorists and theories in traditional texts. Instructors who value both novelty and integration of concepts may find here a way to have their students learn something new in personality theory.

LUCIANO L'ABATE

ACKNOWLEDGMENTS

We are indebted to Frank M. Dattilio, Piero De Giacomo, Cheryl Glickauf-Hughes, and William McCown for a careful, caring, and critical reading of first drafts of selected parts of this work and for helpful comments that allowed us to improve them. We are especially indebted to Richard G. Lambert not only for his thorough evaluation of Chapter 3, but also for performing all of the statistical analyses for the research studies summarized in that chapter. Without his expertise in statistics and computer analyses, completion of those studies would have been very difficult and time-consuming. Lynda Fraizer, Steven Weinstein, and David Russ actively gathered references for Chapter 5. Klaus Schneewind was very helpful in clarifying the distinction between dimensions and prototypes in Chapter 7. We are greatly indebted to Beth Allgood for voluntarily typing and alphabetizing most of the references. Her work allowed the author's time and energy to be devoted to the substance of the text. Howard Cramer's alphabetizing of the final reference list (in a pinch, during the Christmas holidays) was extremely helpful. Thank you Howard! Thanks also to Themis Cramer for lending him to us!

Finally, we are especially indebted to the series editor, Florence W. Kaslow, for her continuous support and leadership, and her invaluable friendship.

Contents

PART ONE

Summary and Expansion of the Theory

CHAPTER 1

The Family as the Context for Personality Development and Socialization

> The challenge for any study of lives in a changing society is to keep both individual and environmental variations in the picture. (Elder & Caspi, 1990, p. 202)

This book delineates a developmental theory of personality socialization that poses the ability to love and the ability to negotiate as the cornerstones of personal and interpersonal competence. In contrast to traditional personality theories, which as a whole have been intrapsychically nonrelational and acontextual, this theory is both relational and contextual. At best, previous theories of personality have touched on the personality–situation interaction. Generally, these theories failed to specify what this interaction consisted of because most of their constructs were internal rather than external. For instance, the abilities to love and to negotiate are relevant only to the extent that each is applicable to a specific setting—usually, the home. The ability to love is more relevant, if not specific, to the home, and it is necessary but insufficient to guarantee functional relationships. The ability to negotiate is equally important and has additional relevance to other settings outside the home.

This theory of the self in the family maintains that we need to find ways and means of determining causal relationships that are relevant at *both* individual and multirelational levels of the family. Interactions are between the subordinate level of the individual and the supraordinate level of the family unit. Both levels are the products and the producers of relationships. Traditional personality theories, however, offer little help because most of them are couched in intrapsychic, nonrelational, acontextual terms that have little relevance to personality socialization and functioning in the family or anywhere else. This position is not intended to dismiss past theories of personality development out of hand; on the contrary, it seeks to highlight the differences without which this theory could not have been constructed.

Developmental competence theory, therefore, would be in some ways isomorphic with existent models of personality socialization that have demonstrated empirical as well as clinical validity (see Chapter 2). The theory described herein should be applicable to individual, dyadic, and family levels of analysis, in ways that are compatible with existing individual and family models, as discussed in Chapter 6. Thus, the theory deals with the individual–family interface *and* the description–explanation dialectic. Rather than getting caught up in the controversial individual–family interface, it seems more useful to focus on *relationships,* and to differentiate them according to specific characteristics. Explanation needs to be distinguished from description. It might be simpler and just as useful to consider both processes as being part of *interpretation*—how one chooses to evaluate personality and its socialization. This theory interprets how individuals deal with each other both within and outside the family, both descriptively and explanatorily.

Developmentally, personal and interpersonal competence is stressed because it defines personality in terms of interactions within settings. The competencies of love and negotiation need to be considered within five specific types of settings: (a) home, (b) school/work, (c) leisure time, (d) transitory, and (e) transit. (Settings are discussed later in this chapter.) Thus, this theory classifies personality socialization in new and different ways—love and negotiation as a whole have not been topics in traditional theories—and it specifies the interaction that takes place continuously between these abilities and specific settings.

METATHEORETICAL FOUNDATIONS OF THE THEORY

Before elaborating on the developmental competence theory proper, it is important to evaluate its metatheoretical foundations. The assumptions and constructs go above and beyond the theory itself. The assumptions (discussed later in the chapter) are common to most personality theories, either implicitly or explicitly (hence, metatheoretical). In this section, these constructs will be considered: (a) personality, (b) development, (c) the depth dimension (levels of interpretation and functioning), (d) the horizontal dimension (the ERAAwC model), and (e) the independent variables of the theory.

Personality: Selfhood and Relationships

Personality is defined by the ability to love and the ability to negotiate. The ability to love is specific to the home; the ability to negotiate is relevant not only to the home but also to other settings (i.e., school/work, leisure time, transition, and transit). These abilities are learned through a process of socialization that derives from familial and cultural contributions, sometimes influenced also by organic and genetic factors. *Selfhood* is defined by how one asserts, expresses, and defines his or her importance in intimate as well as nonintimate relationships. This work elaborates on both definitions. Two models of importance and intimacy are expanded in their multifarious functional and dysfunctional manifestations.

The Intensity Dimension in Socialization and Differentiation: The ARC Model

There are two kinds of development:

1. Chronological and physical progression over time.
2. Intrapersonal and interpersonal competence evidenced in how one deals with oneself and interacts with others.

Most developmental stages are fixed, inevitable, normative, and predictable: (a) childhood; (b) education, formal and informal; (c) job/occupation/career; (d) marriage/nonspousal partnership; (e) parenting; (f) empty nest; (g) retirement; and (h) death. This entire life span is essentially chronological and physical.

Another view of development consists of intraindividually variable and unpredictable phases related to how well and how fast an individual moves through life. For instance, childhood is characterized by dependency. Adolescence may be characterized by a conflict between acceptance and denial of dependency. Adulthood at its best may represent autonomous interdependence, and old age may bring a return to dependency. In its many developmental transformations and trajectories over the life span, dependency may be seen as a theme that requires elaboration because it describes an individual's competence in each stage in life.

Competence is evaluated according to how differentiated an individual is in relation to others. Differentiation is usually achieved by a process of socialization with caretakers and intimate others (parents, partner[s], children, friends, teachers). Hence, this theory of development focuses on how one is socialized rather than how one develops chronologically. One can be 50 years old and extremely undifferentiated personally and interpersonally. Or, one can be 20 years old and already differentiated beyond one's years. This dimension covers the functionality→dysfunctionality continuum as expanded through the ARC (Apathy-Abuse–Reactivity-Repetition–Conductivity-Creativity) model.

The ARC model (explained in greater detail in Chapter 5) consists of six markers along the span of differentiation, beginning with symbiosis at one extreme and ending with alienation at the other extreme. The six markers are:

1. Symbiosis ("I am you and you are me").
2. Sameness ("Be, do, feel, think, and behave like me").
3. Similarity ("Be, do, feel, think, and behave somewhat or a little bit like me, but leave room for being also different from me").
4. Differentness ("I define myself, and I am not like you; I am different from you").
5. Oppositeness or rebelliousness ("I am the opposite of you").
6. Autism or alienation ("I am not").

Combinations of those markers create various styles of relationships. AA represents a relationship style defined by abuse, apathy, or neglect. This personality differentiation is derived from the two extremes of symbiosis and autism. RR, deriving from sameness and oppositeness, represents a style defined by repetitious reactivity. CC is defined as a creative conductivity style, the ability to keep one's counsel and control in spite of stressful circumstances. This style derives from the combination of similarity and differentness. The AA style is the most dysfunctional, the RR style is intermediate between functionality and dysfunctionality, and the CC style is the most functional.

In the RR style, the person behaves by either responding immediately or withdrawing from the situation. The reactive response is either immediate—a verbal retort, for example—or delayed, as is the case with an individual who selects a mate on the basis of oppositeness to his or her parents. Instead of responding, the person may withdraw from the situation, but the withdrawal does not contribute any improvement. Both behaviors result in keeping the interaction essentially the same. Hence, reactive responses are repetitive in nature.

The main difference between the AA and RR styles is the intensity of the response. In the AA style, for instance, a verbal response would be additionally characterized by explosive curse words and derogatory expletives. There would also be a possibility of abusive physical or sexual assault. On the other side of the AA style's dialectical coin is apathy or neglect. The individual gives up, or deals with the situation incompetently, inconsistently, or contradictorily, or does not deal with the situation at all (neglect). Neglect is the reverse side of abuse; one could not exist without the other. Hence, repetition is characteristic of both the RR and the AA styles. In the RR style, one person supposedly wins at another's expense. In the AA style, both the self and the other lose. In the RR style, some attention may be paid to external correction and feedback to change the situation. In the AA style, there is resistance to any external correction or feedback. RR may be amenable to psychotherapeutic intervention. AA, in its most extreme manifestations, might not be.

In CC, the noun "conductor" and the adjective "conductive" combine two metaphors, one musical and one electrical, to describe how one is in charge of self and of situations. Using the musical metaphor, the conductor understands that one can only be in charge of another through manipulation, oppression, or coercion, the methods used in AA and RR. Thus, the conductor *keeps cool* by following a score or a plan that includes: (a) not reacting to provocation or stress, (b) delaying action, (c) gathering relevant information by asking questions of whoever is acting provocatively or stressfully, and (d) if and when action is necessary, following a positive and thoughtful course of action that will enhance self and other. In this style, self and other win because both are acknowledged as important to the situation. In the electrical metaphor, the conductive element keeps cool because of its chemical composition. Instead of overheating or becoming hot, it uses rationality rather than emotionality, thereby keeping the heat down, integrating reason and emotion without denying either, and channeling both capacities in an appropriate fashion to achieve an effective outcome.

Levels of Interpretation: The Depth Dimension

This theory differentiates among four levels of functioning in interpreting personality socialization. The first two levels are descriptive and the next two levels are explanatory. The descriptive levels are comprised of (a) public self-presentation or impression management—how one wants to appear in brief and superficial public contacts (nasty/nice, good/bad, and so on); and (b) the phenotype—how one behaves in private, intimate, close, prolonged, and committed relationships. Both levels can be observed, recorded, and videotaped.

The explanatory levels are comprised of (a) the genotype—how one sees oneself, according to inferred and mostly hypothetical constructs such as self-concept, self-esteem, ego (the theory questions whether inferred and hypothetical constructs at the genotypical level—intrapsychic traits and states, for example—are necessary, except for differentiation and self-determination, which, however, are formed and developed interpersonally) and (b) historical-developmental-situational components. This latter level "explains" how and why one behaves as one does at inferred genotypical and observable descriptive levels. These four levels represent the vertical or depth dimension in personality socialization.

The Horizontal Dimension: The ERAAwC Model

This theory differentiates sharply between what is experienced on the input side and what is expressed on the output side. (For an expanded discussion, see Chapter 4.) These two aspects are not necessarily correlated because the powerful effects of cognition and thinking must be taken into account. What we experience is one process, which involves our feelings. We express our feelings through our emotions, which may or may not be related to the feelings themselves. At best, we experience a limited or circumscribed number of feelings. However, those feelings can be expressed in an infinite number of constructive or destructive ways. The expression of feelings (i.e., emotions) is modulated, modified, amplified, or minimized by how we process the experience of feelings through cognition and thinking (throughput). The experiencing→expressing continuum constitutes the horizontal dimension of behavior and personality, as illustrated by the ERAAwC model, which includes and integrates previous theories of behavior and personality development.

The ERAAwC model ranges from the subjective at the input side to the objective and contextual at the output side. To describe and understand personality, we need to include how one experiences and sees oneself and others (the receptive function) in terms of subjective feelings and perceptions. The elements of the model are:

- **E**motionality or input determines approach-avoidance (withdrawal) tendencies—distances between and among individuals. This view is represented by the humanistic-existential schools, which value the importance of subjectivity in personality. Chapter 2 expands on these tenets.
- **R**ationality determines discharge-delay functions such as control or self-regulation. Classical psychoanalysis and rationally oriented schools value how feelings are processed through rationality or throughput.
- **A**ctivities are what is said and done in observable words and actions. Behaviorism stresses the output side of behavior and its immediate, visible, and quantifiable consequences.
- **Aw**areness of one's behavior, through introspection and reflection, leads to possible change, as feedback to feelings *(E)*, cognitions *(R)*, and, eventually, behavior or activities *(A)* is received. Awareness is a basic corrective change mechanism that allows learning from experience and serves as a feedback function between Context (see below) and Emotionality. When Activity is counterproductive or results in negative outcome (Context), Awareness allows a correction of behavior by going back to *E*, reprocessing it through *R*, and producing a change in *A*. Awareness, therefore, is the outcome of a reflective and introspective process: looking back to one's behavior, considering contextual and relational outcomes, and changing behavior to maximize rewards (i.e., pleasure and enjoyment) and minimize hurts or punishments. This process allows for the development of guilt and shame, regrets and misgivings about one's behavior that produce corrective changes for the better. This characteristic means profiting and using feedback from those who care and those whose judgment and opinion are perceived as important to one's life. Thus, *Aw* relates to the ability to look into oneself within a Context.
- **C**ontext is the internal and external perspective of what desirable or undesirable behavior has taken place. The internal Context refers to how one feels about the behavior being considered. The external Context refers to the immediate, proximal (within each other), or distal outcome that the behavior has produced in relation to others. Information and feedback from others can be accepted or rejected to fit one's view of self and the importance of those imparting the information. Context surrounds the *E, R, A,* and *Aw* processes in their proximal and distal (external and distant) consequences, as stressed by the feminist and family therapy movements.

The ERAAwC model serves a diagnostic function: it characterizes how individuals and families use each of those components primarily, secondarily, and tertiarily. For instance, a person who short-circuits feelings *(E)* may rely on overrational obsessions *(R)* or on impulsive, driven behavior *(A)*. A couple may be polarized, with the man overrelying on Rationality and the woman overrelying on Emotionality. Another function of this model is to serve as a structure to describe and prescribe necessary negotiation skills, either informally in the therapist's office or more formally through systematic written assignments that are to be carried out in the home.

The Independent Variables of Personality Socialization

This theory of development conceives of age and life span, gender differences, socioeconomic status, ethnic origin, culture and race, education, religion, physical status or health, parental rearing and socialization practices, sibling relationships and rivalry, and the psychosocial functioning of the family as exerting powerful influences on socialization, by amplifying or decreasing functionality. Because it would be difficult, if not impossible, to tease out and review all these variables, the theory, by necessity, focuses on select gender differences and parental rearing practices as the two most powerful influences on personality socialization—without denying the influence of other variables.

DEVELOPMENTAL COMPETENCE THEORY

This theory of development was derived in part from social exchange theory, which assumes that six resource classes are continuously exchanged between and among individuals: (a) Status, (b) Love, (c) Information, (d) Services, (e) Money, and (f) Goods (Foa & Foa, 1974), as shown in Table 1.1. These resources are the outcome of a developmental process started by two assumptive dimensions: space and time. From both assumptions flow postulates, modalities, resources, skills, and models, going from the abstract and general to the concrete and specific. Assumptions represent the highest level of abstraction and generality. Skills and models represent the highest level of concreteness and specificity, providing an entry point where the theory can be best evaluated and tested.

Assumptions

Two major features of this theoretical derivation are relevant to elusive links between individual and family socialization: (a) two assumptive dimensions about behavior in general, and (b) the distinction between functionality and dysfunctionality. Two major dimensions of behavior—space and time—are assumed. Space is characterized by approach-avoidance functions that define *distance* between and among individuals. We usually approach and achieve enjoyment with pleasurable people and activities, and we avoid pain and the people and activities that cause it. We approach people whom we love and who love us, and we avoid people whom we do not like or who do not like us. Exceptions to such a generalization must be considered throughout this work. Distance and its extremes in approach-avoidance form the bases for subsequent parent–child and partner–partner attachments. Modulation and modification of approach-avoidance functions lead to amplifications, variations, and

TABLE 1.1 Summary of a Developmental Theory of Interpersonal Competence

Assumptions	Postulates	Modalities	Resources	Skills	Models
1. Space			(Status)*		*Selfhood*
(Distance)			*Importance*		Selfulness
					Selfishness
					Selflessness
					No-self
	Ability to				
	Love	BEING		**PRESENCE**	*Intimacy*
			(Love)*		Communicating values
			Intimacy		Respect for feelings
					Accepting limitations
					Affirming potentialities
					Sharing hurts
					Forgiving errors
Settings: Home, School/Work, Leisure/Surplus Time (Transit, Transitory)					
			Information		*Structure*
					Authority/ Responsibility
		DOING		**Performance**	
					Orchestration/ Instrumentation
			Services		
2. Time	*Ability*				
(Control)	*to Negotiate*			**POWER**	
			Money		*Process*
		HAVING		**Production**	
					ARC
			Goods		ERAAwC
					Priorities: Vertical/ Horizontal

* This term was used in the original resource exchange theory (Foa & Foa, 1974).

failures in attachments that last for the rest of one's life. This assumption, therefore, leads developmentally to attachments, dependencies, and closeness in intimate relationships. These behaviors eventually turn into the ability to love.

Time is characterized by discharge-delay functions that define *control* within and among individuals. Discharge is a sudden—at times, explosive and even destructive—expression toward someone or something that may take place as an attack (verbal or physical, or both). Delay is the time interval between the introduction of an emotionally arousing event and the response to that event. It consists of an inhibition of feelings, thoughts, or actions to prevent their expression through verbal or physical means. Discharge implies little if any control. Delay implies a great deal of control over the expression of feelings, thoughts, or actions. Control and its regulation are important, if not basic, to personality socialization. Both are basic to the development of the *ability to negotiate* and to solve problems in the home as well as in other settings.

The model of distance-control presented here applies to developing children as they differentiate themselves in growing up. The child is born in a world of space and, later, develops in a world of time. Complex dimensions basic to circumplex but static models of personality functioning are developmental outgrowths of distance and control. The notion that love may be a fundamental determinant of personality socialization and family relations has, for whatever reasons, escaped the field of personality theory. Should the reader consider this an extreme and unsubstantiated statement, a simple exercise is recommended. Let the reader pick up any personality theory textbook or family theory/therapy treatise and look up two simple terms: *love* and *intimacy*. How often and for how many pages does either term appear?

Postulates

From these two assumptions of space and time, postulates about the ability to love and to negotiate are derived. The ability to love may be primary in the home but secondary, if not irrelevant, in school/work settings. The ability to negotiate may be primary in the school/work setting and necessary, but secondary to love, at home. In leisure activities, both competencies may be necessary differentially. For instance, in the marketplace, the ability to negotiate may be necessary or even crucial. The ability to love may be necessary in hospitals, clinics, churches, or religious settings.

Functionality in the ability to love results from a balance of approach-avoidance tendencies that is appropriate to the situation at hand. Dysfunctionality in the ability to love results from an imbalance in approach-avoidance functions. Imbalance occurs when one of these functions is greater than the other, or when both functions vacillate or oscillate contradictorily and inconsistently from one extreme to the other. Functional negotiation and problem solving are the outcomes of a balance in discharge-delay functions that is appropriate to the situation at hand. Too much delay is related to overrationality and obsessiveness. Too much discharge is related to underrationality, drivenness, immediacy, and impulsivity. Functional problem solving lies between these extremes; it is the ability to think through various options and to choose the one with the highest rewards and the lowest costs. Dysfunctionality in the ability to negotiate results from an imbalance in discharge-delay functions. Imbalance prevails when one of these functions is greater than the other, or when both functions vacillate or oscillate contradictorily and inconsistently from one extreme to the other (Figure 1.1).

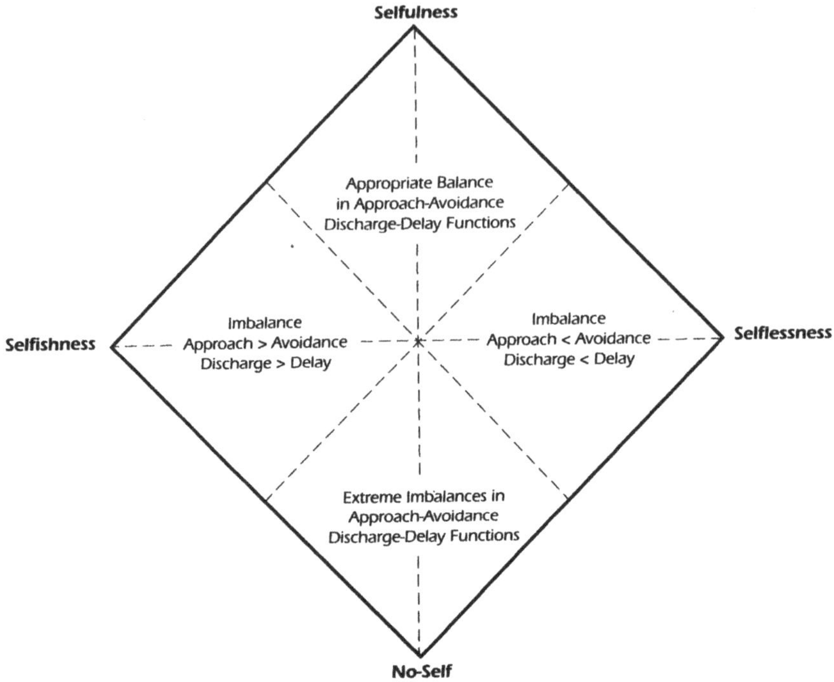

Figure 1.1 A Selfhood Model Derived from Assumptions of Space and Time

Personality Propensities

Balance in both approach-avoidance and discharge-delay functions is represented by a personality propensity called *selfulness.* By the same token, dysfunctionality results from overreliance on one extreme function at the expense of the others, or on contradictory and inconsistent alternation from one extreme function to the other. Extremes in approach (greater than avoidance) and discharge (greater than delay) lead to dysfunctions in externalization, like acting out, impulsivity, aggression, and hostility (Chapter 8). This imbalance tends to produce a personality propensity called *selfishness.* Extremes in avoidance (greater than approach) and delay (greater than discharge) lead to dysfunctions in internalization, like affective disorders, depression, anxiety, fears, and phobias (Chapter 9). This imbalance leads to a personality propensity called *selflessness.* Contradictory and inconsistent vacillations between extremes in approach-avoidance and discharge-delay produce most psychopathological conditions. This imbalance leads to a personality propensity called *no-self* (Chapter 10).

For instance, extremes in approach (greater than avoidance) and delay (greater than discharge) would represent symbiotic overattachment and overdependency, as in so-called codependency. Extremes in avoidance (greater than approach) and discharge (greater than delay) would represent denial of attachment and dependency, possibly leading to isolation and alienation. In many close but dysfunctional relationships, individuals may alternate between extremes. The relationship between approach-avoidance and discharge-delay functions and the four personality propensities named above is shown in Figure 1.1. These personality propensities make up the bulk of this theory.

The foregoing statements need to be qualified, however. The issue with approach-avoidance and discharge-delay functions lies in determining the level at which they take place. For instance, a person may approach another without revealing a hidden agenda that determines the approach. By the same token, one may discharge and attack someone for an insignificant reason or excuse ("You looked at me the wrong way!") when the underlying reason for the attack resides in the attacker's being unable to express verbally the feelings of discomfort that provoked the attack. Hence, both approach-avoidance and discharge-delay need to be qualified by levels of interpretation. The approach-avoidance or discharge-delay one may choose overtly, at the presentational level, does not necessarily reflect what is going on internally at more phenotypical and genotypical levels.

Modalities

From both postulates derive modalities of being, doing, and having. Being derives from the ability to love. Doing and having derive from the ability to negotiate. *Derive* may be an inappropriate term, except to denote a developmental process of differentiation—going from the general and abstract to the specific and concrete. One could just as well argue that the ability to love derives from being, and the ability to negotiate derives from doing and having. This is a chicken-and-egg issue that requires clarification. In functional relationships, being, doing, and having are flexibly and appropriately balanced and enjoyed. In dysfunctional relationships, doing and having are emphasized and heightened at the expense of being. Here, by necessity, daily physical and material survival is primary. Enjoyment is secondary, short-lived, postponed, or nonexistent.

Being, doing, and having may appear at first blush as rather abstract concepts. However, if they are defined by specific resources, they result in observable skills—respectively, presence, performance, and production. All three modalities are necessary to enjoy life and survive. Being involves a developmental process whereby the skill of presence is necessary—that is, being emotionally available to loved ones whose love is reciprocal. It is defined by the combination of two resources: importance and intimacy. Negotiation involves a process of problem solving, bargaining, and decision making, which involves both doing and having. Doing or performance results from the combination of information and services. Production is a skill resulting from having, in this context, goods and money. The combination of doing and having makes up the construct of power. Those who possess these modalities have power over those who do not possess them.

Thus, the two major constructs of interest to this theory of how presence and power are managed in intimate relationships assume that emotionality *(E)* is relevant to the sharing of presence, and that control, or rationality *(R)*, is relevant to the negotiation of power. As shown in Figure 1.2, the two orthogonal dimensions of distance and control are differentiated by the ARC model. *C*C, the most functional interpersonal style, is in the center, followed by *R*R and *A*A styles. The latter is the most dysfunctional, as was explained earlier and will be elaborated in Chapter 5.

In functional relationships, issues of presence are clearly separated from issues of power. Doing and having are negotiated and allocated in a democratic fashion where the relative importance of each individual is acknowledged and affirmed. Presence is not negotiable insofar as it constitutes a receptive feeling of love, a feeling that is nonnegotiable—although *how* love is expressed and shared may become an issue for negotiation. Power is negotiated effectively in functional relationships but inadequately and insufficiently, if at all, in dysfunctional ones. In the latter, presence, feelings, and emotions are inadequately defined and become confused, diffused, and fused with instrumental (power) issues ("If you loved me, you would do . . ."; "If you loved me, you would buy me . . ."). In dysfunctional relationships, issues of power are poorly negotiated or are ignored to the point where authority and responsibility become polarized in either chaotic ("Everything is negotiable") or rigid ("Nothing is negotiable") fashion. Examples of unwillingness to negotiate may be found in

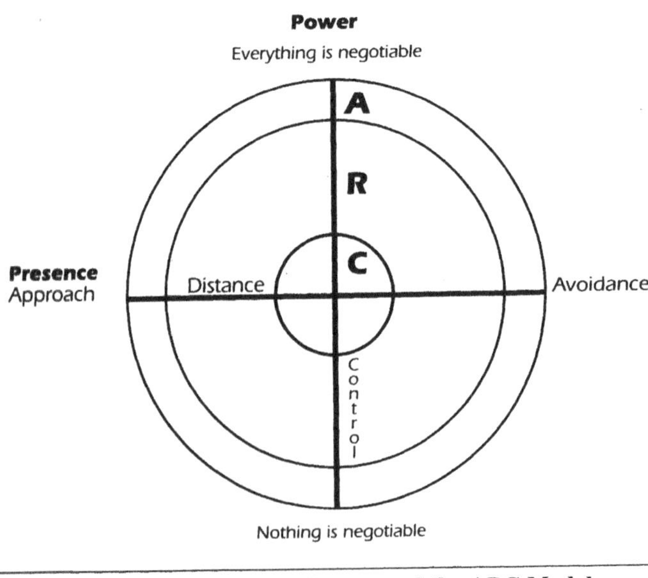

Figure 1.2 Presence, Power, and the ARC Model

addictions and in severe dysfunctionalities. Examples of everything being negotiable may be found in so-called codependent relationships. From the two assumptions of space and time, one can also derive a classification of defenses that are relevant to interpersonal relationships, as discussed in Chapter 6.

More often than not, conflicts over doing and having suggest an inability to be together, that is, to share and to divide stress according to the emotional modality of being and presence rather than modalities of performance (doing) or production (having). In American society it is easier to learn how to do and have than it is to learn how to be. We are trained to do in order to have. Very few individuals are able to share and to teach their offspring how to be by enjoying being together unconditionally. Yet, the modality of being is much more important in sharing stressful events than the modalities of doing and having. Being is crucial in dealing with most stresses *as soon as* they happen. Doing and having are important in dealing realistically with practical issues in the *aftermath* of a stressful event. If family members cannot share being, they will find it even more difficult to negotiate and to solve problems. Most, if not all, stressors have an immediate direct or indirect emotional impact. Unless family members are ready and able to use (that is, to experience, express, and share) their presence by being available emotionally to one another, it is very doubtful that they will be able to negotiate issues of power (performance or production).

These modalities, therefore, define *personality as what one person is, does, and has.* However, these skills are relational in the sense that they do not have meaning separately from the persons who exchange them. In addition, this theory is contextual in the sense that these modalities are necessary not only to function in relationship to others but also in the three major settings necessary for survival and enjoyment: (a) home, (b) school/work, and (c) leisure or surplus time.

Resources

As shown in Table 1.1, the six resource classes are combined into three modalities and their respective skills:

1. Being or presence (importance + intimacy).
2. Doing or performance (information + services).
3. Having or production (money + goods).

Fundamental to developmental competence theory is the concept of status, defined here as "attribution of importance" to self and to selected intimate others, such as spouse, children, parents, siblings, relatives, and friends. *Importance is a process whereby self and selected others are viewed as* necessary *for enjoyment and survival in life.* Enjoyment is more pronounced than survival in functional relationships. In dysfunctional relationships, survival is more pronounced than enjoyment, and enjoyment may be either absent or short-lived.

Attribution of importance to self and other is elaborated in a relational selfhood model to be discussed throughout this work. This model is also "explanatory" of psychopathology and criminality.

Instead of self-esteem, which is an intrapsychic and nonrelational concept, this theory uses *attribution of importance* to self and selected others as the cornerstone of competent socialization. This attribution, when positive toward self and selected others, allows the achievement of *intimacy,* another concept not used in traditional personality theories. This sense of importance is continuously exchanged throughout the life span. It is initially imparted both verbally and nonverbally from one's family of origin. Later in life, it is shared in the family of procreation. Caretakers are positively responsive to and respectful of each other, modeling the same behavior for their offspring. If caretakers are negatively reactive or abusively disrespectful of each other and their offspring, this failure to attribute importance, whether verbal or nonverbal, will repeat itself and become more magnified in the offspring.

Thus, how this sense of importance is attributed and communicated becomes the basic behavior to observe in both intimate and nonintimate relationships. A sense of importance can be attributed and communicated in various ways. Paying attention to and considering another's feelings and opinions is one way to communicate immediately, to that person, a sense of importance. The intrapersonal (i.e., "intrapsychic") outcome of this attributional process is self-esteem, which is widely acknowledged as a "personal resource" (Baumeister, 1993b; Mruk, 1995).

Continually asserted importance is basic to intimate and nonintimate others. Many languages make clear verbal distinctions to communicate the relative importance between two speakers. Latin and Teutonic languages, for instance, use "du" and "tu" to indicate differences in importance in informal relationships, and "Sie" and "Lei," in more formal ones. Many individuals from these cultures find it difficult to discriminate importance on the basis of the seemingly democratic use of "you" in the English language. Consequently, they learn to rely on other cues, as gleaned from the use of titles and nonverbal cues, to understand such a distinction. Asian languages discriminate further among levels of importance. Indonesian languages, for instance, discriminate among at least four, if not more, levels of importance between two speakers. In the Chinese language, among others, there is a continuous reference to how important one is considered within a hierarchical (mostly, a familial) organization.

A sense of importance is also communicated through nonverbal behavior, especially gestures and observance of personal space. Distancing, as shown by ignoring, silence, glances (looking away), rejection, and not paying attention, could be a way to deny a sense of importance. Size of one's office and condition of its furnishings are strong indications of importance in the school/workplace. Clothing and possessions—house, furniture, cars, and gifts—may not be the best way, but they are the clearest way to communicate one's sense of importance. In the military, importance is shown directly and immediately by uniforms, emblems, and protocols denoting rank. Educational and professional titles are indications of one's academic importance. In some cultures in Asia, importance is communicated through deferential gestures such as bowing, walking behind, and never being positioned in a location higher than that of the person in authority. Money is another way to communicate the importance of services performed or goods purchased. Many consider it a misdirected way to indicate love.

Love is a second resource that has been renamed. In developmental competence theory, it is intimacy, defined as the ability to be emotionally available to self and to selected others, especially in times of need—that is, when loved ones are hurting or are fearful of being hurt—without requirements of performance, perfection, problem solving, or production. Thus, the ability to love requires the combination of a sense of self-importance *plus* intimacy; presence is shared with a loved one.

The presence of both importance and intimacy in a relationship will determine its enhancement and growth. Unconditional love is based on commitment, equality, and reciprocity. Importance and intimacy define one's being as shown by the ability to be physically present and emotionally available to one's partner when that partner hurts. Presence, the ability to be emotionally available to self and others, is based on feelings of attachment and interdependence that are not negotiable. We do not negotiate how much we love our partner and the members of our family. In contrast, information, services, goods, and money, the resource classes that altogether define power, are all eminently negotiable—provided they are kept separate and are not confused, diffused, and fused with importance and intimacy, which are not negotiable. There is no negotiation about how family members feel about each other. Negotiation on the other four resource classes, on the other hand, is necessary or even vital if the family is to move forward.

SELFHOOD AND IMPORTANCE: INTRODUCTION TO THE MODEL

Status, defined here as attribution of importance to self and to others, may be considered the flip side of love. Importance or unimportance is learned from one's family of origin. Direct or indirect, verbal and nonverbal, consistent and inconsistent, positive and negative messages are continually given by each family member concerning feelings of importance about the self and others in and outside of the family.

Theoretically and practically, the attribution of importance as the most fundamental exchange between human beings is viewed as a much more useful concept than the inference of self-esteem, self-respect, and other similarly intrapsychic states or traits. At best, esteem can be inferred about oneself but not about another. Unless we ask people how they feel about themselves, we have to infer their self-esteem from their behavior. Self-esteem, an exquisitely intrapsychic process, remains an inference without interpersonal implications. Once we infer, directly or indirectly, someone's level of self-esteem, what interpersonal implications can we draw? Family members do not transact business on the basis of self-esteem. They do it on the basis of how they exchange their importance. Importance, on the other hand, is an attributional process with crucial relational and interpersonal implications. *Love means the attribution of importance to self and to selected significant others.* Grieving does not take place on the basis of the lost person's self-esteem, nor on the basis of the self-esteem of the one who is grieving. Grieving is based on that person's importance to us. Hence, the concept of self-esteem, as one way of defining status, has outlived its usefulness because of its limited, perhaps nonexistent, interpersonal significance and implications.

The sense and attribution of personal importance show a much more definite theoretical and practical significance from a relational viewpoint than does the concept of self-esteem. Once importance is accepted as an attributional process that is based not just on objective reality but also on subjective feelings and perceptions, asserting one's importance and the importance of significant others becomes a lifelong, continuous process. In extreme cases, such attribution may reach symbiotic proportions ("I cannot live without you!"), as in love addictions or in destructive extremes (murder and suicide). This attribution is the very cornerstone of self-socialization and self-definition. It differs on a variety of dimensions:

- *Positive-negative:* The work of Leff and Vaughn (1985) on expressed emotions (EE) in the development of schizophrenia is an example of how negative feelings are expressed in the family. Most families of schizophrenics show a high frequency and duration of negatively abusive comments, reactions, put-downs, insults, blaming, accusations, and name-calling. This research is consistent with the work of Alexander and Parsons (1982), who found two basic styles in families. A supportive style was common in the families of functional adolescents. A negative style of accusations, criticisms, and put-downs was common in the families of juvenile delinquents. Whether working with schizophrenics or with acting-out individuals, one sees clearly that many dysfunctionalities are related to both *AA* and *RR* interpersonal styles magnified from their families of origin.
- *Direct-indirect:* The attribution of importance or unimportance can be direct, as in positive or negative messages ("I love you"; "You are stupid"), or indirect, as in telling someone in the family about the shortcomings of another family member when that member is absent, a favorite device in O'Neill's plays.
- *Verbal-nonverbal-written:* Communication can be spoken, unspoken, or written. Verbal communication is most common, and written is least common, except when physical distance is present. Given the choice, most family members prefer to telephone each other rather than write letters. Consistently positive, directly unconditional messages that differentiate importance (i.e., what one is, one's being) from performance or production tend to produce selful individuals. Consistently or inconsistently negative and directly or indirectly conditional messages of unimportance

or partial importance produce negative and dysfunctional personality propensities.

- *Consistent-inconsistent or contradictory:* This attribution of importance can be consistently positive or consistently negative, or something in between. It can be inconsistent within the same verbal, nonverbal, or written medium, or contradictory, as when a message in a verbal medium is discounted or contradicted by a message in the nonverbal or written media. Who would believe a message like "I am angry at you!" if the person uttering this message is smiling?
- *Conditional-unconditional:* This attribution can be conditional on performance or production (doing, having) or it can be unconditional, as when presence (being) is deemed more important to a relationship than performance or production. An example of this process is visible when the educational achievement of a child becomes the battleground for rewards and punishments, often confusing the child. Here, learning is confused with loving. The parents may well love the child unconditionally. Unfortunately, if stress is put solely on educational achievement, the communication of unconditional love toward the child may become distorted or diluted into a power struggle. The child may learn to feel that the parents' love is conditional on educational achievement and nothing else.
- *Partial-whole:* Messages of importance/unimportance often describe the performance or production of an individual, or they may be generalized to the whole personality. For instance, an individual's feelings, thoughts, or behaviors may be discounted or criticized. An individual with a low sense of self-importance may believe the criticism and generalize it to the whole personality ("If my parent thinks that what I do is bad, then I am bad."), a *pars pro toto* fallacy.

Hence, attribution of importance to self and other (partner, child, parents, friends, neighbors) leads to four personality propensities (Figure 1.3).

1. *Selfulness* is shown interpersonally in the "I win, you win" position, where equal importance ("I am important, you are important") of self is attributed on the basis of "We both must win." Winning represents a process of appreciation and enhancement whereby interactions are pleasurable and productive, and lead to emotional and intellectual growth. Losing represents a process of defeating debasement and discounting devaluation that produces emotional and intellectual deficits. Selfulness consists of committed relationships where reciprocal collaboration, encouragement, mutuality, intimacy, responsiveness, and respect are practiced continuously and culminate in mutually rewarding outcomes. This is the most functional propensity that is basic to personal and interpersonal competence and creativity. It follows the practice of reciprocity and mutuality as exemplified by the Golden Rule ("Do unto others . . ."). Selfulness is equated with commitment, equality, reciprocity, and intimacy in close and prolonged relationships. These qualities make up

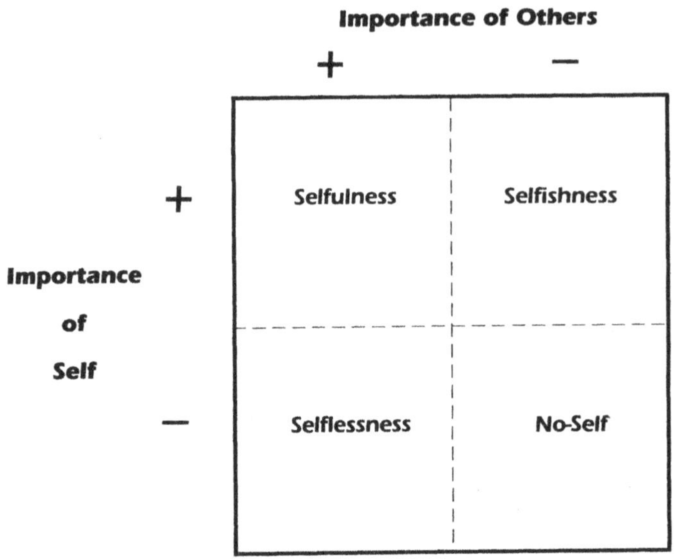

Figure 1.3 Selfhood and Personality Propensities

personal and interpersonal competence as well as marital and familial functionality. Its most common interpersonal style is *CC*.

2. *Selfishness* is shown interpersonally in the "I win, you lose" position, where unequal importance is attributed to the self and denied to other ("I am important, you are either unimportant or not as important as I am"). This propensity is based on an attitude of "I know better than you or anybody else." Here, the individual pushes the limits to get whatever is wanted for self-gratification, regardless of the expense to others. Manipulation, pressure, theft, and cheating are some of the ways used to obtain what is wanted. The ultimate or extreme outcome of this propensity is murder (Chapter 8).

3. *Selflessness* is shown interpersonally in the "You win, I lose" position, where little if any importance is attributed to the self but is attributed to the other instead ("I am not as important as you. You are more important than I am"). When the self is belittled and another's self is enhanced, there is a loss to the self. This propensity is based on an attitude of "I don't known much. You know better than I do." The importance of others is considered before and above self-importance. Selflessness is the primary characteristic of most self-defeating, dependent, and depressed personalities (Chapter 9). The ultimate or extreme outcome of this propensity is suicide, either sudden (physical) or prolonged (emotional). Individuals characterized by Selflessness seem rather naive and gullible. They believe what they are told, and they are unable to draw firm and consistent lines to defend themselves from demands made on them by, usually, selfish others being unable to defend or protect one's body by setting limits (i.e., the "condom line").

Selfish individuals attract and are attracted by selfless ones, where the norm of negative complementarity ("You are weak and I am strong; I am OK, you are not") determines inequality of importance between partners and between parents and children. Selfishness and Selflessness imply relationships marked by manipulation, competitiveness, coercion, conflictful reactivity, and immediate negative rebuttals—tactics designed to diminish the importance of either the self or the other. The most frequent interpersonal style for both Selfishness and Selflessness is *RR*.

4. *No-self* is shown interpersonally in the "I lose, you lose, we both lose" position, where no importance is attributed to either self or other ("Neither one of us is important"). The intrapersonal basis for this propensity is an attitude of "I don't know anything and neither do you." Selfishness and Selflessness are intermediate in their extent of dysfunctionality. The No-self propensity is highly dysfunctional and is basic to the development of most extreme psychopathologies. It is characterized by physical, verbal, and sexual abuse, on one hand, and by apathy and neglect, on the other. Both coexist, often contradictorily, in the *AA* style (Chapter 10).

No-self individuals are socialized to defeat themselves and others. They produce perhaps the greatest number of failures for therapists who use the spoken word as a means of communication. An individual with this propensity tends to marry someone who matches the same level of abuse and apathy; that is, the apathetic, overdependent individual tends to marry the abuser, as in incestuous and battered families. The level of stress in these families is so prolonged and intense that either they seem impervious to it or they tend to break down continually—once a week or more often—through uproars and upheavals.

Competence in the ability to love and to negotiate is produced by modeling parental figures or caretakers who exemplify these abilities to the point that Selful parents or partners will tend to produce Selful children. Parents characterized by Selfishness/Selflessness will tend to produce reactive children because the relationship of these parents will be based on repetitive reactivity, manipulation, and a great deal of conflict. The children will tend to repeat these behaviors in their adult relationships. By the same token, parents characterized as No-self will tend to produce children who will show a mixture of abusive and neglectful behavior—the most frequent and prominent style common to No-self individuals and couples.

The causal antecedents in the sense of importance arise and develop mainly from three interdependent dyads:

1. The marital dyad (i.e., how parents relate to each other as partners).
2. The parent–child dyad (i.e., how parents and children get along with each other).
3. The siblings dyad (how siblings deal with each other as a function of dyads 1 and 2).

Functional personality develops from intact and conductive (CC) marital and parent–child relationships. Criminal and pathological behavior develops from impaired, incomplete, and dysfunctional marital and parent–child relationships (either RR or AA). The basic issue here is how to determine the relation between family type and individual dysfunction, as discussed at length in Chapter 6.

The propensities of Selfulness, Selflessness, Selfishness, and No-self define the boundaries of a domain that includes personality as being contiguous and continuous with criminalities and psychopathologies. As represented in the rhomboid figure repeated throughout this work (Figures 1.4 through 1.9), the major orthogonal dimensions of this model are:

- *Vertical:* Extreme competence in the top center quadrant (Selfulness) and extreme incompetence in the bottom center quadrant (No-self).
- *Horizontal:* Externalization in the left middle quadrant (Selfishness) and internalization in the right middle quadrant (Selflessness).

The vertical dimension of competence can be broken down according to three levels of functionality within each quadrant: (a) creative, (b) intermediate, and (c) adequate. When the additional criterion of *setting competence* is introduced, a creatively competent individual would be defined as functioning extremely well in home, school/work, and leisure settings. For instance, a creative individual may be not only a top-notch partner, parent, or child, as acknowledged by the other partner and other children, but also a top-notch student or employee, as acknowledged by teachers, peers, coworkers, or employers, in addition to being well versed in leisure-time activities. This level of functioning requires balancing all three settings without letting any one setting pay for the importance of the other two. An individual defined as intermediate in competence may function extremely well in one setting but only satisfactorily in the other two. An adequate individual may function satisfactorily in one setting and just appropriately in the other two.

Levels of competence in the Selfishness and Selflessness quadrants depend on, from top to bottom:

- *Occasional conflict* either within the self (i.e., intrapsychic) or with another (i.e., interpersonal), or both, in home, school/work, or leisure settings.
- *Chronic conflict* either within the self or with another, or both, in two of three settings.
- *Intense conflict* within both the self and another, in more than one setting.

In the No-self quadrant, there is little if any competence. Dysfunctionality, ranging from borderline to serious/extreme, is found in all three settings.

As shown in the illustrations, the four propensities furnish the basis of healthy or unhealthy, functional or dysfunctional socialization. Because of these propensities, selful and selfish individuals would show the least change as a result of interventions, but for different reasons. Selful individuals would be less likely to improve on their functionality; selfish individuals would be unwilling or unable to consider and confront corrective feedback, whether psychotherapeutic or otherwise. By the same token, selfless and no-self individuals would improve the most as a result of interventions because they need them, want them, and can profit from them the most. However, it is important to distinguish among levels and types of Selflessness and No-self as well as types of interventions (Chapters 12 and 13).

Selfhood and Gender Differences

This model predicts equal gender ratios for both Selfulness and No-self, but reverse ratios in Selfishness and Selflessness. Many men (at least 25% of the population) in our American culture are socialized for Selfishness. Many women (at least 25% of the population) are socialized for Selflessness. Thus, more men than women would be characterized by Selfishness, and more women than men would be characterized by Selflessness. On the basis of these gender differences, the model can be expanded to psychopathology and criminality. Extremes in Selflessness are represented by affective disorders; suicide is the most extreme expression of denial of self-importance. More women than men are diagnosed with affective disorders. More crimes are committed by men than women, and the ratio of incarcerated male felons to female felons is largely weighted for men. If there is crime in Selflessness, it is usually because the woman wanted to accommodate and comply with her criminal partner. There would be equal ratios of men and women in No-self, depending on what criterion is used. This topic is discussed further in Part Two.

Basic to a definition and differentiation of love is the distinction among three *stages* or *sieves* in the development of love relationships. They relate to the three levels of interpretation mentioned earlier:

1. *Falling in love:* a romantic attraction, an insufficient but possibly necessary condition *at the presentational level.*
2. *Being in love:* knowing someone at more than the superficial or facade level; progressing to the *phenotypical level,* where the public mask is taken away and knowledge is based on behavior in a close, prolonged, and committed relationship.
3. *Staying in love:* being in love with the "inside" of an individual *at the genotypical level,* as summarized in Table 1.2.

Historical, developmental, and situational factors are just as relevant. For instance, it would be difficult for anyone who has not experienced intimacy in one's family of origin to replicate that experience in the family of procreation.

These three sieves require different skills and increasingly more demanding responsibilities. Because of this progression of demands, each sieve has its share of inevitable fatalities. Couples fall along the wayside as they progress

TABLE 1.2 Levels of Personality Functioning and Successive Sieves in the Development of Loving Relationships

Levels of Personality Functioning		
Presentational: Falling in Love	Phenotypical: Being in Love	Genotypical: Staying in Love
Sexual attraction and passion; romantic attraction, infatuation, dreams and fantasies	Fulfillment of earlier requirements plus similarity or commonality of values, interests, and activities; realistic validation	Fulfillment of earlier requirements plus: Commitment, Equality (Selfulness), Reciprocity, Intimacy

from one sieve to another. Even when they reach the third sieve, they are not secure, as our divorce rates attest. The number of people who fall in love every day far exceeds the number of those who are in love. By the same token, only a few of those who are in love stay in love, suggesting that the skills necessary for one sieve are not sufficient for the next sieve. Singer (1987) has suggested such differentiation, elaborating on Grant's (1976) theory of falling in love as a romantic attraction or a sexual attraction, or both. Falling in love may be necessary to start a relationship, but it will not sustain it for the long haul (Branden, 1980; Fine, 1985; Person, 1988; Pope & associates, 1980). Falling in love implies a process of gratification and enjoyment of sexual needs or of fantasies, with a minimum of demands, responsibilities, or requirements. However, neither romantic nor sexual passions alone can support the survival and continuation of a relationship.

To progress from falling in love to being in love may mean retaining the presence of either or both initial factors (sexual attraction and infatuation/idealization), plus common interests, activities, realities, and responsibilities that go beyond the immediate gratification of fantasies or passions. What is suggested here is a continuum ranging from fantasies of passion and infatuation to the realities and responsibilities of everyday life, the mundane and inevitable, as epitomized by what is found in a baby's diaper. Staying in love, in addition to the preceding conditions, requires concern for and interest in the other person's well-being, a factor requiring empathy and self-disclosure, which, concretely, consists of sharing hurts and fears of being hurt, and crying together (intimacy). Joys cannot be shared fully unless there is also a sharing of past and present hurts and of fears of being hurt.

Critical *appraisal* of self and other may be required to move from one sieve to another. This appraisal may be totally absent when falling in love, but it becomes necessary when proceeding from being in love to staying in love and having a successful marriage. A marriage may, however, take place at any point along the continuum defined by these three sieves.

Falling in love, being in love, and staying in love are closely related to how one can preserve or let go of self-boundaries and barriers in a merging of selves, defined as the coming together of two persons to make up another entity, the relationship. Sharing the self may mean giving up the self, especially if individuals subscribe to erroneously romantic or religious fantasies in which each wants to make the other "happy." Eventually, this kind of sharing may mean giving up the self, resulting in symbiotically destructive diffusions, enmeshments, fusions, and confusions, as projective identifications. This process is shown simplistically by abandoning the pronoun *I* and overusing the pronoun *you* (Chapter 13).

The fusion of two selves produces self- and other-defeating overdependencies and counterdependencies—vacillations and waverings between unresolvable dependencies, on the one hand, and denials of dependencies, on the other hand. Only among perhaps 10% of the married population can both partners maintain self-boundaries and limits that allow the self to survive without relying unduly on another for survival. Only under conditions of self-preservation can interdependence take place. Interdependence between partners can take place within the context of spheres of autonomy that allow each of the partners to be a separate human being. There are regions of the self that are left to oneself. Some regions of the self are shared, and other regions of the self are given up. Essentially, this is the issue that Horner (1978) defined as achieving intimacy with another person while retaining one's identity—being together without losing oneself. This ability implies being separate and being together at the same time. Thus, survival of a loving relationship requires an equality of respect and a reciprocal bestowal of value. By acknowledging the principle of the Golden Rule, this reciprocity then becomes fundamental to the exchange of both positive and negative feelings. It is the basis for the achievement of intimacy.

The three modalities of presence, performance, and production can be applied to functionalities and dysfunctionalities in sex and sexuality. For instance, functional sex and sexuality require presence—importance and intimacy (i.e., sharing of sexual anxieties and fears deriving from past events and traumas)—as well as performance *as an act of love* rather than another notch in one's sexual repertoire. Performance alone, without presence, becomes a physical act of sex for the sake of sex, void of intimacy, as in one-night stands or promiscuity (services). Substitute sex can be obtained through pornography (information). Sex can be based on production, buying of sexual paraphernalia (goods), or prostitution (money). Various paraphilias can be understood as extremes in sexual performance or production without presence (L'Abate & Hewitt, 1988).

Selfhood, Attraction, and Selection in Marriage

Marriage can take place at any stage, depending on the personalities of the two partners involved. The decision to marry is less dependent on the stage of development in the relationship than on financial conditions, family circumstances, and personalities. Reactively impulsive persons, for instance, may make more immediate and manipulative decisions concerning their marriage. A conductive, selful individual may tend to make this a more contextual decision that considers the well-being of loved ones in the respective families of origin.

Individuals high in Selfulness tend to attract and marry partners who are at the same level of personality differentiation. This integration of similarity and differentness produces positive and constructive (*CC*) relationships with family members. Because of the couple's inherent equality as individuals, they follow the norm of reciprocity. They respect themselves and each other to the point of allowing individuality, differentiation, growth, and creativity in partners and family members. These couples are characterized by cooperative, harmonious, and loving relationships that enjoy a minimum of conflict and a maximum of effective problem solving and negotiation. At best, only 10% to 15% of the total married population can realistically achieve this position, depending on what criterion is used as a measure. Intimacy is possible within the selfulness context of commitment, equality, and reciprocity. It is difficult if not impossible to find it in the other three personality propensities. If present at all in Selfishness and Selflessness, it is occasional and short-lived, showing up at funerals and similar events. It is practically nonexistent in the No-self context.

Selfish individuals (mostly men), who tend to externalize and push limits to get what they want when they want it, will attract and be attracted by Selfless individuals (mostly women), who will make them more important than themselves and will not be able to set limits to defend themselves and their bodies (i.e., the "condom line"). Hence, these couples will produce the greatest frequency of conflict and, eventually, divorce. Persons characterized by No-self will also tend to attract individuals who, in some way, were abused or neglected. The cycle of abuse and neglect is then repeated in their relationship as well as in their offspring.

Selfish and selfless individuals tend to attract and marry each other, according to the norm of negative complementarity. They operate in the relationship from unequal positions—up or down, right or wrong, true or false—and only rarely as equals. Consequently, there is little room for reciprocity and intimacy. Repetitive reactivity is the norm. Stereotypically, in a ratio of four women to one man, selfless individuals have been socialized to define themselves through a "borrowed" or vicarious identity, taking on the status of their mates (as in codependency) or the identity of the Deity or of a patron saint or martyr. These women tend to attract and be attracted by men who have been socialized to behave selfishly in intimate relationships. Depending on what criterion is used, at least 20% (±5%) in our culture are socialized (perhaps by selfless mothers and selfish fathers) to become self-centered and self-indulgent. One indication of this trend is shown by an emphasis on a "pseudo" self based mainly on occupational identity, material success, or work (doing and having) rather than on being. This extreme is a fertile ground for socially sanctioned and condoned addictions, such as smoking or workaholism, and driven Type-A personalities. Complementary and polarized unions of this type (*R*R) yield the normative context (50% of the population) for family relationships. Most offspring drift along on the same level of reactivity as their caretakers, or, in fewer cases, they gravitate positively upward or negatively downward, depending on other life circumstances.

Selfhood and Parental Styles

In line with the terminology used in this model, parental styles can be classified according to a model developed by Baumrind (1980). Selfulness would be characterized by an *authoritative* style (Figure 1.4), where positive, rewarding child-rearing techniques, including parental example, are used more often than punishment (CC). Selfishness would be characterized by an *authoritarian* parental style, where limits are set rigidly, aversively, and negatively. Selflessness would be characterized by a *permissive* style, where limits are not clearly and firmly set for the child to follow. Both the authoritarian and permissive styles are reactive (RR), in the sense that punishments are seen as being more important than rewards and are directly contingent on the child's behavior. (Punishment is administered immediately or not at all.) No-self would be characterized by a *rejecting-neglectful* style (AA), where extreme variations of aversive and punitive techniques are used contradictorily and inconsistently.

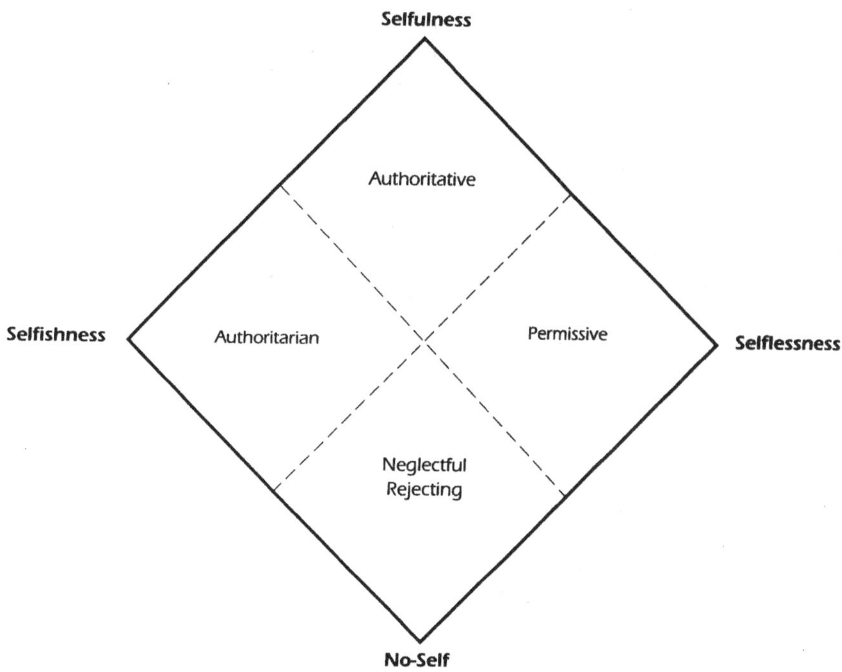

Figure 1.4 Selfhood and Parental Styles (Based on Baumrind, 1980)

Selfhood and Selected Personality Characteristics

Some characteristics associated with personality propensities have been discussed in previous works. This section expands the model to characteristics not considered previously.

Dependency, Trust, and Dominance

If this selfhood model is valid, then a variety of relationships take place within it. For instance, if one considers the interaction of dependency, trust, and dominance (Figure 1.5), when trust is high and dominance is present in both partners, one would predict a relationship based on the acknowledgment and implementation of interdependence (i.e., reciprocity and mutuality). When dominance is high in one partner but low in the other, one dominant partner would deny dependency and the other would be essentially overdependent. When both dominance and trust are low, producing submission and suspiciousness, one would predict contradictory and inconsistent extremes between denial of dependency and overdependency, as occurs in many welfare families or homeless individuals.

From the viewpoint of *dependency,* the selfhood model predicts autonomous interdependence for Selfulness, denial of dependency for Selfishness, and overdependency for Selflessness. In No-self, there is symbiosis or autism/

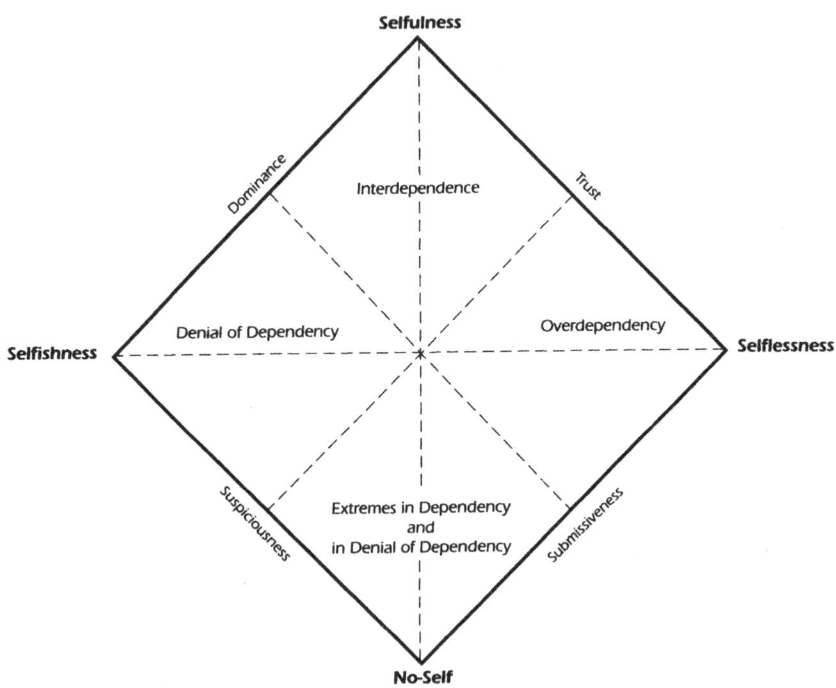

Figure 1.5 Selfhood and Selected Personality Patterns: Dependency, Trust, and Dominance

alienation, or both. Autonomous interdependence produces short-lived and superficial conflict because collaboration and emotional responsiveness are the mainstays in this type of relationship. Denial of dependency is dialectically as well as normatively related to overdependency, where most conflicts will inevitably arise. Ironically, individuals who most intensely deny their dependency—criminals, for example—ultimately become dependent on others or on institutions. In No-self, dependency is so extreme that it loses its normative meaning. Here, terms like symbiosis, autism, and alienation seem more appropriate because hospitalization and continuous care are required.

At the highest level of functioning, interdependence indicates that when two or more people live under the same roof and are related by emotional, legal, or physical bonds and ties, they need to depend on each other in a reciprocal fashion. Synergistic mutuality and reciprocity are present. To obtain such a result, all parties involved in the interaction learn to mediate, modulate, and modify their approach-avoidance and discharge-delay functions to mesh with the same functions in intimate others. Without an agreed-on balance in both functions, there could be no order, continuity, and collaboration. At this level, the conductive-creative (CC) style would be present and functioning.

At an intermediate level of dependency, either denial or overdependency would be producing or being produced by the inability to balance, negotiate, and mediate approach-avoidance and discharge-delay tendencies. Where one would tend to approach, the other would tend to avoid. Where one would tend to discharge, the other would tend to delay. Hence, neither party to the interaction would be able to achieve satisfaction for her or his dependency. Although one may value wanting to be dependent by taking care of the other, the other may not value such a dependency and may view the offered care as a form of control and imposition. The *R*R style would be likely to take place at this level of dependency.

The lowest level of extreme dependency would result in symbiosis, and extreme denial of dependency would result in autism and alienation. Both conditions are seen in extremes, as when a batterer murders the partner who wants to leave the relationship. Physical violence, verbal attacks, and sexual abuse would be more frequent, if not commonplace (AA).

Consequently, the three styles in intimate relationships achieve further elaboration when both approach-avoidance and discharge-delay functions are balanced or unbalanced. Autonomous interdependence is seen in functional relationships where these tendencies are balanced. Conflicts in the denial of dependency and overdependency are relevant to an intermediate level of dependency. Extreme dependency or isolation is seen in symbiotic relationships. Extreme alienation is seen in people who are either unable to live with anyone else or can live only with people similar in their *A*A relationship style.

Selfhood and Impression Management

Self-presentation or impression management varies as a function of personality propensities. For instance, a selful individual tends to make a congruent impression that is appropriate to the situation at hand. A selfish individual may want to make a good impression publicly in front of authorities or in short-lived superficial relationships ("See what a nice guy I am?"). What counts is how this individual functions and performs in prolonged and stressful intimate relationships, where the external facade eventually wears down and the person reverts to type. By the same token, the selfless individual tends to present a "poor me" facade as a victim or as a martyr, putting himself or herself down before others do. In the No-self propensity, the person goes to extremes: making the very best impression in public (as some criminals tend to do in court) or the very worst impression in public and in private (Figure 1.6).

Selfhood and the Five-Factor Model (FFM)

As reviewed in the next chapter, the "Big Five" model of personality (Costa & Widiger, 1994) has recently received a great deal of attention and research support. Hence, it would be useful to show how the selfhood model, which is interactive rather than static, and observable rather than inferred from self-report paper-and-pencil tests, could encompass the five dimensions representing the model: (a) agreeableness, (b) conscientiousness, (c) extraversion, (d) neuroticism, and (e) openness. For instance, selful individuals would be characterized by low neuroticism, high openness, and high conscientiousness. Selfish individuals may be characterized by some openness, high extraversion,

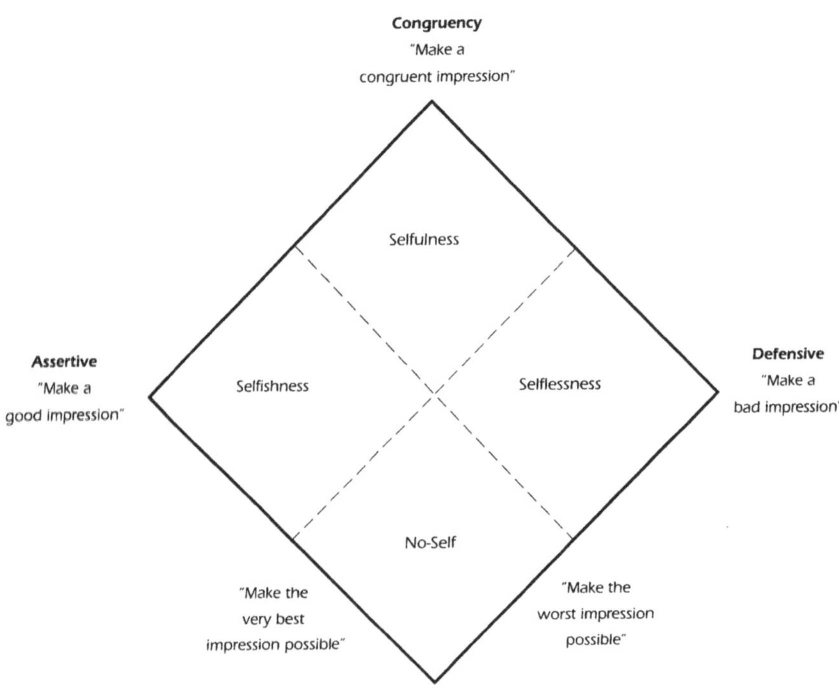

Figure 1.6 Selfhood and Impression Management

low agreeableness, and low conscientiousness. Selfless individuals may be characterized by high conscientiousness, low extraversion, high agreeableness, and low openness. In the No-self propensity, one would predict high neuroticism as well as low conscientiousness in some cases and low openness in others. As discussed in the next chapter, instruments are available to test these predicted relationships (Figure 1.7).

Personality Propensities, Psychopathology, and Internalization/Externalization

The relationships between functionality and dysfunctionality have already been examined. What needs to be stressed here is the direction of intermediate functionality in Selfishness and Selflessness. In the former, one would expect and predict disorders of externalization, which in the extreme would become criminalities (Chapter 8). The terms *secure, dismissing, preoccupied,* and *fearful* (Bartholomew, 1990; Bartholomew & Horowitz, 1991) (Figure 1.8) refer to a model of attachment to be described in Chapter 6. In Selflessness, one would expect and predict disorders of internalization, which in the extreme would become affective disorders. The No-self propensity would be characterized by both externalization and internalization, either coexisting or

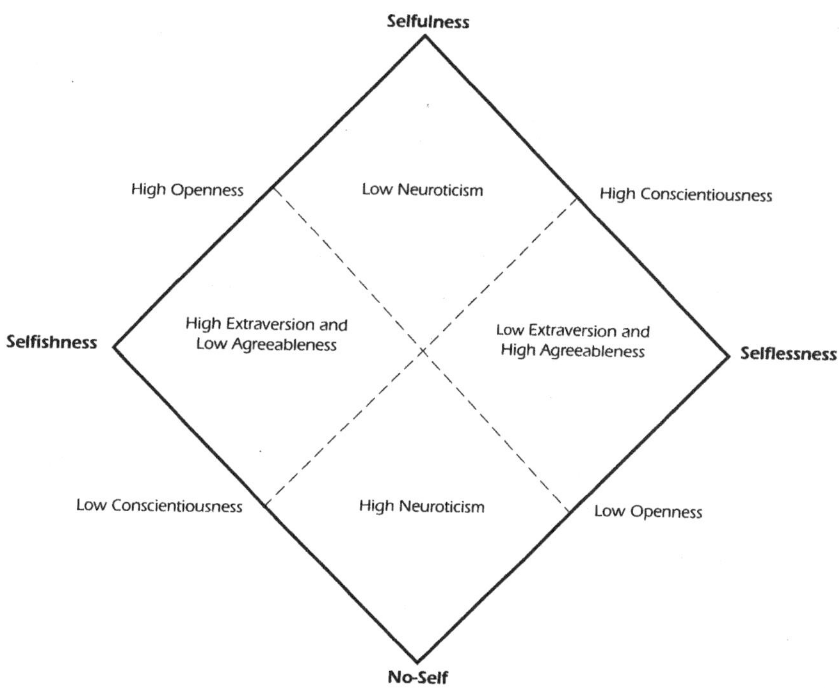

Figure 1.7 Self-Definition and the Five-Factor Model

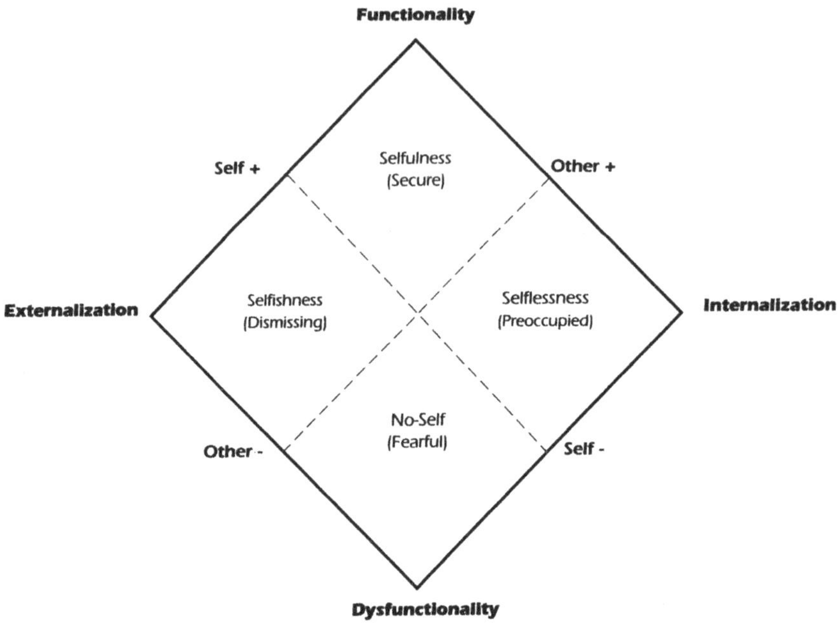

Figure 1.8 Personality Propensities, Psychopathology, and Internalization-Externalization

presenting themselves in a mutually exclusive manner, as in bipolar (manic-depressive) behavior (Figure 1.8).

The horizontal dimension of *externalization-internalization* is also characterized by differences in emotional expressiveness and responsiveness. For instance, in Selfulness, emotions are freely articulated and are clearly differentiated from actions; the self takes responsibility for feelings and actions. In Selfishness, anger is primary among the emotions; in Selflessness, sadness is primary. Repetitive emotional reactivity is the mainstay of both propensities, either internalized or externalized. In No-self, an extremely limited emotional repertoire is composed of primitive feelings, with inadequate emotional awareness. As a result, short-circuiting of feelings will produce contradictory extremes: explosive abuse on one hand, or complete avoidance and withdrawal on the other. Resistance to external feedback is the mainstay of this propensity. Internal feedback is usually extreme (either too much or too little) and very inaccurate or distorted.

A Selfhood Model of Personality, Criminality, and Psychopathology

If all of the relationships among personality propensities described above are valid, then one obtains a model of selfhood, where Selfulness is characterized by problem solving, negotiation, personal power, and agency on one hand, and closeness, unconditional love, presence, and communion on the other. Selfishness is characterized by acting out, and Selflessness by acting in. No-self is characterized by alienation, on one hand, and extreme dependencies produced by both personal and interpersonal ineffectiveness on the other (Figure 1.9). Extremes in Selfishness would overlap with No-self psychopathology, as is common in murder cases, and extremes in Selflessness overlapping with No-self psychopathology would lead to suicide.

Love for the Long Haul: Staying in Love and Intimacy

Intimacy, the second resource class, yielded an early model defined by four processes: (a) seeing the good; (b) physical, practical, and financial caring; (c) forgiveness; and (d) sharing joys and hurts. Intimacy was and is still defined as the sharing of joys, hurts, and fears of being hurt. The ability to love for the long haul—being present without demands for perfection, performance, production, or problem solving—is related to the attribution of importance and to the ability to share joys, hurts, or fears of being hurt. Both resources lead to committed, close, and prolonged relationships.

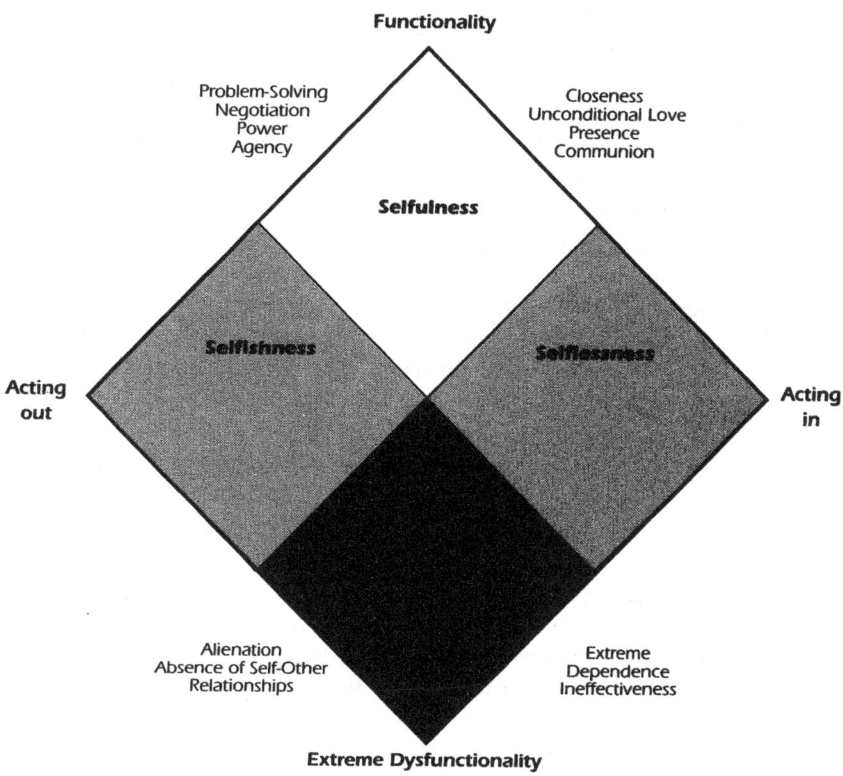

Figure 1.9 A Selfhood Model of Personality, Criminality, and Psychopathology

Being is not negotiable. Attributions of importance to self and other, and emotions, are based on how one feels subjectively. What is chosen to attribute and to affirm to ourselves and our loved ones is based on feelings—how self and others are perceived. These feelings are not negotiable. Both feelings and attributions of importance can be shared when they are expressed positively. Skills necessary for being, as defined by *presence,* require being available emotionally to oneself and to selected others in the time of need (i.e., when either or both are hurting, stressed, or traumatized).

Seeing the good is a cognitive process, a choice that allows valuing self and loved ones. As long as the perceived good overshadows the perceived bad, love is everlasting and unconditional. The process stresses the good, minimizes the bad, and considers the latter as evidence of the imperfection that is a natural characteristic of being human. The idealization of the beloved is an extreme example. Once the balance tips in favor of bad over good, love may become either conditional or withdrawn, culminating eventually in divorce (Gottman, 1994).

Caring includes all the physical acts one performs to show commitment and to ensure the well-being of self and of loved ones. It ranges from making a living to cooking, cleaning, doing chores, and taking care of family members when they are sick. Caring shows in delicate lovemaking, in surprises for birthdays or special occasions, as well as in performance of routine and mundane tasks that are, in the long run, important for smooth family living. Caring is the physical expression of seeing the good.

Forgiveness, in spite of its obviously theological connotation, represents an acceptance of and a tolerance for errors in the self and in loved ones wherein one acknowledges the essentially imperfect nature of human beings. Forgiveness is necessary for unconditional love. It allows one to avoid trying to be perfect or expecting loved ones to be perfect. It is a necessary (albeit insufficient) ingredient of family relations. Its absence, for whatever reason, leads to gunny-sacking, blaming, hurt-collections, tensions, and conflicts. Without forgiveness, all previous errors and traumas are catalogued and preserved so that they can be used against one another. Its absence produces a reactive self- and other-defeating pattern that makes family members simultaneously distant and dependent on each other, because the locus of responsibility is externalized from the self ("It's all your fault!"). This pattern of reactivity is especially evident in couples characterized by Selfishness and Selflessness and the *R*R style.

Being and presence (the skill expressing being) are not for sale or up for bidding and bargaining. When they become commodities to be traded on the open market of the family, they lose their inherent qualities of being freely given and freely shared, as in unconditional love. Both resources constitute the developmental bases for close relationships. The most important and vital of all attachments, the one that defuses and decreases stress, is intimacy—being emotionally available to self and other. The disclosure of these feelings takes place mainly within a context of commitment, equality, and reciprocity. Intimacy means acknowledging one's fallibility, vulnerability, and neediness, and using the "I" pronoun to disclose inner hurts to loved ones.

It takes a strong, selful person to admit what may appear as weaknesses. People who perceive themselves as weak, selfish, selfless, or no-self cannot allow themselves to admit weakness because their admission might be seized on and used against them. They have not experienced it in their families of origin. Hence, intimacy takes place mainly in functional (approximately 25% to 30% of the total population, at best), not in dysfunctional relationships. Unconditional love and a consistent attribution of importance are needed to become intimate with someone. Relationships that cannot share love or attribute importance to one another find it extremely difficult to experience intimacy, and they become dysfunctional.

Physical and interpersonal space between and among family members is the outcome of how importance and intimacy are expressed and shared. Both resources are based on feelings and emotions. Ideally, they should be independent, not controlled or limited by rationally constituted schemes. The former are the bases of emotional attachments that lead to intimacy. Rationally constituted schemes are the bases for negotiation and problem solving, as discussed below.

Without being, and the effects of seeing the good, caring, and forgiveness, it is extremely unlikely that a family can become intimate, sharing individual and family joys as well as hurts and fears of being hurt. Relationships that cannot be intimate overrely on the temporal past or the future rather than on the present. They may be physically close but emotionally distant. People who cry together to share their hurts, when appropriate, represent the ultimate level of intimacy and closeness and the most functional way of withstanding and coping with stress.

Because of the socialization practices mentioned earlier, however, men socialized for Selfishness cannot cry and cannot get in touch with their partners' pain and grief ("Strong men don't cry!"). Their partners, by the same token, may externalize blame onto them for whatever stress or trauma has taken place. A great many people go to great lengths to avoid prolonged intimacy.

Intimacy, then, becomes the basic ingredient for immunization from stress, personal and interpersonal breakdown, trauma, and depression. Those who have not experienced intimacy avoid it because they see it as threatening and therefore dangerous. Individuals who cannot be emotionally intimate make contact with each other through sporadic and sudden ambushes, uproars, upsets, and conflicts over doing and having. They cannot share being with each other because their major orientation to life is one of performance (or the lack of it) or production (or the lack of it). Being, therefore, means being emotionally available to oneself and to loved ones *when the chips are down,* with no demands for performance, production, perfection, or problem solving. If one is unable to feel hurts, it will be very difficult to recognize and share the hurts of others, or to share joys.

A more recent version of the model of intimacy (Figure 1.10) recognizes three prerequisites for intimacy:

1. Commitment to the importance of the relationship.
2. Equality of importance but complementarity of functions.
3. Reciprocity and mutuality in dealing with each other.

From these three requirements flow six self-explanatory processes that produce a positive, upward spiral of growth in the relationship: (a) communicating personal values; (b) respecting personal feelings; (c) accepting personal limitations; (d) affirming respective potentialities; (e) sharing of hurts and fears of being hurt; and (f) forgiving errors.

Intimacy, defined here as the sharing of joys, hurts, and fears of being hurt, is the antidote for depression and many other unpleasant consequences of stress and trauma, as discussed in Chapter 4. Love and hurt are intrinsically intertwined because, through the sharing of hurts, one knows whether one is loved. For instance, parents ache (even fall apart) when they see their children get hurt physically. Some individuals can feel this hurt for their children but cannot feel it for their partners; others can feel it for their partners but not for themselves. Some people can feel hurt for themselves but not for others. From the intertwining of love and hurt, three paradoxes result. Their seemingly contradictory nature makes the attainment of intimacy extremely difficult.

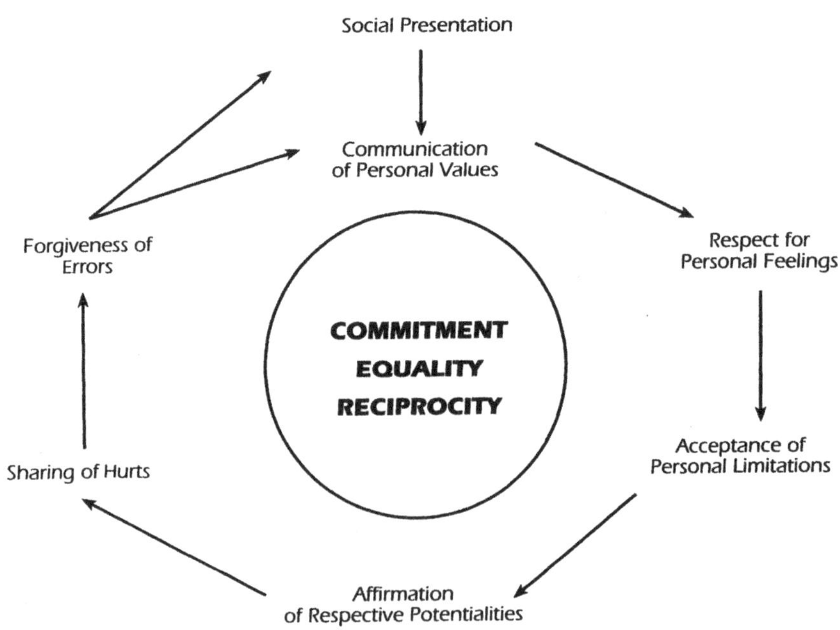

Figure 1.10 The Spiral of Intimacy: A Theoretical Model

1. We only hurt the ones we love because loving gives lovers the freedom to hurt. Negative words or acts from strangers do not hurt. We hurt if someone we love says or does something negative that affects us.
2. We need to comfort and receive comfort from the very persons whom we have hurt or who have hurt us. No one else can comfort us, because no other presence means as much to us as those we love, who love us in return.
3. We need to be separate in order to be together. Only selful individuals, who are autonomously interdependent, can be separate. Being separate and selful allows coming and being together and sharing whatever good or bad comes down the pike.

The first paradox means that love implies giving to and receiving from a loved one a reciprocal power to hurt. Power to hurt is not given to everybody. It is shared only with loved ones who love us in return. There cannot be hurt in seeing a stranger hit by a car, even though there may be shock and sorrow. The body "knows" when a loved one is hurting, physically or emotionally. What makes intimacy difficult to achieve, however, is the need to give comfort to or seek comfort from the very loved ones who have been hurt or have hurt us in return. This position is epitomized by the contradiction of a parent who consoles a child for the pain inflicted from the parent's spanking.

Ultimately, the sharing of hurts in appropriate and enhancing ways represents the ability to be separate and together at the same time. One needs to be strong enough to join another in sharing hurt. However, one needs to be separate enough to be available to the other, without demands for solutions, perfection, performance, or production. Unconditional love is demonstrated by the ability to be available—to just be there to share or to cry together. Crying together is the ultimate demonstration of sharing hurts. Many dysfunctional individuals do not have sufficient or appropriate resources (sense of self-importance, ability to be intimate) to reach this level of sharing. As a result, their children are unable to experience closeness with loved ones. How can they experience closeness or intimacy if they have never seen it in their families of origin? Why are some individuals able to cope while others are broken, even destroyed by stressful events? Without an individual differences approach, one cannot make valid predictions. Once differences in style, resources, personality propensities, and priorities are understood, it will be easier to predict accurately the responses to stress.

Intimacy, when defined as the sharing of joys as well as hurts and fears of being hurt, is mainly present in Selfulness. It is sporadic and short-lived in Selfishness and Selflessness, and it is absent in No-self. It takes fairly mature, selful individuals to share joys and sorrows congruently. Only strong individuals can admit to being "weak," because "weak" individuals find it difficult to admit their vulnerability. This sharing takes place without the need to negotiate anything. It is freely given and freely taken. In selfish and selfless individuals, intimacy is confused with issues of power. Hence, it becomes impossible to share joys or sorrows when the tendency to do or to have is more important than being with someone who hurts. In No-self, issues of love are so confused that it is virtually impossible to be intimate.

Once love is defined as attribution of importance to oneself and to another, intimacy becomes part of the self-disclosure and sharing of pleasurable and painful experiences and events in one's life. Hence, one cannot separate the process of intimacy formation and attainment from one's attribution of importance to self and other. Selful individuals are more self-disclosing and able to be intimate in their relationships with their partners. They are able to communicate their inner values, anxieties, and "hidden" secrets, respecting their feelings as well as those of their partners, accepting personal and marital limitations as inevitable aspects of the human condition, affirming positive potentials in themselves and their partners, sharing appropriately and constructively personal and interpersonal hurts as well as joys, and, finally, forgiving errors. Selfish and selfless individuals allow themselves to be intimate at funerals or whenever there is an important loss in their lives, but at no other times. No-self individuals find it difficult, if not impossible, to be intimate with anybody, including themselves and their partners.

The existential implications of defining intimacy as the sharing of joys, hurts, and fears of being hurt lead to three inevitable, ultimate, bottom-line considerations about the human condition:

1. We are all *vulnerable* to being hurt by those we love, who love us.
2. We are all *fallible* in making judgments and hurting (without meaning to do it!) those we love, who love us (Dahlstrom, 1993; Gilovich, 1991).
3. We are all *needy* in wanting comfort from the very ones we have hurt, and they are *needy* of our comfort if we hurt them.

SETTINGS

A feature of this theory, in addition to its relationality, is a requirement of contextuality. The two orthogonal competencies in the ability to love and the ability to negotiate are functions of three major settings: (a) home, (b) school/work (these are relatively homogeneous), and (c) surplus discretionary leisure-time activities (usually heterogeneous). Leisure time is devoted to: immediate survival needs, such as grocery shopping; delayed survival needs, such as having clothing and furniture; and enjoyable activities, such as enrichment and enlightenment, found in churches, gyms, movies, tennis courts, theaters, hobbies, and so on. These activities are subdivided into transitory and transit settings. Transitory includes all settings necessary for material, spiritual, and aesthetic survival (shops, churches, grocery stores, shopping malls, barbershops or beauty salons, bars, and entertainment venues). Transit includes all settings that are necessary to go from one setting to another (cars, garages, airports, buses, airplanes, hotels, roads and highways, streets, trains, motels, and service stations).

Home

This setting has task requirements that are related to the maintenance of a family as an emotional unit and a home as a physical entity. Most of the responsibilities can be related to four specific roles: (a) caretaker, (b) provider, (c) partner, and (d) parent. Each role demands specific skills. For instance, the responsibilities of the *caretaker* role involve *nurturant* qualities that deal with love (being present and emotionally available), and *instrumental* qualities that deal with the physical and material well-being of the home (cooking, cleaning, purchasing, repairing, and so on). The role of *provider* deals with the economic aspects of family living. Salary, income, credit rating, and mortgage payments are responsibilities of this role. How much money comes into the home and how is it spent? Success in both the caretaker and the provider role is closely connected to the kind of person one is. How well one functions as a *partner* depends on a variety of personality competencies summarized in the selfhood model. In this role, the abilities to love and to negotiate are necessary. The fourth role—*parent*—is probably one of the most difficult and demanding. Most parents have had little if any training in this role, beyond what they learned from watching their own parents. Their parents' errors are perpetuated and their achievements are possibly forgotten because task requirements of today are different from those of any preceding generation. The ability to love and the ability to negotiate become crucial in the parent role. Consequently, an appropriate developmental sequence requires the development of personhood as the basis for partnership. Being able to be a partner is basic to being a parent. Unfortunately, very few parents are lucky enough to follow such an orderly sequence (White, 1991).

School/Work

This setting requires two separate but intertwined sets of skills. The first set consists of specific educational and/or occupational skills that are necessary to perform a job, such as filing, typing, drawing, writing, ditch digging, or managing. The second set of skills consists of extra-job interpersonal skills in getting along with peers, teachers, coworkers, authority figures, clients, or customers. This set of skills may require interpersonal sensitivity, political gamesmanship, and contextual awareness, none of which stems from the substantive job skills necessary for success. Yet these relationship skills may make the difference between promotion or stagnation on the job!

In our Western culture, many people, especially men, identify themselves according to their occupational roles. This role often provides the main source of gratification and therefore may require an investment of energy that diminishes the worker's other roles. Identification by what one *does* or what one *has,* instead of who one *is* as a person, can be dangerous. What happens when one loses his or her job or retires? Is there any self left? How does this role (unemployed or retired) interfere with other roles?

Other Settings

Some skills are neither home- nor work-related. Because they make fewer demands and have fewer requirements, these skills may be considered more discretionary than obligatory.

Leisure Settings

Leisure activity may take place at home, and/or in other settings. It may take place in the company of others, but it can also be solitary; active or sedentary; enjoyed indoors or outdoors; oriented toward people or dependent on apparatus, venue, or personal talent. Working in one's basement on a hobby, participating in the Elks Club, watching TV, going to church, or running a marathon—all are examples of activities in leisure settings. Leisure activities are important for one's enjoyment of life and for personality development. They are an integral part of how we function as individuals, and they specify the value we put on friends and relationships. Leisure settings require skills that are specific to the activity being performed in a particular setting as well as skills to develop and maintain relationships that are formed within each setting.

Transitory Settings

These temporary settings vary in importance from one person to another. Purchasing goods and services, shopping in a mall, going to a beauty salon, or attending a bar may require different amounts of time and energy, depending on how important one considers that activity. Purchasing geniuses may spend a great deal of time plotting how to use coupons to get better bargains, or comparing costs for the same merchandise sold in different stores. Getting the oil changed at the local garage, waiting in an unemployment line, completing the requirements for automobile registration, buying a bottle of aspirin—each activity takes us to a different setting, and each setting has peculiar role demands and codes. Transitory settings may seem less important than other settings, but the ability to perform well in these settings allows survival in the most important setting, the home.

Transit Settings

These settings gained importance when we achieved the capacity to travel long distances in relatively short periods of time. Transit settings include highways, cars, airports, airplanes, terminals, buses, trains, ships, and boats. As perceptions about distance and travel time change, time allotment and activities assigned to these settings may take on their own identity. For instance, increased commuting time requires the acquisition of the skills needed to commute daily and make the best of it. Ease of commuting between settings may also increase the chance of overlap among settings. For instance, having an office in one's home may reduce commuting time. However, it may produce conflicts in fulfilling responsibilities one might not be required to fulfill if one's only office is away from home.

This theory stresses a competence–setting interaction. Competence in itself implies a process of exchange, but this exchange cannot be specified unless the setting in which the competence is expressed is also specified. In addition to the family, there is the influence of school/work, where peers/coworkers and superiors/subordinates will affect one's functioning in both the work setting and at home. By the same token, how one functions at home may affect how one functions at school/work and in other settings.

Settings can be classified according to what resources are exchanged. For instance, the home is the appropriate setting for sharing importance and intimacy. In turn, it provides emotional, interpersonal, moral, and intellectual enjoyment as well as survival functions. Hospitals, offices, hotels, and public institutions provide mostly services, thereby attending to physical, legal, and psychological needs. Schools, libraries, media, bookstores, and publishing houses produce and provide information, which satisfies educational and intellectual needs. Industries, shops, agriculture, and mines produce goods for physical needs. Banks and savings and loan associations exchange money to deal with economic and physical needs.

The variability for conduct in these settings is related to how limited and constrained behavior needs to be. For instance, one needs to strap oneself in a car or plane. Specific goods are in prescribed locations in supermarkets. An agenda of tasks must be performed at school/work. The setting where one has the most freedom from public constraints is the home, although some prescribed chores and responsibilities are present. Home is where the greatest variation occurs in behavior and expressions of personality. The home has no external and public limits set by authorities and no barriers controlling behavior. Hence, most murders, rapes, and instances of verbal, physical, and sexual abuse take place in the home, outside of public observation and control.

ABILITY TO NEGOTIATE DOING AND HAVING

Because the ability to negotiate requires different skills, it yields different models. Performance and production are negotiable commodities. Together, these skills represent *power*. Power is negotiable in democratic relationships, where all the members are equally important, though each member may have different functions. In dysfunctional relationships, where members are unable to show and share their love in enhancing ways, power is misused, abused, or unused. Dysfunctionalities take place when families confuse issues of self-importance, presence, love, and intimacy (being) with issues of performance (doing) and production (having). For instance, many couples try to negotiate issues when they are angry at each other, usually with a disastrous outcome.

Functional families can negotiate more effectively and efficiently than dysfunctional families. The former can process and reach an "I win, you win" consensus, which respects the rights of each individual in the family. Dysfunctional families are unable to reach such a consensus. Whatever the conclusion, it is typically based on manipulation and coercion rather than on genuine problem solving. Someone wins at someone else's expense, achieving only a Pyrrhic victory.

To understand and teach families how to negotiate, the following verifiable models have been found helpful. Negotiation takes place according to two sides of the same coin: structure and process. They need to be considered separately, even though they occur concurrently.

The Structure of Negotiation

Under what structure or context does negotiation succeed, fail, or not take place? In families, where most confusion and conflicts are found, at least three overlapping processes need to be distinguished:

1. Authority versus responsibility.
2. Orchestration versus instrumentation.
3. Exchange of resources, that is, doing (information and services) and having (money and goods or possessions).

Authority versus responsibility concerns who makes the decisions or how decisions are reached (authority), and who carries out those decisions (responsibility). For instance, in one clinical family, the father assumed absolute authority in making decisions about every task, which then had to be carried out by his wife and two children. Decisions ranged from what to buy at the supermarket to what TV programs the children should watch (provided they fulfilled their quota of chores). The wife (a daughter of missionaries) followed her husband's orders unquestioningly and uncritically, and required the same kind of blind conformity from the children. Eventually, in adolescence, both children started to rebel by acting out in various ways. The father remained rigid in retaining his authority (with no responsibilities) and demanding complete assumption of responsibilities (without authority) from the rest of the family. No negotiation on any issue was possible under this regime.

Another useful dimension that clarifies and classifies the structure of negotiation relates to the nature of the decisions to be made by the family. A decision might be crucial, such as a move to another city or a chance to take another job. Decisions of this magnitude require orchestration (i.e., planning, organization, and direction). Other decisions might concern everyday matters, such as what to cook for supper ("What shall we eat tonight?"), and would need instrumentation (i.e., quick implementation without too much planning). Who makes these decisions and who carries them out? If one partner decides to take a job in another city without consulting the other partner, how will this partner feel when left to take care of the move, sell the house, pack, and take care of the children?

In decision making, the content of negotiation needs to be considered. Here, the main modalities are doing and having. Who should carry out which chores (services), which TV channel should be watched, or which books should be bought (information)? How much money is available, and which goods should be purchased (or sold)? How clear are the roles to be assumed by family members, and how are such roles assigned or rejected within the family? Without such clarity of structure, it would be impossible for the family to carry out and complete any type of negotiation and problem solving.

The Process of Negotiation

To understand, describe, and teach negotiation to families, the process needs to be divided into three different subprocesses:

1. The degree of functionality or dysfunctionality. (ILL)
2. The skills that identify the level of competence. (SKILL)
3. The motivation of family members, based on their priorities. (WILL)

Specific features of the coping behavior within each subprocess as well as the processes encompassing both functional (successful) and dysfunctional (unsuccessful) outcomes of negotiation must be described in detail. Therefore, we evaluate the process of negotiation in intimate relationships by considering the following.

Degree of Functionality or Dysfunctionality

This is the coping style at the time of negotiation, as evaluated by the relationship *styles* among intimates. If summarized using the ARC model, the range would extend from dysfunctional styles, such as *AA* to *RR*, to functional ones, such as *CC*. A shortened way to designate this component is ILL.

Skills

The process of negotiation describes the level of competence or mastery of negotiation among the negotiators. The ERAAwC model (*E*motionality, *R*ationality, *A*ctivity, *Aw*areness, and *C*ontext) is employed. A shortened way to designate this component is to use the word SKILL for it. Levels of competence-incompetence relate to the ability to bargain, problem-solve, and make decisions. Although the terms may be different, these processes are very much the same, and they follow an unvarying sequence of steps. For example, creative negotiations and problem solving cannot take place unless certain feelings are expressed at the beginning *(E)*. When these feelings are not expressed and shared (nonjudgmentally), negotiation is detoured, derailed, or even destroyed. After this sharing has taken place, if the situation requires problem solving, it can be accomplished through cognitive brainstorming and give-and-take strategies based on realistic rewards and costs *(R)*. From this brainstorming about choices and options, one course of action may emerge as being more preferable than others. This course of action may be put into effect *(A)*, and feedback about its relative rewards and costs *(Aw)* may produce eventual revisions in that course of action. This corrective, change-oriented feedback is based on an awareness of the internal context (how family members feel about the issue) and external realities defining the issue *(C)*.

Motivation and Priorities

Their desire or willingness to negotiate motivates family members to want to come together to solve problems according to their priorities. A shortened way to designate this component is to use the word WILL for it. What is important to oneself forms the basis of a motivation to negotiate. Emphasis on one priority may make other priorities secondary or even irrelevant. One may be relatively functional and skilled. However, if one does not want to negotiate ("You can take a mule to water, but you cannot make it drink!"), no negotiation will take place.

To understand how time and energy are allocated from one setting to another, the concept of priorities needs to be introduced. This concept is motivational in nature. It represents an aggregate of intentions, expectations, goals, and plans that have determined what the individuals wants or feels is important for survival and enjoyment in life. Priorities involve definite choices about what is important or unimportant in one's life. How important is a person, an object, or an activity? How important is oneself in relation to others? Priorities can be *vertical* or *horizontal*. Vertical priorities can be differentiated into the three modalities of being, doing, and having. Personal, familial, and interpersonal priorities are ranked according to the relative importance given to self and to significant others. Vertical priorities are developmental; horizontal priorities are structural and relate to settings (i.e., house, school/work, leisure time). They exist regardless of a person's level of development. One who values doing more than having or being may become a workaholic, stressing the work setting at the expense of the home and leisure settings. One who stresses being present emotionally in the home may consider work and leisure settings secondary to emotional availability. In other words, vertical and horizontal priorities intersect and interact with each other.

How successful one is in any of the settings considered earlier depends a great deal on priorities. If one defines oneself primarily in occupational terms ("I am an engineer") rather than domestically ("I am a husband and a father"), it follows that one may put more energy into work and perhaps be more successful than at home. By the same token, avocational pursuits may overshadow domestic and occupational roles. Modalities and settings need to be balanced so that no one modality or setting is stressed at the expense of the others.

The salience and satisfaction derived from each modality and setting remain an individual prerogative that determines how each modality and setting is ranked in respect to the others. Each can be reduced in importance by increasing the importance of the others. For example, activities in the leisure area can become direct antidotes for the negative effects of stresses at work or at home. How one juggles and counterbalances demands and difficulties to maintain balance in one's life reflects one's priorities. Priorities motivate people to negotiate, with themselves and with significant others, the important issues in their lives. These priorities can be measured easily by time analysis. How much time does one spend in each of the settings? What modality of expression for being, doing, or having is being used in a primary, secondary, and tertiary manner?

Thus, priorities are hierarchical to the extent that one person, a resource, or a setting is made more important than others. For instance, once the functions of approach-avoidance and discharge-delay are combined with the attribution of importance not only to other human beings but also to activities, one obtains a time management matrix similar to the one developed by Covey (1990, p. 151). First are activities deemed important and urgent (discharge necessary) as in crises, pressing problems, and deadline-driven projects. These activities will be approached before other activities, which by necessity, will be avoided and delayed. Second are activities that are deemed important but not urgent, such as planning, networking, recreation, and exploring new opportunities. Third are activities deemed unimportant but urgent: phone calls, bills, mail, reports, appointments, and meetings. Fourth are activities that are neither important nor urgent, as in trivia work, some mail and phone calls, pleasant activities.

In a continuous balancing act, one needs to prioritize every day what is important and what is urgent. Is being emotionally available to oneself and loved ones (presence) more important than succeeding at school/work (performance and production)? Is winning at a tennis game more important than producing more work than one's colleagues? Some people put home before work. Others put leisure-time activities before anything else. Some car owners value their vehicles more than they value their homes, and so on.

Functionality and successful coping with stress in family living imply a process of negotiation with: (a) reliance on a CC rather than an RR or AA style; (b) a flexible balance of component resources, such as *E, R, A,* and *Aw* of internal and external *C*s, and (c) a flexible and life-stage-appropriate ordering of priorities, both intra- (vertical) and extra- (horizontal) familial, with an even ranking of being, doing, and having over the family life cycle. Under these (ideal) conditions, an individual should be able to cope and can withstand stress with a minimum of breakdown.

Less-than-ideal negotiation and coping abilities and skills produce conflicts, symptoms, and somatizations in family members. Dysfunctionality and a relative inability to negotiate and to deal with stress imply: (a) overreliance on repetitive, defeatingly RR or AA styles; (b) exclusive or extreme reliance on one skill to the exclusion of other skills, such as overrelying on *E* at the exclusion of *R,* or overrelying on *A* at the expense of *Aw;* and (c) mixed-up priorities, such as putting work ahead of family or children ahead of the marriage, or one's family of origin ahead of the family of procreation.

This theory affirms that (ideally), for functional relationships to take place, the ranking of priorities should place selfulness first, partnership second, and parenthood third. One stage of development cannot function effectively unless a previous stage has been achieved. This achievement, however, is never fully reached because there is a feedback loop from one stage to another, at least in selful relationships. Partnership provides grounds for reflection and possible change in selfhood. By the same token, parenthood provides grounds for changes in partnership as well as in selfhood.

Consequently, the ability to negotiate is a multiplicative function of ILL × SKILL × WILL. When all three components of this process are positive, there is a synergistic multiplication that allows smooth and effective negotiation and upward change. When any of these three components is inadequate, negative, deviant, or insufficient, the whole process of negotiation tends to become more inefficient, prolonged and conflictful, subtractive, or devisive of importance in the individuals involved.

THE TRANSMISSION OF FUNCTIONAL AND DYSFUNCTIONAL ABILITIES

What are the mechanisms of transmission within intimate relationships? From the two sets of abilities (to love and to negotiate), at least four levels of personal and interpersonal competence are derived:

Level 1. Ability to love and to negotiate—highest possible level of competence.

Level 2. Ability to love but not to negotiate—second-highest level of competence. This level is a toss-up with the next level as far as functionality is concerned.

Level 3. Ability to negotiate but not to love—third-highest level of competence.

Level 4. Inability to love and to negotiate—lowest level of individual, spousal, family, and relational competence.

Levels 2 and 3 may not differ from each other very much because they depend on the personalities of the partners and the nature of their relationship. In dealing with emotional issues, such as death, one's ability to love may take precedence over one's ability to negotiate. By the same token, the ability to negotiate may then become necessary to deal with serious events such as funeral arrangements and settling of the estate. A family may be rich in love and able to share the finality of death and the loss of a loved one. Yet, either before or immediately after the funeral, the same family may be unable to negotiate practical issues such as the division of goods and money.

How modalities of being, doing, and having (and the resources subsumed by them) are used, misused, and abused derives directly from a family's level of individual and collective competence. If the family members are able to differentiate being from doing or having (i.e., presence rather than power) and keep these modalities separate, they will be able to withstand traumas better than families that cannot keep these modalities separate. Thus, attachments and separations are based on: (a) direct observational learning on the receptive side (input); with (b) self-definitions in the attribution of importance transmitted according to a *continuum of likeness* (Chapter 5); (c) imitation and modeling consequences and reinforcements on the expressive side (output); and (d) repeating the role of gender differences and processing of the continuum of likeness in the family, as, for instance, in "Like mother, like daughter" or "Like father, like son."

The transmission of resources in the *sharing of being* is based on the ability to attribute importance to self and/or other in the caretaking role, as seen through caring and commitment. This process requires seeing: (a) the physical frequency and practical expression of love (carrying the bedpan); (b) the good over the bad—a cognitive decision; (c) forgiveness—another cognitive decision; and (d) intimacy in one's family of origin—the sharing of joys, hurts, and fears of being hurt (i.e., learning emotional availability and presence).

The transmission in the ability to negotiate doing and having is automatically (without awareness) achieved through the structure of negotiation in how authority is differentiated from responsibility and how orchestrated versus instrumental decisions about services, information, goods, and money are made. The process of negotiation is transmitted intergenerationally and developmentally, depending on: (a) which *style* is available and used predominantly (the ARC model); (b) what *skills* are available and used (the ERAAwC model); and (c) which priorities are predominant and how much willingness to negotiate is available.

CONCLUSION

From this theory, it is possible to distinguish differences between personality functioning and dysfunctioning. Previous theories viewed personality development as separate or distinct from criminality and psychopathology. This theory indicates how criminality and psychopathology are related, both in continuity and in contiguity, with each other and with personality socialization. Hence, this is a theory of personality socialization, criminality, and psychopathology. From this theory, it might be possible to look at the fields of personality evaluation and psychological interventions, including prevention and psychotherapy, with new lenses. Furthermore, this theory attempts to integrate humanistic and psychodynamic viewpoints with behavioral and contextual positions that were, heretofore, considered independent of, if not antagonistic with, each other, both conceptually and methodologically. These viewpoints are extremes of a continuum of experiencing and expressing that can be integrated at various levels of functioning.

CHAPTER 2

Corroborating the Theory: Independent and Indirect Evidence

> It seems likely that before long there will be no personality psychology that is not interactionist. (Shaver, 1985, p. 13).

> [T]raditional theories are of "self-out-of-relation," or "self-partly-in-relation." (Bergman, 1995, p. 71)

The purpose of this chapter is to review the supportive evidence for the theory summarized in Chapter 1. Because all the literature that is reviewed here relates to the theory itself, reference will be made only to the part of the theory the evidence applies to. As indicated in the Preface, evidence for the validity of this theory has appeared in greater detail in previous publications and will be reviewed only as necessary throughout this work.

The evidence is given under three major headings: (a) *independent* from but conceptually or empirically similar to the theory, with concepts, constructs, and data that bear close resemblance to the constructs of the theory but have different theoretical or empirical bases; (b) *indirectly* related to the theory, with special focus on evidence generated by Resource Exchange Theory; and (c) *directly* related to and derived from the theory itself. The first two categories of evidence are summarized in this chapter. The third category is summarized in Chapter 3.

EVIDENCE INDEPENDENT OF THE THEORY

Evidence implies tangible proof for the validity of an hypothesis or theoretical statement or prediction. Hence, not all support for this theory can be called evidence, especially if it is extremely general and vague—general systems theory, for example. Instead, one must consider specific theories, models, or viewpoints that are conceptually similar to the assumptions, postulates, modalities, and models of this theory. These similarities cannot and will not be considered as proof in and by themselves. The proof in this case would be equivalent to what is called "face validity": apparent similarities, at first blush, support the validity of a theory or hypothesis, even though they are not considered proof. For this reason, independent evidence is divided into viewpoints that bear *conceptual* resemblance to those making up the theory and *empirical* evidence that seems to be supportive of the very same assumptions, postulates, modalities, and models (see Table 1.1).

CONCEPTUAL RESEMBLANCE

In this section, viewpoints that support the metatheoretical foundations of the theory will be reviewed.

Metatheoretical Foundations of the Theory

These foundations pertain to definitions of personality, development, inferred traits versus visible resources, and the ERAAwC and ARC models.

What Is Personality? Selfhood and Relationships

Helson and Mitchell (1978) concluded their review of the field of personality by stating: "Whether we like it or not, personality psychology is the fundamental discipline, because the psyche comes before any of its most specialized activities" (p. 580). In this respect, they prophesied the "merger of normal and pathological in personality" (pp. 578–579), a merger that is attempted in the present theory. Magnusson and Torestad (1993), on the other hand, insisted that:

> [T]here is no personality as such. What exists is a living, active, and purposeful organism, functioning and developing as a total integrated being . . . personality research is herein defined as the study of how and why individuals think, feel, act, and react as they do. (p. 428)
>
> [E]ssential for further progress in personality theory is a general "model of individual functioning in humans" that integrates the individual and environmental phenomena that operate simultaneously to influence psychological functioning. (p. 432)

They added: "Interaction is a fundamental principle in the functioning of open systems. . . . It is central at all levels of individual functioning . . . in a lawful manner" (p. 437). Their "concept of *lawful interaction* includes: *multidetermination, interdependence, reciprocity, nonlinearity, temporality, and integration*" (p. 439). Most of these principles are present in this theory. One might add multifinality—one cause can have a variety of outcomes.

The dual (self–other) nature of personality in context is supported from a variety of sources. Maddi (1993) argued that "psychology is an extremely fragmented discipline" (p. 86) and "the past 20 years have shown a decline in the influence of personality theorizing" (p. 85). Magnusson and Torestad (1993) agreed with him as far as this fragmentation is concerned (p. 431). Among the reasons for the fragmentation, which he called "a Tower of Babel" (p. 90), Maddi focused especially on the person–situation interaction, a "debate" that "ends inconclusively" (p. 87):

> The reason for this is that it is a false debate in the first place. It takes just a bit of thought to realize that behavior could never be exclusively a function of either person or situation variables. (p. 87)
>
> One way to overcome the fragmentation in our field is for psychologists to spend time and imagination considering entire persons in their social milieu. (p. 91)
>
> One reason why the integrative potential of personality theorizing has not been realized is the result of the very fragmentation and divisiveness itself. (p. 94)

Wrightsman (1994) supported Maddi's arguments by concluding that:

> the emphasis among research psychologists [is] on experimental social psychology and narrow-range, more easily operationalized, concepts. . . . Rather, social psychologists usually derive status among their peers by—if I may exaggerate—the extent to which they carry out highly intricate studies dealing with theory-generated variables in artificial laboratory situations. (p. 15)

In a factor analysis of a questionnaire, which Wrightsman (1994) created to measure assumptions about human nature, he found six dimensions, some of which resemble the two assumptions of the theory and the four personality propensities of the selfhood model:

1. Trustworthiness versus untrustworthiness.
2. Strength of will and rationality versus external control and rationality.
3. Altruism versus selfishness.
4. Independence versus conformity to group pressures.
5. Complexity versus simplicity.
6. Similarity versus variability.

The first dimension implies going toward or away from people, according to whether they are trusted or not; similarly, to approach versus to avoid in the assumption of space. The second dimension of control implies discharge versus delay, as in the assumption of time. The third dimension is similar to the selfishness/selflessness propensities. The fourth dimension of independence versus conformity relates to the distinction made among the levels of dependence. They are: overdependence, denial of dependence, and autonomous interdependence. Even though some people, especially adolescents, may aspire toward independence, there is no such condition in human nature. We are all interconnected in one way or another. The issue is to figure out how dependence is related to personality. The other two dimensions found by Wrightsman will be discussed in the next two chapters in terms of a continuum of likeness in personality development.

Thus, developmental competence theory takes a clear position on the side of socialization *from the outside,* through visible resources, rather than just development *from the inside,* including internal, hypothetical, and inferred biological differences, states, and traits. If these biological or internal differences exist, they are important, but they may have been produced by socialization practices external to the individual rather than the other way around, from inside the individual. This, of course, is a controversial issue. Usually, it is resolved by invoking the interaction of both nature and nurture. For once, however, the position of this theory assumes that nurture modifies, modulates, and may even nullify nature. As Emde (1995) noted in his review of Kagan's (1994) work on temperament, which will be considered in greater detail later in this chapter, "behavior genetics studies indicate that environmental influences account for most of the variance of measured temperamental behavior" (p. 1041).

Socialization and Differentiation: The Intensity Dimension

The dual nature of the self-in-relation-with-other is by now an almost accepted view. Among others, Ogilvie and Ashmore (1991) argued for:

> [a] self-with-other representation as a unit of analysis in self concept research. . . . Our self-with-other unit refers to the internalization of past and present interactions that is fully contained in the minds of individuals. They form the foundation of our being in the world of others and provide us with a sense of continuity between past and present interactive experiences. . . . [These experiences included mother, father,] brothers and sisters, and those members of the extended family which were actively involved in the child's life. (p. 289)

Damon (1988) supported a paradoxical interpretation of life in general and of socialization in particular that relates to the three paradoxical derivations of intimacy as sharing of joys, hurts, and fears of being hurt. We need to be separate in order to be together:

> Social development is a life process built upon a paradox. The paradox is that at the same time we are *both* social and individual beings, connected with others in a multitude of ways, as well as ultimately alone in the world. This dual condition of connectedness and separateness begins at the moment of birth and remains with us all through life. . . . In short, we become more social while at the same time becoming more individual and unique. (p. 3)

According to Damon, social development is comprised of two functions. The first is socialization, which includes:

> all of one's tendencies to establish and maintain relations with others, to become an accepted member of society-at-large, to regulate one's behavior

> according to society's codes and standards, and generally get along well with other people . . . the *integrating* function of social development. (p. 3)
>
> The second function of social development is the formation of the individual's personal identity . . . often called *individuation,* [which] includes the development of one's sense of self and the forging of a special place for oneself within the social order. (p. 4)
>
> In some ways, socialization and individuation are quite distinct processes, even at times operating in opposition to each other. Establishing one's individuality very often requires a different sort of activity from that required for "socialized" behavior in the traditional use of the term. Defining one's distinctness from others and staking out one's unique social position sometimes place one in an antagonistic relation to others. Conversely, being "socially acceptable" sometimes means foregoing personal wishes and habits in deference to the expectations of others. (p. 5)

This dual process of socialization and individuation intersects with another dual process of agency and communion, originally proposed by Bakan (1968). The latter duality has been expanded by McAdams (1990) with two themes that view agency as a *power* motive and communion as an *intimacy* motive. Motive, again, implies an internal, intrapsychic process underlying interpersonal behavior. The process is inferred and hypothetical rather than visible. The power motive operates in an ideology of justice; the intimacy motive operates within an ideology of care. Justice relates to strength, impact, action, and status. Care relates to communication of love, friendship, sympathy, and touch.

From these two themes, McAdams developed a taxonomy (i.e., classification) of imagoes that is somewhat reminiscent of the four personality propensities in the selfhood model: Class 2 (high agency and high communion) produces three positive roles: (a) healer (prophet, artist, protector, organizer, and legislator); (b) counselor (arbiter, therapist, teacher, guide, and peacemaker); and (c) humanist (defender of the weak, revolutionary, and evangelist). Class 1 (high agency) produces three roles: (a) ruler (judge, conqueror, seducer, creator, sage, and celebrity); (b) swift traveler (explorer, adventurer, trickster, rabble-rouser, persuader, gambler, entrepreneur); and (c) warrior (fighter, soldier, policeman). Class 3 (high communion) produces three roles: (a) caregiver (altruist, martyr); (b) loyal friend (spouse, helpmate, chum, confidante, sibling, assistant); and (c) lover (charmer, enchanter). Class 4 (low agency and low communion) produces three roles: (a) homemaker (domestic ritualist); (b) wage earner (craftsperson, laborer); and (c) escapist (pleasure seeker, hedonist, player, epicure, child).

The fit and overlap with the four personality propensities are suggestive but not satisfactory because there is no consideration in McAdams's taxonomy of both themes in Class 1 and Class 3 imagoes. What kind of classification would McAdams produce if, in Class 1, high agency were coupled with low communion? By the same token, what would happen in Class 3 if high communion were coupled with low agency? Within Classes 1, 3, and 4, for instance, there are positive as well as negative roles. As a result of this omission, McAdams failed to differentiate between positively constructive and negatively destructive roles.

In spite of these differences, eventually it will be possible to test out how these internal imagoes (derived from the Thematic Apperception Test) relate to personality propensities.

Among others, Napier (1988), in his subjective account of personal struggles to achieve a lasting marital relationship, used two metaphors: one of closeness and distance (pp. 93–114) and one of power and vulnerability (pp. 115–141). It should be stressed that although most self-report, paper-and-pencil personality tests are designed for adult individuals, the model of distance-control presented here applies to the developing child as he or she differentiates the self in growing up. Dimensions basic to circumplex but static models of personality functioning are developmental outgrowths of distance and control. Developmentally, distance eventually becomes visible in the ability to love, cohesiveness, and intimacy; control eventually becomes visible in the ability to negotiate.

THE INTENSITY DIMENSION: THE ARC MODEL

From the outset of this theory (L'Abate, 1976, 1983), a great deal of evidence to support an intensity dimension in personality socialization, as defined by the ARC model, was reviewed. Evidence and support for such a dimension will be reviewed in Chapters 5 and 6. Gottman (1994), however, provided a similar amount of evidence to support the existence of at least three types of relationships in marriages. His typology consisted of: (a) positively validating couples, whose style of relating seems akin to the CC style; (b) volatile and conflict-minimizing couples, even though at the opposite extremes of externalization and internalization, whose modes of relating seem akin to the RR style; and (c) the possibility that, if observed unobtrusively in their homes rather than in the laboratory, a high number of volatile and conflict-minimizing couples would qualify as showing an AA pattern of relating. Gottman's interpretation of his results in terms of the four "cascade" factors that lead to divorce: (a) complaint/criticism; (b) contempt; (c) defensiveness; and (d) stonewalling—indicates a vicious, reactive cycle of abuse/neglect that escalates into defensiveness and stonewalling. These factors can be encompassed by the approach-avoidance and discharge-delay functions of the theory, as discussed in future chapters.

THE DEPTH DIMENSION: LEVELS OF INTERPRETATION

Descriptive Levels

Descriptive levels are divided into presentational and phenotypical.

Presentational Level

Schlenker and Weigold (1992) summarized the research literature on impression regulation and management—how we want to appear to others. They defined impression regulation as "goal-directed activity of controlling information about some object or event, including self (subsuming the concept of self-identification)" (p. 138). Impression management, on the other hand, was defined as: "the activity of regulating information primarily for real or imagined others (subsuming self-presentation)" (p. 138).

> [P]eople do not just passively react to their social environments; they try to structure and influence their environments so as to construct more beneficial, less threatening surroundings. (p. 134)

These reviewers focused on three major processes to account for impression regulation: (a) self-glorification, consisting of self-esteem maintenance and enhancement as well as self-construction and compensation; (b) self-consistency and self-verification theory; and (c) self-authentication—the quest for accuracy. Notice, however, that these reviewers used the generic and vague term "environments" instead of specifying under which circumstances some people employ self-regulation and maintenance processes and some do not. For instance, many self-presentational processes may work in short-lived, superficial social encounters. However, under the stress of prolonged and intimate relationships, these presentational processes will give way to how people behave phenotypically in the privacy of the home underneath the mask of self-presentation.

Clark, Pataki, and Carver (1996), who studied the effects of three emotions—happiness, sadness, and anger—on self-presentation, found that these emotions are used for purposes of strategic self-presentation, as in ingratiation, supplication, intimidation, and self-promotion. Consequently, these studies support the view that self-presentation is an interpersonal process that derives from the impression one wants to convey to others. Banaji and Prentice (1994) concluded their review of self-presentational strategies as part of "the self in social contexts":

> Thus, people differ considerably in how they want to be seen, but they share in common an active pursuit of those desired self-images. (p. 307)
>
> The literature is replete with examples of how behavior serves to verify, protect, and maintain existing conceptions and evaluations of self. (p. 323)

Phenotypical Level

This level is difficult to evaluate because many people hide in the secrecy and privacy of their homes, not allowing anyone to peek into their lives. Hence, this level must be inferred from how people report on it in terms of their roles as persons, partners, parents, and providers. If occasionally we could place a video camera in homes, there would be a danger of family members behaving in different ways when they feel observed and when they do not feel observed. What is relevant here is not only how people behave phenotypically in their homes but how this level relates to other levels. For instance, how one behaves at home can be evaluated by reports of those who live with that person. One may feel he has been a good father. However, this judgment ultimately has to be rendered by his children. By the same token, one is the judge of how good his or her partner is as a partner. This level of description has to be related to how the person evaluated behaves in public and how that person sees and conceives of himself or herself. One person may be nice outside but nasty inside. Another may be nasty outside the home and nice inside—or nice (or nasty) both outside and inside the home. Unfortunately, evidence of this kind is hard to find because only the extreme cases come to our attention, in public reports of murder, battering, or abusive neglect.

Explanatory Levels

These levels are described as genotypical and historical-developmental-situational.

Genotypical Level

In their review of impression regulation and management, Schlenker and Weigold (1992) included four classes of selective "explanations" for how to account for one's view of reality: (a) defenses of innocence or denial; (b) excuses; (c) justifications; and (d) apologies. From a viewpoint of functionality, one would rate apologies as one of the most functional explanations. The other three would be dysfunctional. Explanation (d) indicates an assumption of responsibility that is avoided in the other three.

Genotypical (Structural) Level: Inferred Traits versus Visible Resources. The best way to evaluate the metatheoretical foundations of developmental competence theory is to compare it with trait theory, which is still the major, pervasively monadic approach influencing current personality theory (Burkitt, 1991; Krahé, 1992; Magnusson & Torestad, 1993; McCrae & Costa, 1990; Pervin, 1990; Wiggins & Pincus, 1992). Developmental competence theory contrasts with traditionally intrapsychic personality theories where inferred, hypothetical, genotypical and internal states and traits are used to "explain" external behavior. As Briggs (1985) suggested:

> Traits can serve as explanations in two related ways. First, a single event can be understood as an instance of a chronic tendency. . . . Traits, however, can also serve as explanations in a second and more profound sense. When we explain an action by pointing to a recurring behavioral pattern (traits as summary concepts), we also point to the individual as the locus of causality. (p. 56)
>
> The trait approach emphasizes the orderliness of a person's behavior. It recognizes the continuities that exist in the lives of individuals and assumes that this coherence reflects an underlying arrangement or process that is both real and enduring. (p. 59)

It is important, therefore, to compare an internal approach with an external, interactional approach. This comparison is summarized in Table 2.1.

TABLE 2.1 Comparison between Trait Approaches and Resources in Developmental Competence Theory

Traits	Resources
1. Inferred/Hypothetical/Derived from paper-and-pencil self-reports	Visible/Recordable
2. Long chain of inferences necessary	Chain necessary in two out of six: importance and intimacy
3. Nonrelational	Relational
4. Acontextual	Contextual
5. Static and nonprocessible	Dynamic and processible
6. Many definitions of the same trait	Importance and intimacy need definitions; other four resources do not
7. Measured in a variety of ways	Limited number of ways to define particularistic resources (information, services, goods, and money)
8. Relationship to theory difficult if not impossible	Relationship to theory possible and relatively direct
9. Many so-called trait measures are state-dependent conditions	Except for importance and intimacy, what you see is what you get
10. "Recipe" model of personality (Gilbert, 1992a)	Two basic abilities: to love and to negotiate

States and traits are remnants of the mysterious and monadic person-within-a-box thinking fostered by views that make internal, intrapsychic, and inferred acontextual and nonrelational conditions (instincts, drives, needs, and dispositions—all reminiscent of the "bad seed" theory) responsible for behavior. This approach is illustrated egregiously by the "self-esteem" movement. This movement makes this internal state the determinant of a great many personal and interpersonal outcomes, even though it is difficult to discriminate between functional and dysfunctional personality types on the basis of self-esteem. As Lott and Maluso (1993) commented: "[H]uman behavior is not well described by traits . . . individuals learn responses to, and in, situations continuously throughout their lives" (p. 104). Magnusson and Torestad (1993) maintained that "many, not to say most, of the variables studied in personality research are hypothetical. . . . The variable-oriented approach presents a static model of how an individual functions and develops" (p. 433). Revelle (1995) concluded:

> Traits are not behavior. They are summary statements describing likelihood of the rates of change in behavior in response to particular situational cues. In addition to their relationship to the probability and latency of response, stable predispositions may be conceptualized in terms of differential sensitivities to

situations and differential response biases. Intervening between traits, situations, and responses are momentary affective and cognitive states. (p. 315)

Historically, internal traits or states were used without giving any consideration to external conditions. This approach is also evident in most theories of emotions, which conceive of emotions as biologically and internally determined—as are other instinctual drives and internal conditions—independent of external determinants or antecedents (Izard, 1991b). Eventually, under criticisms that questioned the tenability of such a position, traits and states were combined with situations to pay lip service to the influence of interactions between internal states or traits and external conditions. Trying to link states and traits with situations is still a chancy enterprise that has not, as yet, led to a solution (Krahé, 1992). One might predict that a solution will not be found as long as a trait approach dominates personality theories. Reasons for such pessimism can be found in the following somewhat overlapping arguments.

1. Traits are inferred, intrapsychic, or hypothetical constructs that need to be guessed at in order to become relevant and eventually reified through paper-and-pencil self-report tests or experimental situations. On the other hand, the abilities, competences, and resources defining the traits are observable and recordable. One does not need to infer any underlying trait or state; what you see is what you get. Even feelings and emotions are the outcome of interpersonal, relational, and contextual determinants. They are learned, modulated, modified, and expressed according to sociocultural norms imparted from intimate relationships. Personal and interpersonal competence cannot be defined by how one responds to a self-report, paper-and-pencil test nor by whatever trait or state one can infer from those responses. Definition comes from how an individual transacts with the most immediate environment, in intimate and nonintimate relationships.

2. The chain of inferences from any trait or combination of traits to what counts as personal and interpersonal competence is a long one. For instance, one could be high in neuroticism and low in the four other traits of the Big Five (agreeableness, conscientiousness, extraversion, and openness). Does it mean that the person is "abnormal"? Is that all it takes to determine the level of functionality of a person? Why not observe how that person behaves in intimate and nonintimate relationships to arrive at a conclusion about that person's competence? Geis (1993) commented on this issue: "Behavior relevant to all traits, including gender stereotypes, is always more or less ambiguous. Trait attribution is always an inference" (p. 30).

3. Traits are nonrelational. They describe people in a vacuum, as though they live and love aside from anybody else, like hermits on top of a mountain. No matter how hard researchers try to link traits to situations, the chain of inferences from one internal trait to an external situation, especially an interpersonal one, is so long that, thus far, little if any success in this area has been achieved (Burkitt, 1991; Krahé, 1992).

4. Traits are acontextual, that is, they supposedly remain the same as they are, regardless of context. It may be a question of their varying as high, low, or in between along a dimensional trait. However, the trait does not link itself to the immediate-delayed, proximal-distal context because traits, by definition, are statically structural. They are constructs that cannot be linked to specific settings, no matter how long the chain of inferences may be or how hard one may try. Stress on traits alone is like looking at individual trees and not looking at the forest surrounding them or at the larger settings outside the forest. As long as we continue to look inside the individuals, we will remain blind to what they do in relevant and important relationships and in home, school/work, and leisure settings.

5. One trait can have multiple meanings, depending on its context. For instance, Stone (1993, p. 117) suggested that the same descriptor, *patriot/rebel,* may have different connotations when applied to different individuals. Hitler may have been a leader to his people. Yet, people in most other countries thought of him as a monster. The same criticism could be leveled against traits like "absent-minded," "sophisticated," or "witty": the same trait can be given positive or negative connotations on the basis of its immediate context: By whom is it being applied and to whom, when, and where? Although there have been attempts to gather this information (Costa & Widiger, 1994), there is still inadequate evidence about the developmental, situational, and intergenerational antecedents of traits.

6. Even though there may be agreement among many researchers (Costa & Widiger, 1994) about the robust and solid foundations of the Big Five personality traits, there is disagreement about what these factors should be called. For instance, Stone (1993, p. 113) wonders whether "extraversion" should be called "surgency" or "social adaptability." Should "agreeableness" be called "confident self-expression"?

7. Traits are infinite. No matter what the theoretical persuasion, there is no limit on how many traits or states one can fathom. Even when a large number of descriptors are factor-analyzed and reduced to a manageable number of traits—say, three, four, five, or seven—this reduction leads to the inevitable Big Five (McCrae & Costa, 1990): agreeableness, conscientiousness, extraversion, neuroticism, and openness. After a finite number of states or traits is established, they still need to be related to a theoretical framework, which so far is nonexistent. There is no personality theory, as yet, that can include traits and states, even though an attempt was made to achieve such a hypothetical link in the previous chapter (Figure 1.7). Consequently, many traits in various empirical models are searching for a theory. If such a theory were to come along, it would be strictly intrapsychic and nonrelational, which would make it irrelevant to recent concerns about the importance of the immediate and proximal environment (i.e., the family) for personality socialization. A trait such as intelligence can be measured in innumerable ways, and no consensus can be found as long as different researchers use different measures.

8. What may appear as traits may be only temporary states, even though trait measures may be reliable and psychometrically sound. What is gained by distinguishing traits from states, except to use length of personal experience to achieve such a differentiation?

9. Gilbert (1992a) has called the trait approach a "recipe" model, whereby different traits, i.e., ingredients for different people, are mixed like a cake mix (p. 253). There is more to personality than a collection and combination of traits.

As discussed in Chapter 6, according to attachment theory, an underlying dimension of security-insecurity at the genotypical level may determine different attachment processes. By the same token, this theory would argue that, whatever security-insecurity may be present at this level, it is very likely a function of how important the individual feels.

Historical-Developmental-Situational Level

At this level, the historical, developmental, and situational conditions are used to "explain" why individuals behave the way they do. Even tribunals accept past negative circumstances in a criminal suspect's background to limit or explain that individual's behavior. The socioeconomic, educational, emotional, and occupational adjustment of one's parents is used to predict or "explain" a person's achievement, behavior, and personality. Developmental traumas, illnesses, accidents, and untoward events become the explanatory antecedents or causes that would account for that behavior according to equipotentiality (one cause can produce different effects) or equifinality (different causes can produce the same effect). Evidence to support this conclusion is so pervasive that it is difficult to select one specific instance to support it.

THE HORIZONTAL DIMENSION: THE ERAAwC MODEL

The ERAAwC model was designed to condense all the various viewpoints relating to personality processes. For instance, in their chapter on personality change and psychotherapy, Messer and Warren (1990) condensed most models of personality and change into:

1. Phenomenological/Experiential, to include those who value subjective *E*xperience over objective reality.
2. Psychoanalytic and cognitive theories based on a *R*ational processing of behavior.
3. Intersubjective theories, including those of Harry Stack Sullivan and Heinz Kohut, which might have been relegated to the historical developments of psychoanalytic theory, but which are the harbingers of interpersonal theories focused on relationships and the family *C*ontext.

The first two components of this model, *E* and *R*, are the subjects of an exhaustive comparison (Epstein, 1991). What Epstein called the *experiential system* was holistic, associationistic, outcome-oriented, mediated from past experiences, marked by concrete images and metaphors, oriented toward immediate action, slow to change, crudely differentiated, crudely integrated, experienced passively, and self-evidently valid ("Experiencing is believing"). The *R*ational system, in comparison to *E*, is more analytic, logical, directed toward cause–effect analysis, more process-oriented, mediated by conscious appraisal of events, capable of encoding reality in abstract symbols, processed more slowly, and oriented toward delayed action. It changes relatively rapidly, is more highly differentiated and more highly integrated, offers active and conscious experience, and requires justification via logic and evidence (p. 123).

Affect (*E*) and cognition (*R*) in close relationship were the subject of Forgas's (1991) analysis. Fitness and Strongman (1991) considered affect in close relationships: "[T]he affective approach is also, without doubt, one of the most difficult areas of psychology to conceptualize, analyze, and theorize about in a meaningful way" (p. 175). On the other hand, Surra and Bohman (1991) as well as Harvey and Orbach (1991) offered a cognitive perspective to the development of close relationships. Both *E* and *R* are necessary but insufficient components of communication in marriage and in close relationships (Noller & Ruzzene, 1992).

Salovey and Rodin (1985) provide support for the circularity of a process that: (a) starts with *E*motionality, (b) moves on to *R*ationality, and (c) then results in social behavior (*A*), which (d) feeds back (*Aw*) to emotionality. They made three assumptions about the connection between feeling states and social behavior:

1. Emotional mood states affect self-cognitions.
2. Changes in self-cognitions will affect subsequent social behaviors.
3. Social behaviors feed back to and affect mood states (*E*) and self-cognitions (*R*).

The only component missing from these assumptions is *C*ontext, a limitation ironically common among many social psychologists, of all people!

Emotionality

Rather than include here evidence in regard to the relevance of this factor (Lewis & Haviland, 1993), it will be partially reviewed and expanded in Chapter 4. Emotionality is closely related to temperament and to approach-avoidance functions, including attachment patterns (Kagan, 1992), and to the development of social competence (Eisenberg & Fabes, 1992). Heron (1992) based a theory of the person mainly on how feelings and emotions are construed, a view that is supported by the work of Salovey and coworkers (cited earlier and again below). Relevant here is Clark and Reis's (1988) review of interpersonal processes in close relationships, defined by interdependence, and focused on emotions, intimacy, and love. They concluded:

> [R]esearchers primarily interested in emotion have typically studied it in nonsocial contexts, examining processes that seem more *intra-* than *inter*personal. . . . Moreover, until recently, relationship researchers have tended to neglect emotion, in large part owing to the tendency . . . to study initial encounters between strangers—interactions characterized by little emotion. (p. 619)
>
> To summarize, emotion clearly plays an important role in natural interdependence. (p. 624)

Additional support for the primacy of emotion and its important influence on behavior is found in the work of Salovey and coworkers (Salovey, Mayer, & Rosenhan, 1991), who maintained that: (a) "(Pleasant) Mood affects attentional focus and thoughts about the self" (p. 219); and (b) "(Pleasant) Mood improves perceptions of situations and of others" (p. 220). "By the same token, unpleasant moods influence the content of thoughts and attentional focus" (p. 222). Salovey and coworkers are responsible for identifying "a set of skills concerning the appropriate recognition of emotions in the self and others and the use of emotional information to solve problems and motivate behavior" (p. 228). They called this set of skills: "*emotional intelligence.* One aspect of emotional intelligence is the recognition, first, that one can regulate mood by behaving in certain ways and, second, that behavior may have long-term as well as short-term affective consequences" (p. 228).

Plutchik (1993) proposed a psychoevolutionary theory of emotions that looks at emotions as:

> communications and genetically based survival mechanisms based on evolutionary adaptations. . . . emotions are hypothetical constructs based on various classes of evidence and complex chains of events with stabilizing feedback loops that produce some kind of behavioral homeostasis. A three-dimensional structural model can represent the relation among emotions that are related to a number of derivative conceptual domains. (p. 55)

Plutchik's theoretical model will be considered in greater detail in Chapter 6. The greatest support for the primacy of *E* over the other components of the model comes from the theorizing of Mayer and Salovey (1995), who made emotional intelligence the basis for the construction and regulation of feelings, to the extent that: "Emotionally intelligent people are defined in part as those who regulate their emotions according to a logically consistent model of emotional functioning" (p. 197). These authors proposed three regulatory models. The first one suggests that "people should (a) optimize their pleasures by forgoing short-term pleasures for longer-term ones, (b) strive toward emotions that are both proindividual and prosocial, and (c) context sensitive" (p. 198). They also considered the construction and regulation of emotions at high and low emotionally intelligent levels, and concluded that "a primary indicator of depression is the active attempt to avoid emotional pain" (p. 202).

Thus, both approach-avoidance and discharge-delay functions are seen as operating in the construction and regulation of emotions. This topic will be developed further in Chapter 4.

Rationality

Feelings regulate distance. Rationality (*R*) regulates how feelings are going to be expressed in words and deeds (Eisenberg & Fabes, 1992). More evidence is being gathered about *R*'s functions in close relationships (Baldwin, 1995).

The importance of this component of the model in the development of intelligence and personality has been summarized, among many others, by Barlon (1985). He linked rationality to the development of cognitive availability, meaningful learning, problem solving, reflective thinking and morality, and the development of an identity and of moral reasoning. Inadequate rationality, the inability to stop inappropriate behavior, is linked to impulsiveness or discharge. Barlon's interpretation, however, failed to stress the role of rationality in close relationships. This step was taken by Duck (1993) and his collaborators, among others, who went one step further in relating "cognition" to interpersonal relationships: "[M]ental structures that individuals bring to relationships [range] from their thought processes and [the] factors that influence those [processes] to the ways they recall and remember relationship events or treat and manipulate relationally relevant information" (p. x).

Andersen (1993) commented on the relationship between *E* and *R*: "Cognitively and emotionally we walk a fine line in our relationships between stressful excitement and boring predictability" (p. 11). Fletcher and Fitness (1993) commented on the relationships between these two processes: "One of the problems with adopting a cognitive approach to personal relationships is that it neglects what surely is a vital and central component of such relationships: the role of affect and emotions . . . affect appears as both a possible eliciting event and an outcome" (p. 140).

E and *R* are sometimes juxtaposed as two sides of the same coin. White (1993), for instance, started with the mind–body duality (p. 30) and attributed affect, feeling, emotional, irrational, unconscious, unintentional, and uncontrolled qualities to the body. To the mind, he attributed cognition, thinking, and reason—conscious, intentional, and controlled qualities. For him, emotions are ultimately part of a social discourse (p. 35) that governs how people relate to each other.

R is the process whereby subjective feelings are processed before they are expressed outwardly as emotions. This process, however, takes place in selfful individuals and not in the other three personality propensities. For instance, in selfish individuals, feelings may bypass *R* and be expressed impulsively and explosively solely through anger, aggression, or attack. In selfless individuals, feelings may be expressed appropriately and shared directly with loved ones, with little if any reliance on *R*. That *R* is necessary for a constructive expression of *E* is supported by the work of Martin, Achee, Ward, and Harlow (1993), who entitled their contribution: "The role of cognition and effort in the use of emotions to guide behavior" (p. 147).

Activity

Most behavioral literature essentially supports the view that observable behavior (*A*) is what is said and what is done, with the consequences and rewards or punishments thereof, and tends to stress the direct study of *A* rather than the study of inferences about it. Unfortunately, most of this literature deals with consequences out of relational contexts. Nonetheless, stress on observables is in agreement with what is stressed here—behavior in interpersonal and intimate relationships.

Awareness

Acitelli (1993) has researched this dimension of relationship awareness probably more than anyone else. She defines it as:

> a person's thinking about interaction patterns, comparisons, or contrasts between himself or herself and the other partner in the relationship. . . . Although relationship awareness is a process and is not defined here as a personality disposition, there is evidence that thinking about relationships may be a personality trait. (p. 151)

Acitelli quoted Snell (1988), who distinguished among three personality dispositions in regard to relationship awareness: "(a) relationship consciousness, the tendency to think about internal dynamic features of a relationship; (b) relationship monitoring, the tendency to think about the public impression created by one's intimate relationship; and (c) relationship anxiety, the tendency to experience anxiety and shyness in an intimate relationship" (p. 151). Acitelli concluded her very important contribution, which unfortunately cannot be described in greater detail here, by suggesting that "although a person's identity can influence whether and how one thinks about relationships, being in and thinking about relationships may also influence one's identity" (p. 174). Fletcher and Fitness (1993), for instance, used the concept of "attributional schemata" to relate knowledge structures (i.e., information) to relationships: "[A]ttributions operate . . . to maintain existing levels of relationship satisfaction regardless of whether positive or negative interactive behavior is produced" (p. 127).

Another source of independent support for the role of awareness is found in the work of Snyder (Gangestad & Snyder, 1985) on self-monitoring. Definite personality differences between individuals who are high or low in this skill are shown: "[I]ndividuals differ in the extent to which they can monitor, through self-observation and self-control, their expressive behavior and self-presentation" (p. 65). This conclusion is supported by Bornstein (1992), who found that awareness produced inhibitory effects on how an individual will respond in an emotional situation.

Context

Context needs to be considered when we try to understand personal and interpersonal competence. Duck (1993), for instance, reflected this viewpoint:

> Individuals bring into relationships their individual characteristics and factors that reflect their point in the life cycle and developmental achievements. Individuals are influenced by the social setting (situational, cultural, linguistic, and societal) in which the relationship takes place; they are constrained and influenced by the structural, transactional, behavioral, and communicative contexts of their relationships; and they sometimes conduct the relationships in dysfunctional environments or disrupted emotional contexts. (p. viii)

Nesselroade (1990) concluded: "Personality development can be conceived as a product of properties of the person and properties of the context" (p. 51). Cohen and Siegel (1991) devoted thirteen contributions to a discussion of development in various contexts (school, home, ecology, and so on). It would be prohibitively time-consuming to summarize all these contributions here, but Siegel and Cohen's (1991) five features of contexts are worth listing:

1. Contexts are constructed by people.
2. Contexts are essentially social.
3. Contexts embody human motives and memories.
4. Context is the appropriate unit of analysis in research.
5. Contexts can change: context involves development (and vice versa).

In an overview of current models and research of organism–environment interaction, Wachs and Plomin (1991) found it "surprising that there is so little emphasis on the process of organism–environment interaction in studies of human development. . . . The classical response of environmental psychologists has been to essentially ignore the possibility of human differences in reactivity, both in their designs and in their models" (p. 2). In other words, not all contexts are the same for all people. We need to differentiate how different people react to different situations in different contexts.

The Independent Variables of Personality Socialization

It would require a separate volume to summarize the evidence that supports the importance of the independent variables listed by the theory. Attention will be paid to gender because this variable is more germain to the theory than the other independent variables, whose ubiquitous role is admittedly general and not specific to this theory.

DEVELOPMENTAL COMPETENCE THEORY

In this section, viewpoints that resemble components of the theory are reviewed.

Assumptions

The two assumptions of space and time are neither new nor original. They have dominated the development of this theory from its inception (L'Abate, 1964). Plutchik (1993) developed a similar framework by assuming two dimensions of territoriality (i.e., space) and temporality. From both assumptions, he developed four existential crises that resemble somewhat the four personality propensities of the selfhood model. Suffice it to say here that his framework intersected a dimension of *hierarchy and dominance versus submission* with *safe personal space and control versus loss of control*—assumptions and dimensions similar to those of the theory.

Birtchnell (1993) developed a theory that in many ways is very close to the present one:

> It has now been established that human relating occurs along two principal axes, one concerned with proximity and one concerned with power. . . . The first of these will be referred to as the horizontal axis (since people move toward or away from each other in a horizontal plane) and the second will be referred to as the vertical axis (since the more powerful person can be conceived of as being above the weaker one). (p. 39)

Birtchnell (1993) cited Hartup (1989), Horney, and Leary as pioneers in this area, as well as Packer and Richardson (1991). The two latter researchers proposed two classes of movement in space: intimacy and status. Birtchnell's concepts will be reviewed in their relation to similar concepts of this theory.

Space and Spatiality

Once distance in space is assumed as the primary dimension along which human socialization occurs, its extremes are defined by approach-avoidance tendencies. These tendencies may occur in humans at various levels: internal-external, emotional-cognitive, acontextual-contextual. Dollard and Miller (1950) and Schneirla (1959) included Miller's (1948) original model of approach-avoidance, as expanded to personality by Taylor-Spence (1963). In the displacement model, the avoidance gradient is steeper than the approach gradient, and conflict is greater where the two tendencies cross each other. This model could be used to observe family interactions from the viewpoint of the distance model, where a Distancer is often approached by a Pursuer, with a Regulator oscillating between approach and avoidance (L'Abate, 1986). The importance of approach-avoidance tendencies has been stressed by Gray (1994) in his Behavioral Activation System, which leads toward approach, and his

Behavioral Inhibition System, which leads toward avoidance. The fine details of Gray's theory can be found in Revelle's review (1995). Unfortunately, Gray—as well as other fine researchers like Kagan (1992, 1994; Kagan & Snidman, 1993; Kagan, Snidman, Reznick, Gibbons, & Johnson, 1989)—confuses the dimension of distance with the dimension of control. Davidson, Ekman, Saron, Senulis, and Friesen (1990) even suggested that approach-withdrawal functions may be related to cerebral asymmetry. If this were indeed the case, this relationship would allow linking developmental competence theory to physical and psychological factors—more than a psychological theorist could hope for.

From these basic approach-avoidance tendencies, the theory expands to nurturance, intimacy, and the ability to love, including attachment and dependency (extreme approach), or the inability to love (extreme avoidance). As Birtchnell (1993) commented on his spatial theory of relating: "In a very fundamental way, people can be conceived of as objects separate from each other by space" (p. 44). He goes on to review approach-avoidance theories, citing various theorists who have used this axis. He mentions intimacy versus solitude and other-interest versus self-interest, without differentiating assumptions from postulates or resources. Birtchnell reviewed theories of closeness and intimacy in regard to "revealing and being revealed to" (pp. 90–91) in a way that is similar to the definition of intimacy as sharing of joys and hurts:

> People vary considerably in the general level of closeness they feel comfortable with. There are those who thrive on closeness, who try to get close to almost everyone they meet; those who avoid it at all costs, and the majority who fit somewhere in between. (p. 101)
>
> Negative closeness assumes the following forms: giving or receiving imposed, invasive, or intrusive closeness; insecure closeness and jealousy; misperceptions of closeness; close behavior resulting from deficiencies of distance such as excessive identification, fear of separation, and fear of being alone; and reactions to the absence of or loss of closeness. (p. 113)

Birtchnell differentiated closeness (becoming involved) from distance (remaining separate) but saw them as extremes of the same axis. However: "Distance should not be viewed as the absence of closeness: it is as much a positive state as closeness is. In distance, the self is built up and related to. . . . Distance closeness involves deriving a degree of closeness from the relatively safe position of distance" (p. 145). He spent much more thought on both concepts than the present theory has been able to do. Distance may be pleasurable to reduce stimuli, meditate, achieve solitude, and relate to the environment and God (p. 118). He conceived of spatial boundaries in the skin and clothes, personal space, privacy, the psychic interior, and personal property. From these qualities, he went on to love of self, ranging from self-indulgence and narcissism to avoidant, schizoid, schizotypal, paranoid, and psychopathic personalities.

Andersen (1993) helped support the concept of distance (approach-avoidance) connecting with love and intimacy: "It is the autonomy/connection of affiliation/avoidance dimension that is the underlying basis of the major theoretical efforts explaining intimacy" (p. 10). Additional support for the dimension of space and whatever behavior derives from it comes from Josselson (1996). She started by differentiating individualism (i.e., self) from relatedness or distance (i.e., others), but focused on the latter as consisting of holding, attachment, passionate experience, eye-to-eye validation, idealization and identification, mutuality and resonance, embeddedness, culminating into caring and love. As expected, no mention was made of problem-solving or instrumental behaviors, a topic that would be considered under the assumption of time.

Time and Temporality

Time and temporal perspective are observed by how slowly or quickly one responds to threatening, painful, or dangerous stimuli (i.e., control). For instance, in functional individuals and relationships, there is a balance of approach-avoidance and discharge-delay tendencies. Psychopathology develops when there are imbalances and extremes in such tendencies. Extremes in discharge are seen in impulsive and driven individuals, and extremes in delay are seen in procrastinators and task avoiders (Ferrari, Johnson, & McCown, 1995). From this dimension of time, the theory expands to the ability to negotiate and to problem solving. Buss (1987) considered the same dimension of control from the viewpoint of arousal. High arousal is present in fear, anger, and sexual arousal, as common to all mammals; love, jealousy, elation, and grief are at the basis of low arousal. Both low and high arousal are present in social mammals such as primates and humans.

Even though, in Chapter 1, time was made synonymous with control and with extremes of discharge and delay functions, implicit to this definition was the conception that each extreme represents differences in temporality; that is, how individuals conceive of time as progression and perspective. For instance, delay represents a view of time where all possible consequences, mostly negative, are considered (thinking before acting), rendering action almost impossible. On the other extreme of discharge, impulsive individuals act with little if any thinking (acting before thinking) as to the consequences of their actions. This temporal perspective is called by Rabin, Zucker, Emmons, and Frank (1990)"a basic assumption of personality theory that is far more commonplace today" (p. 4). This theory would argue that space is even more basic developmentally than time.

Control has received a great deal of attention in recent psychological literature. For instance, in a review of mechanisms of self-regulation or "voluntary action management" (p. 24), Karoly (1993b) commented: "The introduction of self-regulation and related concepts into contemporary psychology has not been restricted to a single discipline" (p. 24), and cited a variety of examples where this concept is necessary. Delay, of course, is too much control or inhibition, and discharge would represent a failure at self-regulation or disinhibition. As Gottman (1994) found, individuals who tend to discharge in their marriages are characterized by negative reciprocity, a process very similar to what this theory calls reactivity.

In a work completely devoted to this topic, Baumeister, Heatherton, and Tice (1994) prefaced this topic by noting: "The aspect of the self as an entity that controls itself . . . has been slower to attract the attention of researchers" (p. ix). Loss of control or discharge (i.e., "self-regulation failure") is considered by these authors as:

> the major social pathology of the present time. . . . All over the country, people are miserable because they cannot control their money, their weight, their emotions, their drinking, their hostility, their craving for drugs, their spending, their own behavior vis-à-vis their family members, their sexual impulses, and more. . . . Self-regulation failure is central to many of the problems that are widely discussed and bemoaned as allegedly hastening the decline and doom of America. (p. 3)
>
> Currently there seems to be a widespread hope, which is probably no more than an absurd and idle fantasy, that raising self-esteem will solve these problems. If only we loved ourselves more, the assumption is, all our problems would vanish. From the perspective of self-regulation theory, this fascination with self-esteem is a pathetic and self-indulgent wish. . . . We cannot, however, go along with the national preoccupation with self-esteem. In our view, America is not suffering from low self-esteem. It suffers from a spreading epidemic of self-regulation failure. (p. 5)

These authors attribute most failures in self-regulation to men, while describing "self-control" as "the quintessential feminine virtue in Western culture" (p. 10). They cite research that supports their conclusion:

> [S]elf-regulatory capacity is a central, powerful, stable, and beneficial aspect of personality. High capacity to delay gratification is linked to being attentive, reasonable, intelligent, resourceful, competent, and cooperative. . . . Children who have low ability to delay gratification tend to be aggressive, restless, unable to deal with stress, prone to feelings of victimization, and likely to be regarded as sulky and whiny. (p. 11)
>
> Thus, self-regulation accounts for roughly half of the adaptive activities of human beings. (p. 12)

For these authors, self-management means taking care of oneself. Failure to control oneself (i.e., discharge) means being unable to control emotions and moods as well as impulses and appetites for alcohol, food, tobacco, gambling, shopping, and aggression. The relation of these addictions to the theory will be considered in Chapter 10.

On a more positive note, Geis (1993) noted:

> Power and control provide personal as well as social advantages. Greater power and autonomy lead to increased motivation and interest, less pressure and tension, greater creativity and cognitive flexibility, better learning, better performance at a task, and better physical and mental health. . . . The greater incidence of depression in women has been attributed to their lesser power and autonomy, especially in the housewife role. . . . Wives who work outside the

home, especially in high-level careers, report greater satisfaction and feelings of well-being. (p. 24)

Wegner and Pennebaker (1993) added to a definition of control in terms of internal rather than external characteristics: "Mental control occurs when people suppress a thought, concentrate on a sensation, inhibit an emotion, maintain a mood, stir up a desire, squelch a craving, or otherwise exert influence on their own mental processes" (p. 1). Hence, their definition tends to look at the delay-constraint extreme of control rather than the other extreme of discharge. Fiske and Emery (1993), on the other hand, concentrated on the loss of mental control and exaggerated social control. Salovey, Hsee, and Mayer (1993) elaborated on the relationship between social intelligence and self-regulation of affect, which implies an accurate appraisal and an appropriate expression of emotions. Watson and Clark (1993) considered delay in terms of "constraint" and discharge in terms of "behavioral disinhibition." A rose by any other name. . . .

Birtchnell (1993) proposed that: "Theories concerned specifically with the vertical axis [which he identified with power] are few" (p. 49). As the two exceptions, he cited Alfred Adler's theory of superiority/inferiority and Eric Berne's striving to achieve objectives. He defined the two extremes of this axis in terms of upperness and lowerness. The former "involves being in a position of advantage or superiority in relation to another or others. . . . Upperness often involves having the power to influence others. . . . Because there are so many ways of being upper, in any particular relationship, one person may be upper in some respects and the other may be so in others. Thus there may be no absolute sense in which either is upper to the other" (p. 147).

Birtchnell, in invoking social comparison theory to indicate how feelings of upperness or lowerness are achieved, listed the main sources of positive (in contrast to negative) upperness as: innate attributes; personal attractiveness; leadership qualities; acquired skills, competencies, experience, and knowledge; academic qualifications; and earning capacity. In this regard, Birtchnell cited status as "an acknowledged social position within a group, community, or society" (p. 153). Instead of an external attribution, the present theory views status as an attribution of importance made to self and other, regardless of social position. One could have a very low social position in a group, community, or society and still feel very important.

Nonetheless, Birtchnell's overall treatment of upperness deserves serious consideration because it amplifies aspects of the present theory that had not been developed as well as in his theory. For instance, he viewed upperness as a defense against or denial of lowerness, as a means of controlling the behavior of others, as abuse for personal gain, and as becoming upper at the expense of the other's lowerness. Criminal behavior is the extreme manifestation of negative upperness. Hence, in this regard, positive upperness would fit within the selful personality propensity, and negative upperness would fit within the selfish personality propensity.

Lowerness, according to Birtchnell, "is not simply the absence of upperness" (p. 182). He expanded on this concept by suggesting, as in the case of upperness, that there are positive and negative manifestations of lowerness. Birtchnell cited the dependent, masochistic, self-deprecating personalities as examples of negative lowerness in a way that would fit them as examples of selflessness. Positive lowerness would fit into the selful personality propensity. From the foregoing framework, he obtained an interpersonal octagon reminiscent of Leary's interpersonal circle and Benjamin's (1993) three-surfaces description of personality. Hence, a future task for research is correlating Birtchnell's self-administered questionnaire (Person's Relating to Others) with the Self Profile Chart found in Appendix A.

Inhibition and uninhibition (delay and discharge in the language of this theory) have been studied by Kagan (1992, 1994; Kagan, Snidman, Reznick, Gibbons, & Johnson, 1989) in terms of temperamental characteristics that are either inherited or acquired in the womb. He found, among other results, that behaviorally inhibited children tend to be more fearful and will avoid unfamiliar situations more than uninhibited children will. Hence, the latter tend to approach more than avoid, and the former tend to avoid more than approach, as predicted by the basic model of the theory (Figure 1.1). Lewis (1989), illustrating how temperamental differences in physiological reactivity vary and are affected by cultural differences, concluded that "although initial individual differences are genetically determined, these different response styles are open to experiential influences" (p. 202).

Burger (1992) identified a personality characteristic—which he labeled "desire for control"—with striking individual differences in high versus low desire for control. High desire for control was related to Type A personality, marked by loud, explosive, rapid, and accelerated speech, potential for hostility, verbal competitiveness, higher levels of education, and preference for control over personal health decisions:

> [D]esire for control is tied to achievement motivation and achievement behaviors in many ways. High desire for control people approach achievement tasks differently than people with a low desire for control. They set higher standards for themselves and are more motivated to overcome challenging tasks in an effort to demonstrate their personal mastery. (p. 98)

How does desire for control relate to developmental competence theory? In the first place, one would need to differentiate levels of functionality before making any predictions. Extremes in desire for control in either direction (high or low) would be dysfunctional; a balanced and differentiated use of control would be functional. In the second place, one needs to establish with whom and under what condition an individual would or would not want control, before making any predictions that would support or fail to support the theory. What Burger described as individuals high on desire to control suspiciously resemble selfish personalities, and those with low desire to control could possibly be selfless.

ABILITY TO LOVE AND TO BE LOVED: BEING PRESENT AND EMOTIONALLY AVAILABLE

The ability to love and to be loved as a legitimate area of psychological inquiry is no longer a questionable pursuit (Aron & Aron, 1996; Berscheid, 1994; Hendrick & Hendrick, 1992a, 1992b; Tzeng, 1992). For instance, Dion and Dion (1985) concluded their review by indicating:

> [T]here are indeed individual differences in the phenomenology of romantic love. An important task is therefore to explain why these differences exist. The pattern of correlates found to date suggests that *responses to intimacy* underlie the relation between personality and the experience of romantic love . . . individuals' reactions to intimacy (for example, responses to another's self-disclosure) should contribute to our understanding of love. (p. 233)

The importance of love has always been proclaimed by poets and writers, never by psychologists, scientists, researchers, or professionals interested in family relations. The correction of past professional and scientific belittlements has taken place mainly during the last generation, as a result of the humanistic impetus toward the fundamental importance of love as well as other emotions (May, 1983). Since the early 1970s, love has received more attention in the professional literature than it had received earlier (Bergmann, 1971). For instance, Curtin (1973) edited one of the first collections on love written by mental health professionals. In her preface, she wrote:

> It has been said that "Love makes the world go 'round," yet not once did I see *love* mentioned in all 23 volumes in the indices of the *Annual Review of Psychology* under Emotion, Motivation, or Love itself. Is love sufficient or even necessary for the aforementioned great task and if so, who talks about it besides poets and novelists and song writers? (p. ix)

The past 25 years have been extremely productive for the study of love and its concomitants. Yet, contributors to Curtin's symposium, exemplifying professional attitudes about love more than a generation go, will be quoted at length as a starting point for an understanding of how love has been viewed in the professional literature in the past. Wright (1973), for instance, argued that love was "neither necessary nor sufficient" for individual adult functioning. Is love necessary for intimate relationships? The answer is affirmative but qualified. *Love is necessary but it is insufficient to sustain prolonged and close (i.e., intimate) relationships within and without the family.* In addition to the ability to love, the ability to negotiate differences is also needed, as explained in the preceding chapter and as elaborated throughout this work.

The main problem that has plagued the study of love as a human emotion worthy of scientific and professional attention has been the search for a definition that is relevant both to individual mental health and to family relations. Can love be defined in ways that would make it a *relational* rather than just an intrapsychic, internal concept? For instance, Freud defined love as the sublimation of unacceptable sexual impulses. Casler (1973) viewed love as "a consequence of the needs for self-esteem, sexual satisfaction, and conformity to social pressure" (p. 8). By contrast, Casler argued the opposite of the position stated earlier:

> There is no evidence that love is either necessary or sufficient for psychological maturity. Indeed, to the extent that love fosters dependency, it may well be a deterrent to maturity. It is not love but the *need* for love that may be pathological, just as it is the need to use a crutch rather than the crutch itself that signifies physical incapacity. The person who seeks love in order to strengthen his self-respect will become, in the style of the alcoholic, increasingly dependent on this illusory source of well-being. (pp. 18–19)

The foregoing quotation contains statements that range from the valid to the invalid. First, Casler related love to intrapsychic, internal concepts without interpersonal impact or relationship, such as self-esteem or self-respect. Second, despite the possible lack of evidence then (in 1973) to substantiate a relationship between the ability to love and emotional maturity, such a relationship may be more tenable now on the basis of new evidence. Third, Casler equated love with dependency, an equation that is as untenable now as it was then. Mature love means interdependence; immature love means denial of dependency, or overdependency, or extreme oscillations between denial of dependency and overdependency. Fourth, whether love or the need for love incapacitates people is irrelevant; a crutch may help someone walk, but it will not heal a broken leg. Fifth, Casler was correct in anticipating what were to be called "love addictions," relationships based on an overwhelming need to be accepted and affirmed through sex and external rather than internal processes (Peele & Brodsky, 1975). Karmel (1973) took a position antithetical to Casler: "[T]o be unable to love is pathological because it reveals an inability of the organism to join forces or relate to another human being, in other words, a fixation at the narcissistic level of development" (p. 75).

Greenfield (1973) questioned whether "to use 'love' as a scientific concept may be self-defeating and unproductive" (p. 39). He referred to love as an observable relationship that includes: "(1) patterned, repetitive . . . and normative behavior; (2) specifiable attitudes; and (3) emotional states between persons of the opposite sex or on occasion of the same sex" (p. 40). As a restrictive cultural attribution, Greenfield believed that "to bring about significant social change, what is needed is not more love, but less, and perhaps none" (pp. 49–50). In other words, love is no solution to many societal problems. It may, indeed, not be a solution, but it may be a start!

Brodsky (1973) criticized the concept of love as representing selflessness from the viewpoint of a feminist: "We cannot continue to promote the clichés about love's selflessness, the intrinsic satisfactions of caring for another, and the notion of love associated with bowing to another's will" (p. 104). Unfortunately, Brodsky was barking up the wrong tree, because, as demonstrated in the selfhood model, love is not, nor need it be, equated with selflessness. As

Horton (1973) discussed, among its many other distortions, love has been equated with "romantic love," a fleeting, superficial, but nevertheless passionate infatuation based on sexual experiences or fantasies unrelated to the mundane routines and responsibilities of everyday life. Romantic love is often based on an unequal relationship. As Horton argued, and as contended here, nothing short of *equality of importance* is acceptable or workable for a prolonged and close relationship. The issue here is equality of what and inequality of what? Basic to equality between two partners is the notion of respect, or any similar notion that implies seeing the good in and bestowing importance on another, as argued by Rawls (1971) and Weigert (1973). Respect for another can take place only when there is respect for oneself.

In the same year that Curtin's symposium was published, Coutts (1973) published a pioneeringly courageous but not very well known book about the relationship between love and intimacy. He was one of the first to use and to elaborate on the word "intimacy," after Fromm (1956), May (1983), and, of course, Erikson (1950). Unfortunately, in defining love, Coutts, like Brodsky (1973) and many other writers with a mystical or magical bent, equated love with *selflessness,* an erroneous and constraining equation. When love is not equated with a romantic infatuation or with selflessness, it is often equated with sex and sexuality (Grant, 1976), another misleading equation among the many diversities and disagreements this concept has created among professionals.

Aron and Aron (1996) suggested an interesting and intriguing view of love as "the expansion of self," a process that implies the inclusion of significant others in the sphere of self-view and functioning. They supported their thesis with a thorough and critical review of the literature on attraction, as already performed by Byrne (1971) and Murstein (1986). More importantly, Aron and Aron, as well as Fine (1985) and many other authors reviewed here, made love a respectable field for scientific and professional inquiry and for clinical applications. This trend culminated with the work of Sternberg and his triadic theory of love (1987), which includes affective, cognitive, and motivational bonds.

The main quality necessary for staying in love, according to McTaggart (1927), as quoted by Singer (1987), is *bestowal:*

> Desirable qualities in another person may explain why we love him or her, if we do, but no quality can guarantee the occurrence of love and none can be a prerequisite for it. In principle everyone could be loved by someone, even if we cannot indicate who that someone might be . . . . Love cannot be deduced from any quality in the object. Without the lover's *bestowal* (underlying ours), no quality will elicit love. (pp. 398–399)

The appraisal of certain loveable qualities interacts with the *bestowal of value* of the other person's worthiness of being loved and feeling loveable enough to receive love from another. The bestowal of value on another may imply the bestowal of value on oneself. By the same token, bestowing value on another is not sufficient for bestowing value on oneself. Bestowing value on oneself must take place before or alongside the bestowal received from another. This bestowal is unconditional to the extent that one can love unconditionally or know experientially what unconditional love is and what it means. What Singer called "bestowal" was changed in this theory to "attribution," a process that takes place in close relationships (Berscheid, 1994; Fletcher & Fincham, 1991).

Clark and Reis (1988) included love in their review of interpersonal processes in close relationships by summarizing most taxonomies related to this topic. They valued Sternberg's (1987; Sternberg & Beall, 1992) tripartite and structural theory of love, including intimacy, passion, and commitment, but also related Hazan and Shaver's (1987) theory to attachment styles, as expanded in Chapter 6. The best support for the relationship of love to an emotionally based as well as a rationally based process is provided by Izard (1991b), who, at the conclusion of his review on emotions, devoted a final chapter to this topic and defined love as "... a pattern of emotions" in the same way that presence was defined in the previous chapter: "Excitement and joy in being with and doing for others is what all types of love have in common" (p. 394). Because no mention was made of problem solving in Izard's chapter, one must assume that this process is separate from the ability to love.

The same conclusion can be drawn from the work of Lazarus and Lazarus (1994) on emotions, which, with Izard's theory, is reviewed in greater detail in Chapter 4. Love was included as one of fifteen emotions and related specifically to emotions provoked by favorable life conditions, together with happiness and pride. The greatest support for the importance of emotional availability comes from the work of Willis (1991), who concluded that:

> results from field studies are notably consistent in finding one function to be important across a broad range of life stressors: emotional support . . . analyses with multidimensional functional inventories have typically shown emotional support to make the strongest unique contribution to well-being . . . supportive relationships are helpful because they provide maintenance of self-esteem. (p. 273)
>
> [C]hanges in self-efficacy may have been more important than changes in self-esteem. (pp. 274–275)

Instead of either self-efficacy or self-esteem, this theory would suggest that being emotionally available, what is euphemistically called "social support," is one way to reaffirm the other's sense of self-importance, which is especially lowered under stress (Baumeister, 1993b).

Hatfield and Rapson (1993) differentiated between passionate and companionate love in a way that is consistent with falling in love, being in love, and staying in love, as discussed in Chapter 1. Passionate love may be necessary in the first two sieves, falling in love and being in love. However, companionate love may be necessary for the long haul. These authors conclude their chapter with support for a link between love and hurt:

The evidence, then, suggests that various states of arousal can spill over and influence one another. Although most of us assume that we love the people we do *in spite of* the suffering they cause us, it may be that, in part, we love them *because of* the pain they cause. Love seems to flourish when it is nurtured by a torrent of good experiences, as well as a sprinkling of unsettling, irritating, and even painful ones. (pp. 600–601)

Winning and Losing

Little can be found in the literature on the notion that relationships can be self–other enhancing as well as self–other debasing. The only reference to winning and losing from an intraindividual rather than an interactive viewpoint can be found in Brim's work about ambition (1992). He conceived of this process in relation to growth and mastery in our lives. Here, the process is applied instead to interpersonal relationships, with outcomes that could be quantified, as amplified in Chapter 14.

Relevant to the whole issue of winning and losing in intimate relationships is the concept of reciprocity (Uehara, 1995), which implies a process of mutually agreed-on responsiveness, verbal or nonverbal. In functional relationships, reciprocity is the ongoing norm—both of the individuals involved in the interaction win, and no one loses. In dysfunctional relationships, reactivity is the norm: either one of the two loses, or both lose.

Modalities

A plethora of references can be found in the modalities of performance and productivity, to the extent that these modalities have been the province of learning theory and work psychology. Relevant evidence for the validity of all three modalities—being, doing, and having—has been reviewed in previous publications. The only reference that escaped previous reviews is one by Fromm (1992), who stressed the importance of being and the relative unimportance of having, especially when the latter is a substitute for the former. For Fromm, "to be" means to be awake, to be aware, to concentrate, and to meditate. He dedicated three chapters to the culture of having: "Living has two dimensions. Man acts, does, produces, creates; in brief, he is active. But man is not acting in a void, not without body and not in an immaterial world: He has to deal with *things*. His acting refers to *objects*, animate or inanimate, which he transforms or creates" (p. 87). Fromm differentiated functional from nonfunctional property. The former is for use, and the latter is for greed and possession.

Burkitt (1991) proposed to view personality as social discourse derived from social relations where *power* is central to interdependencies and "civilized personality." It is unfortunate that Burkitt's interesting proposal does not contain any reference to family socialization or to constructs like love and intimacy. Personality power without presence can only lead to life as a struggle and as competition, where no collaborative reciprocity would be present.

Resources

Button and Collier (1991) are the exception in having asked subjects to rate features, or kinds, of love according to *importance*. Hence, stress on importance as a way to conceptualize (and measure) love is not limited to this theory alone. Because importance as a definition of love has been qualified as "attribution," it might be relevant to find support for this process. The validity of the six resources used in this theory can be sustained indirectly by evidence derived from resource exchange theory, as discussed at the end of this chapter.

Selfhood and Personality Propensities

One cannot separate how one sees oneself from how one relates to others. Grusec (1991), for instance, thought that "socialization also involves learning about relationships, including concepts of the self and of others" (p. 10). The best way to differentiate between self and other is in terms of positivity and negativity, from which one derives the four personality propensities of the selfhood model.

Support for a taxonomy of four personality propensities comes from a variety of sources. Wrightsman (1994) and McAdams (1990) were reviewed earlier. Additional support for the validity of the selfhood model comes from the work of Canary, Cupach, and Messman (1995) on conflict. Combining the models developed by Kilmann and Thomas (1977) and Rahim (1983), they used the dimensions of "concern for self" and "concern for other." From these two dimensions, they derived four styles of managing interpersonal conflict:

1. High concern for self and other produces a collaborating, integrating style that is similar to selfulness and the conductive-creative (CC) style.
2. High concern for self and low concern for other produces a competing, dominating style equivalent to the selfishness propensity.
3. Low concern for self and high concern for other produces an accommodating, obliging style similar to the selflessness propensity. (Styles 2 and 3 use reactively repetitive (RR) patterns.)
4. Low concern for self and low concern for other produces an avoiding style, which in part may describe the no-self propensity, where an AA pattern is likely to occur.

The selfhood model predicts that conflict would be minimal in selfulness, greater in selfishness-selflessness, and extreme, inconsistent, and contradictory in no-self. Canary et al. (1995) clarified that conflict can take place at all levels of behavior. Consequently, it would make sense to think about conflict as occurring vertically at various levels of interpretation (descriptive-explanatory) and horizontally at the level of the ERAAwC model. Furthermore, Canary et al. classified interpersonal conflict into four categories derived from two dimensions of episodic-nonepisodic and specific-nonspecific. From these two types, they obtained the following categories: (a) pervasive conflict (nonepisodic-nonspecific); (b) one type of episode (episodic-nonspecific); as (c) a type of behavior (nonepisodic-specific); and as (d) episodic- and behavior-specific (episodic-specific).

If this classification is valid, then one would predict that perhaps episodic (but short-lived) and specific conflicts—as in (d) above—might be more frequent in the CC relationship style. Conflict categories (b) and (c) would be more frequent in the RR relationship style, and category (d) would be more frequent in the AA relationship style. Indeed, these authors qualify that "opposition, which provides an episode-free but a behavior-specific definition" (p. 9) is one aspect of the RR style, as discussed in Chapter 4.

This model predicts that each of the four rhomboids in Figures 1.4 through 1.9 comprises approximately 25% of the population. In the American population, approximately 25% reach a modicum of selfulness and functionality, as shown in the ability to form lasting and creative intimate relationships. Functional individuals, at their best, cope with stress with a minimum of uproars and with brief prolongation of aftereffects. The left middle rhomboid of Figures 1.4 through 1.9 suggests that 25% of the population is characterized by selfishness. Of this 25%, 80% are males who have been socialized for selfishness, as shown by the prevalence of criminality, addictions, and character disorders among males. The other 20% is made up of women. When one looks at male–female ratios of incarcerated criminals, for instance, one finds five to ten times as many men in jail (Lykken, 1995). When one looks at diagnoses of acting out and character disorders in psychiatric hospitals, one finds a four-to-one ratio of men to women. In the middle right rhomboid, sex ratios are reversed. Many more women than men (four to one!) are diagnosed with depression. Selflessness is the developmental basis for depression, and more women than men are socialized for selflessness (Lemkau, 1984).

Prosocial behavior (Clark, 1980) can be distinguished from altruism and other extremes or deviations of behavior by stressing that constructive prosocial behavior takes place when the self is enhanced while the other is being enhanced as well. Any type of altruism that takes place at the expense of the self would be considered as compulsively and reactively repetitive, and therefore of questionable importance. Eventually, such behavior would be extinguished or would cease to exist because the individual under these conditions would not be able to give continuously without receiving anything in return. In this regard, Grusec (1991) concluded: "Altruism . . . is not always correct and may often be experienced as a mixed blessing by eliciting feelings of failure, inferiority, and dependency in the recipient" (p. 11).

Selfulness expects some kind of reciprocity; selflessness does not. Hence, without any reward, selflessness will eventually be extinguished and the selfless person will probably switch to a selfish position. This switch is seen in many battered wives who eventually are no longer willing or able to withstand their husbands' abuse and either leave them or kill them. This polarization brings about what Clary and Snyder (1991) have called "the egoism-versus-altruism debate":

> The debate over the selflessness versus selfishness of a helper's motives has been vigorous, both in the psychological literature and in the literature on the motivation of volunteers. In both literatures, the argument centers on whether the motivations underlying a helpful act are ever truly altruistic (based on the concern for the other) as opposed to egoistic (based only on concern for the self). . . . Actions taken in the service of altruistic and humanitarian concerns may also be sources of personal rewards and self-affirmation. (p. 141)
>
> Just as one can question whether altruistic motives are purely altruistic, we can wonder whether egoistic constructs are themselves purely egoistic. (p. 142)

One important component of altruism is empathy, feeling for someone's plight or distress: "[A]lthough we humans seem capable of experiencing concern for others, we clearly also care for ourselves" (Batson & Oleson, 1991, p. 82). Mothers who describe themselves as sympathetic and rational have been correlated with children who show the same kind of feelings toward the needy. Mothers who respond to their children's distress seem to produce children who are able to put themselves vicariously in someone else's place and who are socially competent (Eisenberg & Fabes, 1991).

Arguing from the viewpoint of attachment theory, which will be reviewed in greater detail in Chapter 6, Grusec (1991) concluded:

> Securely attached children, whose mothers are sensitive, responsive, and accepting, will see others in the world as trustworthy and reliable and themselves as worthy of care and concern. Insecurely attached children, who have insensitive and rejecting mothers, will develop a model of others as unloving and the self as unworthy. (p. 21)

Arguing on the other side of the selfless propensity, Fiske (1991) attacked the myth of the asocial (or antisocial) individualist (p. 176) on the basis of four elementary types of social relationships:

1. Communal Sharing, without expecting specific reciprocation.
2. Authority Ranking, where both superiors and subordinates look out for each other.
3. Equality Matching, where distribution of goods and resources is balanced to take care of those participating in the exchange.
4. Market Pricing, where competition and economic survival of the fittest are the norms.

The first three types correspond roughly to selfulness, selfishness, and selflessness, respectively. The fourth type would produce individuals who are unable to compete and to survive and would retreat into the no-self position.

Regardless of whether these types relate to the four personality propensities of the selfhood model, Fiske's model is an important elaboration of exchanges, which, until now, were defined as giving and receiving. Fiske breaks down this process according to criteria worthy of further study.

Salovey, Mayer, and Rosenhan (1991) stressed:

> [Selflessness] refers to the performance of charitable acts with no expectation of extrinsic gain. . . . Selflessness-inspired helping may elicit or maintain great joy and relieve guilt. Not adhering to norms of social responsibility can produce shame; pride emanates from doing one's civic duty. When reciprocity is operating, individuals may feel confident and capable, and, when it breaks down, helpless. (p. 230)

Midlarsky (1991) argued that there are at least five "analytically distinguishable reasons" to explain why helping others may actually help the helper:

> even—or perhaps especially—when the help is given by an individual who is experiencing stress but helps, nevertheless, from other-centered motives. These include the capacity of helping (a) to provide distraction from one's own troubles, (b) to enhance the sense of meaningfulness and value in one's life, (c) to increase perceived competence, (d) to improve mood tone, and (e) to promote social integration—all of which can be disrupted by stressful events. (p. 240)

Further support for a selfhood model of personality propensities is found in the work of Vaillant (1977). On the basis of a long-term study of Harvard undergraduates, he proposed the following classification of personalities, each with its own specific defense mechanisms: (a) mature personality, using suppression, sublimation, altruism, humor, and anticipation; (b) immature personality, using acting out, passive aggression, hypochondriasis, fantasy, and projection; (c) neurotic personality, using displacement, intellectualization, depression, reaction formation, and dissociation; and (d) psychotic personality, using denial, delusional projection, and distortion (of reality). Vaillant's mature personality is similar to selfulness, immature to selfishness, neurotic to selflessness, and psychotic to no-self.

Support for the selfhood model from a developmental perspective can be found in the work of Smith, Bowers, Binney, and Cowie (1993) with bully/victim relationships (Figure 2.1) in school-age children. Bullies, of course, represent behavior that is designed to bolster one's own sense of importance at the expense of a victim who is unable to defend himself or herself: "Typically victims of bullying appear to have a low opinion of themselves and to be anxious and insecure" (p. 191). This review suggested that children who are *both* bullies *and* victims may be even more disturbed than either "pure" bullies or "pure" victims. Bullies would fit well within a selfish propensity, victims within a selfless propensity, and bullies/victims may well be found in the no-self propensity.

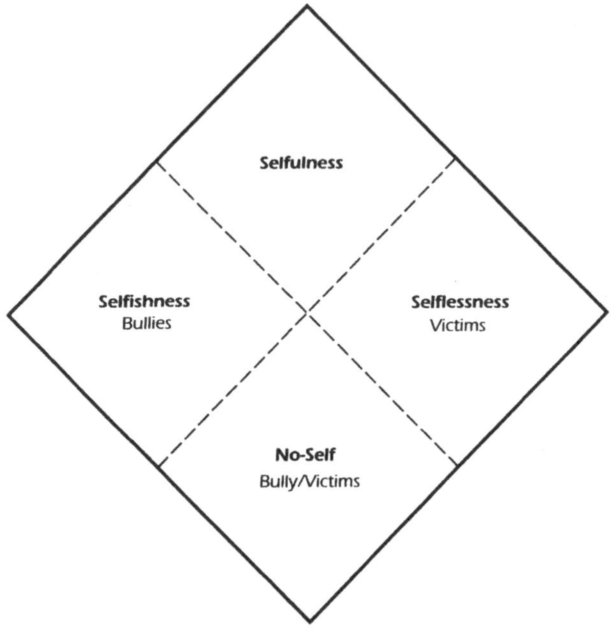

Figure 2.1 Bully/Victim Relationships among School Children (Based on Smith, Bowers, Binney, & Cowie, 1993)

THE IMPORTANCE OF GENDER DIFFERENCES IN SOCIALIZATION

Among the independent variables in the theory, age and gender are probably the most influential. As Geis (1993) commented on this issue:

> [M]uch of one's personal identity is derived from such social group memberships as one's nationality, ethnicity, religion, and occupation—as well as one's sex. . . . [S]ex and gender distinctions are central, important, and pervasive in our culture, [and] gender is the earliest, most central and organizing component of everyone's self-concept. (p. 12)

Cross and Markus (1993) conceived of gender as "a central category for understanding the world" (p. 58). They suggested that men have greater propensity for "separateness" than women, who, in turn, have greater propensity for "connectedness" than men (p. 79). Beall (1993) stressed that "gender is a socially constructed category" (p. 131) whereas sex is a biologically constructed one "because it [gender] differs across cultures in its content and form" (p. 134).

Recently, specific gender differences in interpersonal competence have been pinpointed (Barnett, Biener, & Baruch, 1987; Levant & Pollack, 1995). The crucial importance of these differences has prompted consideration of a selfhood model that distinguishes sharply between genders. At least provisionally, and admittedly stereotypically (as mentioned earlier), we need to acknowledge that many (at least four out of ten) men are socialized to be in many ways different, if not opposite, from women (the same socialization, of course, is true for women). What is the nature and what are the implications of these differences for a theory of interpersonal competence?

Lazarus and Folkman (1984) based part of their model of coping with stress on a major distinction between problem-focused versus emotion-focused strategies. This distinction is consistent with the distinction between the two sets of abilities necessary for survival and enjoyment: the ability to love and the ability to negotiate. Emotion-focused strategies are based on how the individual feels either at the time of stress or after the stressful event. Problem-solving strategies, on the other hand, are based on a rationally controlled, objective view of a stressful situation, a view that leads toward a solution through either performance (services or information) or production (money or possessions). In emotion-focused strategies, no instrumental solution is needed or is even possible. Closeness or emotional availability, comfort, support, and reassurance of personal and relational worth and importance are needed here. Certain painful events (death and taxes) have no solution. Funeral arrangements need to be made, or money must be borrowed to pay a tax assessment. Beforehand, however, the pain of the loss needs to be shared. In stressful situations for which no solution exists (death, rejections, financial reverses, job losses), all that is left is the sharing of hurt feelings, which is the function of bereavement, grieving, and mourning. When partners can join together and share their hurts and their sad feelings about inevitable and painful events, not only do they become available to each other but they give their children a model for how to cope with insoluble events. Unlike stress theory, which emphasizes cognitive appraisal as primary to affective involvement, this theory emphasizes the primacy of emotions as the very basis of love and of family living as well as of competence and coping with stress.

Usually, but not always (and admittedly stereotypically), men who are socialized for selfishness will tend to use problem-focused strategies, and women who are socialized for selflessness will tend to use emotion-focused strategies (Barnett, Biener, & Baruch, 1987; Belle, 1987; Miller & Kirsch, 1987). Most men in our culture, at least in the past, were socialized for the role of, and therefore tended to strive to be, rational problem solvers (i.e., power). Most women in our culture were socialized for and therefore tended to strive toward being in touch emotionally—experiencing, acknowledging, and expressing their feelings (i.e., presence).

Ironically, when one observes which gender in dual-career couples does most work in the house, the woman is invariably more involved than her husband (Levant & Pollack, 1995). Acock and Demo (1994) concluded in their review:

> It appears that many husbands lack sufficient appreciation for the importance of household labor to become more involved themselves. The clear and consistent

> pattern is that, across all family types, mothers (whether employed or not) perform two to three times more housework than their husbands or cohabiting partners. (p. 103)

The irony lies in a discrepancy: those who are more emotion-oriented tend to perform instrumentally in the home; those who are more solution-oriented perform less. Another way to understand these differences stereotypically is through the distinction (Clark & Reis, 1988) of agentic roles for men and communal roles for women.

This major gender difference has profound implications for interpersonal functioning and dysfunctioning. The use of mutually exclusive strategies—what Parsons (Parsons & Bales, 1955) called nurturance (presence or communal) and instrumentality (power or agentic)—represents a deeply ingrained socialization that leads many individuals to respond without much awareness of how their strategies differ from those of their partners. This difference, left unresolved, produces polarizations in couples and becomes counterproductive to joint solutions and resolutions. Emphasizing one strategy at the expense of another not only restricts the repertoire of either partner but, when this emphasis produces mutually exclusive strategies, deters family members from being available to each other in times of need (Levant & Pollack, 1995). The man may tend to maintain his rational facade of instrumental problem-solving performer; the woman may tend to express her emotionality, sometimes blaming the man or at least making him feel guilty for whatever has stressed the couple. She cries; he gets angry!

Additional support for the existence of such stereotypes (as tacit and implicit beliefs) is summarized by Geis (1993). These stereotypes:

> described men as dominant, rational, objective, independent, decisive, competitive, aggressive, capable of leadership, good at science and mathematics, and interested in business, sports, and politics. They described women as submissive, deferent (to men), emotional, subjective, gullible, dependent, sensitive to others, caring, nurturant, able to devote themselves to others, and good at domestic tasks and childrearing. (p. 11)

Both stereotypes apply to selfish and selfless personality propensities, including as well the characteristics of selfulness. From the viewpoint of *gender differences,* the selfhood model predicts that sex ratios are equal in the selfulness and no-self quadrants, but reverse sex ratios are present in selfishness and selflessness. In selfishness, this model predicts an approximate ratio of four men to one woman. The ratio in selflessness is four to one in favor of women.

The detailed rationale, evidence, and consequences for these reverse ratios have been reviewed in previous publications. This evidence supports the relative preponderance of selfishness in men, the relative preponderance of selflessness in women, and their relationship in the etiology of impulsivity and acting out, on one hand, and of depression and affective disorders, on the other.

Another source of independent theoretical support for the selfhood model is found in the attachment model derived from object relations theory, which is reviewed in Chapter 6.

Reasons for these percentages and for the reversal between gender roles along the selfishness–selflessness axis can be found in the following arguments and data:

1. In relation to the pessimistic prediction of only 25% of the population being included in the selfulness propensity—that is, there are no sex differences in either good adjustment (selfulness) or very miserable adjustment (no-self)—a variety of data would support that conclusion. From this model, one would expect that:
   a. Only 25% (±5%, depending on the criterion used) of the U.S. population are free of neurotic symptoms and would show characteristics of the selful personality propensity.
   b. Only 10% (±5%) of long-term marriages will consider themselves to be "happy" or, by external evaluations, "well-adjusted." These judgments depend heavily on what criterion is used.
2. Where the sex ratios in the Selfishness and Selflessness categories are concerned, the following argument suggests that, as a whole, at least in the past, 25% (±5%) of the women have been socialized for Selflessness, and 25% (±5%) of the men have been socialized for Selfishness. These estimates are not as farfetched as they would seem at first blush. Lykken (1995), for instance, stated: "The incidence of Antisocial Personality Disorder is . . . more than five times higher in males than in females" (p. 5). The data to be considered are as follows:
   a. Of all battered individuals, 95% are women and the rest (5%) are men. This percentage means that perhaps 95% of batterers may be men or same-sex lovers (Swift, 1988), in either selfish or no-self propensities.
   b. Most instances of somatic internalizations occur in women rather than in men; the ratio is 5 to 1 (Robins, 1986, pp. 236–237).
   c. More men than women abandon the responsibility of the family by avoiding child support payments. One has only to read newspapers to corroborate this assertion.
   d. More instances of anxiety, depression, and related disorders (self-defeating and/or dependent personalities) take place among women than among men (Barnett, Biener, & Baruch, 1987; Cleary, 1987). Men show higher frequencies of criminalities and of character disorders with acting out than women do. The reasons suggested are:
      i. Women are socialized to give more than to receive (Belle, 1987); in fact, women participate in larger networks and enjoy confiding relationships. Men usually rely on just one person for support, the wife or female partner.

ii. Women are socialized to care about people and their problems, and they are more likely than men to provide help. (How many elementary school teachers, nurses, or social workers are men?) Thus, they are affected by interpersonal stressors more than men are (Wethington, Mcleod, & Kessler, 1987).

iii. There are substance-specific sex differences (Biener, 1987): women use prescription psychotropic drugs more than men do. Alcohol and drug use is higher among men than among women.

iv. As Oulette-Kobasa (1987) concluded, in her review of stress responses and personality:

> The neglect of personality in studies of stress among women and stress and gender differences is somewhat surprising given numerous studies showing that women suffer more symptoms under the impact of stressors, and given the theme prevalent in the psychological and sociological literatures that depicts women as having been socialized in a way that keeps them from developing resilient personalities. . . . While little boys are being taught to be oriented toward problem solving, independent and in control, little girls are learning how to express emotions, be sensitive toward others, and act in a dependent way. (p. 325)
>
> One explanation for the lack of studies may be the inadequacy of current paradigms. (p. 326)
>
> Our choice of personality variables should be guided by a coherent theoretical framework. . . . More expansive theorizing is likely to provoke the need for more complex personality hypotheses . . . . A related recommendation is the elaboration of a contextual focus. (p. 328)

Kobasa's recommendations are relevant to the goals of the present framework, with emphasis on different socialization practices for genders, and the importance of a contextual focus, as shown by the specification of settings relevant to personality development, i.e. home, school/work, and leisure. Her conclusions about gender differences developing since childhood are supported by early studies on sex differences in the awareness and reporting of anxiety in children.

Recent writings on the role of men (Levant & Pollack, 1995) suggest that most men, stereotypically speaking, are socialized to be dominant and selfish, and most women are socialized to be submissive and selfless. These tendencies are respectively present in acting-out, impulsive males, and in depressed, so-called "codependent" women. Normatively speaking, in functional couples, both partners cooperate in ways that are collaborative and that validate the reciprocal importance of each partner. In dysfunctionally reactive couples, the dominant-submissive dimension is more frequent. One partner needs to be on top and needs the other partner to be at the bottom. In the no-self propensity, both partners oscillate inconsistently within and between extremes of dominance and submission.

INTIMACY: CONCEPTUALIZATION AND ASSESSMENT

The importance of intimacy in human relationships has been reviewed by Prager (1995). Her conclusions about the role of intimacy in promoting "well being" are worth citing:

1. Intimate relationships seem to buffer people against the pathogenic effects of stress.
2. Intimate interactions may account for many of the health benefits that intimate relationships provide.
3. People are more likely to seek intimate interactions when they can benefit from them.
4. People who lack intimate relationships are at risk for a variety of ills.
5. Self-concealment has been associated with illness and symptoms of distress.
6. Relationships that do not allow confiding fail to provide the beneficial effects of those that do.
7. Poorly functioning relationships with parents, spouses, and friends have been associated with negative health outcomes (pp. 1–3).

In addition to these seven propositions, Prager stressed that "the effects of intimate interactions and relationships can only be understood in context . . . no behavior or adaptation is effective in all contexts. Context affects behavior directly and modifies its impact on interactions and relationships" (p. 6). Among the concepts related to intimacy are: "love, closeness, self-disclosure, support, bonding, attachment, and sexuality" (p. 13).

As Clark and Reis (1988) concluded in regard to individual differences in close interpersonal relationships: "[A] useful view of personality factors influencing the capacity for intimacy is beginning to emerge . . . a resolved, stable identity is prerequisite to establishing intimate relationships" (p. 636).

A recent review of intimacy, however, failed to find reference to the view of intimacy as sharing of joys, hurts, and fears of being hurt (Van den Brouchke, Vandereycken, & Vertommen, 1995). One would like to think that one reason for this exclusion was publication in family-related journals rather than mainstream American Psychological Association (APA) publications. On the other hand, the significant empirical work of Thelen and his coworkers (Descoutner & Thelen, 1991; Doi & Thelen, 1993), published in a reputable mainstream psychological journal, was also ignored. Hence, one is led to conclude that whatever conceptualization and assessment these authors produced is by necessity limited and possibly selective. Prager (1995), on the other hand, in her recent work in this topic, included the view of intimacy as sharing of hurts and of fears of being hurt.

Since the theory's inception (L'Abate, 1977; L'Abate & Sloan, 1985; L'Abate & Talmadge, 1987), intimacy was defined as the sharing of joys, hurts, and fears of being hurt, a view not even alluded to in Van den Brouchke et al.'s review. Empirical evidence to support this excluded view, at least in part, was sought initially by Frey, Holly, and L'Abate (1979) and developed further in the validation of a Sharing of Hurts Scale (Stevens & L'Abate, 1989). This scale and a spiral model of intimacy were refined further in an Italian edition (Cusinato & L'Abate, 1994). The scale developed and validated by Thelen et al., alluded to above, supports a view of intimacy as the sharing of one's vulnerability, fallibility, and neediness, that is, one's hurts (L'Abate, 1986).

In another instance, the authors of the same review conceptualized marital intimacy (p. 224) in terms of five components: (a) affective, (b) cognitive, (c) instrumental, (d) authenticity and openness, and (e) social group or network level. These components are similar to those of the theory's ERAAwC model, which are necessary to lead toward intimacy. Hence, even on different conceptual and evidential grounds, both conceptualizations agree on what is needed to achieve intimacy, even if defined differently.

By ignoring and excluding possibly significant conceptualizations of marital intimacy and their validation, the conclusions of the review by Van den Brouchke et al. (1995) should be taken as being somewhat limited and certainly selective. In a response to the foregoing criticisms, Van den Brouchke (personal communication, October 9, 1995) concluded:

> On the other hand, we were very pleased to see the many similarities between your model and our conceptualization of marital intimacy. Given that both models were arrived at on very different conceptual and evidential grounds, this similarity may be considered as contributing to the conceptual validity of both. We consider this an important issue, and intend to point out this similarity in any future writings based on our model. We hope that you will also consider this option, and trust that it will add to the further understanding of marital intimacy and its effects.

Further support for the notion of intimacy as sharing of joys, hurts, and fears of being hurt is found in the research of Jones, Kugler, and Adams (1995), whose chapter is aptly entitled: "You always hurt the one you love." This point is elaborated in Chapter 4.

INDEPENDENT EMPIRICAL EVIDENCE RELATING TO THE SELFHOOD MODEL

Independent empirical evidence consists of research that bears epistemological and conceptual similarity to the personality propensities used in this model (selfulness, selfishness, selflessness, and no-self) but is completely unrelated to the original theory. For instance, support for the validity and importance of an externalization-internalization dimension intersecting with a vertical dimension of functionality-dysfunctionality is widespread and derived from a variety of sources, especially developmental ones (Cicchetti & Toth, 1991;

Loeber & Farrington, 1994; McMahon, 1994; Reynolds, 1992). More recently, in a review of personality processes, Revelle (1995) stated: "There is strong agreement that the dimensions of extraversion-introversion and neuroticism-emotional stability are fundamental parts of any personality taxonomy" (p. 307).

Support for the two dimensions of distance and control is found in a variety of sources. The more recent and robust evidence has been introduced by Gondoli and Jacob (1993) for families, and by Benjamin (1993a) and Soldz, Budman, Demby, and Merry (1993) for individuals. Gondoli and Jacob, using the Family Environment Scale, the Family Assessment Measure, and Family Adaptability and Cohesion Evaluation Scales III with 138 families, found three factors: (a) affect-cohesion, (b) family activities, and (c) control. Benjamin stressed an orthogonal circumplex made up of love-hate and enmeshment-differentiation dimensions. Soldz et al. stressed an orthogonal model made up of two dimensions defined by extremes in coldness-overnurturance (i.e., love) and domineeringness-nonassertiveness (i.e., power).

Larsen and Diener (1992) proposed a circumplex model of emotion that bears significant similarity to the two distance and control functions of the theory. Their model has significant implications not only for the role of emotionality (*E*) but also for the role of rationality (*R*) in personality development. These researchers proposed a horizontal axis defined by unpleasant and pleasant extremes and a vertical axis defined by high and low activation. From these two axes, they extracted four dimensions intersecting in the middle of the four quadrants: (a) activated unpleasant affect; (b) activated pleasant affect; (c) unactivated unpleasant affect; and (d) unactivated pleasant affect. Because this approach was strictly intraindividual and nonrelational, the theory would predict that pleasant affect leads to approach, unpleasant affect leads to avoidance, high activation leads to discharge, and low activation leads to delay.

Furthermore, from the two major axes, Larsen and Diener obtained eight distinct clusters of emotions, to which they attached personality characteristics:

Cluster of Emotions	Personality Characteristics
1. Unpleasant affect: unhappy, miserable, sad, grouchy, gloomy, and blue	Anxiety, depression, and somatic complaints
2. Activated unpleasant affect: distressed, annoyed, fearful, nervous, jittery, anxious	Neuroticism and private self-consciousness
3. High activation: aroused, astonished, stimulated, surprised, active, intense	Need for stimulation
4. Activated pleasant affect: enthusiastic, elated, excited, euphoric, lively, peppy	Extraversion and sociability

Cluster of Emotions	Personality Characteristics
5. Pleasant effect: happy, delighted, glad, cheerful, warmhearted, pleased	Subjective well-being, life satisfaction, and happiness
6. Unactivated pleasant affect: relaxed, content, at rest, calm, serene, at ease	Constructive thinking
7. Low activation: quiet, tranquil, still, inactive, idle, passive	Emotional control
8. Unactivated unpleasant affect: dull, tired, drowsy, sluggish, bored, droopy	Social introversion

The issue here, as well as in the rest of the theory, is how to integrate circumplex models of personality with the selfhood model when these models predict different personality arrangements. For instance, although the selfhood model postulates maximum functionality in balance of approach-avoidance and discharge-delay functions, this is not the case in Larsen and Diener's model. These differences could be explained in terms of the intraindividual versus interindividual emphases of the two models, as well as the possibility that there are no one-to-one relationships between internal emotional states and external interpersonal relationships. Nonetheless, this is an area of controversy that will need to be addressed.

A recent study of children and adolescents (McDermott & Weiss, 1995), using a very large (N = 1,400) sample, found four major dimensions that, according to the authors, make up a "taxonomy" of behavior styles:

1. Adjusted and adequately adjusted: inhibition, disruptiveness, apprehension, and indifference.
2. Marginally adjusted: withdrawal, motivation deficit, avoidance, attention seeking, moodiness, nonparticipation, and dependency.
3. At risk: undersocialized aggression, oppositional, provocative attention seeking and manipulation, and attention deficit hyperactive.
4. Maladjusted: instrumental aggression, defiant aggression, avoidant, and schizoid qualities with depressed mood.

These dimensions seem to bear corresponding similarities with the four personality propensities derived from the relational model of selfhood: selfulness for (1), selflessness for (2), selfishness for (3), and no-self for (4).

A study by Swanson et al. (1995) is in line with a view of psychopathology derived from the selfhood model. These investigators developed a short-form test (MMPI-TRI) from items that demonstrated "very high content stability" from both the MMPI and MMPI-2. Three 20-item scales measured: Subjective

Distress, Acting-Out, and Psychosis. After establishing "excellent" internal consistency and sufficient independence from each other, these scales were administered to three groups: (a) 2,831 patients, aged 12 to 84 years, diagnosed as anxious and depressed; (b) 1,060 male prison inmates; and (c) 117 patients diagnosed as schizophrenic and psychotic. The first group yielded highest scores on the Subjective Distress scale (i.e., internalization); the second group yielded highest scores on the Acting-Out scale (i.e., externalization); and the third group yielded highest scores on the Psychosis Scale (i.e., No-self), as a model of psychopathology derived from the selfhood model would predict.

ABILITY TO NEGOTIATE

In a major review of negotiation and mediation, Carnevale and Pruitt (1992) presented a model of dual concerns that looks interestingly similar to the selfhood model. When concern for outcomes to the self and the other are separated into weak and strong, a four-part classification ensues: (a) when concern for self and other is strong, problem solving takes place; (b) when concern for self is strong but for other is weak, contentious tactics take place (i.e., pushing limits?); (c) when concern for self is weak but for other is strong, concession making takes place (i.e., inability to set limits?); and (d) when concern for self and other is weak, inaction takes place (i.e., nobody wins?). Hence, from this model, one would predict that negotiation and problem solving would be most effective in selful (CC) propensities, least effective in no-self (AA), and conflictual in selfish and selfless propensities (RR).

SETTINGS

Elder and Caspi (1990) supported the importance of environmental settings and their variability, especially in settings marked by interdependence, such as the family:

> Environmental variations have behavioral consequences, and individual variations tell us something about how social change is likely to affect behavior and lives. Although a large number of studies have described the behavior patterns of individuals over the life-span, they seldom give equal attention to social context. Moreover, most studies of social context and its influence are carried out as if it did not change. . . . Indeed, studies that begin with the individual seldom do justice to the environment, and studies that begin with macroscopic trends or events often ignore the individual. (pp. 201–202)

Sundberg, Snowden, and Reynolds (1978), in addition to reviewing the field of competence assessment, moved toward the assessment of "situations" by concluding: "At the present time [almost 20 years ago] despite the rapid development of environmental, organizational, and community psychology, along with the behavioral approach, there is little appropriate and practical assessment technology for assessing situations as they related to individuals" (p. 201). Could it be that the field of competence assessment has not progressed as much because it has ignored the very first situation that is fundamental to all following situations—the family?

When one moves on to environmental psychology (Stokols, 1978), one finds reviews of "human spatial behavior" where "The central concern of *proxemics* is the manner in which people use space as a means of regulating social interaction" (p. 270). Under this rubric, one finds concepts such as privacy, personal space, territoriality, and crowding, where "The basic unit of analysis in ecological psychology is the *behavior setting,* a recurring pattern of human activity that takes place within specific time and space boundaries" (p. 276). Stokols concludes his review:

> Transactional views suggest that any attempt to conceptualize the relationship between environment and behavior must account not only for the effects of the environment on people, but also for the reciprocal impact of people on their milieu. . . . The optimization theme emphasizes the attempts of individuals and groups to create environments that are maximally supportive of their goals and activities. The concepts of transactionalism and optimization are relevant to one of the major tasks currently facing the behavioral sciences: namely, the development of a taxonomy of environments. (p. 279)

It is very doubtful whether this goal can be achieved as long as the family is left out of such taxonomy. No mention of the family was made in the two reviews cited above. In an update of the same topic, Stokols (1995) mentioned in passing the importance of the family. However, he did not include it in a classification of environments, a common practice in the field of ecological psychology.

EVIDENCE INDIRECTLY RELATED TO THE THEORY

Most of the indirect evidence to support at least parts of the theory relates to the validity of resource exchange theory, from which the theory is in part derived (Foa, Converse, Tornblom, & Foa, 1993). According to resource exchange theory, status, which has been translated here as attribution of importance, is the most fundamental resource exchanged between and among people. Of the other five resource classes posited by the theory, only love has been changed (to intimacy). The names of the other four resources remain unchanged except for their forming supraordinate modalities (information + services = doing or performance; and money + possessions or goods = having or production).

Besides resource exchange theory, the work of Clark and her associates (Clark & Reis, 1988; Mills & Clark, 1994) is strongly supportive of two different orientations in interpersonal relationships. These orientations are communal and agentic, which are, respectively, equivalent to presence and power in the present theory (Figure 1.9).

Using two coordinates of particularism versus concreteness, Foa (1993) ordered the six resource classes circularly. In this ordering, status, love, and services are defined as more particularistic than information, money, and goods. In turn, the latter three resources are more universalistic and concrete than the first three. Thus, status and love are closer to each other than the other four resource classes (being or presence). Money and goods (having or production) also are closer than information and services (doing or performance), which are opposite and, in fact, negatively correlated with each other. How can these two classes be reconciled under the modality of doing or performance? We might note that those who produce information are also producing a service. However, those who receive the service do not necessarily produce it. For instance, teachers, media, and libraries contain and produce information. Those who receive it do not produce the information themselves. Thus, the exchange is modulated by two processes of giving and taking. Those who give information do not necessarily receive it. Those who give services do not necessarily receive them. Those who receive information and services do not necessarily give either resource.

Another way to understand this negative correlation is to look at academic differences between physicists versus engineers, organic versus inorganic chemists, and experimental versus clinical psychologists. In each pairing, the former are interested in producing information for information's sake. The latter are interested in applying that information as a service. Many liberal arts academicians are quite negative toward those who perform services other than to produce and to propagate information.

In regard to a selfhood model, after studying the relationship between self and other, Foa (1993) concluded:

> [T]o love others requires self-acceptance and it is supported by the repeated finding of a positive relationship between giving love to self and to others. . . . Giving and receiving love cannot be done in a hurry; it requires time. Money, to the contrary, can change hands very rapidly. Love is a relatively long-term investment, with rewards being reaped only after several encounters. (p. 23)
>
> When an individual is denied the most needed resource, he tends to choose the resource which is nearest in the order to the preferred one. . . . Thus a person who needs to be loved and can obtain only money will never be satisfied no matter how rich he becomes. In the same manner, an individual who has been insulted (deprived of status), and can retaliate only by destroying goods belonging to the insulter, will inflict a great deal of damage and still be left with a grudge. (p. 27)

Converse and Foa (1993) focused on how people reciprocate when the preferred resource class is not available to them. If reciprocation cannot take place with the same resource, people will tend to reciprocate with the resource closer in the circular order. If one cannot give love, one may choose to provide status or services. Instead of money, one may exchange goods, according to a norm of distributive justice.

Brinberg and Ganesan (1993) found that the meaning of behavior within an exchange, rather than the behavior itself, determines the outcome of the exchange. For instance, a birthday card from a loved one may be more important than money received from an employer. Resource availability may need to be taken into account in the ordering of resources.

Foa, Salcedo, Tornblom, Garner, Glaubman, and Teichman (1993) studied the internal pattern of relationships among the six resource classes in five cultures (Israeli, Filipino, Mexican American, Swedish, and American). On the basis of intercorrelations, they concluded that this pattern repeated itself cross-culturally. These results support the universality of the six resource classes exchanged among people.

Blieszner (1993) studied the ordering of the six resource classes in older women, arguing that the heavy American emphasis on productivity may make these women feel less satisfied than younger women. It is unfortunate that the author did not use younger women or older men in this study to compare the results. Older women considered it perfectly normal to give to others more than to receive, in line with the gender differences predicted from a selfhood model.

Tornblom and Nilsson (1993) found that particularistic and universalistic resources are seen as being more important for one's life satisfaction when they are provided by a particularistic rather than a universalistic source. Hence, one needs to consider the identity of the giver as well as the receiver in order to understand the nature of an exchange—an issue that is covered by the concept of priorities. Out of eighteen items that included the six resource classes, subjects rated physical and mental health as well as the ability to control their lives as necessary contributors toward life satisfaction. By the same token, love and esteem (i.e., importance) from loved ones were seen not only as necessary but also as sufficient.

Berg and Wiebe (1993) stressed the importance of studying exchanges in natural contexts such as the work setting, rather than paper-and-pencil self-report tests. In two different work settings, one with sophisticated and nonrepetitive tasks, the other with repetitive and routine tasks, they found that indeed the setting and the nature of the task, as well as the resources exchanged among workers, had considerable influence on job satisfaction, including how much context is valued over task demands.

Rettig, Danes, and Sauer (1993) recognized that the family is an important contributor to life satisfaction and consequently used a multidimensional scale that measured subjective perceptions of family life quality that contained resources exchanged among family members. Their subjects were farm families who were experiencing economic hardships that affected how they perceived various resources. The unavailability of money, of course, affected how the other resources were exchanged. Women were much more dissatisfied than men.

Teichman, Glaubman, and Garner (1993) studied the resources exchanged at four developmental stages (early adolescence, adolescence, young adulthood, and middle-aged adulthood) from three sources: family, coworkers, and peers.

Adolescents, more than those in the other three stages, showed greater need for resources, regardless of the source. Except for this finding, no other changes were found over the life cycle.

Berg, Piner, and Frank (1993), after comparing resource exchange theory with similar theories, found that close friends exchange and share more resources of all types than casual friends or acquaintances, especially when one takes into account whether the resource exchanged is particularistic or universalistic. Furthermore, self-disclosure with a partner will correlate positively with the amount of resources received from that partner, especially if the resource is particularistic and selected. Rules of exchange vary according to the degree of closeness in the relationship, as found also by Clark and her coworkers (Clark & Reis, 1988). On the basis of these results, Berg et al., recommended that "need" be added to resource exchange theory as a fundamental dimension along which most resources vary. In other words, this recommendation would support this theory's original definition of subjective and selective perception in deciding who is important to oneself on the basis of "necessity" for survival and enjoyment.

Tornblom, Stern, Pirak, Pudas, and Tornlund (1993) used the six resource classes to elaborate on social comparison theory (reviewed in detail in Chapter 5). People compare themselves with others according to whether they possess a resource (i.e., money) or whether they have the ability to acquire that resource, in addition to the resource used in the comparison. Age and gender were significant sources of differences in these results.

Brinberg and Ganesan (1993) studied the attractiveness of selected resources (a telephone, a kiss, and gold) in variously contrived situations. Their results supported the conclusion that similarity in resources determined the likelihood of their being exchanged. If we do not receive money, we may substitute goods. We may exchange services for money or goods. The authors stressed the importance of resource availability for the ordering of the six classes of resources. Hence, one needs to consider necessity and availability as corollary to which particular resources are exchanged.

CONCLUSION

The independent conceptual evidence was selectively reviewed because one cannot cover all the possible evidence necessary to support this theory. Regardless of the similarity of conceptual and empirical evidence that is both independently and indirectly supportive of the theory, ultimately the validity of this theory will stand or fall on the basis of evidence derived *directly and empirically* from the theory itself, as reported in the next chapter.

CHAPTER 3

Corroborating the Theory: Direct Evidence

> We cannot distinguish what is real about the universe without a theory. (Hawking, 1993, p. 44)

Measurement of theoretical concepts and models should take place, as much as possible, contemporaneously with theory building. The two enterprises cannot be separated from each other, lest theory become fantasy and measurement become goalless and futile, without a theoretical background. Nonetheless, theory usually comes before research because the theory directs and organizes the research. Research to validate this theory was at first conducted psychometrically through paper-and-pencil, self-report instruments. These instruments measured: level of likeness in the family, priorities, intimacy, and similar concepts. However, because many children in families cannot report at the same level as their parents, a visual, self-report battery was developed that could be administered to a whole family, ranging from children 6 years of age to adults. Various doctoral dissertations validated (with different degrees of success) some of the psychometric qualities of these instruments. Other supporting evidence about the validity of certain theoretical constructs in previous versions of the theory were summarized in L'Abate and Wagner (1985) and L'Abate (1994b). However, the most recent research, as summarized below, combines clinical applications with the selfhood model. More recently, a simple, short, easy-to-administer self-report rating scale of self–other importance, the Self-Profile Chart (SPC), was developed (L'Abate, 1992b). (See Appendix A.) This scale derives from, and tests directly, the relational selfhood model.

SELFHOOD AND DEPRESSION: A TEST OF A SELFHOOD MODEL OF RELATIONAL PERSONALITY PROPENSITIES

L'Abate, Lambert, Vardaman, and Lewy (1996) evaluated the relationship between the selfhood model of personality propensities and depression. A relational selfhood model of depression, derived from a developmental theory of interpersonal competence, specifies the relationships among levels of depression (high–low) and personality propensities. This model predicts that individuals who rate themselves high on both self and other(s) (i.e., selfulness) would demonstrate the lowest levels of depression. Individuals who rate themselves low on both self and other(s) (i.e., no-self) would demonstrate the highest levels of depression. Individuals who rate self higher than other(s) (selfishness), or who rate other(s) higher than self (selflessness), would demonstrate intermediate levels of depression, between selfulness and no-self. This final prediction, however, needs qualification because of the role of gender differences.

Gender differences would show equal ratios of men and women in both selfulness and no-self, and, at least stereotypically in the American culture, more men than women in the selfishness personality propensity. The reverse would be found in selflessness: a greater number of women than men would be found. Because women, at least in our culture, are able and willing to admit to and internalize depression while men tend to deny and externalize it, relative to each other, the model would predict that the level of depression of selflessness would be higher than in selfishness; in fact, it would almost approach the level of depression found in no-self.

Additionally, although selflessness predicts a more positive therapeutic outcome than selfishness, the latter, being even more resistant to change than the no-self propensity, would show the lowest amount of change after treatment. Hence, from the viewpoint of therapeutic change, no-self and selflessness would change the most, and selfishness would change the least. Individuals in the selfulness propensity would not show much change because their rating of themselves is already high. However, their change scores would be somewhat greater than those of selfish individuals.

The call sheet for this study specified that subjects had to admit being depressed, detailing many characteristics that are associated with this condition. The study was explained in detail through an informed consent form that described the nature of the study, guaranteed anonymity, and provided no consequences if participants were to drop out from the study. After the consent form was signed, subjects were mailed the test instruments, which they returned to a specially designated drop-box in the Psychology Department. No face-to-face contact between subjects and experimenters took place except by happenstance. Interactions between subjects and experimenters, if necessary and relevant to the administration of the study, took place by telephone. The four experimenters had no knowledge of the theory or models underlying the study.

Subjects were undergraduates (N = 155) who volunteered to participate in a study involving programmed writing about depression, in exchange for course credits. Seventy-eight subjects completed the study; 77 did not. Among the completers, one subject did not complete one inventory but did complete the other two. Subjects were administered four paper-and-pencil, self-report instruments on a pre-/postintervention basis. The three depression instruments administered were: (a) the Beck Depression Instrument (BDI); (b) the Center for Epidemiological Studies Depression Scale (CES-D) (both (a) and (b) have received a great deal of research attention and are considered two of the most useful indicators of depression (L'Abate, Boyce, Fraizer, & Russ, 1992; L'Abate, Hamm, Russ, & Bird, in press)); and (c) the Depression Experiences

Questionnaire (DEQ) developed by Blatt and coworkers (Blatt, Quinlan, Chevron, McDonald, & Zuroff, 1982) to distinguish between two types of depression: dependency and self-criticism. Because the authors of the questionnaire were unwilling to cooperate with the researchers, only one group of subjects had their DEQ scored. Furthermore, the failure to obtain positive correlations between the DEQ and the other instruments used in this research forced the dropping of this questionnaire from the research.

To evaluate self–other propensities, the Self-Profile Chart (SPC) was also administered. The SPC is a short rating scale designed to evaluate oneself on dimensions of personal ("Self") and interpersonal ("Others") roles on a 10-point range, with 1 representing extreme unimportance and 10 representing extreme importance. This instrument is based on Harter's (1993) work on global self-worth. Even though her construct is static, intrapersonal, and nonrelational, it is seen as being very closely related to a sense of importance, which is, however, processible, dynamic, and relational. This sense of importance, according to the model, is continuously exchanged among people—intimates and strangers alike—as seen in language and nonverbal behavior. Harter's scale was revised and amplified to include a temporal perspective (present, past, and future) and to distinguish clearly between dimensions of self and relational roles with intimate others (L'Abate, 1992b, pp. 80–81).

In a previous study with 52 former psychotherapy clients (L'Abate, Hamm, Russ, & Bird, in press), the SPC total Self–Others score was found to correlate positively and significantly with the Tennessee Self-Concept Scale (TSCS; Roid & Fitts, 1989) and the total score of the Coping Resources Inventory for Stress (CRIS; Matheny, Aycock, Curlette, & Junker, 1993), suggesting that all three were measuring overlapping aspects of the self concept. The SPC, however, takes only a few minutes to administer and less than a minute to score. The other two scales take from 30 to 45 minutes to administer and at least 5 to 10 minutes to score. The SPC, therefore, seems to fulfill some of the criteria set to select instruments for treatment outcome assessment (Newman & Clario, 1994). (An item analysis of this instrument is in progress.)

The interventions of this study consisted of two writing programs, focused respectively on the nature of self-criticism, and on dependency. Both programs were administered randomly through the mail. The experimenters knew nothing about the nature of the subjects' depression, because all of the test instruments were scored after completion of these assignments. Both depression programs (or workbooks) consisted of four lessons, administered once a week for four weeks. Each lesson was mailed after the previous one had been completed.

Completers were not significantly different from noncompleters. Both groups combined were, on average, approximately 23 years old. The two SPC measures of Self and Others were dichotomized at the medians for all subjects, completers and noncompleters, to obtain more stable estimates. Four cells were produced: (a) Self and Others ratings were both above the median of the scores distribution (i.e., selfulness); (b) Self was above and Others was below the median score (i.e., selfishness); (c) Others was above and Self was below the median score (i.e., selflessness); and (d) both Self and Others were below the median score (i.e., no-self).

Major differences between these two groups, found in "Self-Now" and "Self-Past" ratings, "Total Self," and CES-D, indicated that noncompleters were more positive toward Self and Others and slightly less depressed than completers. On both the BDI and CES-D, noncompleters' depression scores were slightly lower than those of completers, but not to a notable degree. Completers showed significantly higher scores on Self. On temporal perspective in the SPC, noncompleters produced higher scores than completers on Self-Past. Although completers showed a slightly lower score on Self-Future, the difference was not significant.

Even though differences among the means of the four cells were statistically significant for the Self main effect and for the Others main effect, there was no significant interaction between the two. On the BDI, high-Self/high-Others subjects (selfulness) scored at the lowest level of depression. The low-Self/low-Others (no-self) subjects scored at the highest level of depression, and the high-Self/low-Others (selfishness) and low-Self/high-Others (selflessness) subjects scored in between the two other groups. Subjects in the selfishness cell scored slightly lower than those in the selflessness cell.

The pattern of results found on the BDI was replicated on the CES-D. Mean cell scores were statistically different from each other. Both Self and Others showed significant main effects, with no significant interaction between the two effects. The high-Self/high-Others (selfulness) cell showed the lowest depression score, and the low-Self/low-Others (no-self) cell showed the highest score. The other two groups, high-Self/low-Others (selfishness) and low-Self/high-Others (selflessness) showed intermediate mean scores between the two other groups. However, the mean score for the high-Self/low-Others was lower than the mean score for low-Self/high-Others.

All of the correlations among the independent (SPC) and dependent variables (BDI and CES-D) were highly significant and in the expected directions: SPC Self with SPC Others, SPC Self with BDI, SPC Self with CES-D, with the expected negative correlation between the SPC Others and the two measures of depression, BDI and CES-D. Both BDI and CES-D were also highly correlated. These correlations support the prediction that depression scores are highly related to personality propensities as measured by the SPC. One needs to keep in mind that these results derive from a functional or semifunctional sample of undergraduates whose range in depression scores would not be as great as those in a clinically depressed sample.

The correlation matrix for completers showed significant correlations among the SPC Self–Others measures before and after the programmed writing assignments. The magnitude of these correlations supports the reliability of this rating scale, and its negative and significant correlations with both the BDI and CES-D support its concurrent validity. Depression is indeed significantly correlated with Self–Others ratings. The positive and statistically significant correlations between pre-/postintervention scores for the SPC help to support the reliability of this instrument, even though there was an intervention between the two time periods. Most of the other correlations help to establish the concurrent validity of this instrument, to the extent that it is consistently and significantly correlated negatively with two established measures of depression.

On the BDI, completers who received the Self program, and who rated themselves high (above the median) on Self and Others on the SPC, showed the lowest depression scores and little improvement after treatment. Those who rated themselves low on both Self and Others showed the highest depression scores. However, those who rated themselves high on Self and low on Others showed an intermediate level of depression, and those with low ratings on Self and high ratings on Others showed the highest scores on depression. All three groups showed a significant lowering of scores on the BDI after treatment, and there was significant interaction between high-Self and low-Self ratings and treatment effects over time. Even though, in both cases, high-Self and low-Self groups made significant gains posttest, the significance of this interaction was attributable to much greater gains in the low-Self group. When effect sizes were calculated, the low-Self group showed a much larger effect size than the average size of the high-Self group. There was no other significant effect as a function of treatment. Both Self-directed and Others-directed programs showed significant main effects. For the Others-directed program, the only significant interaction was found with high-Others/low-Self propensity.

On the CES-D, the same pattern of changes after treatment was found. The high-Self groups on the SPC showed a significant main effect and no other significant interaction. Both Self and Others propensities showed independent main effects. Among subjects who were administered the Others program, scores for depression were lowest for those who rated Self and Others the highest. Those who rated low on both Self and Others showed high depression scores, and those who rated high on Others and low on Self scored as high on depression as the previous group. In the low-Self group, a statistical significance was found that was not present in the high-Self group. The effect size for the low-Self group was quite large; for the high-Self group, it was quite small. Among those who rated high on Self and low on Others, the level of depression was intermediate, with all four groups showing improvement after treatment. The effects found on the BDI were also found on the CES-D: low-Others subjects' scores showed greater depression than high-Others subjects' scores, regardless of treatment effects. The same results appeared on both instruments for low-Self over high-Self subjects.

On the CES-D, when the Self program was administered, subjects rating high on both Self and Others on the SPC received the lowest depression scores posttest, and those rating low on both Self and Others showed the highest depression scores. Subjects rating high on Self and low on Others, or low on Self and high on Others, continued to show intermediate depression scores. When the Others program was administered, those rating high on both Self and Others showed the lowest depression scores, compared to those who rated low on both Self and Others. Subjects who rated high on Others and low on Self showed as high a level of depression as those who scored low on both Self and Others. Subjects who rated themselves high on Self and low on Others showed intermediate depression scores and the lowest change scores after treatment.

Effect sizes illustrating and standardizing the reductions in depression scores, as measured by the BDI and CES-D, were calculated using the unbiased method described by Hedges and Olkin (1985). These effect sizes were then used to rank-order cells according to the magnitude of their treatment effects. On the BDI as well as in the CES-D, when both effect sizes were averaged together, the low-Self/low-Others cell, using the Others-directed program, ranked first with the highest effect size of change. The low-Self/high-Others and high-Self/high-Others cells in the Self-directed program were in the second and third places for effect size. The high-Self/high-Others and high-Self/low-Others cells showed the smallest effect size, with both ranking last among the cells. The other cells ranked with intermediate-effect sizes between the two extreme groups, as predicted by the original selfhood model.

A match between SPC scores and treatment interventions based on writing programs was defined by having subjects who scored low (below the median) on Self receive the Self program and subjects who scored low (below the median) on Others receive the Others program. A mismatch between SPC scores and treatment was defined by subjects' scoring high (above the median) on Self and receiving the Self program, and subjects' scoring high (above the median) on Others and receiving the Others program. On the BDI, the difference in mean scores between low-Others and high-Others (matched) groups who were administered the Others program was not statistically significant on pretest, nor was the difference between low-Others and high-Others groups on posttest. In the mismatched groups, where the Self program was administered to low-Others and high-Others groups, the difference in mean scores between the low-Others and high-Others subjects in pretest was significant. The same significant difference was found for the same groups on posttest.

These results may explain the interaction between the Others program and low- or high-Others groups, when subjects assigned to the Self program show the predicted differences. When the effect size was calculated for the matched groups (low-others subjects with Others program), there was a significant effect size. With the mismatched group (low-Others subjects with Self program), the effect size was average. However, these results were not replicated when the low-Self groups received either program. The low-Self group receiving the Others program showed a high effect size; the low-Self group receiving the Self program showed a smaller but significant effect size. Consequently, the effect size for matched groups seems to be greater than for the mismatched groups.

Ratios of men/women in the four cells, derived from median splits, followed predictions from the selfhood model. The overall baseline ratio of 123 women to 32 men was 3.84. There were 10 males and 46 females in the high-Self/high-Others (selfulness) cell, or a ratio of 4.6 women for each man. There were 15 males and 39 females in the low-Self/low-Others (no-self) cell, or a ratio of 2.6 women for each man. The number of subjects in both cells was very close—56 and 54, respectively. In the high-Self/low-Others (selfishness) cell, there were 6 men and 17 women (2.83 women for each man). In the low-Self/high-Others (selflessness) cell, there were 21 women for 1 man, with a near-equal number of subjects in each cell—23 and 22, respectively. The chi-square ratios for gender differences were all highly significant.

These gender differences persisted on posttest. Males were even in the low-Self/low-Others and high-Self/high-Others cells, but there were 4 men in the high-Self/low-Others cell and 2 men in the low-Self/high-Others cell. Women were almost equal in number in both the low-Self/low-Others and high-Self/high-Others cells. There were 8 women in the high-Self/low-Others cell (selfishness) and 12 women in the low-Self/high-Others cell (selflessness). The chi-square ratios for the differences in these cells were all highly significant.

The major implication of these results for intervention strategies stems from the results of the two depression programs and personality propensities. Individuals in the selfishness propensity are highly resistant to written interventions, suggesting that they may be just as resistant to verbal psychotherapy. As shown by L'Abate (1992b), where results from written intervention with two incarcerated felons were reported using a single case-design methodology, 18 to 30 lessons of a social training program expressedly created for impulsive individuals might be required.

A possible shortcoming of this study is the lack of a no-treatment control group. Currently, a control group is being recruited to improve the reliability of these results. At present, it is not possible to conclude that the results of this study tend to support a relational, selfhood model of personality propensities that views depression as a concomitant of such propensities.

TESTING A MODEL OF PSYCHOPATHOLOGY WITH THE MINNESOTA MULTIPHASIC PERSONALITY INVENTORY (MMPI-2)

Another study (L'Abate, Lambert, Townsend, et al., 1996) was designed to determine the validity of a model of psychopathology derived from and related to the relational selfhood model. To link this model of psychopathology to the MMPI-2, one needs to consider that this test was empirically derived from traditional Kraepelinian psychiatric nosology, with few if any ties to theories of personality development and socialization (Ben-Porath, 1995; Butcher, Dahlstrom, Graham, Tellegen, & Kaemmer, 1989). It remains to be demonstrated whether this empirically constructed test and the theoretically derived relational selfhood model can be linked together.

The secondary purpose of this study, therefore, was to evaluate whether programs specifically written for the fifteen Content scales of the MMPI-2 could lower peak scores while a control group would write about trivial topics, as in the methodology developed originally by Pennebaker (1990). In a preliminary study (L'Abate, Boyce, Fraizer, & Russ, 1992), peak and scale elevation scores on the MMPI-2 Content scales could be lowered by administering matching written homework assignments. The sample of subjects and the type of controls used were too small to arrive at conclusive statements. The present study, consequently, is an example of how evaluation can be linked through treatment when programmed writing is used as a medium of treatment. It was designed to determine whether a student's peak score and profile elevation from the Content scales of the MMPI-2 could be lowered by completing programmed writing homework assignments (lessons) developed isomorphically to match each Content scale (L'Abate, 1992b).

A total of 266 undergraduates completed this study either for extra credit in an introductory psychology class or as part of the requirements for an abnormal psychology class. Out of this total number, 221 students completed all the assignments and both pre- and posttest administration of the MMPI-2. Forty-five subjects did not complete the posttest and 4 did not complete the testing in a way that could be used. Of the subjects who completed the study, 162 were females and 59 were males. The median age was 23 years.

All students who agreed to participate, after signing an informed consent form, were administered the MMPI-2 as a pretest and, approximately six weeks later, took the MMPI-2 as posttest, after completion of the written homework assignments. The subjects who returned test protocols initially were randomly assigned to one of three groups: (a) control focused trivia (N = 48); (b) control programmed trivia (N = 56); and (c) experimental (N = 117). The two control groups were combined after it was found that their performance on the before–after testing was not significantly different. Those who received assignments matching their MMPI-2 Content scales were called "matched." Those who received general assignments directed toward supposedly trivial emotionally neutral topics were called "unmatched." All subjects completed four lessons from the workbook for the Content scale based on their peak score, or four assignments directed toward trivial topics, like describing past cars, clothes, places where they had lived, and so on.

The structure of each lesson or homework assignment was generally the same. Respondents were asked to define, in writing, what their particular symptom or problem means to them, and to explain, in detail, how they experience the problem (e.g., social discomfort, depression, cynicism). Various dimensions of the symptom were identified, and respondents were asked to "explain in detail" how each dimension applied to their experience. They were asked to write about specific instances when they experienced the problem and how they felt about those experiences. The next lesson involved evaluating or rating dimensions of the problem that were especially troublesome to them.

The peak or highest score on the Content scales was considered the target score. Where there were two equal peak scores, a coin was flipped to determine which one became the target score. Once the peak score was determined for each participant, lessons specific for each scale were assigned. Respondents were encouraged to take control and assume responsibility for possible change by making appointments with themselves to think and write about each lesson.

Students used their names when they volunteered as subjects. They kept contact with the experimenters through a mailbox set up in the Psychology Department. There was no personal contact with the experimenters. Because students in the abnormal psychology class had personal contact with one of the experimenters, they used five-digit identification numbers to remain anonymous. All test protocols and lessons were received and sent via envelopes with either the participant's name or a code number on the front. All envelopes with names were passed through a box in the Psychology Department. All envelopes with code numbers were passed through a folder of envelopes on the instructor's desk.

To obtain the personality propensities related to the selfhood model, four algorithms were used. These algorithms were reached on the empirical basis and nature of each scale, in keeping with clinical lore (Butcher et al., 1989). Subjects were classified as "normal" if their profile on the Basic clinical scales had no peaks above the 59th scaled score and no score below the 41st scaled score. Subjects were classified as "externalizers" (i.e., selfishness, in the original selfhood model) if they showed: (a) scores higher than the 59th scaled score on at least one of the following scales: F, Pd, Pa, or Ma; or (b) scores below the 41st scaled score on the Si scale; or (c) for men, scores below the 41st scaled score on the Mf scale, with the reverse for women who scored above the 59th scaled score. Subjects were classified as "internalizers" (i.e., selflessness, in the original selfhood model) if they showed: (a) scores above the 59th scaled score on at least one of the following scales: Hs, De, Hy, Pt, or Sc; or (b) scores above the 59th scaled scores on Si; or (c) scores below the 41st scaled score on the Mf, for women, and above the 59th scaled score, for men. Subjects were classified as being severely disturbed (i.e., no-self, in the original selfhood model) if they showed scores that classified them *both* as externalizers and internalizers. This group was called "Both."

Peak scores or spikes were obtained by subtracting the average on the other 14 Content scales from the peak score. In other words, the overall scale elevation was removed by analyzing deviation scores only, regardless of scale elevation. Profile elevation was analyzed separately. Results showed that personality propensities were not significant. The interaction of matched vs. nonmatched with time was significant: the nonmatched group improved more after treatment. The main effect for time decrease due to treatment was significant. The main effect for treatment groups was significant: the nonmatched subjects showed lower overall peak scores across time. No other main effect or interaction was significant.

When Hedges' Unbiased Effect Sizes (UBS) were calculated as a function of matched and nonmatched treatment and personality propensities, the nonmatched group showed a large UBS and the matched group showed a medium UBS. Among the personality propensities, the selful and selfishness groups showed the lowest overall increases, and the other two (selfless and no-self) groups showed the highest.

When scale scores were analyzed for the effect of the four personality propensities, only four Content scales reached statistical significance:

1. Anger: the matched group showed very low UBSs relative to the UBSs of the nonmatched group, and the no-self group showed the lowest UBSs of the four personality propensities, with no change after intervention.
2. Anxiety: in the same pattern, the UBSs for the matched group were lower than for the nonmatched group, and the UBSs for the selfishness and no-self groups were lower than for the other two personality propensities, with selflessness showing the highest UBS value.
3. Bizarre mentation: a reverse pattern compared to the other three scales; selfishness showed the highest UBS relative to the other three scales.
4. Health: selfulness in the matched group reached a medium level in comparison to the other three propensities; in the nonmatched group, selflessness reached the highest UBS value relative to the other three propensities.

In all four scales—anger, anxiety, bizarre mentation, and health—treatment reached significant statistical levels. The matched–nonmatched interaction with treatment reached significance only on anxiety. On the health scale, personality propensities interacted with treatment at a significant level.

The above results are very surprising because of the unexpected changes in the behavior of the control group, which run counter to the original hypothesis. Writing about trivial topics, either focused or programmed, was more effective in lowering peak scores and scale elevations than matched programs with high Content scales peaks. The research assistants who conducted this study reported that students in the two control groups expressed very positive feelings about their homework assignments. The quality of these assignments, which were less task-oriented and probably much less threatening than assignments directed toward lowering peak scores, may have been, paradoxically, somewhat responsible for these results (Segal & Murray, 1994). Furthermore, some of the so-called trivial assignments may not have been as trivial or neutral as was initially thought, especially since some of them dealt with friends, for instance. There is also a possibility that because students were used as participants and they earned school credit for their participation, those in the unmatched group may have felt they "got off easy" by not having to confront relatively threatening topics, which is what the matched group was asked to do. Another possibility: posttest scores might decrease as a result of practice effects.

A better method would be for the control group to make appointments with themselves and write about trivial topics, as was done by Pennebaker (1990). This approach would have alleviated any charge of unfairness from students who might have felt the amount of work was not fairly apportioned, though everyone earned an equal number of credits. It remains to be seen whether clinical clients or patients with higher peaks on Basic and Content scales would respond differentially to the administration of homework assignments matched with their clinical symptoms.

The major criticism that could be leveled against this type of MMPI-2 analysis (using algorithms from the Basic scales to analyze the Content scales) pertains to the inevitable overlap in items and the intercorrelations among the two sets of scales. The analysis of the Content scales tested whether, in addition to benefits regarding the lowering of specific peak scores, subjects received extra benefits by receiving a treatment that generalizes to other areas of functioning. To show the number of items that overlap between the Basic and Content scales, we performed this analysis. The Health Concerns scale showed an overlap of many items on the Hypocondriasis and Psychopathic Deviate Basic scales, and the Bizarre Mentation scale showed overlap on the F (reliability) and Schizophrenia Basic scales. Both Anxiety and Depression Content scales showed a large spread over many of the Basic scales.

Because this is a first attempt to relate the MMPI-2 to a selfhood model, it needs to be replicated. If the results on scale elevation on anger, anxiety, bizarre mentation, and health are substantiated on replication, a significant theoretical and interventional step may have been achieved. These results suggest a two-pronged approach to treatment of symptoms: first, to obtain more information about the client, a focused writing approach using Pennebaker's format (write about traumatic topics for 15 minutes on 4 consecutive days); and second, a programmed writing approach with specific homework assignments to match the clinical condition exhibited at the time of referral. Whether this approach would shorten the length of face-to-face treatment remains to be seen.

VALIDITY OF A TEST WITH TWO MEASURES OF FAMILY FUNCTIONING

There were two purposes to this study (Cox, Lambert, L'Abate, & Stanwyck, 1996). The first purpose was to validate a test derived from a theory of personality development (L'Abate, 1994b) that makes attribution of importance the cornerstone of personal and interpersonal competence. This theory postulates that the two primary interpersonal resources exchanged among people, especially in intimate (close), committed, and prolonged relationships, are the attribution of importance and intimacy—respectively, status and love in the original resource exchange theory (Foa & Foa, 1974). This sense of importance is continuously exchanged among people—intimates and strangers alike—as seen in language and nonverbal behavior. Developmentally, attribution of importance precedes intimacy, becoming, therefore, the primary resource exchanged between caretakers.

The validity of this selfhood model has been evaluated with undergraduates, using a college form of the same test (L'Abate, Lambert, Vardaman, &

Lewy, 1996), but the validity of this model with children needs to be closely examined. If this model is valid, one would expect that description of self/other-importance in children would correlate significantly with descriptions of family functioning.

A second purpose of this study was to evaluate whether the same measure of self–other importance could serve as a brief self-report screening instrument to discover children at risk for future dysfunctionalities. If children describe themselves and others negatively, one would predict that their descriptions of family functioning would be much less positive than those of children who view themselves and others in more positive ways. Children who describe themselves positively and others negatively, as well as children who describe themselves negatively and other positively, would occupy an intermediate position between selful and no-self children.

Subjects were 95 students from an elementary school in a suburb of a large metropolitan area in the southeastern United States. They were drawn from five fifth-grade classes that had approximately 20 students per class. Demographic information (age, race, gender, type of parents in home, and sex/age of siblings) was obtained from each student. Participating were 51 females and 49 males ranging from 9 to 12 years of age (mean age: 10 years). There were 67 Caucasians, 22 African Americans, 5 Caucasian/African Americans, 3 Asians, and 1 Hispanic. The female parenting type, living in the home, included 89 biological mothers, 4 stepmothers, 2 adopted mothers, 1 foster mother, 1 grandmother, and 1 aunt. Two households had no mother type. The male parenting type included 76 biological fathers, 13 stepfathers, 2 adoptive fathers, 1 foster father, 1 grandfather, and 3 uncles. Four households had no father type. Students gave the number and age of siblings (brothers, sisters, stepbrothers, and stepsisters).

To evaluate self–other propensities, the Self-Profile Chart (SPC) was used as a short rating scale designed to evaluate oneself on dimensions of personal ("Self") and interpersonal roles ("Others") on a 10-point scale, from extreme unimportance (1) to extreme importance (10). Rating scales for Self are: intelligence, physical attractiveness, sports success, sense of humor, school achievements, sociability, self-worth or self-esteem. One characteristic is left open to be specified by the respondent. Rating scales for Others are: parents, boy-/girl-friends, relatives, siblings, and friends. One line is left open for anyone not covered by the above list.

The Family Adaptability and Cohesion Evaluation Scale (FACES II), developed by Olson, Portner, and Lavee (1985), is a 30-item instrument designed to measure two main dimensions of family functioning: cohesion and adaptability. Family cohesion assesses the degree to which family members are separated from or connected to their family. It is defined as the emotional bonding family members have for one another. Family adaptability has to do with the extent to which the family system is flexible and able to change. It is defined as the ability of a family system to change its power structure, role relationships, and relationship rules in response to situational and developmental stress. There are 16 cohesion items and 14 adaptability items.

The eight concepts of the items related to the cohesion dimensions are: (a) emotional bonding, (b) family boundaries, (c) coalitions, (d) space/time, (e) friends, (f) decision making, (g) interests, and (h) recreation. The six concepts of the items related to adaptability dimensions are: (a) assertiveness, (b) leadership, (c) discipline, (d) negotiations, (e) roles, and (f) rules. There is a four- to five-week test–retest correlation of .83 for cohesion and .80 for adaptability. FACES II was revised in 1982 to provide a shorter instrument with simple sentences for use by children and adults with limited reading ability (L'Abate & Bagarozzi, 1993). A five-point Likert scale is used, ranging from almost never (1) to almost always (5). FACES II has a fair midrange validity in being able to discriminate among extreme, midrange, and balanced families in several problem categories.

The Self-Report Family Inventory (SFI), developed by Beavers and Hampson (1990), is a 36-item instrument used to provide a quantitative index that distinguishes competent from less competent families by looking at the family members' perceptions of their family's functioning. Its five subdimensions include: (a) family health, (b) family cohesiveness, (c) family expressiveness, (d) directive leadership, and (e) family conflict. The internal consistency of the SFI is .85 using Cronbach's alpha. The SFI has a fair amount of concurrent validity with the subscales of FACES II. The respondent has to choose one of five responses and circle the correct number. Four children failed to complete these two scales, which reduced the number of children in some analyses to 91.

A Parent Permission letter, sent to the parents or caretakers of all subjects, asked permission for their child to participate in the research project. Upon receipt of the signed permission letters from parents, subjects were administered the Self-Profile Chart (SPC), the Family Adaptability and Cohesion Evaluation Scale (FACES II), and the Self-Report Family Inventory. The three instruments were administered by the school counselor in the children's classroom. The tests were read orally to the class, and students marked their responses. This administration took approximately 45 minutes.

Results were evaluated with a correlation matrix among the three tests. This matrix showed that all three measures were significantly intercorrelated, supporting the view that it is difficult to differentiate a child's self-definition from how the child perceives and describes his or her family. On the FACES II, the correlations with the SPC are positive because higher scores on both tests indicate greater functionality. The correlations between the SPC and the SFI were negative because, in the latter test, the higher the score, the greater the dysfunctionality. The correlations between the SPC (as well as the FACES II) and the SFI were negative because scores on the test go in the opposite direction: the lower the score, the greater the level of functionality.

When the students were classified into personality propensities, using median scores to divide their distribution in both Self and Others categories, there were more students in the selfulness and no-self categories than in the selfishness and selflessness categories. The results for both measures of family functioning show that the no-self propensity had lower scores on both Cohesion and

Adaptability of the FACES II than did the other three propensities, indicating lower functionality. On the SFI, where higher scores indicate greater dysfunctionality, the no-self propensity showed higher scores than the other three propensities.

On the Cohesion scale of FACES II, the Others scale of the SPC produced a significant main effect and a significant interaction. At a lower level of significance, the Others scale of the SPC produced a main effect on Adaptability, with a significant interaction between the Self/Others scales of this instrument.

Although not statistically significant, the SFI's Health scale produced similar patterns of the means for the other scales. A significant main effect on SFI Cohesiveness was traced to an interaction between the Self–Others scales. Expressiveness failed to show main effects, but it did produce a significant interaction with the two scales of the SPC. Leadership showed a main effect with Self but not with Others, and no interaction. The Conflict scale failed to show any significant main effects or interaction.

A post-hoc comparison of the SPC's four personality propensities and the scores on FACES II and SFI was conducted using Tukey's HSD to evaluate interaction effects. This procedure demonstrates that, in general, members of categories 2 (selflessness), 3 (selfishness), and 4 (selfulness) scored significantly better on the scales of FACES II and SFI than did members of category 1 (no-self).

On the FACES II Cohesion scale and the SFI Expressiveness scale, the effect size (ES) between the no-self group and the other three personality propensities was "large"—greater than .80, which, according to Cohen (1988), is a large value for social science research. The rest of the effect sizes for the other scales, with the exception of the Leadership scale, are "moderate"—again, according to Cohen.

To test the hypothesis that more boys than girls would be in the selfishness personality propensity and that the reverse would be true for selflessness (more girls than boys), a chi-square test of independence for the four personality propensities was run for each gender. Fourteen boys and 22 girls were in the selfulness propensity, 8 boys and 5 girls were in the selfishness, 5 boys and 7 girls were in the selflessness, and 19 boys and 15 girls were in the no-self. The chi-square value for boys was significant (8.67; df $= 1$; $p < .003$). The chi-square value for girls was also highly significant (12.38; df $= 1$; $p < .000$).

These results suggest that one cannot separate self-description from description of one's family and friends, at least for this age range. The results of this study also tend to support an interpersonal, relational selfhood model that predicts the relation between descriptions of self–other importance and family functioning. In addition, it seems supportive of an attachment perspective, which has shown many consistent results in the research with adults—using, however, rather cumbersome and time-consuming interviews or questionnaires (Doane & Diamond, 1994; Sperling & Berman, 1994; West & Sheldon-Keller, 1994). A model similar to the selfhood one, but derived from attachment theory rather than resource exchange theory, has been proposed by Bartholomew (1990; Bartholomew & Horowitz, 1991), who found strong support for positive views of both self and other that predict a secure pattern of attachment characterized by comfort with intimacy and autonomy.

Having a negative view of self and a positive view of others predicts preoccupation with relationships. Having a positive view of self and a negative view of others predicts dismissal of intimacy and "counterdependency." Negative views of self and of others predict fear of intimacy and social avoidance. These patterns of attachment may derive from similar attachment patterns found in children, which bear some similarities to the four personality propensities measured by the SPC. For instance, selfulness would correlate with a secure pattern of attachment, selfishness would correlate with an anxious resistant pattern, selflessness would correlate with an anxious avoidant pattern, and no-self would correlate with a disorganized-disoriented pattern (L'Abate, 1994b, pp. 135–137). Further research in progress to substantiate these hypotheses is discussed next (Lardieri, 1996).

On the SFI Leadership scale, it is noteworthy to speculate whether both the no-self and the selflessness personality propensities, when compared or contrasted with the other two personality propensities of selfulness and selfishness, may derive from different parental practices, with low leadership for the former two personality propensities and relatively higher leadership for the latter two personality propensities. This hypothesis is not far-fetched, especially when one adapts the Selfhood model to Baumrind's (1980) classification of parental practices: authoritative for selfulness, authoritarian for selfishness, permissive for selflessness, and rejecting-abusive for no-self, as discussed in Chapter 1.

The results of the study imply that fifth-grade children who have positive perceptions of their families also have positive perceptions of the importance of self and others. The no-self personality propensity, defined by a negative sense of importance of self and others, appears related to families perceived as less cohesive and adaptable as well as less healthy.

ATTACHMENT PATTERNS AND SELFHOOD IN AN ITALIAN SAMPLE

Salvo (research in progress, a, b) compared Bartholomew's (1990) model with the selfhood model using the Italian version of the Adult Attachment Questionnaire (AAT) and the Italian Test of Dyadic Relations (TDR) developed by Cusinato (1990) to test the selfhood model. Salvo hypothesized that, given the similarities between the two models at the theoretical level, there should be significant correlations among the four categories postulated by Bartholomew and the four personality propensities postulated by the selfhood model. Her sample consisted of 100 married couples with one or more children, drawn from the schools of a southern Italian middle-sized city. The age range for these couples was between 29 and 49 years (average age: 38.29 years; S.D. = 4.00), with the men (N = 81) being slightly older than the women (N = 78) 40.13 and 36.46 years, respectively. Before administering the Adult Attachment Questionnaire, Salvo validated it with another larger sample of subjects ranging in age from 16 to 90 years. She found significant item-consistency in this scale, using Cronbach's alpha.

Among the correlations for the eight subscales of the two instruments, there were no significant correlations between Secure and Selful subscales nor between Preoccupied and Selfless subscales. There were significant correlations between Dismissing and Selfish ($r = .26$, $p < .01$), and between Fearful and No-Self ($r = .29$, $p < .001$). Salvo stressed that the Secure subscale showed the lowest internal consistency (alpha = .38) in comparison to the other three subscales of the AAT. Hence, she interpreted the Secure prototype as being more multidimensional, a quality that is not sufficiently explained by two self-report, paper-and-pencil instruments.

The absence of significant correlations between Preoccupied and Selfless is somewhat tempered by significantly positive but very small correlations between Preoccupied and Selfishness ($r = .14$, $p < .05$), Dismissing and Selflessness ($r = .12$, $p < .05$), Preoccupied and Dismissing ($r = .14$, $p < .05$), and Selflessness and Selfishness ($r = .12$, $p < .05$). The latter two polarities should show negative correlations because, supposedly, they are opposed to each other to the extent that one could oscillate between the two polarities, as hypothesized by the selfhood model. Furthermore, one cannot expect a one-to-one relationship between internal representations and interpersonal behavior. The latter may be influenced by external self-presentational and social desirability factors that may not influence internal representations. One could have a negative view of self but assume a more positive interpersonal behavior for a variety of reasons: fear of losing a loved one, fear of rejection and ridicule, wanting to make a good impression, and so on. Salvo, in line with the hypothesis about gender differences, found that women in her sample were much more preoccupied and fearful than men, who, in turn, appeared more dismissing on one hand and more selfless on the other. Men showed a more positive view of themselves; women showed a more positive view of others.

PERSONALITY PROPENSITIES, ATTACHMENT STYLES, AND FEAR OF INTIMACY

The purpose of this study (Lardieri, 1996) is to seek experimental validation of a core tenet of the relational selfhood model of personality development posited by L'Abate (1994b). In an attempt to seek empirical validation for the relational selfhood model of personality, this study will examine the relationship between selfhood propensity and the patterns of attachment predicted in the adult attachment literature (Bartholomew, 1990; Bartholomew & Horovitz, 1991; Feeney, 1995; Fuller & Fincham, 1995; Rholes, Simpson, & Blakely, 1995). In the attachment model, an individual's early life experiences culminate in one of four attachment patterns: a relatively healthy and secure pattern of attachment and three less stable, insecure patterns known as avoidant/preoccupied, resistant/dismissing, and disorganized/fearful. Of special interest to this study is the hypothesis that each attachment pattern may correspond to selful, selfless, selfish, and no-self propensities.

Although the study of adult attachment stems from object relations theory, the relational selfhood model is rooted in a developmental theory of interpersonal competence that is derived, in part, from the resource exchange theory of Foa and Foa (1974). Despite originating from divergent theoretical directions, each theory forecasts comparable interpersonal relationships for each of the hypothesized classifications. A great deal of interest has already been shown in the literature for the adult model of attachment (Brennan, Shaver, & Tobey, 1991; Collins & Read, 1990; Feeney & Noller, 1990; Hazan & Shaver, 1987; Kobak & Hazan, 1991; Simpson, Rholes, & Nelligan, 1992). The present study will focus on the relatively untested relational selfhood model to see what it can contribute to understanding personality development and psychopathology. In so doing, it will be possible to determine whether this model warrants further research attention.

This study will also examine the relationships between the four selfhood propensities cited above and fear of intimacy (Descoutner & Thelen, 1991; Doi & Thelen, 1993) to see how each propensity affects the capacity for intimacy. In addition, this research will investigate the relationship between selfhood propensity and emotional experience. After all, one cannot speak of personality development without giving consideration to emotional development.

According to differential emotions theory (Izard, Libero, Putnam, & Haynes, 1993), personal experience is equivalent to emotional experience. One naturally reacts to life's vicissitudes with emotion. The emotional reaction a person has to a situation not only reveals the attendant feelings, but also engenders accompanying thoughts about the experience and guides how it is viewed. According to this perspective, experience leads to an inextricable alliance of emotion, thought, and perception that serves to motivate a person in response to what is occurring. Through recurrent experiences, these emotion-cognition-action sequences become firmly established and result in "a pattern that characterizes the individual's style of adapting to challenging, frustrating, threatening, and other types of emotion-eliciting situations and contribute to the development of personality traits" (p. 848).

Given that an individual's selfhood propensity also arises from repeated interactions with parents/guardians, much like the emotion-cognition-action sequences discussed by Izard and his colleagues, this study will examine the interplay between selfhood propensity and emotionality. Are there predictable patterns of emotional experience that are idiosyncratic to the respective selfhood propensities (Blumberg & Izard, 1985, 1986; Izard, 1991b; L'Abate, 1994b)? Some support of this possibility can be gleaned from the work of Kobak and Sceery (1988). They demonstrated that first-year college students displaying a "dismissing" pattern of attachment were viewed by their peers as being more hostile than students displaying either a secure pattern of attachment or a preoccupied attachment pattern. Students displaying a preoccupied pattern of attachment were rated by peers as being more anxious than either the secure or dismissing groups. Not surprisingly, the type of attachment experiences one is subjected to at home appears to have an enduring impact on one's emotional life. As such, it is reasonable to speculate that there may be characteristic emotional experiences shared by individuals classified with the same selfhood propensities.

Finally, this study will evaluate the use of programmed writing as a psychoeducational intervention for the personality propensities listed above. The inclusion of this intervention is based on a series of studies that suggest that the process of focused writing (i.e., being directed to write in an open-ended fashion about specific experiences) can bring about salutary effects on one's physical health (Esterling, Antoni, Fletcher, Margulies, & Schneiderman, 1994; Francis & Pennebaker, 1992; Greenberg & Stone, 1992; Pennebaker, 1990; Pennebaker & Beall, 1986; Pennebaker, Kiecolt-Glaser, & Glaser, 1988), and programmed writing (i.e., being directed to answer a series of questions divided into lessons devoted to a particular topic) may positively impact one's emotional well-being (Esterling, L'Abate, Murray, & Pennebaker, 1996; Jordan & L'Abate, 1995; L'Abate, 1992; L'Abate, Boyce, Fraizer, & Russ, 1992; L'Abate, Hamm, Russ, & Bird, in press).

For the purpose of this study, programmed writing lessons that focus on the "sharing of hurts" will be employed as the treatment intervention. The decision to utilize this particular intervention is based on the possibility that one's capacity for growth/intimacy rests in large measure on one's ability to deal with one's hurts. In this regard, L'Abate (1986) suggested that the "sharing of hurts" is the binding element that cements nourishing relationships that last. Accordingly, the less an individual is able to come to terms with his or her hurts, the more vulnerable he or she is to emotional upheaval and problems with intimacy. Finally, the use of the "sharing of hurts" intervention is in line with Pennebaker and Francis's (in press) finding that individuals who employ significantly more negative emotion words in their assigned writing tasks exhibit the greatest improvement in their physical health as measured by immune function and decreases in their visits to the doctor. This finding is important because it indicates that the mere act of writing is less beneficial to a person than the act of writing about issues that have emotional gravity (i.e., one's hurts).

In light of the above, this study will examine the following five hypotheses:

1. There will be a positive correlation between a subject's selfhood propensity rating and a pattern of attachment.
2. Subjects displaying the no-self propensity will manifest the greatest fear of intimacy, and individuals in the selful category will exhibit the least fear of intimacy. It is also predicted that individuals displaying the selfish and selfless propensities, respectively, will fall somewhere in between these two extremes.

3. Selful individuals will be more inclined to experience the following emotions: interest, surprise, and joy. Selfish individuals will manifest a preponderance of disgust, anger, and contempt. Selfless individuals will show an inclination toward: shyness, guilt, sadness, and shame. No-self individuals will exhibit significantly greater amounts of fear and anxiety.
4. Programmed writing intervention on the "sharing of hurts" will be significantly more beneficial to selfless and no-self subjects than the "trivial" writing intervention.
5. No-self subjects will benefit most from the programmed writing task (i.e., the "sharing of hurts" lessons) and the selfless subjects will benefit secondarily from this intervention. Given their respective makeups, it is also predicted that the selful individuals and the selfish individuals will benefit the least from the programmed writing intervention.

Subjects (N = 80) for this study will be obtained on a voluntary basis from undergraduate psychology courses and will receive course credit for their participation. Prospective subjects will be asked to sign an informed consent form advising them that they will be participating in a research study that seeks to explore the relationships between the relational selfhood model of personality development, adult attachment style, and fear of intimacy. They will also be told that this study will examine the use of programmed writing as a psychoeducational tool. The subjects in this experiment will be grouped into one of four cells, based on their self and other rating on the "Self Profile Chart—Form CR." This classification will be combined with the type of intervention ("sharing of hurts" or "trivial" writing program) to produce a 2 (self rating) × 2 (other rating) × 2 (type of intervention) factorial design.

An updated version of the "Self Profile Chart—Revised Adult Form" (Appendix A) will serve as the independent variable to assess the subjects' selfhood propensities. The following scales will serve as the dependent measures: (a) the "Fear of Intimacy Scale," to assess comfort with intimacy (Descoutner & Thelen, 1991; Doi & Thelen, 1993); (b) the "Differential Emotions Scale" to assess emotional proclivities (Izard, 1991b; Izard, Libero, Putnam, & Haynes, 1993); and (c) the "Relationship Questionnaire" (Hazan & Shaver, 1987) and the "Relationship Scales Questionnaire" (Griffin & Bartholomew, 1994) to assess levels of attachment.

Subjects who agree to participate in this study will be asked to sign a consent form that outlines the focus of the study. This form will also include a guarantee of anonymity as well as an assurance that there will be no penalty for withdrawal from the study. Upon receipt of the consent form, each participant will receive a packet of test instruments via mail. Included in this packet will be instructions that they are to return the completed materials to a designated mailbox in the Psychology Department. Once the preintervention battery is returned, each subject will be randomly assigned to one of two treatment groups—either a programmed writing lesson that focuses on the "sharing of hurts" (L'Abate, 1986) or a "trivial" programmed writing lesson that would be considered a "control" intervention. All subjects will then be asked to complete a programmed writing lesson once a week for three weeks. Subjects will obtain each lesson through the mail and will not receive a subsequent lesson until the prior lesson is returned to the assigned mailbox. Upon receipt of the final programmed lesson, the postintervention packet will be mailed to each participant with the instruction that it should also be returned to the Psychology Department upon completion. On the basis of these procedures, face-to-face contact between the experimenter and subjects will be avoided, ensuring the anonymity of the participants and no undue influence from the experimenter.

THE RELATIONAL SELFHOOD MODEL AND THE FIVE-FACTOR MODEL

Flowers and Lambert (research in progress) are using the NEO Five-Factor Inventory as the dependent variable for the Self-Profile Chart (SPC), which will be the independent variable. The selfhood model predicts that selful individuals will exhibit low neuroticism, high openness, and high conscientiousness, Selfish individuals will exhibit high extraversion, low agreeableness, high openness, and low conscientiousness, Selfless individuals will exhibit high conscientiousness, low extraversion, high agreeableness, and low openness. No-self individuals will exhibit high neuroticism, low openness, and low conscientiousness. After administering both instruments to a large number of volunteer undergraduates, these researchers plan to perform a factorial MANOVA, crossing gender with self–other importance as measured by the SPC.

Preliminary results from a sample of 71 subjects found acceptable levels of internal consistency for both Self and Others scales, as measured by alpha coefficients of .85 and .89, respectively. In comparison, the five NEO scales yielded the following alpha values: Neuroticism = .86; Extraversion = .66; Openness = .79; Agreeableness = .80; and Conscientiousness = .80. A correlation matrix between Self–Others and the five scales of the NEO yielded a significant correlation between Self and Extraversion = .43, $p < .000$, and the following correlations between Other and Extraversion ($r = .51, p < .000$) and Other and Agreeableness ($r = .35, p < .003$). The Self and Others scales correlated .42, $p < .000$. Larger samples will be needed before substantive conclusions about the relationship of the FFM and selfhood can be reached.

RESEARCH ON A SPIRAL MODEL OF INTIMACY

In partial support for the position that intimacy consists of the sharing of joys, hurts, and fears of being hurt, Frey, Holley, and L'Abate (1979) conducted two experiments to assess the validity of three different methods of dealing with anger: (a) calm rational discussion; (b) "fair fighting"; and (c) sharing of hurts and of fears of being hurt. In the first experiment, videotapes of these three conflict resolution methods, played out by actors, were shown to 36 single undergraduates. Their stated preferences indicated no support for the hypothesis of gender differences in dealing with conflict and some support for differential preferences for each of the three methods. In the second experiment, three structured "enrichment" programs derived from the three theoretical positions were administered at random to 12 married couples. These couples and 10 no-treatment control couples completed the Multiple Affect Check List and the Profile of Mood States. Experimental couples also indicted their preference for each of the three approaches. The fair-fighting method was the most liked, the most preferred for learning, and the method in which they became most involved. Calm, rational discussion was seen as being most suited to interpersonal style and negotiation, and sharing of feelings was viewed as being the most intimate.

Stevens and L'Abate (1989), in a validation of a paper-and-pencil, self-report measure of a Sharing of Hurts Scale, found additional factors such as self-desirability, personal values, vulnerability, and imperfection. In a sample of 37 undergraduate couples, this scale correlated significantly with three scales of marital functioning administered before and after completion of written homework assignments (L'Abate, 1992b, pp. 58–63) with significant reliability (test-retest $r = .69$; $p < .001$). The direction of these correlations supported the concurrent validity of the SOH (Sharing of Hurts) scale in the sense that the greater the sharing of hurts, the better the adjustment and communication of these couples. The SOH correlated significantly ($p < .01$ or .001) on a pre-/posttest basis with the Spanier Dyadic Adjustment Scale, Navran's Primary Communication Inventory, and the Marital Issues Questionnaire. On the basis of this research, Cusinato and L'Abate (1994) are testing an upwardly positive spiral model of intimacy with a 60-item paper-and-pencil, self-report questionnaire. Three central prerequisites—commitment, equality, and reciprocity (mutuality)—are surrounded by factors such as social presentation, communication of personal values, respect for personal feelings, acceptance of personal limitations, affirmation of respective potentialities, sharing of hurts, and forgiveness of errors. If these are necessary and sufficient conditions for the attainment of intimacy, its nonattainment would be found in the opposites of all the factors surrounding it.

CONCLUSION

The research summarized in this chapter illustrates how two models derived directly from a developmental competence theory—attribution of importance, and intimacy—can be evaluated to either corroborate or invalidate the models derived from the theory.

CHAPTER 4

Hurt: A Fundamental but Neglected Feeling

> [I]t is those who most love us who cause us the most pain. (James, 1989, p. 67)

> Emotion was once regarded as a base instinct to be subdued or repressed. Now scientists increasingly view it as a safeguard of survival and an enrichment of experience throughout development. . . . Emotions play an integral role in many major psychological disorders—witness the blunted emotional expression seen in schizophrenia. (National Advisory Mental Health Council, 1985, p. 838)

The thesis of this chapter is that we all hurt human beings, and we hurt and are hurt by people whom we love and who love us. We hurt and are hurt by them more than by strangers. Hurt is a fundamental feeling that is extremely relevant to personal and interpersonal functioning and dysfunctioning. It is not only fundamental to humans, but also to animals, for both humans and animals, as a whole, tend to avoid hurts if they can.

This feeling, however, has been neglected in most secondary references on feelings and emotions (Magai & McFadden, 1995; Zinbarg, Barlow, Brown, & Hertz, 1992), although it is present in many primary references. As Table 4.1 shows, events and experiences that produce hurts could range from put-downs to rejections, criticisms, and various forms of emotional—i.e., verbal, physical, and sexual—abuse. Hurt means any event or experience that is perceived and felt as being not only physically but especially psychologically or emotionally harmful, traumatic, threatening, stressful, destructive, discounting, and debilitating to one's welfare, importance, well-being, and existence. Like all emotions, it derives from an intimate context and it does not develop in a vacuum, as some theorists tried to make us believe in the past.

Thus, when Freud (1953) and other writers (Edelstein, 1990; Pennebaker, 1990) refer to past or early traumas, they are referring essentially to hurtful experiences and events that left a mark, supposedly unconscious, on individuals, sometimes for the rest of their lives. Many forms of sexual, verbal, and physical abuse, suffered as children or as adults, leave long-lasting scars that are sometimes difficult to erase and that influence behavior to a large extent throughout one's life (Everstine & Everstine, 1993; Waites, 1993). This position is bound to be controversial, however, because there is not, as yet,

TABLE 4.1 Antecedent Factors Commonly Associated with Hurt Feelings

Abandonment (Collins & Gabor, 1988).
Anger (Alschuler & Alschuler, 1984; Hall & Kirkland, 1984).
Betrayal (Auerback, 1987).
Body shape and size (Skuse, 1987).
Burnout (Lemkau, Rafferty, Purdy, & Rudisill, 1987).
Conflict and discord (Frankel, 1990).
Deception (Lippard, 1988; Metts, 1989).
Degradation and discounting (Simpson, Lorsbach, & Whitehouse, 1983).
Divorce and broken family (Bonkowski, Boomhower, & Bequette, 1985; Mitchell, 1983; Schlesinger, 1982; Skeen, Covi, & Robinson, 1985).
Embarrassment (Frankel, 1990).
Extramarital affairs (Meyering & Epling-McWherter, 1987).
Failing self-ideal (Lemkau, Rafferty, Purdy, & Rudisill, 1987).
Fear of intimacy (Lutwak, 1985).
Humiliation (Markovitz, 1982).
Physical abuse (Breines & Gordon, 1983).
Physical pain (Gaston-Johansson, Johansson, Felldin, & Sanne, 1985).
Refusals (Lewis & Gallois, 1984).
Rejection (Weiner & Handel, 1985).
Sex role stress (Lemkau, Rafferty, Purdy, & Rudisill, 1987).
Sexual abuse (Collins & Gabor, 1988; Hirsch, 1986).
Shame (Markovitz, 1982).
Verbal or emotional abuse (L'Abate, 1986).
Vulnerability (Willock, 1986).

agreement on what constitutes "basic" emotions (Averill, 1994b; Ekman, 1994; Panksepp, 1994).

CONCEPTUAL AND DEFINITIONAL ISSUES

Once the term "hurt" is used, a host of semantic issues is raised. Freud (1953), as well as most emotion theorists (Izard, 1977, 1979, 1991b; Lazarus, 1991) and researchers (Pennebaker, 1990), using the analytical language of theory and laboratory, avoid using this term and prefer equivalent but scientifically more acceptable terms: trauma, stress, distress, wound, or threat. To quote an anonymous reviewer: "Hurt, on the other hand, is an obviously broad term which is part of the colloquial language of everyday life and of the therapeutic dialogue—no less valuable, but valuable in serving a different purpose." How can one reconcile one domain of discourse—here, the scientific domain—with the supposedly popular domain (Kelley, 1992)? Is hurt a useful concept, both scientifically and clinically, or is the argument about its fundamental importance futile or irrelevant? Evidently, one needs to demonstrate not only that this feeling is scientifically and clinically relevant, but that it is pervasively fundamental to human and even animal functioning. Supposedly, avoidance of hurt has a preventive as well as a protective function for most of us.

When primary references in the scientific and professional literature (Table 4.1) use the term, does that usage contradict the view that hurt is a colloquial term and that equivalent terms such as trauma, stress, distress, wound, or threat are more professional or even more scientific? It is very difficult to draw a line of distinction between the two usages when primary references (Table 4.1) use a term not (yet) used in secondary references (Kelley, 1992). Is there something to be gained when we use a colloquial rather than a scientific term? When most theorists and researchers use terms like trauma, stress, distress, wound, or threat (the five most commonly used euphemistic terms in the scientific and professional literature), all four terms denote experiences and events that have been, are, or have the potential of being hurtful. Trauma indicates a concrete, usually specific injury, wound, or shock that tends to lower the level of functioning. Stress indicates some kind of chronic, pervasive, and prolonged pressure or hassle that is affecting one's functioning. Distress is another term that is used frequently to cover an underlying pattern of emotions that cannot be encompassed by existing classifications. Izard (1991b), one among many, uses it frequently in his text. Yet, this term is not even mentioned in the index of his work. According to Milburn and Watman (1981), a threat is a danger of loss or damage that is outside of our control. Traumas may imply a past occurrence; stresses may imply past and present events; threats imply future dangerous possibilities. All three terms share the common characteristic of being outside of our control.

Wakefield (1992) argued that the only defensible definition of mental disorder is any "harmful dysfunction." He recognized that "harmful is a value term based on social norms," and "dysfunction is a scientific term referring to the failure of a mental mechanism to perform a natural function for which it was designed by evaluation" (p. 373). Harmful, therefore, within this context is synonymous with hurtful. Either term may be a more colloquial term than trauma, stress, wound, or threat, denoting, however, the very same process. Here, one chooses a supposedly colloquial term to refer to the same constructs that in scientific and professional circles have been referred to in different but synonymous terms. By using the term hurt instead of terms like traumas, stress, wound, or threat, one would hope to obtain greater semantic specificity and concreteness and to bridge the gap between colloquial usage and the scientific and professional literature on the same topic (Kelley, 1992). Terms like trauma, stress, wound, and threat have in common the same quality of being hurtful, in the past, present, or future. Cusinato (personal communication, September 5, 1993) suggested a more appropriate term that indicates the interpersonal nature of hurts: "wounds" or "wounded." We do not hurt others nor are we hurt by others in a vacuum. Hence, wounding or being wounded communicates the interpersonal nature of hurts.

The most equivalent, if not synonymous, terms for "hurt" or "harm" found in the literature on emotions are "suffering," "sorrow," "anguish," and "distress" (Blechman, 1990; Frijda, 1986; Izard, 1977, 1979, 1991b; Lazarus, 1991; Mahoney, 1991; Oatley & Jenkins, 1996; Plutchik & Kellerman, 1980). Anguish denotes extreme distress. Distress denotes affliction or suffering, as well as a state of danger. In one instance (Lewis & Haviland, 1993), distress is made synonymous with sadness. Sorrow represents suffering or sadness arising from loss or disappointment. Suffering is considered as being synonymous with distress (Figure 4.1). Hence, these terms, taken altogether, may produce a dimension where they may suggest different degrees of hurtful intensity, going possibly from distress to sorrow, to suffering, and then to anguish (Bakan, 1968; Gilbert, 1992a; Tomkins, 1980).

However, a major distinction needs to be made among these seemingly synonymous terms. Anguish, distress, sorrow, and suffering are usually observable and visible manifestations of hurts. But some hurts have an additional quality of being avoided, remaining unexpressed, and, therefore, being hidden not only from the person who is experiencing them, but consequently also from the observer (Goodwin, 1990). When we look at the common denominator underlying internal fears and phobias, as well as external threats, traumas, wounds, and stresses, we find that all these factors represent ways of dealing with whatever is perceived as hurtful or potentially hurtful to the well-being, existence, welfare, and importance of the individual (Figure 4.1).

Some hurts possess the peculiar quality of being hidden even from the individual who is supposedly experiencing them, forcing one to infer them. Unless

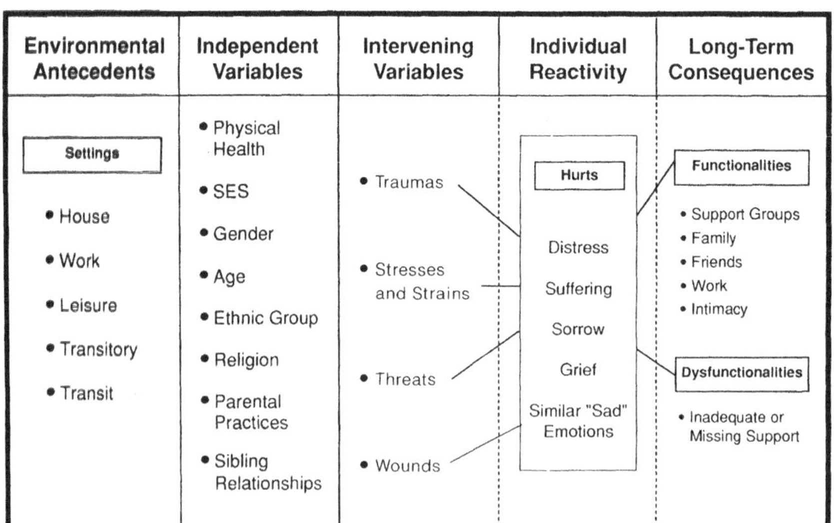

Figure 4.1 A Contextual Definition of Hurts: Antecedents and Consequences

the respondent can experience them, he or she cannot express and report about them. However, experiencing certain hurts is a process that may be distinctly separate from expressing and reporting about them. Some hurts are the most hidden and deepest of all feelings because they are fundamental to our existence. Which hurts are experienced and expressed directly and which are not? Nobody likes to be hurt, even though there may be masochistic individuals who seem to collect hurts more frequently than others.

Many individuals, afflicted with addiction and acting-out character disorders, tend to inflict hurts in others and strongly deny the existence of any personal hurts. It is evident from their reports and behaviors that any slight internal discomfort and distress, let alone a hurt, is short-circuited from experience and avoided. Furthermore, they seem completely unaware that their temporary, abusive pleasure is extremely costly to them and to their loved ones (Daly & McCroskey, 1984; L'Abate & Harrison, 1992; Newman, 1974; Serritella, 1992; Shaines, 1987). Individuals with psychosomatic conditions and strong internalization tendencies find it difficult to experience and express deep feelings of hurt (Sifneos, 1973).

"Grief" and "shame" are not synonymous terms for hurt; they are specifically linked to death and personal losses or perceived inadequacies (Frantz, 1984; Rando, 1984; Schneider, 1984; Tangney & Fischer, 1994; Worden, 1982). By the same token, guilt and shame may be partial components of hurt but do not wholly constitute it. Even depression could be considered a component of, or one avenue of expression for, hurt. However, just as in the case of grief, shame, or guilt, one could be hurt and not be depressed. Hurt, therefore, is a much wider, pervasively encompassing, and ubiquitously underlying feeling that is frequently experienced and reported freely by most functional people (Pennebaker, 1990; Taylor, 1991) as including most traumas, failures, rejections, criticisms, and put-downs (Table 4.1). It is frequently not reported by many dysfunctional individuals for a variety of reasons, as explored in the rest of this chapter and beyond.

We have terms for joy, happiness, and pleasure in the scientific literature, but these terms lack distinct counterparts. Even though the term hurt may fulfill such a requirement in common parlance, a term to describe the opposite of pleasurably nonphysical states is needed. Anger, anxiety, fear, and sadness do not seem to quality as representing the opposite quality of pleasurable or pleasant states, even though they would qualify in their own ways as hurts. The term "pain" is usually reserved for the description of physical experience. We still need a term to describe the opposite of pleasurable experiences. Possibly, this gap could be filled by the inclusion of hurt and hurts as legitimate emotional states worthy of scientific and clinical consideration.

The foregoing arguments are summarized visually in Figure 4.1, where antecedent cultural conditions interact with hurtful external events (traumas, stresses and strains, and threats) and with a host of independent variables to produce feelings of hurt and their similar or synonymous terms. From these feelings emanate functional or dysfunctional consequences, depending on the level of functionality of the individual and of the most available supportive context, usually family and friends.

Most people are able to distinguish reliably among a physical dimension of pain, hurts, aches, and emotional discomfort as well as between sadness and feeling hurt (Gaston-Johansson, 1984; Gaston-Johansson, Albert, Fagan, & Zimmerman, 1990; Gaston-Johansson, Johansson, Felldin, & Sanne, 1985). Most of us, but apparently not those who write secondary references on feelings and emotions, are able to experience and express hurts. Nonetheless, this topic seems to be as widespread in the scientific and professional literature as it is in the culture. We simply avoid dealing with hurtful feelings (Goodwin, 1990; Hayes & Melancon, 1989; Rosenfeld, 1979; Taylor, 1991). Why?

An avoidance of hurtful feelings is not necessarily limited to clinical or deviant populations. The avoidance of hurts and of generally unpleasant topics in general is a fairly widespread cultural phenomenon. For instance, Goodwin (1990) identified cross-cultural similarities in the factor structure of taboo topics in 82 British and 81 Chinese students. Most taboo topics reflected an unwillingness to discuss "family matters" and "hurt feelings." Hayes and Melancon (1989) argued that "a single common denominator, namely, emotional avoidance, underlies many of the diagnostic classifications, client expectations, and therapeutic interventions in clinical psychology" (p. 185). This avoidance pertains to "unpleasant private experiences" (p. 187), which were further defined as being associated with anxiety. Thus, even though Hayes and Melancon's thesis is one step in the direction of finding a commonality of avoidance for painful feelings, they, like many other theorists and clinicians, also avoided dealing with hurt as a fundamental feeling. The similarities (and, one would add, the links) between these two major taboos suggested a great deal of consistency in disclosure across nationalities. Is it the hidden, elusive quality of hurts that fails to make it appear in the secondary "scientific" references on emotions, even though primary references (and common experience!) refer to it?

Upon examination of representative secondary references on emotions (Blechman, 1990; Ekman & Davidson, 1994; Frijda, 1986; Izard, 1977, 1979, 1991b; Lazarus, 1991; Lewis & Haviland, 1993; Magai & McFadden, 1995; Mahoney, 1991; Oatley & Jenkins, 1996; Plutchik & Kellerman, 1980), including many others not cited here, it becomes clear that the term hurt is completely absent from glossaries, indices, and classifications of emotions. At best, grief, guilt, and shame are covered, but no reference can be found for hurt or for synonymous terms like anguish, distress, sorrow, wound, or suffering, or even trauma, stress, or threat (Tangney & Fischer, 1994). How have these terms acquired a greater "scientific" status than hurt? What makes these terms more acceptable in the scientific literature than the term hurt?

When primary references on hurt were explored, several mentioned "hurt feelings" and considered this topic in depth (Tale 4.1). Among secondary references, there are exceptions. Bakan (1968), for instance, was one of the first to stress the importance of suffering in behavior. Blumberg, Hare, Kent, and Davies (1983) included an entire section on "helping and hurting" (pp. 225–275), where coercive power and aggression were related to hurting. It is ironic that textbooks on feelings and emotions and on theories of emotion fail to recognize the existence of hurts. Yet, most of us, as well as our clients, recognize their existence, importance, and influence in our lives and in the lives of loved ones.

Exceptions to the thesis that hurt and similar or synonymous terms have been neglected in primary psychological references are Baumeister (1991), Klinger (1977), and Gilbert (1992a). Baumeister devoted a whole chapter (pp. 232–268) to "suffering and unhappiness," which he characterized as representing a "loss or lack of meaning. Responses to suffering, accordingly, are often designed to find meaning—to make sense of the misfortune itself and to restore a broad sense of meaningfulness that is sometimes threatened by personal suffering" (p. 232). Thus, Baumeister's view puts him squarely in the cognitive camp in viewing feelings of hurt as a cognitive process.

Klinger saw alienation, futility, and discontent (pp. 199–244) as the outcome of "great personal upheavals," "disappointments," disillusionments, defeats, dissatisfactions, costs, and "insurmountable obstacles" in reaching one's strived-for goals (p. 136). As one can see, Klinger, like most theorists about emotions, beats around the bush of hurts without getting into it more directly, as if he, as well as many other writers, were afraid of getting down to concrete specifics. When we deal with affects and emotions that lead to dysfunctionalities, we are confronting and dealing with hurts and fears of being hurt. Gilbert (1992a) makes suffering the bottom line of human nature: It is the basis for functionality when approached and attended to appropriately and for mental illness when avoided and attended to inappropriately.

Clark (1980) argued that empathy is the unique capacity to feel experiences, needs, aspirations, frustrations, sorrows, joys, anxieties, hurts, or hunger of others as if they were our own. The blockage of functional empathy by power drives forms the basis of interpersonal and social tensions, conflicts, violence, terrorism, and war. The control of these destructive forces will require development of techniques to increase functional empathy among all human beings. A great deal of pathology derives from our inability to deal with feelings of hurt in ourselves or to share them with our loved ones. Inability to deal with hurts leads to either internalizations or externalizations (scapegoats). Scapegoats are really strawmen or red herrings that distract and lead attention away from basic issues of hurt. Scapegoats are victims that become scarecrows to be avoided and punished through rejection, incarceration, and hospitalization (L'Abate, Weeks, & Weeks, 1979). This view of pathology is essentially transactional because the process of externalization and internalization of hurts takes place within a family context. Here is where all the members of the same system are intrinsically and interdependently related to one another in producing the hurtful drama triangle, consisting of Persecutors, Victims, and Rescuers (L'Abate, 1986).

Fitness and Strongman (1991) commented on how at least three powerful emotions—love, hate, and jealousy—only recently either have gained the limelight of psychological interest or have been "rarely mentioned in psychology textbooks" (p. 195). One would add hurt to these three emotions, arguing, as discussed below, that, in some way, hurt underlies all three of them. Among twenty most frequent emotions, hurt ranked fifteenth. However, among those twenty emotions were mentioned many that indicated different ways of expressing hurt feelings: regret, worry, anger, hate, fear, depression, embarrassment, upset, sadness, nervousness, shock, and jealousy. Less frequent emotions were grief, loneliness, pride, resentment, and shame (Shimanoff, 1984).

CONTROVERSIAL ISSUES UNDERLYING A CONCEPTUALIZATION OF HURT

Among the controversial issues that must be addressed to support the original thesis of this chapter are:

1. The misleading dichotomy of positive versus negative emotionality.
2. The experiencing–expressing distinction.
3. Levels of description and explanation in emotionality.
4. Individual differences in the experience and expression of hurt.
5. The relationship between hurt and love.

There are many other relevant issues relating to the whole field of emotions, but space limitations do not allow them to be covered here (Ekman & Davidson, 1994; Epstein, 1984; Taylor, 1991).

Positive versus Negative Emotionality: A Misleading Dichotomy

Most textbook classifications of emotions uncritically divide them into positive ones—joy, happiness, pleasure, and contentment, for instance—and negative ones—anger, hostility, fear, resentment, sadness, and worry (Fitness & Strongman, 1991; Frijda, 1986; Izard, 1979; Lazarus, 1991; Oatley & Jenkins, 1996; Shaver, Schwartz, Kirson, & O'Connor, 1987; Taylor, 1991; Watson & Tellegen, 1985). This practice is by now so widespread that we tend to divide feelings into positive and negative emotionality (Belsky, Fish, & Russell, 1991). Where would anguish, distress, hurt, sorrow, and suffering fit? This dichotomy is misleading because its positive–negative quality implies, whether we intend it or not, that positive emotions are "good" and are to be approached and negative emotions are "bad" and are to be avoided.

Lacking objective criteria to make such a distinction, it is easy to conclude that this distinction may be capricious and arbitrary. Furthermore, in most people, the tendency is to equate avoidance with solution, even when a seeming solution would actually compound the problem. The more we avoid dealing with hurts, the more they tend to stay with and within us. Avoidance of an hurtful issue does not *ipso facto* mean that repressing, suppressing, and essentially avoiding it by sweeping it under the rug will automatically make it go away. The more we avoid dealing with our hurts, the more likely they will tend to stay and fester within us.

Additionally, who can say that anger is "better" or more negative than sadness? Why should joy be "better" or more positive than worry? Is all worry negative? Is there a place for realistic and, therefore, positive worry? Is hurt just as negative as anger? What is gained by equating the two emotions by regarding both of them as negative? One could argue about the importance of hurt as a positive, necessary ingredient of any arousal or survival pattern. The positive–negative dichotomy forces us to make unnecessary judgments about the relative value of one emotion over others. If such value judgments are rampant in the research literature cited here, how can we be objective about emotions? This dichotomy may have shown heuristic, research-producing qualities. However, we need to ask whether more specific and less value-laden distinctions might not be more scientifically valid and professionally helpful.

Admittedly, there are negative (harmful) and positive (helpful) events just as there are negative and positive outcomes (Taylor, 1991). However, to extend this line of reasoning to a classification of emotional experience is unnecessary and unwarranted. Suppose pleasant and unpleasant affects are not part of the same continuum, as some investigators insist (Berscheid, 1983; Taylor, 1991). It would then stand to reason (and to empirical scrutiny) that separate consideration would be given to these areas of experience, not in terms of their negative or positive qualities but, instead, in terms of their phenomenologically pleasant–unpleasant, or comfortable–uncomfortable qualities, as Russell (1978) argued on semantic grounds rather than on the basis of value considerations.

Thompson (1981) proposed that reactions to potentially stressful (i.e., hurtful) events depend on their meaning to the individual. She discussed three dimensions of meaning related to controllability or hurtful feelings: (a) endurable vs. unendurable, (b) means to desirable outcomes vs. undesirable outcomes, and (c) planned vs. random events. Hence, there seem to be more descriptive and perhaps more useful distinctions than the positive–negative one. Fitness and Strongman (1991) commented on this dichotomy

> [T]he amount of useful information that can be gleaned from this approach is limited. For example, when researchers speak of "negative affect reciprocity" between distressed marital partners, it is never clear from the global affect codes whether or not the same affect is being reciprocated—does anger evoke anger, or contempt or sadness? (p. 178)

What is the relationship between the negativity–positivity dichotomy and hurt? Why is this dichotomy relevant to the thesis of this chapter? One cannot classify hurt as negative any more than one could classify any other feeling as negative. This dichotomy tends to make unnecessary and unwarranted value judgments that find little if any conceptual or epistemological support. Even though this dichotomy may have received a modicum of heuristic attention, it is time to question its logical and conceptual shortcomings. Furthermore, this dichotomy is clinically dangerous because it suggests, if not implies, that we must avoid negative feelings and approach positive ones. This implication may have destructive developmental, didactic, and clinical consequences. Supposedly, children should be happy and avoid hurts, as if this emphasis would automatically and magically immunize them from dealing with inevitable grief and sorrow. Didactically, this dichotomy suggests that parents and teachers should teach children and adults to avoid hurt feelings and approach happy ones! Clinically, the same course of action would be even more destructive. Has anyone ever met an individual or client who could become happy on command, either implicitly or explicitly?

Despite the foregoing arguments, the evidence suggests the existence of the two polarities (Watson & Tellegen, 1985). This evidence has been replicated successfully even cross-culturally. If one were to regard evidence over conceptual arguments, one could not refute its strength (Almagor & Ben-Porath, 1989; Mayer & Gaschke, 1988; Meyer & Shack, 1989; Watson, Clark, & Tellegen, 1984, 1988). In their review of studies on factor analyses of mood states, Watson and Tellegen (1985) defined unpleasantness using terms like blue, grouchy, lonely, sad, sorry, and unhappy. Negative affect was defined using terms like distressed, fearful, hostile, jittery, nervous, and scornful. However, in going over the lists of terms used in the various studies and in repeated factor analyses, the only terms referring to hurtful or hurt-related feelings were *sorry* and *distressed* and their synonyms (glum, blue, unhappy, down). No terms referring to guilt, shame, or anguish, let alone hurt or harm, were noted. Why would sorry be classified as unpleasant while distressed is classified as negative?

The absence of terms relating to hurt or hurts raises serious questions about the empirical validity, if not the conceptual and human usefulness, of this polarization in affective states. What would happen to Watson and Tellegen's (1985) model if items related to various intensities and kinds of hurt, like harm, anguish, suffering, and pain (including also grief, shame, and guilt) were introduced in their lists? From Watson and Tellegen's analysis, pairings like fearful/hostile, distressed/jittery, and nervous/scornful are mixed together and considered negative. Why should all these descriptors be called negative? Apparently, this classification combines terms that possess completely different characteristics as well as consequences. We may approach someone who is distressed and fearful, but we may tend to avoid someone who is hostile and scornful. Whether we tend to approach or avoid someone who is nervous or jittery depends on many other contextual variables that cannot be included in a factor analysis.

In spite of strong cross-cultural support for Watson and Tellegen's model (Almagor & Ben-Porath, 1989; Watson, Clark, & Tellegen, 1984), Burke, Brief, George, and Webster, (1989) administered Watson and Tellegen's mood scales to three different samples of managerial and professional workers in an insurance firm, retail sales personnel, and a heterogeneous group of students who were employed. Their factor analytic results did not provide a strong fit for the original bipolar model. A first-order model with four descriptively unipolar factors labeled as Positive Arousal (Enthusiasm), Negative Activation (Nervousness), Low Arousal (Fatigue), and Low Activation (Relaxation) provided a better fit across the three samples. These authors interpreted their results as supporting the measurement of positive and negative mood as descriptively unipolar factors. Here is where results from factor analyses need to be evaluated with a large grain of critical salt, lest the proverbial Martian starts to question the uncritical way we accept results from factor analysis that lead us into conceptual and even experiential traps.

However, this issue cannot be considered by itself because it is strongly related to the following distinction, which only recently has been receiving some degree of attention in the literature on emotions.

The Experiencing–Expressing Distinction

The distinction here relates to the qualitative difference between emotional experience and emotional expression (Lewis, 1993), which may not have been sufficiently stressed by most theorists and researchers cited thus far. Feelings are subjectively felt experiences. They lie at a much more deep-seated, genotypical level, often screened from the individual as well as from others. Emotions as objectively manifested are very often visible, phenotypically or presentationally, to others. Yet, the best argument for the existence of levels of emotional experience and expression comes directly from the empirical work of Watson and Tellegen (1985). Commenting on the high correlations between first- and second-order Positive and Negative Affect factor loadings, these authors took these high correlations to mean that "Positive and Negative Affect are not only the two dominant primary factors, but can also be interpreted hierarchically as general dimensions that are superordinate to the more circumscribed discrete emotion factors (anger, fear, and so on)" (p. 230). Could one conceive of a third underlying (i.e., genotypical) level of pleasure–pain, in the psychological sense of hurt and harm, that would underlie even the major four secondary emotions (Table 4.2)?

Even this seeming reconciliation would not be satisfactory once we accept the relevance of the experiencing–expressing distinction. When we experience a feeling, we need to decide whether to approach or avoid it, either internally or externally, by expressing it. In addition to the approach-avoidance dimension, however, we need to consider the importance of rational or irrational factors that control how a feeling is going to be expressed as an emotion, i.e., by discharge or delay. Overreliance on rationality may tend to delay the expression of such a feeling or emotion, and undercutting or short-circuiting rationality may lead to sudden and quick discharge, either in words or deeds (Table 4.2).

Thus, the intervening polarity between experiencing a feeling and expressing it as an emotion depends on whether it is helpful or hurtful to the individual and whether that individual approaches or avoids it internally. If a hurtful feeling is approached internally, then it may or may not be expressed outwardly,

TABLE 4.2 Levels of Emotionality: The Fundamental Hurt-Happiness/Experiencing–Expressing Dimensions

	Levels	Externalization/Expressing/Internalization Discharge ◄——► Delay
DESCRIPTIVE	Presentational	Acting out ---------- Crying Anger ------------- Sadness Hyperactivity -------- Phobias Impulsivity --------- Passivity Drivenness ---------- Calm
	Phenotypical	Approach ------ / --Avoidance
EXPLANATORY	Genotypical	Experiencing Hurt/Happiness: (Pain/Pleasure) (Discomfort/Comfort) (Dissatisfaction/Satisfaction) (Shame and guilt/Pride)
	Historical and Cultural Determinants	Intergenerational family transmission Developmental history Settings and situations

depending on the individual's emotional makeup, level of psychological functioning, personality, and contextual factors (Figure 4.1). If it is avoided internally, it may surface indirectly, possibly in a dysfunctional manner.

This argument is supported in part by the work of Mayer and Gaschke (1988), who proposed that mood experience is comprised of at least two elements: (a) the direct experience of the mood and (b) the meta-level of experience that consists of thoughts and feelings about the mood. In one study, Mayer and Gaschke replicated Watson and Tellegen's (1985) results by obtaining a two-dimensional structure of positive and negative affect from responses of 1,572 subjects. In a second study with 160 subjects, meta-mood experience was conceptualized as the product of a mood regulatory process that monitors, evaluates, and, at times, changes mood. These investigators constructed a scale to measure meta-mood experiences that resulted in finding that levels on meta-mood dimensions differed across moods.

Thus, Mayer and Gaschke concluded that meta-mood experiences may also constitute an important part of the phenomenology of the personal experience of mood. This conclusion would suggest that, once we feel and experience an event, there is another intervening step: the phenotypical level of how to process and express it (Table 4.2). What shall we do with that feeling, especially if it hurts? We can either approach or avoid it. We can either discharge it immediately or delay its expression. If delay is chosen, how long should one hold on to that feeling? If we discharge it, how should we do it? Positively, negatively, or something in between?

This basic differentiation between feelings as subjectively internal experiences versus their expression as objectively external emotions and sometimes representations of internal states is basic to the arguments of this chapter. What we feel is something that happens to us, whether we like it or not (Averill, 1980; Thompson, 1981). What and how we express our feelings is something that we can decide, if indeed cognition and rationality are intermediate processes intervening between the experience and the expression of an emotion. We may have no choices available in feeling hurt. When someone we love dies or rejects us, we are going to be hurt. When someone we care about deceives us, we are going to be hurt (Table 4.1). However, once we are hurt, we have an infinite number of choices about how that hurt can or should be expressed according to: (a) personal and cultural predilections and (b) how much cognitions are used to link subjective, emotional experience with objective, external expression (Pennebaker, 1990).

Given the same emotional experience—in this case, hurt—there is a multitude of ways of expressing it. Engle, Beutler, and Daldrup (1991) made the same point by stressing that "emotions are neutral . . . emotions are neither positive nor negative, good nor bad; they simply exist. Consequently value can only be placed upon what is done with emotions, not upon the class or set of emotions being experienced" (p. 172). According to a differentiation between feelings and emotions, one would qualify these authors' conclusion to the extent that feelings vary along a continuum of pleasant-unpleasant, with a middle point of neutrality. On the other hand, emotions can be either positive or negative, depending on how and in what context they are expressed. One needs to differentiate between hurtful external events—traumas, stresses and strains, wounds, and threats, which constitute the objective reality, versus the experiencing of hurt, which is an internally subjective process. Given the same seemingly traumatic, stressful, or threatening event, two individuals may react in two completely different ways. Their reactions depend on how an event is experienced and how it is processed before it is either expressed or suppressed.

The number of feelings we experience is finite, no matter what theory of emotions we subscribe to. The range is anywhere from eight (Plutchik, 1993) to twelve (Izard, 1991b) or fifteen (Lazarus & Lazarus, 1994). The number of ways in which we can express those feelings is infinite. The expression can take place verbally, nonverbally, or in writing. It can be aggressively harmful. It could be positively and helpfully diffusing in a conflict. Thus, we cannot match or equate subjective experience of feelings with their emotional expression, no matter how hard we try (Plutchik, 1991, 1993). The expression of a feeling—that is, an emotion—could be positive or negative in its interpersonal outcome.

In this fashion, an event provoking any feeling could be classified as pleasant/unpleasant, positive/negative, or emotionally neutral, depending on how the individual chooses to express it (Taylor, 1991). However, feelings cannot be classified according to this dichotomy. Feelings *are*. They exist in our experience. They are part of our being human. No value judgment can or should be made about their alleged positivity or negativity. By the same token, a definite value judgment can be made about their negative (hurtful) or positive (helpful) expression and outcome. Feelings happen to us, even though some theorists argue that we can choose them (Lazarus, 1991). Apparently, these theorists have never experienced the death of a loved one. We can indeed choose how we express the very same feelings *provided we are able to use rational resources (R)*. If these resources are bypassed, then the feelings may be expressed inappropriately through impulsive and possibly destructive actions. There may be no choice as to what feelings are experienced or in what manner. However, there is a great deal of choice as to how and when these feelings can be expressed, if rationality is interposed between the experience of feelings and their expressed emotions.

Consequently, one way of differentiating between experienced/nonexperienced versus expressed/unexpressed hurts may depend on the level of functionality of the individual. The more functional (i.e., selful) the individual, the easier it may be to experience hurts and to express them in appropriate and even self-enhancing ways. By the same token, the more dysfunctional (i.e., noself) the individual, the more difficult it may be to experience and to express hurts in appropriate and self-enhancing ways. It may be that the more dysfunctional the individual, the more one may use self-other-defeating ways of expressing hurt feelings, as argued later on (Oatley & Jenkins, 1996). Some psychosomatic individuals, specifically diagnosed as alexithymic, even avoid experiencing hurt feelings, and if they cannot experience them, how can they express them (Sifneos, 1973)? The experiencing–expressing distinction deals specifically with the width or range of behavior. We need to look at feelings of hurt according to a dimension of depth. Many selfish individuals seem completely unaware of and uninterested in how hurtful their behavior may be. Many selfless individuals, on the other hand, seem to receive their share of hurts, especially if they pick selfish partners.

Levels of Description and Explanation in Emotionality

To understand the topographical position and nomological network of hurt in respect to other feelings, another distinction is needed between levels of description and levels of explanation: the dimension of depth considered in Chapters 1 and 2 (Wakefield, 1989). Description is comprised of presentational and phenotypical levels. Explanation is comprised of genotypical feelings, of which hurt is one, as well as historical and cultural determinants. Presentational describes any emotion that is publicly, obviously, and openly expressed. Its content qualifies its nature, as in anger/hostility or as in crying or sadness. Phenotypical describes the major dimensions through which either hurts or pleasures are channeled and expressed without content, mainly through distance, as measured by extremes in approach-avoidance, and through control, as measured by extremes in discharge-delay. Genotypical describes any experienced feeling that is phenomenologically and subjectively felt. Historical and cultural determinants refer to any contextual past, present, and future events that affected what feelings and emotions were experienced and how they were expressed (Table 4.2).

The presentational level may be still screened from external observers, because most of the emotional passions of life take place within the privacy of our homes (Blechman, 1990; Clark, Pataki, & Carver, 1996; Malatesta & Izard, 1984). Thus, one needs to distinguish further between presentational and phenotypical levels in emotional expression. The presentational level is related to impression formation. It may be short-lived and superficial, relating to the facade or social impression level. The phenotypical level is longer lasting and real, in the sense that the phenotypical underlies the presentational level and takes place more often privately. Who is approached or avoided during anger? Is discharge or delay used when approaching or avoiding someone who hurt us? On the externalization-internalization dimension, for instance, examples of presentational expressions, at the externalization side, are anger (in all of its direct and indirect manifestations, such as sulking, verbal abuse, and explosiveness) and hostility (in its indirect manifestations, such as sarcasm, contempt, or disgust), hyperactivity, impulsivity, and driveness. Sadness, depression, anxiety, fear, and worry are more frequent at the internalization side, where greater frequencies of psychosomatic conditions prevail (Table 4.2).

More specifically, Table 4.2 gives an example of how emotions can be considered at various levels ranging from genotypical experiencing at the bottom to phenotypical expressing intermediately, and to presentational expressing at the top. At the genotypical (bottom) level are dichotomous concepts denoting various dimensions of hurt and related concepts, on the one hand, and happiness-pleasure and related concepts, on the other. These terms represent in their own ways the same fundamental dimension of painful to pleasurable experiencing. At the phenotypical level, these phenomenological experiences are beginning to be expressed through dimensions defined by two major extremes, *discharge* or externalizing, as in impulsivity and hyperactivity, and *delay* or internalizing or withdrawing, as in anxiety, depression, or phobias. Both extremes of discharge-delay (control) interact orthogonally with approach-avoidance (distance) tendencies to form a variety of defenses to deal with feelings of hurt as well as with pleasure-happiness.

Izard (1979, p. 423), among many others, distinguished fundamental from derivative combinations of emotions, using the following criteria: (a) a specific, innately determined neural substrate; (b) a typical neuromuscular expressive pattern; (c) a distinctively subjective, phenomenological quality; (d) a uniquely motivational property; and (e) an inherently adaptive function. To demonstrate the fundamental quality of hurt, one could question whether all of these criteria need to be fulfilled for an emotion to qualify as fundamental. Hurt can fulfill a uniquely motivational property on the basis of how frequently people report behavior that is designed to either inflict or avoid hurt (Table 4.1).

Hurt is a distinctively subjective emotion. Most people are able to know when they hurt. However, this generalization needs qualification. Many people—anexithymic individuals, addicts, and persons with certain character disorders—do not know when they hurt because, often, they have learned to short-circuit feelings of any kind, especially hurtful ones (Hayes & Melancon, 1989; L'Abate, Farrar, & Serritella, 1992; Newman, 1974; Sifneos, 1973). Furthermore, because of its exquisitely subjective quality, hurt is not a feeling that is easily or frequently approached or even expressed. In fact, it is often one of the most avoided emotions (Goodwin, 1990; Rosenfeld, 1979). As Watson and Clark (1991) noted, "[S]ome emotions are more observable than others . . . because some emotional traits are generally easier to judge than others" (pp. 929, 933).

Hurts are unavoidable. We are all destined to be hurt at one time or another, whether we like it or not. However, the expression of hurt feelings is usually avoided and hidden from others. We are all vulnerable to being hurt. Some of us, not willing to accept the inherent vulnerability of the human condition, use denial and other forms of avoidance so as not to deal with our hurts.

We do not know enough about hurts to claim any neural substrate or neuromuscular expressive pattern, although there are definite physiological correlates of hurt and suffering (Bakan, 1968; Frijda, 1986; Laudenslager & Reite, 1984; McAdams & Bryant, 1987; Pennebaker, 1990). Physiological responses depend heavily on how an individual deals with hurt. Some individuals avoid it almost automatically—repressing, suppressing, somatizing, on one hand, or jumping immediately into impulsive and usually destructive actions, on the other. Others may react to hurt by transforming it into compulsive behaviors or obsessive thinking.

Additionally, the avoidance of hurts leads to an avoidance of intimacy, if by intimacy is meant the sharing of hurts and fears of being hurt. If hurts are the other side of pleasure and pleasurable events, then joys, contentment, and other pleasurable emotions cannot be fully experienced unless there is also the sharing of hurts. Even an orgasm—in the complete sense of the word, that is, together with intimacy and mutual sharing—cannot be enjoyed with someone unless there has been a full sharing of past hurts and fears of being hurt. Without intimacy, an orgasm is just performance, no different from going to the bathroom.

Thus, most external and visible manifestations of emotions, either presentational or phenotypical, are direct or indirect expressions of more deeply seated feelings of genotypical hurt, along a basic dimension characterized by hurt on the one hand and pleasure on the other. Feelings of hurt are kept inside and very often are not manifested except through phenotypical expressions, shown stereotypically through anger for men and sadness and fear for women

(Fitness & Strongman, 1991; Lenney, Browning, & Mitchell, 1980; Rosenfeld, 1979). Hurt is a much more intense and fiercely private feeling than all the others mentioned. Another possibility of how hurt is managed internally is through "hurt collection," that is, the hoarding of hurts through gunny-sacking. Saved-up hurts may be unleashed during times of stress or may be clutched even closer, producing even greater distance from others. One individual could, at one extreme, collect all kinds of hurts, without ever expressing them, and then, at the other extreme, explode by committing an extremely harmful act, like murder or suicide.

Either way, hurts are central to our emotional and overall functioning. It is human to have experienced losses, defeats, put-downs, snubs, rejections, criticisms, and discountings. There are differences, however, in how many hurts have been experienced and how they have been stored and interpreted internally. There are differences also in how hurts are expressed—positively or negatively, constructively or destructively. Clark and Watson (1991) suggested that anxiety and depressive syndromes share a nonspecific component of generalized affective *distress.* As soon as this conclusion is reached, a distinction between levels of descriptive and levels of explanation must be made. At the visible and recordable level, anxiety and depression may be "explained" in terms of an underlying, inferred, or hypothetical genotypical state of hurt. Descriptively or explanatorily, theoretically or clinically, nothing is gained and a great deal is lost when distress is labeled as negative affect, lumping it together with terms that determine completely different experiential and interpersonal outcomes.

This formulation about levels of emotional experience (hurt-pleasure) and emotional expression (anger, sadness, fear, and others) is not as far-fetched as may appear at first blush. Johnson and Greenberg (1985), for instance, classified emotional experience according to three types: (a) primary or authentic, like the fear of losing one's partner; (b) secondary or reactive in response to threat or provocation, as when the partner threatens to leave; and (c) instrumental, like crying and tears. These three types of emotional experience and expression match the three levels defined above. The presentational level would match Johnson and Greenberg's instrumental type. The phenotypical level would match their secondary types, and the genotypical level would match their primary or authentic type. Fear of abandonment and rejection is a definite hurt (Table 4.1). The same differentiation was made by Edelhofer, Fabian, and Edelhofer (1988), who distinguished between "surface" and "deep" affect.

Ironically, the strongest support for the hierarchical model presented in Table 4.2 derives from the work and theorizing of Watson and Clark (1991). They proposed a hierarchical model of rated affect that viewed emotional experience as "characterized by two distinct levels: a higher level that consists of general affective dimensions, and a lower level that reflects the unique explanatory and predictive power of specific emotions" (p. 935). In a more detailed version of this model, Clark and Watson (1991) presented a tripartite structure consisting of distress (at the bottom—the genotypical level?), physiological hyperarousal (a control dimension—at the phenotypical level?), and depression (at a presentational level?). The levels used in Clark and Watson's model may be different from the levels in the model suggested here. However, there is agreement in that hierarchical models may be necessary to understand the experience and expression of emotions as taking place at different levels of observation and interpretation.

Hurt and Individual Differences

Once the fundamental centrality of hurt(pain)/pleasure in human experience is assumed, it can be determined how all other emotions derive from or gravitate around it. For instance, the major individual difference in the experience and expression of emotions relates to gender. Most sources conclude that, in response to hurtful experiences, men are more likely to express anger than sadness and fear, and women tend to express sadness and fear more often than anger (Averill, 1982; Bonkowski, Boomhower, & Bequette, 1985; Fitness & Strongman, 1991; Lemkau, Rafferty, Rudisill, & Purdy, 1987; Sprecher, 1986; Wyer & Srull, 1993). When avoided and short-circuited (mostly by men), anger may be expressed and externalized into impulsive acting-out, as in the case of character disorders. When avoided, repressed, or suppressed (mostly by women), internalized hurt is expressed through phobias, sadness, anxiety, and worry. Sprecher's (1986) results, along with those of many other researchers, would tend to support this conclusion concerning gender differences in the expression of emotions.

Rosenfeld (1979), for instance, performed stepwise multiple regression and stepwise multiple discriminant analyses on self-disclosure and self-disclosure avoidance in 220 female and 140 male undergraduates. His results indicated that, although there is similarity in the reasons males and females avoid self-disclosure, coherent gender differences do exist. Generally, males avoid self-disclosure to maintain control over their relationship. Females avoid self-disclosure to avoid personal hurt and problems in their interpersonal relationships. Lenney, Browning, and Mitchell (1980) found that self-confidence is one of the variables moderating these differences. Pennebaker and Roberts (1995) argue that women and men use different cues in defining their emotional states. Women perceive emotions in ways congruent with cognitive appraisal theories, and men define their emotions in ways consistent with William James's peripheralist view. Women tend to perceive emotions on the basis of external cues; men tend to perceive emotions on the basis of internal cues. This important distinction will need to be clarified in order to determine how gender differences in the experiencing of feelings are related to their expression and their functionality.

Individual differences in personality as related to emotional experience and expression, on the other hand, have not been as successfully described or explained because few theorists have attempted to enter this veritable minefield (Fitness & Strongman, 1991; Izard, Libero, Putman, & Haynes, 1993; Magai

& McFadden, 1995). An attempt is made herein, realizing full well that some assumptions must be made before presenting a selfhood model of emotional experience and expression related to personality characteristics.

Briefly, if one assumes that in intimate relationships love is measured by the attribution of importance to self and other (partner, parent, child, friend), then this attribution can take at least four directions: a differentiated, functional direction, and three undifferentiated and dysfunctional directions. As shown in Figure 4.2, for instance, differentiated individuals (in the upper center area of the figure), who are characterized by selfulness in intimate relationships, are able to discriminate among different emotions. They are able to assume responsibility for felt hurts by using the "I" or "We" pronouns instead of projecting responsibility externally or taking too much responsibility internally (and nailing themselves on a cross). By avoiding extremes in approach-avoidance and discharge-delay functions, they balance emotional experience and expression in a nondestructive fashion. These individuals approach and directly confront their hurts as inevitable experiences that can be shared, without reprisal or rejection, with loved ones. Selful, differentiated individuals use hurts to join with, rather than to distance themselves from, loved ones. They

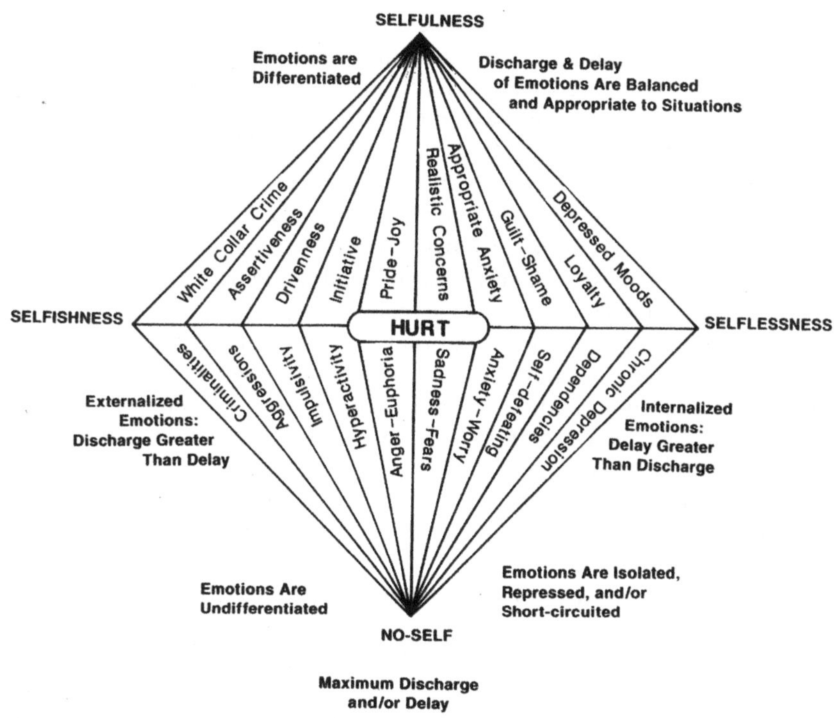

Figure 4.2 Selfhood and Emotions
(Based on L'Abate, 1994b, p. 139)

tend to form autonomously interdependent relationships characterized by care, empathy, forgiveness, and compassion.

In the left middle area of Figure 4.2, individuals characterized by selfishness (mostly men) externalize hurts through the manipulative discharge of anger, acting-out, and hostility to avoid dealing with hurts directly. They deny being threatened by hurts and claim they are invulnerable to what they perceive as an indication of personal weakness, i.e., the admission of vulnerability to hurts. These individuals are so threatened by hurts that they would rather murder someone than deal directly with the hurts, as exemplified by the experience of battering partners (Roberts, 1984; Serritella, 1992). Denial of hurt goes hand in hand with a strong denial of dependency. These individuals will go to great lengths to avoid situations that would put them in a dependent position. Paradoxically, most of them end up in very dependent positions—as jailed criminals and hospitalized addicts.

In the right middle area of Figure 4.2, internalizers of hurt (mostly women), characterized by selflessness, tend to use sadness, anxiety, phobias, worry, and depression rather than deal directly and positively with hurt. Most internalizers would seem to be directly linked to hurt. Often, it is easy to equate depression with hurt. That is not a valid equation. It is unwarranted and misleading. Most depressed individuals avoid dealing with their hurts just as much as externalizers do. While the latter blatantly avoid them, the former tend to become distance regulators to the extent that there is an approach-avoidance conflict as far as hurts are concerned. ("Come here to help. Go away, you did not help me.") These individuals would like to deal with their hurts, but are ultimately unable to face and confront them directly and squarely, sometimes preferring suicide to direct confrontation of hurt feelings. The ultimate result of this handling is overdependency—relying on others more than on self.

Many internalizers, (women, mostly) tend to be attracted to and to attract externalizers (men, mostly). This attraction tends to produce conflicts around the issue of dependency, with one partner overdependent on someone who denies dependency. In contrast to externalizers, who strongly deny hurts, internalizers see themselves as being too vulnerable to handle them. Admission of hurt and vulnerability can only take place in differentiated (i.e., secure) individuals who see themselves as strong enough to admit to their "weaknesses." Undifferentiated (i.e., insecure) individuals do not feel strong enough to admit to being "weak." They see the admission of being hurt as a sign of weakness and vulnerability that would place them even more at risk for additional hurts.

In the lower center area of Figure 4.2 are individuals characterized by no-self, who are unable to deal with the experience of deep hurts. Consequently, they are unable to express them appropriately. Individuals characterized by the no-self personality propensity hurt so deeply and so intensely that to express and speak about their feelings may be seen as a complete loss of self, leading to death. Because emotions are completely short-circuited in awareness, there is no direction or script on how to deal with them. Immediacy of physical expression, via aggression or abuse (discharge), on one hand, and withdrawal, helplessness, passivity, and impotence (delay), on the other, are the only available alternatives.

These individuals go beyond issues of dependency or its denial. Dependency here reaches the level of symbiosis, and its denial becomes autism and alienation. Often, these extremes are used in contradictory fashion, alternating from an extreme of attack (murder) to an extreme of withdrawal (suicide). An example can be found in symbiotic couples where an abusive partner kills the partner who is threatening to leave because he or she "loves" the other too much. Murder is sometimes followed by suicide. Could it be that love and hurt are related?

The continuum of emotions that derives from a selfhood model is supported in part by Schneider's (1990) theorizing. He proposed the same continuum stretching from an extreme of anger and aggression on one end to an extreme of depression and anxiety on the other end. However, he failed to relate feelings and emotions to levels of functionality or dysfunctionality.

The Intrinsic Connection between Hurt and Love

Upon initial consideration, it seems impossible to link love with hurt. However, depending on one's definition of love, such a linkage is existent and strong. If love means attributing importance to self and to other, as defined above, love means granting that other person the power to hurt and to be hurt. We are not hurt by discourteous strangers, rude salespersons, or occasional acquaintances. We may be annoyed or offended by them, but the power to hurt is usually reserved to those few, important individuals, family and friends, who are linked to us by attachment and love ties. We are most vulnerable to hurt by loved ones, and they are vulnerable to our hurting them. We tend to forget the rudeness or discourtesy of an occasional stranger or salesperson. However, we tend to remember and remain affected by a rude or angry remark or discourteous comment by someone we deem important to our welfare and existence. Thus, we are not only *vulnerable* to being hurt by those we love, but we are also *fallible* in hurting them, often without intending to do so.

It could be said that hurt is a family affair. We know how much we love someone according to how much that someone has the potential to hurt us. How much that someone loves us depends on how much that someone has the potential to be hurt by us. There is hurt when someone considered important hurts. Ironically and paradoxically, we are *needy* of comfort and support from the very ones whom we may have hurt and who may have hurt us. No wonder that intimacy, when defined as the sharing of hurts and of the fear of being hurt, is so difficult to achieve and that many want to avoid it as much as possible (Descoutner & Thelen, 1991; Shaines, 1987).

Lutwak (1985), in her study of women with high fears of intimacy, found that they were characterized by: (a) a high resistance to risk taking, (b) a strong need for safety and security, (c) a strong need to appear and behave as if they were emotionally independent, (d) a strong fear of getting hurt in an emotional relationship, (e) a general belief that marriage is a trap, (f) an inability to deal with intense feelings, (g) a feeling that they are unlovable, and (h) a strong need for a career as a way of defending against financial dependence.

These results tend to support a definition of intimacy as a sharing of hurts and of fear of being hurt that allows us to share joys as well. Many multifactorial definitions of intimacy do not even touch on this possibility. Apparently, the existence of hurts in intimate relationships seems either nonexistent or not considered important enough to be addressed in references on this topic (Acitelli & Duck, 1987; McAdams & Bryant, 1987; Perlman & Fehr, 1987; Reis, 1990; Reis & Shaver, 1988).

Gon's (1982) sequential model of the experience of being hurt consisted of four phases: (a) shock, (b) denial, (c) acknowledgment, and (d) adjustment. The first three phases seemed to be oriented toward safety; the fourth phase seemed more oriented toward growth. Responses in these phases were analyzed further in terms of dimensions such as emotional and self experiences, "recipient's" perception of the "donor," cognitive structure, and attitude toward help and sympathy. Because this study was performed with only ten subjects, it needs replication with greater controls and larger samples.

THE SELFHOOD MODEL AND THEORIES OF EMOTION

How does the selfhood model, espoused earlier, fit in existing theories of emotions? Such a comparison is, of necessity, selective, and three theories have been chosen. All three have in common the fact that they are "list" theories of emotions, that is, they list emotions without any grounding in personality characteristics and individual differences; anybody can experience these emotions. However, once the selfhood model is applied to them, some commonalities with the selfhood model of emotions become obvious.

For instance, the twelve emotions that are part of Izard's (1991b) differential theory can be categorized (Figure 4.3) according to the selfhood model: interest, surprise, and joy would be found most likely in the selful propensity; disgust, anger, and contempt would be found most likely in selfishness; shyness, guilt, sadness, and shame would be found most likely in selflessness; and anxiety and fear would be found most likely in no-self.

By the same token, Nathanson's (1992) list would most likely allocate pride, with dimensions of interest-excitement and enjoyment, joy, and surprise in selfulness; anger-rage and attack others most likely in selfishness; dismell (sic!)-disgust [dismay-disgust], shame-humiliation, and avoidance of attack on self most likely in selflessness; and fear-terror and distress-anguish with withdrawal most likely in no-self (Figure 4.4).

Lazarus and Lazarus (1994) differentiated relief and hope under favorable life conditions, where empathetic gratitude and compassion would be found most likely within selfulness; "nasty" emotions, like anger, envy, and jealousy

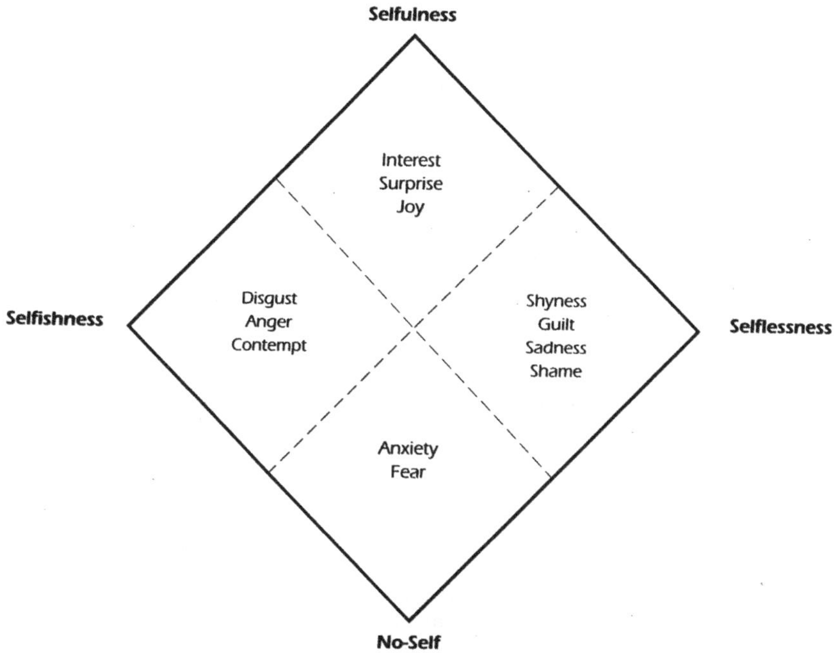

Figure 4.3 Selfhood and Differential Emotions Theory (Based on Izard, 1991b)

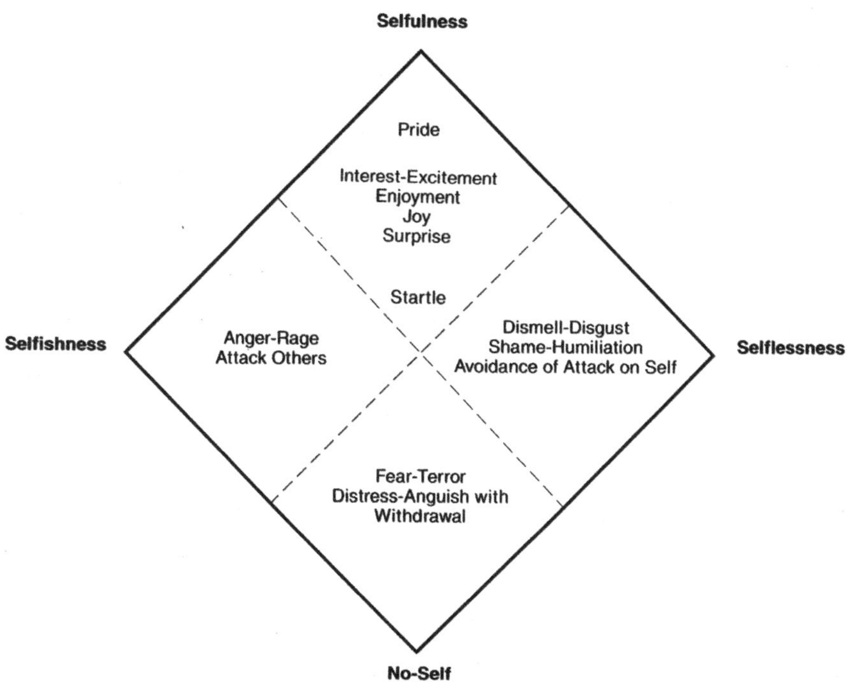

Figure 4.4 Feelings, Emotions, and Personality Propensities (Based on Nathanson, 1992)

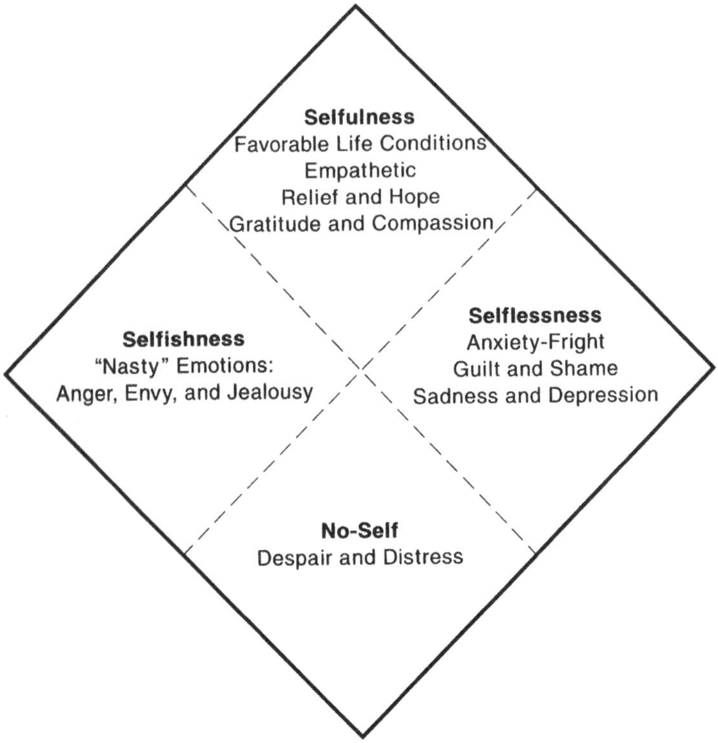

Figure 4.5 Emotions and Personality Propensities (Based on Lazarus & Lazarus, 1994)

would be found most likely in selfishness; anxiety-fright, guilt and shame, and sadness and depression would be found most likely in selflessness; and despair and distress would be found most likely in no-self (Figure 4.5).

Hence, the selfhood model integrates into one encompassing framework seemingly disparate lists of emotions that do not share a common denominator. This conclusion does not mean that the fit is perfect. It means that some integration is possible, and further empirical work, such as Lardieri's research summarized in the previous chapter, is awaited.

IMPLICATIONS: EMPIRICAL VERIFICATIONS

Three possible implications can be derived from stressing the importance of hurt as a fundamental emotion. They relate to: (a) empirical verifications; (b) preventive methodologies (Chapter 12); and (c) psychotherapeutic applications (Chapter 13). Only the first implication is considered here. The other two are considered in the chapters noted.

At least two lines of verification suggest how our thesis about the centrality of hurts could be verified in the laboratory. An early empirical verification of the thesis was performed by Frey (1980), who used an adaptation of visual masking that Erdelyi and Appelbaum (1973) called "emotional masking." This technique involves constructing four slides, each with one of three emotions (distress/crying, anger, and calmness) represented as a schematic drawing of a facial expression. A fourth slide with a neutral stimulus, a large dot, is used as a control. These stimuli are placed in the center of each slide and surrounded by identical orbital arrays of eight neutral stimuli.

In any given experimental condition, one slide was displayed to groups of 160 undergraduates in a single exposure of 250 msec. Following this exposure, two counterbalanced measures of recall and recognition were taken. After this exposure, Witkin's Embedded Figures Test and the Articulated Body Concept Scale were administered together with the Likeness and Sharing of Hurts scales. The first two measures evaluated personality differentiation *à la* Witkin (Witkin, Dyk, Faterson, Goodenough, & Karp, 1974). The other two measures evaluated personality differentiation in the family (L'Abate, 1976). In addition, subjects completed an Emotionality-Rationality-Activity (E-R-A) rating of their priorities for emotions, cognitions, or behaviors.

Results supported the position that emotional stimuli (Angry and Crying faces) disrupted perceptions significantly more than nonemotional stimuli (calm face and large dot). Recognition values were significantly higher for subjects who scored lower on psychological differentiation measures and who rated cognitions highest on the E-R-A scale. There were no significant differences between recall and recognition measures for the Angry or Crying faces, suggesting the learned aspect of both emotions. The emotional system appears to be part of the perceptual system, separate from cognitions and behaviors, according to an experiencing-expressing continuum, as mentioned above.

Another way to test this thesis would be to follow the techniques developed by Power and his associates (Power, Brevin, Stuessy, & Mahony, 1991), who used an Emotional Priming task to investigate the processing of emotion-related material. Names of hypothetical life events of an interpersonal, achievement, and survival nature are presented as primes. Subjects are to respond as to whether a subsequent trait adjective is self-descriptive. In the face of an esteem-threatening life event, normal subjects are slower to endorse negative adjectives. Results from two studies, however, supported affect-regulation rather than more specific esteem-regulation processes.

To verify the present thesis about the sharing of hurts, Pennebaker (personal communication, January 23, 1992) suggested repeating Watson and Tellegen's (1985) review of factor analyses. However, this study would consist of larger groups of subjects rating various emotions, including hurt and similar terms listed in this chapter. Once these ratings are subjected to factor analytic procedures, it would be important to find out how hurt feelings line up with either "negative" or "positive" affectivity. Also, could chronic hurt discriminate differentially psychosomatic health problems from other emotions?

CONCLUSION

This chapter, bolstered by a variety of theoretical arguments and empirical findings, has proposed the centrality of hurt as a fundamental but neglected emotion. Like all new theses, the one argued here needs the critical appraisal of the professional and clinical communities in terms of its consistency, its relevance, and, eventually, its validity. However, the issue raised is whether and how we can find validity for something like hurt, which, as an avoided and hidden emotion, needs to be inferred rather than observed directly. To verify this proposal, we need only ask our subjects or clients. As Pennebaker (1990) has repeatedly demonstrated, they will tell us, especially if they are allowed to reply anonymously in writing.

CHAPTER 5

The Continuum of Likeness in Intimate Relationships: Theory and Research

> Currently, the pendulum is swinging back again to incorporate more interpersonal influences on the self (as well as incorporating motivations, emotions, traits, and personality processes. (Tice, 1995, p. 954)

The purpose of this chapter is to review the theoretical background and evidence underlying the developmental aspects of a psychophysical, dialectical continuum of likeness in intimate (committed, close, and prolonged) relationships, as found usually in families and with friends. This continuum underlies intimate relationships and extends itself from one extreme of symbiosis through sameness, similarity, differentness, and oppositeness to the other extreme of autism or alienation, according to a bell-shaped frequency distribution (L'Abate, 1976, p. 79).*

Because similarity has been found to be present, pervasive, and influential in most human relationships, the guiding hypothesis about the existence and validity of this continuum of likeness is as follows: *If similarity exists as an important variable in relationships, it exists in some degree. Consequently, various gradations of similarity along a continuum of likeness should be detected and determined.* The myriad research in this area affirms, in part, the importance and validity of this continuum in intimate relationships. Because of the immense number of studies, this review can only be sketchy and selective.

Ideally, most of the evidence reviewed here would have been selected on the basis of in vivo situations rather than hypothetical descriptions or ratings of similarity in imagined or contrived relationships. Unfortunately, most of the empirical evidence on similarity-dissimilarity was originally based on presumptive rather than existent intimate relationships (Byrne, 1971; Duck, 1977; Huston, 1974). Nonetheless, again ideally, there should be some consistency between experimental studies in contrived, artificial laboratory conditions and

* The interpersonal implications of these ranges have been expanded in previous publications (L'Abate, 1976, 1994b) and will not be considered in detail here, except to qualify their basic nature.

real-life applications with individuals, couples, and families because this consistency would help validate the importance of this continuum.

The construct of similarity in the continuum of likeness defines an interaction of selves based on commonalities that, in its extremes, may approach identity (a complete overlap between two selves) or symbiosis on the one hand, and complete nonidentity (lack of similarity with anyone) or autism/alienation on the other. Within the continuum defined by these extremes, there is room for differentness and individuality.

Similarity is indeed an all-inclusive concept in everyday life; it has often been the subject of precise definition and analysis. Logicians, mathematicians, biologists, and psychologists have used it to label relationships between objects or events, specifying the exact nature of a relationship according to resemblances, commonalities, and identities. Confusion and ambiguity in measurement and quantification have often been the results. There has also been a paradoxical increase in the usefulness of the concept as an explanatory principle because of its resistance to precise definition (Gregson, 1975).

For purposes of this review, the kinds of similarity considered may be defined as two of the four types postulated by Wallach (1958). Similarity is viewed as:

1. The common properties of two or more phenomena or persons in the environment.
2. The common behavioral response evoked by these properties.

Essentially, similarity as considered here in personal and interpersonal contexts may be termed psychological as opposed to statistical, taxonomical, or logical. What is called similarity is *perceived similarity* because it exists in the eyes of the subjective beholders (including the researchers) rather than in objectively observable behavior.

The continuum of likeness proposed here was derived in part from Festinger's (1954) Social Comparison Theory (SCT) and was extended to include both functional and dysfunctional relationships. Originally, most theorists focused on the importance of similarity (and dissimilarity) as a basic dimension in interpersonal relationships (Griffitt, 1974; Heider, 1958; Schneider, Hastof, & Ellsworth, 1979). However, the two ranges of similarity-dissimilarity seemed too limited to describe or explain intimate relationships. Consequently, Festinger's original dichotomy was expanded to include additional ranges by considering research on conservatism, liberalism, and, especially, the structure of extreme social attitudes (Hansen, 1970; McClanahan, 1971; Rokeach, 1960; Taylor, 1960). This continuum was expanded further by including Mahler's views of symbiotic-autistic parent–child relationships (Edward, Ruskin, & Turrini, 1981; Mahler, 1968; Mahler, Pine, & Bergman, 1975), as the two extremes of the continuum. Figure 5.1 cites a variety of views, mostly consisting of three rather than six ranges, from diverse theorists and researchers who are too many to even cite bibliographically.

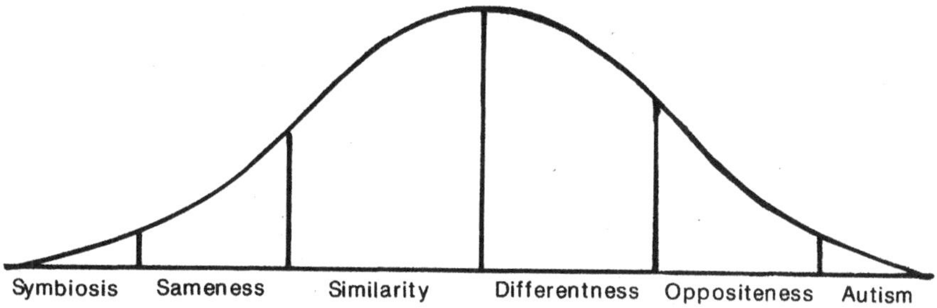

Berne (1964)	Parent	Adult	Child
Harris (1971)	"I'm OK—You're not OK" "I'm not OK—you're OK	"I'm OK, you're OK"	"I'm not OK; you're OK" "I'm OK—you're not OK"
Harvey (1961)	System 1 (conforming)	Systems 3 & 4 (independent)	System 2 (rebelling)
Hegel-Marx	Thesis	Synthesis	Antithesis
Johnson (1972)	Conservatives	Independents	Liberals
Kelly (1955)	Similar	Dissimilar	Contrasting
Kohlberg (1963)	Approval-oriented Authority-rules	Social & moral principles	Instrumental egoism
Loevinger (1966)	Symbiosis	Conscientious-integrative autonomous	Impulse-ridden Self-protective
Lynn (1969)	Parental distance "close"	Higher cognitive functioning	Parental distance "distant"
Mahler (1965)	Symbiotic	Differentiated	Autistic
Peak (1960)	Assimilation	Similarity	Oppositeness/ isolation
Rotter (1966) (Locus of control)	External	Internal	External
Willis (1965)	Yes-man	Independent thinker	no-man
Witkin (1962) cognitive style	Field-dependent (global)	Field-independent (articulated)	Field-dependent (global)

Figure 5.1 The Continuum of Likeness and Compatible Theoretical Formulations

Similarities between two seemingly opposite ways of behaving, hence their dialectical nature (Wrightsman, 1994), would underlie the three ranges of symbiosis-autism, sameness-oppositeness, and similarity-differentness. Each term in each pair is meaningless without the other term. Each range represents two sides of the same coin. Symbiosis and autism link together just as sameness and oppositeness or similarity and differentness. Where there is one, the other will be found, in the sense that symbiosis cannot exist without autism or alienation, or sameness without oppositeness, or similarity without differentness.

Basic to this continuum is the concept of self-differentiation. The self is not defined here in a vacuum, as most theories of personality seem to persist in doing (Pervin, 1990). The self is ultimately differentiated and defined in a continuously reciprocal, ongoing comparison with intimate, important others that follows a continuum of likeness (Banaji & Prentice, 1994). Self-differentiation takes place, therefore, within the context of other family members and important, influential individuals external to the family—friends, teachers, neighbors, mentors, and the like.

According to this curvilinear model, individual differentiation moves along a continuum from symbiosis ("I am you"), sameness ("I am like you"), and similarity ("I am somewhat like you"), to differentness ("I am not like you"), oppositeness ("I am the opposite of you"), and autism ("I am not anyone. Neither you or I exist"). The more differentiated the person, the nearer to the center of the continuum that person will be found. If that person is undifferentiated, he or she will be found at either extreme of the continuum.

Symbiosis means that an individual is unable to live without another, as in *folie à deux* or in relationships where one partner is killed by the other when he or she threatens to leave or indeed has left (Johnson, 1991). In this abusively apathetic and neglectful (AA) style, anger, contradictory and inconsistent withdrawal, and explosive aggression emerge from chaotic lose-lose relationships defined by symbiosis and autism or alienation. Sameness requires blind, uncritical, and rigid adherence to certain arbitrary and capricious rules that produce oppositeness (i.e., rebellion). Combining sameness (a demand for blind conformity) with oppositeness (rebellion), one obtains a reactively repetitive (RR) style. This style is based on immediate revengeful rebuttals and manipulatively coercive patterns of response, as found in 50% to 60% of most marital and family interactions. For instance, with few exceptions, as in the selful position, most parent–child and husband–wife interactions are reactive. This style furnishes the normative context for repetitive sameness and stagnation. In some cases, differentiation takes place upward (toward selfulness and CC) or downward (toward no-self and AA).

The ability to withstand stress and to use intimacy as a buffer and a defense against stress is somewhat more pronounced in the RR style than in the AA style. However, the outcome, with or without stress, is still unsatisfactory because this style increases rather than reduces stress. To a lesser degree than in the AA style, the RR style decreases the level of functioning and the coping resources of those involved in the interaction. Inequality of importance, negative reciprocity, and only sporadic intimacy are found in RR, where win-lose or lose-win outcomes are the norm. This style is found in marital polarizations based on selfless-selfish definitions of partners and in parent–child relationships where a power struggle is present.

Combining similarity with differentness yields a conductively creative (CC) style that indicates commitment to change and to improvement through a variety of positive plans ("Reactors explode, conductors keep cool"). Individuals characterized by this style usually follow a plan or a score (hence a second meaning for conductors) that allows them to think ahead; they ask for and gather relevant information before reaching a decision or going into action. This style is found in individuals, couples, and families whose coping strategies are characterized by democratic decision making, winful interactions, and change-oriented relationships. These CC relationships, characterized by equality of importance but difference in functions, tend to produce reciprocity and intimacy, with positive, prolonged outcomes for family members, in spite of stresses and traumas. These relationships are more resistant to stress than those characterized by AA or RR coping styles, which are transmitted from one generation to another in the same family, with some upward and some downward mobility in a few cases but with RR remaining the norm of most intimate relationships.

Inconsistent and contradictory variations between extremes of immediacy vs. passivity and impulsivity vs. withdrawal are the characteristics of the AA and RR styles. Balance, in both initiative and problem-solving, is the main characteristic of the CC style. The individual is in charge of self by allowing intimate others to give and to receive relevant information before responding. Intimacy is much more likely to be found in the CC style. Stress is handled better because it is shared mutually among family members.

A healthy relationship is based on both similarities and differentness in the individuals involved. Conversely, an unhealthy relationship is one in which partners are either highly similar or highly dissimilar to one another. An integrated balance between similarity and dissimilarity (i.e., differentness) is basic to the ability to form intimate relationships. Intimacy on a prolonged basis can only be found in relationships in which both individuals are able to be separate (dissimilar) yet be together (similar) at the same time.

This functionality-dysfunctionality distinction is additionally elaborated according to three levels of dependence:

1. Contradictory and inconsistent extremes of dependence→denial of dependency in the AA style.
2. Reactive and repetitive conflicts between dependence→denial of dependency at an intermediate level of functionality in the RR style.
3. Autonomous interdependence at the highest level of differentiation in the CC style.

Further elaboration between functional and dysfunctional relationship styles, according to a model derived from the two orthogonal abilities of love and negotiation, is shown in Figure 7.2. Other figures in this chapter will show three styles, ranging from the most functional (CC, in the center of each figure) to the less functional (RR, in the middle ring) and the least functional (AA, on the external ring of each figure).

Differentiation of self, therefore, develops first from how one perceives oneself in constant comparison to the family of origin (parents and siblings). If one becomes aware of positive similarities and differences that exist between oneself and one's family, and if these traits are freely adopted and integrated into one's identity, then one can be considered differentiated from one's parents and siblings. However, if one is reactive to one's parents or siblings—that is, behaves either in a blindly and passively conforming way (sameness) or in an oppositional fashion—that individual is not differentiated and is not free to make responsible decisions and appropriate choices relating to identity, mate selection, parental practices, and occupation. At this RR level, parents request that children comply passively with their commands. If the children behave differently, they are considered oppositional and acting against their parents' stated or unstated expectations and wishes. If the children comply, they are considered obedient and "good." If they do not comply, they are considered rebellious and "bad." In extreme cases of symbiosis and autism, where there is apathy and abuse, parent–child relationships are marred by physical, sexual, and verbal abuse, incest, neglect, or abandonment.

Admittedly, personality, self, and similar constructs are vague and general to the point that one can justifiably ask: "Likeness of what?" If one cannot specify definite characteristics (traits, attributes, behaviors, values) by which people can define themselves, then this continuum is too broad and too indefinite to be evaluated. To be more specific, this continuum applies to a variety of characteristics, but that may be more relevant to the attribution of importance.

HISTORICAL BACKGROUND: SIMILARITY AND SOCIAL COMPARISON THEORY (SCT)

Prior to the 1950s, psychologists avoided theorizing about the concept of similarity because of its apparently obtuse nature and the claim that it was the exclusive domain of logicians. Most references from the literature were passing allusions or philosophical asides that emphasized problems in definition and application. The first empirical test of the hypothesis that similarity influences attraction between people was performed in the early 1800s by Galton, who studied mating patterns in an effort to predict evolutionary changes. In a similar vein, Karl Pearson later studied 1,000 couples and found a tendency toward physical similarity. However, because people tend to marry within their ethnic group and, moreover, ethnic members tend to look alike, early studies are not viewed as proof that similarity necessarily fosters attraction.

Serious consideration of similarity as an area of investigation began primarily with the work of Byrne (1971) and his colleagues in their study of attraction phenomena. His paradigmatic research transferred this concept from the exclusive domain of philosophical inquiry to empirical research. Though not without its critics and some serious methodological restrictions, Byrne's work deserves serious consideration.

One of the major theoretical frameworks in the area of likeness is Social Comparison Theory (SCT), (Festinger, 1954; Schachter, 1959; Suls & Miller, 1977; Suls & Wills, 1991). The key assumption of SCT is that there is a basic drive in the human being to evaluate one's abilities and opinions. When possible, this evaluation is conducted in relation to nonsocial, objective standards—

speed as a runner, target-shooting ability, or opinions about the weather. However, in the absence of objective criteria, Festinger suggested that humans will compare themselves with other persons. Those others are chosen on the basis of similarity to oneself (Wheeler, 1970, 1974). Also, if there is a discrepancy in perceptions, there is an effort to gain congruence by changing the self or others, or ending the comparison. Pressure to conform increases with the respective increase of importance of the opinion or ability of the person or persons with whom one compares oneself. Divergent views are excluded, and there is a unidirectional drive upward in the case of abilities but not of opinions. Similar others will be sought for this comparison. Comparison with dissimilar others would be lacking in validity and stability. When an otherwise similar other is found to differ on an issue, SCT postulates a tendency to change one's evaluation of that opinion or ability. Finally, because the need for evaluation is satisfied by validation with a similar other person, those persons seen as similar are proposed to be rewarding and attractive.

The central concept of SCT is the "similarity hypothesis." Individuals prefer to compare themselves to others who are similar to them. This hypothesis was expanded by Stotland and Canon (1972) to include similarity-interdependence, "groupness" interaction, liking and social acceptance, and proximity-similarity schema, including implications of these schema for parent–child relationships (pp. 270–271). Similarity has often been equated with closeness (Nahemow & Lawton, 1983).

Festinger's hypothesis, however, has been challenged by a number of studies (e.g., Kruglanski & Mayseless, 1990; Wood, 1989). These studies indicated that comparisons are not limited to similarity, but they did suggest that SCT was correct to the extent that comparisons with people who are considered important and who are similar on surrounding dimensions are especially potent sources of self-definition. Comparisons do not take place with people who are unimportant or irrelevant.

Another criticism leveled against SCT relates to the failure to consider functionalities and dysfunctionalities. More recently, Kruglanski and Mayseless (1990), in another review of the evidence surrounding the validity of this theory, concluded that SCT was "found wanting in two respects: (1) It conveys a relatively fixed notion of social comparison, in which people are generally driven to compare, and do so mostly with respect to similar others and predominantly for the sake of accuracy, and (2) Its narrow scope excludes numerous significant issues of interest to social comparison research today" (p. 195). In another review, Wood (1989) concluded that, contrary to the original theory or subsequent research, individuals are not always unbiased in their self-evaluations but may seek many different goals through serial comparison. The social environment cannot be conceived as being inactive in such comparisons; indeed, it may impose unwanted comparisons, producing oppositional outcomes. This process involves more than just selecting a comparison target. It is, as argued previously, a bidirectional process that may vary from individual to individual to fulfill different priorities.

Subsequent studies have offered further support for SCT but have also provided for modifications. For instance, Schachter and Singer (1962), in a well-known study, showed the importance of other persons in an individual's labeling of his or her emotional state. Their results confirmed SCT and suggested that bodily states may be one factor that initiates the comparison process. Gordon (1966) showed that subjects with an experience of success were less likely to rely on social comparison for validation than were subjects with an experience of failure. Hakmiller (1966) found that subjects validated by two others had less need for comparison than subjects validated by a single other person.

Consistent with the findings of Gordon and Hakmiller, Albert (1977) published a revision of SCT called "Temporal Comparison Theory" (TCT). Under certain conditions, one is less likely to compare oneself with other persons and is more likely to use his or her own personal history as a basis for comparison.

> To the extent that a person has a strong sense of self-identity based on comparisons within his own history, contemporary comparisons with others will be less needed; and conversely, to the extent a person's identity is satisfactorily established by his relationship with others, he need not establish his identity by means of temporal comparisons with the past. (p. 502)

In this statement, Albert suggested individual differences in the need for comparison of one's abilities and opinions. The differentiated (i.e., selful) individual possesses a strong sense of identity from inner-directed criteria for self-definition. This person, according to Albert, would have less need for comparison with others. Further, the differentiated individual is involved in intimate, helpful, hurtless, and interdependent relationships from which feedback and support are received, without, however, an increase in dependence. The general feeling or tone of these relationships is positive and growth-oriented. According to Albert, "the tendency to engage in a process of temporal comparison is more likely if the affective quality of the present is negative rather than positive" (p. 580). The differentiated individual would thus be less likely to engage in comparing the present self with the past self. The result of less need for comparison to others and to one's past gives the differentiated individual the freedom to live fully in the present. The issue here is how less differentiated individuals will compare themselves.

THE MEASUREMENT OF PSYCHOLOGICAL LIKENESS

As opposed to comparisons between observable stimuli by a rater, judgments of similarity between people are more complicated and offer complexities of measurement not encountered in "dead" stimuli, like objects. Because people can rate themselves on the same measures used by an observer, judgments by the perceiver of self and others are possible. The majority of studies in similarity research employ rating scales where the scoring is binary or is on an intensity continuum with a number of set values, like a Lickert-scale (Gregson, 1975). There is usually a set of traits on which a person(s) can be scored. As Gregson indicated, traits chosen by an observer can have little validity for a particular ratee because of the different possibilities of disclosure for any one trait. In addition, the significance of how a response on a trait scale can change depends on whether it is the perceiver or the judge who makes it or whether it is to be disclosed to a judge at all.

Perhaps clarity of definition and consistency of nomenclature are more important goals for similarity research at the present time than is scientific precision. In an attempt to clarify presentations of an area known for its lack of clarity, the studies reviewed will be divided into what may be seen as mutually exclusive categories. One-time attributional judgments of assumed similarity hardly resemble a process of likeness comparison. Yet, in some instances, that is all the evidence there is. Consequently, a vast amount of research and theorizing on the role of similarity consists of contrived, single-shot meetings at which undergraduates are asked to react to hypothetical situations that bear little if any resemblance to real-life situations. Typically, the design of these studies entails a subject's rating his or her response of attraction based on information received about a bogus stranger. As much as possible, this review would like to consider research relating to real-life relationships (Hartup & Rubin, 1986), even though it may be necessary at times to refer to contrived research for lack of more adequate sources of evidence.

Likeness and Identification

Lynn (1969) is the most prominent exponent of research in the processes of identification. He saw identification as referring to "a person's similarity to another person, individuals who belong to some body of people, or individuals falling within some category. It is applied to perceived similarity, a motive to become similar, or a state of being similar." The similarity involved may, in turn, be global or limited to gender-typical characteristics; it may also refer to overt behavior or unconscious processes. This plethora of confusing applications of the notion of similarity is but one example of the measurement problem mentioned earlier. Lynn (1969) pointed out how similarity has been used as an explanatory principle for identification, citing Tiller (1963) and Stotland and Dunn (1963) as examples of this use. Tiller considered the perception of sameness to be a necessary step in the development of identification; he viewed people as having a basic need to see themselves reflected in others, to recognize themselves in the environment through a perception of sameness or identity with others, based on characteristics like sex, age, size, and so on. Stotland and Dunn (1963), on the other hand, believed that identification based on similarity occurs when one sees oneself and another as having a trait in common and, in addition, perceives the other as having an additional trait. Identification occurs as the observer believes he or she has a second trait as well.

In Lynn's (1969) description of different degrees of similarity, the highest degree is identification. The lowest degree, *preference,* is described as the desire to adopt the behavioral characteristics of another. More similarity is found in the next higher degree, *perceived similarity,* where one perceives oneself as being similar to another. In *adoption,* one actually acts out the behavior characteristics of another, and *identification* implies the internalization of traits and unconscious reactions similar to the object's reactions. Lynn distinguished between two types of similarity, according to the object identified with. In *parental similarity,* one is similar to a specific parent; in *sex-role similarity,* there is likeness to others of a given sex. Each type of similarity can then be paired with some degree of dissimilarity to yield different combinations, such as perceived sex-role similarity, sex-role preference, parental identification, and so on.

Developmental aspects of identification from childhood through adolescence were discussed by Lickona (1974) in a cognitive-developmental approach to attraction. According to Lickona, a child's definition and experience of social bonds change as he or she becomes cognitively more attuned to similarity. Before the emergence of similarity concepts, a child's feelings of "likeness" may be based on proximity, familiarity, and dependency instead of similarity in role, status, or attributes. Perceived similarity is important in sex-role development, particularly in a boy's orientation to his father during years 4 through 8. This is the first strong physical attachment that cannot be explained as a result of physical caretaking. By the age of 3 or 4, a boy prefers boys' objects because he likes what is similar to himself. At the age of 5 or 6, when the child can sort objects on the basis of similar attributes, he develops the concept of "we." With an increasing interest in male activities comes an increasing need for the father as a model for imitation. This need eventually leads to dependency on and emotional attachment to the father.

A boy's attachment to his father is a result of modeling, which is, in turn, a consequence of the cognition of similarity of sex role. As the boy gets older, he can differentiate interpersonal similarity against a background of dissimilarities. This process, according to Lickona, has implications for friendship formation. A child may like another child because of similar interests or because that child is the only choice available. To a casual observer, a couple's apparent similarity could be obscured by noisy differences. Lickona mentioned an optimal level of similarity, emphasizing that too much similarity may be deleterious. This notion is analogous to that of the likeness continuum, where optimal similarity allows for differentness and too much similarity yields sameness and symbiosis. Unfortunately, Lickona's thinking was not expanded to girls, who would learn to assume feminine roles from their mothers. Kagan (1958) also spoke of "perceived similarity in attributes between the person and the model" as identification. Actual behavior is not considered, only the perception of that behavior. Bronfenbrenner (1958), in work that predated Lynn (1969), considered real and assumed similarity, both in patterns and traits, as important in identification.

Identification appears to be considered an extreme form of likeness or similarity to an important model. This similarity is most often shown in attributes that may be real or assumed, traits that may be inferred, and behavior that can be overt or private. The roots of identification lie in a child's ability to discriminate different types of similarity in people who are closest and most similar. Finally, there is speculation that overidentification can be deleterious. Instead, optimal similarity, consisting of combination and integration of similar and different features, should be sought.

Imitation, another process that has been useful in past theorizing on identification, consists of repeating the same or similar behavior exhibited by a more powerful or bigger human being. However, imitation has been conceptualized as an either-or process. In many instances, imitative behavior does not occur and oppositional behavior occurs instead. These instances cannot be encompassed by the process of imitation. This process may "explain" similar behavior but does not explain oppositional behavior, unless this behavior imitates another adult who is exhibiting such behavior. Hence, the continuum of likeness underlies processes of imitation and identification.

Likeness and Attraction

Mettee and Smith (1977) reported on research suggesting that subjects are most attracted to the group member with the greatest ability. Theoretically, the average-ability subject, by comparison to such an expert, could increase his or her knowledge and gain information leading to expertise. In contrast, when the comparison was to be made public, the subjects were more likely to be attracted to the *least* able group member, which comparison should prove to boost the subject's self-esteem. In both cases, the dissimilar other can be seen as less threatening, possibly because competition and ability comparison to him or her become irrelevant to one's own self-evaluation. Studies in this area (Aronson & Worchel, 1966; Levinger & Moreland, 1969) have shown that the relation of *dissimilarity* to attraction is mediated by the threatening quality of the dissimilar other: the less threat, the more attraction. According to a continuum of likeness, only those individuals in the middle of the continuum have sufficient self-confidence to view differentness as nonthreatening; thus, they can be attracted to a dissimilar other.

Goethals and Nelson (1973) found that attraction was increased for a dissimilar other when he or she, in spite of his or her dissimilarity, agreed with a subject on a given issue. It seems that confirmation of an opinion by a dissimilar other can provide support for that opinion; when a similar other disagrees, this information is taken as simply irrelevant (Berger, 1971; Loh & Nuttin, 1972). For instance, Mettee and Riskind (1974) reported data that supported "the view that a competitor's pronounced superiority in ability can serve the positive function of shielding a person's self-esteem from severe negative comparisons by rendering these comparisons irrelevant." A dissimilar other can provide strong support for an opinion with which one agrees, and cannot affect an opinion with which one disagrees. Is it any wonder that dissimilar others are often attractive? However, this wonderful attraction to the dissimilar is not readily possible for everyone. Some persons are threatened by ambiguity and any disconfirmation of their dogmatic belief system. Thus, in order for a person to be attracted to a dissimilar other, he or she must be nondogmatic, or field-independent, or cognitively complex, or differentiated. If the crucial independent variable is self-definition according to one's "essential similarities and unique differences," then not only is the differentiated individual *capable of* enjoying and being attracted to differentness in another, he or she is also *actively seeking out* such persons to fulfill his or her identity.

Fromkin (1973) argued that, in any given laboratory study, subjects' perception of similarity with another is limited to a very small proportion of traits. He cited several reports that the function reaches a peak and then *follows a rather sharp decline* when similarity is overwhelming or when individual differences are negated. In other words, moderate levels of similarity do indeed increase interpersonal attraction, but after a certain amount of similarity, the sameness seems to possess aversive conditioning value, and attraction sharply decreases.

The hypothesis that similarity in attitudes is related in a direct way to attraction between people is identified mainly with the work of Byrne and his colleagues (1971). Byrne evolved a paradigmatic research strategy where consistent experimental operations were used in a continued setting to study attraction. Typically, subjects were presented with different stimuli in the form of a mimeographed survey with falsified responses. This survey included a bogus stranger whose responses were manipulated to be more or less similar to those of the subject. The subject then made choices of attraction based on the similarity of these surveys to his or her own attitudes. Results showed that greater similarity in attitudes between subject and stimulus (bogus stranger) produced greater attraction for both males and females. This relationship appeared to hold even with stimulus modification (e.g., tape recordings, movies), response modification across subjects (e.g., needs, expectations, and so on), and cross-cultural testing. Byrne also manipulated demand characteristics such as instructions yielding an opposite set of expectations, and found the same results. From this research, he developed a formula to predict and quantify attraction based on similarity.

A number of criticisms have been leveled at the paradigmatic method of Byrne and his followers. Most critics point to the "one-shot" laboratory method as irrelevant to what occurs in ongoing natural relationships (Duck, 1973). In addition, the use of a bogus stranger is an artificial situation allowing for little interpersonal feedback. Duck (1975) saw the presentation of attitudes alone in such a paradigm as obscuring the arrangement of attitudes in a personality constellation and investing them with higher functional importance than in real life. He saw reasons for holding attitudes as important in determining real similarity: dissimilar reasons for holding similar attitudes may indicate this deeper dissimilarity. There are also situations where the relationship appears to be reversed, as when subjects portray mental patients or obnoxious people or drug addicts. Grush, Clore, and Costin (1975) also showed how students dissimilar to their teachers on role-relevant traits liked the teachers more. Evaluation, which Byrne did not consider, appears to be an important component of the attraction relationship.

Nevertheless, within the experimental restrictions imposed by Byrne in his methodology, similarity appears to play a role in attraction. This relationship holds up under different modes of attitude presentation (Byrne, Griffitt, Hudgins, & Reeves, 1969), different populations and issues of varying levels of importance (Clore & Baldridge, 1968), similarity of abilities (Zander & Havelin, 1960), emotional states (Zimbardo & Formica, 1963), and economic status (Byrne, Clore, & Worchel, 1966).

Speculation in this area, as Clore (1975) pointed out, has been rampant. He suggested that similarity of physical attractiveness serves to define a field of eligibles. In work groups and marriage, similarity serves to reduce decision-making time and keeps conflict to a minimum. Similarity may be rewarding because it serves as a cue to the perceiver that similar persons will approve of him or her (Nelson, 1966) or will be attracted in return (Aronson & Worchel, 1966; Insko, Thomson, Stroebe, Shaud, Pinner, & Laytor, 1973). Byrne's explanation of the relationship centers on the idea that similarity leads to attraction when it provides consensual validation of rightness or reasonableness for a subject's actions or opinions (Byrne & Clore, 1967; Johnson, Gormly, & Gormly, 1973). Here, similarity is rewarding when one interprets reality accurately.

Studies concerned with similarity in interpersonal relationships consist of a short-lived meeting (no longer than one hour). They employ dating and/or married couples as subjects. In general, researchers have found that attitudinal similarity leads to attraction (Patzer, 1985). Although generally accepted in the literature, this notion has been challenged by Rosenbaum (1986). Similarity may lead to attraction, but dissimilarity leads to repulsion. Replying to Rosenbaum's criticisms of Byrne's hypothesis linking similarity and attraction, Byrne, Clore, and Smeaton (1986) proposed a two-stage process of relationship formation in which the first-stage dissimilar attitudes lead to repulsion. If the relationship survives the first stage, similarity of attitudes in the second stage leads to attraction. As Applegate and Leichty (1984) commented, regarding the vast research in the area of attraction:

> An inordinate amount of research has been devoted to studying attraction issues based on initial impressions in first encounters. The "longitudinal" research that does exist has originated for the most part in retrospective accounts of the development of commitment in heterosexual relationships. Moreover, little attention has been given to the frequency with which the phenomena typically studied in controlled settings actually occur in everyday life. Without such frequency data we have little indication of whether a particular phenomena [sic!] has much relevance to an explanation of recurring behaviors in relationships. (p. 39)

According to Epstein and Guttman (1984), attraction may involve too many factors to be measured by trait scales. Possibly, couples prefer not to marry their personality clone and select for social variables instead. Even though the correlations are low, the consistent positive replication indicates that selection on the basis of personality characteristics is not entirely random. Howard, Blumstein, and Schwartz (1987) also found evidence that assortment for personality was a smaller factor than assortment for social components. Guttman and Zohar (1987) speculated that self–other centeredness may be of particular importance at the onset of marriage and may reflect actual mate choice. However, their assertion was very tentative. Buss (1985) also identified, via questionnaire, several traits that are desirable in mate selection.

The major finding, considered relevant to an evaluation of a likeness continuum in the attribution of importance, is the consistently positive correlations in self-esteem scores of married couples (Murstein, 1976). If indeed self-esteem is the intrapsychic equivalent of the attribution of importance exchanged between partners, then this finding would support the relation between the selfhood model of personality propensities and relationship styles AA, RR, and CC, which are derived from a continuum of likeness.

According to SCT, similar individuals are rewarding and therefore attractive. This concept is similar to the reinforcement-affect model of attraction (Byrne, 1961, 1971; Byrne & Clore, 1967; Clore, 1975). Byrne and Clore's basic assumption is: What is rewarding is attractive. The two greatest rewards in human interaction are (a) similarity and (b) positive affective communications based on accurate information. The more relevant and researched of these two is similarity. The study of the relationship between similarity and interpersonal attraction comprises one of the largest bodies of literature in psychology. A positive linear relationship between the two has been shown time and time again, including similarity of attitudes, demographic data, needs, physical attractiveness, and self-esteem.

A classic study of attraction and attitude similarity was performed by Byrne (1961). Subjects rated their attraction to strangers who held similar or dissimilar attitudes on 26 issues. On a 14-point scale, attraction to dissimilar strangers produced a mean of 4.41, and attraction to similar strangers produced a mean of 13.00. The difference was highly significant ($p < .001$). A later study (Byrne & Nelson, 1965) revealed that attraction (along the y-axis) is a linear function of the proportion of similar attitudes (along the x-axis). The formula is $Y = 5.44X + 6.62$.

The attraction/similarity relation has been found with repression-sensitization (Byrne, Griffitt, & Stefaniak, 1967), intelligence (Eysenck, 1973), economic similarity (Byrne, Clore, & Worchel, 1966), and similarity of personal constructs (Duck, 1972) as independent variables. The positive linear function between attitude similarity and attraction has been found in children and adolescents, in retired individuals, and in international subject samples.

The study of personality similarity and attraction has been approached from probably as many different directions as there are personality instruments. Using

Rotter's (1966) Internal-External Locus of Control scale, Lombardo, Steigleder, and Fernberg (1975) found that "in spite of the fact that the external subjects described the external stranger in negative terms, they preferred the similar external stranger. Internals also preferred the similar internal stranger." The dimension of cognitive complexity does not seem to predict interpersonal attraction as well as locus of control.

A couple of studies (Fromkin, 1972; Snyder & Endelman, 1979) found evidence for the hypothesized curvilinear relationship between similarity and emotional state. In the first study, by Fromkin (1972), subjects completed a test constructed to appear as if they were completing a questionnaire measuring personality traits, interests, values, and so on. Subjects later received bogus feedback of their results. The feedback that the subject received depended on the "condition" to which the person was assigned. Subjects were led to believe that they were slightly, moderately, highly, or very highly similar to other subjects who had taken the test. After receiving the feedback, each participant completed a mood rating scale. As predicted, Fromkin found a curvilinear relationship between emotional response and degree of similarity. In other words, the emotional response was more positive in the slight to moderate conditions and became less positive in the moderate to high to very high similarity conditions. A curvilinear relationship was found for both sexes, but it was statistically significant only for the males.

The second study (Snyder & Endelman, 1979) utilized a measure of interpersonal distance as a means of assessing the influence of degree of similarity. It was reasoned that the use of a nonverbal indicator is preferable to self-report measures because nonverbal behavior is less susceptible to conscious censoring. Subjects initially completed a self-report inventory by rating themselves on a number of personality characteristics. Each subject then received a bogus inventory concerning a hypothetical other person with whom he or she would shortly meet. The bogus profile was constructed to be 5% similar (mild similarity), 50% similar (moderate similarity), or 95% similar (high similarity) to the subject's own profile. After having a chance to read the bogus profile, each subject was led into a room in which two chairs were pushed up against each other. On one of the chairs were some books and a coat, supposedly the belongings of the person whom the subject was going to meet. The subject was told that the other person must have stepped out, and was invited to take a seat in the empty chair so that interaction could begin as soon as the other person returned. The distance between the two chairs was measured after an interval of approximately five minutes. As predicted by the curvilinear hypothesis, the subjects in the moderate similarity group sat closest to the bogus other person's chair, and the subjects in the mild and high similarity groups sat farthest from the other person's chair.

In summary, at least in the studies reviewed, similarity does appear to promote affiliation. One could speculate from the research of Fromkin (1975) that if the subject group is too large, the opposite reaction might be expected as the need for uniqueness becomes more salient.

Likeness and Mate Selection

When this continuum is applied to an understanding of mate selection and of marital relationships, one would predict that the integration of similarities and differences would lead to greater conductively creative (CC) relationships and greater marital satisfaction than either sameness-oppositeness or abuse-apathy (RR or AA). Does one select a mate based on similarity or complementarity (oppositeness)? Ideally, conductive individuals would be in the middle of this continuum of likeness, integrating in their marital relationship similarities and differences from their families of origin. An ideal relationship is one in which a moderate amount of similarities between partners is complemented by a moderate amount of differences. Intimate relationships characterized by repetitive reactivity and, worse, abuse and apathy, stem from either symbiosis and autism or sameness and oppositeness in the self-differentiation of the partners. Basic to a differentiation model of likeness is the hypothesis that individuals who marry exhibit similar levels of differentiation. Thus, a person in the sameness range will marry someone who fits in either the sameness range or the oppositeness range. Highly differentiated individuals are hypothesized to marry other highly differentiated individuals.

These hypotheses have support in the research literature. For instance, Byrne and Blaylock (1963) found a significant correlation between husbands' and wives' scores on Rokeach's Dogmatism Scale, shown earlier to be possibly related to differentiation. Self-esteem and mate selection warrant presentation in some detail: (a) persons become engaged to partners of similar degrees of self-ideal/self-acceptance; (b) the perception of the partners as similar or different depends on the degree of self-acceptance; (c) persons with low self-acceptance marry persons whom they perceive as less desirable; and (d) the perceived role fit between the perception of fiance(e) and ideal spouse is significantly greater than the actual role fit (Murstein, 1970).

Given that self-esteem is one measure of differentiation, these findings support its interpersonal equivalent, attribution of importance. Support is found for (c). Hutton (1974) found significant correlations between levels of self-esteem and of differentiation in premarital couples. Farley and Davis (1977) found that sensation seeking is possibly related to differentiation. A correlation between husbands and wives was statistically significant ($r = .31$; $p < .01$). This finding was replicated in a cross-cultural sample (Farley & Mueller, 1978).

Murstein (1972) studied similarity of physical attractiveness in premarital couples and found correlations greater than expected. These results were interpreted in terms of stimulus–value role theory, which predicts that the experienced person will be likely to express a maximum degree of effort and obtain the greatest reward at the least cost if he or she directs his or her efforts toward someone of equal physical attraction.

Both Murstein (1972) and Kerckhoff (1974) criticized the extant literature on mate selection. Murstein commented on the tendency of researchers in this area to study only short-term relationships (one to two weeks' duration). Kerckhoff added that subjects are often college-age, middle-class people, and the results must be seen as applying only to this group. Kerckhoff concluded that people tend to marry spouses with whom they share basic values.

Due to the paucity of ongoing-relationship studies in this area, it is difficult to consider generalities on similarity relationships. Physical attractiveness similarity appears to be an important factor. From the literature on dating, one would expect couples at this advanced stage of courtship to have similarity of "deeper" values that have not as yet been specified. Future research must use long-term ongoing relationships to assess these value similarities.

In at least ten areas, likeness in marital selection is present: (a) intelligence, (b) education, (c) personality traits and social characteristics, (d) physical traits and physical attractiveness, (e) age, (f) religion and ethnic background, (g) socioeconomic status, (h) mental retardation and psychiatric disorders, (i) family structure, and (j) personal habits. A review of the literature in each of these areas would distract and detract from the goals of this chapter. There is large overlap of these areas with the independent variables of the theory (Chapter 1).

Apparently, no single theory seems to accommodate all the data concerning mate selection. However, the complex exchange models that try to take most of the data into account are probably on the right track. Similarity plays an important role and should be accommodated into any theory that attempts to explain mate selection.

Likeness and Marital Relationships

Similarity between marriage partners has been demonstrated in several investigations. Byrne (1971) found congruence on a variety of ideals, personality characteristics, and attitudinal topics. Barry (1969), Hicks and Platt (1970), and Levinger and Breedlove (1966) demonstrated that the degree of similarity, both actual and perceived, was related to marital satisfaction. Byrne and Blaylock (1963) earlier hypothesized that this similarity was attributable to a system of reciprocal rewards exchanged by a husband and wife.

More evidence has been found for couple similarity of needs than for couple complementarity. Most likely influenced by the weak support for complementarity, a number of studies after Winch (1955) focused on finding sources of couple similarity. One area that has been investigated is couple similarity in attitudes; two studies have found different results, depending on the type of attitude studied. Byrne and Blaylock (1963) found married couple similarity in political attitudes and dogmatism, as measured by Rokeach's (1960) left opinionation and right opinionation and dogmatism scales. Centers (1975a) failed to find similarity in attitudes on a 16-item scale measuring "the views of the nature of man," which was adapted from the Personal Orientation Inventory. As an example of an item from this scale, subjects were asked to indicate whether they believed humans are naturally cooperative or naturally antagonistic. Centers's subjects consisted of five groups of couples ranging in involvement from "most preferred date" to "married."

A number of other investigators have assessed couple similarity with respect to various personality and cognitive traits, using instruments such as the Eysenck Personality Inventory (Buss, 1984; Price & Vandenberg, 1980), subtests from the Wechsler Adult Intelligence Scale (Watkins & Meredith, 1981), Raven's Progressive Matrices (Price & Vandenberg, 1980; Watkins & Meredith, 1981), and the Embedded Figures Test (Lesnik-Oberstein & Cohen 1984). In general, these studies have found weak to moderate correlations.

A study by Buss and Barnes (1986), investigating mate-selection preference in 92 married couples, included not only general personality tests but also a measure directly related to the marital relationship: the Marital Preferences Questionnaire (MPQ). On the MPQ, the test taker rates 76 items according to how desirable they are in a potential mate. In a factor analysis of the 76 items, Buss and Barnes found nine interpretable factors. Their results on spouse similarity are reported in terms of these factors. Strong significant positive correlations were found for the factors "religious" (.65) and "likes children" (.52). Moderate significant correlations were found for the factors "socially exciting" (.37), "artistic-intelligent" (.39), "politically conservative" (.36), and "easygoing-adaptable" (.35). The remaining factors, "professional status" (.22), "kind-considerate" (.16) and "domestic" (.16), yielded nonsignificant correlations.

Expanding on the findings of couple similarity, a number of investigators have attempted to determine whether couple similarity changes over the course of the relationship. In general, it has been found that similarity does not change over time (Buss, 1984; Eysenck & Wakefield, 1981; Lesnik-Oberstein & Cohen, 1984; Price & Vandenberg, 1980).

A number of clinical theorists have stressed the importance of couple complementarity in marital functioning. For example, in discussing the psychopathology of schizophrenics and their families, Wynne and his colleagues (Wynne, Ryckoff, Day, & Hirsch, 1981) noted that "all interpersonal relations that persist are structured in terms of some kind of complementarity or fitting together" (p. 124). Another theorist, Sager (1976), also argued that complementary couple patterns are crucial for relationship satisfaction: "more good-to-excellent relationships are based on complementarity rather than on congruence" (p. 173). Haley (1963) stressed the importance of both complementarity and similarity in a successful relationship, according to two major types of behavior: (a) symmetrical and (b) complementary. In a symmetrical relationship, two people exchange the same type of behavior. For example, each person can criticize the other, or each person can offer each other advice. This type of relationship tends to be competitive, similar to the RR style.

Complementarity

A complementary relationship exists when two people exchange different types of behaviors. For example, one person in the relationship gives and the other receives. In this type of relationship, one of the persons is in a "superior" or "higher" position than the other. According to Haley, "in a reasonably successful marriage a couple is capable of establishing both complementary and symmetrical relationships in various areas of their marriage" (1963, p. 124). The validity of these notions, however, was seriously questioned by Johnson's (1982) research.

Despite the theoretical support for the importance of both couple complementarity and similarity in interpersonal relationships, most of the findings of empirical studies support the importance of couple similarity for dyadic satisfaction. In fact, couple complementarity is often associated with dyadic dissatisfaction. It is argued, as suggested by other researchers and theorists (e.g., Haley 1963; Snyder & Fromkin, 1980), that both complementarity and similarity are important in dyadic satisfaction. A major problem with previous research is that complementarity and similarity have been looked at in a dichotomous manner. In other words, a person is said to be similar or dissimilar to another. This stance oversimplifies the notion of complementarity and similarity because it fails to consider that one is dealing not with dichotomous variables but with a continuum that has complementarity at one end and similarity at the other. Another problem is that most studies in the mate selection and couple complementarity/similarity area have focused on the assessment of needs, attitudes, or personality characteristics while failing to look at an area that may be even more pertinent to dyadic relationships: couple communication.

The notions that "birds of a feather flock together" and "opposites attract" have existed for some time, but not until the mid 1950s did empirical testing of these notions begin (Murstein, 1976). There seems to be widespread agreement that persons tend to marry others similar in age, proximity, education, socioeconomic status, and intelligence (Murstein, 1980). Research investigating the relationship between personality variables and mate selection is less clear. Studies in this area have yielded conflicting and confusing results (Epstein & Guttman, 1984; White & Hatcher, 1984).

The concept of complementarity implies a process of opposites attracting each other. For this reason, this area is reviewed in its relevance to the likeness continuum. The first empirical testing of a theory of marital choice according to this construct was done in a series of studies by Winch and his colleagues (Winch, 1955). These researchers proposed that people with similar characteristics create a "field of eligibles" from which to choose a mate. Within this field, one chooses as a mate a person whose needs are complementary to one's own. Adapting a classification of needs from Murray's (1938) needs schema, Winch (1955) specified two types of complementary needs. Type I complementarity consists of needs that are different in levels of *intensity*. For example, according to this type of complementarity, if one spouse were high on the need for dominance, the other spouse would be low on the need for dominance. In Type II complementarity, needs are about the same in intensity, but partners differ in the *type* of needs. For example, a highly nurturant person and a highly succorant person might be attracted to each other.

Winch's research has been criticized by a number of other researchers (e.g., Levinger, 1964; Rosow, 1957; Tharp, 1963), in addition to Murstein (1976).

Besides weak statistical support, criticisms included a possible bias in the selection of needs, the bias of raters, and the use of a sample that may be atypical (Murstein, 1976; Tharp, 1963). In a refinement of Winch's theory, Centers (1975b) also found some support for need complementarity. He argued that some needs are more important than others in terms of complementarity. For example, needs such as sex and affiliation were said to be more important than nurturance or dominance. Rejecting the notion of Winch's Type I need complementarity, Centers (1975b) argued that only different needs can be complementary. Need complementarity exists when a person requires, for his or her need gratification, "a different need in another person, which in turn requires for its gratification the kinds of behavior instigated by the first person's need" (p. 121). Centers administered a revised version of the Edwards Personal Preference Scale (EPPS) to 71 engaged college students. A total of 239 hypotheses was created concerning the relationship of female–male needs. Centers found 208 of 225 correlations to be in the predicted direction; 62 of them were statistically significant. However, Murstein (1986) characterized Centers's theory as "sketchy." His data were sometimes analyzed incorrectly, and his hypotheses predicted the null hypothesis.

A number of other researchers have attempted unsuccessfully to replicate Winch's findings (e.g., Banta & Hetherington, 1963; Becker, 1964; Blazer, 1963; Bowerman & Day, 1956; Katz, Glucksberg, & Krauss, 1960; Murstein, 1961; Schellenberg & Bee, 1960) using the EPPS. Not only was little support found for either Type I or Type II complementary needs, but some evidence was found for the opposite outcome—the similarity (or homogamy) for needs.

Winch (1974) placed much of the responsibility for the failure to replicate his results on the use of an "unvalidated" instrument, the EPPS. The use of the EPPS cannot be solely blamed, however. Researchers using other assessment measures have also generally been unable to replicate Winch's findings. Other assessment instruments used in studies have included Murray's (1938) need scale, the Rorschach (Murstein, 1972), and value inventories (Murstein, 1972).

The first and strongest support for complementarity of needs came from a study by Kerckhoff and Davis (1962). In this study, 94 undergraduate dating couples who were "seriously attached" served as subjects. The couples were administered the FIRO-B (Schultz, 1958) and Index of Consensus (Farber, 1957). The FIRO-B was used as a measure of need complementarity. This test assesses the need for inclusion, control, and affection. The Index of Consensus, which involves the ranking of ten standards of family success, was used as a measure of value consensus. Seven months after the initial testing, Kerckhoff and Davis also gave the couples a questionnaire in which they asked how serious they felt their relationship was at that time, compared with the seriousness of their relationship during the initial testing. The researchers referred to this factor as "progress toward permanence." It was hypothesized that both degree of need complementarity and value consensus would be positively related to progress toward a permanent union. In other words, these researchers predicted that courtship progress is positively related to complementarity in needs and similarity in values.

In their initial analysis, the researchers found support for similarity in values. Although in the predicted direction, need complementarity was not found to be significantly related to courtship progress. When a further analysis was done, however, dividing the couples into long-term (those who had dated for 18 months or more) and short-term (those who had dated for less than 18 months), support was found for need complementarity only in the long-term couples. On the other hand, value consensus was related to courtship progress in the short-term couples, but not for the long-term couples.

The findings from this study led the researchers to propose a filter theory of mate selection. They hypothesized that, in the first stage in a couple's relationship, the similarity in backgrounds attracts partners to each other. Once the couple passes through this stage (or filter), they enter a stage in which similarity in values determines whether the couple will remain attracted to each other. If the couple is still together after passing through the similarity in values filter, need complementarity becomes an important determinant in the further progression of the relationship.

For a number of years, the findings of Kerckhoff and Davis were widely cited in the literature as providing support for the evidence of need complementarity. Then a study by Levinger, Senn, and Jorgensen (1970) failed to replicate their results. A total of 330 couples went through the same procedure as in the Kerckhoff and Davis study. In addition to the FIRO-B and Index of Value Consensus, these researchers included a number of supplementary questionnaires assessing aspects of the couple's relationship and background. These researchers found that *neither* value consensus nor need complementarity was related to courtship progress. In an attempt to account for their failure to replicate Kerckhoff and Davis's findings, Levinger et al. discussed differences in subject cohort and geographical location, as well as the current appropriateness (or inappropriateness) of the FIRO-B and Index of Value Consensus in light of the changes in social values and courtship patterns that have occurred in the intervening years between the two studies.

Wilson (1989) suggested a possible resolution between similarity and complementarity. In some dimensions, similarity is desired mixed with just enough difference to create a comfortable contrast in the correct direction. Wilson used height as the variable that would determine whether his theory was correct. He theorized that similarity and complementarity cannot be inferred from positive or negative correlations alone, and that the distribution of scores must be taken into account. Complementarity will not be found in extreme scores but it is present in moderate differences that reflect true complementarity. In other words, moderates will attract moderates. The amount of complementarity or similarity can be determined by the bimodal distribution of the scores. This position is supported by Snyder and Fromkin (1980), who stressed the importance of *both* similarity and dissimilarity in a relationship.

Most of the foregoing elements would seem to fall into a continuum of likeness, where individuals on opposite ends of the continuum (symbiotic or autistic) would be so similar that they would become enmeshed and actually fused, producing an extremely dysfunctional relationship. This notion is supported in the literature (Bentler & Newcomb, 1978; Cattell & Nesselroade, 1967; Hill, Rubin, & Peplau, 1976) in that dissimilar relationships tend to be more likely to be problematic, and similarity tends to aid the continuance of the relationship. However, when does too much similarity become dysfunctional sameness and symbiosis? The ideal would be found toward the center of the continuum, where both similarities and differences are appreciated and accepted. Wilson's (1989) contrast model would support a moderate level of complementarity in interactions between partners.

Data to support the theory of complementarity are scant, but there is enough face validity to its relevance to make it garner attention (Wilson, 1989). The problem is probably not with its relevance but with the models or instruments that have been used to measure it. Also, the notion of change, toward either convergence or divergence across marriage, seems well supported in the literature. Social and family theories would add the interactive nature of relationships so that one does not fall victim to seeing personality or marital choice as happening in a vacuum.

What is the role of complementarity in dysfunctional couples? For instance, Cattell and Nesselroade (1967) compared stably and unstably married couples and found that the stable group had significant positive correlation across several of the personality factors in the 16 Personality Factor Questionnaire (16PF). The unstably married couples had only two positive correlations (on guilt proneness and radicalism) as well as some significant negative correlations. A continuum of likeness would predict that couples integrating moderate degrees of similarities and differences would function well, and couples unable to achieve such an integration would respond in a repetitively reactive fashion or, in extreme cases, an abusively apathetic fashion. More evidence will be necessary to unravel this dilemma. What are more relevant: anecdotal, clinical, and commonsense views, or empirical evidence? This issue will be considered below.

Couple Complementarity/Similarity and Marital Adjustment

Failing to replicate Winch's theory of complementary needs, Bowerman and Day (1956) suggested that researchers look for couple complementarity in terms of needs and level of marital adjustment. Since Bowerman and Day's paper, a number of investigations, using a variety of assessment instruments, have been conducted on the relationship between couple complementarity/similarity and marital adjustment. As we will see, most of this research has supported a positive relationship between couple similarity and marital adjustment.

One of the first researchers to attempt to assess the relationship between need complementarity and marital adjustment was Blazer (1963). In his study, 50 "emotionally well-adjusted" married couples (defined as couples with no history of mental illness and success in everyday interpersonal relationships), were administered the EPPS and an early unpublished version of the Locke-Wallace Marital Adjustment Test (MAT), (Locke & Wallace, 1959). No evidence for a relationship of complementary needs to marital satisfaction was found. Instead, the results suggested a relationship between similar needs and marital adjustment.

Other researchers, using measures other than the EPPS, have also found a positive association between couple similarity and marital adjustment. For example, Murstein and Beck (1972) found a significant positive correlation between couple similarity and marital adjustment using as assessment instruments a 20-item bipolar checklist, the Edmonds Marital Conventionalization Scale, and the MAT. Levinger and Breedlove (1966) found a significant positive correlation between couple similarity in attitudes toward family life and marital adjustment.

Responding to Winch's (1974) criticism that the EPPS has not been proved to be a valid instrument, Meyer and Pepper (1977) attempted to measure need compatibility and marital adjustment using an "empirically demonstrated reliable and valid" measure of needs, a modified version of the Personality Research Form (PRF; Jackson, 1967). The PRF was designed to measure 20 of Murray's (1938) needs (12 of these are duplicated on the EPPS). Some rewording was done to make the measures more relevant to the marriage. A slightly revised version of the Marital Adjustment Test (MAT) was used as the measure of marital adjustment. A total of 66 couples participated in the study. Using the cutoff score suggested by Locke and Wallace (1959), couples were divided into a low (N = 15) and high (N = 51) adjustment group. As in the Blazer (1963) study, support was found for the relation between need similarity and marital adjustment, but no support was found for a relationship between either Type I or Type II complementarity and marital adjustment.

Not only have studies shown that marital adjustment is positively related to greater similarity, but there is also some evidence to suggest that complementarity is negatively correlated with marital adjustment. Goodman (1963) used a test of self-acceptance (Hill Index of Adjustment and Values) as his measure of adjustment. Subjects were also administered the EPPS. Based on the self-acceptance measure, 75 couples were divided into high (N = 38) and low (N = 37) self-acceptance groups. Goodman hypothesized that couples in self-acceptance would have similar needs, and couples low in self-acceptance would have complementary needs. In general, support for both hypotheses was found. With respect to the complementary needs, low self-acceptance couples were significantly more complementary in both Type I and Type II needs.

Pickford, Signori, and Rempel (1966) found similar results using the Guilford-Zimmerman Temperament Survey and the Burgess and Wallin (1943) General Satisfaction Scale as their measures of marital satisfaction. Subjects in this study comprised three groups: happily married, having trouble, and on the "verge of separation." Each group consisted of 35 couples. Happily married couples were recruited through a local church by other church members who described them as happily married. The having-trouble and near-separation groups were referred to the experimenters by marriage counselors, lawyers, and social workers. Of these couples, those who stated they were planning to separate and were taking steps to do so, were placed in the separation group. Pickford et al. hypothesized that similar personality traits are related to marital happiness and dissimilar or unrelated personality traits are related to marital unhappiness. For the most part, the researchers' hypotheses were supported. In the happily married group, four out of ten traits on the Guilford-Zimmerman Temperament Survey were significantly positively correlated. These were: General Activity, Restraint, Friendliness, and Personal Relations. The other six traits in the survey, although nonsignificant, were all in the predicted direction. For the having-trouble group, six of the traits were negatively correlated. Two of these traits, Emotional Stability and Objectivity, were significantly negatively correlated. Finally, for the near-separation group, only one of the traits (Emotional Stability) was significantly negatively correlated, but seven of the other traits were in the predicted direction. Although not providing overwhelming evidence, this study does offer some support for the notion that maritally adjusted couples may have more similar personality traits and unhappy couples may have more complementary traits.

The study by Cattell and Nesselroade (1967), already cited, investigated the link between complementarity and marital dissatisfaction. Couples were divided into "stable" (N = 102) and "unstable" (N = 37) groups. The stable group comprised couples who had made no known step toward the dissolution of the marriage. In the unstable group were couples who were separated or were seeking counseling for marital difficulties. Couple complementarity/similarity was assessed through the 16 PF. General support was found linking marital satisfaction with similarity. In the stable group, 15 of the 16 factor correlations between husband and wife were positive; of these, 8 were significant. Little support was found for the association between complementarity and marital dissatisfaction. For the unstable group, of 8 negative correlations, 3 were significant. Of the remaining 8 variables, 2 were significantly positively correlated.

The studies described above provide at least marginal support for the positive relation of complementarity in unhappy couples. Another study, (Katz, Glucksberg, & Krauss, 1960), however, has found some support for a link between complementarity and marital happiness, supporting the notion that *both* similarity and complementarity may be necessary in a functional marriage! In the study by Katz et al., 56 couples were administered an abbreviated version of the EPPS. Satisfaction was measured through a questionnaire that required subjects to rate the extent to which the spouse needed to satisfy or thwart the needs measured by the EPPS. The subject's self-ratings of satisfaction for the needs were added together to yield a total satisfaction score. Based on their satisfaction scores, the 20 couples with the highest scores were placed in a high-satisfaction group and the 20 couples with the lowest satisfaction scores were placed in a low-satisfaction group. These researchers selected 21 combinations of EPPS variables that they felt were relevant to the hypothesis of complementarity. Thirteen of these were Type I needs and 8 were Type II needs. Among the wives, complementarity was not generally related to total satisfaction. For the men, however, some evidence for a positive relationship between complementarity and marital satisfaction was found. Two Type I needs (Achievement-Achievement and Succorance-Succorance) showed significantly more complementarity in the high-satisfaction group than in the low-satisfaction group. There was also a trend toward greater complementarity on the Dominance-Dominance need pairing in the high-satisfaction group. Only one Type II need (Husband Succorance-Wife Nurturance) revealed greater complementarity among the husbands in the high-satisfaction group.

In summary, most evidence points to a positive relationship between similarity and marital satisfaction. Some evidence for a link between complementarity and marital dissatisfaction has been found, and very meager research supports a link between complementarity and marital satisfaction. The fact that previous research has often associated complementarity with marital dissatisfaction cannot be interpreted as meaning that all differences in couples are detrimental to the relationship. The studies mentioned previously have, for the most part, used inventories of needs or values, or various personality measures. What has largely been ignored, however, is the assessment of couple complementarity/similarity on measures of affect. It may be helpful for couples to be similar on these cognitive measures, but there is some evidence to support the notion that complementary affective processes (specifically, nonverbal communication patterns) are associated with greater dyadic satisfaction (Rosenthal, Hall, Di Matteo, Rogers, & Archer, 1979; Weinstein, 1989).

Weinstein's (1989) study examined the relationship of couple complementarity/similarity to couples' levels of dyadic adjustment and intimacy. In addition to the traditional measure of attitudes, couple complementarity/similarity was assessed through an examination of the subjects' nonverbal communication-processing skills. Much of the clinical literature focuses on ineffective communication patterns as a cause of marital distress, so it is particularly important to examine this variable as it relates to mate selection. In addition, as Snyder and Endelman (1979) noted in their use of their nonverbal measure of physical distance, a non-self-report measure is less susceptible to conscious censoring. The measure of nonverbal receiving ability used was the Profiles of Nonverbal Sensitivity (PONS), a non-self-report measure.

Weinstein's study was not designed to be solely a replication of Rosenthal, Hall, Di Matteo, et al.'s studies; it expanded on their research in a number of important ways. First, Rosenthal, Hall, Di Matteo, et al.'s (1979) support for complementarity came only from dating couples. Weinstein's study included both dating and married couples. Second, Rosenthal, Hall, Di Matteo, et al. used a crude measure of relationship satisfaction. Standardized measures were not used. Weinstein's study included standardized measures for both dyadic satisfaction and intimacy. Third, a major difference between Rosenthal, Hall, Di Matteo, et al. and Weinstein's study was that the latter assessed only nonverbal receptive skills. Weinstein included a measure of expressive nonverbal skills and a measure of attitudes.

Weinstein (1989) investigated differences in nonverbal communication skills within dating and married couples, and their relationship to the couples' levels of dyadic adjustment and intimacy. Although previous research, utilizing variables other than nonverbal communication, had primarily supported the role of couple similarity and marital happiness, the underlying hypothesis in this study was that previous research failed to find a link between couple complementarity and dyadic satisfaction because of the variables that were studied.

Differences in nonverbal communication skills are crucial to dyadic satisfaction and intimacy. Of the eight hypotheses proposed, three were relevant to the similarity/dissimilarity distinction: (a) Couples who are in the middle of a continuum of similarity-complementarity in attitudes and receptive and expressive nonverbal communication skills will be the most satisfied with their relationship; (b) couples who are in the middle of a continuum of similarity-complementarity in attitudes and receptive and expressive nonverbal communication skills will have a higher level of intimacy; and (c) greater complementarity (dissimilarity) in nonverbal receiving ability will be associated with higher levels of dyadic adjustment (satisfaction) and intimacy. Five additional hypotheses were made, based on peripherally related issues.

Participants in this study were 32 dating and 32 married couples who were recruited from either introductory psychology classes or acquaintances of the researcher. Couples were run in groups. The number of couples in each group varied, depending on how many were available for any given experimental session. Groups ranged from one couple to eight couples.

Nonverbal communication instruments used in this study consisted of the PONS (Rosenthal, Hall, Archer, et al., 1979; Rosenthal, Hall, Di Matteo, et al., 1979) which is a videotape measuring nonverbal decoding skills, and the Affective Communication Test (ACT), (Friedman, Prince, Riggio, & Di Matteo, 1980) a self-report questionnaire measuring nonverbal expressiveness. Two self-report measures of dyadic adjustment utilized in the present study were: the dyadic satisfaction subscale from the Dyadic Adjustment Scale (DAS), (Spanier, 1976) and the Kansas Marital Satisfaction Scale (KMS). Wording of both scales was revised so that they could be used with both married and dating couples. Two measures of intimacy were the Personal Assessment of Intimacy in Relationship (PAIR), (Schaefer & Olson, 1981) and the Sharing of Hurts Scale (SOH), (Stevens & L'Abate, 1989). Both are self-report measures. Finally, a self-report inventory of attitudes, adapted from an attitude scale developed by Byrne (1971), was also included.

After reading and signing a consent form, couples were first administered the PONS, after which they were given a packet of questionnaires containing the self-report measures. Couples were instructed to fill out each questionnaire separately, without consulting with his or her partner. Each packet of test instruments displayed a code number on the outside. Couples were told that, to preserve anonymity, they should not put a name on the test instruments, but rely only on the code number given on the outside of the packet.

Findings did not support a curvilinear relationship between couple similarity/complementarity in nonverbal communication skills and dyadic adjustment and intimacy. Some support was found for a relationship between dissimilarity on the nonverbal measures and greater levels of dyadic adjustment in dating couples. For married couples, greater support was found for the link between similarity in nonverbal decoding skills and higher levels of dyadic adjustment and intimacy. These results suggested instead a developmental or evolutionary theory of mate selection.

Results indicated that similarity in attitudes is positively related to dyadic satisfaction and intimacy, a finding that supports previous studies in this area. In a question that was added to the DAS (Dyadic Adjustment Scale), couples were asked to rate themselves on how similar or complementary they felt they were to their partners. Evidence indicated a positive relationship between reports of being complementary to one's spouse and higher levels of dyadic adjustment and intimacy. Because of a possible misunderstanding of the wording of this item, however, conclusions from this finding are questionable. More questions may have been raised than were answered by this investigation, but it addressed an area that has been largely neglected in the mate-selection literature: the role of nonverbal communication in the selection of a mate.

Differences between the studies may explain why these hypotheses were not supported. Neither Fromkin (1972) nor Snyder and Endelman (1979) used actual couples. Instead, subjects were given information about bogus strangers. Not only were actual couples not used, these studies investigated a different stage of a relationship than in the study under discussion. Fromkin and Snyder and Endelman were looking at initial attraction; the subjects in Weinstein's study had passed that stage. The importance of the relationship stage has already been discussed in terms of the difference between dating and married couples.

This study has a number of limitations that must be addressed. One limitation pertains to the dyadic adjustment instruments used in the present study (DAS and KMS). As noted previously, these instruments had to be reworded so they could be used with dating couples. The reworded scales are believed to be applicable to both dating and married couples, but further research is necessary to establish the validity of the subscales for dating couples.

Perhaps the most important limitation pertains to the nature and generalizability of the subject population used. Most of the dating couples were college freshmen or sophomores enrolled in an introductory psychology course. The majority of the married couples were acquaintances of the researcher and were involved in some psychology-related profession. Most were college graduates. Because the sample was probably not representative of the general population, issues of generalizability of results arise. Another issue involving the subject population is the fact that the dating couples had been together for a relatively short time. Over 50% of the dating couples had been together less than five months, and 25% had been dating less than three months. Future research might compare results for longer-term dating couples. Nonverbal communication skills of couples in different stages of courtship would appear to be a fruitful avenue of research, especially when a number of mate-selection theories are based on different stages of courtship (e.g., Kerckhoff & Davis, 1962; Murstein, 1976).

In addition to dividing couples into nondistressed and distressed groups, future researchers might consider dividing the subjects according to couple types. For instance, based on a factor analysis of her Relational Development Instrument (RDI), Fitzpatrick (1988) identified three types of married couples: (a) traditional, (b) independent, and (c) separate. Future research might investigate similarities and differences of nonverbal communication skills based on marital types such as those reported by Fitzpatrick or by Gottman (1994).

Results from Weinstein's study suggest a number of other areas for future research. In the area of self-report of partner complementarity/similarity, there was, as noted earlier, a possibility of the couples' misunderstanding the question. Future research might reword the question on how similar or *different (dissimilar)* couples felt they were to their partners. Results from this question can then be compared with the overall levels of satisfaction and intimacy. Findings from Weinstein's study, along with trends found in Hall's (1984) research, also point toward future research in the area of sex differences. Future investigations might look for sex differences in verbal and nonverbal communication as a function of cultural changes in sex roles (Surra, 1990).

Likeness in Parent–Child/Sibling Relationships

Limited information is available concerning personality development, social development, similarity, and differentiation in reference to parent–child relations. For instance, of the approximately 40,000 journal articles on development, half were related to personality development but only 43 articles related to personality development in reference to parent–child relations. The numbers were even smaller for sources relating the concepts of likeness, similarity, differentiation, conformity, and rebelliousness to parent–child relations. No articles that related the term "family" with any of the above concepts were available.

In an attempt to discuss parent–child relations over a lifetime, Atkinson (1989) suggested three dimensions or variable criteria for studying parent–child relationships. The three dimensions were chosen because of Atkinson's criticism of Bengtson's (1976) concept of family solidarity, which relies on similarities between group members to bond them together. Atkinson argued that family members are very different in age, socioeconomic status, generational status, and value orientation. Therefore, relying on the influence of sameness in order to develop a focus of study does not seem feasible. Atkinson suggested using the concepts of attachment, crescive bonds, and identity salience in studying parent–child relations.

> Attachment theory has been widely accepted in the field of mother–child interactions and has been used in research that addresses later-life relationships,

> as discussed in the next chapter. Crescive bonds address later-life relationships and develop over time. They exist when an individual feels bonded or connected to another, when no other individual can be substituted, and when the relationship is expected to be ongoing (Atkinson, 1989). These bonds are contingent on interaction that enhances self-esteem. They are formed when a person assimilates the qualities of another into his or her self concept. Children often identify with parents because they see the parents' positive attributes, which they would in turn possess through bonding with them. Because these crescive bonds are expected to be lifelong, parents and children invest in each other and make commitments that are future-oriented. Atkinson included identity salience because she saw children and parents as being connected to and part of each other's self concept: "[A] child's self concept is formed in the context of the family and even when a child rebels against a parent, the parent is helping to further define the child's self-concept by providing a standard to oppose." (p. 90)

In this way, children are constantly affirming themselves in relation to their parents. They often reflect parental characteristics in an effort to be "just like them." One reason parents and children interact throughout their lives is because they reciprocally provide information about each other.

Atkinson's formulation seems to follow a continuum of likeness, specifically in the similarity-differentness ranges, leading to conductive-creative relationships. If there is successful bonding of parents and infants, attachment develops. Parents can then relate to their children because they are part of them in their similarities, as well as being different from them because they are part of the other partner and his or her family of procreation, as well as being individuals in their own right. Atkinson did not specifically address the negative aspects of parent–child relationships because she wanted to "provide a framework for understanding why relationships continue for lifetimes" (p. 91).

However, using her examples, it is easy to see where the rebelling child could be discouraged from developing characteristics different from those of his or her parents. Without positive affirmation of a child's differentness, it can be seen as oppositeness and may even be punished. This punishment may lead to a negative self concept and interfere with crescive bonding. In the extreme, a child who perceives himself or herself as being different from the parents, and expects that the differentness will be punished, may decide to inhibit his or her individual growth, which could result in the development of an apathetic or autistic way of relating to the world. The converse of that process would be a child who is completely enmeshed with the parents and fails to see where his or her own self begins or ends (sameness and symbiosis).

Strong support for a likeness continuum in parent–child relationships is found in Rossi and Rossi's work (1990) across the life course. Focusing on the qualities in children that parents consider important, they found three constructs—autonomy, conformity, and status—to represent parental values. The qualities they associated with autonomy were independence, self-reliance, and open-mindedness. Conformity was defined by respectfulness toward adults, obedience to parents, neatness, cleanness, and good manners. With status they associated competitiveness, ambition, success, and athletic prowess. Although it appears that conformity (sameness) and autonomy (differentness) may be polarized characteristics, both qualities could be stressed when considering behavior appropriate at home, at school, and in the work setting. For instance, conformity to parents' wishes would not be viewed as a negative trait, whereas conformity to peers' wishes would be. The respondent's age determined which values would be highlighted. The older generation valued conformity higher; the younger generation valued autonomy or independent thinking higher than conformity. In relation to the continuum of likeness response styles, conformity and autonomy are not viewed as polarized concepts at the CC level. Rather, there is a balance between the two that is acceptable to both parents and children. However, these traits would become polarized at the two dysfunctional levels of RR and AA styles.

Rossi and Rossi also found cross-generational transmission of quality of marriage (1990), supporting Martin's (1990) investigation of whether marital relationship difficulties are transmitted from parents to their adolescent children's romantic relationships. Martin believed modeling of conflict behavior by the parents, in interaction with the son or daughter and between the two parents, relates to how adolescents handle conflict in their romantic relationships. He contended that there is a path of intergenerational influence from interparent conflict to child–parent avoidance behaviors to troubled romantic relationships. In terms of a continuum of likeness, it is easy to see how parental styles, functional (conductive-creative) or dysfunctional (abuse-apathetic or reactive-repetitive), can be imitated and repeated by the children. In an atmosphere where similarities and differences are affirmed, the ability to negotiate in times of conflict is what parents would be modeling. In turn, adolescents would choose romantic partners out of free choice rather than in reaction to their parents' relationships.

Olson (1989) defined family cohesion as the "emotional bonding that family members have toward one another" (p. 9) and included variables of boundaries, coalitions, time, space, whether friends are shared, decision making, mutual interests, and shared recreation. Their Circumplex Model of Family Functioning has four levels of *cohesion*—disengaged, separated, connected, and enmeshed—as described in Chapter 6. Family adaptability is described as "the ability of a marital or family system to change its power structure, role relationships, and rules in response to situational as well as developmental stress" (p. 12). The four levels of *adaptability* are: rigid, structured, flexible, and chaotic. Smart and Chibucos (1990) hypothesized that the central levels, or more "balanced" ones, are more conducive to optimum marital and family functioning. The extremes are more problematic. This research, using nonclinical families, supported the hypothesis that extreme family functioning is related to greater risk of substance use among adolescents.

The Circumplex Model may relate to the continuum of likeness. In the extremes of functioning and relating, symbiosis-autism would again be comparable to enmeshed-disengaged families, which would have adaptation styles of rigidity and chaos. At the midrange (comparable to sameness-oppositeness) would be separated-connected families, which would have structured and flexible adaptation styles. At the optimum level of functioning, similarity-differentness would compare to a balance between structured and flexible adaptation styles. This balance would include the ability to move from one style to another, as needed by the particular situation. In respect to the continuum of likeness, an individuated relationship would be one that functions at the similarity-differentness level. A symbiotic-autistic relationship would be indicative of the enmeshment and disengagement extremes.

In a study of the impact of conflict on the cohesion and power structures of families, Gehring, Wentzel, Feldman, and Munson (1990) found that conflict decreased cohesion and changed power relations in the family structure. In respect to adolescents, conflict was more prevalent in issues relating to autonomy. In issues relating to power, the changes could be indicative of various problem-solving and communication styles such as those mentioned in Nobel, Adams, and Openshaw (1989). Their three styles of conflict resolution—withdrawal, authoritarian demands, and negotiation—seem to fit into a continuum of likeness. Withdrawal could be related to autism and apathy. Authoritarian demands for conformity to a parent's wishes are similar to sameness: "Do as I say (not as I do)." Negotiation is mainly possible for those who communicate at the CC level, where similarity and differentness in the relationships are pronounced, valued, and integrated.

Each parenting style can be described in the context of the continuum of likeness, with the optimum level of parenting being present where encouragement is stressed. Compensatory permissiveness and conditional permissiveness are both indicative of the RR styles of communicating at the level of sameness-oppositeness. Indifferent permissiveness, the AA style, can lead to neglect or abuse, which is indicative of the symbiotic-autistic level.

Another line of research supporting an underlying continuum of likeness in intimate relationships is found in studies of parents and adolescents (Archer, 1987, pp. 163–178) using the Minnesota Multiphasic Personality Inventory (MMPI). In summarizing the conclusions from a variety of sources, Archer noted that:

> [I]nvestigations of intrafamily personality similarities have substantial importance and relevance to theoretical models of psychological development, as well as implications for applied treatment issues such as the selection of intervention setting (inpatient or outpatient) and the type or combination of therapies (e.g., individual or family). (p. 163)

One test of the similarity of test profiles pertains to relationships between parents and adopted children as compared with parents and biological children. Most studies reviewed by Archer on this point showed contradictory results. The major consistency of results was found for siblings: "Substantial and impressive correlations in personality features between siblings are found only under conditions in which both identical genetic inheritance and similar family environments are present" (p. 168).

When psychopathology is used as an independent variable to evaluate similarity of profiles between parents and their children, "The results of these investigations have consistently shown evidence of greater psychopathology among the MMPI profiles of parents of psychiatrically disturbed children in contrast to adults in normal populations" (p. 169). The same finding can be applied to the profiles of parents of disturbed and nondisturbed adolescents: "Maternal-adolescent correlations showed stronger relationship than did interrelationships between psychiatrically disturbed adolescents and their fathers" (p. 174). As a whole, "maternal features seem to be much more centrally related to both male and female adolescent characteristics than may be noted in the relationships of fathers to their offspring" (p. 176).

Even more relevant to the validity of an underlying continuum of likeness was the finding that acting-out adolescents seem to show profile patterns that are opposite to the patterns evidenced by their parents. This outcome would be predicted on the basis of Forehand and associates' work with noncompliant children (Forehand & McCombs, 1988). The more the parents, particularly the mother, demand blind conformity and obedience, the more the children, especially the boy, will tend to rebel against the mother's demands and oppose her. If the boy sees that the father is nonsupportive of the mother or even is using oppositional *(RR)* practices to relate with her, his rebellion may intensify. Girls, on the other hand, tend to conform to the demands of the same-sex parent.

Cohen (1983), in describing incestuous fathers, used many adjectives indicative of abusive and apathetic individuals: moralistic, alcoholic, violent, depressed, emotionally immature, seeking to control others by whatever means necessary, and denying of others' rights. Mothers of incestuous families are usually weak, submissive, indifferent, or promiscuous; often, they are depressed and withdrawn from the family. These characteristics reflect the abusive-apathetic styles of the individuals involved. Their relationship is characterized by symbiosis and autism at the level of self-differentiation in likeness.

Research into parent–child similarity grew out of the developmental literature, especially the work of Lynn (1969). It was most often called *identification.* However, the high degree of similarity implied by this term excludes other similarities of lesser intensity. Interestingly, mother–son dyads were the only parent–child relationships to have significantly similar cognitive styles. If one is to believe the attraction literature, this would imply stronger attachment.

Personality similarity was investigated by Peck and Everson (1975) using 28 male and female offspring, ages 11 to 42, and their parents. The researchers administered the Adjective Inventory Diagnostic Scale and found greater similarity among peers than between offspring and either or both parents.

Similarity in cognitive styles, as evidenced in intellectual functioning, appears to be strongest in cross-sex parent–child dyads. Identification, as we have seen, is more same-sex-oriented.

Likeness and Friendship Choice

Likeness is present in many friendship choices (Blieszner & Adams, 1992; Derlega & Winstead, 1986). Poe and Mills (1972) divided 67 females into two groups: (a) subjects who knew each other well and (b) subjects who had recently met. They measured interpersonal attraction, popularity, similarity of personal needs, awareness of others, self-awareness, and personal needs. Their goal was to determine whether interpersonal attraction choice of peer is related more to similarity of a subject's and peer's personal needs than to the pattern of needs manifested by the peer. Results showed a significant positive relationship between interpersonal attraction and awareness of others. Similarity manifested by a peer was important here in determining friendship choice.

Duck (1975) noted that most studies investigating naturally occurring relationships, such as friendship, use the correlational method, and attention is usually directed to similarity or some personality dimension. However, in an interesting departure from the relationship as predicted by Byrne (1971), Duck argued that gross personality similarity, assessed at an early stage of acquaintance, may mediate the attraction choices at that time but, with increasing interaction, concentration on deeper and more personal evaluations usually results. He studied two groups of females, those previously acquainted and those newly acquainted. Results with the California Personality Inventory and Reptest (constructs) showed that they could differentiate newly acquainted friendship pairs from other pairs, but at the stage of formed friendships, only the Reptest differentiated in this manner. Duck concluded that because the similarity that mediates acquaintance may change over time, personality tests should be administered with this in mind. One must evaluate with a progressively more specialized set of criteria as the relationship develops, because what may appear as similarity may, on a deeper construct level, be dissimilarity.

La Gaipa and Werner (1971), in apparent confirmation of Duck's results, found that attraction was influenced more by the level of agreement, whether it concerns the meaning of friendship or other interpersonal issues. Bailey, DiGiacomo, and Zinser (1976) studied same-sex friendship pairs, asking them to estimate their own intelligence, a friend's intelligence, the intelligence of an ideal friend, the intelligence attributed to them by a friend, and the intelligence attributed to them by people in general. Results showed that perceived intelligence similarity was a reliable feature only for long-term friendships. However, the most important relationship discussed, according to the authors, was that between the perception of one's own intelligence and the view of one's intelligence held by a friend. These were similar for all friendship pairs.

The authors conclude that this self-concept support is the basis for friendship attraction.

In summary, it appears that similarity in friendship needs to be assessed with the duration of the friendship in mind, and that levels of similarity need to be taken into account, because deeper dissimilarity may often exist. Similarity appears to foster self-concept support, which may form the basis of friendship formation.

Likeness and Oppositeness

In studying dissimilarity as the opposite of similarity, one does not know whether this construct means differentness or oppositeness. Hence, it is important to distinguish between two constructs because completely different predictions can be made. Differentness coupled with similarity leads to a *CC* style; oppositeness coupled with sameness leads to an *RR* style. For instance, Stewart and Zaenglin-Senger (1982) defined adolescent defiance as the "acting out of personal stresses" often developed in the context of family discord. Defiant behavior, they believed, can be generated through psychological aberrations between the adolescent and destructive parenting. They defined three types of parenting: (a) compensatory permissiveness, where parents give their children everything they did not have, thereby enjoying vicarious gratification; (b) conditional permissiveness, where the teenager gets what he or she wants so long as parental demands are satisfied; and (c) indifferent permissiveness, where parents give numerous material gifts and then feel released from emotional attachment. During this developmental phase of individuation, teenagers are experimenting with behaviors that symbolize independence from parental control. Parents need to accept and be comfortable with the emerging ability of their children to make decisions for themselves. They should not interpret adolescent decision making as defiance but should encourage an ability to make choices and strive for autonomy.

CONCLUSION: THE UBIQUITY OF THE LIKENESS CONTINUUM

Evidence to support the existence and influence of an underlying continuum of likeness in intimate relationships is fraught with many theoretical and empirical issues. Such a continuum may indeed exist; however, how influential is this continuum? How does the continuum of likeness stack up against criteria of validity and reliability? How it can be tested in the future? And how it is related to other relevant personality propensities, relationship styles, functionalities, and dysfunctionalities? The answers to these questions remain open.

CHAPTER 6

Linking Individual with Family Behavior: Seven Models in Search of a Theory

> An approach that emphasizes an integration of individual characteristics and family systems ideas may have the potential . . . to be far more productive than models that reject individual characteristics. . . . [I]f we incorporate ideas of vulnerability and individual characteristics into family models, it is possible that specific links between family functioning and different types of psychopathology will be uncovered. (Dadds, 1995, p. 35)

The purpose of this chapter is to link individual socialization and the selfhood model with seven models of family functioning and dysfunctioning according to the theory and models summarized in Chapter 1. Two psychoanalytic models are included: (a) one derived from self-psychology and (b) one derived from object relations theory. The other models are: (c) the elementary pragmatic model (De Giacomo, 1993, 1995); (d) a model of family defense mechanisms (Schwebel, 1993); (e) an analytical model of family paradigms (Constantine, 1986, 1993); (f) a circumplex model (Olson, 1993; Olson, 1989); and (g) family types and strengths over the life cycle (McCubbin, Thompson, Pirner, & McCubbin, 1988).

Finding possible links and reconciling similarities between a model of selfhood derived from developmental competence theory and models of family functioning should strengthen such a linkage, even though the models originated from different theoretical, experiential, and empirical sources. If the model is applicable to all seven models, it would strengthen the model as well as the validity of the theory. Furthermore, a theory contains a variety of models; a model, on the other hand, stands alone and does not contain any other model, unless it is part of the same theory.

The first three models deal with individuals or with relationships between individuals. The remaining four models operate at the level of family functioning *qua* family as a whole system, rather than as a unit of interacting personalities. At this level of analysis, the personality of individual family members is subordinate to the family. Here the individual's contribution is secondary to the study of the total family's variance as the major unit of analysis. This view is shared by most family theorists, researchers, and sociologists

(Boss, Doherty, LaRossa, Schumm, & Steinmetz, 1993; Broderick, 1993; Brubaker, 1993; Burr, Day, & Bahr, 1993; L'Abate & Bagorozzi, 1993; White, 1991), as well as many family therapists (Gurman & Kniskern, 1991). These professionals consider the family at the group level of analysis and pay less attention to individual members' contributions. At best, they may focus on the bidirectional or multidirectional influence or interactions of family members on each other, without specifying the personal characteristics that determine, and are determined in part from, these interactions.

A different viewpoint, derived from family psychology rather than family sociology or family therapy, makes the individual both the product and the producer of family relationships. Here, the focus of analysis is the individual as a member of the family unit rather than the family unit as a whole (Gross, 1992). Furthermore, although most sociological or therapeutic models of families are mainly descriptive rather than explanatory (Constantine, 1986, 1993; McCubbin, Thompson, Pirner, & McCubbin, 1988; Olson, 1989), the theory attempts to "explain" family variance by exploring personal and interpersonal characteristics and interactions of individuals who are interdependent by virtue of commitment as well as prolonged and close involvement. Thus, family *qua* family theorizing explains present interactions as a function of previous interactions among family members and usually avoids dealing with explanations using the individual level. This theory, on the other hand, places the individual's contribution at the same level as the family's contribution.

To expand on how explanation differs from description (terms that have been used liberally heretofore), the latter concerns itself with *what* are a family's functions or *how* a family fails to function, i.e., the content and structure of a family. Explanation concerns itself with *why* a family functions or fails to function on the basis of developmental characteristics of individual family members *plus* their interactions (Gross, 1992). Thus, family psychology maintains that explanation is found in the developing personalities of individual family members, whose interactions may well correspond with various descriptive patterns that have been captured by many family sociologists, theorists, and therapists. This, of course, is an issue of reductionism. Total family variance, therefore, is the summative, subtractive, divisive, or multiplicative outcome of individual, dyadic, and multirelational variance.

The present theory maintains that there is a need to find ways and means of determining causal characteristics that are relevant *both* at the individual *as well as* at the multirelational level of the family, moving from one level of analysis to the other, i.e., from the subordinate level of the individual to the supraordinate level of the family (and, of course, vice versa). Traditional personality theories, however, are not helpful here because most of them are couched in intrapsychic, nonrelational terms that have little, if any, relevance to personality socialization and functioning in the family (Dunne & L'Abate, 1978).

Developmental competence theory, therefore, should be in some ways isomorphic with existent models of family functioning that have been shown to possess empirical as well as clinical validity. This theory should be applicable to individual, dyadic, and family levels of analysis, in ways that are compatible with existing family models. Family psychology and developmental competence theory differ from family sociology or family therapy perspectives on two thorny and controversial issues: the individual–family interface and the description–explanation dialectic. Rather than getting caught up in the controversial individual–family interface, it seems more useful to focus on *relationships,* and to differentiate them, perhaps, according to qualities of intimacy, harmony, and so on. Once this differentiation is followed, however, one needs to define what is meant by intimacy or harmony. These characteristics are to be found in any relationship characterized, among other features, by mutual commitment, equality of importance, prolonged and close emotional involvement, responsiveness, and emotional availability to partner and children. Instead of dichotomizing the issue of explanation versus description, it might be simpler and just as useful to consider the process as interpretation.

Once the positive characteristics of functional relationships are specified, identifying the dysfunctional ones becomes relatively easy. They either do not show positive characteristics or they show their opposites:

1. The marital relationship is fraught with overt conflict, or else such conflict is denied or hidden covertly from outsiders.
2. Communication is unclear, inconsistent, and contradictory; individuals do not say what they mean and do not mean what they say.
3. Little if any responsive emotional support or responsible, effective problem-solving is present.
4. The outlook is generally pessimistic; life is colored in inherently negative terms.
5. Few encouragements or intimacies are present, in contrast with the many discounting put-downs, blamings, and insults, which escalate into explosions or withdrawals.

Negative rebuttals and counteractions are the order of the day. No one knows who is in charge, and whoever needs or wants to be a leader is subject to criticisms and discouraging remarks. If someone is in authority, that position may be achieved through coercion, emotional blackmail, or physical, emotional, or sexual abuse. No one is a real winner because everyone wins at someone else's expense. Perceived victories are Pyrrhic victories: one wins while losing, or at someone else's expense.

Dysfunctional relationships may be classified according to various criteria, including the nature of the pathology in the identified patient, the symptom bearer, the nature of family interactions, or the personality patterns of the parents (L'Abate & Bagarozzi, 1993; L'Abate, 1994c). In addition to the negative characteristics listed above, dysfunctional relationships exhibit at least eight specific characteristics that are derived from assumptions of space and time, and three styles of intimate relationships (Figure 6.1). In the *AA* style of relating: (a) rejection is defined by inconsistent and contradictory extremes in

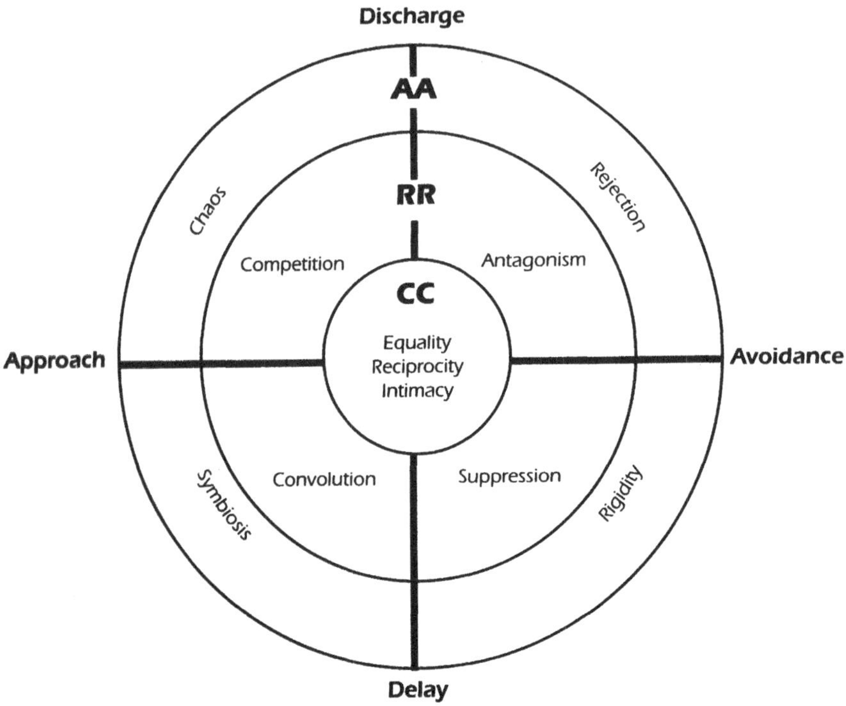

Figure 6.1 A Model of Relationship Functionality and Dysfunctionality

discharge and avoidance; (b) symbiosis is defined by inconsistent and contradictory extremes in approach and delay; (c) rigidity is defined by inconsistent and contradictory extremes in delay and avoidance; and (d) chaos is defined by inconsistent and contradictory extremes in approach and discharge.

To elaborate on Figure 6.1, in the *AA* style, *rejection* is defined by extremes in discharge and avoidance. Here, the bonding between partner and partner, as well as between parent and child, is damaged. The child is seen as an intrusion, a foreign object that is interfering with the gratification of the caretaker(s) and, possibly, the rest of the family. Individuals growing up in this type of family do not feel accepted, let alone loved. There is little or no emotional involvement among members, a pattern that leads to early disengagement and distancing. Members from this type of family, as well as the other dysfunctional families discussed above, show a lifelong pattern of low self-importance that does not allow them to love themselves or others. Apathy, withdrawal, and isolation are the prevalent lifestyles. On the continuum of likeness, these families would tend to gravitate toward the autistic, alienated extreme.

On the opposite quadrant, *symbiosis* is defined by extremes in approach and delay. There is a pattern of emotional overinvolvement among family members; conflict is avoided or denied. Personal boundaries are brittle and highly permeable, making for emotional enmeshment and an inability to extricate oneself from relationships except through conflict. No one knows where the personal sphere of self ends and another begins. With conflict being avoided, denied, or repressed because each member needs other members desperately, pseudo-mutual patterns develop, like sticking together even though being together means a denial of the self. No one is entitled to his or her own feelings, thoughts, or actions. No one is allowed to be different, and no one knows what it feels like to become and be separate and independent, because survival is mostly dependent on the other(s) and not on the self. Abuse is the earmark of rejecting relationships; apathy is the earmark of symbiotic relationships. Underneath both extremes, there is an inability to experience, express, and share hurts and fears of being hurt. There are also feelings of helplessness, hopelessness, despair, confusion, emptiness, guilt, and sadness that are very difficult to express unless there is external intervention.

On the quadrant of *rigidity*, defined by extremes in delay and avoidance, there is a pattern of authoritarianism. Criticalness, characterized by discipline, control, and scapegoating, is the norm. The primacy of the parents takes place at the cost of impaired individuality in their children. Uncritical and unquestioned obedience and submission produce poor decision-making skills and inadequate judgment. A possible result is that family members may learn to steal, act out, and lie rebelliously. Control is achieved through direct orders, criticisms, and verbal abuse, as well as through indirect sarcasm and innuendos. This atmosphere, demanding sameness and blind conformity, ultimately produces opposition and rebellion, either active or passive.

The characteristic of *chaos*, defined by extremes in approach and discharge, implies that there are no rules, routines, or rituals that give predictable direction and meaning to the family. Instead, there is erratic discipline, and inconsistent and contradictory messages lead to inadequate self-control and excessive self-centeredness. Closeness brings crisis. Confusion is the order of the day. Stability and predictability are frightening, because they are unknown and only precede another crisis. The message in this situation is: "Better keep things stirred up so that no one can get the upper hand over anyone else!"

By contrast, in the *CC* style of relating, equality of importance, reciprocity, mutuality, and responsiveness lead to intimacy. All these characteristics are short-lived, sporadic, or not found in either *AA* or *RR* styles. In the *CC* style, the individual does not respond to provocation but seeks, first, to understand the situation by asking for information from all parties involved, and, second, to produce a positive response, plan, script, or solution that does not discount but actually may enhance whoever is involved in the situation at hand (Gottman, 1979).

In the *RR* style of relating: (a) suppression is defined by an intermediate level of delay and avoidance; (b) antagonism is defined by an intermediate level of discharge and avoidance; (c) competition is defined by an intermediate level of approach and discharge; and (d) convolution is defined by an intermediate level of approach and delay.

In the *RR* style, the characteristic of *suppression* takes place in families where repetitive reactivity is the norm. Anything that anyone says and does is followed by discounting repercussions and consequences. No one can feel or think without being challenged and questioned. As a result, no one can express real feelings and emotions, because of the concomitant distrust and distortions in both feeling and thinking.

The characteristic of *antagonism* indicates that conflicts, arguments, and confrontations are the norm. The family lives in a continuous state of uproar, fights, anger, and hostility. No one can get close to anyone because such closeness is too risky. One can be attacked at any moment. Ambushes provoke the family into being like an armed camp under a constant state of siege. No one can stay calm and relaxed under these conditions. There may be a capricious and wanton attack at any time. Insofar as it exists, closeness is achieved through fighting and arguments.

Competition makes success the ultimate goal of survival and acceptance in such relationships. Perfectionism is accepted as worthwhile. Love is always conditional, because performance and production are the bases for bestowal of rewards. Goods and money are the sure indications of success. Lack of money is an indication of failure. Feelings are expressed in terms of being superior or inferior to some arbitrary standard set by authorities, with little tolerance for imperfections or mistakes. Dependency is denied; independence—that is, the denial of dependency—is glorified. Strong is better than weak. To succeed means to be strong. To fail means to be weak.

Convolution implies that the family cannot communicate directly and openly. Instead, indirect patterns are acknowledged, accepted, and encouraged. No one can focus on a relevant issue. Everybody needs to read the mind of everybody else, with a concomitant overreliance on inevitably inaccurate, incomplete, and distorted information. Everyone makes assumptions about others. However, if these assumptions were to be checked out, they typically would turn out to be inaccurate.

Consequently, the model described in Figure 6.1 is an elaboration of developmental competence theory that is compared with the seven models described below. By using two assumptions of space and time and three degrees of functionality–dysfunctionality, possible links may be obtained between the theory and the models.

SELF PSYCHOLOGY

Self psychology is composed of a variety of subschools and viewpoints that will not be reviewed here. The major expression and summary of this psychoanalytic school is found in the area of "ego defenses" as represented best by the work of Plutchik (1993). He developed (within the historical context of psychoanalytic theory) basic propositions for a psychoevolutionary theory that postulated eight emotions: (a) fear, (b) anger, (c) joy, (d) sadness, (e) acceptance, (f) disgust,

(g) expectation, and (h) surprise. From these "subjective" emotions, he derived a variety of "ego defenses," described in a circular "approximate circumplex" which he "obtained empirically using similarity scaling methods" (1993, p. 61).

Through these methods, Plutchik obtained four clusters of defenses:

1. Sublimation, rationalization, intellectualization, and isolation (of affect).
2. Regression, reaction formation, and denial.
3. Repression, undoing, compensation, identification, introjection, and fantasy.
4. Acting out, displacement, and projection.

As shown in Figure 6.2, these clusters characterize the two basic and orthogonal functions of space and time: specifically, cluster 1 is characterized by avoidance, cluster 2 is characterized by approach, cluster 3 is characterized by delay, and cluster 4 is characterized by discharge.

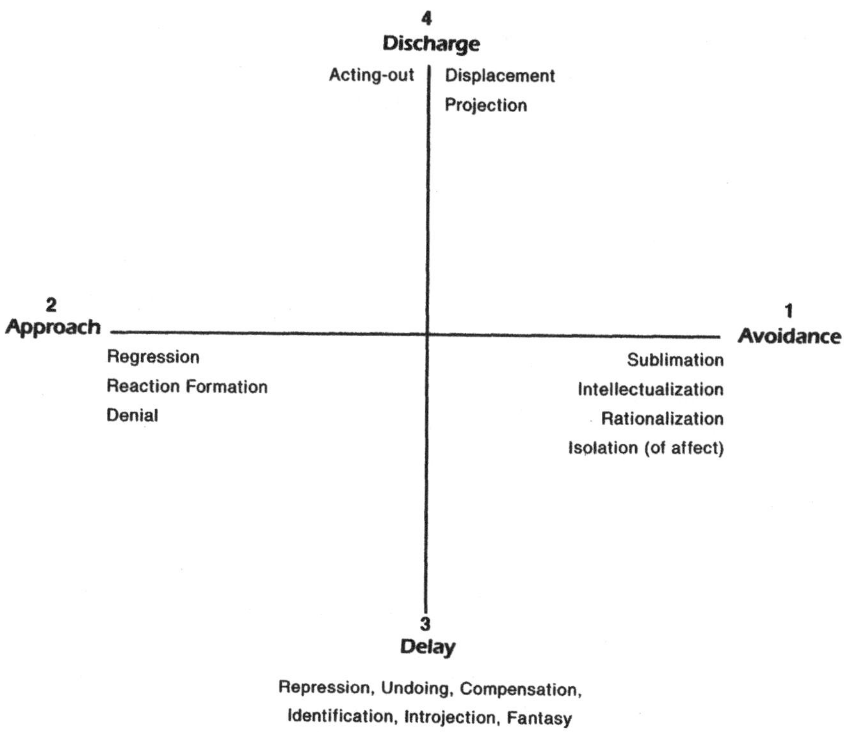

Figure 6.2 Selfhood Model and Ego-Defenses (Based on Plutchik, 1993, p. 61)

OBJECT RELATIONS THEORY

Object relations theory has been summarized and condensed by the attachment model, which has received a great deal of attention in the research literature. The attachment model is fast becoming a leading paradigm that is bridging much-needed gaps between theory and research and between research and clinical practice. It fills connections between the theoretical and the applied fields of endeavor, a long-awaited goal of the psychological community. The amount of current research to validate this model is indeed staggering, to the point that it is impossible to summarize all the relevant literature that has proliferated in the past few years. Reference can be made only to recent, selected secondary sources, among many (Bartholomew & Perlman, 1994; Bloom-Feshbach & Bloom-Feshbach, 1987; Doane & Diamond, 1994; Kerns, 1994; Sharabany, 1994; Sperling & Berman, 1994; West & Sheldon-Keller, 1994), and to selected primary research projects, among many (Bartholomew, 1990; Bartholomew & Horowitz, 1991; Fuller & Fincham, 1995; Hertsgaard, Gunnar, Erikson, & Nachmias, 1995; Horowitz, Rosenberg, & Bartholomew, 1993; Rholes, Simpson, & Blakely, 1995; Solomon, George, & De Jong, 1995), as well as to some possible clinical applications (Byng-Hall, 1995; Rutter, 1995).

Object relations theory, therefore, finds its exemplary summary and best representation in an attachment model of human relationships derived from Ainsworth's Stranger Situation (Ainsworth, Blehar, Waters, & Wall, 1978). The original model postulated one secure pattern and two insecure patterns: anxious and avoidant. More recent expansions of this model have been proposed by Bartholomew (1990; Bartholomew & Horowitz, 1991; Griffin & Bartholomew, 1994) and by Steele and Steele (1994). The first expansion to adult attachment is based on a self–other dimension intersecting with a positive–negative dimension. This intersection produces four cells: (a) secure, for positive self–other, (b) preoccupied, for positive other–negative self, (c) dismissing, for positive self–negative other, and (d) fearful, for negative self–negative other. Borrowing from similar models proposed in the past, the second expansion to children repeated a secure pattern, and three insecure patterns: avoidant (A), resistant (C), and disorganized (D). Harwood, Miller, and Irizarry (1995), in comparing middle- to lower-class Puerto Rican women living in their native country and in the United States, raised some questions about this classification. Secure and insecure patterns of attachment may be a function not only of socioeconomic status but also of culture.

Supposedly, a secure pattern in childhood produces or results in a secure pattern in adulthood; an avoidant pattern in childhood produces or results in a preoccupied pattern; a resistant pattern in childhood produces or results in a dismissing pattern; and a disorganized pattern in childhood produces or results in a fearful pattern. This brief summary does not do justice to the richness of the model and of the research findings derived from it. Yet, the four categories delineated by this model overlap significantly with similar categories in the next two models.

THE ELEMENTARY PRAGMATIC MODEL

The pragmatic elementary model proposed by De Giacomo (1993, 1995) was derived in part from systems theory. It has been reviewed (L'Abate, 1994d) and commended for a specificity not achieved heretofore by existing and traditional systems theory and for its originality. Systems theory has been criticized for its vagueness and generality; it fails to specify what kind of interactions take place within families as well as outside families. Moyer (1994) is just one of the many critics who, recently, leveled these charges. Additional references critical of systems theory are found in L'Abate's review (1994d). The specificity of the pragmatic elementary model overcomes many of these criticisms and adds new luster to systems theory.

The pragmatic elementary model is based on four possible coordinates that derive, for instance, from subject A's (husband) and subject B's (wife) interactions. An interaction is composed of elements that form the content of the shared (common) worldview of the participants: (a) elements internal-external to the worldviews of the two interacting subjects; (b) one's worldview; (c) the other's worldview; and (d) whatever is common between the two worldviews. Thus, the two major dimensions of this model—internality versus externality to one's worldview, and common versus not common to the same worldview—produce a 2 × 2 matrix.

The four coordinates of the model are (De Giacomo, 1993, pp. 14–15):

1. *Acceptance.* Something that did not exist in the husband's world but existed in the wife's world is made part of the interaction. For instance, the husband says, "I don't want to watch TV." The wife replies, "Come on, in a little while a great program will be on." The husband acquiesces to his wife's proposal and watches TV.
2. *Maintenance* of one's own world. Something that existed in the husband's world but did not exist in the wife's world is accepted. For instance, the husband suggests, "I want to watch TV," and the wife replies, "I want to go out." She then acquiesces and eventually watches TV.
3. *Sharing* of one's world with another. Something existing in both the wife's world and the husband's world is accepted. For instance, he says, "Tonight I want to watch TV," and the wife replies, "Me too, dear," and they both watch TV.
4. *Antifunction.* They accept a proposal that is in neither one's world nor the other's world. For instance, the husband says, "I do not want to watch TV," and the wife replies, "Neither do I," but they both end up watching TV.

This model does not address individual characteristics but stresses interactions between individuals who are interdependent.

From the merging of the four coordinates (4 × 4) are derived 16 relational styles, or interaction characteristics, according to Boolean logic. This logic requires arranging the four basic possibilities given above (accepting, maintaining, sharing, and antifunction) in different ways, ranging all the way from no to yes in all four coordinates and producing 16 possibilities, such as: "no, yes, yes, no" or "yes, no, yes, no." Extreme positions would be: "yes, yes, yes, yes" and "no, no, no, no." Thus, the 16 logical possibilities describe 16 relational styles. For instance, the four-no sequence corresponds to an extreme negative style of function, F0; pure sharing would produce a positive style, F1; an accepter of only one's own world would be F2, and so on, as summarized below. When all the 16 styles of function are described, they make up a taxonomy of human interactions and its changes.

F0. Emptiness of mind, when nothing is accepted in one's world nor in the world of the other, nor in external elements. An example is a comatose person or an individual who goes blank during an interaction and loses contact with the other.

F1. Sharing part of one's world when another is sharing a part and when only what is common to both worlds is accepted. Two coworkers may work on the same project during work hours but then go their separate ways after leaving work; or, two sex addicts may share a one-night stand without knowing anything about each other and without any plan to meet again.

F2. Exclusive acceptance of one's world but not of the other's nor of whatever may be common to the two worlds. A self-centered individual may ignore, dismiss and discount the proposal of another and whatever they share in common in the relationship. For example, a partner who wants a computer gives the computer as a gift to the partner who does not want it, thus ignoring the receiver's lack of interest in owning a computer. The giver follows exclusively his or her own interest, regardless of the partner's wishes.

F3. Maintenance of one's world through the acceptance not only of one's own world but also of whatever is shared in common with the world of the other. Extremely selfish and rigidly unbending individuals take from the other what is already in his or her world. They do whatever they want, regardless of the wants and desires of an intimate other.

F4. Accepting the world of another without sharing it. A passive individual yields uncritically and flexibly to the other's world, surrendering his or her world to the world of the other. An example is a partner who is willing to accede to the other's sexual wishes or practices, no matter how kinky or extreme they may be, without expressing or paying attention to his or her own desires.

F5. Accepting only the other's world and what is common to both worlds. Some individuals altruistically and gratefully give active acceptance of the proposals of others. In cases of extreme identification, individuals are transformed by taking on the characteristics of their partners.

F6. Accepting one's world and the other's world without sharing it. Selfish altruists ambivalently hesitate to share either world. They oscillate between accepting and refusing their own world, or the world of the other, without connecting the two worlds. These individuals cannot make decisions one way or another because they have an underlying agenda that has not been faced by either partner. For example, a girl has been raped; her family members, who know about it, do not want to talk about it. A great deal of oscillation is produced and may manifest itself in conflicts over decisions. Or, one partner has had an affair and both partners are aware of it. The ensuing silence produces a distortion in the relationship.

F7. Accepting one's own and the other's world and mediating the two worlds harmoniously without getting lost in either one. A very close couple is mutually available to the other in any possible way, yet neither loses his or her world.

F8. Accepting only what does *not* exist in one's own or in the other's world, but accepting external elements of the outside world that were not present previously in the interaction and were not common to both worlds. An example: uttering words or engaging in acts that are irrelevant or outside the context of an interaction, such as asking about the price of eggs in China during sexual intercourse.

F9. Accepting only what exists and what does not exist in one's own and the other's world. For instance, unquestioning and uncritical sharing of what is common in their internal and external worlds is visible in an extremely symbiotically enmeshed couple. One partner cannot accept the other partner's world separate from his or her own and cannot accept his or her own.

F10. Accepting only what exists in one's internal world and in the external world but rejecting what exists in the other's world or whatever is shared. "Mary, Mary, quite contrary" personalizes the active, systematic opposer, the spiteful negativist and obstructionist. This is the individual who does exactly the opposite of what is proposed by intimate others.

F11. Accepting one's own world, whatever is shared with the other's world, and whatever is foreign to one's own world and the other's world. Some people go to exaggerated extremes to stick to and defend their own world while attempting to expand toward the world of others. Faced with opposition, however, these individuals become confused and emerge as bullies, dictators, and arrogant egotists who continue to push limits to the extreme. Eventually, they meet strong opposition that they can no longer control or dominate. Richard Nixon and some contemporary dictators come to mind.

F12. Accepting only what is in the other's world without sharing it, but accepting also whatever does not exist in one's own world or in the other's world. An example is the pseudo-altruist who appears to accept the other's world but, who, in reality, maintains his or her own world. Self-proclaimed martyrs sacrifice themselves for their own sake and not for the sake of others. A sexually unsatisfied partner may receive pleasure vicariously after giving pleasure to the other.

F13. Accepting the other's world and whatever is common that does not exist in one's own and the other's world, but not what is part of one's own world. This behavior is seen in amplification of the world of the other while refusing to accept what exists exclusively in one's own world. For example, a partner who hates pets gives the other, who likes pets, a cat or a dog as a gift.

F14. Total acceptance of one's own world, the other's world, and the external world of both, without accepting shared elements. This behavior is seen in individuals who lack the focus needed to complete interactions successfully. They are subject to premature ejaculation, and, to avoid addressing issues directly, they may speak in metaphors instead.

F15. Total acceptance of whatever exists, internally and externally, in one's own world and the other's world. These individuals unselectively and inconclusively accept whatever exists at both extremes of any situation, without any boundary or discussion. Everything is negotiable.

By predicting the kinds of interaction that take place as a consequence of two similar or different styles in two interacting individuals, this model facilitates the organization of specific guidelines for specific interventions. Consulting a matrix of possible combinations and permutations of styles between and among individuals or members of a family, a therapist can follow certain designated routes available in a computer program written by the author. For instance, if an individual with a F10 style needs to be changed to an F3 style, the therapist or a member of the family, acting according to the therapist's prescription, may use an F12 style. By the same token, a partner in a couple interacting with an F14 style can be changed to follow an F3 when the other partner follows an F12 style. When an individual with an F6 style interacts with an individual who has an F5 style, the former may follow an F3 style.

Many studies have attempted to evaluate the validity of this model (De Giacomo, 1995). A representative one (De Giacomo, Pierri, Lefons, & Mich, 1990) illustrates how the model was validated from its beginning through a three-step presentation of Holtzman's (1961) 90 inkblot tables and, later, through a five-step presentation of Holtzman's 80 tables (Pierri, 1992). These tables were administered in an interactive fashion by showing them in slides to single subjects or to groups of subjects. First, subjects viewed each slide and were instructed to indicate a preference for one slide among the 90. Next, 40 slides, chosen at random from the 90, were shown again with the information (set) that these were the most popular ones chosen by most subjects. In this presentation, subjects were asked to reselect which slides they liked best. In a third presentation, subjects were instructed again to select 40 slides from the 90 slides originally presented, without any other information. From these selections, it was possible to find out: (a) how much each subject accepted the world of the other (acceptance coordinate), (b) how much each one maintained his or her own world (maintenance coordinate), (c) how much each one shared his or her own world (sharing coordinate), and (d) how much each one accepted whatever was not in the first and the second presentations (antifunction coordinate). Among normal subjects, maintenance was the most frequent style. Antifunction was the least frequent, except among schizophrenic subjects.

Another study (De Giacomo et al., 1986) evaluated how interaction patterns change as a function of drug administration, again using Holtzman's tables in an interactive fashion. Silvestri, Lefons, De Giacomo, and Corfiati (1988), also measuring changes with Holtzman's test administered interactively, studied how communication patterns change as a function of age.

In the most recent application of this model, a computer program has been developed to foster creativity in problem-solving and greater awareness of the various interpersonal possibilities available through a presentation of the 16 styles (De Giacomo, 1995). To make validation of the model more accessible to researchers and clinicians, adjective lists have been created that will allow comparative testing of this model with other models.

FAMILY DEFENSE MECHANISMS

Schwebel (1993) developed a framework consisting of four family defense mechanisms (FDMs):

1. Escape, through (a) physical withdrawal, (b) psychological distance, or (c) substance abuse (drugs and alcohol).
2. Goal-drivenness, through team problem solving.
3. Mood swings, through provocation, resignation, and buying-off.
4. Multihousehold FDMs, through escape and goal-driven FDMs.

This framework can be encompassed by the four possibilities derived from the two assumptions of distance and control: (a) approach-discharge, (b) approach-delay, (c) avoidance-discharge, and (d) avoidance-delay. According to the model derived from developmental competence theory, Schwebel's escape FDMs involve avoidance-discharge, his goal-driven and mood-swing FDMs involve approach-discharge, and his multihousehold FDMs involve either avoidance-discharge or avoidance-delay.

In contrast to the previous three models, this model concentrates on family patterns without an expansion to dysfunctional units. It fails to answer a question that can be raised with all family-oriented models: "Where do these family defense mechanisms come from and how do they develop?" According to Schwebel (personal communication, May 20, 1993), the answer to this question is: "Families happen upon them [FDMs] after some of their intentional efforts to solve family problems have failed." This is an insufficient answer to the original question. Better exploration and explanation are needed to understand how overall family defenses (if existent) develop in relation to functionalities and dysfunctionalities in individuals and families.

AN ANALYTICAL MODEL OF FAMILY PARADIGMS

Constantine (1986, 1993) created a very complex and well-developed model of family functioning that is an elaboration of Kantor and Lehr's (1975) original contribution. The latter authors distinguished among closed, random, and open families. Constantine added a synchronous type and elaborated on the characteristics of each family type. The closed type favors hierarchy and reliance on authority to regulate interaction processes and determine solutions. The random type favors divergence and relies on the diverse and independent actions of individual family members as the most acceptable method for deriving group solutions. The open type favors reflexivity and reliance on exploration and examination of the family's own structure and process for developing solutions and making decisions. The synchronous type favors alignment, relies on preexisting tacit agreements, and has a shared set of values, goals, and ideas to regulate process and determine solutions.

In dealing with dysfunctionality, Constantine differentiates between two levels, with the first being somewhat more functional than the second. In the open type of family, the first level is cooperatively democratic and the second is chaotically enmeshed. In the random type, the first level is creatively laissez-faire and the second is chaotically disengaged. In the closed type, the first level is stably authoritarian and the second is rigidly enmeshed. In the synchronous type, the first level is quietly consensual and the second is rigidly disengaged. The two orthogonal dimensions crossing the four types are enmeshment versus disengagement and chaos versus rigidity.

By using the two assumptions of distance and control, it is possible to classify Constantine's four family types (see Figure 6.3). The open type falls into the approach-discharge quadrant. The random type falls into the discharge-avoidance quadrant. The synchronous type falls into the avoidance-delay quadrant, and the closed type falls into the delay-approach quadrant. The two dimensions of enmeshment vs. disengagement and chaos vs. rigidity would correspond respectively to two dimensions of distance, defined by approach and avoidance, and of control, defined by discharge and delay.

If the selfhood model developed from developmental competence theory (Figure 6.2) is valid, then Constantine's open type would lead toward competition and extreme chaos. The random type would lead toward antagonism and rejection; the synchronous type, toward suppression and rigidity; and the closed type, toward convolution and symbiosis. The major disagreement between the two models lies in whether the random type should fall into the approach-discharge quadrant or the discharge-avoidance quadrant, and whether the synchronous type should fall into the delay-avoidance quadrant. This and other disagreements between the theory and the models would need detailed clarification on more comparative conceptual and empirical grounds.

THE CIRCUMPLEX MODEL AND DEVELOPMENTAL COMPETENCE THEORY

The sixth model (Olson, 1989) is well known and widely cited (L'Abate & Bagarozzi, 1993), and it has been introduced already in the previous chapter. It consists of two dimensions of cohesion and adaptability that are orthogonal

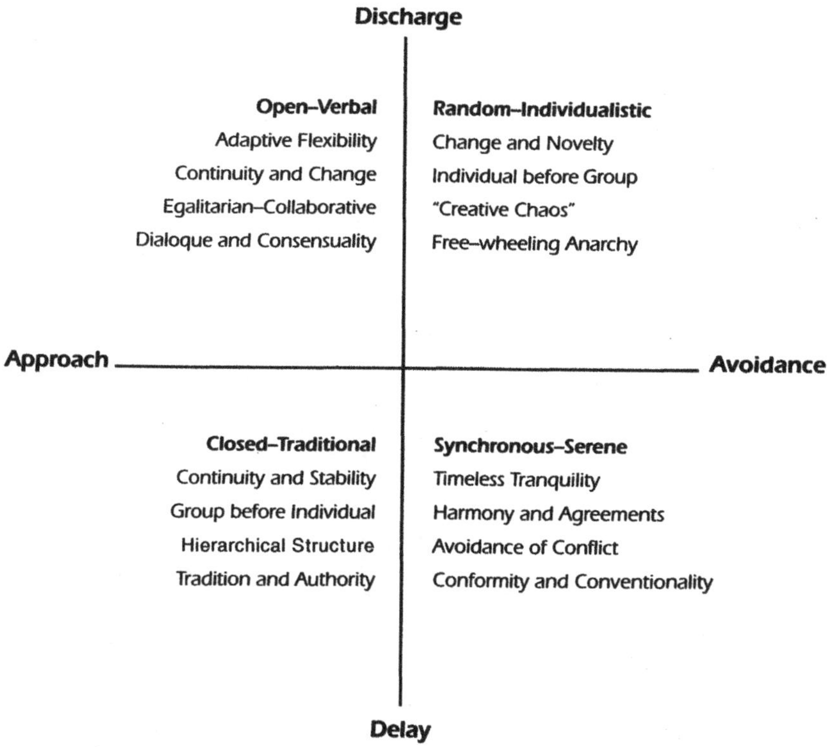

Figure 6.3 A Circumplex Model of Family Paradigms (From Constantine, 1986, 1993)

to each other. Cohesion is defined by four ranges going from low to high: disengaged, separated, connected, and enmeshed (Figure 6.4). Adaptability is defined by four ranges: chaos, flexibility, structuredness, and rigidity. In each dimension, the first and fourth ranges are dysfunctional, and the middle two are functional.

When this circumplex model is compared to the two dimensions of distance and control, cohesion coincides with an assumption of distance, and adaptability coincides with an assumption of control. Thus, this circumplex model (Figure 6.4) can be compared with the theory-derived model (Figure 6.2) by classifying the circumplex as follows: the disengaged-chaotic would fall into the avoidance-discharge quadrant; the chaotically enmeshed, into the discharge-approach quadrant; the rigidly enmeshed, into the delay-approach quadrant; and the rigidly disengaged, into the avoidance-delay quadrant.

The circumplex model yields three types of families according to the functionality–dysfunctionality distinction: (a) balanced and functional; (b) midrange or semifunctional; and (c) extremely dysfunctional. This typology predicts that the style most used by balanced families would be *CC,* midrange families would use *RR,* and extremely dysfunctional families would use *AA.* Again, these comparisons need to be verified empirically.

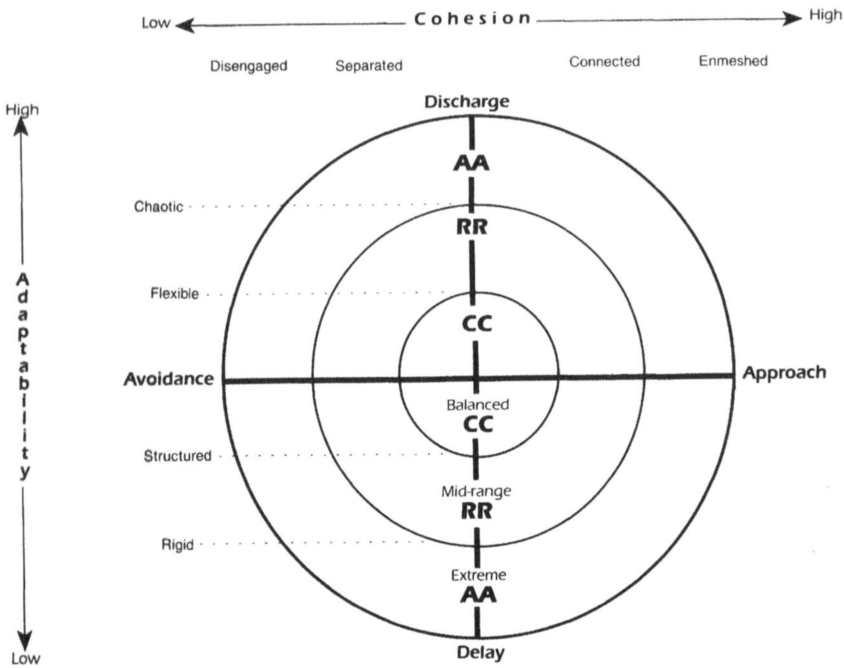

Figure 6.4 The Circumplex Model and Competence Theory

FAMILY TYPES AND STRENGTHS

McCubbin, Thompson, Pirner, and McCubbin (1988) developed a classification of families according to three degrees of functionality within a life-cycle, ecological perspective (Figure 6.5). They designated the basic functional types of families as: resilient, regenerative, rhythmic, and ritualistic (Figure 6.5). Resilient families value bonding and flexibility and develop a bonded-pliant pattern at an intermediate level of functionality that can become fragile under extreme circumstances. Similarly, regenerative families value coherence and hardiness. They may move through a secure-durable pattern at an intermediate level of functionality, which in its extreme makes families become vulnerable. Rhythmic families stress valuing and routines, giving origin to a structured-intentional pattern at an intermediate level of functionality, which in the extreme becomes unpatterned. Ritualistic families value traditions and celebrations, which give origin to a traditionalistic-celebratory pattern at an intermediate level of functionality. In the extreme, the pattern becomes situational.

Developmental competence theory would predict that the four basic functional types would use *CC* styles of relating, and patterns at the intermediate level would relate according to an *RR* style. Extreme outcomes would typically use the *AA* style (Figure 6.5). For example, resilient families would be

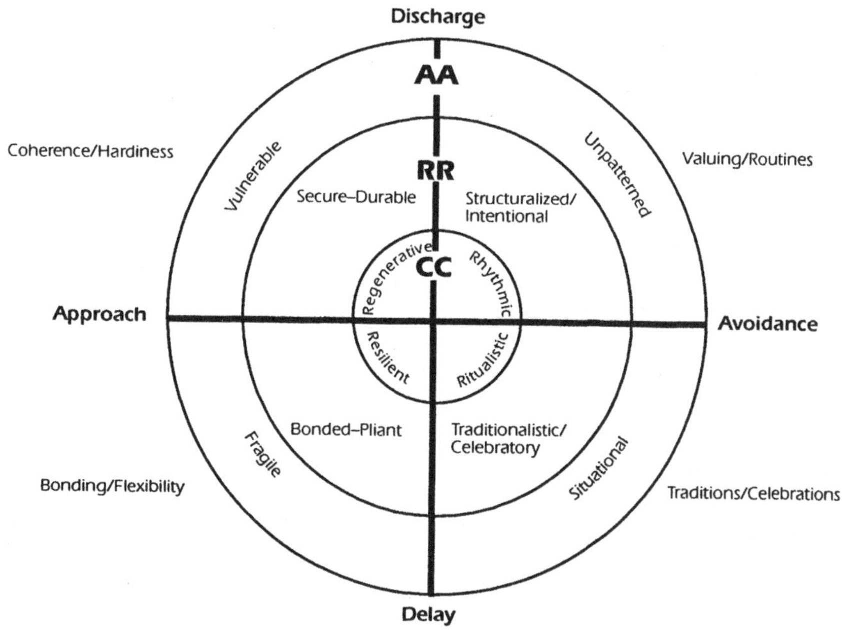

Figure 6.5 A Circumplex Classification of Families at Three Levels of Functionality (Adapted from McCubbin et al., 1988)

characterized by approach-delay and would fall into that quadrant. Regenerative families would fall into the approach-discharge quadrant; rhythmic families, into the discharge-avoidance quadrant; and ritualistic families, into the avoidance-delay quadrant.

This model is the most difficult to compare with the theory. Preceding models have quite a few points of commonality with developmental competence theory, but this model's language makes it difficult to compare it with the theory or with the three preceding models. However, unless conceptual comparisons and contrasts are made, even erroneously, it will be impossible to develop a classification of individual or family behavior that reconciles these models within an overarching theoretical framework.

OVERLAPS AND SIMILARITIES AMONG ATTACHMENT, RELATIONSHIP STYLES, AND THE SELFHOOD MODEL

De Giacomo and L'Abate (1996) proposed that there are many similarities and overlaps among the attachment model and two other models of human interaction developed by the two authors. The relational selfhood model and the attachment model (L'Abate, 1994b, pp. 135–137) predict the same patterns. Consequently, in both children and adults, selfulness would be equated with secure pattern B; selfishness, with insecure, resistant/dismissing pattern C; selflessness, with avoidant/preoccupied pattern A; and no-self, with disorganized/fearful pattern D.

How can the elementary pragmatic model be related to the other two? The four coordinates bear similarities to the four attachment categories and to the four personality propensities discussed above. For instance, the accepting coordinate resembles the preoccupied/selfless pattern; the maintaining coordinate resembles the dismissing/selfish pattern; the sharing coordinate resembles the secure/selful pattern, and the antifunction coordinate resembles the fearful/no-self pattern (Figure 6.6).

To elaborate on these relationships, the secure/selful pattern reflects the following styles, ranging from the most functional to the semifunctional: F7, F1, F6, and F9 (see Figure 6.6). This secure/selful style, however, under certain conditions, may overlap with the fearful/no-self pattern. The dismissing/selfish pattern reflects the following styles, listed in order of increasing dysfunctionality: F3, F12, F11, F10, and F2. Under certain conditions, F12 may overlap with the preoccupied/selfless pattern. This latter pattern is comprised of the following styles: F12, F5, F13, and F4. The fearful/no-self pattern includes the following styles: F15, F14, F8, and F0.

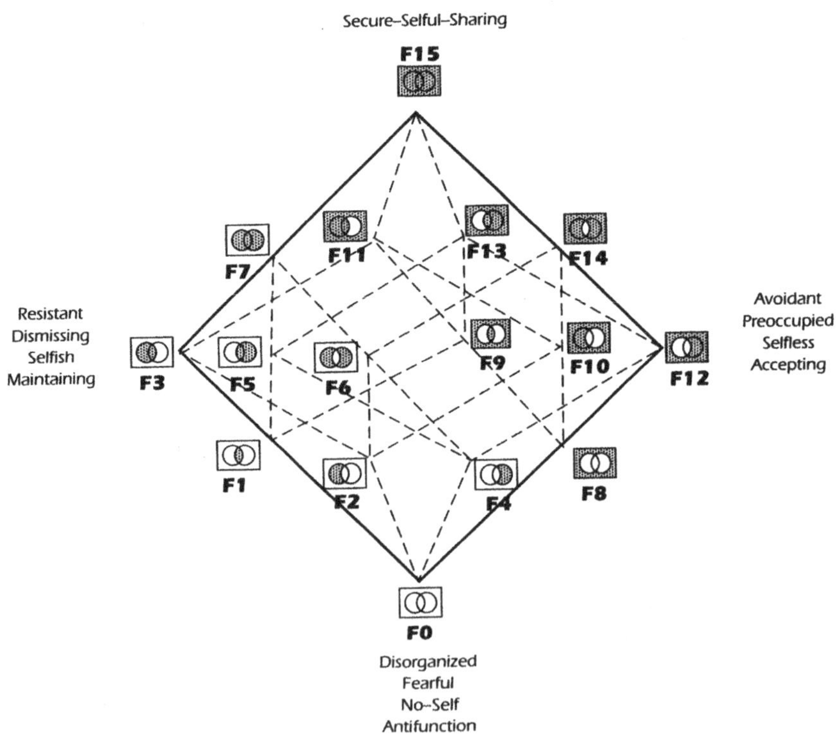

Figure 6.6 Attachment, Relationship Styles, and Personality Propensities

The three models (attachment, elementary pragmatic, and selfhood) are derived from completely different theoretical viewpoints. For instance, the attachment model has followed an inductive process based strictly on empirical evidence that assumes internal states, like security-insecurity, that are, however, derived from external interactions. The elementary pragmatic model follows a completely interactive viewpoint, without any inferences about intrapsychic processes, and is the product of a deductive approach. It stresses the changes that will take place in relationships rather than inside individuals. The relational selfhood model also follows a deductive approach from clinical and from epistemological sources, but considers only three internal processes: (a) attribution of importance to self and others, (b) self-differentiation, and (c) self-determination. These three processes, however, are all relationally derived. Consequently, by interrelating these three models, it will be possible to amplify their respective descriptive and explanatory powers.

These similarities need to be ascertained empirically. Both the attachment and the relational selfhood models have available self-report, paper-and-pencil tests, but that is not the case for the elementary pragmatic model.* However, one could replicate the Holtzman tables' interactive presentations with greater controls, where all subjects would have completed a battery of tests that derive from the attachment model (Bartholomew & Perlman, 1994) and from the relational selfhood model (Chapter 3).

There are other stylistic rather than substantive similarities among these models. For instance, all three models: favor visual representations of their characteristics; make predictions about which pattern will be more successful as a result of psychological interventions; and have been verified empirically in one way or another. The amply influential attachment model has been verified by a variety of researchers across the world. The elementary pragmatic model and the relational selfhood model await further verification outside of their respective proponents.

COMPARISONS AMONG FAMILY MODELS AND DEVELOPMENTAL COMPETENCE THEORY

When McCubbin et al.'s model (Figure 6.5) is compared with the three previous ones (Figures 6.2 through 6.4), similarities and differences become apparent. In the upper-left quadrant of approach-avoidance, the chaotic and competitive quality of the theory-derived model (Figure 6.1) seems consistent with the random quality of Constantine's model (Figure 6.3) but not consistent with the same quality in Olson's circumplex (Figure 6.4). The upper right quadrant of avoidance-discharge, antagonism-rejection (Figure 6.2) does not seem consistent with the other two models (Figures 6.3 and 6.5), which are, however, consistent with each other in the sense of describing similar patterns

* Self report adjective checklists derived from De Giacomo's model are available from this author.

of rhythmicity and synchronicity. In the lower left quadrant of approach-delay, convolution and symbiosis (Figure 6.2) may be consistent with the bonded-pliant and fragile qualities of McCubbin et al.'s model (Figure 6.5), but perhaps not consistent with the open quality of Constantine's model (Figure 6.3). In the lower right quadrant of avoidance-delay, suppression-rigidity seem to compare well with the traditional-ritualistic quality of McCubbin et al.'s model as well as with the closed quality of the model derived from developmental competence theory (Table 6.1). A comparative evaluation of all models is summarized in Table 6.1.

Constantine's and Olson's models are worded in structurally static, cross-sectional terms. Developmental competence theory, on the other hand, employs dynamic, process-oriented, relational terms. Only Olson's and McCubbin et al.'s models include a life-cycle and ecological perspective that is dynamic in nature. These models, however, are unable to distinguish or "explain" what makes a family functional or dysfunctional, because they are unable to use the individual contribution of each family member. In addition, there is the danger that abstraction of various patterns may overlook the multifaceted nature of real families. For instance, Constantine (1993) gave the example of a single-parent, chaotic family with six children. The "explanation" for the characteristics of this family needs to be located, at least in part, in the developmental and generational history of the mother, who eventually was referred for individual psychotherapy. The individual is not considered within the last four models. However, when one addresses the reality of actual families, the importance of the individual must be recognized.

In comparing the origin of developmental competence theory and the seven models, some additional comments are necessary. The theory is grounded in a process of abstraction from the literature as well as from clinical experience. The family defense mechanism and family paradigm models seem based on similar grounds—a mixture of theoretical and clinical—and the last two models (circumplex model and family types and strengths) were empirically derived from paper-and-pencil, self-report tests. These tests are usually insensitive to styles of relating because respondents are either unaware of these patterns or, if they are aware, as in the case of *AA* styles, they are not going to admit and disclose them.

Thus, paper-and-pencil, self-report tests may be questionable as a basis for classificatory systems of family interactions. This conclusion is relevant not only to paper-and-pencil, self-report tests but also to most classificatory systems derived from laboratory studies of family interactions using complex coding schemes (L'Abate & Bagarozzi, 1993). Both approaches, thus far, have failed to capture extreme ranges of family dysfunctionality. For instance, *AA* or *RR* styles in intimate relationships cannot be captured by paper-and-pencil, self-report tests nor by laboratory observations, in which families are going to try to present an acceptable facade. These styles may be captured at the presentational and phenotypical levels, once specific tests are developed to measure them. Most families, no matter how dysfunctional, would want to make a

TABLE 6.1 Summary Comparison of Developmental Competence Theory (DCT) with Seven Models of Individual and Family Behavior

Theoretical Assumptions: Distance = Approach (Ap)—Avoidance (Av)
Time = Discharge (Di)—Delay (De)

Model	Styles	Ap-Di	Ap-De	Av-Di	Av-De
DCT	*AA*	Chaos	Symbiosis	Rejection	Rigidity
	RR	Competition	Convolution	Antagonism	Suppression
	CC	Appropriate balance of Ap-Av and Di-De resulting in Equality, Reciprocity, Mutuality, Responsiveness, Intimacy			

	Selfulness	Selflessness	Selfishness	No-self
Selfhood	Appropriate balance of Ap-Av/Di-De	Av > Ap De > Di	Ap > Av Di > De	Extremes in Ap/Av//Di/De

	Approach	Avoidance	Discharge	Delay
Self Psychology	Sublimation	Regression	Acting out	Repression
	Rationalization	Reaction/	Displacement	Undoing
	Intellectualization	Formation	Projection	Compensation
	Isolation of affect	Denial	Identification	Introjection

Attachment (Object Relations)				
	Secure		Insecure	
Children	Secure	Avoidant	Resistant	Disorganized
Adults	Secure	Preoccupied	Dismissing	Fearful
Elementary Pragmatic	Sharing	Accepting	Maintaining	Antifunction

DCT	Ap-Di	Av-Di-De	Ap-Di	Av-Di-De
FDMs	Problem-solving Goal-drivenness	Multihousehold	Mood swings Provocations	Escape Withdrawal

DCT	Ap-Di	Ap-De	Av-Di	Av-De
Paradigms	Open	Closed	Random	Synchronous

DCT	Ap-Di	Ap-De	Av-Di	Av-De
Circumplex Styles				
Extreme	Chaotically	Rigidly	Chaotically	Rigidly
	Enmeshed		**Disengaged**	
Mid-range	Flexibly	Structurally	Flexibly	Structurally
	Enmeshed		**Disengaged**	
Balanced	Flexibly	Structurally	Flexibly	Structurally
	Connected		**Separated**	

DCT	Ap-Di	Ap-De	Av-Di	Av-De
Types and Strengths				
Extreme	Vulnerable	Fragile	Unpatterned	Situational
Mid-range	Secure	Bonded	Structuralized	Traditionalistic
Balanced	Regenerative	Resilient	Rhythmic	Ritualistic

good impression by masking or avoiding unpleasant and unsavory characteristics for external consumption, unless they are forced, under pressure, to do otherwise. In cases of abuse, for instance, the knowledge that criminality may be involved and even reportable by law may be a further deterrent to disclosure.

Regardless of the validity of the developmental competence theory or the seven models, this comparative overview of individual and family models can serve as a basis for future, more critically evaluative analyses. From such comparative evaluation might emerge a more sophisticated view of individual and family functioning that will yield greater specificity in prediction. This specificity would allow greater possibility of verification, because specific predictions can be verified much more easily than general ones. Furthermore, this specificity should answer questions like: "What kind of individual will result from what kind of family?" This comparison is just the first step toward reconciling individual and family characteristics. Future conceptual and empirical work will perhaps help clarify some of the consistencies and inconsistencies found among different classifications of families.

Ultimately, the validity of either the theory or the models will be judged by clinicians in the front line. They will diagnose whether families are fitting, in part, into the theory or any of the models. Therapeutically, either the theory or the models could furnish blueprints for more specific treatment plans that would attempt to answer the question: "What kind of intervention will be most effective with what kind of individual, and what kind of therapist will be best suited to work with his or her family?" Instead of one type of therapy for all families, these blueprints would allow therapists to consider applying more differentiated therapies that are more appropriate for particular families. For instance, an extremely disturbed, random, unpatterned, abusive, apathetic, and neglectful family with an identified, certified schizophrenic patient would need a completely different approach than a midrange, reactive, but traditionalistic family. Up to the present, therapists have been unable to make clear-cut differentiations among types of treatments. Using the funnel approach, one treatment has been prescribed for all families. If the field of therapy is to differentiate, like any growing system, it will need to specify and demonstrate that different individuals and their families need different therapeutic approaches.

CONCLUSION

This chapter has attempted to compare and contrast the selfhood model derived from developmental competence theory with two models of individual functioning, one model of relationships, and four models of family functioning. This tentative process will need constant revision through consultation with the originators of the models and empirical verification by independent researchers. Many patterns described here are abstractions. More empirical evidence is needed to substantiate this or any typology through clear-cut, prototypical cases that illustrate extremes of *AA* or *RR* styles. In real life, dysfunctional relationships evidence mixed patterns of *AA* and *RR*. Borderline or midrange relationships, using an *RR* style of relating, are likely to vary the most. They range from an almost quasi-functional *CC* style to a quasi-*AA* style—for instance, using verbal rather than physical, sexual, or substance abuse. Their true nature, however, is unveiled under stress. *CC* styles of relating will not be available clinically. They will be found in the community; we need only look for them.

PART TWO

Expansions of the Theory to Personality, Criminality, and Psychopathology

CHAPTER 7

Linking Personality with Criminality and Psychopathology

> Although these topics are often not presented in tandem, it is my view that theories of personality, that is, normal development, and models of psychopathology, that is, abnormal development, are inextricably linked. (Brown, 1992b, p. 111)

> . . . evidence [bears] on the hypothesis that normal and abnormal personality can be conceptualized using the same set of personality constructs. (Helmes & Jackson, 1994, p. 341)

> . . . a list of variables hardly amounts to a theory of individual personality development. . . . a list of variables does not a theory of personality make. (Magai & McFadden, 1995, pp. 193, 214)

The proposal in this chapter is not the first, nor will it be the last, to suggest a comprehensive model for personality, criminality, and psychopathology. Past theoretical systems (humanism, psychoanalysis, and behaviorism) developed and proliferated because of their encompassing ability to interrelate these three fields, at least rhetorically. Frances and Widiger (1986) reviewed contributions of Cattell, Eysenck, Leary, and Millon, who, together with Benjamin (1993), Blashfield (1986), and Lorr (1986), among many others, have submitted proposals based mainly on factor-analytical methodology. These contributions have influenced, in various ways, the genesis and development of this proposal.

A historical review of current models of psychiatric classification (Blashfield, 1991) started with the pioneering Kraepelinian classification and ended with the DSM-IV (American Psychiatric Association, 1994) classification as its remnant. Structural models of classification included categorical, dimensional, and hierarchical ones. The notion that a prototypical model of psychopathology is an improvement over the traditionally categorical Kraepelinian model was introduced.

CRITIQUE OF EXISTING CLASSIFICATIONS

In considering the field of personality theory and research, this field is firmly separated from criminality and somewhat inconsistently and tenuously connected with psychopathology. This conclusion is based on the following evidence.

Personality

In a survey, conducted through citation indexing, of 34 representative textbooks on personality (Table 7.1), criminality was never mentioned, with the exception of Peterson (1988). Links between personality and psychopathology were made in approximately half of these references. Where mention of various psychopathological conditions was made, the range of citation usage varied from at least 1 reference in most texts to 72 references in Rotter, Chance, and Phares (1972), 73 in Ewen (1988), 55 in Kluckhohn, Murray, and Schneider (1953), and 36 in Murphy (1947). In the latter case, index citations were mostly related to narcissism, a characteristic that presently could fall within the field of criminality or character disorders. The unit of analysis used in the survey—a subject index citation—may have been a full page, a paragraph, or just a short mention; it was not compared with the ratio of total pages written. In spite of its obvious weaknesses, this unit still remains a rough estimate of how much attention or coverage criminality and psychopathology are given in personality texts—almost nil and inconsistently variable, respectively.

Fortunately, the foregoing trend has been corrected by the work edited by Strack and Lorr (1994). In the foreword to this work, Tellegen (1994) states: "Most contemporary psychology textbooks and training programs treat personality psychology and psychopathology as separate areas, historically connected and adjacent, but essentially independent" (p. ix). In their introduction, the editors of this work state:

> In trying to define what is pathological, we have come to understand that we must examine the nature of normal personality and the relationship between normality and pathology. . . . However, there are virtually no books to address the interface between normal and abnormal personality from a multitheoretical, multimethod perspective. (p. xiii)

In the same work, Eysenck (1994) argues in favor of a three-factor model of personality that would differentiate normality from abnormality. McCrae (1994) factors a five-factor model, as reviewed in Chapter 1. Cloninger and Svrakic (1994) advocate a seven-factor model. All of these theorists provide cogent research data to support their arguments. Whether three, five, or seven factors, all models would need to fit into the selfhood model to either support or discount it. In their summary and perspective on the various contributors to their volume, Strack and Lorr conclude:

> The modern tradition of examining healthy and disordered personality separately may be viewed by future psychologists as a scientific detour necessitated by the psychoanalytic conceptions that dominated the field in the first half of the century . . . a wealth of theories, methods, and measures is available to clinicians and researchers to address the interface between normality and psychopathology. (p. 421)

TABLE 7.1 Subject Index References to Criminality and Psychopathology (or Related Terms) in a Representative Sample of Personality Textbooks

		Number of References	
Author(s)	Year	Criminality	Psychopathology
Allport	1968	None	1
Babladelis/Adams	1967	None	10
Burton	1974	None	None
Byrne	1974	None	None
Carson	1969	None	None
Cartright	1979	3	None
Carver/Scheier	1988	1	4
Carver/Scheier	1992	None	8
Dollard/Miller	1950	None	2
Ewen	1988	1	73
Fiske	1971	None	None
Fransella	1981	None	None
Freedman/Kaplan	1971	None	32
Hall/Lindzey	1978	None	None
Kluckhohn/Murray/Schneider	1953	3	55
Levy	1970	None	None
Lidz	1976	None	None
Liebert/Spiegler	1990	None	None
Maddi	1980	None	6
Maddi	1989	None	None
Massey	1981	None	None
McAdams	1990	None	None
Mischel	1986	None	None
Murphy	1947	None	36
Pervin	1980	None	2
Pervin	1990	None	10
Peterson	1988	34	4
Phares	1988	None	10
Rotter/Chance/Phares	1972	None	72
Rychlak	1981	None	21
Sarason	1962	None	2
Schultz	1990	None	None
Smith	1968	2	3
Staub	1980	None	None

> Of course, developing a taxonomy that encompasses normal and abnormal traits will not be easy. The population of abnormal persons is much smaller than that of normal persons, and changing definitions continue to shift the boundaries of psychopathology. (p. 423)

There are at least two fallacies in the foregoing conclusions—or, if not fallacies, two sources of disagreement and controversy. The first disagreement originates in the editors' emphasis on inferred, hypothetical, and reified traits, indicating their identification with internal rather than external observable interpersonal processes in intimate relationships. The second source of disagreement is their statement that there are more healthy than unhealthy persons. The selfhood model, as well as the rest of this theory, would suggest instead a much more pessimistic outlook about this conclusion. If the selfhood model and the theory behind it are valid, there would seem to be more disordered (i.e., unhealthy) than healthy personalities, as discussed in the first two chapters. This argument hinges on what criteria are used to arrive at such a differentiation.

Another significant contribution to the relationship between personality and psychopathology is found in the feminist contributions edited by Brown and Ballou (1992). In her foreword, Walker (1992) stated:

> . . . no longer can we strip context from the understanding of who we are, what we do, and why we do it. (p. vii)
>
> Despite the new data presented by both women and men scholars, those who control the standards have ignored pleas for adding external context to the understanding of human behavior, and instead have continued to focus on internal deficits, either with biology or personality. (pp. vii–viii)

The two editors introduced the thesis of their work by stating:

> [T]raditional or mainstream personality theories and views of psychopathology are not adequate from the standpoint of feminist theory. . . . Ideological domination is not absent from personality theory and models of psychopathology. . . . As long as personality theories focus solely on the individual in a decontextualized state, the links with politics-power and assignment of status will not be seen. . . . The social fabric, with its multiple systems, contains oppressive structures that deeply affect and define individuals. Until these structures are defined, not just in clinical practice but in theories of distress and human nature and development, the fullest depths of oppression will remain unexcavated, and theories that provide optimum life spaces will not have been built. (pp. xi–xiii)

Developmental competence theory attempts to redress deficiencies in past personality theories by making gender differences a cornerstone of the selfhood model. In selfulness and no-self, both genders are equally represented, for different reasons. In selfulness, both partners (or parents and children) affirm each other's equality of importance and difference in functions. In no-self, neither gender can affirm self- or other-importance. In selfishness, one gender (usually male) affirms its importance at the expense of the other gender (usually female), and in selflessness, one gender (usually female) puts itself down, denying its own importance and allowing the other gender (usually male) to assert its importance at the female's expense.

Criminalities

When the field of criminality is surveyed, a reverse trend is observed. Many criminologists (Gibbons, 1988; Gibbs, 1987, 1991; Lykken, 1995; Raine, 1993; Yochelson & Samenow, 1977a, 1977b), and especially Eysenck (1977; Eysenck & Gudjonsson, 1989), support a psychological explanation of criminal behavior. In some cases, the family contexts is even referred to as one of the antecedents for such behavior. This explanation is related to personality factors, including classifications of criminalities using the MMPI (Zager, 1988) and Jesness's inventory (Jesness, 1988); Quay's AIM approach (Levinson, 1988); the interpersonal maturity level (Harris, 1988); the cognitive style and defensiveness (Gacono & Meloy, 1988); and a conceptual matching model (Reitsma-Street & Leschied, 1988). Most psychological classifications, based on the MMPI, or AIM, or the cognitive Interpersonal level, received some support when compared with each other (Van Voorhis, 1988).

Psychopathologies

In considering the present-day classification of psychopathology, as exemplified by DSM-IV (American Psychiatric Association, 1994), three inadequacies relevant to the purpose of this proposal stand out:

1. The obviously categorical nature of most classifications of psychopathology, which are simply lists of symptoms or syndromes.
2. The consistent omission of criminalities from classifications of psychopathology.
3. The in-vacuum (i.e., nonrelational and acontextual) nature of existing classifications, not only in psychopathology, but in personality and criminality as well (see Table 7.1).

There have been a great many criticisms about the rationale, validity, reliability, or usefulness of psychiatric classification (Carson, Butcher, & Coleman, 1988; Clark, Watson, & Reynolds, 1995; Kutchins & Kirk, 1986; Millon & Klerman, 1986), but they are beyond the scope of this chapter. What is relevant, however, is the categorical nature of such nosology. Different psychopathologies are presented like a laundry list or a test in naming the bones of a skeleton. Entries appear unrelated to each other, as if one were studying the anatomy of the body by memorizing its various parts (Quay, 1986). For instance, how are the schizophrenias related to paranoias? How are the depressions related to obsessive-compulsive disorders? What is the overlap among various psychopathological conditions? Each disorder is listed separately from all others, and no linkages among disorders are possible or potentially reachable, given the ordinal nature of the classification (Barlow, 1985; Cooper, Frances, & Sacks, 1986; Millon, 1967, 1969; Millon & Klerman, 1986; Quay, 1986). Millon (1986c) described this inadequacy and indicated what corrections could be made to it:

> Although the DSM-III [a precursor of DSM-IV] offers a multiaxial schema in which relationships that exist among clinical categories can be noted, each syndrome is still organized as if it were a discrete entity of clustered clinical signs independent and distinct from other syndromes. A framework that would spell out the inevitable overlap occurring among diagnostic groups would enable the clinician to immediately identify the extrinsic covariations that do exist among clinical disorders. Especially valuable would be the illumination of relationships between personality vulnerabilities and coping styles, on the one hand, and specific clinical symptom disorders, on the other. What is likely to be needed to achieve this end is more than a format that merely organizes the fragmented nature of the current nosology, but one, as noted previously, that is based on theoretical principles that furnish the logic and point out the bases for commonalities and interconnections observed in the clinical world. (p. 64)

Carson, Butcher, and Coleman (1988), commenting on the same issue, stated that the DSM classification seems "more appropriate to medical diseases than to human behavior" (p. 15). Eysenck (1986), a vocal critic of the categorical method of classification, raised the question of *continuity* among classes of disorders. One could also raise the issue of *contiguity*. How are these classes continuous and contiguous with each other?

The second inadequacy consists of the persistent omission of most criminalities, except for one type of psychopathology—a syndrome consisting of impulse disorders (American Psychiatric Association, 1994). These disorders are limited to explosiveness or intermittent explosive disorder, pyromania, kleptomania, pathological gambling, and trichotillomania. (Since when is pulling one's hair a crime?) No other type of criminality is included. By what criteria were these five disorders included and others excluded? Is criminality a completely different field, unrelated to psychopathology and mental health? How is criminality, for instance, related to psychopathology? In many cases, the two conditions overlap (Hochstedler, 1987; Lurigio & Lewis, 1987; Lykken, 1995; Posey, 1988; Raine, 1993). Many criminals show paranoid tendencies (Toch, Adams, & Greene, 1987), emotional disturbances (Gibbs, 1987, 1991; Walters, Mann, Miller, Hemphill, & Chlumsky, 1988), hyperactivity, and sensation-seeking (Jefferson & Johnson, 1991), among other psychological dysfunctions.

Rothblum, Solomon, and Albee (1986) cited Wootton's (1978) thesis concerning antisocial behavior as psychiatric illness:

> [P]ersons who commit antisocial acts can be divided into two classes: those who have a mental disorder and those who do not . . . if it is established that a mental

> disorder exists in a person who has committed antisocial acts, then it is also possible to ascertain whether these acts are caused by the disorder. (p. 186)

As shown in Table 7.1, most personality texts leave criminality completely out of their coverage, as if it were a completely independent field from personality or psychopathology (Carson, Butcher, & Coleman, 1988; Hersen & Turner, 1991; Millon & Klerman, 1986; Rosenhan & Seligman, 1984).

In DSM-IV (APA, 1994), however, there is a well-developed classification of addictions. It is not clear how addictions—drug dependency or substance abuse, alcoholism, and smoking, among others—are related to criminality. True, one cannot be a drug addict without committing a felony by buying an outlawed substance. Also, driving while intoxicated and committing a murderous car accident is judged as a criminal act (Walfish, Massey, & Krone, 1989). But one can drink or smoke to excess without committing an illegal or criminal act. A compulsive smoker may ultimately commit slow suicide. How is suicide resulting from compulsive smoking, or any other substance abuse, different from a sudden suicide with a handgun (L'Abate, Farrar, & Serritella, 1992)?

The third inadequacy of most classifications in the fields of personality, criminality, and psychopathology relates to their in-vacuum nature (Mahrer, 1970; Millon, 1967, 1969; Rosenhan & Seligman, 1984). Personalities, criminalities, and psychopathologies seem to arise and develop on their own, separate and independent from their most natural, immediate, and proximal social contexts. If an etiology is given, genetic and physiological antecedents are quoted.

Fortunately, this trend toward finding the deus ex machina inside individuals has been corrected by recent treatises (Lilly, Cullen, & Ball, 1995; Lykken, 1995; Raine, 1993). When ten publications on personality were analyzed for the number of references to family, marriage, parenting, and parent–child relationships, less than half of one percent of the pages were related to these topics (Dunne & L'Abate, 1978), as though personality development took place aside from a family context. A more recent survey, of personality textbooks published since the original survey, yielded the same results (L'Abate, 1994a). Two recent scholarly reviews of personality and social psychology (Burkitt, 1991; Krahé, 1992), for instance, failed to mention marriage, family, or parenting, even though both texts stressed the *social* nature of personality. What is more social than the family?

Carson, Butcher, and Coleman (1988) commented on this inadequacy in the DSM-III classification in regard to:

> . . . the propensity to localize disorder *within* (italics in original) individuals . . . we shall consider not only disturbed individuals but also pathogenic families and larger groups that are implicated in the causation and maintenance of maladaptive behavior. Such behavior does not occur in a vacuum but is rather in part a response to factors of context, particularly social context. (p. 15)

The most immediate and pervasively influential social context for behavior and personality socialization, functional and dysfunctional, is the family.

Many psychiatric texts (Bebbington, 1986; Cooper, Frances, & Sacks, 1986; Helzer & Guze, 1986) or theories (Millon, 1967, 1969) may have vague references to environmental factors, but more direct and specific linkages among family functioning, personality, criminality, and psychopathology remain few and far between. Work such as was done by Jacob (1987) and L'Abate (1994d, in press), where the evidence for the relationship between psychopathology and family functioning is thoroughly reviewed, may help correct this inadequacy (Perris, Arrindell, & Eisenmann, 1994).

Consequently, one is led to conclude that existing classifications of psychopathology are not linked consistently with personality. Criminality is sometimes linked with personality variables, but the reverse situation is rarely found. Furthermore, all three fields—personality psychology, criminality, and psychopathology—share the same characteristic of being described, with noted exceptions, as arising from a vacuum. At best, the generic and vague influence of social factors is invoked, but direct links with the family context are not.

Clark, Watson, and Reynolds (1995), in their review of diagnosis and classification of psychopathology, challenged the clinical usefulness of the categorical DSM approach on the grounds of: (a) clinical utility, (b) research facilitation, and (c) scientific understanding. They expanded on this critique by introducing data from comorbidity—the "co-occurrence of two or more disorders in the same individual" (p. 128). As discussed in Chapter 11, what seemed to be an exception in the past is the rule now. Most deviant individuals can be labeled according to two or even three diagnoses. One cannot put people in diagnostic pigeonholes by excluding other characteristics without detracting from understanding them: "One major problem was that the architects of DSM-III offered virtually no theoretical rationale of empirical evidence to justify exclusionary rule . . . comorbidities had important diagnostic and treatment implications . . . . Individuals with comorbid conditions are more likely to seek treatment than are those with a single disorder" (pp. 128–129).

A second challenge to categorical classification comes from: (a) the "within-category heterogeneity of defining features" (p. 132) and (b) the "mixed symptom presentations that fall between diagnostic boundaries," as in the "Not Otherwise Specified" category: "It is worth noting that comorbidity and heterogeneity are related issues. Problematic comorbidity exists, in part, because patients differ widely (i.e., they show within-group heterogeneity) in diagnostic features that are shared across diagnoses" (p. 137). All of the above means that calling someone schizophrenic does not help because another individual with the same label may show completely different features.

A third source of challenge for the DSM approach, as found by Clark, Watson, and Reynolds, relates to the internal organization of the DSM categories according to the different axes, I and II, where clinical syndromes (Axis I) are separated from personality disorders (Axis II) rather than seen as extensions of each other. As these reviewers concluded: "In the long run . . . the most clinically useful system will be one that has maximal predictive power regarding course and treatment because it is based on a scientific understanding of the relevant parameters" (p. 147).

REQUIREMENTS FOR A NEW, COMPREHENSIVE CLASSIFICATION

To correct the inadequacies found in these classifications, a new classification of the psychopathologies is needed that is continuous and contiguous not only with personality functioning but also with the criminalities. This new classification should be: (a) prototypical; (b) contextual; (c) relational-interpersonal; (d) inclusive, integrative, and comprehensive; and (e) verifiable. Let us examine each of these requirements.

Prototypical

Of the possible approaches to classification (i.e., categorical, dimensional, structural/factor-analytic, and prototypical), the latter is the least used but the most preferable. Carson, Butcher, and Coleman (1988) stated:

> According to this [prototypical] model, few if any pure types exist in nature, and any category boundaries we establish should be viewed as blurred at best. Hence, a given type blends imperceptibly into another with which it shares many similarities and we would expect few *perfect* prototypes among the members of a given type or class. . . . Prototypically, membership in a class is not dependent on a perfect match with rigorous and exclusionary criteria, but merely on a relatively strong correlation between the defining criteria and member characteristics. . . . Everything considered, then, the [prototypical] approach has much to recommend it in the area of classifying abnormal behavior, including a high degree of compatibility with dimensional thinking. (pp. 25–26)

Cantor and Genero (1986) called the prototypical approach "successful" (p. 240) because they saw it as being "based on a similarity-matching procedure whereby category membership is determined by the degree of similarity between a particular instance and a standard of comparison" (p. 241). They suggested many instances of how this approach might have been applied even to DSM-III. The work of Horowitz and his associates was cited as being fundamental to its development (Horowitz, Post, French, Wallis, & Siegelman, 1981; Horowitz, Wright, Lowenstein, & Parad, 1981).

Blashfield (1991) listed six tenets that would be required for a model to qualify as being prototypical (p. 11):

1. Nominalism in the diagnostic categories or concepts is used in the real world by most mental health professionals.
2. Nondiscrete categories can blur together and even overlap.

3. A graded membership exists among different instances of a concept: "[N]ot all members of a category are equally good representatives of the concept" (p. 11).
4. Categories are defined by exemplars rather than by lists.
5. Salient features, like symptoms, are neither necessary nor sufficient to determine membership. "[T]he degree of membership [in] a category is correlated with the number of features [characteristic of a member]" (p. 12).
6. Membership in a category is correlated with the number of features or symptoms shown by an individual.

Thus, a prototypical model will have to fit into these six tenets to earn that definition. Criteria that would contribute to classification, using a prototypical model, would be: (a) *similarity of symptoms,* measured by correlations between and among symptoms—for instance, anxiety and depression would tend to correlate with each other and with other internalization tendencies rather than with externalization tendencies, like impulsivity, acting out, or drivenness, which, in turn, would correlate more with each other than with other clinical conditions; and (b) *proximity of location,* defined by continuity and contiguity, criteria that would derive from the degree of similarity (i.e., correlations) between and among symptoms—anxiety, for instance, would be located nearer topologically to depression than to acting out or criminality. If there are different kinds of anxiety or depression, for instance, they would still be located nearer to each other than to symptoms of a different nature, such as acting out. Thus, the two basic criteria for a prototypical model are *correlations* and *location,* where diagnoses of similar symptoms will be placed together (proximity) on the basis of degree of similarity, as measured by correlations.

An example of how a prototypical approach is relevant to the selfhood model is given in Figure 7.1. Within each rhomboid defined by the two orthogonal dimensions of ability to love and ability to negotiate, there are circles that define prototypes. The prototype for selfulness would be an individual who is extremely satisfied and successful at home, at school or work, and in leisure-time activities both externally and internally. The prototype for selfishness would be a rapist/murderer (Chapter 8). The prototype for selflessness would be a suicidal or extremely depressed individual (Chapter 9). A prototype of no-self would be a schizophrenic individual or someone who commits suicide after killing others (Chapter 10).

Contextual

Aside from psychopathologies with clear organic origins, personality and most psychopathologies, including criminalities, grow out of a family context (Hetherington & Martin, 1986; Jacob, 1987; Litz, 1992) and eventually generalize to other settings. This classification, then, needs to acknowledge that

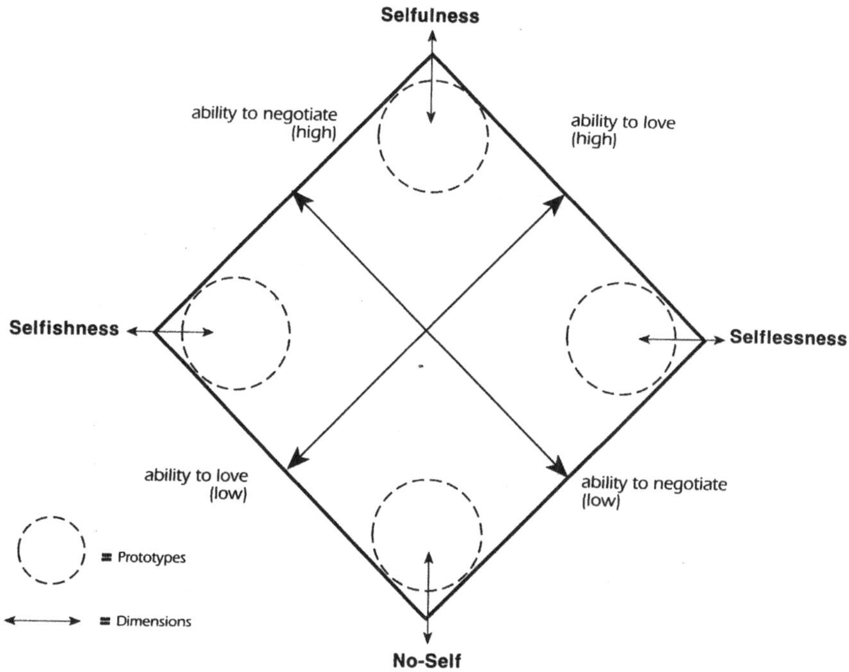

Figure 7.1 A Selfhood Model: Dimensions and Prototypes

personalities, criminalities, or psychopathologies do not develop in a vacuum. The term *context* is still too general; in some ways, it is just as vague as terms like *environment, culture,* or *society.* These general terms must be differentiated into more concrete and specific settings, in addition to the family, that may be equally or more influential, depending on the life cycle and priorities of the individual.

Relational-Interpersonal

This new classification seeks not only contextual relevance but also relational correlates (Millon, 1986c). Individuals are products and producers of interpersonal, intimate relationships, whether functional, criminal, or dysfunctional. Again, to cite all the research in support of this requirement invites entanglement in a controversial quagmire and is contrary to the aims of this chapter.

Inclusive, Integrative, and Comprehensive

The aim of this proposed model is to include and integrate personality with criminality and psychopathology as comprehensively as is possible with any model (see Figure 7.2).

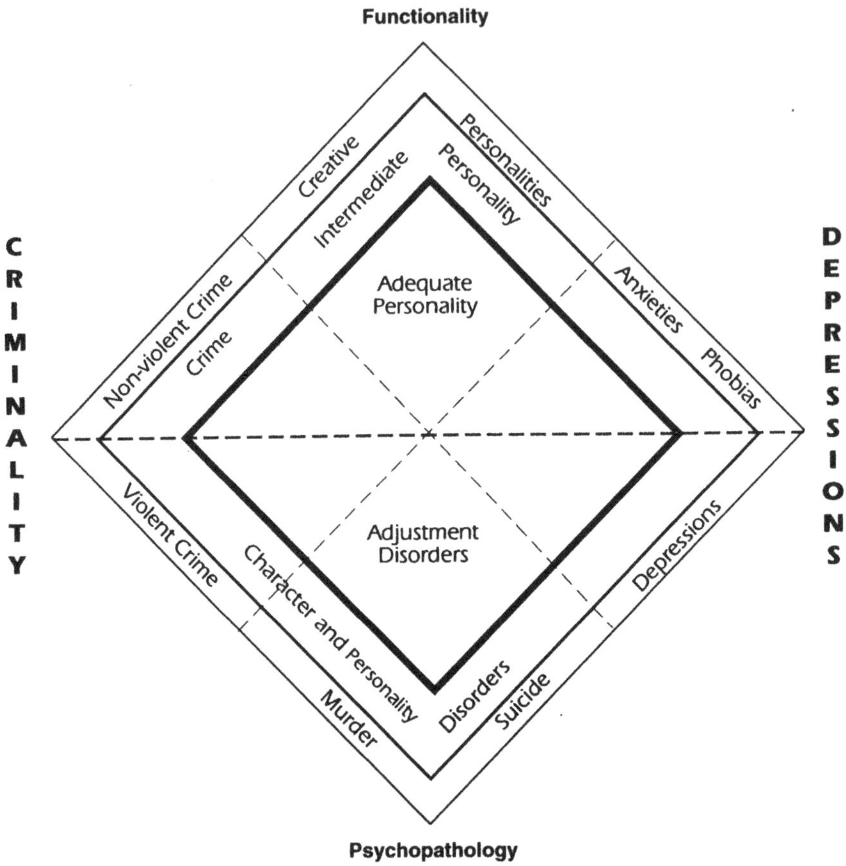

Figure 7.2 Personality Propensities and DSM-IV

Verifiable

Ultimately, the major requirement of this proposal lies in its being verifiable. How can it be evaluated and tested? This question has been answered by the evidence cited in Chapter 3. However, the most important aspect of this proposal is that both functional and dysfunctional relationships are *observable*. They can be videotaped, recorded, and analyzed. There is no need to invoke mysterious and mystical internal states or traits to describe and to understand relationships.

THE SELFHOOD MODEL AND DSM-IV

When positive characteristics of functional relationships are specifiable—for example, in the *CC* style—it becomes relatively easy to identify dysfunctional relationships, as already accomplished in Chapter 6. When DSM-IV is used as a basis for classification with one member of the family, who is the symptom carrier and is identified as a patient, the model shown in Figure 7.2 illustrates how functionalities and dysfunctionalities are related. Figure 7.2 makes it possible to view personality, criminalities, (depressions, affective disorders), and psychopathology as being all included in the same model.

Among selful personalities, one can differentiate three levels of functionality: (a) adequate, (b) intermediate, and (c) creative-superior. Adequate individuals may function relatively well in one setting (i.e., work) but not as well in other settings (i.e., family or social activities). Intermediate individuals may function extremely well in one setting (i.e., family) and acceptably well in the other two settings. Creative-superior individuals function extremely well in all three settings, as judged by subjective ratings of personal satisfaction and by external ratings of success in the three modalities of Being or presence, Doing or performance, and Having or production. One cannot separate the level of satisfaction from the particular setting in which that satisfaction is felt. In addition, personal satisfaction is not sufficient to arrive at a definite conclusion, especially if personal satisfaction is discrepant from observations and conclusions from people familiar with the individual in a particular setting (family, teachers, peers, friends, bosses, coworkers).

Adjustment disorders are located below the center and the middle of Figure 7.2. In the second rim of the figure, below and outside of functionality, are character and personality disorders. In the external rim, nonviolent crimes are located above and violent crimes below an imaginary horizontal line in the middle of the figure. Depressions are located in the middle right side. Severe psychopathologies are located in the lower central (i.e., no-self) part of the figure.

Adjustment Disorders

In the three rhomboids in the center of Figure 7.2 are disorders identified by stressors that have occurred within the near past (three to four months). They include: (a) in the middle-right rhomboid, disorders of internalization, like depressed mood, or anxiety; (b) in the middle-left rhomboid, disorders of externalization, like disturbances in conduct; and (c) in the lower rhomboid, mixed disturbances of emotions and conduct that would be more dysfunctional than the first two adjustment disorders.

Personality Disorders

A plethora of arguments have been generated concerning the number and types of disorders that should be included under this rubric (Benjamin, 1993; Costa & Widiger, 1994; Johnson, 1994; Millon, 1981; Stone, 1993; Turkat, 1990). Instead of becoming entangled in the controversy concerning the nature and number of personality disorders, the goal of the selfhood model is to project these disorders as extensions of functional characteristics. Oldham and Morris

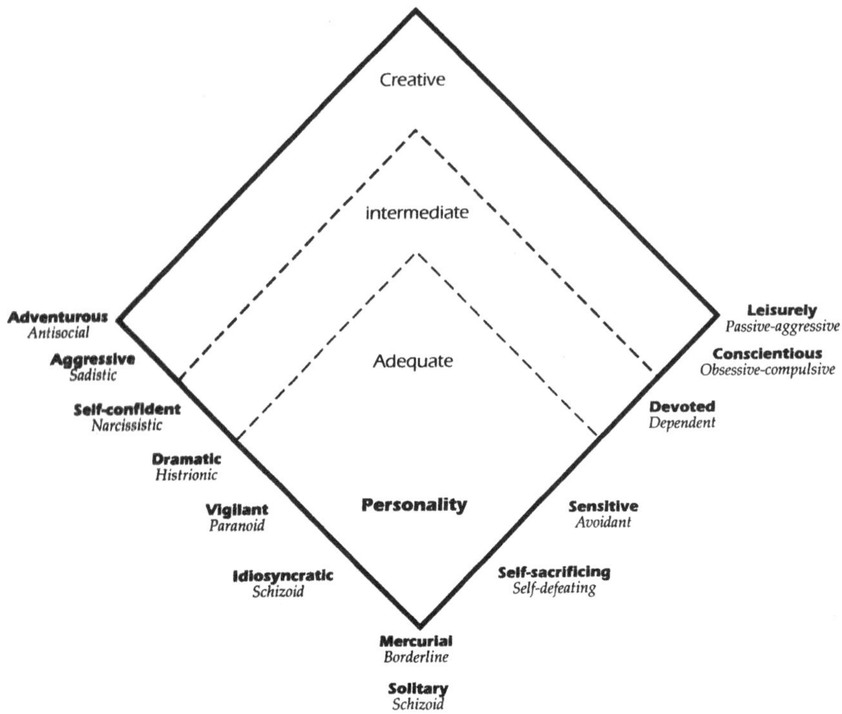

Figure 7.3 Personality Propensities and Personality Self-Portrait (Based on Oldham and Morris, 1990)

(1990) developed a list of adjectives that are descriptive of normal personality characteristics (printed in boldface in Figure 7.3). Abnormal characteristics, extensions of normal ones, are in italics. Thus, adventurous may be represented by an antisocial counterpart, leisurely by a passive-aggressive component, and so on. In the selfhood model, an order is applied to this list of adjectives by ranking them on the left side of the figure according to an agentic perspective, from the most functional (top) to the least functional (bottom). On the right side of the figure, communal characteristics are ranked the same way, from the most functional (top) to the least functional (bottom).

In the same vein, character and personality disorders can be classified according to the selfhood model. By using Johnson's (1994) classification, it is possible to localize his "character styles" (Figure 7.4). Selfishness encompasses histrionic, narcissistic, and obsessive-compulsive styles. Selflessness contains oral, symbiotic, and masochistic styles. No-self consists of various shades and types of the schizoid style, ranging from borderline to schizo-affective. Stone (1993, pp. 297–308) quoted a variety of sources in concluding that there are four sections within the selfishness rhomboid: (a) upper center, impulsive, one-time aggression, transitory; (b) middle left, continuous repeated

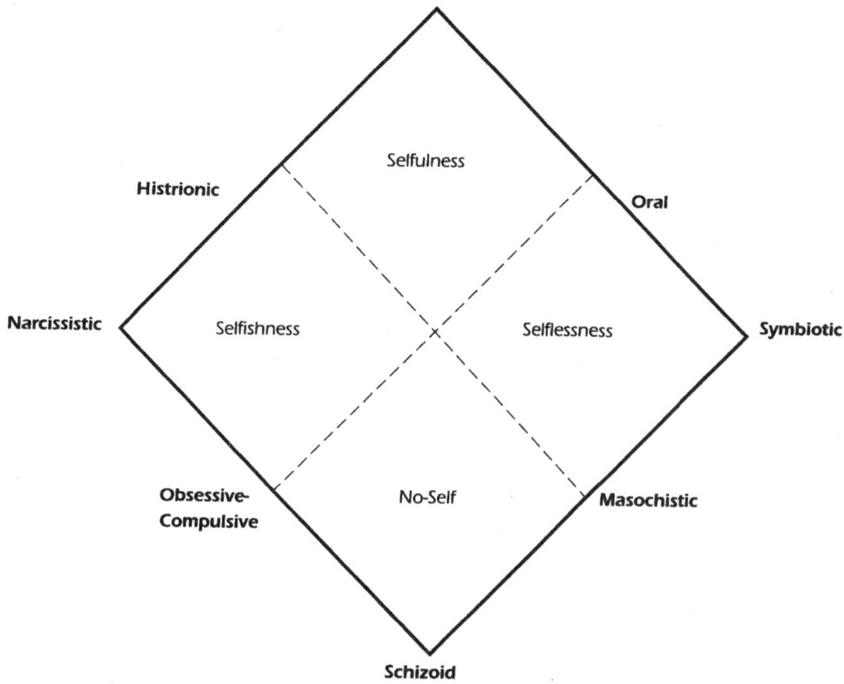

Figure 7.4 Selfhood and Personality Styles (Based on Johnson, 1994)

aggression and callousness; (c) middle right, passivity and parasitism; and (d) bottom, paranoia, revengefulness, suspiciousness, and aloofness. According to the selfhood model: (a) impulsive, one-time, transitory aggression is located to the left, above the middle horizontal line of the rhomboid; (b) continuous, repeated aggression and callousness are located to the left, below the middle horizontal line; (c) passivity and parasitism are located to the right, either above or below the horizontal line, depending on severity; and (d) paranoia, revengefulness, suspiciousness, and aloofness are located in the middle, lowest section of the rhomboid.

The natural extension of this thinking, as reflected in the previous figures and arguments, culminates in a classification of personality, criminalities, affective disorders, and psychopathology into one encompassing model, as shown in Figure 7.5. In this figure, the major vertical axis ranges from selfulness, defined by autonomy-interdependence and personal and interpersonal competence (top), to extreme no-self dependence (bottom). No-self is defined by symbiosis and autism, with extreme dependence and alienation, where personal and interpersonal incompetence are visible. In the selfulness rhomboid, at least three levels of competence can be discriminated: (a) creative (top), (b) intermediate (middle), and (c) adequate (bottom). In the no-self rhomboid, borderline

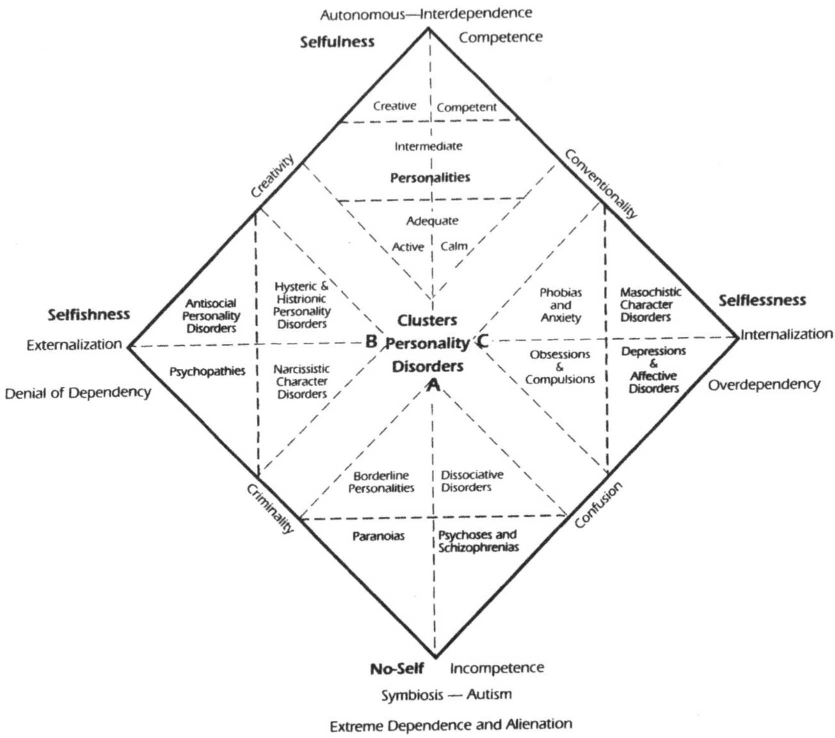

Figure 7.5 A Selfhood Model and Its Extremes

personalities are on the left side; on the right side are dissociative disorders or multiple personalities. At the bottom left are the paranoias and on the right are psychoses and schizophrenias. When the dimensions mentioned above operate within the boundaries that define this model (Figure 7.5), it is possible to locate various criminalities and psychopathologies within it. The three shaded areas represent the most extreme deviations in each polarity.

The horizontal axis crossing the vertical axis in the middle of the figure contains externalizations on the left side and internalizations on the right side. In the selfishness rhomboid, antisocial personality disorders are located on the left, above the horizontal line. Selfishness describes most criminalities, where externalization, impulsive acting out, anger, aggression, pushing the limits set by society, and denial of dependence are the major characteristics. Most are based on the enhancement of self at the expense of others (Cicchetti & Toth, 1991; Mak, 1991; Millon, 1986a, 1986b). Within this rhomboid, criminalities and antisocial personalities without murder fit in the top left section, and *most* (not all) hysteric and histrionic personality disorders fit in the top right section. Criminalities and psychopathies with murder are located in the bottom left, and character and narcissistic personality disorders are located in the bottom right section (Marshall & Barbaree, 1991).

One noteworthy clarification in the model pertains to the location of criminalities without murder, on the left side of creativity. At first blush, this placement would appear far-fetched. However, Agnew (1989) argued that creativity, whatever its definition, can be used positively or negatively. Especially in adolescents, delinquency, instead of being produced by biological, psychological, or societal constraints, "may best be viewed as a creative enterprise" (p. 98). If white-collar crimes were to be placed on the top of that section, it is conceivable that these crimes possess a somewhat creative flavor. Furthermore, many criminals are more creative in eye–hand coordination than in verbal processing and output (Walsh, Petee, & Beyer, 1987), a possible reason why many criminals drop out of school. They are required to excel in their area of greatest weakness—verbal processing. Their motor skills, however creative, are used negatively. Furthermore, a certain degree of narcissism might be necessary in any creative endeavor.

Selflessness describes most internalizing disorders (Reynolds, 1992), where acting in, belittlement of self-importance, martyrdom, despair, anxiety, fears, and phobias are the earmarks (Baumeister, 1993b). Within this rhomboid, phobias and anxiety disorders fit in the top left section, and masochistic character disorders, like codependency (L'Abate & Harrison, 1992), fit in the top right section. Affective disorders fit in the lower right section of this rhomboid, and obsessive and compulsive conditions are located in the lower left section. Manic-depressive disorders would be seen as alternations between extremes of selfishness and selflessness.

Selfish individuals, characterized by acting out and criminal behavior, relate to selfless individuals, characterized by affective disorders, by the *norm of complementarity* in marriage. Selful individuals tend to marry other selful individuals, following the *norm of reciprocity*. In the two middle polarities of the model, selfish individuals, mostly men, tend to attract and marry their opposites, selfless individuals, mostly women. The evidence to support this conclusion is fairly well established by many lines of independent research. Depressed women tend to marry impulsive men. In four out of five cases, their sons will tend to be like their fathers, and their daughters will tend to be like their mothers. Among these couples, one finds the greatest extent of marital strife and the highest number of divorces.

This line of thinking is endorsed by self-verification theory (La Ronde & Swann, 1993), which includes the notion that people are attracted to like people on the basis of support of their self-views:

> [W]hen people with negative self-views choose interaction partners, they display a relative preference for those who think poorly of them. Moreover, people with negative self-views prefer partners who appraise them unfavorably whether the self-view is relatively global or specific. . . . Even when people with negative self-views happen to wind up in relationships in which they are appraised favorably by their partners, they tend to withdraw from the relationship . . . people will gravitate toward social relationships in which they anticipate self-confirmatory feedback and avoid relationships in which they expect self-discrepant feedback. (p. 148)

If this conclusion is as valid as its proponents believe it to be, it would explain why selful individuals will be attracted toward similarly selful individuals, selfish individuals will be attracted to selfless ones, and individuals with no-self will be attracted by individuals at the same lowest level of self-esteem. Another way of looking at the same conclusion would be through the continuum of likeness (Chapter 5). Selful individuals would be attracted to each other on the basis of similarities and differences, and selfish and selfless individuals would be attracted to each other on the basis of complementary sameness and oppositeness.

No-self individuals would be attracted to each other on the basis of autism and symbiosis. In the no-self rhomboid, borderline personality disorders fit in the top left section. Reviews of this condition found it to be quite heterogeneous in etiology, in response to treatment, and in short- and long-range outcome, with many self- and other-defeating characteristics of other groups in the same rhomboid (Gutsch, 1991; Heard & Linehan, 1993; Zanarini, Chauncey, Grady, & Gunderson, 1991). Whether borderline personality disorder is relatively less pathological than narcissistic personality disorder remains to be seen (Plakun, 1991). This model predicts that the overall level of dysfunctionality may well be the same for both disorders. However, the direction and nature of the dysfunctionality might be different. There may be more manipulation and acting out in narcissism than there would be in borderline disorders. Dissociative disorders/multiple personalities would fit in the top right section. In terms of externalization, paranoias would fit in the lowest left section, and psychoses and schizophrenias, with greater internalization, would fit in the lowest right section (Nicholson & Neufeld, 1993). Similarity of an abusive or neglectful background, and repetition of the same behavior, would be characteristic of marital couples who follow the norm of "Misery loves company."

In line with the DSM-IV, the no-self contains Cluster A personality disorders: paranoia, schizoid, and schizotypal. Selfishness contains Cluster B: antisocial, borderline, histrionic, and narcissistic personality disorders. Selflessness contains Cluster C: avoidant, dependent, and obsessive-compulsive personality disorders.

The major inconsistency between this classification and the one interpreted from Johnson (Figure 7.4) involves obsessive-compulsive disorders, which are found in the lower left side between selfishness and no-self in the interpretation of Johnson's list, but are located in the selflessness propensity in the selfhood model and its extremes (Figure 7.5). Undoubtedly, more inconsistencies will be discovered once this integration is reviewed more critically than its authors' present scope allows. In line with the thinking summarized in Chapter 1, the upper left dimension of creativity represents positive interpersonal relationships in the upper part, but this creativity may represent white-collar schemes and flim-flamming in the lower part. By the same token, in the upper right dimension of conventionality, lesser conventionality is predicted in the upper part and greater conventionality of thinking and behavior is predicted in the lower part. The dysfunctional counterpart of creativity is confusion

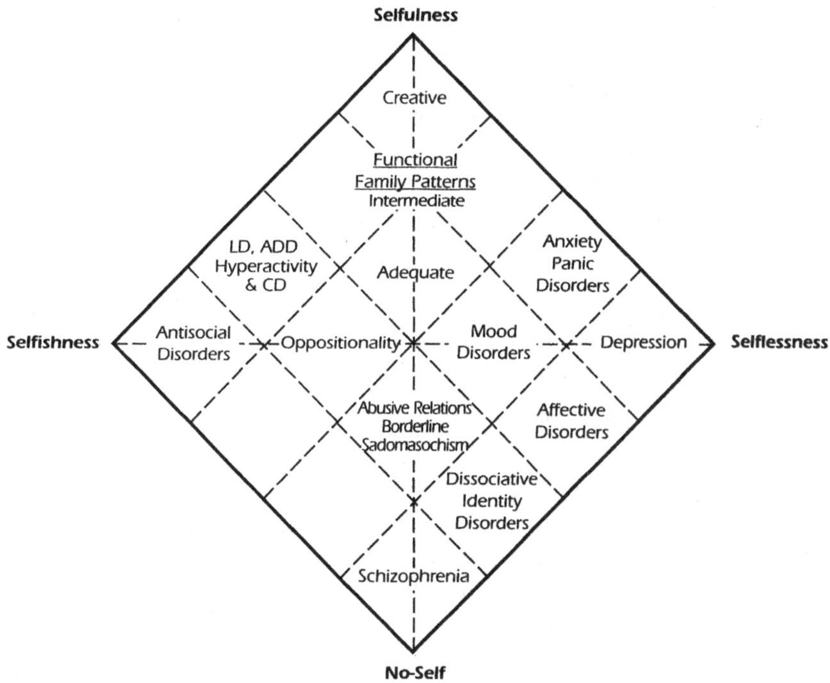

Figure 7.6 Relational Diagnosis and Dysfunctional Family Patterns (Based on Kaslow, 1996)

(lower right side of the figure), and criminality is the dysfunctional counterpart of conventionality.

A more recent work on relational diagnosis and dysfunctional family patterns (Kaslow, 1996) includes a variety of patterns that follow a list approach rather than a theoretical model. When dysfunctional patterns are considered from the viewpoint of a selfhood model, they fit well within the model just as individually oriented dysfunctional patterns (Figure 7.6). Even though some categories within each rhomboid were not filled—for instance, paranoia—by the same token, dissociative identity disorders (a more recent term for multiple personality disorders) and sadomasochism were filled, supporting the position that a relational selfhood model can and should apply to relationships just as it does to individuals and families.

Thus, this model seems to fulfill the first four requirements listed. It is:

1. *Prototypical:* characteristics of similarity, proximity, continuity, and contiguity among personality, criminality, and psychopathology are observed.

2. *Contextual:* specific settings are identified as being in interaction with specific competencies; that is, the family is the major setting responsible for the beginning socialization of individual personality propensities.
3. *Relational:* the four polarities in the attribution of importance in the selfhood model have meaning in relationships and not in a vacuum.
4. *Comprehensive:* personalities, criminalities, and psychopathologies are linked together within one integrated domain.

The major issue, then, becomes one of verifiability. In addition to its face validity (i.e., whether it makes sense conceptually), can this model be verified? Direct verification of the model's validity would indirectly speak also to the validity of the theory from which it is derived. Verification can take place at various levels and with different approaches. At least three levels of verification are possible: (a) epistemologically independent, (b) indirect (Chapter 2), and (c) direct (Chapter 3).

At the *epistemological level,* one needs to check whether the conceptual bases of the model are in agreement with independent sources dealing with similar constructs that are completely unrelated to the model. For instance, what theoretical or empirical support would validate the process of importance attribution? Some support was found for this model in self-verification theory. At the level of *indirect* verification, or *relatedness,* the question is: What is the validity of the status construct in resource exchange theory from which the attribution of importance is derived? For instance, how would methods of measurement developed by resource exchange researchers to assess status support the process of importance attribution (Foa, Converse, Tornblom, & Foa, 1993)? At the level of *direct* verification, a level of complete derivation from the theory itself, the question is: What is the validity of measures derived from this model? This topic is discussed in Chapter 3.

Among the different approaches to test this model is epidemiological verification. Early versions of this model (L'Abate, 1994b; L'Abate & Harel, 1993) made predictions about the distribution of individuals in the four rhomboids of the model. Each rhomboid—depending, of course, on what criterion is used—contains approximately 25% of the population. This prediction—that approximately only 25% of the population would fit into the selfulness polarity—would make this a rather pessimistic model. However, the conclusion would not be too far off the mark when one considers the results of the Manhattan study (Srole et al., 1962), where only 20% of the respondents were found to be symptom-free. Other evidence was reviewed in the first two chapters.

Applying this prediction to the other three rhomboids would unduly strain the validity of this model. Its validity should not be judged by how many people fit into a rhomboid or into the four sections that make up each rhomboid. Instead, the validity of this model should hinge on the *location* of each diagnostic category—its proximity (continuous and contiguous) to similar or related categories. It cannot be expected, much less predicted, that an equal number of individuals is in each of the four sections that make up each quadrant. For instance, when all addictions are totaled, approximately 75 million Americans might be affected (L'Abate, Farrar, & Serritella, 1992). Thus, some sections would differ in their number of individuals, depending on the particular culture where dysfunctionalities develop. More refined criteria would be needed to reach that level of precision. Again, *sections within larger rhomboids predict location and not number of people contained therein.* Indeed, one of the tasks of the future will be to fit numerical approximations of individuals into the four rhomboids and into the sections internal to the rhomboids. Eventually, sections and rhomboids in different sizes may have to be drawn, depending on the number of individuals located in each particular section and the criterion used to categorize them.

The major issue for verification depends on the operational definition and the measurement of the four personality propensities and their criterion validity (L'Abate & Wagner, 1988). This issue has been confronted in two ways. First, a rating scale, the Self-Profile Chart, was created (see Appendix A) to measure the extent of self- and other-importance. In this scale, respondents rate themselves on dimensions that describe their self (intelligence, health, physical attractiveness, moral goodness, and spiritual status) and their social roles (son or daughter, student, friend, and so on). The validity of this instrument to discriminate among levels of depression was reviewed in Chapter 3.

A second way to verify this model psychometrically is to create two scales that measure the four personality propensities (in addition to 20 other conflictual dimensions) in couples. One scale, the Problems in Relationships Scale, consists of 240 items rated on a five-point Lickert scale, which also yields scores on four scales measuring the four propensities. These scores have meaning only in relationship to a partner; they are meaningless for individuals unless more norms are gathered. A second, parallel scale follows a semantic differential format on the selful–no-self and selfish–selfless polarities. Both instruments have been administered to clinical and nonclinical couples. An early version of the Self-Profile Chart, the Problems in Relationship Scale, and its semantic differential version have already been published (L'Abate, 1992b).

Although empirical methods have been used to verify this model, there is no substitute for determining the level of importance attribution from one's history. Patterns of selfishness, selflessness, or no-self are readily available, once this model is applied to the history of an individual. These patterns are made clearer through direct questioning about a person's sense of importance, even though clear-cut results cannot be expected. Nonetheless, asking people directly how they feel about their sense of importance may be another way to verify this model. Most depressed people answer in negative terms; they deny their importance. Most acting-out individuals (criminals or persons with character disorders) answer in terms of feeling quite important. Whether this assertion represents self-protectiveness rather than real self-importance or whether a sense of importance is part of the self-presentational facade of acting-out individuals remains to be seen (Kernis, 1993). To these individuals, the possibility that their sense of self-importance is achieved at the expense of others is irrelevant. These individuals achieve a sense of self-importance through negative rather than positive means. For instance, the greater the crime, the greater will be the sense of importance and the status among peers in jail. Most individuals who fit into the no-self propensity answer that they do not know whether or how they are important. This approach, of course, is strictly impressionistic and limited to clinical experience. Yet, this individual questioning of people remains the most direct and simplest method of verifying this model.

CONCLUSION

The extension of the selfhood model includes three levels of personality functioning in the selfulness propensity; various Cluster B personality disorders in selfishness; Cluster C in selflessness; and Cluster A in the no-self propensity. Each of these clusters, in their extensions to criminalities, affective disorders, and psychopathologies, will be considered in greater detail in later chapters.

CHAPTER 8

Criminalities

> [T]wo parental role models are essential for the normal development and well-being of children. (Acock & Demo, 1994, p. 180)

> Criminals are not obviously distressed or personally unhappy. . . . Criminal behavior fits the extended aspect of this definition in that it clearly creates distress; people do not enjoy being robbed or assaulted. . . . The fact that criminals fail to report any discomfort should not therefore be taken as evidence that they are untroubled in their lives. (Raine, 1993, p. 9)

Criminal behavior has been described according to a variety of viewpoints (Binder, 1988; Doren, 1987; Fowles, Sutker, & Goodman, 1994; Hirschi & Gottfredson, 1994; Le Blanc & Loeber, 1993; Lilly, Cullen, & Ball, 1995; Lykken, 1995; Raine, 1993) and is a controversial area. Discussion of it would detract from the purpose of this chapter: to describe criminalities in terms of developmental competence theory. Criminal refers to any behavior that results in the ultimate loss of life, limb, possessions, money, or services to others for the benefit of the perpetrator. Criminal behavior is composed of extremes that are the culmination of a set of characteristics resulting from externalization, impulsivity, anger, aggression, and extraversion (Dodge, 1993). The ultimate prototype in externalization is murder/rape. From this extreme emerges a myriad of less severe behaviors designed to bring benefits to the perpetrator at the expense of someone else. Externalizations may vary from mild, everyday manipulations to coercion, cheating, lying, robbing, and, in the extremes, rape and murder.

The thesis of this theory is that criminal behavior is characterized by externalizations, a term that denotes two different but overlapping meanings. The first and more common meaning implies making others outside of the self responsible for the behavior that has taken place. For instance, in response to the question: "How did you get in jail?" the answer may vary from "The judge [jury] sent me here" to "The dude who did it snitched on me and I'm taking his rap." The second meaning of externalization implies the use of external targets—other people, goods, or money—as scapegoats. In answer to the question: "Why did you shoot him?" the response may vary from "He looked at me the wrong way; he did not show me respect" to "He reached in his pocket and, before he shot me, I shot him." Thus, externalizations are coupled with impulsive, thoughtless, and destructive behavior that needs examination at various levels of interpretation. Raine (1993) invoked the concept of "selfish gene" to describe ruthless behavior that is designed to increase chances of survival, even at the expense of the survival of another human being (pp. 29–30).

METATHEORETICAL ASSUMPTIONS

These assumptions refer to various dimensions (continua and levels) included in the theory but not exclusive to the theory: intensity, continuum of likeness, depth, and horizontal behavior.

The Intensity Dimension

Externalization signifies a process of impulsive, driven behavior that is based on the immediate expression of unpleasant, painful, and short-circuited feelings through either words or actions designed to minimize the importance of the other person and maximize the importance of the self. Externalization is marked by immediacy, extraversion, and impulsivity; there is little if any ability to introspect, reflect, and use corrective feedback from either self or others. Externalization, therefore, is used here as a catchall rubric to include various extreme characteristics commonly found in aggressive, violent criminals (rapists/murderers), as well as less extreme characteristics found in individuals who cheat, rob, intimidate, lie, and manipulate others—through emotional blackmail, bribery, and coercion—to get what they want when they want it.

Continuum of Likeness

Personality differentiation in criminality takes place along a continuum of likeness, with specialization in the oppositeness range, which is dialectically linked to sameness (Chapter 5). Even though their behavior is based on oppositeness to everyday rules and regulations, criminals learn to conform to a common criminal code, where revenge, attack, manipulation, and coercion are the major ways or relating. People are opportunistically useful to obtain what is wanted, regardless of the outcome to them.

Lykken (1995) differentiated the following continuum of severity in what he called antisocial personalities:

1. Sociopathic personalities are the most extreme in their externalization and acting out; they produce the majority of violent crimes and are divided into common, alienated, aggressive, and dyssocial.
2. Psychopathic personalities, whose acting out may range from white-collar crime to theft and flim-flam, are divided into primary, secondary, distempered, and charismatic.
3. Character neuroses—which Lykken called "a wastebasket collection of persons who break the rules, usually in a rather small way, for reasons of

> personal or social maladjustment. This is one group of antisocial personalities that is likely to benefit from some form of counseling or psychotherapy" (p. 39)—is made up of (a) super-ego lacunae, (b) punishment seekers, (c) adolescent rebels, (d) paranoid personalities, and (e) inadequate personalities.

If Lykken's continuum is valid, it would suggest that sociopathic personalities fall into a classification reflecting a symbiotic-autistic internal definition that is expressed mainly through an *AA* style in relationships. Psychopathic personalities, as well as character disorders, fall into a category characterized by same–opposite, either–or self-definition. Their interpersonal style would tend to be mainly *RR* but would, under pressure, revert to *AA*. Within this style, it would be important to distinguish character neuroses from psychopathic personalities, especially in predicting outcome to psychological interventions. This distinction may be reached in terms of how much internalization is available. Are introspection and reflection present to indicate remorse, guilt, and sorrow?

The Depth Dimension

Descriptive Levels

These levels merely describe what the behavior consists of and the difference between what is presented in public in front of authority figures and what is done when public or external controls are nonexistent.

Self-Presentational Level

Self-presentation in selfish, acting-out individuals is devoted to making a good impression in front of authority figures or during social events. However, under pressure or stress, especially in prolonged interpersonal relationships, including psychotherapy, this facade can give way very quickly to anger, rebellion, and even attack, if the desired goal is not reached: "I want whatever I want, whenever I can get it, however I can get it." If and when they have to present an acceptable facade in public or in front of an authority figure, externalizers are able to make a good impression to avoid punishment and augment their chance to achieve desired gains.

Phenotypical Level

When impression management is no longer necessary or useful at the presentational level, the style of relating at the phenotypical level is either reactive *(RR)* or abusive-neglectful *(AA)*. One might argue that some criminals—white-collar criminals, for instance—exhibit conductive and creative behavior in their planning of a crime. This is not the case. The theory states that for the *CC* style to take place, both participants have to be enhanced. In a crime, someone wins at someone else's expense. Consequently, no criminal behavior is contained within the *CC* style.

Explanatory Levels

These levels consist of inferred or hypothetical constructs that are used to account for behavior at descriptive levels.

Genotypical Level

The self concept of the acting-out individual is either negative or chaotic, with little differentiation except for being "bad" or nasty or strong to avoid any possibility of being thought a sissy or weak. Any vulnerability, neediness, fallibility, or dependency is denied. Denial is one of the many defenses that are part of externalization.

Historical-Developmental Level

Background factors for the genesis of criminal behavior are discussed below in the section on parental styles.

The Horizontal Dimension: The ERAAwC Model

The elements of this model have been explained in detail in Chapter 2. The abbreviations are used here to facilitate the discussion.

E

Feelings as a whole are avoided through blatant denial or through immediate response, regardless of the consequences. Avoidance of *E,* especially of hurt and sad feelings, does not allow acting-out individuals to get too close to anybody or to give and accept love (Doren, 1987). The avoidance of unpleasant, depressive (sad, dysphoric) feelings in psychopaths has been addressed by many authors (Doren, 1987). Reid (1978) noted:

> The psychopath is not, cannot allow himself to be, truly aware of his depression. Indeed, avoidance of it plays a major role in his symptomatology. When forced into depression (a rare event) he still remains far from a conscious viewing of his emptiness. . . . He will have expended tremendous psychic energy fighting off emptiness. (pp. 9–10)

This conclusion is in agreement with Averill's (1994a) distinction between subjective experience and objective expression, which parallels the same distinction made in Chapter 4. This distinction refers specifically to the experience of feelings in externalizers: ". . . the subjectivity of feelings does not necessarily imply conscious awareness. . . . Both subjective and objective judgments can, and on occasion do, proceed outside of awareness" (p. 384).

Patrick (1995) contributed a summary of research on the emotional and temperamental antecedents of psychopathic (i.e., delinquent) behavior. He found two distinct but correlated factors: (a) emotional detachment, consisting of superficial charm, manipulativeness, shallow affectivity, and absence of guilt or empathy; and (b) antisocial behavior, consisting of deviance (from an early age), aggressiveness, impulsivity, irresponsibility, and boredom.

Raine (1993) commented about the "distress/suffering to self and others" in a way that is relevant to the thesis of Chapter 4 about the function of hurts, but also refers to the relationship of distress/suffering to criminal behavior:

> . . . a considerable degree of stress and suffering that criminals experience in their childhood, and in later adolescence and adulthood . . . is supplemented by school and occupational failure, downward social mobility, homelessness, disturbed marital relationships, and social isolation. (p. 9)

Raine, however, argued that:

> The distress/suffering of self or others criterion, like the deviation from social norms criterion, has a high degree of face validity but suffers from four important limitations. . . . many people are distressed and unhappy, but such distress is appropriate to their life circumstances and is not a sign of underlying pathology . . . people differ with respect to how much distress they can put up with before they acknowledge that they are suffering. Criminals may feel distress and unhappiness but do not express it because it does not fit with their macho image. . . . the relationship between degree of distress and severity of illness is less likely to be linear and more likely to be described by an inverted U-shaped function. . . . a number of debilitating mental disorders . . . . are associated with a lack of insight into the disorder itself, while distress to *others* may be much higher. Similarly, criminals with a psychopathic personality or who have some of the characteristics of psychopathy lack insight into their disorder and into their personal state of well-being. . . . In summary, criminal behavior fulfills this definition in that it creates distress for those in contact with criminals. (pp. 9–10)

Delinquents tend to avoid unpleasant or hurtful internal emotional tensions. This avoidance at the genotypical level is coupled at the presentational and phenotypical levels with approach toward other people in a negative, destructive fashion, perhaps to distract and to avoid dealing with unpleasant feelings. Patrick, like Lykken (1995), differentiated psychopathy from antisociality or common criminality, because "distinct subtypes of antisocial offender exist, and . . . these subtypes can be delineated on the basis of temperament-related traits" (p. 7). Temperament relates to the ability or inability to control oneself (Hirschi & Gottfredson, 1994). This characteristic results from an inability to use *R* to process *E* so that the outcome can be modified from an understanding of possible consequences deriving from one's behavior (i.e., *A*). Changing behavior may involve an *Aw*areness of *C*ontext in order for *E* to be analyzed appropriately. This process might be equivalent to what Lazarus (1991) has called appraisal. Contrary to this position, however, appraisal occurs *after* and not *before* emotional experience, as shown by *R* following *E*. How can appraisal take place if the individual does not feel anything?

R

Cognitive deficits in criminal behavior can be interpreted as arrested or delayed development. Inadequate rational controls result in discharge and a parallel inability to delay gratification—the hallmark of criminal behavior. Kegan (1986) concluded that, behind the mask of sanity, one does not find "insanity, but a child, captive of concrete thinking, with an orientation to others as short-term supplies to the self, embedded in its own goals and purposes, unable to coordinate more than a single point of view internally and interpersonally" (p. 75).

Cleckley (1976) understood and explained psychopathy as "semantic aphasia," that is, "an extensive and deep loss of understanding of meaningful language, a loss that may not at first be evident to the casual observer because the dysfunction may be disguised by intact superficial functions" (p. 98).

On the basis of what is known about criminal behavior, these conclusions are warranted: (a) criminality may be seen as a deficit in thinking; (b) this deficit seems related to a difficulty in using words to control behavior, especially nonverbal behavior (i.e., there is no transfer from the language system—ear-mouth relationships, as in most noncriminal persons—to the nonverbal system—eye-hand relationships; and (c) impulsive and eventually criminal behavior seems based on an inability to learn from experience and express feelings and emotions positively. Instead, feelings are short-circuiting and bypassing cognitive processes, jumping instead directly and swiftly into destructive or self-destructive behavior.

The foregoing, admittedly brief, description of characteristics of acting-out behavior indicates an individual with inadequate if not deviant cognitive controls and inappropriate understanding of social situations and consequences. Thus, inadequate *R* is the most important deficit in acting-out individuals, coupled with deficits in *E* both in experience and in expression.

A

Immediate and thoughtless reactivity—acting before thinking, and discharging rather than delaying—is a major characteristic of selfish behavior. Impulsive behavior may not be criminal in itself, but it may eventually culminate in criminal extremes when these types of behavior are added: (a) learning or modeling through blind conformity or conventional sameness, a characteristic of the depressed individual (Chapter 9), and (b) learning through oppositeness or rebelliousness. The former implies straightforward copying of the behavior of persons seen as worthy or as the only available examples of desirable behaviors, even if those behaviors are destructive. The latter implies an avoidance of and a reaction to situations or persons perceived as personally frightening, threatening, and dangerous.

For instance, many impulsive children, especially boys, learn to avoid sad and depressed feelings shown by their (usually selfless) mothers, because, like their (usually selfish or absent) fathers, they view sad and depressed feelings as indications of weakness and vulnerability. These perceived weaknesses invite susceptibility to persecution, ridicule, and rejection at the whims of others. Impulsive boys may model avoidant behaviors from their fathers and avoid their mother's sad and self-defeating behavior, just as their fathers do. Anger, then, becomes the main avenue of emotional expression. Unable to process sad and fearful feelings, acting-out individuals rely instead on anger or superficial expressions of happiness and euphoria, even if they have to rely on drugs to obtain this result (L'Abate, Farrar, & Serritella, 1992).

Impulsivity is the basic characteristic of most character-disordered persons. As Barratt (1985) concluded in his review of what he called impulsiveness, persons high in this characteristic show seven consistent behavior patterns:

1. Inability to keep appointments or be on time.
2. A good first impression, which, however, does not last.
3. Difficulty in sustaining interpersonal relationships.
4. Acting and speaking without thinking.
5. Jumping to decisions (i.e., making up one's mind too quickly).
6. Taking great risks.
7. Not planning ahead.

Diagnostically, these characteristics are found in a high score on the Psychopathic Deviate Scale 4 of the MMPI-2. Scale 4 is used as a criterion to evaluate initial and final levels of impulsivity in persons who have undergone any form of psychological intervention. When mothers of acting-out children or adolescents are evaluated with the same instrument, they may obtain high scores on Scale 2, Depression.

In impulsive individuals, who prefer acting out to thinking, the eye-hand relationship becomes the preferred modality of expression (in contrast to the ear-mouth relationship, which would be the preferred modality of expression for internalizing individuals). Exclusive use of the ear-mouth relationship at the expense of the eye-hand relationship can be dysfunctional if it is used exclusively (for example, by obsessive individuals). Compulsive individuals, by the same token, tend to use the eye-hand relationship at the expense of the ear-mouth relationship. Hence, there is usually a pattern of Performance-higher-than-Verbal on intelligence tests, such as the Wechsler scales, for externalizing individuals. The opposite pattern, Verbal-greater-than-Performance, may be found among internalizing individuals.

Conning, deceiving, and manipulating become almost automatic responses—ways to survive in dealing with depressive and painful affect. Language is used as a form of manipulation or distraction from relevant issues—a smoke screen for maintaining one's distance, making a good impression on the listener and getting away with it, or pulling the wool over the other's eyes. One aspect of poor cognitive controls and a limited understanding of social situations and consequences is retarded moral development (Arbuthnot & Faust, 1981; Blasi, 1980; Jurkovic & Prentice, 1977; Raine, 1993). Most acting-out individuals fail to understand the consequences of ignoring norms of reciprocity, responsibility, and other basic concepts of moral development.

Aw

This factor, which is missing in many acting-out individuals, is usually referred to as an inability to show remorse or regret about destructive behavior, i.e., an impaired or absent conscience. This deficit derives from the inability to introspect and reflect on the consequences of any action. Thus, without this corrective change mechanism, behavior continues its course repeatedly, with little deviance from established behavioral patterns that may continue for a lifetime.

C

The only context that matters to the criminal is immediate gratification: whatever the individual can get, whenever it is wanted, regardless of consequences to others.

According to the ERAAwC model, therefore, criminalities consist of *A* being more pronounced, with little if any importance given to *Aw*, *C*, or *E*. *R* is used only for the purposes of conning, deceiving, manipulating, and trying to obtain what is desired. Whatever feelings may be experienced are limited and short-lived, if not completely short-circuited—except for anger, the most prominent emotion expressed by criminals. Thus, avoidance of emotional experience is a hallmark. Externalizers jump immediately into action *(A)* without relying on thinking *(R)* or *Aw*areness of self or of *C*ontext to correct their behavior. The consequences of impulsive behavior are not considered and are not part of this immediacy.

DEVELOPMENTAL COMPETENCE THEORY

How can criminal behavior be described, if not understood and explained, from the present theory? The description and outline used in the first two chapters follow here and in the next two chapters, in an effort to obtain clarity and consistency from the theory and its expansions.

Assumptions

Space

Criminals avoid internal feeling states, but most will approach other persons more frequently than avoid them (Gray, 1994; Revelle, 1995). As Lykken (1995) has indicated, there are exceptions who are completely isolated from others. These individuals belong in the no-self personality propensity (Chapter 10). Thus, at the internal level, an avoidance of unpleasant and hurt feelings precipitates an inability to reflect on and to be introspective about one's own behavior. Externally, however, in interpersonal situations, approach is greater than avoidance. Intimacy is nonexistent except as an artificial and short-lived tool to con or manipulate others.

Time

Discharge is greater than delay, and anger, immediacy of action, inability to delay gratification, and attack are part of this pattern. The consequences of one's impulsivity are not considered. Controls are inadequate, and the temporal perspective, which, in the impulsive person, is based on fantasy and wishful thinking about immediate gains and gratifications, is limited. This restricted thinking stems from a denial of reality, without which the impulsive individual could not operate. Immediacy is the goal; consequences are discounted or minimized; or, the self is seen as the exception to any rule ("I know better" and "I won't be caught"). The completion of tasks focused on thinking and reflection, or even on writing, is very difficult for impulsive persons, unless it is coupled with technology, such as computers.

Postulates

The ability to love and the ability to negotiate are inadequate in criminals. Life is a struggle characterized by winning and losing: the more powerful and dominant wins at the expense of the meek and the submissive. If negotiation takes place, it is aimed to obtain a personally desired end and to discount the desires of others. Often, negotiation is viewed as a form of manipulation, and dissimulation, cheating, and conning are part of the game.

Criminals possess deficits in the ability to love others and in the ability to negotiate and problem-solve. Where do these deficits come from? By definition, any criminal behavior is based on an assertion of self-importance over the importance of other persons (whether this assertion focuses on persons, goods, or money), and is therefore characterized by *selfishness.* This personality propensity is learned; it is not genetically transmitted from the family of origin. As Lykken (1995) put it: "Crime runs in families" (p. 206).

Selfishness, Attraction, and Selection in Marriage

Depending on the severity of their externalization and pathology, selfish men tend to attract similarly selfish, complementarily selfless, or no-self partners, according to the level of functionality involved. Newspapers report cases of women writing to and "falling in love" with incarcerated murderers, whom these women want to marry in the confines of a penitentiary.

Modalities

Doing (performance and services) and having (products, possessions, and money) are stressed more than being (importance and intimacy). Being is the major area of deficit in individuals who avoid and deny sadness, hurt feelings, and dysphoric affects. Presence and being emotionally available and responsive to intimate others are impossible because no one ever modeled these behaviors in the delinquent's family life.

Resources

Importance is established through power over others rather than through closeness to them. Thus, importance is established in terms of negative behaviors. The "top gun" in a cell block is the one who has the highest number of murders or has committed the greatest number of attacks or robberies. Intimacy is threatening because it implies sharing hurt feelings and fears of being hurt. How can one share what is not felt or understood?

Parental Styles

Most authors (Brody & Forehand, 1986; Doren, 1987; Hirschi & Gottfredson, 1994; Lykken, 1995; Patterson & Dishion, 1988) cite inconsistent parental disciplinary practices as a key factor in the lives of acting-out individuals. They learned to receive negative attention and reinforcement—that is, attention and punishment for inappropriate rather than appropriate behavior, a pattern related to neglect. Receiving attention, even if negative, through acting-out is better than conformity, because the latter fades into nothingness. Better to be noticed than to be ignored. Being noticed, even being chased, especially by the police, is very gratifying, even if one is caught. Receiving attention from guards, juries, judges, bailiffs, and other authority figures is more gratifying than being completely ignored.

Maternal inconsistency, ranging from permissiveness to harsh punishment, has some history here. Neither extreme is necessarily relevant or even contingent to the behavior. A poor or inadequate marital coalition is usually characterized by reliance on punitive immediacy (i.e., reactivity) rather than on expression of feelings or the use of rational problem solving and decision making in parenting. Impulsive criminal behavior develops within a familial context of conflicts between a selfish father and a selfless mother. The father, if present, usually models self-centered behavior and stereotyped masculine characteristics of dominance, self-reliance, and limit-pushing, including aggression and attack. Often, because the father is absent, the fathering role is rendered nonexistent or extremely variable and inconsistent. The mother usually models the role of the put-upon martyr who does not know how to set limits on the father's or the child's behavior. Boys' behavior especially will mirror and resemble the father's, i.e., sameness.

According to the selfhood model, acting-out behavior may be the outcome of rejecting, abusive, and neglectful parental practices (Figure 1.4). No-self is the major level of functioning and produces the most extreme forms of acting-out. Acting before thinking results from impulsivity (discharge > delay), a characteristic that is related to the avoidance of sad or dysphoric feelings as experienced by the mother or by the original caretaker (Brody & Forehand, 1986). Depressive and similar feelings result from inconsistently abusive and neglectful parental disciplinary practices, which may range from extreme apathy to extreme emotional, physical, and sexual abuse, and will produce a person who is essentially resistant to any form of discipline, external or internal (Patterson, 1982). Acting-out becomes the only solution, the only survival method when faced with such extremes. A vicious circle results: avoidance of depressive feelings (sad, unpleasant, painful, dark, empty) through acting-out, followed by punishment, which brings on more acting-out, and so on.

Depressive feelings can be conceptualized in part as being expressed interpersonally through two triangles: Victim-Rescuer-Persecutor and Distancer-Regulator-Pursuer (L'Abate, 1986). Combining both triangles, the depressed caretaker, usually a woman, plays the Victim-Regulator role, asking intimates to come close to help, but rejecting their rescuing efforts, thus regulating distance by inconsistent approach-avoidance tendencies. This inconsistency eventually proves one's worthlessness and helplessness. The Rescuer-Pursuer, who tries to get close to the Victim-Regulator, is rejected and becomes the Victim-Distancer. In turn, the Victim-Distancer becomes a Persecutor, either by increasing the Pursuer role or by becoming a Distancer.

The child involved in such pathogenic family triangles either becomes silently mystified, internalizing the most painful experiences, or acts out impulsively to avoid dealing with these confused, chaotic, and inconsistent relationships. The acting out is the main modality for receiving attention and some form of importance and status (i.e., punishment is better than neglect), where no attention is available because abuse and neglect are the order of the day.

Lykken (1995) expressed a very frightening thought in regard to future parental skills of delinquents: "... because unsocialized people tend to become incompetent parents themselves, the number of sociopaths is growing faster than the general population, faster indeed than we can build reform schools and prisons" (p. 12).

Selfhood and Selected Personality Characteristics

Selfishness is visible along a continuum of severity and a variety of types. For instance, at the most severe extreme, selfishness is expressed by criminal behavior; rape and murder are prototypical. Next to criminality is narcissism, with or without sadism or criminal behavior. Narcissism is followed by egoism, a lesser form of selfishness without acting-out. Egoism is manifest in wanting to win arguments and control negotiation outcomes to reflect personal ends. Next to egoism is self-centeredness, as seen in some creative individuals and charismatic leaders. At the least severe extreme is self-involvement, which may border on selfulness when it enhances others.

Dependency in selfishness is usually denied because the self is incapable of admitting basic human conditions like fallibility, vulnerability, and neediness. Trust is practically nonexistent because trusting anyone would elicit rejection, betrayal, cheating, and being used: "Better to get others before they get me." If life is a power struggle between the weak and the strong, it is better to be strong according to traditional stereotypes of macho behavior. Being weak means being cheated, and, at worst, obliterated from existence.

Dominance—being superior or above others—is the only way to live because it is the only way to survive and to enjoy life. Any other alternative is unknown or unacceptable.

Major support for a conceptualization of criminality as determined from selfishness (defined as attribution of importance to self and unimportance to others) is found in a review by Baumeister, Smart, and Boden (1996). Although written from an intrapsychic position, using self-esteem as an explanatory construct, it includes an internally consistent explanation of criminal behavior:

> Conventional wisdom has regarded self-esteem as an important cause of violence, but the opposite view is theoretically viable. An interdisciplinary review of evidence about aggression, crime, and violence contradicted the view that low self-esteem is an important cause. Instead, violence appears to be most commonly a result of threatened egotism—that is, highly favorable views of self that are disputed by some person or circumstance. Inflated, unstable, or tentative beliefs in the self's superiority may be most prone to encountering threats and hence cause violence. The mediating process may involve directing anger outward as a way of avoiding a downward revision of the self-concept. (p. 5)

If one were to substitute attribution of importance as the interpersonal process underlying self-esteem, terms like selfishness and egotism would support the thesis that a great deal of criminal behavior is one way to bolster one's sense of self-importance at the expense of the sense of importance of others.

Selfishness and Gender Differences

Because this issue has been repeated throughout the previous chapters, suffice it here to stress that the ratio of selfish behavior is higher among men, with the exact numbers depending on the criterion that is used. If incarceration is a criterion, the ratio of incarcerated men to women may vary between seven and ten to one.

Ability to Negotiate

Criminals have limited ability to negotiate because thinking is dichotomous, i.e., one is either a winner or a loser, strong or weak, dominant or submissive, friend or foe, with few if any analogical possibilities existing between these extremes. Negotiation is an all-or-nothing process in which only either-or possibilities are considered feasible. Nothing is negotiable or everything is negotiable; there are no intermediate choices. Under these conditions, a constructive process of negotiation is impossible because only performance or production is negotiable. Presence is usually absent, so the outcome is incomplete. One wins and the other loses; there is no other acceptable solution. The notion of both participants winning at the same time is alien to the criminal mind.

If the interpersonal style is either *AA* or *RR* (= ILL), where *A* is dominant over *E, R, Aw,* or *C* (= SKILL), and priorities (intentions, expectations, goals, and motivations) are confused, suspect, or questionable (= WILL), any interpersonal process, including negotiation, will be lopsided, incomplete, and unsatisfactory.

CONCLUSION

This chapter has described prototypical criminalities as extreme extensions of selfishness within the context of developmental competence theory. The same set of concepts and constructs used to describe and explain functional behavior has been used to describe and explain criminal behavior.

CHAPTER 9

Affective Disorders

> There is general agreement that rates of depression are about twice as high in women [as in] men. . . . From an epidemiological perspective, the observed sex differences in depression must be accounted for if we are to claim an understanding of depression. (Hamilton & Jensvold, 1992, p. 116)

> [P]reliminary results highlight the importance of viewing clinically significant depression as a disorder of the transactions between the person and the environment. (Hammen, 1995, p. 5)

The previous chapter considered disorders of externalization. This chapter covers disorders of internalization, usually called affective disorders. The purpose here is to show how disorders of internalization, including depressions, fears, phobias, obsessions, and anxieties (Zinbarg, Barlow, Brown, & Hertz, 1992), can be accounted for by developmental competence theory. Internalization refers to any disorder in which the individual keeps inside whatever is hurting, without acting out or expressing any hurt outwardly and directly—acting in, so to speak. Internalizing individuals are unable to speak about whatever past hurts may have undermined their sense of self-importance and increased the attribution of greater importance to others than to self. They collect hurts and keep them carefully inside because all these hurts contribute to their need to behave as martyrs and to deny their self-importance (Dodge, 1993). The prototypical condition for internalization is chronic, refractory depression (Nolen, Zohar, Roose, & Amsterdam, 1994) characterized by powerlessness (Gilbert, 1992a) and by "demoralization, hopelessness, suicidal ideation, impairments in social adjustment, . . . a 'self-medicating' pattern of substance abuse" (Thase, 1994, p. 84), and suicide.

Original predictions (see Chapters 1 and 2) that affective disorders of internalization—disturbances where selflessness, the major characteristic, includes depressions, phobias, obsessions, and anxiety disorders—encompass 25% of the population (±0.5%) are not off the mark.

> Approximately 20% of the people in the United States will experience clinical depression in their lifetime. (President's Commission on Mental Health, 1978)

> Bipolar disorder will affect from 0.4% to 1.2% of the adult population. . . . At some time in the course of their lives, 18% to 23% of females and 8% to 11%

of males will experience a major depressive episode. (Haas & Clarkin, 1988, pp. 3, 10)

It has been finally recognized that depression arises from specific family constellations and not from unspecifiable physiological or genetic conditions (Clarkin, Haas, & Glick, 1988; Hammen, 1991). The issue here is: What kind of family will more likely produce depressed, internalizing individuals? The answer is found in Chapter 6, where links between individual and family behaviors are discussed. Any family where *AA* and *RR* styles are present or predominant will tend to produce at least one offspring with depression. More specifically, if the maternal caretaker is a model of selflessness and is married to a man characterized by selfishness, it is likely that the daughter will model her behavior after the mother and the son will model his behavior after the father, if present and available. The former will tend to internalize, and the latter will tend to externalize, along same-sex lines. Even without a father present, sons will behave as much as possible in opposite (contrary, noncompliant, rebellious, nonconforming) ways to their depressed, selfless mothers, who are unable to set firm, consistent, and clear limits for any rule infraction or acting out. If the selfish father discounts the selfless mother, verbally or behaviorally, the son will learn to discount the mother accordingly.

Most treatises on depression (Gilbert, 1992a, 1992b; Hamilton & Jensvold, 1992; Hammen, 1991) agree that the major characteristic of depressed individuals is low self-esteem. In Chapters 1 and 2, it was argued that self-esteem is not a visible, interpersonal concept. It is intrapsychic and nonrelational—an internal manifestation of interpersonal processes where the individual has learned to see the self as being important, depending on the interactions predominant in the family of origin *(CC, RR,* or *AA).* Hamilton and Jensvold argue, for instance, that a great deal of depression derives from a process of victimization. What is this process but one aspect of *AA* relationships? A variation on the theme of victimization also is related to the genesis of selflessness: *parentification,* that is, giving to the oldest sibling caretaking responsibilities over the younger children.

METATHEORETICAL ASSUMPTIONS

The Intensity Dimension: The ARC Model

The internalizing individual functions interpersonally with either an *RR* or an *AA* style. However, this individual may perform and produce relatively well in work settings that do not require close involvement with others. Some selfless individuals are extremely responsible persons who are generous with their time and energy, provided that little if any emotional attachment is needed. Newspapers do report instances of seemingly penniless, mostly alone individuals who have secretly amassed fortunes and left them to others to enjoy.

The Depth Dimension: Levels of Interpretation

Descriptive Levels

1. *Self-presentation.* The presentation of the internalizing individual varies with the severity of the condition and the reactions received from intimate others. Many want to present a heroic, jolly facade, deceiving others about their internal turmoil. Many masked depressions are hidden from the view of others for fear of criticism and rejection. Inevitably, this turmoil emerges under stress. The facade gives way to how the individual actually feels—sad, fearful, anxious, or panic-stricken. Often, the inability to express any of these bottled-in feelings leads to suicide, which shocks and surprises loved ones, who never suspected anything was amiss. Other internalizers tend to dramatize their condition in order to be accepted and helped. They may want to appear in worse condition than is supported by facts and symptoms. However, a discounting of how they feel subjectively would only increase the severity of their condition (Higgins, Snyder, & Berglas, 1990).

2. *Phenotypical level.* At this level, most internalizers need to become perfectionists in order to foreclose any possible criticism (Blatt, 1995). The self, perceived negatively, has to prove that it is acceptable by a performance or production that is perfect or as close to excellent as possible. Shades of gray do not exist if the thinking is dichotomous: good or bad, perfect or imperfect. Imperfection means badness. Only perfection may give short and temporary relief to feelings of inadequacy. As a result, a great deal of procrastination and task avoidance controls the individual, to the point of precluding the ability to perform or produce (Ferrari, Johnson, & McCown, 1995).

Explanatory Levels

1. *Genotypical.* The self is perceived negatively: bad, weak, incomplete, and, therefore, imperfect. Only external proof of performance or production may temporarily bolster the inadequacy of the self. Unfortunately, such bolstering can only be temporary and ephemeral because this individual, under these conditions, has become dependent on others for approval and approbation. He or she may become codependent, seeking out partners or people who may be able to bolster a low and negative sense of self-importance. Most treatises on depression refer to "low self-esteem" as one of the characteristics of internalizing individuals (Ferrari et al., 1995; Gilbert, 1992a). What is low self-esteem but an internal manifestation of a negative attribution of self-importance?

2. *Historical-developmental-situational.* According to the continuum of likeness, selfless individuals are influenced by both sameness (in blind, conventional, and uncritical conformity to an idealized caretaker, usually the mother), and oppositeness (to a feared and even hated paternal figure, a source of critical and abusive put-downs and discountings). A negative and depressed family climate is very likely in the background of anyone who does not value self and values others more than self.

The Horizontal Dimension: The ERAAwC Model

E

Emotionality is expressed directly because the internalizer is extremely aware of all the many hurts that have taken place in her or his life. Yet, even the outward expression of these hurts seems insufficient because the immediate environment, i.e., loved ones, is unable to accept and share these feelings. Consequently, even though the expression of these feelings is frequent and even intense, no one seems to be listening. This is the case especially if the selfless individual has selected a selfish partner who is unable and unwilling to recognize and affirm the importance and validity of feelings in general and the selfless individual in particular. If these feelings are criticized, put down, and even ignored, they persist and even amplify to the point of despair and hopelessness: "No one is listening to me!"

R

Rationality is usually not impaired as far as performance and production are concerned. It is impaired, however, in the area of presence; the individual is unable to assert self-importance. Indeed, self-importance is mainly achieved by performing and producing for others.

A

Activity may range from extremes of driven, perfectionistic, and compulsive overactivity (i.e., working continuously with no breaks except to go to sleep) to an inability to perform and produce at all. The notion of enjoyment as doing nothing is completely alien to the compulsive performer and producer. The selfless individual is able to give love, information, goods, money, and services. However, he or she is unable to receive reciprocally. Consequently, the process of exchange is inequitable. Giving is more blessed than receiving. And why should a worthless person receive anything of value? Performance and production are for the purpose of proving oneself worthy in the eyes of others rather than in the eyes of the self. Consequently, there is never sufficient activity to please others. Even if they appreciate the activity, their appreciation is never sufficient to fill and fulfill the unworthy self.

Aw

Awareness of past and present hurts is acute, and a negative outlook is the outcome. Hurts occupy such a prominent place in the internalizer's awareness, there is little room for anything else. The hurts of others are of concern because the individual feels powerless in dealing with her or his own hurts. Concentrate on the hurts of others and perhaps they will better appreciate one's hurts. However, if others do not appreciate or affirm the importance of sharing hurts, it is better to keep them inside and not share them, because ridicule and rejection may be the outcomes.

C

Context is not helpful because it is the source of negative criticisms and abusive put-downs.

Continuum of Likeness

Internalizing individuals, mostly women, are fairly conventional and conforming. They accept social dogmas and doctrines as given, without critical appraisal, which suggests that, on the continuum of likeness, selfless individuals are defined by sameness—at times, very rigid sameness. Internalizers are so conventional and conforming that they find it necessary to attract and be attracted by selfish individuals who complement them. They define themselves through oppositeness, as demonstrated in unconventional and nonconforming, if not rebellious, behavior. Internalizers are unable to draw lines and set definite, firm, and clear limits to defend their bodies ("the condom line") and themselves. Their low sense of self-importance pushes them to select individuals who, instead, push lines and ignore limits sexually, physically, mentally, emotionally, economically, and in any other ways they can.

DEVELOPMENTAL COMPETENCE THEORY

Assumptions

Internalizers tend to avoid rather than approach and to delay rather than discharge. Many are worriers and ruminators; they focus on self-defeating and self-debasing aspects of their behavior by worrying about the welfare of others rather than themselves. They tend to accept responsibility, and even blame, for the errors of others, and are quick to assume the victim role to prove their unworthiness.

Postulates

The ability to love and the ability to negotiate are impaired because the foundation for loving others is love of self. If this love for self is in low supply or is negative, concentration on the welfare of others may serve only as a distracting maneuver to avoid looking inside. In negotiation, internalizers operate from a down position. They accept uncritically, and often gullibly, whatever conditions are set by others. They are willing to give love to others, but they are not able to accept love because they feel unworthy of it. They select selfish partners, who, by definition, are willing and able to receive and take love but are not able to give it. Under these conditions, love becomes a one-way street, paving the way for ultimate imbalance in the relationship. Any attempts by others to convince internalizers of their inherent worth and intrinsic importance are denied. The self is bolstered through perfectionistic performance and overresponsible production of goods and services. However, even under positive and rewarding circumstances, any bolstering of self-importance is short-lived. Whoever affirms the importance of the internalizer must be lying or motivated by devious and self-serving needs. No matter how much others may want to convince an internalizer of his or her intrinsic worth, they are not going to be believed. They may even be considered liars by the internalizer.

Modalities

The depressed individual is able to give love but is unable to receive it because the self is unworthy of love. Even giving love in an altruistic, martyr-like fashion is defective because love is equated with not setting any limits: "If I let you do whatever you want, then you will know how much I love you." Unconditional love is confused with permissiveness and not setting any limits. An inability to set limits for either a partner or one's offspring is one of the antecedents of impulsive and selfish behavior (L'Abate, 1994a). As a result of this imbalance in the ability to love, the ability to negotiate is impaired. Hammen (1995), for instance, found that depressed young women were dysfunctional in problem-solving strategies, which suggests that depressed women may not be able to take responsibility and initiative in interpersonal relationships. They depend on others to lead and to conclude negotiations.

If the style in intimate relationships is either *RR* or *AA* (ILL) and *E, R, A, Aw,* or *C* is restricted (SKILL), and if motivation to change is very poor (WILL), then, inevitably, negotiation and problem solving will be derailed, detoured, and incomplete. On the other hand, many selfless and depressed individuals *do* want to change. Their only possible route to change requires a move from extreme selflessness to extreme selfishness. Most women murderers received a great deal of abuse and neglect but, eventually, were able to redress the balance by killing their abusive partners, usually in a fit of anger, during a fight, or as a way of defending themselves from physical or sexual attacks.

Resources

If self-importance is denied or diminished, achieving a modicum of intimacy becomes very difficult. Consequently, only perfect performance and unlimited production remain as avenues of affirmation and validation. However, even they are not enough because, as external sources, they cannot fill the internal void produced by a low sense of self-importance. Information, services, money, and possessions may become substitute goals, as seen in addictions (Chapter 11).

Varieties of Selflessness

Selflessness is not exclusively evident in depressions. It can be seen in extreme self-criticism as well as in overdependence or so-called codependence (Blatt et al., 1982). Masochistic is another term commonly applied to individuals who supposedly like to suffer, as in the Victim-Martyr complex. Self-defeating/ self-handicapping patterns of behavior are common in depressed individuals (Higgins, Snyder, & Berglas, 1990).

Selflessness and Gender Differences

A great many of the gender differences in depression have been related to the "status inequality . . . that the male gender role is more valued in our society than the female role. . . . One implication is that women's sense of identity develops within a framework that devalues women" (Hamilton & Jensvold, 1992, p. 119). Status is a Latin word that means importance. It may also mean condition, as in the "status of my car," but this is not the meaning intended here. Rather than accepting "status inequality" as being the result of vague and generic societal failures, as Hamilton and Jensvold contend, it is more parsimonious and specific to concentrate on families rather than blame deficiencies on society or culture at large.

There are unquestionably families where status inequalities for women do exist. However, in other families, women may be given higher status than men. Consequently, it is preferable to distinguish among different families rather than make society a scapegoat. In selful families, for instance, males and females receive and give the same level of positive importance, regardless of gender, although there may be differences in functions. There are families where one gender is favored over the other, producing imbalances in either selfish or selfless offspring with an *RR* style of relating. Neither gender is important in some families; both genders are put down and discounted equally, no one can win, and no-self *AA* relationship styles are the norm.

Selected Personality Characteristics

Internalizing individuals, in general, are dependent on the opinions of others because their own self is devaluated. They tend to trust others to the point of gullibility and impressionability, believing uncritically what they are told if the source is authoritative or powerful enough. They tend to be submissive rather than dominant; they want to convey the impression of being good even though their internal self-concept is bad or negative. Their public impression management may vary from trying to create a facade of being normal to making a very bad impression to convey how bad they really are.

Because they have picked selfish individuals who are afraid of intimacy, selfless individuals are just as afraid of intimacy as their partners, even though they crave it more than their partners do. They want it but do not know how to get it because they never experienced it in their families of origin. The major personality characteristic of selfless individuals is self-defeating behavior.

CONCLUSION

Selflessness, the attribution of greater importance to others than to self, is related to a self-defeating/self-handicapping internalization of hurts that leads to depressive, dysphoric preoccupation with hopelessness and helplessness. Masked and refractory depressions are so pervasive, especially in women, that preventive approaches need to be found at the psychological level before biological approaches take over.

CHAPTER 10

Psychopathologies

> Family interactions comprise an important source of stress that cannot be documented as a life event; they contribute nonspecifically to liability in already vulnerable individuals. (Fowles, 1992, 321)

> [I]n general, the shared family environment contributes little if anything to the similarity of children growing up in the same home. That is, within a similar culture, biologically related children growing up together tend to be similar on most personality traits as they would be growing up apart, and unrelated children growing up together tend to be no more similar than unrelated children in general. (Revelle, 1995, p. 309)

Psychopathology represents an extremely large gamut of dysfunctional conditions or psychopathologies. In their most encompassing meaning, psychopathologies include affective disorders (Chapter 9), borderline personality disorders, schizophrenias, paranoias, and dissociative disorders. Schizophrenias represent one prototype of the no-self personality propensity. "Neither you nor I is important. Neither you nor I is going to win." The other prototype is represented by the murderer-suicide who kills a loved one, usually a partner or child, and then self-destructs.

Most recent reference texts or treatises on psychopathology contain lists of psychiatric disorders, without rhyme or reason for inclusion or exclusion of addictions or other clinical conditions. For instance, Ammerman and Hersen (1993) edited two chapters for each of the following conditions in children and adults: major depression, separation and panic disorders, simple phobias, obsessive-compulsive disorders, anxiety disorders, posttraumatic stress disorders, conduct and antisocial personality disorders, schizophrenia, mental retardation, substance abuse, and obesity. Hersen and Last (1990) followed the same format of one chapter for children and one for adults in the following areas: major depression, bipolar disorder, schizophrenia, anxiety disorder and agoraphobia, social phobia and simple phobia, obsessive-compulsive disorder, overanxious and generalized anxiety disorder, posttraumatic stress disorder, conduct disorder and antisocial personality, mental retardation, alcohol abuse and dependence, and obesity.

Bellack and Hersen (1993) listed all the above syndromes but added a chapter on bipolar disorders and sexual dysfunction and deviation. Hersen and

Turner (1991) added chapters on organic mental disorders and dissociative disorders—topics that are not contained in two of the previously cited sources. Could it be concluded that inclusion or exclusion of psychopathology-related conditions is a matter of arbitrary whim? Can a psychiatric syndrome be added or withdrawn at will? Without a theory to direct a listing of psychiatric conditions, the selection is destined to be capricious.

Of the four reference works cited above, only Bellack and Hersen (1993) contained references to the role of family background in depression, eating disorders, schizophrenia, sexual dysfunction, and substance abuse. The other three works, including the two addressing psychopathology in children and adults (Ammerman & Hersen, 1993; Hersen & Last, 1990), failed to mention the family as being related in any way to the genesis of psychopathology. Credit should be given, however, for their consistent inclusion of character disorders and antisocial personalities, which are topics typically excluded in abnormal personality texts, as discussed in Chapter 7.

Two major issues in the diagnosis of psychopathology, especially schizophrenia, are: (a) subtype heterogeneity or boundaries among various psychopathologies versus a continuum of severity, and (b) comorbidity overlap not only with affective disorders but also with criminalities (Costello, 1993a, 1993b; Fowles, 1992). Both issues have been addressed in this proposal. As explained in Chapter 7, included under the rubric of psychopathologies are borderline disorders and dissociative disorders, which, if treated, have a somewhat more positive prognosis than paranoias and schizophrenias. However, variability within each of these four conditions is sometimes so great that overlap with either internalizing or externalizing conditions is inevitable.

Externalization (Chapter 8) and internalization (Chapter 9) are related to fairly distinct clinical conditions (i.e., criminalities as disorders of externalization versus affective disorders as disorders of internalization). In the psychopathologies, *both* externalizations and internalizations coexist. This dialectical coexistence is marked by contradictory and inconsistent reversals and oscillations from one extreme of externalization to another extreme of internalization, as found in bipolar affective disorder (manic-depression) or murder-suicide.

PSYCHOPATHOLOGIES AND THE FAMILY

The major controversial issue concerning the psychopathologies lies in their etiology. How much does the family contribute to their genesis? Some reviewers of the literature, plus three of the four reference texts cited above, either do not consider the family altogether (Haynes, 1992) or deny its influence, making heredity the major cause of behavior (Rowe, 1994). Just as many other scholars propose the opposite influence of the environment. Functionalities and dysfunctionalities develop from family backgrounds (Frude, 1991; Goldstein, 1988; Goodyear, 1990; Helmersen, 1983; Jacob, 1987; L'Abate, 1994b; White,

1993). Because of this controversy, a selective review of the evidence, slanted toward external, interactive influences rather than internal ones, is included. Hence, the term socialization rather than personality development is employed in this presentation. Could not this controversy be laid to rest once the evidence for or against nature or nurture is gathered under one cover (L'Abate, in press)?

Parenting and Psychopathologies

The theory predicts that, under the no-self personality propensity, parental styles would be either abusive or rejective with abandonment, neglect, and emotional and behavioral reactivity. In an issue of the *Infant Mental Health Journal* (Musick & Cohler, 1983) entirely devoted to the relationship between parental psychopathology and infant development, the editors noted: "Psychiatric illness among mothers of infants and young children is believed to have serious implications for the child's cognitive and socio-emotional development, and presents a continuing crisis in the provision of reliable parental care" (p. 140). In the same issue, Sameroff, Seifer, and Barocas (1983) found that, in children whose mothers were diagnosed with a variety of psychiatric disturbances, there were "few unique effects on child performance" (p. 237). In addition to the importance of social status, which affects the child's cognitive development, "The severity of the mother's disturbance was the most important factor affecting the child's social-emotional competence" (p. 237).

More recently, Perris, Arrindell, and Eisemann (1994) edited a collection of studies relating psychopathology to dysfunctional parental rearing. This work is perhaps the most important source of evidence to support the relationship between parental dysfunctionality and the development of psychopathology. More pages than is feasible would be needed to fully summarize this work. However, no serious student of psychopathology can ignore this contribution, especially because most of the research was performed outside of the United States.

Pettit and Mize (1993) found that stylistic qualities of parenting were related to children's competence with peers (pp. 121–127) and that the substance of parental teaching consists of explicit structuring and coaching (pp. 128–133). Style and substance in parenting are two pathways to the socialization of children. These qualities are inadequately represented in deviant parents: "[A]ccumulating evidence suggests that young children develop social skills in the context of adult-mediated experience" (p. 151). Direct parental influences affect how young children relate with their peers (Ladd, Le Sieur, & Profilet, 1993). Children who behave as bullies (i.e., persecutors) seem able to select children who behave as victims. Both types derive from specific family constellations (Smith, Bowers, Binney, & Cowie, 1993).

Putallaz, Costanzo, and Klein (1993) reviewers results from the literature on parental abuse and concluded that, in retrospective studies, there is "support for . . . abusive parents . . . having some aberrant personal characteristic that leads them to abuse their children" (p. 66).

In prospective studies, the same reviewed found that:

> Similar to findings from retrospective abuse research is that evidence exists for intergenerational continuity of abuse for many, but not all parents. (p. 68)
>
> [G]ender is an important variable. (p. 74)
>
> Parents rated as secure in their own attachments with their parents . . . tended to value attachment relationships and to view them as affecting personality development. . . . Parents rated as insecure in their attachments to their own parents not only lacked these [positive] qualities but also displayed some of the following three patterns. They (a) dismissed attachment relationships as unimportant, (b) seemed preoccupied with their dependency on their parents and ability to please them, or (c) had not yet resolved the death of an attachment figure they lost during childhood. (pp. 75–76)

In addition, these reviewers concluded that "a troubled marriage is an important condition of continuity with regard to problematic mothering, and inversely, . . . a good marriage can serve as a buffer against the intergenerational transmission of maternal negative affect" (p. 80).

Frik et al. (1992) found that, in children between 7 and 13 years of age diagnosed as conduct disordered, there was an association between their diagnosis and "several aspects of family functioning: maternal parenting (supervision and persistence in discipline) and parental adjustment (paternal antisocial personality disorder and paternal substance abuse)." Children with oppositional defiant disorder differed from control children in having a higher rate of paternal substance abuse and paternal antisocial personality disorder. Parental antisocial personality disorder was significantly associated with conduct disorder. It is unfortunate that this study did not assess the level of depression in mothers, because the theory would predict that if the father was antisocial (i.e., a selfish externalizer), the mother was more likely to be either depressed or acting out, like the husband.

Greenwald (1992), after reviewing the research that related the onset of schizophrenia to specific family communication patterns, concluded: "[P]arents of schizophrenics have difficulty in clearly establishing their focus of attention and their opinions and thoughts, though they can communicate when the focus is set and unambiguous" (p. 158). Not only is affect usually negative but personal power is also discounted so that the self becomes powerless. Criticism, as a form of abusive discounting, is one of the major characteristics of communication in families of schizophrenics.

Gotlib and Avison (1993) reviewed the evidence that predicted risk for psychopathology in children: (a) family milieu, (b) social disadvantage, (c) family structure, (d) separation/divorce of parents, (e) unmarried mothers, (f) death of a parent, especially the mother, (g) parental psychiatric disturbance, including depression, schizophrenia, and alcoholism, (h) marital/family discord, and (i) parental emotional unavailability. In other words, psychopathology does not develop mysteriously in a vacuum. It develops from specific and recognizable family antecedents, especially the personality propensities of parents.

The Influence of Siblings in the Development of Psychopathology

There are many instances where sibling parentification, sibling rivalry, and sibling abuse (physical, sexual, or emotional) may cause irreparable psychopathology. Sibling abuse may result from incomplete and neglectful parental practices, where either parent is not aware of or cannot stop any deleteriously negative sibling–sibling pattern. As discussed in Chapter 6, abuse and neglect are dialectically related and are transmitted intergenerationally. One style cannot exist without the other at both the intraindividual and interindividual levels. If a child is behaving in destructive ways toward another child or sibling, it means that parents or caretakers are being neglectful in their care and supervision of their offspring. By the same token, this neglect may derive from a weak, apathetic, and conflictful marital relationship.

METATHEORETICAL FOUNDATIONS OF THE THEORY

Socialization and Differentiation: The ARC Model

The most intense style of relating in psychopathology is, by definition, *AA*, which ranges from abuse, at one extreme, to apathy, emotional atrophy (i.e., unavailability or nonresponsiveness) and neglect at the other extreme. However, this dimension cannot be separated from the depth dimension.

The Depth Dimension: Levels of Interpretation

It is difficult for many no-self individuals to present a socially acceptable facade, but it is possible, provided that demands on these individuals are limited and do not tax already depleted emotional resources. Millions of individuals are able to survive economically by keeping their jobs and limiting themselves strictly to survival skills, with little if any enjoyment. This range includes what Depue and Zald (1993) called "nonpsychotic psychopathology." Thus, the self-presentational level may appear acceptable within circumscribed conditions, but the individual's intimate context at the phenotypical level may match the level of the parent or partner, in the sense that selection is on the basis of a similarly abusive/neglectful background. Although the marriage may last for a lifetime, it would be strictly instrumental in nature; intimacy would be very difficult to achieve under these conditions. Presentationally, the union may even pass as being normal. However, what matters is how both partners behave phenotypically within the confines of their home. Child rearing would be characterized by *AA* and *RR* styles, and the offspring will repeat the style of the parents. An adult child of alcoholic parents may not become an alcoholic but may become a religious fanatic instead. The best that can be said about self-presentation and impression management is that these processes are very weak and nonexistent under stressful conditions. Self-presentation is negative and self- and other-defeating.

The selection of the no-self label for psychopathologies evolved from a preference to encompass the whole range from functional to dysfunctional—from seemingly normal cases who fake being normal at the presentational level, to unquestionably dysfunctional cases at the same level. No-self lacks a gyroscope—an internal, positive sense of self to direct and guide behavior. At best, behavior is repetitively reactive (*RR* versus proactive which is *CC*). At worst, *RR* becomes *AA*. There is barely enough energy to cope with immediate daily needs, let alone to enjoy life or plan for the future. At the phenotypical level, these individuals function to meet immediate survival needs and little else. Genotypically, whatever sense of self-awareness may exist is chaotic, negative, and confused. Historical, developmental, and situational antecedents would be of a severe *RR* style and a clear *AA* style in the family of origin as well as in the family of procreation (Gilbert & Connolly, 1991; Magnussen & Ohman, 1987).

Greenwald (1992) noted that "not only may there be multiple pathways to schizophrenia, but there may be no one-to-one correspondence between the pathway and the form and course of the illness" (p. 148). This conclusion applies not only to schizophrenia but to psychopathologies in general.

The Horizontal Dimension: The ERAAwC Model

E

This component is extremely limited or avoided in its subjective feeling aspects, and there is inappropriate or inadequate expression in its objectively visible aspects. Because *E* is responsible for determining approach-avoidance functions, the whole process of RAAwC is going to be inadequate, incomplete, and/or inappropriate.

R

Dobson and Kendall (1993) devoted a whole volume to the relationships between cognition and psychopathology, and it would be impossible to summarize all of the many contributions to this important area. Kendall and Dobson (1993) distinguished between "*cognitive deficits* or *deficiency*" and "*cognitive distortions*": "Deficiencies refer to the lack of certain forms of thinking (e.g., the absence of information processing where it would be beneficial) whereas distortions refer to active but dysfunctional thinking processes" (p. 10). These authors proposed a model based on emotional intensity, which reflects "the fact that cognitions are associated with emotional reactions and behavior across time (e.g., cognitions occur before, during, and after behavioral events). Because events do not occur in a vacuum and because behavior is determined by multiple causes, the model must allow for the feedback that results from multiple, sequential behavioral events" (p. 12).

If one conceives of *Aw* and *C* as being part of what these authors call feedback and events not occurring in a vacuum, respectively, their model contains all five components of the ERAAwC model.

Costello (1993a) proposed that "cognitive processes and contents play a causal role in the occurrence of psychopathology" (p. 321). After presenting relevant evidence to support his proposal (too detailed to summarize here), he concluded:

> The fundamental problem seems to be that psychopathologists have, for the most part, investigated cognitive contents rather than processes. If a case is to be made for cognitive causes of psychopathology, then one must demonstrate that people are more likely to develop psychopathological conditions if they show some peculiarity in cognitive processes, such as the way of perceiving or remembering things, and not simply in the things they perceive or remember. (p. 347)

A

Criteria for psychopathological activities are: (a) inadequacy and inappropriateness in behavior, coupled with (b) disturbance value to others. As long as an individual is able to appear adequate and appropriate in public, there is no limit on what that individual can do within the privacy and secrecy of his or her home. When the inadequacy or inappropriateness of *A* reaches or disturbs loved ones, authorities, or neighbors, it becomes necessary to label that behavior as sick and requiring hospitalization. As long as an acceptable facade of normality is kept in public, few if any consequences will occur.

Aw

Because *Aw*areness is intrinsically related to *R*, even though it may occur after *A*, it possesses the same two characteristics of *R:* deficiencies and distortions. More important, however, *Aw* cannot be used for corrective purposes. Feedback from others, including well-meaning and experienced therapists, cannot be used. Any form of correction is viewed as an encroachment on and invasion of a restricted sense of self. Hence, with no-self conditions, it may often be necessary to use paradoxical interventions to avoid an out-and-out rejection of corrective feedback from well-intentioned others, whether loved ones or therapists.

C

When little if any *Aw* of self is present, then *C*ontext is undoubtedly incompletely defective and negatively distorted to the point of denial and rejection.

DEVELOPMENTAL COMPETENCE THEORY

Assumptions

Space

Developmental competence theory predicts an extreme imbalance in approach-avoidance functions. Reversals in either approach or avoidance will be present. Distance is used through either extreme in approach-avoidance, as in aggression and overdependence. Aggression may result ultimately in hospitalization or incarceration—conditions that imply overreliance on the wishes and rules of others.

Time

The theory predicts an extreme imbalance in discharge-delay functions, where reversals in either discharge or delay are present. Control is either extreme (to a point where fantasy, hallucinations, and other indications of distorted feelings and thinking might indicate exaggerated delay functions) or sudden (to a point where unexpected and unpredictably destructive acting out may take place). For example, consider the disgruntled, fired employee who returns to the place of former employment to kill whoever was thought to be responsible for the dismissal. Paranoid individuals may hide their distortions internally until a triggering event results in an explosive manifestation of their deviant thinking.

Postulates

In the no-self personality propensity, the ability to love and the ability to negotiate are either impaired or nonexistent. This statement does not mean that no-self individuals cannot meet and marry other similarly impaired individuals. Schizophrenics manifest inadequate and limited social skills, but there is a whole range of psychopathologies wherein little ability is needed to meet and marry someone with the same limited range of social skills (Gilbert & Connolly, 1991). Under these conditions, the same inabilities are transmitted to the offspring. Because of positive life-circumstances outside of the family, some offspring may be able to elevate themselves to a more functional level. By the same token, another offspring may become even more dysfunctional. Hence, the theory predicts that no-self parents might produce some offspring who are more functional than themselves, some who remain at the same level, and some who are more dysfunctional.

Modalities

In the no-self individual, limited performance and production may take place, but presence is almost nonexistent, especially in schizophrenia. Keeping in mind that an *AA* style derives from symbiotic-autistic-alienated personality differentiations, the prediction is that it would be difficult to help individuals who have reached this level of functioning. By definition, these individuals are not able to relate to others in positive ways. Even if they begin psychotherapy, whether under duress or voluntarily, the outcome would be unpredictable. The question also arises as to whether psychotherapy is the treatment of choice. Less threatening media of treatment, like writing or nonverbal interventions, may be needed to establish a successful therapeutic relationship (see Chapters 12 and 13).

Resources and the No-Self Personality Propensity

How can a person function if he or she denies not only the importance of the self but also the importance of the other? The answer: Very poorly. Intimate relationships with others would be either very distant or very conflictual. It is not unusual for no-self individuals and their families to have daily or weekly upsets and uproars, among themselves as well as outside the home. A continuum of no-self, in order of least to most severe, would be: borderline, dissociated, paranoid, schizophrenic, and psychotic.

Selfhood and Gender Differences

Greenwald (1992) concluded:

> [T]here are numerous gender differences in schizophrenia. Female schizophrenics tend to develop the disorder later in life, experience higher premorbid and recovery level of functioning, need fewer rehospitalizations, show more clear evidence of important environmental influences, and display more florid and affective symptomatology. . . . males show a more physiologically based predisposition to schizophrenia, whereas, for females, schizophrenia may be more environmentally based. . . . There are distinct male and female patterns in schizophrenia. (p. 167)

Selected Personality Characteristics

Any personality characteristic considered in Chapter 1 would be either defective to the point of nonexistence, or exaggerated to the point of inappropriateness and destructiveness. For instance, dependence may be extreme, as shown in chronic overreliance on welfare agencies. However, such dependence may be coupled with denial, as shown in concomitant criminal behavior such as selling welfare coupons. Under these circumstances, it would be practically impossible to trust anybody. If trust is given, it is difficult to separate it from issues of dependence. Where does trust end and naive gullibility (overreliance on someone who cannot be trusted otherwise) begin?

Dominance is either extreme or related to excessive subservience and submission. One extreme cannot take place without the other. One cannot dominate unless someone allows the dominance to occur. For instance, decision making becomes an all-or-nothing, either-or process. Power, in whatever form, is not shared. Whoever has it does not want to give it away or is not able to negotiate it. On the other end of the power continuum, everything is negotiable and no boundaries exist or can be negotiated. According to the Five Factors Model, the level of negativism would be highest with low openness and almost no agreeableness.

Comorbidity

How can drastically different psychopathological conditions coexist? This model accounts for coexistence of different diagnostic conditions. For instance, in manic depression, there is a switch from a complete polarity of selfishness to a polarity of selflessness. Externalization and internalization are dialectically related to the process of importance attribution. In the combination of externalization and internalization, confused, inconsistent, and contradictory messages emerge from equally confused, inconsistent, and contradictory role models. For instance, an acting-out adolescent may pattern after his or her self-centered, driven, and angry father. However, at the same time, the adolescent has to contend with a selfless, passive, and depressed mother. Acting out and depression are coexistent in the adolescent's experience. The question is: Which of these conditions will manifest itself first? Acting out may manifest itself first, but when the adolescent is incarcerated because of criminal behavior, depression may set in and suicide may become possible.

Another way to understand coexistence is to understand the dialectical nature of polarities. For instance, selfishness cannot develop without a selfless caretaking setting. Abuse of any kind cannot develop without an apathetically neglectful caretaking setting. Both extremes are contradictorily but dialectically related; one cannot take place without the other. Confusion and contradiction are the hallmarks of dysfunctional behavior, where extremes can and do coexist.

Suicide

When the model predicts that more women suffer from depression than men, it may seem logical to conclude that more women would commit suicide than men. But this is not the case. Suicide is the product of a variety of personal and interpersonal antecedents, and multiple meanings are attached to it. There are different kinds of suicide. One type may be the result of selfishness (not thinking of others; thinking only of oneself). Another type may be the result of extreme avoidance of unpleasant, uncomfortable, and painful feelings. Actually, more men than women, worldwide, commit suicide because, as discussed in Chapter 8, they are more impulsive, less likely to ask for help, and more self-centered than women. They do not realize nor reflect on how much suffering their act will produce for loved ones. Hence, suicide cannot be thought of as a selfless act. There are many ways to kill the self, and suicide is just one of them. Suicide is a multidetermined act, sometimes precipitated not only by depression but also by an impulsive personality propensity. It has meaning within the context of the no-self personality propensity rather than in selflessness or selfishness.

CONCLUSION

Psychopathologies may be described, if not explained, by developmental competence theory. However, the issue is whether they are accurately and reliably described, a judgment that can only be reached by people external to the theory.

CHAPTER 11

Addictions and Psychosomatic Illnesses

> [A]ddictions need to be treated differentially, not only on grounds of multiple causality and levels of analysis, but also on grounds of individual differences. (L'Abate, 1992a, p. 4)

This chapter will evaluate addictions and psychosomatic illnesses from the viewpoint of developmental competence theory. If the theory (cl)aims to understand personality, criminality, affective disorders, and psychopathology, then it should be able to encompass addictions and psychosomatic illnesses. To achieve this purpose, both terms should be defined. An addiction is an overinvolvement with, overdependence on, and abuse of a specific substance, a specific object, a specific individual, or a specific behavior to the point of emotional, financial, and occupational detriment to the individual and to his or her intimates (L'Abate, Farrar, & Serritella, 1992; Marlatt, Baer, Donovan, & Kivlahan, 1988). Substances could be food, alcohol, inhalants, or drugs. Objects could be cigarettes, goods, or money, when one gambles or buys excessively. Individuals could include those who are used to satisfy a sexual craving without any emotional involvement. Behavior could range from physical abuse to excessive exercise. Thus, most if not all addictions have in common the quality of *externalization;* they overrely on external sources or resources to gratify the self. A certain degree of impulsivity is characteristic of many addictions, to the point that it is difficult, sometimes, to differentiate them from criminalities.

Sources used in addictions are identical with the resources of the theory. Abuse can take place in the resources of importance and intimacy (persons), services and information (performance), or money and goods (production). Addictions indicate an inability to control oneself, a reliance instead on external sources or resources to satisfy unmet, unspoken, and unfulfilled emotional hurts rather than unspecified needs (Fairburn & Wilson, 1993). These (re)sources become substitute—albeit temporary, ephemeral, and superficial—forms of gratification for emotional hurts that the individual has been unable to express and share appropriately in the family of origin or the family of procreation. Very likely, these hurts were produced by family members, and this relationship made it difficult to express and share the hurts.

Addictions do not constitute a discrete, homogeneous category or class of psychopathology (Meyer, 1986). As seen in dual diagnoses, for instance, addictions can cover the whole gamut of psychopathological conditions (Allen & Frances, 1986; Evans & Sullivan, 1990; Solomon, Zimberg, & Shollar, 1993). They are distributed among different diagnostic (i.e., DSM-IV) categories. Therefore, addictions cannot be placed in one single location in a prototypical model, even though some overlap with diagnostic psychiatric categories may be inevitable.

Psychosomatic illnesses, on the other hand, exist at the other side of the externalization–internalization spectrum (Frank & Powell, 1967). Addictions are disorders of undercontrol; psychosomatic illnesses are disorders of overcontrol (Dantzer, 1993). The individual is unable to rely on either external or internal sources of gratification, legitimate or illegitimate, to deal with past hurts. The term *psychosomatic,* however, carries at least three meanings. A wider meaning implies that all physical and physiological processes, functional or dysfunctional, possess psychological components or concomitants. One cannot be physically sick and not be somewhat depressed or at least unhappy. This meaning, therefore, applies to emotional *correlates* of physical illnesses. A second, more specific and usual meaning of psychosomatic, refers to the possibility that some physical illnesses may have psychological *antecedents*—precursors, or causes. A third meaning consists of *somatizing,* a process of becoming overly involved and interested in one's body or becoming oversensitive to every little nuance of the body as a possible or potential indication of illness. Somatization may increase or at least exacerbate the severity of any physical illness.

Where and how would psychosomatic illnesses fit within this theory? The answer to this question is proposed in this chapter. If they are heterogeneous as addictions, perhaps one would have to consider what personality characteristics or psychopathological conditions would locate them within this model, regardless of specific psychosomatic patterns. Thus far, it has not been sufficiently demonstrated that one specific personality disorder or characteristic predicts a specific psychosomatic pattern.

Even if the family may not be directly responsible for producing any of these conditions, it is still concomitantly affected by them. It pays for some of the economic and emotional ripple effects of the addiction or the psychosomatic disease (Meissner, 1974). Ultimately, the family assumes the responsibility for taking care of the addicted or psychosomatically ill individual. For instance, any addiction that leads to health problems and sickness has definite somatic, psychosomatic, and contextual effects; hence the necessity to consider both conditions in the same chapter.

Among many illnesses that are considered psychosomatic in various degrees are: (a) eating disorders—anorexia-nervosa (Grigg, Friesen, & Sheppy, 1989), binge eating (Fairburn & Wilson, 1993), bulimia (Giat, 1986; Johnson & Flach, 1985), and obesity (Swift, Andrews, & Barklage, 1986); (b) respiratory asthma, especially in children; (c) high blood pressure; (d) some types of ulcers; (e) some types of cancer (Andersen, Kiecolt-Glaser, & Glaser, 1994; Katz & Jay, 1984; Temoshock, 1995); (f) diabetes; (g) enuresis and encopresis

(Bemporad, Pfeifer, Gibbs, Cortner, & Bloom, 1971); (h) chronic pain; and (i) coronary heart disease.

Adler and Matthews (1994), in trying to answer the question: "Why do some people get sick and some stay well?" considered social environmental contributors to disease: stress and social connections. Some people can reduce stress if they are proactive and positive, as in the *CC* style. Personality predispositions also contribute to disease: (a) type A personality, the driven person, and hostility; (b) depression, distress, and exhaustion; (c) neuroticism and negative affectivity; and (d) optimism, explanatory style, and self-esteem. The first three factors increase the likelihood of disease. The fourth factor tends to attenuate this likelihood, which means that a positive and high sense of self-importance, coupled with intimacy, would lessen the likelihood of physical illness.

ISSUES OF COMORBIDITY AND DUAL DIAGNOSIS

Most psychopathologies, as discussed in Chapter 7, cannot be pigeonholed behind a ready-made diagnostic label because there is too much variability within one label and among different labels (Evans & Sullivan, 1990; Solomon, Zimberg, & Shollar, 1993). Hence, an individual may possess other characteristics that force professionals to use additional labels that encompass the complexity of his or her behavior. Dual diagnoses recognize this inherent complexity and attempt to add diagnostic—and, hopefully, predictive—labels that will have some therapeutic effectiveness, if indeed psychological treatments can be that specific. Dual diagnosis in psychiatric classification was once considered the exception rather than the rule. Now, it is acknowledged that dual diagnosis is the rule rather than the exception (Clark, Watson, & Reynolds, 1995).

METATHEORETICAL ASSUMPTIONS

Levels of Intensity: The ARC Model

According to the ARC model, both addictions and psychosomatic illnesses represent functioning mostly at the *AA* or *RR* level, depending on the severity of the condition. For instance, many individuals with psychosomatic illnesses may seem to function well in intimate relationships, but these seemingly unimpaired relationships are conducted with a great deal of unexpressed internal tension. Many addicted individuals are able to conduct themselves properly (almost in a seemingly *CC* style) in order to make a good impression socially. When their condition reaches unacceptable levels of severity, however, whatever social facade may exist will crumble under pressure.

In psychosomatic illnesses, as in the affective disorders, self-presentation and phenotypical behavior may vary according to the type and severity of the illness. For instance, in bulimia, self-presentation may be deceptively acceptable or even praiseworthy. However, in both addictions and psychosomatic illnesses, self-presentation, no matter how positive, is short-lived and superficial. There may be a great discrepancy between an individual's social self-presentation and that same individual's private behavior, at the phenotypical level. The nasty/nice dimension may be relevant here, to the point where the individual may be nice on the outside and nasty on the inside, in the family setting.

The Depth Dimension: Levels of Interpretation

Approach and discharge in addictions and avoidance and delay in psychosomatic illnesses may appear evident at self-presentational and phenotypical levels, but this is not the case when addictive and psychosomatic behaviors are examined at the genotypical level. As with most dysfunctionalities, the experience and expression of hurt feelings are avoided at this level. These feelings have been either avoided completely or incorrectly processed so that their expression is either inadequate or inappropriate.

External approach toward something or someone, as in addictions, may be caused by an internal avoidance of painful feelings. In psychosomatic illnesses, external approach-avoidance tendencies are confused, chaotic, and unsatisfactory. Internally, there is a strong avoidance of feelings. Delay in the expression of feelings is the norm, as is the case in many dysfunctions, including criminality. The thesis of this theory is: Avoidance of hurt feelings accumulated in the past and not properly processed, expressed, and shared, both in the past and in the present, leads to dysfunctionality. The problem here is to differentiate more clearly, as in previous chapters, what feelings are attached to what type of dysfunctionality.

The Horizontal Dimension: The ERAAwC Model

E

In most dysfunctionalities, there are deficits in how feelings are approached or avoided. If feelings are avoided, physiological processes might take over and these feelings might not be expressed, as in extreme repression or alexithymia (Sifneos, 1973). If feelings are avoided and short-circuited, as in the criminalities, impulsive action or obsessive behavior may be the outcome. If feelings are approached but not processed properly, the outcome will be incomplete, inadequate, or inappropriate expression. Thus, *E* is the cornerstone of either functional or dysfunctional behavior, depending on how feelings are approached, avoided, processed, expressed, or shared.

What happens when *E* is exaggerated, that is, when it is either inflated or magnified? The outcome depends on how *R* is used: Is *R* introduced in the process to reduce magnification, or is *R* avoided? If the latter is true, there is an impulsive jump from *E* to *A*, with little *Aw*areness of either self or *C*ontext.

R

When *E* is avoided, short-circuited, or processed improperly, this component becomes either decreased, as in the criminalities, or exaggerated, as in obsessive disorders or in behavior such as compulsions *(A)*. If addictions are interpreted as compulsions, *R* is not being used appropriately to control and regulate *A*. In psychosomatic illnesses, *R* may become magnified to the point of becoming obsessive intellectualization and rumination.

A

When both *E* and *R* are inadequately processed, the outcome in *A* will be inadequate (incomplete or inappropriate) as well. Consequently, *A* can become limited, as in psychosomatic illnesses; or impulsive, as in the criminalities; or compulsive, as in the addictions. Repetition in *A*, therefore, is the earmark of a disorder, whether internal or external.

Aw

When the three previous components of the model are inadequately processed, *Aw* might become restricted and therefore limited as a change mechanism. The individual is unable to use *Aw* to reflect, introspect, and dialogue within the self. At best, there is an internal monologue. However, this monologue is, by nature, inadequate because the individual does not have sufficient *Aw* of self, other, or *C*ontext. Nor is external feedback used to change. Consequently, *Aw* is impaired. Either there is no feedback loop back to *E* to improve the process, or the loop will not be strong enough to change the process.

C

When all four components of this model are inadequate, it cannot be expected that *C*ontext will even be acknowledged or considered. At best, it will be denied or rejected as irrelevant or unimportant.

DEVELOPMENTAL COMPETENCE THEORY

How does the theory deal with both addictions and psychosomatic illnesses?

Assumptions and Postulates

In addictions, the self is loved and hated at the same time. Self-gratification is a substitute for a negative or incomplete attribution of importance either to self or to intimate others. In psychosomatic illnesses, others are loved more than self. In either condition, there is little if any intimacy. Consequently, the ability to negotiate, especially regarding emotional issues, is also impaired. The individual is unable to be present (available emotionally) to self or to loved ones, and, when able, concentrates mainly on performance or production. Being, therefore, is impaired.

In addictions, discharge is greater than delay, and approach toward a specific substance, object, individual, or behavior is greater than avoidance. However, this generalization needs to be qualified by specifying the level of interpretation at which such an approach-avoidance conflict takes place, as discussed earlier. In psychosomatic disorders, delay is greater than discharge, and avoidance is greater than approach. Hence, they represent one extreme of *internalization.*

Evidence for this conclusion, when delay as a process is usually called inhibition in other sources, is derived from the work of Pennebaker and his coworkers (Francis & Pennebaker, 1992; Pennebaker, 1993a, 1993b; Pennebaker, Barger, & Tiebout, 1989; Pennebaker & Beall, 1986; Pennebaker & Susman, 1988; Petrie, Booth, Pennebaker, Davison, & Thomas, in press) as well as other investigators who have verified many of Pennebaker's original findings (Esterling, Antoni, Fletcher, Margulies, & Schneiderman, 1994; Esterling, Antoni, Kumar, & Schneiderman, 1990). Essentially, Pennebaker and his associates found that writing for fifteen minutes a day, for four consecutive days, about one's past unexpressed traumas (i.e., hurts) that had been avoided until then, produced significant health benefits, not only in immune functions but also in decreased visits to medical facilities. These findings, replicated in a variety of settings and with different populations, have implications not only for psychosomatic theory but also for prevention, as discussed in the next chapter.

The only point of difference here relates to the use of the term *delay* instead of its synonym, *inhibition.* Delay is an observable process that can be measured; inhibition is an internal process inferred from delay. In delay, one can see how long it takes from the beginning of an emotional event surrounding an individual to when (and how) that individual reacts. If the reaction is quick and the response is fast, one assumes impulsivity and/or drivenness. If the reaction is slow (i.e., delayed) or does not appear, then one infers some form of inhibition like in obsessions. Thoughtless impulsivity is one of the characteristics of addictions. Thoughtful inhibition is one of the characteristics of psychosomatic illnesses.

Modalities

The theory, however, accounts for addictions according to the modality or resource class used to the extreme. For instance, emotional, verbal, physical, and sexual abuse are ways of denying the importance (status) of another individual. Multiple or addictive love relationships indicate disturbances in the area of intimacy (i.e., love). Both classes of addiction indicate disturbances in the modality of presence. Extreme TV watching, reading, or religious fanaticism, at the exclusion of other activities, indicates disturbance in receiving or giving information. Excessive exercise derives from an imbalance in services. Both classes of addictions indicate disturbance in the modality of performance at the expense of presence. Substance abuse, alcoholism, and eating disorders are based on the extreme use of goods. An additional category (omitted from the previous classification of addictions, and indicative of an extreme use of possessions), is hoarding (Frost & Gross, 1993; Greenberg, 1987). Gambling and excessive spending derive from the abuse of money. Both classes of addictions indicate disturbance in the modality of production, again without presence.

Selfhood and Personality Propensities in Addictions

Figure 11.1 illustrates how the selfhood model relates to addictions. In selfulness, addictions manifest themselves as behaviors that indicate positive overinvolvement with certain objects or individuals, as seen in art collections, hard work, making money, providing pro-bono services, or volunteering for charitable causes. In positive addictions, therefore, the behavior is self- and other-enhancing rather than debasing (Figure 11.1). Addictions proper are represented by all three dysfunctional personality propensities. However, selfishness, with its imperviousness to corrective, external feedback, would be more likely to be found in addictions. Selflessness would more likely be found in psychosomatic illnesses. Both personality propensities overlap with no-self, depending on the severity of the addiction and of the psychosomatic illness. For instance, sexual addictions involving incest and many paraphilias belong in the no-self category. The relationship between psychosomatic illnesses and no-self is still unclear and needs further conceptual and empirical work.

Figure 11.1 Toward a Classification of Addictions from a Model of Selfhood

Selfhood and Gender Differences

There are definite gender differences in addictions (L'Abate, Farrar, & Serritella, 1992). For instance, alcoholism and gambling tend to be more pronounced in men, and excessive shopping or hoarding tend to be more frequent among women. The role of gender differences in psychosomatic illnesses may not be as prominent as it is in addictions. However, if psychosomatic illnesses are more likely to be found in selflessness, then it follows that these conditions would be more frequent in women than in men.

CONCLUSION

This chapter has considered addictions and psychosomatic illnesses from the viewpoint of developmental competence theory. The former derive from externalization processes, where approach is greater than avoidance and discharge is greater than delay. The latter derive from internalization processes, where avoidance is greater than approach and delay is greater than discharge.

PART THREE

Applications of the Theory to Psychological Interventions

CHAPTER 12

Prevention

> To my mind, the most important development in psychoanalysis in recent years has been the growing recognition that intrapsychic phenomena must be understood in the context of the larger interactional systems in which they take form. (Stolorow, 1991, p. 17)

If the developmental competence theory is valid, then the goal of any psychological intervention, whether preventive or psychotherapeutic, is to help people learn how to love and to negotiate better than they have done heretofore. Love and intimacy may make the world go 'round, but most dysfunctional people (*AA* and *RR* relationship styles) do not know how to love or how to negotiate effectively. They may undoubtedly love (there is no question about its receptive, input aspects). However, there are many questions about their ability to love expressively, on the output side. Most dysfunctional individuals do not know how to attribute importance to self or others, or how to be intimate in constructive ways. If therapists do not teach them, who will?

This chapter introduces the reader to the context of change, a differentiation of psychological interventions, and suggestions about applications of long-distance writing (LDW) and computer-assisted training (CAT) as preventive, secondary interventions. Nonverbal and verbal interventions are discussed in the next chapter.

THE CONTEXT OF CHANGE: THE MAGICAL NUMBER 3

Once a definition of *what* constitutes change is developed and the conditions necessary for change are specified, the question arises as to *where* change is to take place. This question is answered, in part, in Stolorow's statement at the beginning of this chapter: "larger interactional systems." Next, a definition of what comprises these systems is needed. It is a given that change must take place within intimate relationships and within the individuals who determine those relationships. Furthermore, change should be specified to occur in relationships that matter—those that are enduring, committed, close, prolonged, and based on interdependence. This specification is not sufficient: these relationships are embedded into a cultural context that needs specification as well.

Contextually, dysfunctionality takes place at various individual, dyadic, or multirelational levels, especially in the family, which is a whole unit of interacting personalities. Change at the individual level does not take place without impinging on and influencing change in those who live close by or who are related by blood, legal, or emotional ties.

A more comprehensive viewpoint, above and beyond interdependent relationships, would pinpoint where change is to take place when larger interactional systems are considered as representing the context for change. By breaking down the rather general and encompassing term *context* into three specific settings, a matrix of three larger interactional systems is obtained. This matrix includes: (a) communication media through which nonverbal, verbal, and written resources are exchanged; (b) settings—home, school/work, and leisure time; and (c) resource modalities (Figure 12.1).

Communication Media

The three media of communication—verbal, nonverbal, and written—as summarized in Table 12.1, are fairly well defined inside and outside a professional help-giver's office. In addition to the three media mentioned here, there is the kinesthetic medium, which is as important as the other three but which is included in the nonverbal medium. Ideally, an isomorphic process should be going

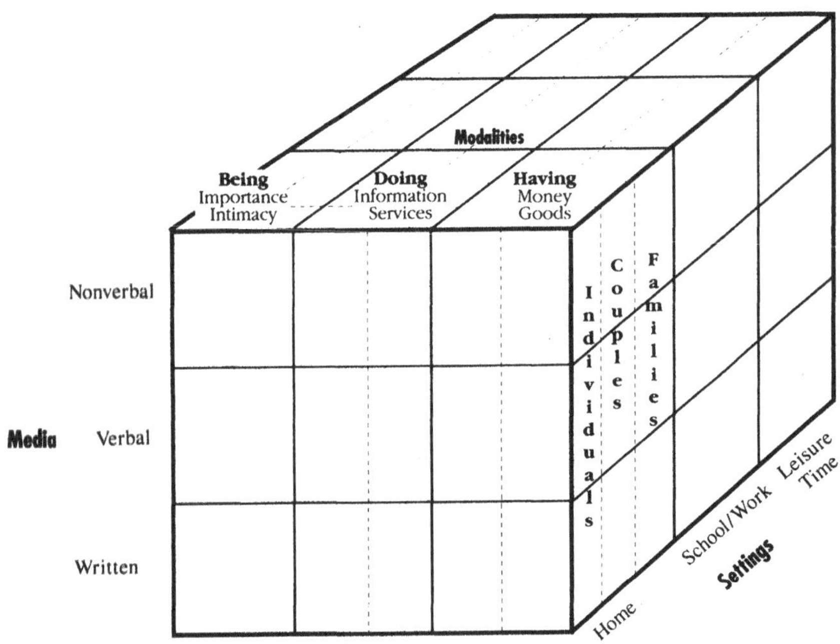

Figure 12.1 The Context of Change

TABLE 12.1 Media of Communication and Functions of Intervention Settings

Media of Communication	Functions of Intervention Settings: Professional's Office — Inside	Professional's Office — Outside
Verbal	Evaluation Direction of Intervention Emotional Support Confrontation of Issues Motivation for Change Generalization to Outside	Dialogue with: self, partner, relatives and family of origin, friends, children, and coworkers
Nonverbal	Awareness exercises Calisthenics, aerobics Dance, art, play Biofeedback Kinesiology	Sports and exercise Nutrition-diet Vitamins Meditation

Written	Structure	Content	Goals	Abstraction
	Open Focused Guided Programmed	Traumatic vs. Trivial	Cathartic vs. Prescriptive	Concrete vs. Abstract

Adapted from L'Abate, 1994b.

on between the therapist's office and the other three settings: home, school/work, and leisure. As Table 12.1 shows, psychological interventions, thus far, have been used in one of the three available communication media. The traditional overreliance on the verbal medium at the expense of the other two has severely curtailed the options available to therapists and their clients, either in prevention or crisis intervention. In the future, change for mental health professionals will include learning how to use judiciously the other two media of communication—nonverbal and written—in addition to the verbal. Once these two media are added to the preventive and therapeutic armamentarium, the other changes will consist of decreasing the number of individual sessions and increasing group, couple, and family sessions. With these two changes in place, it will be easier to help more people per unit of professional time than ever before.

Selfhood and Reactions to Interventions

If the selfhood model is at all valid, it would be expected and predicted that selful and selfish individuals would respond minimally to external interventions, whether preventive or psychotherapeutic, but for different reasons. Selful individuals would profit from enrichment-oriented interventions. However, their basic propensity would not need to change because it is positive toward self and other. Selfish individuals, on the other hand, would resist external interventions, believing that others need to change, not themselves. Selfish people can be given help only if they want it. However, because the chances of failure with them are so high, it would be important to consider inexpensive and mass-oriented ways of helping them within the context of the immediate and structured rewards found only in detention homes and jails.

Selfless individuals would profit from any form of intervention because their need to change is as intense as their personal pain. No-self individuals need help the most, but, by the very nature of their inherent propensity to produce defeat in both self and other, engaging them in a meaningful and successful dialogue is exceedingly difficult. Hence, ways and means must be found to help those who need and want help the most: selfless and no-self people.

Settings

The family, the most immediate and major focus of intervention, may be assumed to be the primary setting for change, but it is not necessarily the only setting available. Other settings, each with its own peculiar and specific task demands, also influence people. School/work and leisure-time activities, for instance, have a great deal of influence. Depending on one's priorities, they may have more influence than the family setting. Participation in religious activities or in addiction-like sports regimens, such as running, can have a stronger influence than either family or work settings (Yates, 1991). Leisure time refers to whatever time is left after taking care of home and work responsibilities. This time includes transitory settings that are necessary for enjoyment and survival but do not have the permanency and primary survival value of home and school/work.

From this vantage point, psychological interventions help people change their investments in performance and production into investments in presence, i.e., the ability to love and to be intimate. Admittedly, performance and production are necessary for survival but they are not sufficient for full enjoyment. Dysfunctional people need help to increase presence, that is, to become more emotionally available to themselves and to important others. Changes need to be made in how clients prioritize the relative values of media, modalities, and settings. By changing one part of the context, change may reverberate to other parts, producing the ripple effect so dear to systems thinking.

Given three communication media, three settings where exchanges take place, and three exchange modalities, a more specific framework of larger interactional systems is obtained. This framework defines the overall context of change (Figure 12.1). When this context is specified, one can delineate in greater detail the major maxim of systems thinking: *Change in one part of this context may affect other parts of the same context.* Interconnectedness and wholism are useful systems concepts that are represented concretely by the analogy of the ripple effect.

The framework summarized in Figure 12.1 demonstrates some advantages over traditional systems thinking that were not possible before. Manageably *finite* and *limited* processes are proposed rather than infinite and unlimited ones. These processes are more *specific* and *detailed*, compared to systems thinking's general, undefined, and vague concepts. They are also more *concrete* than the abstract notions of systems thinking (L'Abate & Colondier, 1987; Merkel & Searight, 1992; Searight & Merkel, 1991). The characteristics of finiteness, specificity, and concreteness make this framework more verifiable than systems thinking, which, as a whole, is difficult to evaluate and verify.

How can people who hurt but who do not see themselves as needing professional help be reached? Pennebaker (1990) found that a great many seemingly well-functioning undergraduates admitted to many more hurts ("traumas") than he was expecting—an indication that hurts are widespread in the general population. Instead of psychotherapeutic applications, some mass-oriented, preventive, psychoeducational, or paratherapeutic methodologies are needed. There are not enough preventers or psychotherapists to deal with all the people who hurt. The methodology used by Pennebaker (1990) (asking people to write about their hurts for fifteen to twenty minutes a day for four days) can be applied to as many people as are willing to follow this focused instruction. Writing is a more cost-effective medium than spoken words, especially when one must reach large masses of people.

A CONTINUUM OF INTERVENTIONS

Any positive intervention should improve the well-being and functioning of any individual, couple, or family. This section is devoted to practical ways of discriminating, at least conceptually, among three types of interventions that are differentiated according to the *type of activity* demanded by each level. For instance, primary prevention can be defined as *proactive*, tertiary prevention as *reactive*, and secondary prevention as *paraactive*, that is, taking place alongside activities that are either proactive or reactive but fall somewhere between the two. Secondary prevention practices may be used while the symptomatic behavior is occurring, even though a crisis requiring more severe interventions may not have taken place. Thus, long-distance writing (LDW) and computer-assisted training (CAT) are secondary prevention activities that can take place alongside preventive and psychotherapeutic activities.

The distinction among the three types of interventions—pro-, para-, and reactive—applies also to a definition of therapeutic practices, that is, face-to-face interactions between people in crisis and professional helpers, as discussed in the next chapter. Using the notion of therapy as a tertiary prevention, there can be: *pre*therapeutic practices in primary prevention, *para*therapeutic practices in secondary prevention, and therapeutic practices proper in tertiary prevention. How can these practices be differentiated further?

By designating types of prevention according to activity and practices, a tentative list of at least 14 qualitative criteria (thus far, admittedly, subjective and tentative) emerges. This list allows distinctions and differentiations among the three types of preventive interventions, according to the degree and extent of:

1. Risk and impairment.
2. Reversibility of behavior.
3. Probability of breakdown.
4. Characteristics of the population.
5. Ability to learn.
6. Goals.
7. Type of involvement.
8. Recommendations.
9. Cost.
10. Effectiveness.
11. Personnel.
12. Types of intervention.
13. Structure.
14. Specificity.

An elaboration of each item on this list follows.

1. A traditional way of differentiating the three types of prevention is according to the degree of *risk and impairment.* To decrease the chances of future breakdown, most individuals, couples, and families, even functional ones, need improvement in their competencies, coping skills, functionalities, and enjoyment of life. As many as half to two-thirds, if not three-fourths, of this population do not cope as well as the rest. They are at greater risk than the others, as the assumption of individual differences would predict. Hence, risk assessment is necessary to discriminate highly competent from less competent individuals and families. In an at-risk population, a certain percentage (depending on criteria yet to be determined, and according to the behavior targeted) will need specific help to prevent further acting out (and incarceration), addictions, depression, mental illness, and suicide. These individuals and their families may not be willing or able to use tertiary prevention approaches, which deal rehabilitatively with emotional crises and dysfunctionalities *after* breakdown has taken place. Families in crisis have an identified patient and are not able to cope by themselves. Examples are: a family that has discovered incest, an adult child of an alcoholic who has developed an addiction, or an emotional disturbance precipitated by an impending divorce.

A more specific example, provided to sharpen this differentiation, is prevention of sexual abuse. The primary prevention of sexual abuse would consist conceptually in helping *all children,* because all are at risk for sexual abuse. By the same token, most adults who were abused as children are at risk for being sexual abusers of children. Out of these two general populations—the ones at risk for abuse and the potential abusers—secondary prevention would take place with children who have been abused at least once and with perpetrators who may have been caught at least once, before they go to jail or receive harsher punishment. Both groups need help, but this help need not be therapeutic; it could be paratherapeutic. Tertiary prevention deals with people who have abused or have been abused and who are now in crisis because this behavior has come to the attention of authorities or has reached a similar extreme.

2. *Reversibility of behavior* refers to the probability that a temporarily disturbed or disturbing behavior may go back to its original normal (i.e., not disturbed or disturbing) state. What may start as a temporary reaction, if handled improperly, may increase in duration, frequency, and intensity and thus become resistant to intervention. The more resistant to intervention a particular behavior becomes, the greater the difficulty in returning to an original state of functionality. For instance, an adult child of alcoholic parents, just by being so labeled, is at much greater risk of becoming an alcoholic or an addict with some other form of dependency. After the addiction becomes a reality, it may be much more difficult to treat than if help had come earlier, during the formative years (L'Abate, Farrar, & Serritella, 1992). During childhood, however, the individual would not have been capable of realizing the dangers transferred from the family of origin.

In any random population, one can expect that, without intervention, 33% of that population, at best, will continue to function relatively well, even under stress, or will be able to go back to a satisfactory level of functionality after a crisis. Of the remaining 67%, 33% to 67% would be at risk for some type of breakdown. Without intervention of any kind, the disturbing condition might get worse and produce a crisis, which then may or may not be reversible. There is no reversibility after a murder or suicide. Thus, the odds in favor of reversibility decrease as pathology and dysfunctionality increase.

3. Many of the listed criteria overlap when one is dealing with the *probability of breakdown.* In primary prevention, attention is given to populations in which everybody has *potential* for breakdown, i.e., children of alcoholic parents would be at greater risk for future addictions than would children of nonalcoholic parents. Secondary prevention is for populations in need, such as children of alcoholics who have already started to drink or who show indications of incipient addictions. Their behavior indicates that breakdown is now a much greater *possibility* than in primary prevention. In tertiary prevention, where a breakdown of some kind has usually taken place (a crisis), the possibility has become a *reality.*

Compared to secondary prevention, primary prevention deals with a much larger pool—even up to 100%, when education is used as a preventive approach. Out of this large pool, some persons may not profit from primary prevention and may need secondary prevention instead. Examples are: (a) abused and neglected children; (b) children of divorce, of unwed mothers, or of psychiatrically ill parents; (c) children from single-parent families; (d) families who have lower socioeconomic status (SES) or are unemployed; or (e) children and adult children of alcoholics, criminals, or addicts.

Secondary prevention deals with dropouts who do not or cannot profit from primary prevention approaches. Among them are: (a) acting-out or runaway adolescents (and their families); (b) depressed children and adolescents (and their families); (c) learning-disabled or underachieving children and adolescents (and their families); and (d) adult children of alcoholics.

Tertiary prevention deals with populations that cannot use either primary or secondary prevention approaches. With appropriate help, however, many critical and clinical families may eventually be able to learn from secondary and even from primary prevention approaches, especially after their crisis has been successfully resolved.

4. As far as *characteristics of the population* are concerned, the key factor is an ability to identify individuals and families who are more at risk than others. Degree of risk can be ascertained fairly easily when certain predictors are present. For instance: (a) SES may be a predictor of a higher possibility of acting out or of psychopathology; (b) gender differences may be predictors of greater risk for acting-out disorders in males and depression in females; and (c) children of single-parent families may be at greater risk for delinquency or addictions than children from intact families. If these predictors are compounded (e.g., low SES plus a single-parent family with an alcoholic parent), being *at risk* changes to being *in need.* The population may still be nonclinical if there is no identified patient and no one is in crisis. For example, the adult child of an alcoholic parent may be labeled ACOA but not yet diagnosable as alcoholic or addicted. An adolescent child of an alcoholic single parent with a low SES may be *in need,* especially if his or her academic performance is weak and school conduct is poor. If this adolescent is diagnosable as a status offender or a prejuvenile, it may be only a question of time before he or she acts out to the point of requiring the attention of authorities.

When this possibility becomes reality, a label becomes a diagnosis. Children from single-parent families with low SES are at greater risk for delinquency or addiction than are children from intact families. A population may be nonclinical in the sense of not yet having an identified patient (IP), and not being in a crisis or requiring professional help. However, this population may already have a label, which often is a precursor to a clinical classification.

5. An *ability to learn* from experience, from training, and from education is another important way of discriminating among the three types of preventive interventions. The greater the degree of psychological health, the greater the ability to learn. The greater the degree of pathology and dysfunctionality, the greater the inability to learn. Populations at risk in general can learn from almost any experience and training. However, at risk is a very wide criterion; it includes practically everybody. Out of this population, a certain percentage of individuals, couples, and families cannot profit from primary prevention approaches because they are too troubled, too conflictual, too disturbed, or too stressed. They will need secondary or even tertiary prevention approaches.

After these families have been helped to decrease stress, disturbance, and conflict, they may profit from secondary or primary prevention.

6. What are the *goals* of the three types of prevention? The main goal of primary prevention is to increase interpersonal competence and resistance to stress and breakdown. The goal of secondary prevention is to decrease stress and the chance of a probable crisis while increasing competence through learning to curb problem behavior. The goal of tertiary prevention is to restore individuals, couples, and families to their original (or at least a minimal) level of functionality, or to help them achieve a greater level of functionality than they had in the past.

All preventive approaches share the same goal of helping people learn new and more positive ways of interacting, that is: *to love each other better and to negotiate conflictul issues with a minimum of acrimony.* These ways of interacting should eventually translate into greater competence and resistance to breakdown. This newly acquired level of functionality will help clients during the long haul. If clients learn new and more positive ways of relating with one another, these new ways should allow them to withstand future stresses with a minimal possibility of breakdown.

7. What *type of involvement* can be asked of people who need help? In primary prevention, this involvement can only be voluntary; it certainly cannot be forced by external pressures. Families should be informed of their possible choices. For instance, the community may offer various parenting classes. A couple that does not like one class may switch to another class that offers a different approach. The degree of choice begins to disappear if the behavior of one family member starts to disturb the rest of the family or the community (school, neighborhood, and so on). The behavior may not have reached a critical level, but it may be unpleasant and worrisome. A problem may be denied by the family ("Boys will be boys"), and especially by the member who is exhibiting the disturbing behavior, and the denial may exacerbate the situation to the point of producing a crisis. The family may then deny any awareness of precursors that should have alerted them to a need for help—a pattern found in the families of many suicides.

Although involvement may not be obligatory in primary prevention, the degree of forced choice increases with need and crisis. A functional family may choose not to participate in a primary prevention program; a semifunctional or dysfunctional family may find itself without a choice. For example, the school principal may recommend that both parents participate in a parent-training group or that their acting-out youngster receive tutoring. If the disturbing behavior continues in spite of the parents' receiving parenting training, the whole family may be referred to a mental health clinic for crisis intervention.

8. Clergy, teachers, physicians, and lawyers are among the professionals who make *recommendations* for the best welfare of the community. They need to be educated about the preventive efforts available in the community to address a particular problem. Many families refuse to follow recommendations because of fear of and resistance to change and because they need to protect

themselves. The greater the degree of resistance to recommendations, the greater the likelihood of eventual serious disturbance and a need for crisis intervention. How people use feedback from informed and caring professionals tells a great deal about their level of functionality. Inability to follow recommendations and resistance to change are two of the many criteria used in reaching conclusions about anyone's functionality.

9. *Costs* are usually much less in primary prevention because most approaches at this level are based on groups of individuals, couples, or families. These approaches, to be effective, are mass-oriented and relatively inexpensive per unit of professional time. Exercise and diet are much cheaper than a heart by-pass operation that could have been prevented if precautions had been taken years before surgery was needed. Secondary prevention may be a bit more expensive than primary prevention. However, secondary prevention has not been practiced long enough to be evaluated for its efficiency. Tertiary prevention costs more because the time of professionals is more expensive, treatment takes longer, and it is much more difficult to treat symptomatic behavior that often took years (even generations!) to develop. At best, tertiary prevention may help as many as two-thirds of the people in crisis who come for help. What happens to the other third, who cannot be helped or do not want any help? Secondary prevention approaches may become helpful here, although certain types of families may not want to change and may refuse help of any kind. Hospitalization, incarceration, or lifelong medication may then become inevitable.

10. *Effectiveness* and the cost/effectiveness ratio deserve serious consideration. Although psychotherapy and crisis intervention are expensive because of the degree of professional expertise and the time required, primary and secondary prevention approaches need not be extremely expensive if competent middle-level, paraprofessional, preprofessional, and nonprofessional personnel are available. Effectiveness would be even greater if therapists relied on primary and secondary prevention approaches to boost families' levels of competence. Integrating all three approaches and combining them synergistically would create a much greater impact than a single approach could have.

11. We need to rely on new and different types of *personnel.* A professional middle-level, para-, and preprofessional hierarchy alerts us to the need for different levels of expertise. The sheer number of people at risk, in need, and in crisis makes it impossible for existing professional preventers and therapists to help them all. The number of people in crisis alone is sufficient to keep existing professionals busy for some time to come. The newcomers to the profession might be less highly credentialed, but their human qualifications would allow them to learn to administer specific pre- and paratherapeutic programs under the supervision, support, and direction of higher professionals.

12. *Types of intervention* or prevention must be sensitive to differences in ability to learn. The degree of functionality is directly related to the ability to learn and to retain learning. The more functional the individual, the greater the ability to learn. Dysfunctional people in crisis have a deficit in their ability to learn. Remedial methods that may work with one person may not work

with another. Very likely, individual differences, predicated on SES, motivation, and personality propensities make it possible for some people to learn and create barriers for others. Hence, different methods need to be applied. Operationally, it should be possible to distinguish what could be called an enrichment approach for primary prevention and a more specific approach (i.e., programmed materials) for secondary prevention. As discussed in Chapter 3, personality propensities do predict how individuals will react to interventions. Selfless and no-self individuals may react well to verbal and nonverbal interventions, but both types of intervention may be useless with selfish individuals, who are more interested in conning a professional than in changing themselves.

The relevant issue among the various modalities of learning is *interchangeability.* For instance, although many primary prevention programs, such as structured enrichment (L'Abate & Weinstein, 1987; L'Abate & Young, 1987), were originally designed to be administered orally, by a trainer or a facilitator, to functional and semifunctional families, they can be administered in writing, as though they were programmed materials, or by computer. In their written format, these programs are designed to be self-administered and self-instructional. The intent is to have families complete them on their own at home. Programmed materials are administered in addition to or as alternatives to crisis-oriented face-to-face therapy or primary prevention approaches. Structured enrichment or programmed materials can be administered orally by mental health assistants, provided they are willing to use *verbatim* a script that follows a clear and definite plan.

This interchangeability suggests that the three different types of prevention can be distinguished, among other criteria, on the basis of the medium of communication. In writing, both structured enrichment and programmed materials can be administered as self-instructional approaches that would be complementary to any face-to-face approach, either primary or tertiary. Primary and secondary prevention programs rely mostly on written blueprints. Tertiary prevention usually relies on the immediately exchanged spoken word, with little if any structure to program this exchange. If no structure is present, it is nearly impossible to record the process and study it. However, the media of exchange—the oral and the written—can be used interchangeably. Both impinge on the third medium of interpersonal and therapeutic exchange, the nonverbal.

13. Differences in methods should clarify the three types of prevention. For instance, the degree of *structure* is quite high in primary prevention programs. The intended audience knows beforehand the general topic (e.g., parenting), the number of sessions it will take to complete the course, and the cost. These characteristics may be difficult or impossible to state in tertiary prevention. No topic is stated beforehand, except: how the client defines a problem. The number of sessions is hard to predict, and the cost (if not to the client, to the agency providing the help) is high because of the professional time required.

14. Concerning the degree of *specificity,* the topic to be addressed in primary prevention programs is very pointed (e.g., parenting). All parents taking

the course are subjected to the same treatment: parenting, in all its practical principles and applications, is considered in terms of parenting in general, not the needs of a particular couple. This focus on generality can be called a "funnel approach"; that is, everyone who attends this course gets the same treatment. In secondary and tertiary prevention, which includes LDW and CAT, the approach is much more individualized, reflecting the specific needs of a particular individual, couple, or family.

Using Preventive Practices before, during, or after Psychotherapy

By enlarging and expanding therapeutic practices through the addition of nonverbal and written media, rather than relying only on the spoken word, a much wider range of problems may be addressed. For instance, nonverbal approaches may help individuals who are lower in their intellectual and educational functioning, and who are not as comfortable relying on the spoken word as professionals are or for whom English is a second language. This population could include clients with lower SES or with character disorders, who are action rather than introspection-oriented.

Evaluation as Standard Operating Procedure

The normative state of affairs in the mental health field consists of professionals intervening without objective evaluation and researchers concentrating on evaluation instruments without interventions. There is a great deal of research on evaluative instruments independent of interventions. One really does not need to present evidence to support this conclusion; a perusal of the majority of mental health and clinical psychology journals will support it. However, more often than not, research for evaluation instruments is performed without pairing it with interventional processes and outcomes. As a result, neither the field of evaluation nor the field of psychological intervention can profit from the experience of the other. They are two completely separate fields of experience with little if any mutual feedback. Combinations of both into one process are few and far between. Usually, a research grant is needed to combine them.

Briefly, no matter how much we may justify and rationalize the importance of evaluation, this practice has failed in being an integral part of psychological interventions. Most mental health professionals still rely on the interview alone (the spoken medium) to arrive at an understanding of what is going on in their clients. They fail because of the inadequacy of the speech medium for direct treatment. As long as evaluation is based on the spoken word, treatment planning and treatment in general will be based on a catch-as-catch-can basis and not on rational or even empirical grounds. Only if part of the treatment consists of written homework assignments can evaluation be linked successfully with treatment.

Evaluation performed before intervention, to meet external demands or routines, is limited in its value unless performed again at the end of the intervention.

However, unless a contract to this effect is made at the very outset, many clients who quit prematurely will not be reexamined at the end. Is a rationale for reevaluation necessary? How can an assessment be made on whether clients have been helped? How can therapists distinguish whether their clients have improved by feeling better or by negotiating a better life style? How can therapists rely on self-reported comfort when no external criterion can indicate whether changes have indeed taken place?

Is the interview sufficient in suggesting treatment planning and predicting treatment progress? It is definitely necessary, but is it sufficient? Without some objective ways of verifying whether change has taken place, how can professionals document their competence? A solution to this problem would be to charge clients for both pre- and posttreatment evaluation from the very beginning of therapy. If they drop out of treatment without reevaluation, they lose the amount prepaid. Pre- and posttreatment evaluation would not, of course, be the only means of evaluating clinical practice. Number of sessions, rates of dropouts and no-shows, and self-reports of clients' satisfaction could all be used as indicators of substantive professional competence.

A major issue in psychological interventions, both preventive and psychotherapeutic, involves the conditions under which a specific linkage between evaluation and intervention can be achieved. As long as psychological interventions are based solely on the verbal medium, this linkage will be difficult and expensive—if not impossible—to establish, except among a handful of specialized researchers (Haynes, 1993; Haynes, Spain, & Oliveira, 1993; Karoly, 1993a; Mash & Hunsley, 1993; Neru & Neru, 1993). Like the search for the Holy Grail, this linkage will remain a hoped-for but unattainable and expensive chimera reserved for few (re)searchers. Only when intervention is based, at least in part, on the written medium can this specific linkage be established easily and inexpensively, as demonstrated in Chapter 3.

If clients were evaluated on a pre- and posttreatment basis as a standard operating procedure, the need to make clinical procedures open to scrutiny and inspection from outsiders might be obviated. Lacking this practice, however, the question arises as to how professionals are credentialed by state agencies and how these credentials allow practice to occur within existing legal and ethical guidelines. Practitioners' credentials have been granted on the basis of paper-and-pen examinations rather than visible, observed, hands-on practice, as is required, for instance, for advanced certification as a board diplomate. Opening clinical files to external scrutiny would raise a great many issues of confidentiality. Yet, without such scrutiny, the whole issue of professional competence is left open and unanswered.

LONG-DISTANCE WRITING AND COMPUTER ASSISTED TRAINING

Long-distance writing (LDW) and its most immediate applications to computer-assisted training (CAT) have the potential to become the third avenue of service delivery (behind psychotherapy and medication) in mental health prevention. By now, the evidence for the beneficial effects of writing, in its many parapreventive and paratherapeutic applications, is well established. Most of this research has used a focused type of writing. Respondents are asked to either talk into a microphone or write about traumatic events in their lives (experimental groups) or about trivial topics (control group). This format has been used extensively in the variety of studies cited previously. Talking into a microphone or writing about traumatic events in one's life improves immune system functioning and reduces the number of titers in the Epstein–Barr virus (Esterling et al., 1994).

A more structured type of writing—programmed writing—is a recent trend that has produced a variety of workbooks about many mental health problems in individuals, couples, and families, including depression, anxiety, and conflict resolution, among others (L'Abate, 1986, 1992b, 1996a; L'Abate, Boyce, Fraizer, & Russ, 1992; L'Abate, Hamm, Russ, & Bird, in press).

The major difference between focused and programmed writing, beyond their respective formats, lies in the latter being more amenable to testing hypotheses because of its greater structure. For instance, a recent study, reviewed in Chapter 3, tested the hypothesis that personality propensities were related to different levels of depression and differential outcome to two depression writing programs. The greater structure of programmed writing, regardless of the topic, allows for greater control and specificity than are possible with focused writing. This comparison should not be interpreted as a criticism of focused writing, which is still an important avenue of cathartic expression and information gathering worthy of widespread parapreventive and paratherapeutic applications.

Programmed writing lends itself to comparative theory testing (Stiles, 1994) in ways that would be difficult to achieve with less structured forms of writing (open, focused, or guided). As demonstrated in Chapter 3, programmed writing can be made isomorphic with specific models, a feature that is absent in less structured forms of writing. Programmed writing helps standardize interventions in a more uniform and economic way than is possible with traditional alternatives such as psychotherapy treatment manuals, stage models of psychotherapy, and standardized intervention modules (Kiesler, 1994). The issue here, regardless of writing structure, is to find out what kind of personality characteristics correlate with improvement or nonimprovement in writing assignments, as discussed in Chapter 3.

As long as psychological interventions continue to rely on the medium of speech, progress will be slow and difficult. Verbal messages from a professional, no matter how beneficial in their intent and quality, can be distorted, demeaned, and forgotten by upset people. Hence, progress can take place in a more cost-effective way if interpretations and homework assignments are administered in writing rather than orally. People are in trouble because they have relied heavily on the words spoken in anger or during periods of stress or conflict. To help establish or reestablish a sense of control, clients need to learn to deal with themselves and with each other *by regular appointments and in writing.*

The results from programmed interventions also support the use of writing as a parapreventive and paratherapeutic alternative or adjunct. As shown in Chapter 3, most subjects improve their depression scores regardless of whether the program is matched or mismatched to their particular depression. LDW and its computer applications (CAT), therefore, could join medication and psychotherapy to form a trio of cost-effective, mass-oriented avenues of service delivery.

Background and Rationale for LDW and CAT with Criminal Offenders

Applying traditional psychotherapy to the treatment of delinquency and criminality evokes an illustrative analogy. Efforts to teach primates to talk like human beings occupied quite a few researchers for quite a few years, but were extremely limited by the physiology of the animals' vocal cords. Researchers wanted them to behave like human beings, and the primates simply were not able to do so! When these efforts were abandoned and the primates were trained to perform according to their asset modalities of eye-hand coordination, a tremendous explosion in successful research efforts occurred. Similarly, with acting-out criminal behavior, therapists have tried to use the therapeutic modality (ear-mouth) that is applied to mostly normal or neurotic people. Instead, why not use the eye-hand modality preferred by action-oriented criminals? It leads toward more cost-effective use of computers rather than time-consuming and expensive face-to-face verbal contact with a professional counselor.

The need for cost-effective programs was spotlighted by the inadequacies, if not the failures, of traditional face-to-face talk-psychotherapy with offenders and character-disordered persons (Barley, 1986; Doren, 1987; Kadzin, 1984; Lester, 1981; Lion, 1978; Watkins, 1983). Barley (1986) noted: "Unfortunately, the empirical support for these forms of cognitive or cognitive-behavioral treatment is not extensive" (p. 166). Even when recommending these forms of treatment, Barley qualified the recommendation by observing that the "research base with these persons is limited" (p. 183).

This conclusion is shared by many other investigators and reviewers (Doren, 1987; Hirschi, 1969; Lester, 1981; Reid, 1978). Frustrations with traditional face-to-face individual psychotherapy are present, whether the inpatient or the outpatient treatment of psychopaths is considered (Lion, 1978; Steadman, *undated*). Sources of these frustrations are the high attrition rates and the failures in using what is considered an inappropriate and expensive treatment for impulsive and acting-out individuals. Psychotherapies based on face-to-face contact with verbal interaction may well be the treatment of choice with neurotic, depressed, and internalizing (i.e., selfless or no-self) individuals. However, different modalities of prevention and treatment need to be considered with impulsive or acting-out individuals.

The human element of direct, face-to-face relationships needs to be minimized with acting-out individuals, although it cannot and should not be eliminated. Anyone working with or attempting to work with acting-out individuals knows that prolonged face-to-face oral contacts need to be minimized. These contacts are too expensive (i.e., time-consuming) and, ultimately, too ineffective for the professional time and energy that they require. They are not cost-effective (Barley, 1986; Watkins, 1983).

In reviewing the outcome studies of behavioral and cognitive therapies, Watkins (1983) noted that most of these studies suffer from three main methodological deficits: (a) too little follow-up, (b) high rates of relapse, and (c) confounding of a specific treatment with concomitant interventions: "The change mechanisms are poorly understood, even in the studies producing the most impressive outcome and maintenance" (p. 626). This conclusion begs the question that any rehabilitative program needs to specify: What assumptions are made to explain what Watkins (1983) called "change mechanisms"? Among the many change mechanisms needed for working with acting-out individuals, cognitive control (R) and awareness (Aw) are of paramount consideration. Acting-out individuals uniformly demonstrate an inability to delay and to think before they act (Doren, 1987). Deficits in cognitive control need to be viewed within the context of overall assumptions about criminal behavior.

These pessimistic conclusions are reinforced by Kazdin's (1984) review of treatment approaches for early conduct disorders in childhood and adolescence:

> The plethora of available techniques might be viewed as a healthy sign that the field has not become rigidly set on one or two techniques. On the other hand, the diversity of available procedures suggests that no particular approach has been shown to ameliorate antisocial behavior. Although there are many different techniques, relatively little well-controlled outcome evidence can be presented on their behalf. . . . At present, no treatment has been clearly shown to . . . controvert the untoward consequences to which it often leads. (p. 74)

In commenting on the necessity for specification of treatment, Kazdin (1984) considered the importance of treatment conceptualization. Treatment procedures should be specified in a manual that includes written materials to guide the therapist in attaining the specific goals of treatment. In this manual, the therapist would find procedures, techniques, topics, themes, therapeutic maneuvers, and activities because: "With few exceptions, treatments for antisocial behaviors are rarely specified in a format that would permit their careful evaluation or training of other therapists" (p. 92).

Given the less-than-optimistic results, one is bound to conclude that talk in general (and, in particular, talk therapies with acting-out individuals) has failed to produce the hoped-for outcome. As in all generalizations in human behavior, exceptions can be found. No proposed approach has yet identified which acting-out individuals profit by a form of intervention and which do not. In the absence of specific identification, therapists may need to adopt a successive-sieves approach, starting with the least expensive protocol. If it is not successful, a more expensive approach is adopted, and attempts progress from the least to the most expensive available. Perhaps no acting-out individual should receive individual or group psychotherapy unless he or she has mastered successfully the less expensive forms of treatment, such as LDW or CAT.

In addition to being questionably effective with offenders, traditional talk-oriented therapies are expensive because they demand a great deal of professional and semiprofessional time and effort. Costly professional involvement and energies could be used more advantageously and effectively if different and less expensive approaches were considered first. There is a need for inexpensive (i.e., non-time-consuming) for the helping professional or semiprofessional) approaches that will maximize changes in most aspects of personal and interpersonal functioning, affect, cognition, and behavior. To achieve this goal, self-administered, self-paced, criterion-oriented workbooks may be administered. Their written instructions must require written responses, and the behavioral criteria for improvement must be concrete and specific. These programs would require learning that can be translated into appropriate behavior. Critical thinking would be stressed, and progress would be directly linked to behavioral applications.

Popular ways of dealing with criminals—restitution, fines, specialized probation, electronically monitored confinement, and carefully organized volunteer efforts (Steadman, *undated*)—have two negative characteristics in common: (a) they put the offender in a passive position, and others, usually authority figures, take responsibility for the offender's actions, and (b) nothing new and positive—no novel pattern of thinking, behaving, or feeling—is taught to the offender. Under these conditions of forced inaction, it is practically impossible for the offender to learn anything constructive. How is the offender to change if all change is external and no effort is required to learn new and more helpful ways of behaving? All these conditions could be helpful, however, if, as part of a program of rehabilitation, the offender had to start working actively on change. Cost-effective, mass-produced workbooks in LDW and CAT could help offenders to learn new and better ways of behaving and relating. Like all modes of intervention, not all workbooks will work with all offenders. The task will be to find out which offenders will be helped by LDW and CAT and which ones will not. Perhaps workbook exercises could direct specific behaviors to take place in specific settings (behavioral in addition to written words), such as home, school/work (jail), and leisure. Maybe a reward for engaging in these behaviors may be built into the system of change. Just as criminal behaviors have rewards (and consequences, especially if the criminal is apprehended), non-criminal behavior might also be taught and rewarded.

To minimize costs and personal contacts and to maximize reflectivity and criticalness toward one's behavior, talking cannot be the main medium of reception, expression, and communication with offenders. Reliance on LDW and

CAT is imperative. Hence, the primary issue in a mass-oriented, public health approach to increasing reflection and introspection lies in reducing impulsivity. This issue assumes that reflection and impulsivity are inversely related. The main guideline with impulsive individuals consists of remembering that immediate, clear, and concrete consequences are the best way to increase motivation. For instance, motivation to change is highest among incarcerated criminals who want to get out of jail. They will complete any workbook if they think that completing it will increase their chances of freedom. Next in motivation are persons waiting for an appearance in court. If professionals make it clear that they will not appear in court with any client who has not completed a written program based on pre- and postprogram testing, compliance might be higher. A third level of motivation is money. For nonincarcerated offenders whose families are concerned about their impulsivity and acting out, it helps to have the total fee paid before the program is administered. A portion of the fee, usually one-third, is then refunded on completion. Because prolonged face-to-face contact with acting-out persons is time-consuming and usually unsatisfactory, it is often more practical to administer workbooks through the mail or via e-mail, with written feedback but with no face-to-face contact. Safeguards should be instituted to make sure that the writing is done by the offender and no one else. Perhaps concomitant behavioral changes, in addition to written assignments, could be built into the program and used as one resultant measure of success.

Cleckley (1976) maintained that individuals with poor impulse control are defective in their understanding of verbal symbols. To try to help them by using a talk method is a very expensive and quite futile proposition. Relatively inexpensive media, like LDW and CAT, can be applied with a minimum of a therapist's time and effort. Writing has been used as a mass-oriented education method for the creation and cultivation of critical thinking (Meyers, 1986; Stonewater, 1980). LDW and CAT, then, are the least expensive, most underutilized media in mental health and offender rehabilitation.

Stonewater (1980) commented that "the self-paced mastery instructional approach provides an effective way of teaching for problem solving . . . . Self-paced mastery instruction is a solution" (p. 54). Meyers (1986) suggested criteria for the design of effective written assignments that essentially follow a programmed instruction methodology: (a) gradual, stepwise development of skills; (b) a focus on real and relevant problems and issues; and (c) clear, unambiguous instructions. To be stressed is the importance of (a) concrete and specific instructions and information, and (b) wording that forces active generalization from the written word to behavior.

The technology of programmed instruction in LDW and CAT offers hope that this approach might ameliorate delinquent, resistant behavior patterns in a mass-oriented and cost-effective fashion. This inexpensive and replicable technology can be administered to as many people as can read and write. Those who profit by this approach i.e., those who have completed a program successfully can help other offenders who cannot read and write.

Workbooks for Impulsive or Acting-Out Individuals

Two social training workbooks (L'Abate, 1992a, 1996a) are available to improve internalization and decrease impulsivity. These workbooks should not be administered in groups because group discussion increases smoke screening and other manipulative and distracting functions of talking. A group approach also detracts from the participants' learning how to think and reflect. Workbooks should be administered individually, with just five minutes of face-to-face contact (at the most) allowed after completion or through visual, e-mail, or computer. Avoidance of *any* face-to-face contact is even better. Each lesson should be evaluated: Should it be done over, or can the offender proceed to the next lesson? When workbooks are administered through the mail or via computers, feedback should be given in writing, not verbally. In institutional settings, it is crucial that social training take place with the staff's full knowledge and support, and with a defined, specific plan of agreed-on consequences (positive and negative) for the completion or noncompletion of each lesson. Perhaps specific behavioral changes may also be required.

The purpose of the two social training workbooks is to help individuals who have deficits in their comprehension of social situations and express them, either potentially or actually, in impulsivity and acting out. More than likely, these individuals need to be under a court order, on probation or parole, or incarcerated. Without these restrictions, it would be difficult to obtain their cooperation. The workbooks are based on principles of semantic reconditioning that recognize and stress the power that certain key words (e.g., *self, control, law, love*) have over behavior. Each lesson ends with homework assignments that must be completed before the person proceeds to the next lesson. For offenders who cannot read and write, these workbooks might be administered by someone who has successfully completed both workbooks, either through LDW or CAT.

The workbooks constitute a self-administered, self-paced program for acting-out individuals. The first workbook (L'Abate, 1992b) consists of 16 basic terms or concepts that seem to govern a great deal of behavior, plus four optional terms that can be administered if needed. Each term forms a lesson that is explicated question by question. Requirements to fulfill specific behavioral criteria for the satisfactory completion of each lesson are stated. The second workbook (L'Abate, 1996a) consists of eight lessons that replicate how criminals think. For instance, one lesson deals with thinking: "I will not be caught." Another lesson consists of "Pushing the limits to the limit," and the next lesson deals with "I know better than anyone else." All are characteristic statements in the thinking of selfish individuals.

Like any new and possibly promising program, social training does not claim any magic cure or extraordinary treatment gains. In reviewing various behavioral and cognitive therapeutic approaches applied to individuals with deficits in impulse control, Watkins (1983) concluded by asking the crucial question that has been repeated for years: "For which type of client, with which impulse-control disorder, of what magnitude or severity, should each of the above treatment procedures be prescribed or warranted?" (p. 625). It can no longer be required that any therapeutic or rehabilitative program must achieve unqualified success for any population it claims to serve. Given that acting out, or criminal behavior, can be divided into at least ten personality groupings (Megargee & Bohn, 1979), an identification needs to be made: Which offenders would profit most from particular programs and which offenders will not be helped?

Effectiveness is just one criterion for evaluating any intervention; cost is equally important. Any self-administered program would ultimately be chosen over one that is just as effective but more expensive. A program that requires prolonged, face-to-face contacts between offenders and professionals could be made less expensive by using subprofessionals to fulfill the contact functions. Costs become the paramount consideration after equal effectiveness in programs has been demonstrated.

CONCLUSION

Compared to face-to-face contact methods, LDW and CAT offer the possibility of reaching more people for preventive purposes and, in some cases, substituting a cost-effective alternative or an adjunct to psychotherapy, especially when linked to personal computers and to interactive technologies. With impulsive, acting-out offenders, LDW and CAT may be the only viable alternatives where many other approaches have failed.

CHAPTER 13

Crisis Interventions and Psychotherapies

> The most needy, particularly those lacking in education, are least likely to receive treatment in the psychotherapeutic service delivery system. (Howard, Lueger, & Schank, 1992, p. 164)

The purpose of this chapter is to demonstrate how the theory presented in previous chapters is, as much as is humanly possible, isomorphic with clinical practice (Beutler, Williams, Wakefield, & Entwistle, 1995; Peterson, 1995; Stricker, 1992; Stricker & Trierweiler, 1995). This purpose implies explaining theory and practice as they are conceived here. A major implication of developmental competence theory applies to the conduct of individual therapy, which, up to the present time, has been the preferred mode, even the rule of psychological intervention in the United States. If the text of the preceding chapters is correct, it is time-consuming and inefficient to see individuals alone without intimate others present. It would be more efficient, and perhaps more effective, to see the individuals involved in ongoing relationships. Information gathered in this fashion would allow a faster understanding of the referral problem or symptom. Seeing individuals alone in psychotherapy is very expensive because of the time needed to understand them outside of their natural contexts. Seeing them alone, without their families present, produces inevitable distortions without corrective feedback from close intimates.

Compared to individual therapy, the group, marital, and family therapies are more economical and perhaps more effective ways to reach people in trouble. Even individuals who do not have their families available would profit from the reactions of strangers in ongoing, face-to-face group therapy (Szapocznik, Kurtines, Foote, Perez-Vidal, & Hervis, 1983). Hence, individual therapy should be an exception reserved to very special cases. Even though individuals may be able to pay for individual therapy sessions, the important issue here is not only how they relate to a therapist, but how they relate to, confront, and are confronted by, other people who are hurting as much as they are.

CRISIS INTERVENTION AND PSYCHOTHERAPY

A strong conviction about the importance of research for the growth of the profession is shared by only a small percentage of therapists—a percentage that mirrors most mental health professions. No matter how strong this conviction is, it will be ignored, as were similar convictions proposed at the beginning and during the development of the field of crisis intervention and psychotherapy. To understand why the percentage of mental health professionals interested in research is so small, one has to understand the strong presence and influence of different value systems. The values of therapists are different from those of researchers. Unless common ground between the two disciplines is found, it will be difficult if not impossible to integrate them. The disciplines will continue on two separate tracks that criss-cross accidentally during occasional calls to action. This schism between researchers and therapists should not be surprising to anyone who has seen the same separation in even more traditional and supposedly more scientific professions in the physical sciences. Engineers do not talk to physicists. Organic chemists do not talk to inorganic chemists.

As a whole, professions interested in providing services are not as interested in creating new information, let alone sharing it. Nor are they interested in changing clinical practices learned during their professional training. The need of service providers is for immediacy. For a fee, they give help to those who need it, as soon as is possible. When people hurt, they need immediate relief. They cannot wait for an indeterminate period of time. To perform their services, professional helpers will adopt, adapt, beg, steal, or borrow from whatever theoretical or therapeutic approach fits their immediate needs. Any theory or therapy that seems plausible and attractive enough to fit into these immediate needs is adopted, often uncritically and wholesale. Eventually, in a few instances, a therapeutic position adopted blindly on faith may reach a level akin to a cult or religion, without evidence as to its validity or empirical foundation.

The needs of researchers are more transcendental; they encompass requirements for accountability and verifiability. Immediacy be damned! Reliable and verified methods are needed to help clients in need. What criteria should be used to adopt any theoretical or therapeutic approach? Critical selectivity and delayed judgment become paramount to helping. The validity of any therapeutic technique should be known before it is applied. These two positions, set diametrically apart, are very difficult to unite. As Foa and Foa (1974) found, correlation between services and information is significantly negative, which means that those who are interested in services are not equally interested in acquiring or disseminating new information. Conversely, those who are interested in information may be less interested in providing services than in acquiring and sharing the information.

A variety of theorists have suggested two main routes to knowledge creation and acquisition: a dialectical route and a demonstrative route. The former relies mainly on the strictly aesthetic, subjectively impressionistic approach shown by the typical style of the therapist: warmth, unconditional positive regard, and empathy; that is, emotional availability to people who are hurting. The latter route relies instead on the pragmatic, objectively verifiable importance of method over style.

Some may consider these two routes mutually incompatible and even antagonistically exclusive, but both are necessary because they complement each other; one cannot survive without the other. Style alone, without method, may seem effective with some individuals but may fail in dealing with hurt couples and families. Method alone, without style, as argued by early behaviorists, is just as untenable in providing helpful services. A client in crisis needs emotional support and affirmation, as received through the style of the help-giver, but new and helpful ways to solve problems and decrease conflicts and hurts must also be found.

Recognizing the helpfulness of writing about traumatic events in one's life (Pennebaker, 1990) and a similar theoretical position about the fundamental importance of hurts in human existence (Chapter 4), the first author asks all his clients, as a standard operating procedure, to write about their hurts from the very beginning of a therapeutic contract. This practice seems well documented not only by Pennebaker's (1990) work but also by supporting replications of many sources cited in Chapter 12. This is likely to be one of the most convincing validated approaches thus far gathered about the practice of psychotherapy. Perhaps the use of writing for parapreventive and paratherapeutic purposes, in its four levels of structure (open-ended, focused, guided, and structured), may be the bridge that will link practitioners with researchers.

Greater Differentiation and Specialization

The more a system grows and differentiates itself, the greater will be the specialization of its component parts. Thus, therapeutic intervention may be predicted to continue not only to proliferate but also to break up into smaller and smaller specializations that will concentrate on the various psychopathologies. Even now, some therapists specialize in dealing with acting-out behavior and delinquency, and others specialize in various addictions (L'Abate, Farrar, & Serritella, 1992).

Mandated Limitations on Services

The psychotherapy field was at one time subsidized by insurance companies because of its claimed cost-effectiveness in decreasing medical referrals and treatments. However, its tremendous growth (to billions of dollars yearly) is producing a retrenchment in third-party payments. Insurance companies and managed care companies are becoming increasingly leery and suspicious of the costs and the effectiveness of the various psychotherapies, no matter what the composition of the patient may be (individual, couple, family, or group). These companies are beginning to monitor and, in some cases, to limit the work of therapists by asking for peer reviews, monthly or periodic progress reports, indications of improvement, and even evidence of outcome. With an economy that makes insurance an expensive proposition for many employers, obtaining mental health benefits in insurance contracts will become increasingly difficult and expensive. The results may be dangerous if not disastrous for the whole psychotherapeutic community. If a universal, nationwide insurance network is ever created, political avenues will need to be pursued to ensure that mental health benefits become part of any insurance package. Group, marital, and family therapies might become the treatment of choice, with individual psychotherapy reserved for special cases or for people who can afford to pay for it themselves.

Integration of Therapies with Paratherapies

As more and more therapeutic practices become subject to scrutiny and questioning by external parties, it is important to ensure that these practices become more cost-effective than they have been in the past. This development may require a blend or integration of traditional psychotherapies with prevention-oriented methods that have received more documented evidence. As suggested in Chapter 12, the introduction of the written medium, either alone or in combination with the verbal and the nonverbal media, may be more cost-effective.

Thus, the informal, free-floating, individualized, and often unstructured nature of many therapeutic approaches may increasingly incorporate, as useful adjuncts, more structured, psychoeducational, social skills training approaches that have been found useful in the fields of primary and secondary prevention. The extreme variability of psychotherapeutic approaches may be decreased through the use of treatment manuals and structured techniques learned from the paratherapies (Levant, 1986; McFarlane, 1991).

Creating and Adopting New Theories or Therapeutic Approaches

As a result of third-party demands for positive and documented returns for each dollar of insurance expenditure, therapeutic practices may be adopted and adapted in a more selective and critical fashion than in the past. Consequently, these practices may become more competitive with each other. The question that will be raised more often will be: "Given the same outcome, which therapeutic approach is less expensive than another comparable approach?" The challenging question, for the last quarter of this century, has been, "Which client(s) will benefit by which therapeutic approach?" In the first quarter of the next century, the question of *comparative effectiveness* among various and multiple therapeutic approaches may be raised.

As long as therapeutic practices are based on the spoken word, it will be difficult and expensive to answer the latter question. Only the few researchers who will receive the diminishing research grants will be able to obtain the support needed to code and analyze therapist–client(s) interactions. Even if this time-consuming task is accomplished, the coding system used will become questionable if it fails to include patterns of abuse and neglect that occur in families but are screened out when these families are investigated in the laboratory (L'Abate & Bagarozzi, 1993).

The evaluation-treatment match, long the chimera of the psychotherapies, is difficult and expensive to reach as long as treatment is based on the verbal modality. If and when this goal is attempted, it will be a laborious and difficult task. Thus, inevitably, issues of comparative effectiveness among the psychotherapies will become issues of greater treatment specificity. However, such specificity is difficult to obtain verbally, because the verbal medium is not as explicit and replicable as writing (L'Abate, 1992b).

Psychotherapy is and remains a humanly exciting and challenging pursuit. No matter how many issues and problems it creates among its practitioners, it still remains a way of helping people in trouble that, thus far, is unsurpassed by any other available or imaginable approach, including medication. However, psychotherapists cannot rely on psychotherapy exclusively. Past experiences with the other paratherapeutic media, nonverbal and written, can increase the therapeutic repertoire, perhaps allowing therapists to help more clients than was possible in the past.

WHY PEOPLE ASK FOR HELP

Why do people ask for help? Because they love themselves and each other! Once we establish the fundamental importance of love in family relations, even though this attribution may be expressed destructively, it becomes axiomatic that love acquires motivational properties that need to be claimed, reclaimed, and proclaimed in therapy. Unless individuals, couples, and family members care about themselves and each other, they are incapable of asking for help and wanting change for the better. Love may be present receptively. However, because it is usually expressed destructively, it invites the inevitable confrontation of psychotherapy.

Love, and its proper experience and expression among family members, is the primary goal of any therapy. Day in and day out, among family members as well as between families and therapists, feelings and attributions of importance or unimportance are communicated. Directly or indirectly, positively or negatively, partially or wholly, consistently or inconsistently, a sense of importance is continuously exchanged. Individuals and families in trouble come to therapy to receive a different, positive, consistent affirmation that their asking for help is an expression of love for themselves and each other. Their sense of importance is increased indirectly by the therapist's positive comments and structuring of the therapeutic process. An even better approach is to affirm clients positively and directly for their asking for help.

Love, of course, is not enough. As the developmental competence theory points out, people also must learn to negotiate. Whether this negotiation needs to be taught by therapists directly remains to be seen. Rather than leaving clients to learn this important process on their own, it is much more practical and relevant to help them learn problem solving and negotiation directly. Ultimately, the goal of all therapies is to help people to love, become more intimate, and negotiate in better ways than they used before they came for help.

Love as a Motivation to Ask for Help

Love becomes the reason clients ask for help. Unfortunately, many dysfunctional clients have forgotten the importance of love and have learned to use negative explanations for the misbehavior of its members. Usually, the opening question, "Why did you come here?" is answered in terms of negative characteristics attributed to the problem member of the family or to the negative consequences of one's behavior (lying, stealing, setting fires, misconduct in school, not achieving educational potential). For a therapist to accept negative explanations is tantamount to self-defeat. Passive acceptance of an unacceptable negatively tinged or perceived reality can only affirm the negativity of the reason for referral. From the very beginning, a negative reason for asking for help needs to be contradicted without demeaning or discounting the client. Furthermore, when the contradiction is positive—that is, explained in terms of the love the clients have for each other, they usually accept the positive reframing: "You came here because you care for each other and you care especially for ________ . Is that right?" In 40 years of practice, not once has this assertion been denied by clients. Love for self and for each other as the reason to ask for professional help needs to be asserted boldly and clearly by therapists from the very beginning, because most dysfunctional clients are not able to do it.

Most therapies give or increase a sense of self-importance to clients *indirectly.* Just by receiving attention, affirmation, and support, clients are given a sense of importance that may be translated into a better way of loving and of negotiating. This is why some positive outcomes in psychotherapy cannot be attributed either to methods or to the therapist's style. Just coming face to face with someone who shows interest and concern for one's problems can be sufficient to allow generalization from problems to self, from incomplete or negative importance to positive self-importance. "If this professional (therefore important!) person is interested in my problems, then she or he is interested in me as an important human being." Such a result, however, is usually indirect and unclear. Why not deal with the effects of therapy in terms of importance and intimacy? Why not state the relevance of both factors directly and unambiguously from the very outset of therapy?

Love as a Motivation for Change

Once the intrinsic connection between love and hurt has been established (Chapter 4), a great deal of pathology can be related to clients' inability to share their feelings of love toward themselves and others. This inability is derived from the avoidance of experiencing hurts, a tactic learned from one's caretakers or family of origin. If caretakers avoided pain within and between themselves, how can their child learn to do what the adults could not do? Behind this defeating position is found a common error in thinking: If these hurts are not approached, confronted, and dealt with, they will go away. These hurts may be avoided—that is, denied, repressed, suppressed, or sublimated—but because they are imprinted in our physical experience, they do not and will not go away. They need to be acknowledged and asserted from the very beginning of therapy, but dealing directly with them at that stage is probably premature. More often than not, clients cannot confront the experience and expression of intimate feelings at the beginning of therapy. They need to learn to trust the therapist and experience a few successes before they can share their hurts and thus experience intimacy. L'Abate (1986) suggested this progression of interventions: (a) dealing with the presenting problem, the symptom or reason for referral, which means paying attention to past traumas and stresses; (b) helping clients learn to negotiate in the present and for the future; and (c) eventually, after a sense of mastery has been achieved, confronting issues of intimacy that will allow clients to go forward on their own for the long haul.

Love and Positive Reframing

Therapists must show their care by using an unrelentingly positive reframing of their clients' negativity. The same reality can be perceived in positive and negative ways. Therapists need to stress positives without putting down, negating, discounting, or ignoring clients' perceptions and explanations. At least at the beginning of therapy, the focus should be on positively reframing the reason for referral ("You asked for help because you love each other and want the best for all of you") and the symptomatic behavior, within the context of its genesis. The symptom did not arise from nowhere, even though its cause may be a mystery to family members who are unaware of (or unwilling to confront) the contextual nature of any symptom.

From the very first meeting, the professional's personality should include a high degree of positivity—seeing the good in everything, especially in the clients who need help. This positivity is communicated readily in positive injunctions and interpretations ("There must be a horse here somewhere"). Rather than accepting the client's negative interpretation of a symptom or of an identified patient, the client's asking for help is reframed as an example of love. The therapist's positive plan must be one that can be readily followed conceptually as well as behaviorally. Its positivity has to be powerful enough to make a difference in people's lives. To match the regularity of appointments, there must be consistent regularity in the therapist's presence.

Helping People to Negotiate

A second goal of therapy is to help clients learn to negotiate—which assumes that the therapist has a clear idea of the nature and components of negotiation. One cannot help clients learn to negotiate when they are in crisis or are just beginning therapy. Before teaching negotiation skills, the therapist has to help with the symptom or the problem behavior at hand. After clients learn to negotiate solutions, they can more easily deal with issues of intimacy, which usually are difficult to confront at the beginning or in the middle of therapy. Intimacy issues may have to be left until the end of therapy. The process of therapy would then include: (a) caring for the symptomatic behavior, whatever it may be; (b) teaching negotiation skills; and (c) dealing with issues of intimacy and termination.

THE NEED FOR ISOMORPHISM BETWEEN THEORY AND PRACTICE

The main issue here is one of *isomorphism*—how theory and practice are related to each other. How is professional practice helpful to dysfunctional (*AA* and *RR*) relationships within the context of developmental competence theory? Three possibilities are available. First, one could theorize without practice. One could then be a theorist, a researcher, or a scholar; but without (psychotherapeutic) practice, one could not be called a therapist. Theorizing or researching without practice is eminently possible. One could theorize about behavior and not practice at all. For instance, researchers and theorists may be interested in experimenting with dysfunctional relationships but may not be interested in helping them.

Second, one could practice without theory, as family members, friends, or neighbors do when they help each other in times of trouble. This process, although very important, does not make these people therapists. This possibility takes place every day, but the process, however helpful, humane, and widespread, is not therapy. It would seem impossible to practice crisis intervention and psychotherapy without some notions, no matter how vague and ill-defined, about the nature of behavior, especially behavior in intimate relationships. Thus, the second possibility may be ruled out.

Third, one could attempt to relate theory and practice. All three possibilities are logically valid, but only the third is acceptable for crisis intervention and psychotherapeutic practice. What *is* the relationship between theory and practice? Why do we need isomorphism? How can clinical practice occur without it? It seems inconceivable that responsible practice of any kind, when people who hurt are involved, could take place without a theoretical background, a theory-drivenness.

What Is a Theory?

A theory can mean different things to different people. Usually it means (a) a coherent body of generally accepted, more or less verified, established propositions or statements used as principles of explanation for a specific class of events, factors, or variables; or (b) a proposed explanation based on provisional and conjectural principles or hypotheses. Theory is thinking about how relationships work or fail to work, how problems are solved, how people enjoy life, how to contribute to society or depend on it, functionally or dysfunctionally.

However, there are two other problems to contend with here:

1. What is the relevance of any theory to intimate behavior?
2. How verified or verifiable is that theory?

There are different criteria for theories. At one extreme, one could select uncritically a very appealing, elegantly seductive theory that is not validated or verifiable. An example is systems theory. At the other extreme, one could reject a rather unappealing, even boring, theory that is validated and verifiable, as exemplified, in part, by behavioral learning theory. In real life, one does not find theories in such black-and-white extremes. The issue here is selection. How is one to choose a theory for use in therapeutic practice? Should a theory be chosen on the basis of elegance, appeal, and the emotional recognition of relevance to one's practice, or should a theory be chosen on the basis of whether it can be empirically validated or is verifiable? Aesthetic preferences contend with pragmatic considerations. Does one wish to practice as an artist, or as a scientist/researcher? Is it possible to do both?

Two sets of value systems exist in most mental health professionals. In one system, the receptive input side (*E* and *Aw*), there is an exquisitely aesthetic, intuitively artistic reliance on feelings and emotions, subjective experiences and perceptions. In the other system, the expressive output side (*R* and *A*), a calculatingly pragmatic, orderly, and coolly rational aspect favors planning, predictability, and objectivity in the structure of what is done to help others. The former system wants to help immediately whoever is in trouble. The latter system wants to wait, think, plan, and plot before helping. Can these two sides be reconciled?

In addition to the issue of whether a theory is verified or verifiable, there is an issue of consistency. Does one practice according to one theory or a combination of theories? How is what is said and done in the therapist's office related to what and how that therapist thinks theoretically? Is it possible to discriminate what is said and done and what is thought? Some relationship between theory and practice must be supported on the following grounds. Theory and practice need to be related to each other to fulfill at least four functions: (a) to derive practice from theory; (b) to use practice to evaluate, verify, and change theory; (c) to use theory to change practice; and (d) to achieve a greater degree of consistency among what is felt (*E*), thought (*R*), and said and done (*A*), with sufficient awareness (*Aw*) to change practice on the basis of its proximate and distal context (*C*). Why should anyone change therapeutic practices?

Clinical Practice

Practice is the clinical application of a theory to diminish suffering and hurtful behavior. The goal of professional practice, whether preventive or psychotherapeutic, is to help troubled people learn to love themselves and selected others in more constructive ways than they were using before they asked for professional help. A second goal of professional practice is to help troubled people learn to negotiate and problem-solve effectively. By practice is meant any approach or intervention designed to help people function better than they did before they sought professional help. Verbal psychotherapy is not the only way to intervene and help troubled people. Professional helpers should be aware of at least two other media—the nonverbal and the written—that can be used to help.

Therapy: Helping People Change for the Better

Generally, therapy means any face-to-face professional relationship established between a help seeker and a help giver. Orlinsky (1989) contended that therapy represents at least four images: (a) a mental health treatment; (b) personal (or family!) education; (c) a reform or correctional process; and (d) moral or spiritual redemption. Each of these images has a different historical antecedent, possible differences in therapeutic emphasis, and, very likely, different therapeutic consequences or outcomes.

Although Orlinsky did not refer to it, his classification is very similar to one independently developed by Brickman et al. (1982). These authors assumed two basic dimensions of help seeking: (a) the extent of responsibility for causing the problem, ranging from all to none, and (b) the extent of responsibility for solving the problem, ranging from all to none. These two dimensions give rise to a fourfold classification of therapeutic models:

1. *Medical,* the equivalent of Orlinsky's "treatment," in which the responsibility of causing and solving the problem is low, and a professional is responsible for the change.
2. *Compensatory,* or the equivalent of education, in which the responsibility for causing the problem is low, but personal responsibility for solving it is high.
3. *Enlightenment,* reforming or correctional, in which personal responsibility for causing the problem is high but responsibility for solving it is low.
4. *Moral* or spiritual, in which personal responsibility for causes and solutions is high.

Dunst, Trivette, and Deal (1988) believed that only the compensatory or educational model increases a sense of empowerment and enhances well-being; the other three models, according to these authors, result in negative consequences. The medical model leads to passivity, dependency, and learned helplessness. The enlightenment or correctional model leads to lowered self-esteem, incompetence, and submissive tendencies. The moral model leads to loneliness and physical exhaustion. These authors failed to provide evidence to support such direly negative consequences. Thus, as useful and overlapping as both classifications may be in defining therapeutic practices, they fail to discriminate among different types of interventions. Furthermore, neither distinguishes the skills necessary to administer psychotherapeutic interventions.

Can Practice Be Derived from Theory?

An affirmative answer to this question means that practice, in some way, is or should be essentially isomorphic with theory. This is an extremely difficult position to defend. As long as practice is based on the personality of the professional helper and the medium of exchange between the helper and clients remains the spoken word, it is virtually impossible to verify whether a relation between theory and practice is indeed taking place. Even though the person of the therapist and the spoken word are necessary to start and maintain therapeutic exchanges, they are not sufficient to help people change. Clients can be helped to change when all three media of exchange are employed: the oral, the nonverbal, and the written (see Table 12.1). If the professional helper operates as an artist, helping intuitively, immediately, and empathetically through verbal interpretations, reflections of feelings, commiserations, commentaries, rational understanding, and support, it will be difficult, expensive, and virtually impossible to see how the helper's actions are derived from any theory.

Typically, to examine this link, a recording or videotape of what transpires between the professional helper and clients is made. The videotape is then converted to a written transcript for analysis and coding of content and of content-free and nonverbal behavior patterns. This very expensive process may require up to 30 hours of analysis for every hour of therapy. It is available to only a few researchers who qualify for highly competitive grants that have produced interesting classification systems (Gottman, 1994; L'Abate & Bagarozzi, 1993).

Using Practice to Verify and Change Theory

If what professional helpers say and do is based on what is felt and thought, and if what they say and do with their clients actually works, supposedly it reflects how adequate, accurate, and effective the theory is. This would be the conclusion one would draw if the relationship between theory and practice were indeed, point by point, isomorphic. Unfortunately, behavior is not that simple. For instance, helpers have many ways to rationalize failures to help; usually, they attribute negative qualities to clients who refuse or cannot use their help (i.e., diagnostic categories). Therapeutic failures are rationalized on grounds that psychotherapy is a service, and, as with all services, one cannot expect to help everybody who asks for help. There is no way of knowing beforehand which clients will benefit from professional services and which ones will not. Thus, psychotherapists try to help whoever seeks their services, knowing full well that it is impossible to help everybody who comes in. From therapy outcome studies, data which has become common knowledge in the field of psychotherapy indicates that at best, one-third of all clients who seek help can be helped. Another third may be helped somewhat. Very likely, another third will not be helped. Helping is a very unpredictable process!

Although some practitioners attempt to justify therapeutic failures by attributing negative qualities to clients who fail to benefit from professional services, there is another view. The failures may be caused by limitations in the therapeutic methods used rather than in the clients who were not helped. A more appropriate view would be that limitations may exist in therapeutic theories, in professionals' practices, and in the attitudes and behaviors of clients. If the range of therapeutic and practical choices available to professional helpers is expanded, a larger therapeutic armamentarium may help to encompass a wider range of problems and populations.

To the extent that therapeutic practices derive from a theory, they reflect how accurate, encompassing, and useful that theory is. If the practices do not work effectively or fail to work in some instances, one must ask whether the theory under which one presumably operates is valid: Does it reflect what is going on in and around the clients, and does it explain why they were not helped?

Using Theory to Change Therapeutic Practice

The relation between theory and therapeutic practice is, in varied instances, tenable, tenuous, or untenable. The relation is especially tenuous or untenable when the theory, the practice, or both, are vague, general, and unspecifiable. To the extent that a theory is clear and specific, it may generate valid methods of intervention and practice. Theoretically, it is preferable to be specific and wrong than to be general and right. However, this criterion cannot be applied to clients. They deserve better theories and better psychological interventions. Consequently, the three feasible and acceptable possibilities for isomorphism between theory and practice, stated at the start of this section, can be reframed. First, the theory is completely independent of the practice, as when a professional helper does intuitively what needs to be done, on the spur of the moment, without any relationship to theory—that is, with *no isomorphism.* Second, the practice is somewhat related to the theory, but the connection is vague and ill-defined, as in most therapeutic, verbally based practices, which have *some isomorphism.* Third, the practice is completely derived from the theory, with the *point-by-point isomorphism* that is partially possible in LDW and CAT (Chapter 12). This approach detracts from the earlier mentioned improvement due to attribution of importance to a client whose situation is closely listened to and addressed.

The third possibility is ideal but is difficult to achieve verbally, given the variability of the factors involved—the theory, the practice, the therapist, the client(s), and the relationship between client(s) and therapists. An approach like this would be cold, mechanical, and impersonal. If the client feel this, will he or she have a good relationship with the therapist? Because human nature is variable, the best and most realistic goal may be the second possibility, some isomorphism. Point-by-point isomorphism between theory and practice is extremely difficult if not impossible to achieve, even when LDW and CAT are employed.

Achieving Greater Consistency between Theory and Practice

How is the goal of greater isomorphism to be achieved? The answer: Gradually and carefully! Available theories need to be examined in detail to see how they relate to clinical practices. Who is going to judge the degree of consistency (i.e., isomorphism) between theory and practice? If there is unclear structure, both theoretically and practically, how can the therapeutic profession obtain any clear relation between theory and practice? The clearer (i.e., more structured) the theoretical and practical structures, the clearer should be the clinical processes derived from them—a goal that is easier said than done! Perhaps the best tactic is to choose clients with whom reciprocal liking is present. But how does one define liking, on the part of the therapist and the client? When is structure considered cold, impersonal, and uncaring to the point that the client feels treated unimportantly, like the masses, rather than like an important individual?

If the goal of therapy is to change clients for the better, what does this change mean? Does it mean leaving behind, giving up, or going past self- and other-defeating and hurtful patterns of feeling, thinking, and behavior, and replacing them with novel and comfortable patterns for the client and intimate others? To obtain therapeutic progress, one needs to apply practices that will produce it. Various theories claim to produce that progress and outcome.

WHAT THEORY SHALL BE SELECTED AND ON WHAT GROUNDS?

Most theories of crisis intervention and psychotherapy can be broken down into the same classical viewpoints and schools that have influenced the field of psychology (Hansen & L'Abate, 1982). These theories cannot be given here the full coverage they deserve. There are more treatises on theories of psychotherapy than there are treatises on therapeutic methods. Nonetheless, some basic information on these theories is essential to introduce criteria by which each theory can be evaluated and eventually selected.

Criteria for Evaluation of a Theory for Therapeutic Practice

The criteria listed below can be used to evaluate developmental competence theory, as well as other theories.

1. *Comprehensiveness and integration.* How comprehensive is the theory, and how well does it integrate past or present theories? The range may vary from functionality to dysfunctionality, and from individuals to families. It may

apply to many areas of individual functioning but not to couples or families. It may include other theories or ignore them. For instance, psychodynamic theory seems very comprehensive. However, it may be at odds with other theories, which makes integration with them difficult.

2. *Simplicity.* Are there patterns in the complexity of behavior that allow use of just a few principles? Would these principles allow description and explanation of a wide range of functional and dysfunctional behaviors?

3. *Reducibility and continuity.* How well is the theory related to psychology as a science and a profession? Can complex behaviors be reduced in continuity with well-known and validated psychological concepts derived from monadic, individually oriented psychology but expanded to relational and contextual factors?

4. *Verifiability.* How is the theory testable? In the laboratory? In the therapy office. In statistical analysis? Should a theory be verifiable? Some therapists regard antagonistically, even suspiciously, anything remotely related to empiricism and research. *Reducibility* (from family patterns to individually meaningful psychological constructs) and *verifiability* are tantamount to dirty words that go against the *zeitgeist* of many therapeutic ideologies. The concept of verifiability should be differentiated from the concept of accountability. Verifiability deals with whether a theory or parts of a theory are empirically testable. Accountability deals with the kinds of outcome and results obtained from a therapy derived from a given theory, regardless of its verifiability.

5. *Accuracy.* How precise and accurate is the theory? Does it describe and explain functional and dysfunctional patterns, making them recognizable by both the therapist and the client? If they recognize that what is said and done in therapy is relevant to their experience, then, to that extent, the theory may be accurate. However, people in crisis may be so confused that they accept as accurate and valid whatever a therapist says and does.

6. *Usefulness.* Kurt Lewin's often quoted dictum, "There is nothing as useful as a good theory!" applies here. Many theories describe human behavior well, but how many of these theories can be applied to help troubled people change for the better? One aspect of usefulness is *fruitfulness.* What has the theory done to influence and produce programs and plans to help? For instance, in the field of mental health prevention, many parental and marital programs have been derived from a humanistic perspective, while both psychoanalysis and systems theory have failed to produce any preventive program.

7. *Accountability.* Regardless of the criteria listed above, does a theory yield practices that produce results? If results are obtained, how are they demonstrated—subjectively, objectively, experientially, experimentally? As explained above, this criterion is different from verifiability. A therapeutic theory could be eminently verifiable and still produce negligible results, and another theory might not be verifiable but might produce unexpected results. Because no therapeutic theory, thus far, has shown superiority over other theories, as long as the therapist provides a *CC* context that is new, positive, predictable,

and different from the past experience of the client, these conditions will provide grounds for improvement.

Current Theories of the Therapeutic Relationship: A Summary

Most theories of therapy are theories of how people function or fail to function. However, before proceeding any further, the composition of a therapeutic relationship needs to be determined. Committed, prolonged, and intimate relationships are usually found in families. The family is a unit or set of individuals who are linked by physical (blood), legal, economic, or emotional ties and who may or may not live under the same roof. Theories may stress one or many of these qualities, yet the major interest may be the emotional bonds that link family members together. In contrast, therapeutic relationships are professional arrangements in which clients pay for services. The exchange is agentic, not communal, although some therapists prefer to stress the latter quality rather than the former (while still accepting the fee for their services).

Theories of therapy have been classified in many ways. Torgenrud and Storm (1989) identified the following schools: psychodynamic, intergenerational, contextual, experiential, structural, strategic, functional, and behavioral. Gurman, Kniskern, and Pinsof (1986) listed 15 different schools of therapy, which overlapped with and expanded on those given by Torgenrud and Storm. Hansen and L'Abate (1982) used a classic division for therapy theories: (a) humanism; (b) psychoanalysis; (c) behaviorism; and (d) systems. A recent textbook of psychotherapy (Bongar & Beutler, 1995) contained separate chapters on psychodynamic, behavioral, experiential, cognitive-behavioral, and systems theories. A similar classification was made by Bergin and Garfield (1994), who identified major therapeutic approaches as being behavioral, cognitive, cognitive-behavioral, psychodynamic, and experiential.

Humanism is a widespread school that encompasses similar viewpoints such as phenomenology, existentialism, and experientialism. This school stresses the importance of the immediate present, that is, the subjectively available, phenomenologically personal experience of the individual as expressed verbally and nonverbally. In this school, the client's emotional reactions as well as the therapist's contribution are considered paramount to the process of change. This school is relevant to *A*wareness of *input* variables—how clients and therapists process subjectively felt events (*E*). Representatives of this school eschew the importance of theories and theorizing, stressing instead the therapist's gut feelings about particular clients.

In terms of comprehensiveness, the humanistic school integrates just one part of an individual's experience: subjectivity. In some cases, it belittles the importance of reason and rationality while emphasizing the metaphorical, the symbolically experiential, and the role of perceptual input in personality functioning. It is not as much concerned with output as is, for instance, the behavioral school. Because of its stress on subjectivity and experience, humanism is not a simple school to understand and to master. Its reducibility and continuity can be traced to influential individually oriented therapists such as Carl Rogers, and theorists such as Abraham Maslow and Rollo May, among others.

Verifiability and accountability are dirty words to some humanistic therapists. These words smack of mechanical accounting and engineering qualities that deny and dehumanize the therapeutic process. Accuracy may be relevant to the reflection of feelings and subjective experiences, but it remains limited when applied to behavior patterns. Its usefulness lies in furnishing a relevant way to recognize and help clients express warm, positive feelings toward themselves and others. Using the criterion of fruitfulness, this school has helped produce and shape many, if not most, of the psychoeducational marital and parenting programs in primary and secondary prevention (L'Abate, 1986, 1990; Levant, 1986; McFarlane, 1991).

Psychoanalysis is an established school of therapy that has spawned, among others, self psychology and the object relations school reviewed in Chapter 6. Like any school, it includes less influential viewpoints, like orthodox psychoanalysis and combinations thereof. This theory stresses the importance of past, unconscious experiences in the family of origin, as understood by genograms, intergenerational family history, and developmental traumas and experiences. Its methods focus on a rational, step-by-step understanding of these past experiences. Its stress on a rational approach is shared by subschools that give similar importance to rational factors, such as rational-emotive therapy, reality therapy, and the so-called cognitive school of therapy, a more recent offshoot of behaviorism.

For the criteria of comprehensiveness and integration, psychoanalytically oriented therapies can claim to cover a wide range of phenomena, both overt and covert, to deal with unconscious and conscious behaviors. They can rationalize (verbally) most, if not all, behaviors in terms of past experiences and defense mechanisms acquired during development. They stress the importance of how experience is processed rationally (throughput). Psychoanalysis is not a simplistic school to learn and to master. It is, however, reducible to individual factors and is in continuity with ego psychology and object relations schools. Unfortunately, psychoanalysis is not an easy theory to verify. Its accuracy is questionable because what one therapist selects as important for verbal interpretations may not be seen as important by another therapist of the same school. Furthermore, given its costs and the present climate surrounding economic clinical procedures, as well its questionable accountability, one wonders how long this school will survive.

Myriad viewpoints and practices fall under the rubric of the psychodynamic-psychoanalytic school. On the surface, going back to one's family of origin seems to be useful; many clients seem to benefit from going back to past individual experiences. But how far into the past does one need to go? For how long shall one deal with it? How does rehashing of past history relate to change in the present? Would it not be more economical to include intimate others who have shared the same past with the client? These questions may be answered by trying the family-group approach, because all therapists need to be aware of their own past history as they probe into a client's family's history. Psychoanalysis has influenced a great many individually oriented, group, and marital therapists, to the point that no therapist worthy of any clinical salt can readily dismiss it.

The major shortcoming of psychoanalysis relates to the criterion of fruitfulness. It has failed to produce psychoeducational marital and family programs that can be used in primary and secondary prevention. The exception to this conclusion is the followers of Alfred Adler, who have been very influential in generating and producing many marital and parenting programs (Dinkmeyer, Pew, & Dinkmeyer, 1979).

Behaviorism, like all the schools reviewed, includes a variety of smaller viewpoints, and each has its representative and influential theorists. The main contribution of this school lies in its unrelenting stress on observables and measurables in terms of activities (*A*) and consequences resulting from either internal drive states (e.g., anxiety) or external reinforcers. It stresses the output side of behavior while belittling hypothetically inferred internal factors, such as feelings and thoughts. Its stress on empiricism may have made it a psychology of rats, stats, and graphs. It was, at least in the beginning, devoid of the awareness of possibly relational and contextual factors. Its most recent offshoot, the cognitive-behavioral school, is now quite influential. Eventually, there will be an experiential-behavioral school because the therapeutic field, in its necessary eclecticism, has spawned combinations and permutations of different schools.

From the criteria of comprehensiveness and integration, behaviorism stresses the output side at the expense of input (*E*), throughout (*R* and *Aw*), and *C*ontextual factors. It is relatively simple to understand and implement—perhaps deceptively so. Sometimes in focusing completely on one controlled factor, concomitant but important fall-out factors are ignored, such as when reinforcing a child for good behavior the locus of control established becomes external rather than internal. Therefore, even though the specific behavior in the specific instance is addressed, generalized, and more important metalevel behavior (locus of control) for the future has been adversely influenced. Its reducibility to frequencies and reinforcements allows it to be in continuity with accepted individually oriented behavioral principles, and it is highly verifiable by being selectively accurate in its methodology and clinical applications. However, in its stress on immediate solutions, it has forgotten the importance of dealing with subtly critical factors, such as the style of the therapist and the importance of this style in dealing with initial crises and resistances (Patterson, 1985). It is unquestionably useful in many situations, and it has been fruitful in producing a variety of psychoeducational marital and family programs in primary and secondary prevention. This school stresses the importance of skill training, especially in problem solving and negotiation, an area neglected by other schools.

Systems thinking attempts to deal with individuals as irreducible parts of the whole family. Individual behaviors are understood and described mainly as the result of transactions among family members, inseparable from individual contributions to those transactions. This school, like most therapeutic schools, has been subdivided into structural, strategic, and communication approaches. Its wholistic thinking has pervaded and influenced almost every professional who works with families. No one can deny that families operate as systems in which one member is interdependent with other members. This wholeness is stressed as the outcome of complexity at the expense of reducibility. Circularity in causality is stressed rather than the traditionally linear, step-by-step, one-cause-one-effect viewpoint. One cause may produce many different outcomes (equipotentiality); one outcome may be the result of many different causes (equifinality). The reflexivity or feedback functions of family transactions produce circular loops that defy empirical measurement but are visible to the naked eye of many family therapists.

The undeniable face validity of these concepts should not blind one to their inherent shortcomings. One should be able to derive the same principles from the same assumptions. This is not true of systems thinking. Various approaches claim direct derivations from systems thinking. Systems thinking is not a theory; it does not have the formal, hierarchical structure of a theory, in which one concept or construct is derived from another superordinate construct. It is not verifiable, as a theory should ideally be. It fits the second definition of a theory given at the beginning of this chapter. It consists of a set (some would say a hodge-podge) of beliefs based on conjectural, provisional, and hypothetical constructs. However, its greatest shortcoming lies in its being separate and discontinuous from psychological constructs and not verifiable. Hence, it may be a paradigm, but it is not a theory.

L'Abate and Colondier (1987) argued that:

1. Much of what is accepted as systems thinking is mostly a metatheory unrelated to the field of psychology. It may be vaguely connected to psychology, but it does not appear so because its constructs are nonpsychological in nature. Systems thinking lacks connectedness with established psychological theories because its generally vague notions lack specificity.
2. Much of what passes for systems thinking is untestable, or, at best, is an unrelated set of unverifiable hypotheses, some of them without substance.
3. A great deal of what is found in systems theory is methodologically sterile and vacuously unproductive. In short, it lacks empirical productivity and practical fruitfulness. It has not fulfilled its early promise of a revolution in mental health.

Consequently, systems thinking may work as a metaphor, a paradigm, or a metatheory, but not as a theory per se. Furthermore, this way of thinking was developed from the metaphors of gunsights in cybernetics and the thermostat in heating and air-conditioning. How are these two metaphors applicable to human behavior? Systems thinking has been very critical of past theories proclaiming a new revolutionary era, a novel ecosystemic epistemology that would replace shopworn theories and outdated linear practices with more circular practices. As Gurman, Kniskern, and Pinsof (1986) concluded, in their review of the results of family therapy:

> Unfortunately, the passion with which advocates of the "new epistemology" criticize the continuing use of family therapy research methods based on the "old" epistemology has been rarely translated into the development of experimental designs more consistent with ecosystemic views. . . . To our knowledge, there does not yet exist a single outcome study of family therapy whose design has been perceptibly influenced by such ecosystemic ideas. (p. 569)

The systems view sees itself as discontinuous from psychology as a science and as a profession. Thus, the attempt at comprehensiveness and integration claimed by this thinking may have been a goal achieved at the cost of giving up other goals, such as parsimony, reducibility, and continuity with psychology, and denying verifiability and accountability as important criteria in theory building. Accuracy, if it exists, lies in the eye of the beholder—the therapist's eye and no one else's—because objective, external empirical verifications are considered puerile and unnecessary.

From the viewpoint of usefulness, systems thinking scores high for providing certain new paradoxical modes and strategies of intervention. From the viewpoint of fruitfulness, however, it has failed to produce any marital or parental programs for primary and secondary prevention. On the plus side, systems thinking has spawned hybrid theories and therapeutic approaches that include an eclectic mixture of systemic and humanistic, systemic and psychodynamic, and systemic and behavioral schools.

What can one learn from this extremely brief review? All these theories can be integrated into one diagnostic model of negotiation—the ERAAwC model. All these schools have contributed significantly to our understanding of behavior as a continuum composed of experiencing, on the receptive internal input side (*E*); processing, in the middle (*R*); and expressing, external output at the end (*A, Aw,* and *C*). All contributed a vast number of techniques that have enlarged the necessary therapeutic armamentarium to unyielding levels that can no longer be learned by any single therapist.

Humanism has contributed the importance of input factors in subjectively felt emotions (*E*). Psychoanalytic-psychodynamic schools have stressed the importance of the rational (*R*) processing of these emotional experiences (throughput). Behaviorism has stressed the importance of output—expressive activities, with their external reinforcements (*A*). The Gestalt school has stressed the feedback function of awareness as a change mechanism (*Aw*), which may or may not work with families. The family therapy field has stressed the undeniable importance of contextual (*C*) factors in behavior. The humanistic and behavioral schools, however, have been more fruitful than the psychodynamic and systems schools in their contributions to primary and secondary prevention programs.

Theoretical and Practical Implications

The primary purpose of this theoretical framework, as expanded in previous chapters, is to link individual with family psychology, in both its functional and dysfunctional aspects. The secondary purpose is to bridge the inevitable gaps between theory and practice; theory building and theory testing; and theory and types of crisis intervention and psychotherapy. To fulfill multiple purposes, this theory attempts to meet two formal requirements—*reductionism* and *verifiability*. How (and how much) can one reduce family functioning and dysfunctioning to psychological principles and constructs relevant to individuals? Or, as family systems thinking suggests, is the family an irreducible whole that is greater than its parts and that, therefore, should not be considered in terms of its parts? Is reductionism necessary to ensure verifiability? The answer to these questions seems affirmative: One cannot exist without the other.

Reducibility: Links between Individual and Family Psychology

This first requirement is met by using psychological terms that are both interactional and relational. Love and negotiation, for instance, imply the presence of a partner to love and to negotiate with. Both sets of abilities are necessarily vital for individual, dyadic, and family functioning. Most dysfunctionalities are the product of deficits in either or both of these abilities. This framework is consistent, continuous, and reducible, if not indeed isomorphic, with monadic models of behavior. One can thus expand systematically on relationships between individual and family functioning and dysfunctioning.

This theory seems continuous and consistent with monadic psychology through at least five links. The first link is found in the emphasis on constructs such as self or personality, which, although derived from individual psychology, have been redefined here according to relational and interrelational concepts (e.g., being, doing, and having). A second link is found in the spatial assumption of approach-avoidance and the development of the dependencies, overdependencies, and interdependencies basic to intimacy. The third link is found in the temporal dimension of discharge-delay control functions basic to the development of the ability to negotiate. The fourth link lies in the emphasis on individual differences, especially gender differences, that distinguish the strategies for dealing with stress: presence-related and performance-related.

The fifth link is found in sex and sexuality, which form the biological and social bases for the formation and socialization of the individual in the family. Presence (being) and power (performance and production) help to classify sexual functions and dysfunctions. Most sexual dysfunctions are based on an inability to feel important and to be intimate, or on achieving self-gratification at the expense of the other. Our culture stresses sexual performance and production at the expense of sexual and emotional presence. Functional sex and sexuality imply an ability to be available emotionally to one's partner before one can be available sexually. Performance or production—that is, the physical act of intercourse at the expense of emotional presence—is bound to produce deviations and disturbances in sexuality.

WHY CHANGE?

Why should change take place when it is not wanted? There are reluctant clients, mostly in the selfish and no-self propensities, who do not want change even though other family members and professionals observe the need for change. One needs to deal with denial (i.e., avoidance) from the outset as the major defense against change. What prompts an individual, couple, or family to deny the referral problem, and, by extension, possibly the reality and painfulness of the situation? Underneath the denial there may be fear of the unknown, hopelessness, a threat to feelings of self-worth and self-esteem, and inadequacy. There may be fear of confronting oneself as a perpetrator or persecutor rather than as a victim. The process of denial, then, has little to do with any rational basis, but it has a great deal to do with an emotional basis. In dealing with hurt human beings, there is either too little or too much rationality. The bottom line, however, is fallibility, vulnerability, and neediness.

Wanting to Change

Why and when do people want change? People want change for at least two reasons: (a) necessity and (b) conflict. Change is wanted when the costs of staying the same are higher than the costs of changing. When one is faced with alternative outcomes such as hospitalization, incarceration, divorce, financial or emotional bankruptcy for self or for loved ones, and there are no other alternatives except therapy, necessity dictates accepting the inevitable choice that seems less costly than others. In spite of this argument, many dysfunctional people still refuse help, no matter how serious the consequences may be. Some people prefer murder or suicide to professional help. When conflict, either internal or external, is present and is too high and, again, too costly, then one might consider cheaper alternatives.

Types of Therapeutic Skills

Forty years ago, Rogers (1957) considered three necessary and sufficient conditions for change—(a) empathy, (b) warmth, and (c) unconditional regard. Rogers's original considerations need further expansion by adding necessary, and probably insufficient, conditions for personal change that were not considered at that time. His original conditions may have been necessary from a monadic, humanistic viewpoint, but they seem rather insufficient now, in view of the developments in the field of psychotherapy that stress attention to contextual factors. The three sine qua non conditions stressed by Rogers may be necessary and sufficient for certain individuals, but they seem both limited and limiting in view of more recent developments in marital and family therapy. They may be necessary, but they are definitely insufficient to help severely dysfunctioning individuals, or deeply entrenched, conflictful couples, or dysfunctional families. With character disorders, for instance, these conditions may be counterproductive. These individuals may be suspicious of empathy, warmth, and unconditional regard as being too seductive and too manipulative. These stylistic conditions by themselves do not work with schizophrenics (i.e., no-self individuals). Couples and families in trouble want immediate solutions rather than warmth, empathy, and unconditional regard.

Rogers's conditions refer to the *style of the therapist,* but have little, if anything, to say about *structuring skills in psychotherapy.* Style represents the relational skills that are fundamental in starting the process of therapy. Structuring represents the *method* that is necessary to help people change independently of the therapist's style. *Both* skills are necessary for change, especially in couples and families. Hence, professional change means not only reconsidering style as a necessary but insufficient condition for psychotherapeutic change, but also reconsidering method as another necessary but insufficient condition to obtain change. When style and method are successfully combined, they become necessary and sufficient to help clients change for the better. (Issues of style remain outside the purpose of this chapter, which is to stress the relation between theory and method.)

The literature on psychotherapy (Bergin & Garfield, 1994; Garfield & Bergin, 1986; Orlinsky, 1989) recognizes the importance of these two basic but different sets of skills to help clients improve. Relationship skills consist of reflective, relatively passive, and nurturing nondirective techniques that tend to give clients a sense of being supported, understood, and even affirmed. They are shown by a warm smile, a firm handshake, a pleasing comment, or a genuinely empathetic reaction to their plight ("I can see you are in a real pickle"; "I am sure that all of you are really hurting"; "There must be a lot of caring in this family"). These skills have been stressed by humanistically oriented therapists, sometimes at the expense of structuring skills. In fact, Gurman et al. (1986) commented that, at least in family therapy, relationships skills are necessary but not sufficient. On the basis of their review of research on the process and outcome of marital and family therapy, they concluded:

> A therapist's "style" of providing little structuring of early treatment sessions, and confrontation of highly affective material may be reliably associated with observed deterioration effects and is clearly more deterioration promoting, in general, than a style of stimulating interaction and giving support. (p. 572)

This is an important distinction between *support,* which is to be given from the moment clients walk into the therapy office, and *intimacy,* a tremendously strong emotion that is to be confronted toward the end of therapy. Structuring skills are actively prescriptive and directively pragmatic approaches that range from techniques specific to a therapist to methods available intersubjectively to many therapists. These skills consist of suggestions, recommendations, prescriptions, and assignments given to clients. These assignments may range in structure from ad hoc, individualized, spur-of-the-moment intuitions to systematic, step-by-step programs that are manual-driven and less individualized. Behavioristic therapists have stressed the structuring importance of these assignments, sometimes at the expense of relationship skills.

Why are there different paths to change and no demonstrated differential effects providing that one therapeutic approach is better than others? Common elements in the process must share similarities among different interventional approaches. Hence, it is important to list what these common elements are.

The Necessary (but Insufficient!) Conditions for Change

Regardless of the therapeutic persuasion employed, five conditions are necessary for change:

1. Admitting the existence of problematic issues, problems, or symptoms that have persisted regardless of any attempts to change for the better.
2. Asking for external intervention to help change existing dysfunctional patterns.
3. Receiving positive, direct/indirect communications about one's sense of importance.
4. Achieving hope that change is possible and that it can take place, if one wants it and works for it.
5. Establishing a sense of control where controls have been defective, extreme, or missing.

In any physical, human (individual, dyadic, or multirelational, like a family), philosophical, or other system, the first condition necessary for change is to admit that the system needs external intervention because it can no longer cope or survive with its existing resources. This admission leads to the second step in producing change: calling a professional and asking for help. Sometimes, the first step may be all that is necessary. The admission in itself may provoke a critical reexamination of the system's assets and liabilities that may result in a change. Most therapists recall potential clients who have called for help but who, when contacted because they failed to follow up on the initial call, indicated that they no longer needed the sought-after help. After the initial call, apparently they came up with some new conclusion about or solution for their problem. These people may be a minority; nevertheless, they suggest that admission of a problem is the first step toward its solution. Admission of one's vulnerability, fallibility, and neediness, as indicated even by a simple phone call, takes a lot of strength and may lead toward a reexamination of one's way of living. Very dysfunctional systems—addicted, borderline, criminal, no-self, and psychotic systems—may be too weak and unable to ask for help.

A necessary condition for change in an ailing, dysfunctional system, therefore, is to ask for and obtain external intervention. Most frequently, in functional conditions, this intervention may consist of talking with a friend or family member, reading a self-help book, going to a concert, meditating and reflecting, taking a trip, or attending a lecture. When confronted by more dysfunctioning conditions, differentiation among degrees of dysfunctionality is needed. For instance, most shy individuals could benefit from an assertiveness training workshop or similar social skills training. Shy, withdrawn, and fearful individuals, however, will need more than preventive, psychoeducational interventions. They may need therapeutic interventions in their various compositions (individual, group, marital, or family).

The next condition necessary for change in any system is for intervention to come from outside that system. Like any other dysfunctional units, human systems may need an expert's evaluation and a possible change, realignment, or replacement of defective parts. Both human and physical systems need external intervention to change. It is relatively easy to admit that a machine needs an external replacement or realignment to keep on working; it is more difficult to admit to the same principle for human beings. "Marriages are made in heaven" and many other clichés of the same ilk testify to self-defeating, fatalistic optimism. Somehow, no matter how terrible things may be, relationships (and individuals) are expected to be fixed by themselves, without external intervention. Behind this thinking, one finds apathy, helplessness, and tremendous fear of change and of confrontation of the unknown ("The devil I know is better than the devil I don't know!").

No dysfunctional system, whether physical or human, abstract or concrete, can adjust, fix itself, and survive from the inside. The analogy drawn between human and physical systems may not be palatable, but there is no evidence that dysfunctioning human systems have a greater or different ability to fix themselves. This thesis relies heavily on the nature of what constitutes external intervention. It does not need to be only psychotherapy. Any positive, external intervention or service of sufficient intensity and regularity may produce change. Interventions may help, provided that they match the immediate and transcendent needs of clients, and that the clients themselves are able and willing to absorb and assimilate the help given. This optimal match has been the golden fleece of psychotherapeutic theory and research since its very beginning.

The third necessary condition is to give clients a sense of importance or status. This is basic to the establishment of and the exchanges within intimate human relationships. Without communicating this sense of importance directly and indirectly, verbally and nonverbally, consistently and continuously, it is difficult to help people who want help. Direct communication consists of listening to someone's problems and plight, affirming the validity of someone's perceptions, and asserting the seriousness of the problem as perceived by the one reporting it. Verbal communication reframes positively the request for help: "Only people who care for themselves ask for help"; "You must care a lot about yourself [or each other] if you were strong enough to ask for help"; "You must be very strong because mostly strong people ask for help; weak people are too weak to ask." Further communication is effected by behaving toward clients as if they were guests and accepting their plight unconditionally.

The fourth condition necessary for change is to give a sense of hope that, through appropriate help, change for the better can and will take place. Thus, clients need to be reassured that admitting there is a problem, asking for help, and acknowledging the importance of the problem, regardless of its objective seriousness, are relevant and important issues to the professional helper. The subjective estimation of the seriousness of the problem itself, rather than its objective outcome, is necessary to give reassurance that the problem can be solved and that change will bring about such a solution: "This is a very serious problem, but with your help, I think we can work on it."

The fifth necessary condition for change is to give clients a sense of control and mastery over their lives. People want help because their own life or someone in their life is out of control. How is a sense of control and mastery to be achieved? This topic is too important to be capsuled here. Later in the chapter, greater attention will be given to its therapeutic applications.

What Does Change Imply?

Much has been learned about change in the past generation of practice and research in the field of psychotherapy (Ehrenwald, 1991; Freedheim, 1992). A summary of what change means is appropriate here. For change to take place at all, four basic components are necessary, though they may be insufficient by themselves. Change takes place when there is a *new* response that is both *positive* and *strong enough* to be incorporated into one's repertoire of responses and to make a distinct difference and give *direction* to one's life (Prochaska, DiClemente, & Norcross, 1992). The first component, *newness* or *novelty,* is defined as any attitude, feeling, or behavior that was not previously experienced and that becomes presently available in one's emotional, cognitive, and behavioral repertoire. This new experience is therefore different from past ones; even if it has been potentially available, it has not been used before. Talking about oneself to someone who listens, and who evidences caring by responding to one's inner feelings, is a new, positive, and exciting experience for people who have not been listened to in the past. In some clients' past, feelings and subjective perceptions may have been discounted or even punished.

The second component of change requires a new response to be of a *positive* nature, that is, a self-enhancing and rewarding behavior that does not damage anyone else. After all, one can change for the worse by either doing nothing or using negative means. Any new positive behavior helps one feel good, enhanced, important, and whole as a human being, to the extent that no one gets hurt by this new behavior. A sense of positivity is achieved through: (a) hearing someone in authority affirm the validity of one's perceptions as determined by attendant feelings; and (b) affirming the validity and importance of past, painful experiences that have been negatively influential in one's life. Regularity of meetings and talking, in and by themselves, may be sufficient to make a difference in one's life. Positive affirmation and reframing may be new experiences where negativity has been the hallmark in the past.

As Cantor and Kihlstrom (1987) suggested, effecting change is based on avoiding "old scripts" and learning new ones (pp. 227–234), while persisting in change efforts and reflecting on the self. Persistence means frequent repetition, practice, and rehearsal in order to increase the habitual preeminence of this new behavior.

The third component of change is *strength.* This quality is added when one's perceptions and experiences are affirmed and validated *repeatedly.* Strength refers to behavior that is forceful, intense, and powerful enough to make a difference in how one is going to live the rest of one's life. This difference is seen in Rogers's "corrective emotional experience," in "peak experiences," or even in routine repetition and repetitive practice of new and positive behaviors. These three components of change can be reframed as being based on *frequency and duration* of appointments and positive affirmations, and on *intensity*—the emotional experience of meeting with a professional to share deep and painful feelings and emotions.

A fourth component, *direction,* is necessary to learn, from past experiences, how to change toward more rewarding and realistic priorities. One can have novelty, positiveness, and strength. Without direction in how to use these components, however, one could go around in circles endlessly, unable to direct one's energy and efforts toward rewarding goals (i.e., becoming more selful and asserting one's importance without putting anyone else down).

Thus, the psychotherapeutic experience allows for the acquisition and emission of new responses that were not experienced or present emotively, cognitively, or behaviorally in one's past repertoire. For instance, preset appointments help achieve some sense of regularity, predictability, and stability where none was present in the past. This regularity is important to establish or reestablish a sense of control where controls, in the past, were not present or, at best, weak and inadequate or too rigidly strong.

Given these components of change, why are so many people afraid of it? Among the many possibilities that exist, the following are derived from clinical practice:

1. Change places too many demands on one's limited resources.
2. Change is a threat that may prove one's badness, craziness, or inadequacy; it carries a threat of possible banishment and hospitalization.
3. Inability to change in general is a lifelong pattern that has in itself produced and compounded the problem, as seen in addictions, borderline cases, and psychoses.

4. Rejection of treatment is part of overall denial of dependency and proclamation of independence, without considering that the human condition is characterized by *inter*dependence; independence does not exist because all human beings are, in one way or another, interdependent.
5. Loss of power occurs, especially in dyadic and family relationships, where the one who has the most power, with little or no responsibility (stereotypically, the man), sees change as a threat to that position. Selfish men feel threatened by change and find it difficult to accept psychotherapy as a positive and benign process.

Change is no different from other behavioral dimensions. It has:

1. *Duration,* as seen in the length of a therapy session and a sequence of sessions, however short or long.
2. *Frequency* of positive experiences—the peak experiences that take place inside and outside the therapist's office—and rate of appointments.
3. *Intensity* of depth and strength in the experience.
4. *Direction,* which is just as important as any other component.

All four components intermingle in the therapeutic experience.

PRINCIPLES OF CONTROL

Past behavioristic positions have simplistically stressed the importance of immediate consequences with contingent reinforcements. However, this position has been shown to be practically, philosophically, and empirically limited in helping complex human systems. Control is established by external reinforcements as well as by internal emotional attitudes and cognitions that direct behavior above and beyond immediate, concrete reinforcements. Many people work for internal and abstract, if not transcendental, reasons. Behavioral positions deal strictly with the output of behavior, not with the input and throughput. In this regard, they remain incomplete and wanting. Control is achieved when the access, input, beginning, output, and end of any behavioral sequence, as well as what happens during that sequence, are regulated. It is just as important to help people establish a sense of control at the input or beginning of the undesirable behavior as at the output or end.

How is control established in real life? In everyday reality, control consists of beginning a behavior (say, going to work) at a certain, predetermined time and ending it (exiting from work) at a given, preestablished time. Employers control their employees by requiring them to show up at an established time and to leave the place of work at a later, already predetermined time. If employees are late, they should have a reasonable excuse, and if they wish to leave early, they must request permission. In some companies, employees are penalized for any deviation from the agreed-on starting and ending times. Thus, control is established through regulation of inputs (entrances, beginnings, accesses), throughputs, and outputs (exists and endings).

This real-life analogy is also a rationale for establishing controls during the process of psychotherapy. Clients receive present appointment times for which the duration is established in a predictable, regular, and repeatable sequence. Sometimes, this sequence may not be sufficient, or it may be too expensive, chancy, and lengthy. Consequently, a parallel process of homework meetings and written assignment is required at preset, prearranged times, to increase repetitive predictability and establish regularity. The quality of *regularity,* found in activities such as brushing the teeth every day, having set mealtimes, and traveling to and from work at the same time daily, helps establish a sense of control. The establishment of regularity for the beginning and ending of any behavioral sequence, plus directions over what should happen in between, *is* control. Very likely, without a sense of repetitive regularity, a sense of control would not be established.

The regularity of therapy appointments is doubled by requiring clients to have regular home meetings that parallel the frequency and time frame of therapy sessions. When required of individuals, couples, or families, home meetings, although based on personal impressions, produce a sense of mastery more quickly than when therapy sessions are used alone. If this double regularity (at home and at the therapist's office) is accepted and agreed on from the beginning of the therapeutic relationship (through a written contract), the therapist must administer written homework assignments that make the home meetings relevant. The therapy hour then becomes more effective and productive by enlarging and strengthening the sphere of therapeutic influence to include the home.

An important part of structuring skills consists of helping clients who are out of control to learn new ways of controlling themselves. The following principles are suggested for therapists' application in their practice.

Principle 1. Teach Control without Appearing to Control

This is a tricky principle to implement. To help out-of-control clients (individuals, couples, or families) achieve control without their knowing it, one must consider at the outset that many clients want change but are also afraid of it. They would like things to be better but do not want to face themselves in the process. Often, the identified patient, who has or exhibits the problem, is the one who must change. The rest of the family professes to be OK ("If it weren't for ______, we would be all right!") and feels no need to change. This is a very unrealistic attitude; it does not work. A family member will find it very difficult (impossible, some therapists would maintain) to change unless the other family members change as well.

Thus, the therapist must follow a thin line of helping without seeming to help, controlling without appearing to control, and not taking any kudos for improvement nor any blame if things get worse! If they change for the better, clients take all the credit.

Principle 2. Take Control, Then Give It Away

The therapist must realize that control is limited to oneself. It is virtually impossible to control anybody else without using coercion or manipulation. Follow the client's lead for how much control the client may allow the therapist to have, and never threaten the client's need to avoid being controlled. Before taking control or giving it back, understand that control consists of persuasion and decision making, as well as directions, suggestions, and recommendations for beginning and ending a task assignment.

Principle 3. Control the Problem, or It Will Control You

If the therapist cannot take control and then relinquish it to the client, defeat for both of them will be the outcome. Many clients are so set in defeating self and others that they are also capable of defeating the therapist. Each therapist must choose *how* (not *whether*) to control a problem, while recognizing that, ultimately, the choice belongs to the client. Even though clients may claim they want to control a problem, very likely they do not know how. It is up to therapists to teach clients to understand the nature of control and regulation, by providing a positive plan of treatment implementation developed beforehand.

Principle 4. Start a Behavior if You Want to Learn to Stop It

Up to the time the client asks for professional help, most of the energy of the individuals involved has very likely been invested in stopping the problem, no matter what or how drastic the process or the consequences. One family, in a desperate effort to stop a child's sucking his index finger, had a dentist build a metal mouth cage (more like a trap!) that would not allow the child to insert his finger into his mouth. Most people—and families—want to stop what they perceive as bad behaviors at the end rather than at the beginning of the behavior. The behavioral school has not helped; it has stressed a view of control based on reinforcement or avoidance *after* the undesirable behavior has taken place rather than *before* it happens. Instead, the undesirable behavior should be started, provided it is not lethal or toxic to anyone. This principle can be broken down into specific steps.

Step 1. Make the behavior happen in the way it naturally happens. By making the unacceptable behavior happen, the problem remains in the hands of the therapist rather than in the hands of the one who has the problem. For instance, in dealing with temper tantrums or sibling rivalry, it is possible to induce these behaviors in an environment that closely resembles the conditions that have brought them forth in the past. Specific instructions and programmed materials for these two problem patterns and others are available elsewhere (L'Abate, 1992b, 1996a).

Step 2. Determine where, when, and how the behavior is going to happen. By regulating where, when, for how long, and how the problem behavior is to take place, control can be achieved, provided the family members follow the instructions to the letter. If they do not, explore the reasons for their continuing choice of self-defeat. If the family so chooses to defeat itself, the defeat can be proscribed at specific times and in specific ways.

Step 3. Control through planning. To achieve control, one needs a plan: a blueprint to read, a score to follow, a program to submit, or a model to implement. Just having an ad hoc single-shot idea or a gimmick is not enough, even though a great deal of therapy seems to consist of one-time remedies. A plan implies a systematic sequence of steps that is written down and included in the therapeutic contract.

Step 4. Control through regulation. To regulate means to set spatial and temporal boundaries and limits to behavior *once it has started.* Consequently, this step is translated into specific times for family conferences. Appointments should be set up at least twenty-four hours in advance, for a duration of at most one hour. Thus, regulation means having times for meetings whose duration and content are determined and agreed on beforehand.

Step 5. Control through writing. A Latin proverb, "*Verba volant, scripta manent,*" translates to "The spoken word flies away, but the written word remains." A client who is really interested in changing will need to do a lot of writing—*open,* as in a diary; *focused,* as in describing past and even secret hurts; or *programmed,* as in systematic homework assignments (L'Abate, 1986, 1992b, 1996a).

Step 6. Change the context of the problem. By prescribing certain problematic behaviors, one changes the context of the problem. Instead of taking place randomly or under out-of-control circumstances, the problem takes place under controlled conditions, within preset spatial and temporal boundaries. The problematic behavior does not take place at the whim of one or more family members. It is no longer at the mercy of moods, impulses, and other questionable and destructive motivations or habits.

Step 7. Change the direction of the problem. The direction of a problem changes as soon as it is started at prearranged times. However, it may be preferable to make sure that, instead of going from the one who carries the problem, who is called the *identified patient* (IP) or the *symptom carrier,* to the rest of the family, the direction is changed. By setting someone other than the IP in control (by starting a meeting, by prescribing the symptom), the direction and context of the symptom are changed. This change can take place in at least four ways: (a) changing from the one who has the problem and who has in some way control of the problem to those who are controlled by it (e.g., from the problem child to the parents); (b) changing from the one who is most involved to the one who is least involved (e.g., from the mother of an acting-out child to the father of the child); (c) breaking the deadly lock of the drama triangle by having all family members take turns playing the same self-defeating parts: the victim, the rescuer, and the persecutor (these parts or roles can be assigned for homework if the instructions are in writing, or they can be played out in the therapist's office); and (d) prescribing the defeating patterns themselves ("Keep on defeating each other, either at will or at preset times, whichever is easier.").

How are these principles of control related to the theory enunciated earlier? The therapist must see through the distracting smoke of conflict, acrimonious recriminations, and passionate accusations, and reframe them positively ("You are certainly involved with each other"; "You must love each other very dearly, if you are so passionate for each other"; "You are not indifferent to each other"). Once an understanding of the partners' or parents' respective self-definitions has been reached (it may take from one session to one year without specific writing assignments), the therapist must make sure that everyone is involved in the prescribed transaction. If written homework assignments are completed and conferences are attended, the therapist produces at least three positive feedback loops: (a) from the written questions to their answers; (b) from one individual (the IP) to the other individuals; and (c) from the other individuals to the therapist.

NONVERBAL TECHNIQUES IN CRISIS INTERVENTION AND PSYCHOTHERAPY

This section introduces nonverbal techniques in the practice of crisis intervention and psychotherapy (Druckman, Rozelle, & Baxter, 1982; Fisher, 1970; Knapp, 1972; Patterson, 1984; Scheflen, 1972; Seraganian, 1993; Waxer, 1978; Weitz, 1974; Wieman & Harrison, 1983). Nonverbal behavior is the first medium of communication; it occurs prior to the development of talking and writing. A child is born into a nonverbal world of space where approach and avoidance tendencies are modulated by how rewarding or punitive the child's caretaker is (Birdwhistell, 1970; Markus-Kaplan & Kaplan, 1984). The use of nonverbal behavior for therapeutic or paratherapeutic purposes has had, thus far, limited applications in clinical circles (Kepner, 1993; Kramer & Akhtar, 1992; Middleman, 1968, Steere, 1982; Waxer, 1978). Marriage and family therapists not trained in using this approach may be leery of using it in conjunction with and in addition to the verbal medium. Furthermore, there is very little information or evidence about its short- or long-term benefits. According to the advocates cited above, nonverbal awareness of their bodies seems to make people feel good. However, how does this feeling, no matter how positive, transfer to other behaviors, both verbal and nonverbal, especially outside of the therapist's office? And if this medium is not used in therapy, how can one find out whether it is effective?

A Brief Historical Background about Nonverbal Techniques

Of all the texts cited above, only Waxer (1978) reminds the reader that emphasis on nonverbal behavior goes as far back as Charles Darwin, William James, and Carl George Lange scientifically, and as far back as Sigmund Freud, Theodor Reik, and Wilhelm Reich clinically. Waxer acknowledged the contributions of: Virginia Satir (1972), concerning the importance of nonverbal cues in family therapy; Fritz Perls, in Gestalt therapy; body therapists Albert Pesso, Magda Proskauer, Ida Rolf, William Schutz, and Bernard Gunther; and Alexander Lowen's bioenergetics. Among those who conducted clinically descriptive studies, Waxer cited Karl Lewin, Albert Scheflen (1972), and Paul Ekman and Wallace V. Friesen. Unfortunately, Waxer omitted from his otherwise competent review the contributions of pioneers like Ray L. Birdwhistell (1970) in the descriptive realm and Ruth R. Middleman (1968) in the clinical realm. The latter was the first to provide a complete survey of these techniques in working with groups. She stressed the important role that "doing-oriented activities" play in group work. There is no reason why such activities should not work with couples and families as additions to verbally oriented psychotherapy.

All of the contributions mentioned above should be taken as presenting and representing the necessary scientific and historical background to validate the use of nonverbal techniques in psychotherapy. Hence, therapists should not feel uneasy about using these techniques, provided they are administered responsibly and within the context of ethical and professional boundaries. In spite of a distinguished history, however, few rationales have been presented in the literature about the use of these techniques in psychotherapy. Such a rationale is now given.

A Rationale for Nonverbal Techniques in Psychotherapy

What is the purpose of using nonverbal techniques in psychotherapy? The major reason for using them is to increase clients' awareness of their bodies and their concentration on themselves rather than on anybody else. Often, clients' awareness (*Aw*) is restricted and limited. Why not deal with it directly through body work rather than talk? There are actually two distinct rationales for the use of nonverbal techniques in psychotherapy. They are: (a) a *developmental* rationale and (b) a *structural* rationale. The developmental sequence of communication media progresses from nonverbal to verbal and then to writing. This sequence is universal and constant. It is very doubtful whether a verbal medium can develop before a nonverbal one is adequately established. There are paralyzed individuals who learn to talk and write in spite of their physical handicap. Normatively speaking, however, the nonverbal–verbal–writing sequence is fairly standard. Each medium is pretty well differentiated along a variety of dimensions. Each medium's special characteristics distinguish it from the other two. It is no accident that all three media are needed to survive and to enjoy life.

The use of writing in therapy has been discussed in Chapter 12. The nonverbal medium may not lend itself equally well to preventive approaches because of the need for a face-to-face relationship with a trainer. The writing medium, as discussed in the previous chapter, does not need such a presence. It can take place long-distance through letters or e-mail (L'Abate & Torem, 1996). The nonverbal medium can be administered through videotapes or computers, which free therapists from giving time-consuming instructions. However, to obtain feedback from the therapist, a group of individuals, couples, or families would need to be videotaped. This approach is possible, but is it feasible? It would be described through writing or questionnaire completion.

The structural rationale implies that all three media of communication are needed to ensure that behavior generated or initiated in the therapist's office will generalize or transfer to home, school/work, and leisure-time settings. This structure only reinforces the need for therapists to operate at all three levels of communication to help people in trouble. Stressing the importance of the body and of body work may strengthen the use of the body for exercise outside of the therapist's office. Seraganian's work (1993) covers all of the many psychological benefits that can be derived from exercise. Plante (1993) also showed how aerobic exercise can be used for the prevention and treatment of psychopathology. The issue here lies in how clients can be motivated to pay attention to physical aspects of their behavior. It is doubtful (but not impossible) whether this motivation can be established verbally, through exhortation. Even though such a possibility cannot be excluded, would it not be better to demonstrate in the professional's office how body exercises may help one's awareness and one's feelings of mastery over the immediate environment (i.e., one's own body) in addition to making one feel better?

Preparing Clients to Use Nonverbal Techniques

Any deviation from mainstream verbal psychotherapy should be approached carefully, lest the therapist be accused of practicing in ways that are not part of the accepted armamentarium of the profession. Hence, to protect oneself from possible complaints from clients or other professionals, clients should be informed at the beginning, during the first interview, that the therapist plans to use techniques that do not rely only on the verbal medium. In the initial session, after this information is shared and before a therapeutic contract is concluded, clients should be able to express whatever doubts or reservations they may have. To avoid pressuring clients to agree, they should be allowed to "sleep on" the decision to include these techniques in the course of their psychotherapy. The decision to use writing in the practice of therapy should be given the same leeway. After possible doubts and reservations are discussed fully, a written, informed consent form should be drawn, either to be signed in the therapist's presence, if clients are ready, or to be taken home for further consideration and eventual signature. More discussion of this issue appears later in the chapter.

Nonverbal Exercises in the Therapist's Office

Table 13.1 lists a variety of simple exercises to administer to groups of individuals and, under certain conditions, to groups of couples or a few families together. Due to their intimate nature, exercises E and F should be done with only one couple or one family present. The final decision on how many people to include, however, rests with the therapist. Relationship and contextual factors will contribute to his or her decision.

TABLE 13.1 Examples of Nonverbal Exercises for Groups of Individuals, Couples, and Families

The purpose of these exercises is to help each of you become more aware of yourselves, your bodies, and how to use your bodies for your benefit by receiving information from the inside and outside of your bodies.

Instructions	Commentary
A. Standing exercises (stand behind a chair; use the back of the chair as a prop to balance and to protect against falling down)	The symbolic meaning of this exercise is that life is a balancing act. Ask how it feels to learn to stand on one foot. The learning curve is fast with practice.
1. Try to stand on one foot only, and count how many seconds you can stand. Repeat standing on the same foot until you can stand for at least 30 seconds or more. Switch from one foot to another, and try to increase the time spent standing on each foot.	
2. For those who can stand well on one foot, bend the other knee upward 33% and move the portion of the leg below the knee up and down three times. Switch to standing on the other foot and, with the knee bent, repeat the procedure. Continue switching from one foot to the other for at least five minutes or more.	This is another way to relax the body and to become more confident of ones' control and use of one's own body.
3. Stand with the feet a few inches apart, close the eyes, and release all tension from the body. Let the head fall forward to experience complete relaxation.	Many people do not know how to relax standing up. After a few minutes, when everybody seems relaxed, ask for reports on how they feel.
4. Without changing position, bring the shoulders up and down a few times to increase relaxation.	This movement increases relaxation in the neck and shoulder muscles. Ask for additional feedback.

TABLE 13.1 *(Continued)*

Instructions	Commentary
5. Keeping the eyes closed, become aware of breathing. Breathe fast for a few minutes, breathe slowly for a few minutes, and then breathe normally.	After a few minutes, ask for reports. Is everyone aware that they can control their breathing?
6. Tense the muscle in the lower left leg . . . and let go. Tense the muscle in the lower right leg . . . and let go. Use the same approach for thighs, stomach muscles, arms, neck, and shoulders. How does the body feel after a complete tour of tension/relaxation?	This is a traditional exercise that can be repeated sitting or lying down.
B. Sitting exercises Except for exercises 1 and 2 above, all of the standing exercises can be repeated while sitting or lying down.	
C. Lying down exercises In addition to performing exercises 3 through 6 lying down, the prone position allows a variety of additional movements of arms and legs: up and down, sideways, and back and forth.	If the trainer is of a different gender than the group, it is suggested that a second professional be present to avoid any possibility of misinterpretation.
D. Couples' relationship exercises	
1. *Blaming.* Both partners stand facing the therapist with feet apart and with one arm extended and raised at shoulder level toward the other partner. The index finger on the extended hand is directed toward the other partner. When this position is achieved, partners take turns shouting to each other: "It's all your fault!" They can stop when they become tired of holding the arm up.	This stance mimics what goes on in many dysfunctional couples, where individuals are not able to take responsibility for themselves and indulge, instead, in finding fault with the other, without any awareness or admission of personal error.
2. *Placating.* One partner keeps the blaming stance. The other kneels down on one knee, keeping the other foot flat. The hands are joined in a pleading, prayerful	A variation on this exercise has the placating partner assume a martyr position by standing against a wall and extending the arms as though crucified. Stereotypically, more women than men are willing

(continued)

TABLE 13.1 *(Continued)*

Instructions	Commentary
stance, and he or she says repeatedly: "Be nice to me, please be nice to me." The other partner keeps on saying: "It's all your fault." After some repetitions, the stances are reversed. The blaming partner assumes the placating stance and the placating partner assumes the blaming stance.	to assume this stance. In the next exercise, more men than women value being "reasonable."
3. *Intellectualizing or computerizing.* The therapist can illustrate this stance by assuming a rigidly straight standing position with the feet together, arms down on the side of the body, and head up high. After the couple assumes this stance, each partner keeps on saying: "I am reasonable and if we used reason and logic in our marriage [or relationship] things would be a lot better."	As these stances are performed, allow the partner to comment on how they apply to them outside of the therapist's office.
4. *Distraction or irrelevance.* With legs wide apart, feet turned inward, and arms raised up, the upper torso should turn around while each partner says: "It's not my fault! It's not my job! I have nothing to do with it! I am innocent!"	Verbal statements can be tailored to the specific utterances heard by the therapist in talking with each couple.
E. Couples' intimacy exercises	
1. The partners sit in front of each other and, with the eyes closed, take turns to touch hands, forearms, and face, describing what they feel as each area is touched and after completion.	This is something that many couples do not do, even though it can be a very pleasant experience. This exercise could be preparatory for the next one.
2. The therapist then says: "With eyes closed, get in touch with all your hurts that you have received in your life and start becoming aware of how these hurts are represented in different ways in your body. When you can no longer	This is a diagnostic as well as a cathartic exercise. It allows a couple to see whether they can share hurts and are or can become intimate (L'Abate, 1986).

TABLE 13.1 *(Continued)*

Instructions	Commentary
contain or control these hurts, say: 'I hurt.' See what the other partner says or does in response to this message.	
F. Families' exercises	
1. *Sculpting the family as one sees it* The therapist says: "I need a volunteer to help me sculpt this family. Does anybody know what sculpting means? [Pause for answer; accept whatever answer indicates an understanding of the process.] Now that you know what sculpting means, who will help me sculpt this family? [After there is a volunteer, continue.] I want you to move your family around without saying one word, and I want the rest of you to move as [name of volunteer] wants you to move, in any position [volunteer] wants. Each of you will get your turn (to be sculptor). Make sure you move and sculpt your family *the way you see it.*" (This whole process should take place without words from anyone in the family. Once the family has been sculpted, ask the sculptor to describe what positions were given to each family member and why. Ask for the same exercise to be performed by every member of the family who is willing.	This exercise is described in detail in L'Abate, Hansen, and Ganahl (1986), where most of the relevant references on this exercise can be found. The therapist must pay attention to the affect generated by this exercise, because it may create powerful feelings. Consequently, it should be administered only when a great deal of time is available to pay attention to forthcoming feelings. It should be followed immediately by the next exercise, which will allow the session to end on a more positive note.
2. *Sculpting the family as one would like it to be.* The instructions for this exercise are the same as for the one above, except that the family should now be sculpted according to how each family member would like it to be. As in the previous exercise, go from nonverbal to verbal expression.	This is a good exercise to end a family session, because it is much more positive than the previous one and will counteract any possible negative effects.

Note: Exercises D, E, and F are after Satir (1972).

Most of the exercises listed in Table 13.1 are fairly standard and are easy to administer. It is beneficial if the therapist first experiences them directly, as a way of learning about their effectiveness in improving the therapeutic relationship and the awareness of one's own clients. The wording of the instructions is not cast in concrete. It can and should be changed to fit the therapist's own style and the clients' particular needs. During and after the administration of these exercises, detailed notes should be taken either by the therapist or by a cotherapist assistant.

Ethical and Professional Issues in the Practice of Nonverbal Techniques

It is wise, in this day and age of litigation, to limit one's physical contact with clients to a warm handshake. If a hug is initiated by a client, it can be accepted with a minimum of warmth and gestures and a maximum of circumspection, limiting oneself at best to reciprocate with a pat on the back, preferably in the presence of other people. *Nonverbal techniques should not be used with single individuals who are alone with the therapist,* especially when these clients are of a different gender from the therapist. These techniques lend themselves well to groups of individuals, couples, and families. Because of their nonmainstream nature, as recommended above, therapists planning to use them or already using them should get a written, informed-consent form signed by clients or by adult caretakers if families with children are involved. This recommendation is for therapists' self-protection. Unfortunately, issues of professional liability and credibility cannot be ignored. No matter how careful and circumspect a therapist may be, especially if one's practice is very large, it is crucial that a written contract be signed before initiating any nonverbal technique.

Nonverbal techniques in psychotherapy may enlarge the therapist's repertoire to include aspects of behavior that would be otherwise hidden or unavailable to the observation and understanding of individuals, couples, or families. Especially in family therapy, children love to participate in nonverbal exercises. They would get bored and lose interest if all contacts with the therapist where limited solely to the verbal medium. For the therapist, nonverbal techniques have the advantage of varying the clinical practice and making it more interesting than if it were limited to the verbal medium.

SUCCESSFUL (*CC*) AND UNSUCCESSFUL (*RR* & *AA*) COMMUNICATION

As described by the developmental competence theory, there are successful (selful) and unsuccessful (selfish, selfless, and no-self) patterns of communication. By successful is meant any pattern of communication that increases the functionality of oneself and of another. This communication enhances all respondents involved in intimate (committed, close, and prolonged) relationships, such as couples and families. Enhancement comes from any acts and verbal communications that lead to a positive upward spiral of growth and advancement in all respondents. Unsuccessful communication means any act, verbal or nonverbal, that debases, discounts, and devalues respondents, exacerbating and escalating communication in a negative, downward direction.

For instance, given the same kind of provocation by one partner—"Why are you so late?"—the other partner can answer in ways that will defuse the provoking statement and enhance the relationship or that will debase it. A successful reply might be: "I am sorry . . . but didn't you get my message in the phone secretary? I called you at 4:00 o'clock to tell you that an emergency had arisen in the office and that I would be unavoidably detained." The provoking partner would then listen to the phone message and would apologize for not listening to the phone and jumping to an unwarranted conclusion without giving the partner the benefit of the doubt—"I am sorry, Honey. I should have listened to the phone before jumping on your case. Please forgive me." Here, the secret lies in asking questions without reacting to the provocation (by saying, e.g., "Didn't you listen to the phone?") and giving relevant and contextual information about the behavior. In this instance, neither partner was put down or devalued except in the opening statement, which was defused by the question, and, as a result, was then ameliorated by an apology.

The successful communicator stops, asks questions to obtain relevant information, and answers in a way that affirms the importance of whoever is involved in the provocation, as in "I can understand you were upset because I was late. But, did you listen to the phone messages?" This response asks, gets, and gives relevant information without making an emotional mountain out of an inflated molehill.

The Seven Unsuccessful (Suicidal and Murderous) Errors of Communication

Suicidal describes whatever kills the importance of the self. *Murderous* describes whatever is said or done to kill the importance of the other. Both patterns include *AA* and *RR* relationship styles. Unsuccessful communication could lie in the answer to the same provoking statement: "Why are you so late?" especially if this statement is accompanied by curses, name-calling, negative "You" statements (Error no. 1) or generalizations qualified by absolutes. Murderous statements contain absolute words like "never" or "always" as in "You are *always* late" or "You *never* call me to let me know you are going to come home late." Here, the respondent increases the escalation by getting "hooked" by the provocation and answering at a similarly emotional level: "What difference would it make? You always bitch whether I come home early or late." Unsuccessful communication is immediate and thoughtless. It is characterized by responses that are reactive rather than proactive, repetitive rather than one-word occurrences.

In unsuccessful communication, the reactor answers in kind; the emotional provocation, when met by another emotional response, can only escalate into a full-fledged argument, fight, or explosion. Thus, a partner either responds immediately in kind or does not answer at all—withdrawing instead of verbalizing the response, as in: "If you are stupid enough not to listen to my phone messages, you do not deserve an answer. Good-bye." This *RR* style (immediate answer in the same emotional tone, or withdrawal) can become abusive, including not only negative "You" statements as in "You are such a [expletive] because you never call me to let me know when you're coming home," but any of the other seven suicidal and murderous errors of abusive communication.

Bringing up the painful past (Error no. 2) is another way to escalate into unsuccessful communication, as in: "You never did call me. You [expletive], you did not call me three years ago when mother came to visit or six years ago when your mother came to visit."

Mind-reading (Error no. 3) is another abusive pattern, as in: "I know why you did not call me, you [expletive], you do not care for me or your children." Name-calling is a well-known murderous sin of communication, especially when the other's abuse or neglect is used to justify one's own abuse or neglect. One then makes excuses (Error no. 4) for self but allows no excuses for the other, as in: "I can call you names because you called me a name six weeks ago, when I forgot to call you"; or "My behavior is excusable, but yours is not."

Emotional blackmail or bribery (Error no. 5) is another suicidal and murderous pattern of communication, as in: "If you loved me you would buy me ______" or "If you loved me you would stop drinking yourself stupid." The other side of the same pattern is: "I will give you what you want if you do [say, act] what I want you to do."

Ultimatums and deadlines (Error no. 6) is another form of blackmail that forces, coerces, and manipulates the other to capitulate to the partner's demands or wishes, taking away any self-determination of the self: "If you do not stop drinking by next Sunday, I will see a lawyer on Monday."

The last pattern is more subtle, but just as destructive: answering in ways that detract and distract from the issue at hand (Error no. 7). This pattern implies bringing in irrelevant, tangential issues that do not pertain to the present situation. For example: "I may be late, but did you get the mail and the newspaper?"

Teaching Successful Communication

Given the destructiveness of these patterns, how can clients be helped to communicate better? The answer: "In many ways." First, clients need to become repeatedly involved in unsuccessful patterns as a method of learning to communicate better. Clients need to practice negative patterns—all of the seven errors and more—as a way to abandon them and learn positive substitutes. They are not going to quit communicating unsuccessfully by *fiat* of the therapist, even after an explanation of the seven erroneous patterns. They need to be trained to achieve successful communication. Hence, to become aware of destructive patterns, they need to continue practicing them. Only through repetition can they become painfully and hopelessly aware of the destructiveness of their errors.

One way to increase this awareness is to prescribe and tape-record a fight after they receive a written list of the seven errors. They are asked to fight according to these seven patterns. After the fight has been recorded, they are asked to listen individually to the tape at home, recording how many times each erroneous pattern has been used. A program on how to fight more successfully is available for professionals to administer to couples or families who demonstrate unsuccessful communication patterns (L'Abate, 1992b). A lesson concerning the same pattern is available in a second work (L'Abate, 1996a).

An additional and complementary way to teach couples to learn to communicate successfully is to put rubber bands on their wrists and instruct them to give themselves a jolt with it anytime they are having negative thoughts about their partners. These thoughts usually include negative "You" statements qualified by "never" and "always." Thus, the "You" pronoun is banned from use unless used in positive thoughts, seeing the good rather than the bad in the partner, as in: "I love you." To discourage partners from using the negative "You" pronoun and other errors of communication, they have to learn better ways to communicate successfully by using three little words: "I," "It," and "We."

Using "I" Statements

After clients have given up unsuccessful, abusive, and repetitive patterns, they need to learn how to speak for themselves and not for others. Taking responsibility and speaking for oneself is demonstrated by use of the pronoun "I." Clients can learn to use the pronoun "I" by working on written homework assignments that require completion of at least ten stems starting with "I am ______." These completions help them to see how their self is depleted and devalued by speaking about the other partner or their parents and not about themselves.

After this homework is completed and discussed by the couple or by family members, a second homework assignment consists of ten feeling statements, starting with the stem: "I feel ______ when ______." Each stem requires matching a feeling word with an emotional event. If necessary, clients may practice making feeling statements in front of each other.

Another assignment that teaches the use of the "I" pronoun is to ask clients to write down all the hurts received in a lifetime for 15 or 20 minutes a day, on 4 consecutive days. Afterward, this list can be shared with a support or therapy group or with a professional helper. To learn greater control over their lives, clients are asked to meet at home at a prearranged time to complete this task. To communicate better, it is necessary to become aware of all the hurts accumulated over a lifetime and share them reciprocally with important others. Without this sharing, it is difficult to share joys. Once awareness of hurts occurs, more helpful (successful) ways of communication may be learned, and hurtful (unsuccessful) ones can be relinquished.

Using "It" Statements

In parallel, or after the negative "You" pronoun is given up, clients need to speak about noxious or unpleasant behavior (performance) rather than about the person. They need to speak in a nonjudgmental, impersonal (rather than personal) manner. This is a much more difficult undertaking because it requires discrimination between what is done (performance) and who one is (person). Sometimes, even perfectly wonderful people make errors of omission and commission that impact others unpleasantly or hurtfully. Clients need to learn to speak about unpleasant, painful, unacceptable behavior in ways that are self- and other-enhancing rather than debasing of both. Hence, reference to unpleasant behavior is made through the impersonal "It" pronoun. Whatever is upsetting becomes "It" as in: "It is very upsetting to have you come home late. Can we do something to avoid that upset?"

Using "We" Statements

The interdependence of people living in intimate relationships, where the behavior of one impacts on everybody else, needs to be affirmed. To assert this interdependence, clients need to speak about "us" rather than "them" and "we" rather than "you." For instance: "I thought we agreed together on the time when we should eat. However, if I am mistaken, please correct me. Let's discuss whether and why we should honor our agreements or whether we should ignore them. Is it acceptable to you?" By jumping from the specific behavior (i.e., time of eating) to the general issue of whether agreements should be honored, the whole situation is viewed from a different perspective. Hence, the unpleasant or obnoxious behavior is put within a greater context of honoring agreements rather than just being on time.

In conclusion, before they can learn successful communication, clients need to be disabused from using unsuccessful communication through its repeated practice, to the point where they become painfully aware of how hurtfully they communicate. The secrets of successful communication consist of three small words: "I," "It," and "We."

EXPERIENCING AND EXPRESSING HURTS

Clients are hurt and suffering individuals or fellow travelers. Whether they admit it or not, and whether they like it or not, they are all, in some way, hurt human beings. We cannot exist and not be hurt. We all have our accumulation and depository of past and present rejections, put-downs, losses, and failures. The sooner this existential reality is recognized, the earlier—and the better—clients are going to help themselves. Hurts can be approached, confronted, and dealt with properly, leading to functional uses of most emotions and positive outcomes, or they can be avoided, discounted, and short-circuited, leading to dysfunctional uses of emotions and negative outcomes. The approach, confrontation, and consideration of hurts relate to how empathic therapists can be with themselves and with those they love.

The major therapeutic implication of this position, if valid, would be that therapists need to help people approach, rather than avoid their hurts from the very outset of therapy. Once therapists connect with them at that level, clients can be helped toward an appropriate balance of rational discharge-delay functions. Therapists themselves may need to have approached, confronted, and worked through their hurts before helping clients deal with theirs (Izard, 1991a). This is a different and more specific rationale for therapists receiving therapy than previous blanket rationales.

Major references on the role of emotions in psychotherapy (Greenberg & Safran, 1987; Nichols & Zax, 1977; Pierce, Nichols, & DuBrin, 1983; Safran & Greenberg, 1991) fail to refer to hurt or closely similar terms such as anguish, sorrow, distress, and suffering. The sole exception to this conclusion is contained in the review by Engle, Beutler, and Daldrup (1991) of Greenberg and Safran's (1987) work. Although in the original work the term *hurt* does not even appear in the subject index, Engle et al. considered the distinction between hurt and anger an important task of therapy (pp. 185–186).

Is this not the reason why people seek therapy—to find ways and means of learning how to cope with hurt feelings (Pennebaker, 1990)? Most of the foregoing references explored extensively the importance and use of feelings and emotions in psychotherapy. Yet these references failed to mention that the majority of clients want help in coping with their hurts. Apparently, the view of hurt human beings seems quite difficult to confront and to digest. Most psychopathology may be the true outcome of an "inability to express intense affect" (Beutler, Engle, Oro'-Beutler, Daldrup, & Meredith, 1986). What does intense affect consist of? In addition to rage, anger, and hostility, most intense affect consists of deep hurts that are the outcome of past abuses, disappointments, and all other antecedents.

Once the therapeutic dialogue starts with listing all past hurts in writing (Pennebaker, 1990), then whatever anger, hate, and hostility may be present tend to decrease considerably. Clients no longer need to present themselves as angry, put-upon, victimized human beings. Dealing with hurts from the very outset of psychotherapy seems to undercut whatever anger and hostility may have been generated from past hurts, leading to a qualitatively different dialogue. Therapists then fulfill a primary function as healers rather than as fixers or, worse, mechanics or engineers.

Some clients whose past hurts are extremely intense and deeply buried internally may resist dealing with them except through hypnosis. Even then, one must be very careful in uncovering deeply hurtful feelings whose experience and expression may be seen as destructive to the client's existence. In dealing with clients whose past hurts are so intense that dissociation was the inevitable outcome, as in multiple personalities (dissociative identity disorders), one would need to rely on hypnosis to explore the nature of hurts that have been completely repressed (Edelstein, 1990). Through hypnosis, one can find that most dissociative disorders are the outcome of an extreme avoidance of past, intense, and destructive hurts and traumas, consisting mostly of verbal, physical, and sexual abuses and neglects, as originally posited by Freud (1953). A future task for the prescription of a written list and elaboration of past hurts, as suggested by

Pennebaker (1990), lies in finding whether the same, but more cost-effective outcome of uncovering past hurts can be reached through the written medium rather than through hypnosis or other existential, nonverbal media.

There are a variety of ways to help clients express their hurts (Bertman & Krant, 1977). With children and adolescents, one may use drawings of make-believe trees (Hall & Kirkland, 1984) and other artistic expressions. With adults, it has been found useful to have them write about traumatic events in their lives for 20 minutes each day for 4 days (Pennebaker, 1990), a practice that can be prescribed from the very outset of therapy. Men may need body work to help them approach and deal with their hurts or their grief (Brownell, 1981). That approach may not be needed with women (Stroebe & Stroebe, 1991). It is useful to have couples share their hurts by holding each other's hands, closing their eyes, and concentrating on all their accumulated past and present hurts, as described in Table 13.1. Once they cannot hold hurts inside any longer, each partner is to express them directly by admitting them. In group therapy, one may need to establish the kind of group cohesiveness that is a necessary prerequisite for sharing of hurts (Macaskill, 1980).

One important therapeutic issue relates to helping clients take responsibility for hurts they have inflicted on others and for how they have responded to hurts they received from others. Above and beyond techniques or gimmicks to "access" clients emotionally (Edelhofer, Fabian, & Edelhofer, 1988), there is no substitute for the therapist's being emotionally available for clients. What does it mean to be emotionally available? It means making it easy for clients to share their hurts, not only cathartically, but by giving them a framework whereby they can learn to: (a) let go of past hurts, (b) avoid collecting new ones, and (c) go on with their lives free of past emotional baggage (Collins & Gabor, 1988).

Another important issue in helping clients deal with hurts refers to forgiveness of hurts inflicted and received. Although forgiveness of errors may smack of theological implications (Ritzman, 1987; Walters, 1984), no equivalent process functions in the same fashion. Tolerance or acceptance may imply the same process and avoid the theological undertones of the term *forgiveness*. Unconditional positive regard may include the same process, because many clients have not experienced either unconditional love or intimacy in their past. Whatever term one may choose, the process implies letting go of demands for perfection, production, performance, and problem-solving in themselves before they can let go of the same demands in others. To forgive means to give up all claims on whoever has produced the hurt, including letting go of the emotional consequences of the hurt. The issue here is how often should one forgive? We have two cheeks. How often will we allow others to slap them?

Walters (1984) postulated the following stages in the process of forgiving: preparation, decision, action, closure, and follow-through. Patients who have been abused, for instance, need to forgive the abuser by showing that they can conduct themselves better than the abuser. Without forgiveness, one would continue to attract and collect hurts throughout one's life. The process is not for the benefit of the one being forgiven, who by now may have either passed away or be unreachable (Ritzman, 1987). The process of forgiveness is necessary for the welfare of the one doing the forgiving, lest a store of hurts, anger, resentment, and many other unpleasant emotions remain in the client's system. To help clients forgive themselves, for whatever they may have done to hurt themselves and loved ones, is more of a process goal than something that can take place at the beginning of therapy. With genuine forgiveness there should be the cathartic experience of crying, which is basic to the establishment of intimacy. Without the sharing of tears, there would be some doubt as to whether hurts are congruently felt and expressed.

SELFHOOD AND REACTIONS TO INTERVENTION

Selful individuals or couples will not see the need for therapy but will enjoy and benefit from the enrichment and self-enlightenment offered in preventive programs. However, they will be able to ask for professional help when necessary. Selfish individuals will tend to dismiss any need for treatment because of their strong need to deny dependency and avoid any form of confrontation that may produce internal conflict. Hence, they are poor prospects for psychotherapy, even though they may be amenable to the use of computers for self-improvement, especially if this use may get them out of jail or other sticky situations, as described in Chapter 12. Selfless individuals form two-thirds of the outpatient caseload in mental health. They represent the conventional, obedient client who follows instructions and feedback from an authority figure such as a therapist. If they are expected to talk, they will talk; they will be good patients who will make their therapists feel successful in their enterprise. Some no-self patients will improve and others will not. Hence, a more specific differentiation of individuals according to the selfhood model is necessary, in terms of who will be a success or failure in psychotherapy.

This proposal may raise more questions than it will answer. However, one possible implication, among others, relates to the role of preventive and psychotherapeutic interventions. One cannot use the same method of intervention when dealing with fundamentally different individuals. For instance, although the verbal medium may be relatively successful with selfless individuals, who admit to their condition almost too quickly, it may not be successful with selfish individuals, who deny their condition and externalize it onto other sources. Other media of treatment may be necessary. In dealing with selfish persons, nonverbal, physically based group approaches may be more appropriate than individual psychotherapy based on the verbal medium. In dealing with no-self individuals, structured, psychoeducational, social skills training approaches may be more appropriate and effective than verbal psychotherapies.

Consequently, from the viewpoint of personality propensities, a suggested sequence of interventions may be as follows:

1. Selfulness: Sequence and approaches may not matter; there is improvement no matter which sequence or modality is followed.

2. Selfishness: Initially, long distance writing (LDW) or computer-assisted training (CAT) and nonverbal (group) therapy are recommended; ultimately, verbal psychotherapy may be possible, but only if sufficient changes and motivation for change have been demonstrated beyond a shadow of a doubt.
3. Selflessness: initially, verbal therapy may establish rapport; later, it may be combined with both written (individualized) and nonverbal (group) approaches.
4. No-self: Initially, nonverbal (group) therapy would be used, then written, and eventually verbal therapy, if justified by sufficient change and demonstrated motivation for change.

CONCLUSION

This chapter has attempted to show some isomorphism between the theory of developmental competence and clinical applications. Whether a goal of isomorphism has been achieved will be difficult to prove as long as therapeutic interventions are based on the verbal medium. If people are to learn how to love and how to negotiate, they first must learn how to become aware through nonverbal means, to achieve control over their lives through principles of control, and to take responsibility for how they have managed their past hurts, using the "I," "It," and "We" pronouns in relating to intimate others.

PART FOUR

Conclusion

CHAPTER 14

Toward a Simple Arithmetical Model for Interpersonal Relationships

The relative strength of causal variables may be affected by psychosocial learning experiences. (Haynes, 1992, p. 110)

This final chapter suggests that it is possible to begin conceptualizing interpersonal relationships, and especially intimate interpersonal relationships characterized by interdependence (marriage, parent–child, and sibling–sibling relationships), according to simple arithmetical rules involving addition, subtraction, multiplication, and division. This chapter is an arithmetical statement of a simple model (L'Abate, 1976, pp. 11, 188) that was elaborated later on (L'Abate, 1985a) in terms of the function that victories and defeats have in keeping family members close and dependent on each other, whether they like it or not.

Attempts to use arithmetic and mathematics to conceptualize psychological functions go back far in the history of psychology; for some decades, there has been a specialized field of mathematical psychology (Coombs, Dawes, & Tversky, 1970; Lawing, 1973; Luce, 1995), although an elaboration of it is above and beyond the scope of this chapter or this theory. This field concerns itself with quantifying intrapsychic, individual functions, and is beginning to enter the field of interpersonal relations. Lewin (1935) was one of the early pioneers who attempted to reduce social relationships to mathematical formulas through his well-known equation (Behavior = Person × Environment).

Recently, there have been at least two attempts, among many, to quantify relationships according to algebraic and mathematical formulas. Rapoport (1972) developed two differential equations to predict how a social system, such as members of a family, reacts to keep the status quo by deescalating or escalating their behavior to change the balance of the system. Bernard (1964) and Broderick and Smith (1979) used these equations to predict increased hostility in couples (Broderick, 1993, pp. 71–75). Silvestri (1993) has attempted the same task as Rapoport, perhaps in a more complex manner. Unfortunately, these attempts have not been very successful in convincing many theorists—or therapists—to use arithmetical or algebraic means to conceptualize interdependent relationships. These earlier attempts used advanced mathematical symbols that are well beyond the skills of the average theorist or therapist (and the author). Thus, one should begin with a very simple arithmetical approach that is well within the comprehension of the average theorist or therapist.

Characterizations of interpersonal relationships according to game theory (Ashmore, 1987; Coleman, Coleman, & Thomas, 1990; Pruitt, 1983) allow condensing these relationships according to either positive (+) or negative (−) outcomes (Lindsay, 1976). The positivity or negativity of interdependent interactions depends on the phenomenological experience, the perception of each participant in that interaction. Thus, any simple arithmetical formulation would need to consider the subjective aspects of an interaction from the receptive side of the experiencing–expressing continuum. What may appear as a victory objectively to an external observer on the expressive side may be perceived and felt as a defeat subjectively by either participant on the receptive side. Furthermore, what may be perceived subjectively as a victory by one participant may be perceived subjectively as a defeat by the other.

Positivity is defined by a successful conclusion of any exchange, where a feeling of progressive advancement and enhancement is experienced by both participants or partners. A positive (+) outcome may consist of a compliment or a smile, an agreement, a gift, a simple card, a token reward, or just an unspoken feeling of relief and contentment. The satisfaction of being acknowledged by another as being important as an individual in one's own right, may be more relevant than any material manifestation of that importance. In a negative (−) experience, either one or the other or both participants experience or perceive a sense of debasement, denigration, degradation, discounting, emptiness, loss, and, in extreme cases, annihilation or mystification and hurt.

More specifically, positively perceived and felt experiences can be computed as additions (+), and negative experiences can be computed as subtractions (−). Additions and subtractions apply to individual experiences and are personal characteristics of individuals. Personal victories, as subjectively felt and perceived, are computed as pluses (+). Personal defeats, as subjectively felt and perceived, are minuses (−). Participants can define whether the outcome is positive or negative according to their personal perceptions. Neutral outcomes, where neither a victory nor a defeat is felt or perceived, do not matter because they do not influence the ultimate outcome of intimate, interdependent interactions. Furthermore, there are very few neutral outcomes in intimate relationships, where even trivial molehills may grow and become enormous, defeating, interfering mountains.

Positivity and negativity in intimate relationships imply a view that makes these qualities the outcome of either cooperative or competitive processes. In cooperation, the outcome in intimate relationships is usually positive for both participants. A small percentage of interactions—perhaps 25% to 30%—are cooperative. Approximately one-fourth of most intimate relationships, therefore, are positive for both participants (++)*(CC)*. In competition, the outcome is usually positive for one participant and negative for the other; one wins and the other loses. The majority of interdependent relationships—perhaps 50% to 60%—are *RR:* one participant wins competitively and manipulatively at the other's expense. Approximately one-half of intimate relationships are *RR*, positive for one participant and negative for the other (+−) or vice versa (−+). Approximately one-fourth of most intimate relationships are *AA*, or negative for both participants (−−).

Cooperation implies that life and intimate relationships are viewed as harmonious, self- and other-enhancing endeavors; competition implies a view of intimate behavior as a struggle. The battle, life-as-a-struggle, or conflict metaphor is not too extreme in conceptualizing competitive, reactively repetitive, and abusive-apathetic or neglectful relationships. The metaphor of struggle may apply to a great many intimate relationships between marital partners and between parents and children, but it is not universal. It cannot be used for everyone and for all relationships. It can be used in competitive relationships where the outcome is either 0 (a plus (+) for one participant cancels a minus (−) for the other) or a split or division (/) produced by two minuses (−−). Although the poet laureate Archibald MacLeish conceptualized life as "a fight, and if you pretend you are not in a fight you aren't talking about life," this metaphor applies only to those relationships where competition, animosity, anger, manipulation, coercion, or antagonism leads to a negative outcome. Once this outcome is achieved, it may repeat itself, as in the status quo, or in a breakdown at the individual or at the relationship level. There are cooperative dyads where the outcome of two pluses (++) produces a synergistically multiplicative (×) growth in the relationship.

On the basis of the foregoing considerations, (+) and (−) apply to individuals, and multiplications (×), zeros (0), and divisions (/) apply to ultimate outcomes of relationships. The outcome of a relationship is: (a) *multiplicative* (×), where both participants win together (++), signifying growth, enhancement, positive change, and progress; (b) *unchanged* (0), signifying status quo, where the victory for one participant (+) takes place with a parallel loss for the other (−); one's victory cancels the other's defeat, and the defeating outcomes are repeated with no change in the relationship; or (c) *divisive* (/), where both participants lose (−−), signifying deterioration, regression, destruction, and breakup, whether personal, dyadic, or systemic, as seen in extreme psychopathology, addictions, murder, and suicide.

Consequently, intimate relationships may be conceptualized as following rules that do enter into the formal realm of arithmetic. They follow a process that culminates in either a victory or a defeat. There is nothing in between because there is very little room in these relationships for neutrality. Both participants win, or one wins at the expense of the other, or both lose. It is difficult for many people to understand that, in the heat of the battle, at least in intimate relationships, the defeat of another (−) might ultimately be a defeat of oneself (−). Relationships are enhanced by reciprocal enhancement of both participants. Relationships are diminished by belittlement of each participant.

This seeming simplification of interpersonal relationships is not as far-fetched as it may seem at first blush. Dabbs (1992), for instance, related the whole process of winning and losing in relationships to the measurement of testosterone indicating that studies with animal and human subjects show testosterone levels rising with winning and declining with losing. Examples of winning and losing were drawn from tennis players, officer candidate schools, incarceration, prison internment, hostages, chess tournaments, and soccer games, among others. Hence, if testosterone levels in conflictful couples, where losing is the major characteristic, are measured and compared with testosterone levels of relatively peaceful couples, a link between intimate interpersonal relationships and physiological functioning could be undertaken.

VICTORIES AND DEFEATS

It follows from the above arguments that the reciprocal or mutually positive expression—whether nonverbal, verbal, or written—by both participants in an intimate interaction results in a growth of the relationship as in the following symbolic equation:

$$\{(+)(+) = \times\}. \tag{1}$$

A positive expression by one participant and a negative expression by the other results in a static no-change outcome, as shown by the symbolic equation:

$$\{(+)(-) = 0\}. \tag{2}$$

The same outcome is predicted by a reversal of positions. If the participant who was positive becomes negative, and the other becomes positive after being negative, the eventual outcome remains the same symbolic equation:

$$\{(-)(+) = 0\}. \tag{3}$$

When both participants behave negatively, the eventual outcome may be a division, as observed by a breakdown at the personal, relational, or systemic level, as shown by the symbolic equation:

$$\{(-)(-) = /\}. \tag{4}$$

In equation (1), there is an elevation in functioning. In equations (2) and (3), there is no change in functioning. In equation (4), there is lowering and eventual deterioration in functioning, either in those who are involved in the relationship or in their offspring.

RESOURCES EXCHANGED

If one assumes, as Foa and Foa (1974) did, that six classes of resources are exchanged among us, this exchange results in positive, neutral, or negative outcomes. These classes of resources are: status and love; information and services; money and possessions. The resource class of status was changed to attribution of importance. This attribution leads to a sense of personal importance or positive self-esteem, if one wants to use this term. The resource class of love was renamed and reconceptualized as intimacy, defined as the sharing of joys and hurts and fears of being hurt (Chapter 4).

Thus, the ability to exchange (give and receive) importance is a multiplicative, summative, subtractive, or divisive function of these resources being exchanged. If both partners give (+) and receive (+) importance, that is, attribute importance to the self and to the other (partner, parent, child, relative, friend), the outcome is ×. If one partner gives importance (+) to the other but does not receive it in return (−), then the outcome is 0. The outcome is also 0 if one participant gives importance to the other (+) but denies importance to the self (−). If both participants fail to give (−) or to receive (−) importance, the outcome is (/). For example, if intimacy is expressed cooperatively and hence, unconditionally [equation (1)], there will be an enhancement of the relationship. When intimacy is sporadically and erratically shared, the outcome is 0 [equations (2) and (3)]. If intimacy does not exist in a relationship at all, the eventual outcome will very likely result in a breakdown (/) [equation (4)].

The other four classes of resources (information and services; money and goods) follow the same process of exchange. One may give information for services, money, or goods. Without an even or equitable exchange among these classes, a relationship cannot continue. Conceivably, one could exchange either services or information for just importance or intimacy, but eventually the outcome would be inequitable and negative. Unless there is a reciprocal and mutual exchange of information, services, goods, or money, one partner will ultimately feel short-changed, will indicate dissatisfaction with this outcome, and, if not heard, will eventually sever the relationship. For instance, suppose one partner works full-time by providing services or goods for money, and the other does not, for whatever reason, and there is no exchange of importance or intimacy from the nonworking partner. The working partner may eventually feel taken advantage of. The relationship may last, but it will be repetitively marred by status quo or by abusive and apathetic (i.e., neglectful) interactions. When that happens, a (− +) or (+ −) process may deteriorate into an abusive-neglectful relationship that will, in the long run, produce a break at the intraindividual, dyadic, or multipersonal level. If the relationship is competitive, there will be reactivity on both sides, with consequent repetition of the same behavior [equations (2) and (3)].

From the foregoing considerations, it becomes possible to develop the following equations for the two abilities that are fundamental to an enjoyable existence within a context of intimate relationships—the ability to love and the ability to negotiate:

$$\text{ability to love} = \{\text{importance} + \text{intimacy}\}$$

$$\text{ability to negotiate} = \{(\text{information} + \text{services}) \times\text{-0-/}\ (\text{money} + \text{goods})\}$$

When these two equations are in place, the functionality of a relationship can be predicted to the extent that both participants show and share the abilities to love and to negotiate. The result is a multiplication $\{(+)+(+) = \times\}$. Dysfunctionality represents the reverse: inability to love $(-)$ + inability to negotiate $(-)$ results in a division $\{(-) + (-) = /)\}$. In functional relationships, the ability to love is sharply separated from the ability to negotiate, to the point where the outcome will be × for both abilities. In dysfunctional relationships, both abilities are confused, fused, and diffused to the point where the outcome will be either 0 or / ("If you loved me you would do . . ."; "If you loved me you would buy me . . ."). To develop this line of thinking further, the same kind of arithmetic can be applied to more complex relationships.

There are two different routes for reducing relationships or relationship potentials to arithmetical formulations. One route is to conceptualize the outcome as a ratio between positives and negatives, as in an equation with a numerator and denominator. The other route is to conceptualize the outcome as the total summation of various components.

A POSITIVE AND INTERPERSONAL RECONCEPTUALIZATION OF ALBEE'S ALGORITHM

The closest one can get to a potential quantification of complex interpersonal relationships is through Albee's (1982) original algorithm, which has been taken for granted in the prevention field as having a great deal of descriptive currency and factual validity (Lorion, 1990). It was developed as a shorthand formula to describe and predict dysfunctionalities. By its very purpose, this formula was not concerned with functionalities because it was composed of negatives. Furthermore, it was formulated from a monadic viewpoint—at least some of its terms, especially coping skills and self-esteem, were considered from an individual-in-the-vacuum viewpoint. To revise and update Albee's undeniably creative formula and introduce more relationally positive terms, the original terms of the formula have been changed to the prediction of functionalities instead of dysfunctionalities. Some of its monadic (i.e., intrapsychic) terms, such as *self-esteem,* have been changed into relational terms. Albee's original algorithm consisted of:

$$\begin{array}{l}\text{Incidence of} \\ \text{psychopathology}\end{array} = \frac{\text{organic factors} + \text{stress} + \text{exploitations}}{\text{coping skills} + \text{self-esteem} + \text{support groups}}$$

APPLICATION OF ALBEE'S ALGORITHM TO THE PRESENT THEORY

The problem here consists of reframing predictors of dysfunctionalities into predictors of functionalities. Instead of incidence of dysfunctionalities, how can one predict incidence of functionalities? Albee's formula would become:

$$\text{Relationship potential} = \frac{\text{physical condition(ing)s (age, diet, exercise, health)} + \text{stress} + \text{hurts (including abuse)}}{\text{competence level (ARC} \times \text{ERAAwC} \times \text{priorities)} + \text{importance (selfhood)} + \text{family support (intimacy)}}$$

When Albee's original algorithm is reframed in terms of positive, interpersonal functionalities, it can be reduced to more specific factors. In the numerator, organic factors, stress, and abuse, according to Albee, are constants that cannot be changed. However, they can be reduced to more specific factors, not just the organic. For instance, physical conditioning is the outcome of summative, subtractive, multiplicative, or divisive relationships among: (a) age; (b) exercise or lack thereof; (c) diet and weight; and (d) physical health. Stress, as a subjectively felt experience, can be reduced to total of hurts experienced or feared (Chapter 4). Extent of abuse, like any other variable, can be measured just as well by using an ordinal scale or reducing any distribution of raw scores on any self-report test or rating sheet of extent of abuse (verbal, physical, or sexual) to standard scores or z-scores with a mean of 0 and a range varying between +3 and −3.

How can this formula be reduced to arithmetical terms? Standard scores could be obtained easily from either outsiders' ratings or insiders' self reports. Negative values would represent a deficit or shortcoming, and positive values would represent assets and strengths. Each of the terms in this equation can be reduced to standard scores varying between +3 and −3. In the numerator, physical condition(ing)s could be broken up into age (+3 or −3), exercise (+3 or −3), diet (+3 or −3), weight (+3 or −3), and physical health (+3 or −3). Stress could be evaluated according to socioeconomic status (SES) and number of children in the family, with a range from +3 (middle to upper SES and few children) to −3 (lower SES and more than three children). Abuse could be broken up into number of hurts and fears of being hurt (+3 or −3), for a total numerator value ranging from −18 to +18.

In the denominator, coping skills, self-esteem, and support groups cannot be defined by resource exchange theory, because it makes no assumptions about competence level. It does define status as an interpersonal resource exchanged as a substitute for self-esteem, and support could be measured by reports of intimacy exchanged (i.e., "How often have you cried together when one of you lost a loved one?"). However, definitions of coping skills could be added in terms of: (a) competence level of individual participants, plus (b) individuals' sense of self- and other-importance, and (c) the influence of the family as the major support system, as measured by intimacy.

The ability to love is made up of the sense and attribution of importance to self and other plus the ability to be intimate. The ability to cope is measured by the ability to negotiate performance (information + services) and production (money + goods). This ability is the outcome of:

1. Style, functional or dysfunctional, in intimate relationships, as described by the ARC model *(Ill)*. The ARC model describes intimate relationships in terms of three styles: *AA* or neglectful, *RR*, and *CC*. The *AA* style leads to negative outcomes for both parties in a relationship (−− = /), varying anywhere between −3 and −2. The *RR* style leads to a positive outcome for one partner and a negative outcome for the other (−+ or +− = 0), varying between −1 and +1. The *CC* style leads to positive outcomes for both participants. (++ = ×), varying between +2 and +3.
2. Skills, as described by the ERAAwC model *(Skill)*. The second ERAAwC model is defined by how emotionality *(E)*, rationality *(R)*, activity *(A)*, awareness *(Aw)*, and context *(C)* are used by each participant, defining, therefore, each participant's level of competence to negotiate.
3. Motivation to negotiate, as described by the priorities model *(Will)*. Willingness to negotiate is defined by the priorities chosen by each participant. These are developmental, intrafamily priorities, such as self, marriage, children, extended family and in-laws, friends, and leisure, and structural priorities, such as home, work, and leisure settings. Some of these priorities are functional and some are not, depending on the stage of personal, dyadic, and family life cycles. Using the same standard scores, the total number of points could vary between +21 and −21.

The second class of factors in the denominator could be the attribution of importance or a sense of self-importance, which is a more relational concept than self-esteem. Standard scores could be derived from a variety of paper-and-pencil tests of self-esteem (which could be viewed as the internal representation of the interpersonal exchange of importance between participants), or from Foa and Foa's (1974) paper-and-pencil measurement of Status, or from the self–other profile chart discussed in Chapter 3 (Appendix A). The range would be between −3 and +3. Selfulness could be measured by assigning +3 to creative, +2 to intermediate, and +1 to adequate personality propensities. Zero could be assigned to either selfish or selfless individuals, and −1, −2, or −3 could be assigned to three levels of no-self, according to severity of psychopathology.

The third class of predictors in the denominator—family support—relates to the ability to be intimate, based on factors such as commitment, equality of importance but difference in functions, and reciprocity, through communication of personal values, respect for personal feelings, acceptance of personal limitations, affirmation of respective potentialities, sharing of hurts, and forgiveness of errors. There are definite ways of quantifying the first three variables, whereas many self-report, paper-and-pencil questionnaires assess the last six variables (L'Abate, 1994c; L'Abate & Bagarozzi, 1993). Intimacy and commitment could be measured according to Rusbult's original equation (1980). She defined commitment according to an equation where (satisfaction + investments) − alternatives would yield the amount of commitment. Recently, Worthington (1991) defined satisfaction by adding five subcomponents: closeness + communication + conflict resolution + cognitions + confession/forgiveness. Worthington then defined operationally each term in his equation, making it much more complex than initially. For instance, closeness can be defined according to a paper-and-pencil self-report test, the PAIR, which yields five areas of closeness: (a) emotional, (b) sexual, (c) social, (d) intellectual, and (e) recreational. Thus, closeness would be measured by the total points obtained in each of the five areas. However, one could use whatever instrument is relevant to one's perception of closeness or intimacy.

Communication can be measured by at least three different elements: (a) accuracy and timing; (b) self-disclosure; and (c) metacommunication, the process of communicating in contrast to the content. Conflict resolution can be assessed by frequency, duration, and intensity of conflict together with the style of conflict. This last part, left undefined by Worthington, relates to the ARC model in intimate relationships: (a) abusive/apathetic (neglectful); (b) reactive/repetitive; and (c) conductive/creative. To define cognitions, Worthington used Baucom and Epstein's (1990) classification of cognitions: (a) perceptions; (b) causal attributions; (c) expectancies; (d) assumptions; and (e) standards. More than definitions are needed to arrive at a quantitative score for all of the five classes. Confession/forgiveness is assessed through the amount of inevitable hurts that have been produced in the relationship. If these hurts are left unresolved, they fester inside the partners and inside the relationship unless there is forgiveness.

Thus, assuming that commitment, equality, and reciprocity were also assessed, the total number of points could vary between −27 and +27. Adding the total number of points for each of the factors in the denominator, one would produce a hypothetical range between +51 and −51 points. The ratio of total points in the numerator (between −18 and +18) divided by the total points in the denominator (between −51 and +51) would yield a measure of individual relationship potential ranging from −.35 to +.35. In this fashion, one can begin to transform a qualitative algorithm into a mathematical equation.

The outcome of following this route is quite complex, as one can readily see. Starting with a simple equation, one would need to define each term in the equation in terms of component and subcomponent parts in both the numerator and denominator. Adding them up would result in an incredible number of factors whose numerical values would be rather questionable. Furthermore, the outcome—the ratio between numerator and denominator—would result in one limited, single value that varies between small negative and positive numbers.

The result suggests that, if this route were followed, one would need to use component parts that represent each dimension in the most efficient manner. For instance, a test of equality in intimate relationships would need to be found, together with a test for reciprocity to complete the whole equation. This route would lead to a never-ending struggle concerning which factors to use in either the numerator or the denominator of the equation. There are no finite factors, as in the case of physical variables, so the result would never end, although it would not be impossible. What would the result be for a different route that relates to a summation of parts rather than an equation?

SUMMATION OF COMPONENT PARTS

Instead of an equation, with its attendant shortcomings, it is possible to use the same component parts and add them according to their standard scores. For instance, each of the components given in the previous equation could be added or subtracted from the summation. The weights of these factors, which would be part of the numerator in the equation, would be added to or subtracted from the weights obtained for the components in the denominator, yielding a hypothetical range varying, for instance, from −69 to +69. This total would represent the relationship potential for each individual and would predict how that individual would relate to another in an intimate relationship. This summation total would be much larger, and therefore more variable, than the score obtained from a ratio.

CONCLUSION

Applying game theory in terms of victories (+) and defeats (−) permits a conceptualization of interdependent relationships according to multiplicative (×), no-change (0), and divisive (/) outcomes. Additions and subtractions apply to the subjective view of each individual participant as well as to the positive or negative outcome of an interaction. Multiplication, zero-sum, and division apply respectively to the growth-enhancing, repetitively static, and deteriorating qualities of the interaction itself. Developmental competence theory is applied to Albee's (1982) algorithm by changing from a negative to a positive statement. A different route consists of using an additive or subtractive model of relationship potential that would predict quantitatively the positive or negative outcome of a relationship.

This proposal is very hypothetical. However, it does suggest that it is possible to quantify interpersonal relations if one quantifies all of the components parts of any human equation with a summation of its parts. Any model of interpersonal relationships can conceptualize them arithmetically if they are reduced to ordinal and eventually quantitative dimensions.

APPENDIX

Self-Profile Chart—Revised Adult Form (RAF)

ID #_______________

Sex _______ Age _______ Date _________________

Please rate how much each of the following qualities gives you a sense of importance.
Lowest Importance = 1 Highest Importance = 5

1. School achievement	Now	1	2	3	4	5	NA
	Past	1	2	3	4	5	NA
	Future	1	2	3	4	5	NA
2. Work achievement	Now	1	2	3	4	5	NA
	Past	1	2	3	4	5	NA
	Future	1	2	3	4	5	NA
3. Physical attractiveness	Now	1	2	3	4	5	NA
	Past	1	2	3	4	5	NA
	Future	1	2	3	4	5	NA
4. Athletic activity	Now	1	2	3	4	5	NA
	Past	1	2	3	4	5	NA
	Future	1	2	3	4	5	NA
5. Intelligence	Now	1	2	3	4	5	NA
	Past	1	2	3	4	5	NA
	Future	1	2	3	4	5	NA
6. Creativity	Now	1	2	3	4	5	NA
	Past	1	2	3	4	5	NA
	Future	1	2	3	4	5	NA
7. Sense of humor	Now	1	2	3	4	5	NA
	Past	1	2	3	4	5	NA
	Future	1	2	3	4	5	NA
8. Morality	Now	1	2	3	4	5	NA
	Past	1	2	3	4	5	NA
	Future	1	2	3	4	5	NA
9. Self-esteem	Now	1	2	3	4	5	NA
	Past	1	2	3	4	5	NA
	Future	1	2	3	4	5	NA

Please rate how much each of the following people
gives you a sense of self-importance.

SD = Strongly Disagree **D** = Disagree **N** = Neutral **A** = Agree
SA = Strongly Agree **NA** = Not Applicable

1. Partner/Mate or Boy/Girlfriend	Now	SD	D	N	A	SA	NA
	Past	SD	D	N	A	SA	NA
	Future	SD	D	N	A	SA	NA
2. Children (if applicable)	Now	SD	D	N	A	SA	NA
	Past	SD	D	N	A	SA	NA
	Future	SD	D	N	A	SA	NA
3. Parents	Now	SD	D	N	A	SA	NA
	Past	SD	D	N	A	SA	NA
	Future	SD	D	N	A	SA	NA
4. In-laws (if applicable)	Now	SD	D	N	A	SA	NA
	Past	SD	D	N	A	SA	NA
	Future	SD	D	N	A	SA	NA
5. Siblings	Now	SD	D	N	A	SA	NA
	Past	SD	D	N	A	SA	NA
	Future	SD	D	N	A	SA	NA
6. Friends	Now	SD	D	N	A	SA	NA
	Past	SD	D	N	A	SA	NA
	Future	SD	D	N	A	SA	NA
7. Co-workers	Now	SD	D	N	A	SA	NA
	Past	SD	D	N	A	SA	NA
	Future	SD	D	N	A	SA	NA
8. Neighbors	Now	SD	D	N	A	SA	NA
	Past	SD	D	N	A	SA	NA
	Future	SD	D	N	A	SA	NA
9. Relatives	Now	SD	D	N	A	SA	NA
	Past	SD	D	N	A	SA	NA
	Future	SD	D	N	A	SA	NA

References

Acitelli, L. K. (1993). You, me, and us: Perspectives on relationship awareness. In S. Duck (Ed.), *Individuals in relationships* (pp. 121–174). Thousand Oaks, CA: Sage.

Acitelli, L. K., & Duck, S. (1987). Intimacy as the proverbial elephant. In D. Perlman & S. Duck (Eds.), *Intimate relationships: Development, dynamics, and deterioration* (pp. 297–308). Newbury Park, CA: Sage.

Acock, A. C., & Demo, D. H. (1994). *Family diversity and well-being*. New York: Oxford University Press.

Adler, N., & Matthews, K. (1994). Health psychology: Why do some people get sick and some stay well? *Annual Review of Psychology, 45,* 229–259.

Agnew, R. (1989). Delinquency as a creative enterprise: A review of recent evidence. *Criminal Justice and Behavior, 16,* 98–113.

Ainsworth, M. D. S., Blehar, M. C., Waters, E., & Wall, S. (1978). *Patterns of attachment: A psychological study of the Strange Situation*. Hillsdale, NJ: Erlbaum.

Albee, G. W. (1982). Preventing psychopathology and promoting human potentials. *American Psychologist, 37,* 1043–1050.

Albert, M. (1977). Temporal comparison theory. *Psychological Review, 84,* 485–503.

Alexander, J., & Parsons, B. (1982). *Functional family therapy*. Monterey, CA: Brooks/Cole.

Allen, M. H., & Frances, R. J. (1986). Varieties of psychopathology found in patients with addictive disorders: A review. In R. E. Meyer (Ed.), *Psychopathology and addictive disorders* (pp. 17–38). New York: Guilford.

Allport, G. W. (1968). *The person in psychology: Selected essays*. Boston, MA: Beacon Press.

Almagor, M., & Ben-Porath, Y. S. (1989). The two factor model of self-reported mood: A cross-cultural replication. *Journal of Personality Assessment, 53,* 10–21.

Alschuler, C. F., & Alschuler, A. S. (1984). Developing healthy responses to anger: The counselor's role. *Journal of Counseling and Development, 63,* 26–29.

American Psychiatric Association. (1994). *Diagnostic and statistical manual of mental disorders (DSM-IV)*. Washington, DC: Author.

Ammerman, R. T., & Hersen, M. (Eds.). (1993). *Handbook of behavior therapy with children and adults: A developmental and longitudinal perspective*. Boston, MA: Allyn & Bacon.

Andersen, B. L., Kiecolt-Glaser, J. K., & Glaser, R. (1994). A biosocial model of cancer stress and disease course. *American Psychologist, 49,* 389–404.

Andersen, P. A. (1993). Cognitive schemata in personal relationships. In S. Duck (Ed.), *Individuals in relationships* (pp. 1–29). Newbury Park, CA: Sage.

Applegate, J. L., & Leichty, G. B. (1984). Managing interpersonal relationships: Social cognitive and strategic determinants of competence. In R. N. Bostrom (Ed.), *Competence in communication: An interdisciplinary approach* (pp. 33–55). Beverly Hills, CA: Sage.

Arbuthnot, J., & Faust, D. (1981). *Teaching moral reasoning: Theory and practice*. New York: Harper & Row.

Archer, J. (1987). Beyond sex differences: Comments on Borrill and Reid. *Bulletin of the British Psychological Society, 40,* 88–90.

Aron, A., & Aron, E. N. (1996). Self and self-expansion in relationships. In G. J. O. Fletcher & J. Fitness (Eds.), *Knowledge structures in close relationships: A social psychological approach* (pp. 325–344). New York: Guilford.

Aronson, E., & Worchel, P. (1966). Similarity versus liking as determinants of interpersonal attractiveness. *Psychonomic Science, 5,* 157–158.

Ashmore, T. M. (1987). The prinsoner's dilemma: A computer's adaptation. *Western Journal of Speech Communication, 51,* 117–126.

Atkinson, M. P. (1989). Conceptualizations of the parent-child relationship: Solidarity, attachment, crescive bonds, and identity salience. In J. A. Mancini (Ed.), *Aging parents and adult children* (pp. 81–98). Washington, DC: Lexington Books.

Auerback, S. (1987). Groups for wives of gay and bisexual men. *Social Work, 32,* 321–325.

Averill, J. R. (1980). A constructivist view of emotion. In R. Plutchik & H. Kellerman (Eds.), *Emotion: Theory, research, and experience* (pp. 305–339). New York: Academic Press.

Averill, J. R. (1982). *Anger and aggression: An essay on emotion.* New York: Springer-Verlag.

Averill, J. R. (1994a). I feel, therefore I am—I think. In P. Ekman & R. J. Davidson (Eds.), *The nature of emotion: Fundamental questions* (pp. 379–385). New York: Oxford University Press.

Averill, J. R. (1994b). In the eyes of the beholder. In P. Ekman & R. J. Davidson (Eds.), *The nature of emotion: Fundamental questions* (pp. 7–14). New York: Oxford University Press.

Babladelis, G., & Adams, S. (1967). *The shaping of personality: Text and readings for a social-learning view.* Englewood Cliffs, NJ: Prentice-Hall.

Bailey, R. C., DiGiacomo, R. J., & Zinser, O. (1976). Length of male and female friendship and perceived intelligence in self and friend. *Journal of Personality Assessment, 40,* 635–640.

Bakan, D. (1968). *Disease, pain, and sacrifice: Toward a psychology of suffering.* Boston: Beacon Press.

Baldwin, M. W. (1995). Relational schema and cognition in close relationships. *Journal of Social and Personal Relationships, 12,* 547–552.

Banaji, M. R., & Prentice, D. A. (1994). The self in social contexts. *Annual Review of Psychology, 45,* 297–332.

Banta, T. J., & Hetherington, M. (1963). Relations between needs of friends and fiances. *Journal of Abnormal and Social Psychology, 66,* 401–404.

Barley, W. D. (1986). Behavioral and cognitive treatment of criminal and delinquent behavior. In W. H. Reid, D. Dorr, J. I. Walker, & J. W. Bonner, III (Eds.), *Unmasking the psychopath: Antisocial personality and related syndromes* (pp. 159–190). New York: Norton.

Barlon, J. (1985). *Rationality and intelligence.* Cambridge, UK: Cambridge University Press.

Barlow, D. H. (Ed.). (1985). *Clinical handbook of psychological disorders.* New York: Guilford.

Barnett, R. C., Biener, L., & Baruch, G. K. (Eds.). (1987). *Gender and stress.* New York: Free Press.

Barratt, E. S. (1985). The authoritarian personality: A proposed systems theory analysis. *The High School Journal, 68,* 114–119.

Barry, W. A. (1969). Marriage research and conflict: An integrative review. *Psychological Bulletin, 73,* 41–54.

Bartholomew, K. (1990). Avoidance of intimacy: An attachment perspective. *Journal of Social and Personal Relationships, 7,* 147–178.

Bartholomew, K., & Horowitz, L. M. (1991). Attachment styles in young adults: A test of a four-category model. *Journal of Personality and Social Psychology, 61,* 226–244.

Bartholomew, K., & Perlman, D. (Eds.). (1994). *Attachment processes in adulthood.* London: Jessica Kingsley.

Batson, C. D., & Oleson, K. C. (1991). Current status of the empathy-altruism hypothesis. In M. S. Clark (Ed.), *Prosocial behavior* (pp. 62–85). Newbury Park, CA: Sage.

Baucom, D. H., & Epstein, N. (1990). *Cognitive-behavioral marital therapy.* New York: Brunner/Mazel.

Baumeister, R. F. (1991). *Meanings of life.* New York: Guilford.

Baumeister, R. F. (1993a). Conceptions of self and identity: A modern retrospective on Allport's view. In K. H. Craik, R. Hogan, & R. N. Wolfe (Eds.), *Fifty years of personality psychology* (pp. 177–186). New York: Plenum.

Baumeister, R. F. (Ed.). (1993b). *Self-esteem: The puzzle of low self-regard.* New York: Plenum.

Baumeister, R. F., Heatherton, T. F., & Tice, D. M. (1994). *Losing control: How and why people fail at self-regulation.* San Diego, CA: Academic Press.

Baumeister, R. F., Smart, L., & Boden, J. M. (1996). Relation of threatened egotism to violence and aggression: The dark side of high self-esteem. *Psychological Review, 103,* 5–33.

Baumrind, D. (1980). New directions in socialization research. *American Psychologist, 35,* 639–652.

Beall, A. E. (1993). A social constructionist view of gender. In A. E. Beall & R. J. Sternberg (Eds.), *The psychology of gender* (pp. 127–147). New York: Guilford.

Beavers, W. R., & Hampson, R. B. (1990). *Successful families: Assessment and intervention.* New York: Norton.

Bebbington, P. E. (1986). Psychological etiology of schizophrenia and affective disorders. In J. E. Helzer & S. B. Guze (Eds.), *Psychoses, affective disorders, and dementias* (pp. 115–124). New York: Basic Books.

Becker, G. (1964). The complementary-need hypothesis: Authoritarianism, dominance, and other Edwards Personality Preference Schedule scores. *Journal of Personality, 32,* 45–56.

Bellack, A. S., & Hersen, M. (Eds.). (1993). *Psychopathology in adulthood.* Boston: Allyn & Bacon.

Belle, D. (1987). Gender differences and the social moderators of stress. In R. C. Barnett, L. Biener, & G. K. Baruch (Eds.), *Gender and stress* (pp. 257–276). New York: Free Press.

Belsky, J., Fish, M., & Russell, I. (1991). Continuity and discontinuity in infant negative and positive emotionality: Family antecedents and attachment consequences. *Developmental Psychology, 27,* 421–431.

Bemporad, J. R., Pfeifer, C. M., Gibbs, L., Cortner, R. H., & Bloom, W. (1971). Characteristics of encopretic patients and their families. *Journal of the American Academy of Child Psychiatry, 10,* 272–292.

Bengston, V. L. (1976). *The social psychology of aging.* Indianapolis, IN: Bobbs-Merrill.

Benjamin, L. S. (1993). *Interpersonal diagnosis and treatment of personality disorders.* New York: Guilford.

Ben-Porath, Y. S. (1995). The MMPI and MMPI-2: Fifty years of differentiating normal and abnormal personality. In S. Strack & M. Lorr (Eds.), *Differentiating normal and abnormal personality* (pp. 361–401). New York: Springer.

Bentler, P. M., & Newcomb, M. D. (1978). Longitudinal study of marital success and failure. *Journal of Consulting and Clinical Psychology, 46,* 1053–1070.

Berg, J. H., Piner, K. E., & Frank, S. M. (1993). Resource theory and close relationships. In U. G. Foa, J. Converse, Jr., K. J. Tornblom, & E. B. Foa (Eds.), *Resource theory: Explorations and applications* (pp. 169–195). San Diego, CA: Academic Press.

Berg, J. H., & Wiebe, F. A. (1993). Resource exchange in the workplace: Exchange of economic and interpersonal resources. In U. G. Foa, J. Converse, Jr., K. J. Tornblom, & E. B. Foa (Eds.), *Resource theory: Explorations and applications* (pp. 97–122). San Diego, CA: Academic Press.

Berger, S. M. (1971). Observer perseverance as related to a model's success: A social comparison analysis. *Journal of Personality and Social Psychology, 19,* 341–350.

Bergin, A. E., & Garfield, S. L. (Eds.). (1994). *Handbook of psychotherapy and behavior change.* New York: Wiley.

Bergman, S. J. (1995). Men's psychological development: A relational perspective. In R. F. Levant & W. S. Pollack (Eds.), *A new psychology of men* (pp. 68–90). New York: Basic Books.

Bergmann, M. S. (1971). Psychoanalytic observations on the capacity to love. In J. McDevitt & C. Settlage (Eds.), *Separation-individuation: Essays in honor of Margaret S. Mahler* (pp. 15–40). New York: International University Press.

Bernard, J. (1964). The adjustment of married mates. In H. T. Christensen (Ed.), *Handbook of marriage and the family* (pp. 321–387). Chicago, IL: Rand McNally.

Berscheid, E. (1983). Emotion. In H. H. Kelley, E. Berscheid, A. Christensen, J. H. Harvey, T. L. Huston, G. Levinger, E. McClintock, L. A. Peplau, & D. R. Peterson (Eds.), *Close relationships* (pp. 110–168). San Francisco: Freeman.

Berscheid, E. (1994). Interpersonal relationships. *Annual Review of Psychology, 45,* 79–129.

Berscheid, E. (1995). Help wanted: A grand theorist of interpersonal relationships, sociologist or anthropologist preferred. *Journal of Social and Personal Relationships, 12,* 529–533.

Bertman, S., & Krant, M. J. (1977). To know of suffering and the teaching of empathy. *Social Science and Medicine, 11,* 639–644.

Beutler, L. E., Engle, D., Oro'-Beutler, E., Daldrup, R., & Meredith, K. (1986). Inability to express intense affect: A common link between depression and pain? *Journal of Consulting and Clinical Psychology, 54,* 752–739.

Beutler, L. E., Williams, R. E., Wakefield, P. J., & Entwistle, S. R. (1995). Bridging scientist and practitioner perspective in clinical psychology. *American Psychologist, 50,* 984–995.

Biener, L. (1987). Gender differences in the use of substances for coping. In R. C. Barnett, L. Biener, & G. K. Baruch (Eds.), *Gender and stress* (pp. 330–349). New York: Free Press.

Binder, A. (1988). Juvenile delinquency. *Annual Review of Psychology, 39,* 253–282.

Birdwhistell, R. L. (1970). *Kinesis and context: Essays on body motion communication.* Philadelphia: University of Pennsylvania Press.

Birtchnell, J. (1993). *How humans relate: A new interpersonal theory.* Westport, CT: Praeger.

Blashfield, R. K. (1986). Structural approaches to classification. In T. Millon & G. L. Klerman (Eds.), *Contemporary directions in psychopathology: Toward the DSM-IV* (pp. 363–380). New York: Guilford.

Blashfield, R. K. (1991). Models of psychiatric classification. In M. Hersen & S. M. Turner (Eds.), *Adult psychopathology and diagnosis* (pp. 3–22). New York: Wiley.

Blasi, A. (1980). Bridging moral cognition and moral action: A critical review of the literature. *Psychological Bulletin, 88,* 1–45.

Blatt, S. J. (1995). The destructiveness of perfectionism: Implications for the treatment of depression. *American Psychologist, 50,* 1003–1020.

Blatt, S. J., Quinlan, D. M., Chevron, E. S., McDonald, C., & Zuroff, D. (1982). Dependency and criticism: Psychological dimensions of depression. *Journal of Consulting and Clinical Psychology, 50,* 113–124.

Blazer, J. A. (1963). Complementary needs and marital happiness. *Marriage and Family Living, 25,* 89–95.

Blechman, E. A. (Ed.). (1990). *Emotions and the family: For better or for worse.* Hillsdale, NJ: Erlbaum.

Blieszner, R. (1993). Resource needs and life satisfaction. In U. G. Foa, J. Converse, Jr., K. J. Tornblom, & E. B. Foa (Eds.), *Resource theory: Explorations and applications* (pp. 67–79). San Diego, CA: Academic Press.

Blieszner, R., & Adams, R. G. (1992). *Adult friendship.* Thousand Oaks, CA: Sage.

Bloom-Feshbach, J., Bloom-Feshbach, S., & Associates. (1987). *The psychology of separation and loss.* San Francisco: Jossey-Bass.

Blumberg, H. H., Hare, A. P., Kent, V., & Davies, M. F. (1983). *Small groups and social interaction* (Vol. 1). New York: Wiley.

Blumberg, S. H., & Izard, C. E. (1985). Affective and cognitive characteristics of depression in 10- and 11-year-old children. *Journal of Personality and Social Psychology, 49,* 194–202.

Blumberg, S. H., & Izard, C. E. (1986). Discriminating patterns of emotion in 10- and 11-year-old children. *Journal of Personality and Social Psychology, 51,* 852–857.

Bongar, B., & Beutler, L. E. (Eds.). (1995). *Comprehensive textbook of psychotherapy: Theory and practice.* New York: Oxford University Press.

Bonkowski, S. E., Boomhower, S. J., & Bequette, S. D. (1985). What you don't know can hurt you: Unexpressed fears and feelings of children from divorcing families. *Journal of Divorce, 9,* 33–45.

Bornstein, R. F. (1992). Inhibitory effects of awareness on affective responding. In M. S. Clark (Ed.), *Emotion* (pp. 235–255). Thousand Oaks, CA: Sage.

Boss, P. G., Doherty, W. V., LaRossa, R., Schumm, W. R., & Steinmetz, S. K. (Eds.). (1993). *Sourcebook of family theories and methods: A contextual approach*. New York: Plenum.

Bowerman, C. E., & Day, B. B. (1956). A test of the theory of complementary needs as applied to couples during courtship. *American Sociological Review, 21*, 602–605.

Bowlby, J. (1980). *Attachment and loss: Vol. 3. Loss, sadness and depression*. New York: Basic Books.

Branden, N. (1980). *The psychology of romantic love*. Los Angeles, CA: J. P. Tharcher.

Breines, W., & Gordon, L. (1983). The new scholarship on family violence. *Signs, 8*, 490–531.

Brennan, K. A., Shaver, P. R., & Tobey, A. E. (1991). Attachment styles, gender, and parental problem drinking. *Journal of Personal and Social Relationships, 8*, 3–35.

Brickman, P., Rabinowitz, V. C., Karuza, J., Coates, D., Cohen, E., & Kidder, L. (1982). Models of helping and coping. *American Psychologist, 37*, 368–384.

Briggs, S. R. (1985). A trait account of social shyness. In P. Shaver (Ed.), *Self, situations, and social behavior* (pp. 35–64). Beverly Hills, CA: Sage.

Brim, G. (1992). *Ambition: How to manage success and failure throughout our lives*. New York: Basic Books.

Brinberg, D., & Ganesan, S. (1993). An application of Foa's resource exchange theory to product positioning. In U. G. Foa, J. Converse, Jr., K. J. Tornblom, & E. B. Foa (Eds.), *Resource theory: Explorations and applications* (pp. 219–231). San Diego, CA: Academic Press.

Broderick, C. B. (1993). *Understanding family process: Basics of family systems theory*. Newbury Park, CA: Sage.

Broderick, C. B., & Smith, J. (1979). The general systems approach to the family. In W. R. Burr, R. Hill, F. I. Nye, & I. L. Reiss (Eds.), *Contemporary theories about the family* (Vol. 2, pp. 112–129). New York: Free Press.

Brodsky, A. M. (1973). Perspectives of a feminist therapist. In M. E. Curtin (Ed.), *Symposium on love* (pp. 95–106). New York: Behavioral Publications.

Brody, G. H., & Forehand, R. (1986). Maternal perceptions of child maladjustment as a function of the combined influence of child behavior and maternal depression. *Journal of Consulting and Clinical Psychology, 54*, 237–240.

Bronfenbrenner, U. (1958). The study of identification through interpersonal perception. In R. Tagiuri & L. Petrullo (Eds.), *Person perception and interpersonal behavior* (pp. 110–130). Palo Alto, CA: Stanford University Press.

Brown, L. S. (1992a). A feminist critique of the personality disorders. In L. S. Brown & M. Ballou (Eds.), *Personality and psychopathology: Feminist reappraisals* (pp. 206–228). New York: Guilford.

Brown, L. S. (1992b). Introduction: Feminist perspectives on psychopathology. In L. S. Brown & M. Ballou (Eds.), *Personality and psychopathology: Feminist reappraisals* (pp. 111–114). New York: Guilford.

Brown, L. S., & Ballou, M. (Eds.). (1992). *Personality and psychopathology: Feminist reappraisals*. New York: Guilford.

Brownell, A. J. (1981). Counseling men through body work. *Personnel and Guidance Journal, 60*, 252–255.

Brubaker, T. H. (Ed.). (1993). *Family relations: Challenges for the future*. Newbury Park, CA: Sage.

Burger, J. M. (1992). *Desire for control: Personality, social, and clinical perspectives*. New York: Plenum.

Burgess, E. W., & Wallin, P. (1943). Homogamy in social characteristics. *American Journal of Sociology, 69*, 109–124.

Burke, A. P., Brief, J. M., George, L. R., & Webster, J. (1989). Measuring affect at work: Confirmatory analyses of competing mood structure with conceptual linkage to cortical regulatory systems. *Journal of Personality and Social Psychology, 57*, 1091–1102.

Burkitt, I. (1991). *Social selves: Theories of the social formation of personality*. London, UK: Sage.

Burr, W. R., Day, R. D., & Bahr, K. S. (1993). *Family science.* Pacific Grove, CA: Brooks/Cole.

Burton, A. (Ed.). (1974). *Operational theories of personality.* New York: Brunner/Mazel.

Buss, A. (1987). Personality: Primate heritage and human distinctiveness. In J. Aronoff, A. I. Rabin, & R. A. Zucker (Eds.), *The emergence of personality* (pp. 13–48). New York: Springer.

Buss, D. M. (1984). Marital assortment for personality dispositions: Assessment with three different data sources. *Behavior Genetics, 14,* 111–123.

Buss, D. M. (1985). Human mate selection. *American Scientist, 73,* 47–51.

Buss, D. M., & Barnes, M. (1986). Preferences in human mate selection. *Journal of Personality and Social Psychology, 50,* 559–570.

Butcher, J. N., Dahlstrom, W. G., Graham, J. R., Tellegen, A., & Kaemmer, B. (1989). *Manual for the restandardized Minnesota Multiphasic Personality Inventory: MMPI-2. An administrative and interpretive guide.* Minneapolis: University of Minnesota Press.

Button, C. M., & Collier, D. R. (1991). *A comparison of people's concepts of love and romantic love.* Paper presented at the Canadian Psychological Association Conference, Calgary, Alberta, Canada.

Byng-Hall, J. (1995). Creating a secure family base: Some implications of attachment theory for family therapy. *Family Process, 34,* 45–58.

Byrne, D. (1961). Interpersonal attraction and attitude similarity. *Journal of Abnormal and Social Psychology, 62,* 713–714.

Byrne, D. (1971). *The attraction paradigm.* New York: Academic Press.

Byrne, D. (1974). *An introduction to personality: Research, theory, and applications.* Englewood Cliffs, NJ: Prentice-Hall.

Byrne, D., & Blaylock, B. (1963). Similarity and assumed similarity of attitudes between husbands and wives. *Journal of Abnormal and Social Psychology, 67,* 636–640.

Byrne, D., & Clore, G. L. (1967). Effectance arousal and attraction. *Journal of Personality and Social Psychology, 6,* (No. 4, Whole No. 638).

Byrne, D., Clore, G. L., & Smeaton, G. (1986). The attraction hypothesis: Do similar attitudes affect anything? *Journal of Personality and Social Psychology, 51,* 1167–1170.

Byrne, D., Clore, G. L., & Worchel, P. (1966). Effect of economic similarity-dissimilarity on interpersonal attraction. *Journal of Personality and Social Psychology, 4,* 220–224.

Byrne, D., Gouax, C., Griffit, W. B., Lamberth, J., Murakawa, N., Pradad, M. B., & Ramirez, M. (1971). The ubiquitous relationship: Attitude similarity and attraction. A cross-cultural study. *Human Relations, 24,* 201–207.

Byrne, D., Griffitt, W. B., Hudgins, W., & Reeves, W. (1969). Attitude similarity-dissimilarity and attraction: Generality beyond the college sophomore. *Journal of Social Psychology, 79,* 155–161.

Byrne, D., Griffitt, W. B., & Stefaniak, D. (1967). Attraction and similarity of personality characteristics. *Journal of Personality and Social Psychology, 5,* 82–90.

Byrne, D., & Nelson, D. (1965). Attraction as a linear function of proportion of positive reinforcements. *Journal of Personality and Social Psychology, 1,* 659–663.

Canary, D. J., Cupach, W. R., & Messman, S. J. (1995). *Relationship conflict.* Thousand Oaks, CA: Sage.

Cantor, N., & Genero, N. (1986). Psychiatric diagnosis and natural categorization: A close analogy. In T. Millon & G. L. Klerman (Eds.), *Contemporary directions in psychopathology: Toward the DSM-IV* (pp. 233–256). New York: Guilford.

Cantor, N., & Kihlstrom, J. F. (1987). *Personality and social intelligence.* Englewood Cliffs, NJ: Prentice-Hall.

Carnevale, P. J., & Pruitt, D. G. (1992). Negotiation and mediation. *Annual Review of Psychology, 43,* 531–582.

Carson, R. C. (1969). *Interaction concepts of personality.* Chicago: Aldine.

Carson, R. C., Butcher, J. N., & Coleman, J. C. (1988). *Abnormal psychology and modern life.* Glenview, IL: Scott, Foresman.

Cartright, D. S. (1979). *Theories and models of personality.* Dubuque, IO: Wm. C. Brown.

Carver, C. S. M., & Scheier, M. F. (1992). *Perspectives on personality.* Boston: Allyn & Bacon.

Casler, L. (1973). Toward a re-evaluation of love. In M. E. Curtin (Ed.), *Symposium on love* (pp. 1–36). New York: Behavioral Publications.

Cattell, R. B., & Nesselroade, J. N. (1967). Likeness and completeness theories examined by sixteen personality factor measures on stably and unstably married couples. *Journal of Personality and Social Psychology, 7,* 351–361.

Centers, R. (1975a). Attitude similarity-dissimilarity as a correlate of heterosexual attraction and love. *Journal of Marriage and the Family, 37,* 305–312.

Centers, R. (1975b). *Sexual attraction and love: An instrumental theory.* Springfield, IL: Charles C. Thomas.

Cicchetti, D., & Toth, S. L. (Eds.). (1991). *Internalizing and externalizing expressions of dysfunction.* Hillsdale, NJ: Erlbaum.

Clark, K. B. (1980). Empathy: A neglected topic in psychological research. *American Psychologist, 35,* 187–190.

Clark, L. A., & Watson, D. (1991). Tripartite model of anxiety and depression: Psychometric evidence and taxonomic implications. *Journal of Abnormal Psychology, 100,* 316–336.

Clark, L. A., Watson, D., & Reynolds, S. (1995). Diagnosis and classification of psychopathology: Challenges to the current system and future directions. *Annual Review of Psychology, 46,* 121–153.

Clark, M. S., Pataki, S. P., & Carver, V. H. (1996). Some thoughts and findings on self-presentation of emotions in relationships. In G. J. O. Fletcher & J. Fitness (Eds.), *Knowledge structures in close relationships: A social psychological approach* (pp. 247–274). New York: Guilford.

Clark, M. S., & Reis, H. T. (1988). Interpersonal processes in close relationships. *Annual Review of Psychology, 39,* 609–672.

Clarkin, J. F., Haas, G. L., & Glick, I. D. (Eds.). (1988). *Affective disorders in the family: Assessment and treatment.* New York: Guilford.

Clary, E. G., & Snyder, M. (1991). A functional analysis of altruism and prosocial behavior: The case of volunteerism. In M. S. Clark (Ed.), *Prosocial behavior* (pp. 119–148). Newbury Park, CA: Sage.

Cleary, P. D. (1987). Gender differences in stress-related disorders. In R. C. Barnett, L. Biener, & G. K. Baruch (Eds.), *Gender and stress* (pp. 39–72). New York: Free Press.

Cleckley, H. (1976). *The mask of sanity.* St. Louis, MO: Mosby.

Cloninger, R. C., & Svrakic, D. M. (1994). Differentiating normal and deviant personality by the seven-factor personality model. In S. Strack & M. Lorr (Eds.), *Differentiating normal from abnormal personality* (pp. 40–64). New York: Springer.

Clore, G. L. (1975). *Interpersonal attraction: An overview.* Morristown, NJ: General Learning Press.

Clore, G. L., & Baldridge, B. (1968). Interpersonal attraction: The role of agreement and topic interest. *Journal of Personality and Social Psychology, 9,* 340–346.

Cohen, J. (1988). *Statistical power analysis for the behavioral sciences.* Hillsdale, NJ: Erlbaum.

Cohen, R., & Siegel, A. W. (Eds.). (1991). *Context and development.* Hillsdale, NJ: Erlbaum.

Cohen, T. (1983). The incestuous family revisited. *Social Casework, 64,* 154–161.

Coleman, A. A., Coleman, A. C., & Thomas, R. M. (1990). Cooperation without awareness: A multiperson generalization of the minimal social situation. *Behavioral Science, 35,* 115–121.

Collins, D., & Gabor, P. (1988). Helping children with cathartic disclosure of trauma. *Journal of Child Care, 3,* 25–38.

Collins, N., & Read, S. (1990). Adult attachment, working models, and relationship quality in dating couples. *Journal of Personality and Social Psychology, 58,* 644–663.

Constantine, L. L. (1986). *Family paradigms: The practice of theory in family therapy.* New York: Guilford.

Constantine, L. L. (1993). The structure of family paradigms: An analytical model of family variation. *Journal of Marital and Family Therapy, 19,* 39–70.

Converse, J., Jr., & Foa, U. G. (1993). Some principles of equity in interpersonal exchanges. In U. G. Foa, J. Converse, Jr., K. J. Tornblom, & E. B. Foa (Eds.), *Resource theory: Explorations and applications* (pp. 31–39). San Diego, CA: Academic Press.

Coombs, C. H., Dawes, R. M., & Tversky, A. (1970). *Mathematical psychology: An elementary introduction.* Englewood Cliffs, NJ: Prentice-Hall.

Cooper, A. M., Frances, A. J., & Sacks, M. H. (Eds.). (1986). *The personality disorders and neuroses.* New York: Basic Books.

Costa, P. T., & Widiger, T. A. (Eds.). (1994). *Personality disorders and the five-factor model of personality.* Washington, DC: American Psychological Association.

Costello, C. G. (1993a). Cognitive bases of psychopathology. In C. G. Costello (Ed.), *Basic issues in psychopathology* (pp. 320–355). New York: Guilford.

Costello, C. G. (1993b). Introduction: Conceptual and methodological issues in the sciences of psychopathology. In C. G. Costello (Ed.), *Basic issues in psychopathology* (pp. 1–18). New York: Guilford.

Coutts, R. L. (1973). *Love and intimacy: A psychological approach.* San Ramon, CA: Consensus.

Covey, S. R. (1990). *The seven habits of highly effective people.* New York: Fireside.

Cox, S. E., Lambert, R. G., L'Abate, L., & Stanwyck, D. J. (1996). *The concurrent validity of a screening test for fifth graders with two measures of family functioning.* Manuscript submitted for publication.

Cross, S. E., & Markus, H. R. (1993). Gender in thought, belief, and action: A cognitive approach. In R. J. Sternberg & A. E. Beall (Eds.), *The psychology of gender* (pp. 55–98). New York: Guilford.

Curtin, M. E. (1973). *Symposium on love.* New York: Behavioral Publications.

Cusinato, M. (1990). *Test di relazione diadica.* Universitá a gli Studi, Departimento di Psicologia Generale, Padova, Italy.

Cusinato, M., & L'Abate, L. (1994). A spiral model of intimacy. In S. M. Johnson & L. S. Greenberg (Eds.), *The heart of the matter: Perspectives on emotion in marital therapy* (pp. 108–123). New York: Brunner/Mazel.

Dabbs, J. M. (1992). Testosterone measurements in social and clinical psychology. *Journal of Social and Clinical Psychology, 11,* 302–321.

Dadds, M. R. (1995). *Families: Children, and the development of dysfunction.* London: Sage.

Dahlstrom, W. G. (1993). Tests: Small samples, large consequences. *American Psychologist, 48,* 393–399.

Daly, J. A., & McCroskey, J. C. (Eds.). (1984). *Avoiding communication: Shyness, reticence, and communication apprehension.* Newbury Park, CA: Sage.

Damon, W. (1988). Socialization and individuation. In G. Handel (Ed.), *Childhood socialization* (pp. 3–10). New York: Aldine de Gruyter.

Dantzer, R. (1993). *The psychosomatic delusion: Why the mind is not the source of all our ills.* New York: Free Press.

Davidson, R. J., Ekman, P., Saron, C., Senulis, J., & Friesen, W. V. (1990). Approach/withdrawal and cerebral asymmetry. *Journal of Personality and Social Psychology, 58,* 330–341.

De Giacomo, P. (1993). *Finite systems and infinite interactions: The logic of human interactions and its applications to psychotherapy.* Norfolk, CT: Bramble Books.

De Giacomo, P. (1995). *Mente e creativitá.* Milano: Franco Angeli.

De Giacomo, P., & L'Abate, L. (1996). *Relationship styles: Integrating models of human interaction.* Manuscript in preparation.

De Giacomo, P., Pierri, G., Lefons, E., & Mich, L. (1990). A technique to simulate human interaction: Relational styles leading to a schizophrenic communication pattern and back to normal. *Acta Psichiatrica Scandinavica, 82,* 413–419.

De Giacomo, P., Silvestri, A., Pierri, G., Lefons, A., Corfiati, L., & Tangorra, F. (1986). Research on the effects of psychodrugs on human interaction. *Acta Psichiatrica Scandinavica, 74,* 417–424.

Depue, R. A., & Zald, D. H. (1993). Biological and environmental processes in nonpsychotic psychopathology: A neurobehavioral perspective. In C. G. Costello (Ed.), *Basic issues in psychopathology* (pp. 127–237). New York: Guilford.

Derlega, V. J., & Winstead, B. A. (Eds.). (1986). *Friendship and social interaction.* New York: Springer-Verlag.

Descoutner, C. J., & Thelen, M. H. (1991). Development and validation of a fear-of-intimacy scale. *Psychological Assessment, 3,* 218–225.

Dinkmeyer, D. C., Pew, W. L., & Dinkmeyer, D. C., Jr. (1979). *Adlerian counseling and psychotherapy.* Monterey, CA: Brooks/Cole.

Dion, K. K., & Dion, K. L. (1985). Personality, gender, and the phenomenology of romantic love. In P. Shaver (Ed.), *Self, situations, and social behavior* (pp. 209–239). Beverly Hills, CA: Sage.

Doane, J. A., & Diamond, D. (1994). *Affect and attachment in the family: A family-based treatment of major psychiatric disorder.* New York: Basic Books.

Dobson, K. S., & Kendall, P. C. (Eds.). (1993). *Psychopathology and cognition.* San Diego, CA: Academic Press.

Dodge, K. A. (1993). Social-cognitive mechanisms in the development of conduct disorder and depression. *Annual Review of Psychology, 44* 559–584.

Doi, S. C., & Thelen, M. H. (1993). The fear-of-intimacy scale: Replication and extension. *Psychological Assessment, 5,* 377–383.

Dollard, J., & Miller, N. E. (1950). *Personality and psychotherapy: An analysis in terms of learning, thinking, and culture.* New York: McGraw-Hill.

Doren, D. M. (1987). *Understanding and treating the psychopath.* New York: Wiley.

Druckman, D., Rozelle, R. M., & Baxter, J. C. (1982). *Nonverbal communication: Survey, theory, and research.* Thousand Oaks, CA: Sage.

Duck, S. (1972). Friendship, similarity, and the reptest. *Psychological Reports, 31,* 231–234.

Duck, S. (1973). Personality similarity and friendship formation: Similarity of what, when? *Journal of Personality, 41,* 543–558.

Duck, S. (1975). Attitude similarity and interpersonal attraction: Right answers and wrong reasons. *British Journal of Social and Clinical Psychology, 14,* 311–312.

Duck, S. (1977). *Theory and practice in interpersonal attraction.* New York: Academic Press.

Duck, S. (1993). *Individuals in relationships.* San Diego: Academic Press.

Dunne, E. E., & L'Abate, L. (1978). The family taboo in psychology textbooks. *Teaching of Psychology, 5,* 115–117.

Dunst, C., Trivette, C., & Deal, A. (1988). *Enabling and empowering families: Principles and guidelines for practice.* Cambridge, MA: Brookline Books.

Edelhofer, F. E., Fabian, K. J., & Edelhofer, S. F. (1988). Directed affective treatment: A step beyond empathy. *Psychotherapy in Private Practice, 6,* 47–57.

Edelstein, M. G. (1990). *Symptom analysis: A method of brief therapy.* New York: Norton.

Edward, J., Ruskin, N., & Turrini, P. (1981). *Separation-individuation: Theory and applications.* New York: Garner.

Ehrenwald, J. (Ed.). (1991). *The history of psychotherapy.* Northvale, NJ: Aronson.

Eisenberg, N., & Fabes, R. A. (1991). Prosocial behavior and empathy: A multimethod developmental perspective. In M. S. Clark (Ed.), *Prosocial behavior* (pp. 34–61). Newbury Park, CA: Sage.

Eisenberg, N., & Fabes, R. A. (1992). Emotion, regulation, and the development of social competence. In M. S. Clark (Ed.), *Emotion* (pp. 109–150). Thousand Oaks, CA: Sage.

Ekman, P. (1994). All emotions are basic. In P. Ekman & R. J. Davidson (Eds.), *The nature of emotion: Fundamental questions* (pp. 15–19). New York: Oxford University Press.

Ekman, P., & Davidson, R. J. (Eds.). (1994). *The nature of emotion: Fundamental questions.* New York: Oxford University Press.

Elder, G. H., & Caspi, A. (1990). Studying lives in a changing society: Sociological and personological explorations. In A. I. Rubin, R. A. Zucker, R. A. Emmons, & S. Frank (Eds.), *Studying persons and lives* (pp. 201–247). New York: Springer.

Emde, R. N. (1995). Syndromes of temperament: A review of Galen's prophecy. *Contemporary Psychology, 40,* 1039–1041.

Engle, D., Beutler, L. E., & Daldrup, R. J. (1991). Focused expressive psychotherapy: Treating blocked emotions. In J. D. Safran & L. S. Greenberg (Eds.), *Emotion, psychotherapy, and change* (pp. 169–196). New York: Guilford.

Epstein, S. (1984). Controversial issues in emotion theory. In P. Shaver (Ed.), *Emotions, relationships, and health* (pp. 64–88). Newbury Park, CA: Sage.

Epstein, S. (1991). Cognitive-experiential self-theory: An integrative theory of personality. In R. C. Curtis (Ed.), *The relational self: Theoretical convergences in psychoanalysis and social psychology* (pp. 109–137). New York: Guilford.

Epstein, E., & Guttman, R. (1984). Mate selection in man: Evidence, theory, and outcome. *Social Biology, 31,* 243–278.

Erdelyi, M. T., & Appelbaum, A. G. (1973). Cognitive masking: The disruptive effect of an emotional stimulus upon the perception of contiguous neutral items. *Bulletin of the Psychonomic Society, 1,* 59–62.

Erikson, E. H. (1950). *Childhood and society.* New York: Norton.

Esterling, B. A., Antoni, M. H., Fletcher, M. A., Margulies, S., & Schneiderman, N. (1994). Emotional disclosure through writing or speaking modulates latent Epstein-Barr virus reactivation. *Journal of Consulting and Clinical Psychology, 62,* 130–140.

Esterling, B. A., Antoni, M. H., Kumar, M., & Schneiderman, N. (1990). Emotional repression, stress disclosure responses, and Epstein-Barr viral capsid antigen titers. *Psychosomatic Medicine, 52,* 397–410.

Esterling, B. A., L'Abate, L., Murray, E. J., & Pennebaker, J. W. (1996). *Empirical foundations for writing in prevention and psychotherapy: Mental and physical health outcomes.* Manuscript submitted for publication.

Evans, K., & Sullivan, J. M. (1990). *Dual diagnosis: Counseling the mentally ill substance abuser.* New York: Guilford.

Everstine, D. S., & Everstine, L. (1993). *The trauma response treatment for emotional injury.* New York: Norton.

Ewen, R. B. (1988). *An introduction to theories of personality.* Hillsdale, NJ: Erlbaum.

Eysenck, H. J. (1973). *The measurement of intelligence.* Baltimore: Williams & Wilkins.

Eysenck, H. J. (1977). *Crime and personality.* London: Routledge and Kegan Paul.

Eysenck, H. J. (1986). A critique of contemporary classification and diagnosis. In T. Millon & G. L. Klerman (Eds.), *Contemporary directions in psychopathology: Toward the DSM-IV* (pp. 73–98). New York: Guilford.

Eysenck, H. J. (1994). Normality-abnormality and the three-factor model of personality. In S. Strack & M. Lorr (Eds.), *Differentiating normal and abnormal personality* (pp. 3–25). New York: Springer.

Eysenck, H. J., & Gudjonsson, G. H. (1989). *The causes and cures of criminality.* New York: Plenum.

Eysenck, H. J., & Wakefield, J. A. (1981). Psychological factors as predictors of marital satisfaction. *Advances in Behavior Research and Therapy, 3,* 151–192.

Fairburn, C. G., & Wilson, G. T. (1993). *Binge eating: Nature, assessment, and treatment.* New York: Guilford.

Farber, B. (1957). An index of marital integration. *Sociometry, 20,* 117–134.

Farley, F. H., & Davis, S. A. (1977). Arousal, personality and assortative mating in marriage. *Journal of Sex and Marital Therapy, 3,* 122–127.

Farley, F. H., & Mueller, C. B. (1978). Arousal, personality, and assortative mating in marriage: Generalizability and cross-cultural factors. *Journal of Sex and Marital Therapy, 4,* 50–53.

Feeney, J. A. (1995). Adult attachment and emotional control. *Personal Relationships, 2,* 143–159.

Feeney, J. A., & Noller, P. (1990). Attachment style as a predictor of adult romantic relationships. *Journal of Personality and Social Psychology, 58,* 281–291.

Ferrari, J. R., Johnson, J. L., & McCown, W. G. (1995). *Procrastination and task avoidance: Theory, research, and treatment.* New York: Plenum Press.

Festinger, L. (1954). A theory of social comparison processes. *Human Relations, 7,* 117–140.

Fine, R. (1985). *The meaning of love in human experience.* New York: Wiley.

Fisher, S. (1970). *Body experience in fantasy and behavior.* New York: Appleton-Century-Crofts.

Fiske, A. P. (1991). The cultural relativity of selfish individualism: Anthropological evidence that humans are inherently sociable. In M. S. Clark (Ed.), *Prosocial behavior* (pp. 176–214). Newbury Park, CA: Sage.

Fiske, D. W. (1971). *Measuring the concepts of personality.* Chicago: Aldine.

Fiske, S. T., & Emery, E. J. (1993). Lost mental control and exaggerated social control: Social-cognitive and psychoanalytic speculations. In D. M. Wegner & J. W. Pennebaker (Eds.), *Handbook of mental control* (pp. 171–199). Englewood Cliffs, NJ: Prentice-Hall.

Fitness, J., & Strongman, K. (1991). Affect in close relationships. In G. J. O. Fletcher & F. D. Fincham (Eds.), *Cognition in close relationships* (pp. 175–202). Hillsdale, NJ: Erlbaum.

Fitzpatrick, M. A. (1988). *Between husbands and wives: Communication in marriage.* Newbury Park, CA: Sage.

Fletcher, G. J. O., & Fincham, F. D. (1991). Attribution processes in close relationships. In G. J. O. Fletcher & F. D. Fincham (Eds.), *Cognition in close relationships* (pp. 7–35). Hillsdale, NJ: Erlbaum.

Fletcher, G. J. O., & Fitness, J. (1993). Knowledge structures and explanations in intimate relationships. In S. Duck (Ed.), *Individuals in relationships* (pp. 121–143). Newbury Park, CA: Sage.

Fletcher, G. J. O., & Fitness, J. (1996). *Knowledge structures in close relationships: A social psychological approach.* Hillsdale, NJ: Erlbaum.

Flowers, C., & Lambert, R. G. (1996). *Correlating a selfhood model of personality with the five-factor model.* Research in progress.

Foa, U. G. (1993). Interpersonal and economic resources. In U. G. Foa, J. Converse, Jr., K. J. Tornblom, & E. B. Foa (Eds.), *Resource theory: Explorations and applications* (pp. 13–30). San Diego, CA: Academic Press.

Foa, U. G., Converse, J., Jr., Tornblom, K. J., & Foa, E. B. (Eds.). (1993). *Resource theory: Explorations and applications.* San Diego, CA: Academic Press.

Foa, U. G., & Foa, E. B. (1974). *Societal structures of the mind.* Springfield, IL: C. C. Thomas.

Foa, U. G., Salcedo, L. N., Tornblom, K. Y., Garner, M., Glaubman, H., & Teichman, M. (1993). Interrelation of social resources. In U. G. Foa, J. Converse, Jr., K. J. Tornblom, & E. B. Foa (Eds.), *Resource theory: Explorations and applications* (pp. 57–64). San Diego, CA: Academic Press.

Forehand, R., & McCombs, A. (1988). Unraveling the antecedent-consequence conditions in maternal depression and adolescent functioning. *Behavior Research and Therapy, 26,* 399–405.

Forgas, J. P. (1991). Affect and cognition in close relationships. In G. J. O. Fletcher & F. D. Fincham (Eds.), *Cognition in close relationships* (pp. 151–174). Hillsdale, NJ: Erlbaum.

Fowles, D. C. (1992). Schizophrenia: Diathesis-stress revisited. *Annual Review of Psychology, 43,* 303–336.

Fowles, D. C., Sutker, P., & Goodman, A. H. (Eds.). (1994). *Progress in experimental personality and psychopathology research: Special focus on psychopathy and antisocial personality, a developmental perspective.* New York: Springer.

Frances, A., & Widiger, T. A. (1986). Methodological issues in personality disorder diagnosis. In T. Millon & G. L. Klerman (Eds.), *Contemporary directions in psychopathology: Toward the DSM-IV* (pp. 380–400). New York: Guilford.

Francis, M. E., & Pennebaker, J. W. (1992). Putting stress into words: The impact of writing on physiological, absentee, and self-reported well-being measures. *American Journal of Health Promotion, 6,* 280–287.

Frank, I., & Powell, M. (Eds.). (1967). *Psychosomatic ailments in childhood and adolescence.* Springfield, IL: Thomas.

Frankel, K. A. (1990). Girls' perceptions of peer relationship support and stress. *Journal of Early Adolescence, 10,* 69–88.

Fransella, F. (Ed.). (1981). *Personality: Theory, measurement, and research.* London, UK: Methuen.

Frantz, T. T. (Ed.). (1984). *Death and grief in the family.* Rockville, MD: Aspen.

Freedheim, D. K. (1992). *History of psychotherapy: A century of change.* Washington, DC: American Psychological Association.

Freedman, A. M., & Kaplan, H. I. (Eds.). (1972). *Interpreting personality: A survey of twentieth-century views.* New York: Atheneum.

Freud, S. (1953). *Complete psychological works of Sigmund Freud.* London: Hogarth Press.

Frey, J. H., III. (1980). *Personality correlates of emotional masking.* Unpublished doctoral dissertation. Georgia State University, Atlanta.

Frey, J. H., Holley, J., & L'Abate, L. (1979). Intimacy is sharing hurt feelings: A comparison of three conflict resolution methods. *Journal of Marital and Family Therapy, 5,* 35–41.

Friedman, H. S., Prince, L. M., Riggio, R. E., & Di Matteo, M. R. (1980). Understanding and assessing nonverbal expressiveness: The affective communication test. *Journal of Personality and Social Psychology, 39,* 331–351.

Frijda, N. H. (1986). *The emotions.* New York: Cambridge University Press.

Frik, P. J., Lahey, B. B., Loeber, R., Stouthamer-Loeber, M., Christ, M. A. G., & Hanson, K. (1992). Familial risk factors to oppositional defiant disorder and conduct disorder: Parental psychopathology and maternal parenting. *Journal of Consulting and Clinical Psychology, 60,* 49–55.

Fromkin, H. L. (1972). Feelings of interpersonal undistinctiveness: An unpleasant affective state. *Journal of Experimental Research in Personality, 6,* 178–182.

Fromkin, H. L. (1973). *The psychology of uniqueness: Avoidance of similarity and seeking of differentness.* West Lafayette, IN: Purdue University.

Fromm, E. (1956). *The art of loving.* New York: Harper.

Fromm, E. (1992). *The art of being.* New York: Continuum.

Frost, R. O., & Gross, R. C. (1993). The hoarding of possessions. *Behaviour Research and Therapy, 31,* 367–381.

Frude, N. (1991). *Understanding family problems: A psychological approach.* Chichester, UK: Wiley.

Fuller, T. L., & Fincham, F. D. (1995). Attachment style in married couples: Relation to current marital functioning, stability over time, and method of assessment. *Personal Relationships, 2,* 17–34.

Gacono, C. B., & Meloy, J. R. (1988). The relationship between cognitive style and defensive process in the psychopath. *Criminal Justice and Behavior, 15,* 472–483.

Gangestad, S., & Snyder, M. (1985). "To carve nature at its joints": On the existence of discrete classes in personality. *Psychological Review, 92,* 317–349.

Garfield, S. L., & Bergin, A. E. (1986). *Handbook of psychotherapy and behavior change.* New York: Wiley.

Gaston-Johansson, F. (1984). Pain assessment: Differences in quality and intensity of the words pain, ache, and hurt. *Pain, 20,* 69–76.

Gaston-Johansson, F., Albert, M., Fagan, E., & Zimmerman, L. (1990). Similarities in pain descriptions of four ethnic-culture groups. *Journal of Pain and Symptom Management, 5,* 94–100.

Gaston-Johansson, F., Johansson, G., Felldin, R., & Sanne, H. (1985). A comparative study of pain description, emotional discomfort, and health perception in patients with chronic pain syndrome and rheumatoid arthritis. *Scandinavian Journal of Rehabilitation Medicine, 17,* 109–119.

Gehring, T. M., Wentzel, K. R., Feldman, S. S., & Munson, J. (1990). Conflict in families of adolescents: The impact on cohesion and power structures. *Journal of Family Psychology, 3,* 290–309.

Geis, F. L. (1993). Self-fulfilling prophecies: A social psychological view of gender. In A. E. Beall & R. J. Sternberg (Eds.), *The psychology of gender* (pp. 9–54). New York: Guilford.

Giat, L. G. (1986). Bulimia: The transgenerational view. *Journal of Marital and Family Therapy, 12,* 231–240.

Gibbons, D. C. (1988). Some critical observations on criminal types and criminal careers. *Criminal Justice and Behavior, 15,* 8–23.

Gibbs, J. J. (1987). Symptoms of psychopathology among jail prisoners: The exposure to the jail environment. *Criminal Justice and Behavior, 14,* 288–310.

Gibbs, J. J. (1991). Environmental congruence and symptoms of psychopathology: A further exploration of the effects of exposure to the jail environment. *Criminal Justice and Behavior, 18,* 351–374.

Gilbert, D. G., & Connolly, J. J. (1991). *Personality, social skills, and psychopathology: An individual differences approach.* New York: Plenum.

Gilbert, P. (1992a). *Human nature and suffering.* New York: Guilford.

Gilbert, P. (1992b). *Depression and the evolution of powerlessness.* New York: Guilford.

Gilovich, T. (1991). *How we know what isn't so: The fallibility of human reason in everyday life.* New York: Free Press.

Goethals, G. R., & Nelson, R. E. (1973). Similarity in the influence process: The belief-value distinction. *Journal of Personality and Social Psychology, 25,* 117–122.

Goldstein, M. J. (1988). The family and psychopathology. *Annual Review of Psychology, 39,* 283–299.

Gon, M. (1982). The meaning of being hurt: A study of social-emotional relation. *Indian Journal of Clinical Psychology, 9,* 237–244.

Gondoli, D. M., & Jacob, T. (1993). Factor structure within and across three family-assessment procedures. *Journal of Family Psychology, 6,* 279–289.

Goodman, M. (1963). A pilot study of the relationship between degree of expressed self-acceptance and interpersonal need structure in the mate selection process. *Dissertation Abstracts, 24,* 867–868.

Goodwin, R. (1990). Taboo topics among close friends: A factor-analytic investigation. *Journal of Social Psychology, 130,* 691–692.

Goodyear, I. M. (1990). *Life experiences, development and childhood psychopathology.* New York: Wiley.

Gordon, B. F. (1966). Influence and social comparison as motives for affiliation. *Journal of Experimental Social Psychology* (Suppl. 1) 55–56.

Gotlib, I. H., & Avison, W. R. (1993). Children at risk for psychopathology. In C. G. Costello (Ed.), *Basic issues in psychopathology* (pp. 271–319). New York: Guilford.

Gottman, J. M. (1979). *Marital interaction: Experimental investigations.* New York: Academic Press.

Gottman, J. M. (1994). *What predicts divorce? The relationship between marital process and marital outcomes.* Hillsdale, NJ: Erlbaum.

Grant, V. W. (1976). *Falling in love: The psychology of romantic emotion.* New York: Springer.

Gray, J. A. (1994). Framework for a taxonomy of psychiatric disorder. In S. H. M. van Goozen, N. E. van de Poll, & J. Sergeant (Eds.), *Emotions: Essays on emotion theory* (pp. 29–59). Hillsdale, NJ: Erlbaum.

Greenberg, D. (1987). Compulsive hoarding. *American Journal of Psychotherapy, 41,* 409–417.

Greenberg, L. S., & Safran, J. D. (1987). *Emotion in psychotherapy: Affect, cognition, and the process of change.* New York: Guilford.

Greenberg, M. A., & Stone, A. A. (1992). Writing about disclosed versus undisclosed traumas: Immediate and long-term effects on mood and health. *Journal of Personality and Social Psychology, 63,* 75–84.

Greenfield, S. M. (1973). Love: Some reflections by a social anthropologist. In M. E. Curtin (Ed.), *Symposium on love* (pp. 37–51). New York: Behavioral Publications.

Greenwald, D. (1992). Psychotic disorders with emphasis on schizophrenia. In L. S. Brown & M. Ballou (Eds.), *Personality and psychopathology: Feminist reappraisals* (pp. 144–176). New York: Guilford.

Gregson, R. A. M. (1975). *Psychometrics of similarity.* New York: Academic Press.

Griffin, D. W., & Bartholomew, K. (1994). The metaphysics of measurement: The case of adult attachment. In K. Bartholomew & D. Perlman (Eds.), *Attachment processes in adulthood: Vol. 5. Advances in personal relationships* (pp. 17–52). London, UK: Kingsley.

Griffitt, W. (1974). Attitude similarity and attraction. In T. L. Huston (Ed.), *Foundations of interpersonal attraction* (pp. 285–308). New York: Academic Press.

Grigg, D. N., Friesen, J. D., & Sheppy, M. I. (1989). Family patterns associated with anorexia nervosa. *Journal of Marital and Family Therapy, 15,* 29–42.

Gross, P. R. (1992). The crisis in family therapy: Paradigmatic family therapy solutions. *Child and Family Behavior Therapy, 14,* 39–62.

Grusec, J. F. (1991). The socialization of altruism. In M. S. Clark (Ed.), *Prosocial behavior* (pp. 9–33). Newbury Park, CA: Sage.

Grush, J., Clore, G. L., & Costin, F. (1975). Dissimilarity and attraction: When difference makes a difference. *Journal of Personality and Social Psychology, 32,* 783–789.

Gurman, A. S., & Kniskern, D. P. (1991). *Handbook of family therapy* (Vol. 2). New York: Brunner/Mazel.

Gurman, A. S., Kniskern, D. P., & Pinsof, W. M. (1986). Research on the process and outcome of marital and family therapy. In S. L. Garfield & A. E. Bergin (Eds.), *Handbook of psychotherapy and behavior change* (pp. 565–624). New York: Wiley.

Gutsch, K. U. (1991). *DSM-III-R* and psychotherapy. In M. Hersen & S. M. Turner (Eds.), *Adult psychopathology and diagnosis* (pp. 441–462). New York: Wiley.

Guttman, R., & Zohar, A. (1987). Spouse similarities in personality items: Changes over years of marriage and implications for mate selection. *Behavior Genetics, 17,* 179–189.

Haas, G. L., & Clarkin, J. F. (1988). Affective disorders and the family context. In J. F. Clarkin, G. L. Haas, & I. D. Glick (Eds.), *Affective disorders and the family: Assessment and treatment* (pp. 3–28). New York: Guilford.

Hakmiller, K. L. (1966). Threat as a determinant of downward comparison. *Journal of Experimental Social Psychology, 2,* 32–39.

Haley, J. (1963). Marriage therapy. *Archives of General Psychiatry, 8,* 213–234.

Hall, C. H., & Lindzey, G. (1978). *Theories of personality.* New York: Wiley.

Hall, E., & Kirkland, A. (1984). Drawings of trees and the expression of feelings in early adolescence. *British Journal of Guidance and Counseling, 12,* 39–45.

Hall, J. A. (1978). Gender effects in decoding nonverbal cues. *Psychological Bulletin, 85,* 845–857.

Hall, J. A. (1984). *Nonverbal sex differences: Communication accuracy and expressive style.* Baltimore, MD: Johns Hopkins University Press.

Hamilton, J. A., & Jensvold, M. (1992). Personality, psychopathology, and depression in women. In L. S. Brown & M. Ballou (Eds.), *Personality and psychopathology: Feminist reappraisals* (pp. 116–143). New York: Guilford.

Hammen, C. L. (1991). *Depression runs in families: The social context of risk and resilience in children of depressed mothers.* New York: Springer-Verlag.

Hammen, C. L. (1995, Fall). Interpersonal vulnerability on the generation of stress. *Clinical Science,* 4–5.

Hansen, D. (1970). Dogmatism and political ideology. *Journal of Human Relations, 18,* 995–1002.

Hansen, J. C., & L'Abate, L. (1982). *Approaches to family therapy.* New York: Macmillan.

Harris, P. W. (1988). The interpersonal maturity level classification system: I-level. *Criminal Justice and Behavior, 15,* 58–77.

Harter, S. (1993). Causes and consequences of low self-esteem in children and adolescents. In R. F. Baumeister (Ed.), *Self-esteem: The puzzle of low self-regard* (pp. 87–115). New York: Plenum.

Hartup, W. W. (1989). Social relationships and their developmental significance. *American Psychologist, 44,* 120–126.

Hartup, W. W., & Rubin, Z. (1986). *Relationships and development.* Hillsdale, NJ: Erlbaum.

Harvey, J. H., & Orbach, T. L. (1991). Cognition in close relationships: Overview and integration. In G. J. O. Fletcher & F. D. Fincham (Eds.), *Cognition in close relationships* (pp. 331–348). Hillsdale, NJ: Erlbaum.

Harwood, R. L., Miller, J. G., & Irizarry, N. L. (1995). *Culture and attachment: Perceptions of the child in context.* New York: Guilford.

Hatfield, E., & Rapson, R. (1993). Love and attachment processes. In M. Lewis & J. M. Haviland (Eds.), *Handbook of emotions* (pp. 595–604). New York: Guilford.

Hawking, S. (1993). *Black holes and baby universes and other essays.* New York: Bantam Books.

Hayes, S. C., & Melancon, S. M. (1989). Comprehensive distancing paradox and the treatment of emotional avoidance. In L. M. Ascher (Ed.), *Therapeutic paradox* (pp. 184–218). New York: Guilford.

Haynes, S. N. (1992). *Models of causality in psychopathology: Toward dynamic, synthetic, and nonlinear models of behavior disorders.* New York: Macmillan.

Haynes, S. N. (1993). Treatment implications of psychological assessment. *Psychological Assessment, 5,* 251–253.

Haynes, S. N., Spain, E. H., & Oliveira, J. (1993). Identifying causal relationships in clinical assessment. *Psychological Assessment, 5,* 281–291.

Hazan, C., & Shaver, P. (1987). Conceptualizing romantic love as an attachment process. *Journal of Personality and Social Psychology, 52,* 511–524.

Heard, H. L., & Linehan, M. M. (1993). Problems of self and borderline personality disorder: A dialectical behavioral perspective. In Z. V. Segal & S. J. Blatt (Eds.), *The self in emotional distress: Cognitive and psychodynamic perspectives* (pp. 301–325). New York: Guilford.

Hedges, L. V., & Olkin, T. (1985). *Statistical methods for meta-analysis.* Boston: Academic Press.

Heider, F. (1958). *The psychology of interpersonal relations.* New York: Wiley.

Helmersen, P. (1983). *Family interaction and communication in psychopathology: An evaluation of recent perspectives.* London: Academic Press.

Helmes, E., & Jackson, D. N. (1994). Evaluating normal and abnormal personality using the same set of constructs. In S. Strack & M. Lorr (Eds.), *Differentiating normal and abnormal personality* (pp. 341–360). New York: Springer.

Helson, R., & Mitchell, V. (1978). Personality. *Annual Review of Psychology, 29,* 555–585.

Helzer, J. E., & Guze, S. B. (Eds.). (1986). *Psychoses, affective disorders, and dementia.* New York: Basic Books.

Hendrick, S., & Hendrick, C. (1992a). *Liking, loving, & relating.* Pacific Grove, CA: Brooks/Cole.

Hendrick, S., & Hendrick, C. (1992b). *Romantic love.* Thousand Oaks, CA: Sage.

Heron, J. (1992). *Feeling and personhood: Psychology in another key.* London: Sage.

Hersen, M., & Last, C. G. (Eds.). (1990). *Handbook of child and adult psychopathology: A longitudinal perspective.* New York: Pergamon.

Hersen, M., & Turner, S. M. (Eds.). (1991). *Adult psychopathology and diagnosis.* New York: Wiley.

Hertsgaard, L., Gunnar, M., Erikson, M. F., & Nachmias, M. (1995). Adrenocortical responses to the Strange Situation in infants with disorganized/disoriented attachment relationships. *Child Development, 66,* 1100–1106.

Hetherington, E. M., & Martin, B. (1986). Family factors and psychopathology in children. In H. C. Quay & J. S. Werry (Eds.), *Psychopathological disorders of childhood* (pp. 332–389). New York: Wiley.

Hicks, M., & Platt, M. (1970). Marital happiness and stability: A review of research in the sixties. *Journal of Marriage and the Family, 32,* 553–573.

Higgins, R. L., Snyder, C. R., & Berglas, S. (1990). *Self-handicapping: The paradox that isn't.* New York: Plenum.

Hill, C. T., Rubin, Z., & Peplau, L. A. (1976). Breakups before marriage: The end of 103 affairs. *Journal of Social Issues, 32,* 147–167.

Hirsch, I. (1986). Sexual disorders: A perspective. *American Journal of Psychoanalysis, 46,* 239–248.

Hirschi, T. (1969). *Causes of delinquency.* Berkeley: University of California Press.

Hirschi, T., & Gottfredson, M. R. (1994). *The generality of deviance.* New Brunswick, NJ: Transaction.

Hochstedler, E. (1987). Twice cursed? The mentally disordered criminal defendant. *Criminal Justice and Behavior, 14,* 251–267.

Holtzman, W. H. (1961). *Inkblot perception and personality: Holtzman Inkblot Technique.* Austin, TX: University of Texas Press.

Horner, A. (1978). *Being and loving.* Northvale, NJ: Aronson.

Horowitz, L. M., Post, D., French, R., Wallis, K., & Siegelman, E. (1981). The prototype as a construct in abnormal psychology: A clarifying disagreement in psychiatric judgments. *Journal of Abnormal Psychology, 90,* 575–585.

Horowitz, L. M., Rosenberg, S. E., & Bartholomew, K. (1993). Interpersonal problems, attachment styles, and outcome in brief dynamic psychotherapy. *Journal of Consulting and Clinical Psychology, 61,* 149–160.

Horowitz, L. M., Wright, J. C., Lowenstein, E., & Parad, H. W. (1981). The prototype as a construct in abnormal psychology: A method for deriving prototypes. *Journal of Abnormal Psychology, 90,* 568–574.

Horton, M. (1973). Alternatives on romantic love. In M. E. Curtin (Ed.), *Symposium on love* (pp. 107–121). New York: Behavioral Publications.

Horvitz, A. V. (1990). *The logic of social control.* New York: Plenum.

Howard, J. A., Blumstein, P., & Schwartz, P. (1987). Social or evolutionary theories? Some observations on preferences in human mate selection. *Journal of Personality and Social Psychology, 53,* 194–200.

Howard, K. I., Lueger, R., & Schank, D. (1992). The psychotherapeutic service delivery system. *Psychotherapy Research, 2,* 164–180.

Huston, T. L. (Ed.). (1974). *Foundations of interpersonal attraction.* New York: Academic Press.

Hutton, S. P. (1974). *Self-esteem, values and self-differentiation in premarital couples.* Unpublished doctoral dissertation, Georgia State University, Atlanta.

Insko, C. A., Thompson, V. D., Stroebe, W., Shaud, K. F., Pinner, B. E., & Layton, B. D. (1973). Implied evaluation and the similarity-attraction effect. *Journal of Personality and Social Psychology, 25,* 297–308.

Izard, C. E. (1977). *Human emotions.* New York: Plenum.

Izard, C. E. (Ed.). (1979). *Emotions in personality and psychopathology.* New York: Plenum.

Izard, C. E. (1991a). Perspectives on emotions in psychotherapy. In J. D. Safran & L. S. Greenberg (Eds.), *Emotion, psychotherapy, & change* (pp. 280–289). New York: Guilford.

Izard, C. E. (1991b). *The psychology of emotions.* New York: Plenum.

Izard, C. E., Libero, D., Putnam, P., & Haynes, O. (1993). Stability of emotional experiences and their relations to traits of personality. *Journal of Personality and Social Psychology, 64,* 847–860.

Jackson, D. N. (1967). *Personality Research Form Manual.* Goshen, NY: Research Psychologists Press.

Jacob, T. (Ed.). (1987). *Family interaction and psychopathology: Theories, methods, and findings.* New York: Plenum.

Jefferson, T. W., & Johnson, J. H. (1991). The relationship of hyperactivity and sensation-seeking to delinquency subtypes. *Criminal Justice and Behavior, 18,* 195–201.

Jesness, C. F. (1988). The Jesness inventory classification system. *Criminal Justice and Behavior, 15,* 78–91.

Johnson, C., & Flach, A. (1985). Family characteristics of 105 patients with bulimia. *American Journal of Psychiatry, 142,* 1321–1324.

Johnson, C. D., Gormly, J., & Gormly, A. (1973). Disagreements and self-esteem: Support for the competence-reinforcement model of attraction. *Journal of Research in Personality, 7,* 165–172.

Johnson, J. R. W. (1982). *The logical typing of the symmetrical complementary, and parallel relationship typology: A follow-up study.* Unpublished doctoral dissertation, Georgia State University, Atlanta.

Johnson, S., & Greenberg, L. (1985). Emotionally focused couples therapy: An outcome study. *Journal of Marital and Family Therapy, 11,* 313–317.

Johnson, S. M. (1991). *The symbiotic character.* New York: Norton.

Johnson, S. M. (1994). *Character styles.* New York: Norton.

Jones, W. H., Kugler, K., & Adams, P. (1995). You always hurt the one you love: Guilt and transgressions against relationship partners. In J. P. Tangney & K. W. Fisher (Eds.), *Self-conscious emotions: The psychology of shame, guilt, embarrassment, and pride* (pp. 301–321). New York: Guilford.

Jordan, K. B., & L'Abate, L. (1995). Programmed writing and therapy with symbiotically enmeshed patients. *American Journal of Psychotherapy, 49,* 225–236.

Josselson, R. (1996). *The space between us: Exploring the dimensions of human relationships.* Thousand Oaks, CA: Sage.

Jurkovic, G. J., & Prentice, N. M. (1977). Relation of moral and cognitive development to dimensions of juvenile delinquency. *Journal of Abnormal Psychology, 86,* 414–420.

Kadzin, A. E. (1984). *Behavior modification in applied settings.* Homewood, IL: Dorsey.

Kagan, J. (1958). The concept of identification. *Psychological Review, 65,* 296–305.

Kagan, J. (1992). Temperamental contributions to emotion and social behavior. In M. S. Clark (Ed.), *Emotion* (pp. 99–118). Thousand Oaks, CA: Sage.

Kagan, J. (1994). *Galen's prophecy: Temperament in human nature.* New York: Basic Books.

Kagan, J., & Snidman, N. (1993). Temperamental contributions to styles of reactivity to discrepancy. In R. D. Cocking & K. A. Renninger (Eds.), *The development and meaning of psychological distance* (pp. 81–89). Hillsdale, NJ: Erlbaum.

Kagan, J., Snidman, N., Reznick, J. S., Gibbons, J., & Johnson, M. (1989). Temperamental inhibition and childhood fears. In P. R. Zelardo & R. G. Barr (Eds.), *Challenges to developmental paradigms: Implications for theory, assessment and treatment* (pp. 191–202). Hillsdale, NJ: Erlbaum.

Kantor, D., & Lehr, W. (1975). *Inside the family.* San Francisco: Jossey-Bass.

Karmel, L. J. (1973). The case for love. In M. E. Curtin (Ed.), *Symposium on love* (pp. 69–87). New York: Behavioral Publications.

Karoly, P. (1993a). Goal systems: An organizing framework for clinical assessment and treatment framework. *Psychological Assessment, 5,* 273–280.

Karoly, P. (1993b). Mechanisms of self-regulation: A systems review. *Annual Review of Psychology, 44,* 23–51.

Kaslow, F. W. (1996). *Handbook of relational diagnoses and dysfunctional family patterns.* New York: Wiley.

Katz, E. R., & Jay, S. M. (1984). Psychological aspects of cancer in children, adolescents, and their families. *Clinical Psychology Review, 4,* 525–542.

Katz, I., Glucksberg, S., & Krauss, R. (1960). Need satisfaction and Edwards PPS scores in married couples. *Journal of Consulting Psychology, 24,* 205–208.

Kegan, R. G. (1986). The child behind the mask: Sociopathy as developmental delay. In W. H. Reid, D. Dorr, J. I. Walker, & J. W. Bonner, III (Eds.), *Unmasking the psychopath: Antisocial personality and related syndromes* (pp. 45–77). New York: Norton.

Kelley, H. H. (1992). Common sense psychology and scientific psychology. *Annual Review of Psychology, 43,* 1–24.

Kendall, P. C., & Dobson, K. S. (1993). *On the nature of cognition and its role in psychopathology* (pp. 3–17). San Diego, CA: Academic Press.

Kepner, J. I. (1993). *Body process: Working with the body in psychotherapy.* San Francisco: Jossey-Bass.

Kerckhoff, A. C. (1974). The social context of interpersonal attraction. In T. L. Huston (Ed.), *Foundations of interpersonal attraction* (pp. 61–78). New York: Academic Press.

Kerckhoff, A. C., & Davis, K. I. (1962). Value consensus and need complementarity in mate selection. *American Sociological Review, 27,* 295–303.

Kernis, M. H. (1993). The role of stability and level of self-esteem in psychological functioning. In R. F. Baumeister (Ed.), *Self-esteem: The puzzle of low self-regard* (pp. 167–182). New York: Plenum.

Kerns, K. A. (1994). A developmental model of the relations between mother-child attachment and friendship. In R. Erber & R. Gilmour (Eds.), *Theoretical frameworks for personal relationships* (pp. 129–156). Hillsdale, NJ: Erlbaum.

Kiesler, D. J. (1994). Standardization of intervention: The tie that binds psychotherapy research and practice. In P. F. Talley, H. H. Strupp, & S. F. Butler (Eds.), *Psychotherapy research and practice: Bridging the gap* (pp. 143–153). New York: Basic Books.

Kilmann, R. H., & Thomas, K. W. (1977). Developing a forced-choice measure of conflict-handling behavior: The "MODE" instrument. *Educational and Psychological Measurement, 37,* 309–325.

Klinger, E. (1977). *Meaning and void: Inner experience and the incentives in people's lives.* Minneapolis: University of Minnesota Press.

Kluckhohn, C., Murray, H. A., & Schneider, D. M. (1953). *Personality in nature, society, and culture.* New York: Knopf.

Knapp, M. L. (1972). *Nonverbal communication in human interaction.* New York: Holt, Rinehart and Winston.

Kobak, R., & Hazan, C. (1991). Attachment in marriage: The effects of security and accuracy of working models. *Journal of Personality and Social Psychology, 60,* 861–869.

Kobak, R., & Sceery, A. (1988). Attachment in late adolescence: Working models, affect regulation, and representations of self and others. *Child Development, 59,* 135–146.

Kohlberg, L. (1969). Stage and sequence: The cognitive-developmental approach to socialization. In D. A. Goslin (Ed.), *Handbook of socialization theory and research* (pp. 347–480). Chicago, IL: Rand McNally.

Krahé, B. (1992). *Personality and social psychology: Towards a synthesis.* London: Sage.

Kramer, S., & Akhtar, S. (Eds.). (1992). *When the body speaks: Psychological meanings in kinetic clues.* Northvale, NJ: Jason Aronson.

Kruglanski, A. W., & Mayseless, O. (1990). Classic and current social comparison research: Expanding the perspective. *Psychological Bulletin, 108,* 195–208.

Kutchins, H., & Kirk, S. (1986). The reliability of *DSM-III*: A critical review. *Social Work Research Abstracts, 22,* 3–11.

L'Abate, L. (1964). *Principles of clinical psychology.* New York: Grune & Stratton.

L'Abate, L. (1976). *Understanding and helping the individual in the family.* New York: Grune & Stratton.

L'Abate, L. (1977). Intimacy is sharing hurt feelings: A reply to David Mace. *Journal of Marital and Family Therapy, 3,* 13–16.

L'Abate, L. (1983). Styles in intimate relationships: The A-R-C model. *The Personnel and Guidance Journal, 63,* 227–233.

L'Abate, L. (1985a). Descriptive and explanatory levels in family therapy: Distance, defeats, and dependence. In L. L'Abate (Ed.), *Handbook of family psychology and therapy* (pp. 1218–1248). Pacific Grove, CA: Brooks/Cole.

L'Abate, L. (1985b). The status and future of family psychology and therapy. In L. L'Abate (Ed.), *Handbook of family psychology and therapy* (pp. 1417–1435). Pacific Grove, CA: Brooks/Cole.

L'Abate, L. (1986). *Systematic family therapy.* New York: Bruner/Mazel.

L'Abate, L. (1990). *Building family competence: Primary and secondary prevention strategies.* Newbury Park, CA: Sage.

L'Abate, L. (1992a). Excessive spending. In L. L'Abate, J. E. Farrar, & D. A. Serrittela (Eds.), *Handbook of differential treatments for addictions* (pp. 253–270). Boston: Allyn & Bacon.

L'Abate, L. (1992b). *Programmed writing: A self-administered approach for interventions with individuals, couples, and families.* Pacific Grove, CA: Brooks/Cole.

L'Abate, L. (1994a). A family theory of impulsivity. In W. McCown, J. L. Johnson, & M. B. Shure (Eds.), *The impulsive client: Theory, research and treatment* (pp. 93–117). Washington, DC: American Psychological Association.

L'Abate, L. (1994b). *A theory of personality development.* New York: Wiley.

L'Abate, L. (1994c). *Family evaluation: A psychological approach.* Thousand Oaks, CA: Sage.

L'Abate, L. (1994d). Book review: De Giacomo's "Finite Systems and Infinite Interactions: The logic of human interaction and its application to psychotherapy." *American Journal of Family Therapy, 22,* 88–93.

L'Abate, L. (Ed.). (1994e). *Handbook of developmental family psychology and psychopathology.* New York: Wiley.

L'Abate, L. (1996a). *Long distance writing and computer assisted training: Programs for individuals, couples, and families to be administered by mental health professionals.* Manuscript submitted for publication.

L'Abate, L. (1996b). *Attachment, personality propensities, and fear of intimacy.* Research in progress.

L'Abate, L. (Ed.). (in press). *Handbook of family psychopathology.* New York: Guilford.

L'Abate, L., & Bagarozzi, D. A. (1993). *Sourcebook of marriage and family evaluation.* New York: Brunner/Mazel.

L'Abate, L., Boyce, J., Fraizer, L., & Russ, D. (1992). Programmed writing: Research in progress. *Comprehensive Mental Health Care, 2,* 45–62.

L'Abate, L., & Colondier, G. (1987). The emperor has no clothes: A critique of systems thinking and a proposal. *American Journal of Family Therapy, 15,* 19–33.

L'Abate, L., Farrar, J. E., & Serritella, D. A. (1992). *Handbook of differential treatments for addictions.* Boston: Allyn & Bacon.

L'Abate, L., Hamm, J., Russ, D., & Bird, G. (in press). Programmed writing: Two follow-ups and one application with clinical outpatients. *Contemporary Psychodynamics.*

L'Abate, L., Hansen, J. C., & Ganahl, G. (1986). *Methods of family therapy.* Englewood Cliffs, NJ: Prentice-Hall.

L'Abate, L., & Harel, T. (1993). Deriving, developing, and expanding a theory of developmental competence from resource exchange theory. In U. G. Foa, J. Converse, Jr., K. Y. Tornblom, & E. B. Foa (Eds.), *Resource theory: Explorations and applications* (pp. 23–269). San Diego, CA: Academic Press.

L'Abate, L., & Harrison, M. G. (1992). Treating codependency. In L. L'Abate, J. E. Farrar, & D. A. Serritella (Eds.), *Handbook of differential treatments for addictions* (pp. 286–307). Boston: Allyn & Bacon.

L'Abate, L., & Hewitt, D. (1988). Toward a classification of sex and sexual behavior. *Journal of Sex and Marital Therapy, 14,* 29–39.

L'Abate, L., & L'Abate, B. L. (1979). The paradoxes of intimacy. *Family Therapy, 6,* 175–184.

L'Abate, L., Lambert, R. G., Townsend, J., Madison, S., Ling, M., & Billehus, A. (1996). *Testing a model of psychopathology with the MMPI-2.* Research in progress.

L'Abate, L., Lambert, R. G., Vardaman, P., Lewy, L., DaLee, D., & Hunter, L. (1996). *Selfhood and depression: A test of a selfhood model of relational personality propensities.* Research in progress.

L'Abate, L., & Odell, M. (1996). Enlarging practices and roles of family clinicians. In M. Harway (Ed.), *Treating the changing family: Handling normative and unusual events* (pp. 321–339). New York: Wiley.

L'Abate, L., & Sloan, S. Z. (1985). Intimacy. In L. L'Abate (Ed.), *Handbook of family psychology and therapy* (pp. 305–329). Pacific Grove, CA: Brooks/Cole.

L'Abate, L., & Talmadge, W. C. (1987). Love, intimacy, and sex. In G. R. Weeks & L. Hof (Eds.), *Integrating sex and marital therapy* (pp. 23–34). New York: Brunner/Mazel.

L'Abate, L., & Torem, M. S. (Eds.). (1996). *Long distance writing and computer assisted training in psychiatry and mental health.* Manuscript submitted for publication.

L'Abate, L., & Wagner, V. (1985). Theory-derived, family-oriented test-batteries. In L. L'Abate (Ed.), *Handbook of family psychology and therapy* (pp. 1152–1177). Pacific Grove, CA: Brooks/Cole.

L'Abate, L., & Wagner, V. (1988). Testing a theory of developmental competence in the family. *American Journal of Family Therapy, 16*, 23–35.

L'Abate, L., Weeks, G., & Weeks, K. (1979). Of scapegoats, strawmen, and scarecrows. *International Journal of Family Therapy, 1*, 86–96.

L'Abate, L., & Weinstein, S. E. (1987). *Structured enrichment programs for couples and families.* New York: Brunner/Mazel.

L'Abate, L., & Young, L. (1987). *Casebook of structured enrichment programs for couples and families.* New York: Brunner/Mazel.

Ladd, G. W., Le Sieur, K. D., & Profilet, S. M. (1993). Direct parental influences on young children's peer relations. In S. Duck (Ed.), *Learning about relationships* (pp. 152–183). Thousand Oaks, CA: Sage.

La Gaipa, J. J., & Werner, R. E. (1971). Effects of topic relevancy and attitude similarity on two measures of affiliation. *Psychonomic Science, 24*, 67–68.

Lardieri, L. (1996). *Attachment styles, personality propensities, and fear of intimacy.* Atlanta: Georgia State University, Department of Psychology. Research in progress.

La Ronde, C., & Swann, W. B., Jr. (1993). Caught in the crossfire: Positivity and self-verification strivings among people with low self-esteem. In R. F. Baumeister (Ed.), *Self-esteem: The puzzle of low self-esteem regard* (pp. 147–165). New York: Plenum.

Larsen, R. J., & Diener, E. (1992). Promises and problems with the circumplex model of emotion. In M. S. Clark (Ed.), *Emotion* (pp. 25–59). Thousand Oaks, CA: Sage.

Laudenslager, M. L., & Reite, M. L. (1984). Losses and separations: Immunological consequences and health implications. In P. Shaver (Ed.), *Emotions, relationships, and health* (pp. 285–312). Newbury Park, CA: Sage.

Lawing, D. (1973). *Mathematical psychology.* London: Academic Press.

Lazarus, R. S. (1991). *Emotion and adaptation.* New York: Oxford University Press.

Lazarus, R. S., & Folkman, S. (1984). *Stress, appraisal, and coping.* New York: Springer.

Lazarus, R. S., & Lazarus, B. N. (1994). *Passion and reason: Making sense of our emotions.* New York: Oxford University Press.

Le Blanc, M., & Loeber, R. (1993). Precursors, causes, and the development of criminal offending. In D. F. Hay & A. Angold (Eds.), *Precursors and causes in development and psychopathology* (pp. 233–263). Chichester, UK: Wiley.

Leff, J., & Vaughn, C. (1985). *Expressed emotions in families.* New York: Guilford.

Lemkau, J. (1984). Reflections on selflessness in the lives of women. *Women and Therapy, 3*, 31–36.

Lemkau, J. P., Rafferty, J. P., Purdy, R. R., & Rudisill, J. R. (1987). Sex roles stress and job burnout among family practice physicians. *Journal of Vocational Behavior, 31*, 81–90.

Lenney, E., Browning, C., & Mitchell, L. (1980). What you don't know can hurt joy: The effects of performance criteria ambiguity on sex differences in self-confidence. *Journal of Personality, 48*, 306–322.

Lesnik-Oberstein, M., & Cohen, L. (1984). Cognitive style, sensation seeking, and assortative mating. *Journal of Personality and Social Psychology, 46*, 112–117.

Lester, D. (1981). *Psychotherapy for offenders.* Jonesboro, TN: Pilgrimage.

Levant, R. F. (1986). *Psychoeducational approaches to family therapy and counseling.* New York: Springer.

Levant, R. F., & Pollack, W. S. (Eds.). (1995). *The new psychology of men.* New York: Basic Books.

Levinger, G. (1964). Note on need complementarity in marriage. *Psychological Bulletin, 61*, 153–157.

Levinger, G., & Breedlove, J. (1966). Interpersonal attraction and agreement: A study of marriage partners. *Journal of Personality and Social Psychology, 3*, 367–372.

Levinger, G., & Moreland, J. (1969). Approach-avoidance as a function of imaginal shock threat and self-other similarity. *Journal of Personality and Social Psychology, 12,* 245–251.

Levinger, G., Senn, D. J., & Jorgensen, B. W. (1970). Progress toward permanence in courtship: A test of the Kerckhoff-Davis hypotheses. *Sociometry, 33,* 427–443.

Levinson, R. B. (1988). Developments in the classification process: Quay's AIMS approach. *Criminal Justice and Behavior, 15,* 24–38.

Levy, L. H. (1970). *Conceptions of personality: Theories and research.* New York: Random House.

Lewin, K. (1935). *Dynamic theory of personality.* New York: McGraw-Hill.

Lewis, M. (1989). Culture and biology: The role of temperament. In P. R. Zelardo & R. G. Barr (Eds.), *Challenges to developmental paradigms: Implications for theory, assessment and treatment* (pp. 203–223). Hillsdale, NJ: Erlbaum.

Lewis, M. (1993). The emergence of human emotions. In M. Lewis & J. M. Haviland (Eds.), *Handbook of emotions* (pp. 223–235). New York: Guilford.

Lewis, M., & Haviland, J. M. (Eds.). (1993). *Handbook of emotions.* New York: Guilford.

Lewis, P. N., & Gallois, C. (1984). Disagreements, refusals, or negative feelings: Perception of negatively assertive messages from friends and strangers. *Behavior Therapy, 15,* 353–368.

Liberman, R. P., DeRisi, W. J., & Mueser, K. T. (1989). *Social skills training for psychiatric patients.* Boston: Allyn & Bacon.

Lickona, T. (1974). A cognitive-developmental approach to interpersonal attraction. In T. L. Huston (Ed.), *Foundations of interpersonal attraction* (pp. 31–59). New York: Academic Press.

Lidz, T. (1976). *The person: His and her development throughout the life cycle.* New York: Basic Books.

Liebert, R. M., & Spiegler, M. D. (1990). *Personality: Strategies and issues.* Pacific Grove, CA: Brooks/Cole.

Lilly, J. R., Cullen, F. T., & Ball, R. A. (1995). *Criminological theory: Context and consequences.* London: Sage.

Lindsay, J. S. (1976). Balance theory: Possible consequences of number of family members. *Family Process, 15,* 245–249.

Lion, A. (1978). Children's needs and parents' rights: Legal and psychological dilemmas. *Mental Health and Society, 5,* 314–324.

Lippard, P. V. (1988). "Ask me no questions, I'll tell you no lies": Situational exigencies for interpersonal deception. *Western Journal of Speech Communication, 52,* 91–100.

Litz, T. (1992). *The relevance of the family to psychoanalytic theory.* Madison, CT: International Universities Press.

Locke, H. J., & Wallace, K. M. (1959). Short marital-adjustment and prediction tests: Their reliability and validity. *Marriage and Family Living, 21,* 251–255.

Loeber, R., & Farrington, D. P. (1994). Problems and solutions in longitudinal and experimental treatment studies of child psychopathology and delinquency. *Journal of Consulting and Clinical Psychology, 62,* 887–900.

Loh, W. D., & Nuttin, J. M., Jr. (1972). Effects of interethnic-group comparison and attitudes on task performance. *Journal of Personality and Social Psychology, 24,* 291–300.

Lombardo, J. P., Steigleder, M., & Fernberg, R. (1975). Internality-externality: The perception of negatively valued personality characteristics and interpersonal attraction. *Representative Research in Social Psychology, 6,* 89–95.

Lorion, R. P. (1990). Basing preventive interventions on theory: Stimulating field's momentum. In R. P. Lorion (Ed.), *Protecting the children: Strategies for optimizing emotional and behavioral development* (pp. 7–31). New York: Haworth.

Lorr, M. (1986). Classifying psychotics: Dimensional and categorical approaches. In T. Millon & G. L. Klerman (Eds.), *Contemporary directions in psychopathology: Toward the DSM-IV* (pp. 331–345). New York: Guilford.

Lott, B., & Maluso, D. (1993). The social learning of gender. In A. E. Beall & R. J. Sternberg (Eds.), *The psychology of gender* (pp. 99–123). New York: Guilford.

Luce, R. D. (1995). Four tensions concerning mathematical modeling in psychology. *Annual Review of Psychology, 46,* 1–26.

Lurigio, A. J., & Lewis, D. A. (1987). The criminal mental patient: A descriptive analysis and suggestions for future research. *Criminal Justice and Behavior, 14,* 268–287.

Lutwak, N. (1985). Fear of intimacy among college women. *Adolescence, 20,* 15–20.

Lykken, D. T. (1995). *The antisocial personalities.* Hillsdale, NJ: Erlbaum.

Lynn, D. B. (1969). *Parental and sex role identification: A theoretical formulation.* Berkeley, CA: McCutchan.

Macaskill, N. D. (1980). The narcissistic core as a focus in the group therapy of the borderline patient. *British Journal of Medical Psychology, 53,* 137–143.

Maddi, S. R. (1980). *Personality theories: A comparative analysis.* Homewood, IL: Dorsey Press.

Maddi, S. R. (1993). The continuing relevance of personality theory. In K. H. Craik, R. Hogan, & R. N. Wolfe (Eds.), *Fifty years of personality psychology* (pp. 85–101). New York: Plenum.

Magai, C., & McFadden, S. H. (1995). *The role of emotions in social and personality development: History, theory, and research.* New York: Plenum.

Magnusson, D., & Ohman, A. (1987). *Psychopathology: An interactional perspective.* Orlando, FL: Academic Press.

Magnusson, D., & Torestad, B. (1993). A holistic view of personality: A model revisited. *Annual Review of Psychology, 44,* 427–452.

Mahler, M. S. (1968). *On human symbiosis and the vicissitudes of individuation.* New York: International Universities Press.

Mahler, M. S., Pine, F., & Bergman, A. (1975). *The psychological birth of the human infant.* New York: Basic Books.

Mahoney, M. J. (1991). *Human change processes: The scientific foundations of psychotherapy.* New York: Basic Books.

Mahrer, A. R. (Ed.). (1970). *New approaches to personality classification.* New York: Columbia University Press.

Mak, A. S. (1991). Psychosocial control characteristics of delinquents and nondelinquents. *Criminal Justice and Behavior, 18,* 287–303.

Malatesta, C. Z., & Izard, C. E. (Eds.). (1984). *Emotion in adult development.* Beverly Hills, CA: Sage.

Mangen, D. J., Bengtson, V. L., & Landry, P. H., Jr. (1988). *The measurement of interpersonal relations.* Newbury Park, CA: Sage.

Markovitz, E. (1982). Aggression: An overview. *Psychoanalytic Inquiry, 2,* 11–20.

Markus-Kaplan, M., & Kaplan, K. J. (1984). A bidimensional view of distancing: Reciprocity versus compensation, intimacy versus social control. *Journal of Nonverbal Behavior, 8,* 315–326.

Marlatt, G. A., Baer, J. S., Donovan, D. M., & Kivlahan, D. R. (1988). Addictive behaviors: Etiology and treatment. *Annual Review of Psychology, 39,* 223–252.

Marshall, W. L., & Barbaree, H. E. (1991). Personality, impulse control, and adjustment disorders. In M. Hersen & S. M. Turner (Eds.), *Adult psychopathology and diagnosis* (pp. 360–391). New York: Wiley.

Martin, B. (1990). The transmission of relationship difficulties from one generation to the next. *Journal of Youth and Adolescence, 19,* 181–199.

Martin, L. L., Achee, J. W., Ward, D. W., & Harlow, T. F. (1993). The role of cognition and effort in the use of emotions to guide behavior. In R. S. Wyer, Jr., & T. S. Srull (Eds.), *Perspectives on anger and emotion* (pp. 147–158). Hillsdale, NJ: Erlbaum.

Maruish, M. E. (Ed.). (1994). *The use of psychological testing for treatment planning and outcome assessment.* Hillsdale, NJ: Erlbaum.

Mascie-Taylor, C. G., & Vanderberg, S. G. (1988). Assortative mating for IQ and personality due to propinquity and personal preference. *Behavior Genetics, 18,* 339–345.

Mash, E. J., & Hunsley, J. (1993). Assessment considerations in the identification of failing psychotherapy: Bringing the negatives out of the darkroom. *Psychological Assessment, 5,* 292–301.

Massey, R. F. (1981). *Personality theories: Comparison and syntheses.* New York: Von Nostrand.

Matheny, K. B., Aycock, D. W., Curlette, W. L., & Junker, G. N. (1993). The Coping Resources Inventory for Stress: A measure of perceived resourcefulness. *Journal of Clinical Psychology, 49,* 815–830.

May, R. (1983). *The discovery of being.* New York: W. W. Norton.

Mayer, J. D., & Gaschke, Y. N. (1988). The experience and meta-experience of mood. *Journal of Personality and Social Psychology, 55,* 102–111.

Mayer, J. D., & Salovey, P. (1995). Emotional intelligence and the construction and regulation of feelings. *Applied and Preventive Psychology, 4,* 197–208.

McAdams, D. P. (1990). *The person: An introduction to personality psychology.* San Diego, CA: Harcourt Brace Jovanovich.

McAdams, D. P. (1990). Unity and purpose in human lives: The emergence of identity as a life story. In A. I. Rubin, R. A. Zucker, R. A. Emmons, & S. Frank (Eds.), *Studying persons and lives* (pp. 148–200). New York: Springer.

McAdams, D. P., & Bryant, F. B. (1987). Intimacy motivation and subjective mental health in a nationwide sample. *Journal of Personality, 55,* 395–413.

McClanahan, L. D. (1971). Social maturity and multivariate discriminant analysis for personality descriptions of conservatives, activists, and radicals. *Measurement and Evaluation in Guidance, 10,* 135–144.

McCrae, R. R. (1994). A reformulation of AXIS II: Personality and personality-related problems. In P. T. Costa & T. A. Widiger (Eds.), *Personality disorders and the five-factor model of personality* (pp. 303–317). Washington, DC: American Psychological Association.

McCrae, R. R., & Costa, P. T., Jr. (1990). *Personality in adulthood.* New York: Guilford.

McCubbin, H. I., Thompson, A. I., Pirner, P. A., & McCubbin, M. A. (1988). *Family types and strengths: A life cycle and ecological perspective.* Edina, MN: Burgess International Group.

McDermott, P. A., & Weiss, R. V. (1995). A normative typology of healthy, subclinical, and clinical behavior styles among American children and adolescents. *Psychological Assessment, 7,* 162–170.

McFarlane, W. R. (1991). Family psychoeducational treatment. In A. S. Gurman & D. P. Kniskern (Eds.), *Handbook of family therapy* (Vol. 2, pp. 363–395). New York: Brunner/Mazel.

McMahon, R. J. (1994). Diagnosis, assessment, and treatment of externalizing problems in children: The role of longitudinal data. *Journal of Consulting and Clinical Psychology, 62,* 901–917.

McTaggart, J. E. (1927). *The nature of existence.* Cambridge, UK: Cambridge University Press.

Megargee, E. I., & Bohn, M. J. (1979). *Classifying criminal offenders.* Newbury Park, CA: Sage.

Meissner, W. W. (1974). Family process and psychosomatic disease. *International Journal of Psychiatry in Medicine, 5,* 411–430.

Merkel, W. T., & Searight, H. R. (1992). Why families are not like swamps, solar systems, or thermostats: Some limits of systems theory as applied to family therapy. *Contemporary Family Therapy: An International Journal, 14,* 33–50.

Messer, S. B., & Warren, S. (1990). Personality change and psychotherapy. In L. A. Pervin (Ed.), *Handbook of personality: Theory and research* (pp. 371–398). New York: Guilford.

Mettee, D. R., & Riskind, J. (1974). Size of defeat and liking for superior and similar ability competitors. *Journal of Experimental Social Psychology, 10,* 333–351.

Mettee, D. R., & Smith, G. (1977). Social comparison and interpersonal attraction: The case of dissimilarity. In J. M. Suls & R. L. Miller (Eds.), *Social comparison processes: Theoretical and empirical perspectives* (pp. 69–102). Washington, DC: Hemisphere.

Metts, S. (1989). An exploratory investigation of deception in close relationships. *Journal of Social and Personal Relationships, 6,* 159–179.

Meyer, G. J., & Shack, J. R. (1989). Structural convergence of mood and personality: Evidence for old and new directions. *Journal of Personality and Social Psychology, 57,* 691–706.

Meyer, J. P., & Pepper, S. (1977). Need compatibility and marital adjustment in young married couples. *Journal of Personality and Social Psychology, 35,* 331–342.

Meyer, R. E. (1986). How to understand the relationship between psychopathology and addictive disorders: Another example of the chicken and the egg. In R. E. Meyer (Ed.), *Psychopathology and addictive disorders* (pp. 1–16). New York: Guilford.

Meyerling, R., & Epling-McWherter, E. A. (1987). Decision making in extramarital relationships. *Lifestyles, 8,* 115–129.

Meyers, C. (1986). *Teaching students to think critically.* San Francisco, CA: Jossey-Bass.

Middleman, R. R. (1968). *The nonverbal method in working with groups.* New York: Association Press.

Midlarsky, E. (1991). Helping as coping. In M. S. Clark (Ed.), *Prosocial behavior* (pp. 238–264). Newbury Park, CA: Sage.

Milburn, T. W., & Watman, K. H. (1981). *On the nature of threat: A social psychological inquiry.* New York: Praeger.

Miller, N. E. (1948). Theory and experiment relating psychoanalytic displacement to stimulus-response generalization. *Journal of Abnormal and Social Psychology, 43,* 155–176.

Miller, S. M., & Kirsch, N. (1987). Sex differences in cognitive coping with stress. In R. C. Barnett, L. Biener, & G. K. Baruch (Eds.), *Gender and stress* (pp. 278–307). New York: Free Press.

Millon, T. (1967). *Theories of psychopathology.* Philadelphia, PA: Saunders.

Millon, T. (1969). *Modern psychopathology: A biosocial approach to maladaptive learning and functioning.* Philadelphia, PA: Saunders.

Millon, T. (1981). *Disorders of personality DSM-III: Axis II.* New York: Wiley.

Millon, T. (1986a). A theoretical derivation of pathological personalities. In T. Millon & G. L. Klerman (Eds.), *Contemporary directions in psychopathology: Toward the DSM-IV* (pp. 639–669). New York: Guilford.

Millon, T. (1986b). Personality prototypes and their diagnostic criteria. In T. Millon & G. L. Klerman (Eds.), *Contemporary directions in psychopathology: Toward the DSM-IV* (pp. 671–712). New York: Guilford.

Millon, T. (1986c). On the past and future of the *DSM-III*: Personal recollections and projections. In T. Millon & G. L. Klerman (Eds.), *Contemporary directions in psychopathology: Toward the DSM-IV* (pp. 29–70). New York: Guilford.

Millon, T., & Klerman, G. L. (Eds.). (1986). *Contemporary directions in psychopathology: Toward the DSM-IV.* New York: Guilford.

Mills, J., & Clark, M. S. (1994). Communal and exchange relationships: Controversies and research. In R. Erber & R. Gilmour (Eds.), *Theoretical frameworks for personal relationships* (pp. 29–42). Hillsdale, NJ: Erlbaum.

Mischel, W. (1986). *Introduction to personality.* New York: Holt, Rinehart and Winston.

Mitchell, A. K. (1983). Adolescents' experiences of parental separation and divorce. *Journal of Adolescence, 6,* 175–187.

Moyer, A. J. (1994). Cybernetic theory does not explain family and couple process: Systems theory and dialectical metatheory. *American Journal of Family Therapy, 22,* 273–281.

Mruk, C. (1995). *Self-esteem: Research, theory, and practice.* New York: Springer.

Murphy, G. (1947). *Personality: A biosocial approach to origins and structure.* New York: Harper & Brothers.

Murray, H. A. (1938). *Explorations in personality.* New York: Oxford University Press.

Murstein, B. I. (1961). A complementary need hypothesis in newlyweds and middle aged married couples. *Journal of Abnormal and Social Psychology, 63,* 194–197.

Murstein, B. I. (1970). Stimulus-value-role: A theory of marital choice. *Journal of Marriage and the Family, 32,* 464–481.

Murstein, B. I. (1972). Interview behavior, projective techniques, and questionnaires in the clinical assessment of marital choice. *Journal of Personality Assessment, 36,* 462–467.

Murstein, B. I. (1976). *Who will marry whom?: Theories and research in marital choice.* New York: Springer.

Murstein, B. I. (1980). Mate selection in the 1970's. *Journal of Marriage and the Family, 42,* 777–792.

Murstein, B. I. (1986). *Paths to marriage.* Beverly Hills, CA: Sage.

Murstein, B. I., & Beck, G. D. (1972). Person perception, marriage adjustment and social desirability. *Journal of Consulting and Clinical Psychology, 39,* 396–403.

Musick, J. S., & Cohler, B. J. (Eds.). (1983). Parental psychopathology and infant development. *Infant Mental Health Journal, 4,* 140–164.

Nahemow, L., & Lawton, M. P. (1983). Similarity and propinquity: Making friends with 'different' people. In H. H. Blumberg, A. P. Hare, V. Kent, & M. Davies (Eds.), *Small groups and social interaction* (Vol. 1, pp. 279–292). New York: Wiley.

Napier, A. Y. (1988). *The fragile bond: In search of an equal, intimate, and enduring marriage.* New York: Harper & Row.

Nathanson, D. L. (1992). *Shame and pride: Affect, sex, and the birth of the self.* New York: Norton.

National Advisory Mental Health Council. (1995). Basic behavioral science research for mental health: A national investment, emotion and motivation. *American Psychologist, 50,* 838–845.

Nelson, D. (1966, May). *Attitude similarity and interpersonal attraction: The approval-cue hypothesis.* Paper presented at the meeting of the Southwestern Psychological Association, Arlington, TX.

Neru, A. N., & Neru, C. M. (1993). Identifying and selecting target problems for clinical interventions: A problem-solving model. *Psychological Assessment, 5,* 254–263.

Nesselroade, J. R. (1990). Adult personality development: Issues in assessing constancy and change. In A. I. Rabin, R. A. Zucker, R. A. Emmons, & S. Frank (Eds.), *Studying persons and lives* (pp. 41–85). New York: Springer.

Newman, D. E. (1974). The personality of violence: Conversations with protagonists. *Mental Health and Society, 1,* 328–344.

Newman, F. L., & Clario, J. A. (1994). Criteria for selecting psychological instruments for treatment outcome assessment. In M. E. Marvish (Ed.), *The use of psychological testing for treatment planning and outcome assessment* (pp. 98–110). Hillsdale, NJ: Erlbaum.

Nichols, M. P., & Zax, M. (1977). *Catharsis in psychotherapy.* New York: Gardner.

Nicholson, I. R., & Neufeld, R. W. J. (1993). Classification of the schizophrenias according to symptomatology: A two-factor model. *Journal of Abnormal Psychology, 102,* 259–270.

Nobel, P. S., Adams, G. R., & Openshaw, D. K. (1989). Interpersonal communication in parent-adolescent dyads: A brief report on the effects of a social skills training program. *Journal of Family Psychology, 2,* 483–494.

Nolen, W. A., Zohar, J., Roose, S. P., & Amsterdam, J. D. (1994). *Refractory depression: Current strategies and future directions.* Chichester, UK: Wiley.

Noller, P., & Ruzzene, M. (1992). Communication in marriage: The influence of affect and cognition. In G. J. O. Fletcher & F. D. Fincham (Eds.), *Cognition in close relationships* (pp. 203–233). Hillsdale, NJ: Erlbaum.

Oatley, K., & Jenkins, J. M. (1996). *Understanding emotions.* Cambridge, MA: Blackwell.

Ogilvie, D. M., & Ashmore, R. D. (1991). Self-with-other representation as a unit of analysis in self-concept research. In R. C. Curtis (Ed.), *The relational self: Theoretical convergences in psychoanalysis and social psychology* (pp. 282–314). New York: Guilford.

Oldham, J. M., & Morris, L. B. (1990). *The personality self-portrait.* New York: Bantam Books.

Olson, D. H. (1993). Circumplex model of marital and family systems. In F. Walsh (Ed.), *Normal family processes* (pp. 104–137). New York: Guilford.

Olson, D. H., Portner, J., & Lavee, Y. (1985). *FACES III.* San Paul, MN: University of Minnesota, Family Social Science.

Olson, D. H. (1989). Circumplex model of family systems VIII: Family assessment and intervention. In D. H. Olson, C. S. Russell, & D. H. Sprenkle (Eds.), *Circumplex model: Systematic assessment and treatment of families* (pp. 7–49). New York: Haworth.

Orlinsky, D. E. (1989). Researchers' images of psychotherapy: Their origins and influence on research. *Clinical Psychology Review 9*, 413–441.

Oullette-Kobasa, S. C. (1987). Stress responses and personality. In R. C. Barnett, L. Biener, & G. K. Baruch (Eds.), *Gender and stress* (pp. 308–329). New York: Free Press.

Packer, M. J., & Richardson, E. (1991). Analytic hermeneutics and the study of morality in action. In W. M. Kurtines & J. L. Gewirtz (Eds.), *Handbook of moral behavior and development* (pp. 335–371). Hillsdale, NJ: Erlbaum.

Panksepp, J. (1994). The basics of basic emotion. In P. Ekman & R. J. Davidson (Eds.), *The nature of emotion: Fundamental questions* (pp. 20–24). New York: Oxford University Press.

Parsons, T., & Bales, R. F. (1955). *Family socialization and interaction processes.* Glencoe, IL: Free Press.

Patrick, C. J. (1995, Fall). Emotion and temperament in psychopathy. *Clinical Science,* 5–8.

Patterson, G. R. (1982). *Coercive family process.* Eugene, OR: Castalia.

Patterson, G. R. (1985). Beyond technology: The next stage in developing an empirical base for parent training. In L. L'Abate (Ed.), *Handbook of family psychology and therapy* (pp. 1344–1376). Pacific Grove, CA: Brooks/Cole.

Patterson, G. R., & Dishion, T. J. (1988). Multilevel family process models: Traits, interactions, and relationships. In R. Hinde & J. Stevenson-Hinde (Eds.), *Relationships within families: Mutual influences* (pp. 283–310). Oxford, UK: Clarenson.

Patterson, M. L. (1984). Nonverbal intimacy and exchange. *Journal of Nonverbal Behavior, 8,* 233–293.

Patzer, G. L. (1985). *The physical attractiveness phenomena.* New York: Plenum.

Peck, R. E., & Everson, J. E. (1975). Similarities between parents and offspring on a personality inventory. *American Journal of Psychiatry, 132,* 453–454.

Peele, S., & Brodsky, A. (1975). *Love and addiction.* New York: New American Library.

Pennebaker, J. W. (1990). *Opening up: The healing power of confiding in others.* New York: Morrow.

Pennebaker, J. W. (1993a). Putting stress into words: Health, linguistic, and therapeutic implications. *Behavioral Research and Therapy, 31,* 539–548.

Pennebaker, J. W. (1993b). Social mechanisms of constraint. In D. M. Wegner & J. W. Pennebaker (Eds.), *Handbook of mental control* (pp. 200–219). Englewood Cliffs, NJ: Prentice-Hall.

Pennebaker, J. W., Barger, S. D., & Tiebout, J. (1989). Disclosure of traumas and health among Holocaust survivors. *Psychosomatic Medicine, 51,* 577–589.

Pennebaker, J. W., & Beall, S. K. (1986). Confronting a traumatic event: Toward an understanding of inhibition and disease. *Journal of Abnormal Psychology, 95,* 274–281.

Pennebaker, J. W., & Francis, M. E. (in press). Cognitive, emotional, and language processes in writing: Health and adjustment to college. *Journal of Personality and Social Psychology.*

Pennebaker, J. W., Kiecolt-Glaser, J., & Glaser, R. (1988). Disclosure of traumas and immune function: Health implications for psychotherapy. *Journal of Consulting and Clinical Psychology, 56,* 239–245.

Pennebaker, J. W., & Roberts, T. A. (1995). Toward a his and hers theory of emotions: Gender differences in visceral perception. *Advances in Experimental Cognitive Psychology, 27,* 143–176.

Pennebaker, J. W., & Susman, J. R. (1988). Disclosure of traumas and psychosomatic processes. *Society for Scientific Medicine, 26,* 327–332.

Perlman, D., & Fehr, B. (1987). The development of intimate relationships. In D. Perlman & S. Duck (Eds.), *Intimate relationships: Development, dynamics, and deterioration* (pp. 13–42). Newbury Park, CA: Sage.

Perris, C., Arrindell, W. A., & Eisenmann, M. (Eds.). (1994). *Parenting and psychopathology.* New York: Wiley.

Person, E. S. (1988). *Dreams of love and fateful encounters: The power of romantic passion.* New York: W. W. Norton.

Pervin, L. A. (1980). *Personality: Theory, assessment, and research.* New York: Wiley.

Pervin, L. A. (Ed.). (1990). *Handbook of personality theory and research.* New York: Guilford.

Peterson, C. (1988). *Personality.* Fort Worth, TX: Harcourt Brace Jovanovich.

Peterson, D. R. (1995). The reflective educator. *American Psychologist, 50,* 975–983.

Petrie, K. J., Booth, R. J., Pennebaker, J. W., Davison, K. P., & Thomas, M. G. (1995). Disclosure of trauma and immune response to an hepatitis B vaccination program. *Journal of Consulting and Clinical Psychology, 63,* 787–792.

Pettit, G. S., & Mize, J. (1993). Substance and style: Understanding the ways in which parents teach children about social relationships. In S. Duck (Ed.), *Learning about relationships* (pp. 118–151). Thousand Oaks, CA: Sage.

Phares, E. J. (1988). *Introduction to personality.* Glenview, IL: Scott, Foresman.

Pickford, J. H., Signori, E. I., & Rempel, H. (1966). Similar or related personality traits as a factor in marital happiness. *Journal of Marriage and the Family, 28,* 190–192.

Pierce, R. A., Nichols, M. P., & DuBrin, J. R. (1983). *Emotional expression in psychotherapy.* New York: Gardner.

Pierri, G. (1992). Methods for evaluating normal and pathological couples and families according to the elementary pragmatic model. *Annali dell'Istituto Superiore di Sanita', 28,* 177–184.

Pietropinto, A. (1985). Effect of unhappy marriages on children. *Medical Aspects of Human Sexuality, 19,* 173–181.

Plakun, E. M. (1991). Empirical perspectives on narcissism. In S. M. Mirin, J. T. Gossett, & M. C. Grob (Eds.), *Psychiatric treatment: Advances in outcome research* (pp. 195–211). Washington, DC: American Psychiatric Press.

Plante, T. G. (1993). Aerobic exercise in prevention and treatment of psychopathology. In P. Seraganian (Ed.), *Exercise psychology: The influence of physical exercise on psychological processes* (pp. 358–379). New York: Wiley.

Plutchik, R. (1993). Emotions and their vicissitudes: Emotions and psychopathology. In M. Lewis & J. M. Haviland (Eds.), *Handbook of emotions* (pp. 53–66). New York: Guilford.

Plutchik, R., & Kellerman, H. (Eds.). (1980). *Emotion: Theory, research, and experience.* New York: Academic Press.

Poe, C., & Mills, D. H. (1972). Interpersonal attraction, popularity, similarity of personal needs, and psychological awareness. *Journal of Psychology, 81,* 139–149.

Pope, K. S., & Associates. (1980). *On love and loving.* San Francisco: Jossey-Bass.

Posey, C. D. (Ed.). (1988). Special Issue: Correctional classifications based on psychological characteristics. *Criminal Justice and Behavior, 15,* 3–136.

Power, M. J., Brevin, C. R., Stuessy, A., & Mahony, T. (1991). The emotional priming task: Results from a student population. *Cognitive Therapy and Research, 15,* 21–31.

Prager, K. J. (1995). *The psychology of intimacy.* New York: Guilford.

Price, R. A., & Vandenberg, S. G. (1980). Spouse similarity in American and Swedish couples. *Behavior Genetics, 10,* 59–71.

Prochaska, J. O., DiClemente, C. C., & Norcross, J. C. (1992). In search of how people change: Applications to addictive behaviors. *American Psychologist, 47,* 1102–1114.

Pruitt, D. G. (1983). Experimental gaming and the goal/expectation hypothesis. In H. H. Brumberg, A. P. Hare, V. Kent, & M. F. Davies (Eds.), *Small groups and social interaction* (Vol. 2, pp. 107–121). New York: Wiley.

Putallaz, M., Costanzo, P. R., & Klein, T. P. (1993). Parental childhood social experiences and their effects on children's relationships. In S. Duck (Ed.), *Learning about relationships* (pp. 63–97). Thousand Oaks, CA: Sage.

Quay, H. C. (1986). Classification. In H. C. Quay & J. S. Werry (Eds.), *Psychopathological disorders of childhood* (pp. 1–34). New York: Wiley.

Rabin, A. I., Zucker, R. A., Emmons, R. A., & Frank, S. (Eds.). (1990). *Studying persons and lives.* New York: Springer.

Rahim, M. A. (1983). A measure of styles of handling interpersonal conflict. *Academy of Management Journal, 26,* 368–376.
Raine, A. (1993). *The psychopathology of crime: Criminal behavior as a clinical disorder.* San Diego, CA: Academic Press.
Rando, T. A. (1984). *Grief, dying, and death: Clinical interventions for caregivers.* Champaign, IL: Research Press.
Rapoport, A. (1972). The uses of mathematical isomorphism in general systems theory. In G. J. Klir (Ed.), *Trends in general systems theory* (pp. 42–77). New York: Wiley.
Rawls, J. (1971). *A theory of justice.* Cambridge, MA: Harvard University Press.
Reid, W. H. (1978). *The psychopath: A comprehensive study of antisocial disorders and behaviors.* New York: Brunner/Mazel.
Reis, H. T. (1990). The role of intimacy in human relations. *Journal of Social and Clinical Psychology, 9,* 15–30.
Reis, H. T., & Shaver, P. (1988). Intimacy as an interpersonal process. In S. Duck, D. F. Hay, S. E. Hobfoil, W. Ickes, & B. M. Montgomery (Eds.), *Handbook of personal relationships: Theory, research and interventions* (pp. 367–389). New York: Wiley.
Reitsma-Street, M., & Leschied, A. W. (1988). The conceptual-level matching model in corrections. *Criminal Justice and Behavior, 15,* 92–108.
Rettig, K. D., Danes, S. M., & Sauer, J. W. (1993). Gender differences in perceived family life quality among economically stressed farm families. In U. G. Foa, J. Converse, Jr., K. J. Tornblom, & E. B. Foa (Eds.), *Resource theory: Explorations and applications* (pp. 123–155). San Diego, CA: Academic Press.
Revelle, W. (1995). Personality process. *Annual Review of Psychology, 46,* 295–328.
Reynolds, W. M. (Ed.). (1992). *Internalizing disorders in children and adolescents.* New York: Wiley.
Rholes, W., Simpson, J., & Blakely, B. (1995). Adult attachment styles and mothers' relationships with their young children. *Personal Relationships, 2,* 35–54.
Ring, F. O. (1967). Testing the validity of personality profiles in psychosomatic illness. In I. Frank & M. Powell (Eds.), *Psychosomatic ailments in childhood and adolescence* (pp. 43–54). Springfield, IL: Thomas.
Ritzman, T. A. (1987). Forgiveness: Its role in therapy. *Journal of Medical Psychoanalysis, 2,* 4–13.
Roberts, A. R. (Ed.). (1984). *Battered women and their families: Intervention strategies and treatment programs.* New York: Springer.
Robins, L. N. (1986). Epidemiology of antisocial personality. In G. L. Klerman, M. M. Weissman, P. S. Appelbaum, & L. H. Roth (Eds.), *Social, epidemiologic, and legal psychiatry* (pp. 231–244). New York: Basic Books.
Rogers, C. R. (1957). The necessary and sufficient conditions of therapeutic personality change. *Journal of Consulting Psychology, 21,* 95–103.
Roid, G. H., & Fitts, W. H. (1989). *Tennessee Self-Concept Scale: Revised manual.* Los Angeles: Western Psychological Services.
Rokeach, M. (1960). *The open and closed mind.* New York: Basic Books.
Rosenbaum, M. (1986). The repulsion hypothesis: On the nondevelopment of relationships. *Journal of Personality and Social Psychology, 51,* 1156–1166.
Rosenfeld, L. B. (1979). Self-disclosure avoidance: Why I am afraid to tell you who I am. *Communication Monographs, 46,* 63–74.
Rosenhan, D. L., & Seligman, M. E. P. (1984). *Abnormal psychology.* New York: Norton.
Rosenthal, R., Hall, J., Archer, D., Di Matteo, M., & Rogers, R. (1979). *The PONS test manual: Profile of Nonverbal Sensitivity.* New York: Irvington Press.
Rosenthal, R., Hall, J., Di Matteo, M., Rogers, R., & Archer, D. (1979). *Sensitivity to nonverbal communication: The PONS test.* Baltimore: Johns Hopkins University Press.
Rosow, I. (1957). Issues in the concept of need-complementarity. *Sociometry, 20,* 216–233.
Rossi, A. S., & Rossi, P. H. (1990). *Of human bonding.* New York: Aldine de Gruyter.

Rothblum, E. D., Solomon, L. J., & Albee, G. W. (1986). A sociopolitical perspective of *DSM-III*. In T. Millon & G. L. Klerman (Eds.), *Contemporary directions in psychopathology: Toward the DSM-IV* (pp. 73–98). New York: Guilford.

Rotter, J. B. (1966). Generalized expectancies for internal versus external control of reinforcement. *Psychological Monographs, 80* (Whole No. 609).

Rotter, J. B., Chance, J. E., & Phares, E. J. (1972). *Applications of a social learning theory of personality.* New York: Holt, Rinehart and Winston.

Rowe, D. C. (1994). *The limits of family influence: Genes, experience, and behavior.* New York: Guilford.

Rusbult, C. E. (1980). Commitment and satisfaction in romantic associations: A test of the investment model. *Journal of Experimental Social Psychology, 16,* 172–180.

Russell, J. (1978). Evidence of convergent validity on the dimension of affect. *Journal of Personality and Social Psychology, 36,* 1152–1168.

Rutter, M. (1995). Clinical implications of attachment concepts: Retrospect and prospect. *Journal of Child Psychology and Psychiatry, 36,* 459–571.

Rychlak, J. F. (1981). *Introduction to personality and psychotherapy.* Boston, MA: Houghton Mifflin.

Safran, J. D., & Greenberg, L. S. (Eds.). (1991). *Emotion, psychotherapy, and change.* New York: Guilford.

Sager, C. J. (1976). *Marriage contracts and couple therapy: Hidden forces in intimate relationships.* New York: Brunner/Mazel.

Salovey, P., Hsee, C. K., & Mayer, J. D. (1993). Emotional intelligence and the self-regulation affect. In D. M. Wegner & J. W. Pennebaker (Eds.), *Handbook of mental control* (pp. 258–277). New Jersey: Prentice Hall.

Salovey, P., Mayer, J. D., & Rosenhan, D. L. (1991). Mood and helping: Mood as a motivator of helping and helping as a moderator of mood. In M. S. Clark (Ed.), *Prosocial behavior: Review of personality and social behavior* (pp. 215–237). Newbury Park, CA: Sage.

Salovey, P., & Rodin, J. (1985). Cognition about the self: Connecting feeling states and social behavior. In P. Shaver (Ed.), *Self, situations, and social behavior: Review of personality and social psychology* (pp. 143–166). Beverly Hills, CA: Sage.

Salvo, R. (1996a). *Il questionario di attaccamento tra adulti: Un primo studio sulla validita' e fedelta' dello strumento.* University of Padua, Italy, Department of General Psychology. Manuscript in preparation.

Salvo, R. (1996b). *L'attacamento nelle relazioni adulte: I primi modelli.* University of Padua, Italy, Department of General Psychology. Manuscript in preparation.

Sameroff, A. J., Seifer, R., & Barocas, R. (1983). Impact of parental psychopathology: Diagnosis, severity, or social status effects? *Infant Mental Health Journal, 4,* 236–249.

Sarason, I. G. (Ed.). (1962). *Contemporary research in personality.* Princeton, NJ: Van Nostrand.

Satir, V. (1972). *Peoplemaking.* Palo Alto, CA: Science and Behavior Books.

Schachter, S. (1959). *The psychology of affiliation.* Stanford, CA: Stanford University Press.

Schachter, S., & Singer, J. E. (1962). Cognitive, social, and psychological determinants of emotional state. *Psychological Review, 69,* 379–399.

Schaefer, M. T., & Olson, D. H. (1981). Assessing intimacy: The PAIR Inventory. *Journal of Marital and Family Therapy, 7,* 47–60.

Scheflen, A. E. (1972). *Body language and the social order: Communication as behavioral control.* Englewood Cliffs, NJ: Prentice-Hall.

Schellenberg, J. A., & Bee, L. S. (1960). A re-examination of the theory of complementary needs in mate selection. *Marriage and Family Living, 22,* 227–232.

Schlenker, B. R., & Weigold, M. F. (1992). Interpersonal processes involving impression regulation and management. *Annual Review of Psychology, 43,* 133–168.

Schlesinger, B. (1982). Childrens' viewpoints of living in a one-parent family. *Journal of Divorce, 5,* 1–23.

Schneider, D., Hastof, A., & Ellsworth, P. (1979). *Person perception.* Reading, MA: Addison-Wesley.

Schneider, J. (1984). *Stress, loss, & grief.* Baltimore: University Park Press.

Schneider, K. J. (1990). *The paradoxical self: Toward an understanding of our contradictory nature.* New York: Insight Books.

Schneirla, T. C. (1959). An evolutionary and developmental theory of biphasic processes underlying approach and withdrawal. In M. R. Jones (Ed.), *Nebraska Symposium on Motivation* (pp. 1–42). Lincoln: University of Nebraska Press.

Schultz, D. (1990). *Theories of personality.* Pacific Grove, CA: Brooks/Cole.

Schultz, W. C. (1958). *FIRO-B: A three dimentional theory of interpersonal behavior.* New York: Holt, Rinehart and Winston.

Schwebel, A. I. (1993). Family defense mechanisms: The concept and its utility to family scientists, practitioners, and educators. *The Family Journal: Counseling and Therapy for Couples and Families, 1,* 31–41.

Searight, H. R., & Merkel, W. T. (1991). Systems theory and its discontents: Clinical and ethical issues. *The American Journal of Family Therapy, 19,* 19–31.

Segal, D. L., & Murray, E. J. (1994). Emotional processing in cognitive therapy and vocal expression of feeling. *Journal of Social and Clinical Psychology, 13,* 189–206.

Seraganian, P. (Ed.). (1993). *Exercise psychology: The influence of physical exercise on psychological processes.* New York: Wiley.

Serritella, D. A. (1992). Domestic violence as addiction. In L. L'Abate, J. E. Farrar, & D. A. Serritella (Eds.), *Handbook of differential treatments for addictions* (pp. 113–122). Boston: Allyn & Bacon.

Shaines, N. (1987). Masochism—or self-defeating personality? *Journal of Personality Disorders, 1,* 174–177.

Sharabany, R. (1994). Continuities in the development of intimate relationships: Object relations, interpersonal, and attachment perspectives. In R. Erber & R. Gilmour (Eds.), *Theoretical frameworks for personal relationships* (pp. 157–178). Hillsdale, NJ: Erlbaum.

Shaver, P. (1985). Editor's introduction. In P. Shaver (Ed.), *Self, situations, and social behavior* (pp. 7–13). Beverly Hills, CA: Sage.

Shaver, P., Schwartz, J., Kirson, D., & O'Connor, C. (1987). Emotion knowledge: Further exploration of a prototype approach. *Journal of Personality and Social Psychology, 52,* 1061–1086.

Shimanoff, S. B. (1984). Commonly named emotions in everyday conversations. *Perceptual and Motor Skills, 58,* 514.

Siegel, A. W., & Cohen, R. (1991). Why a house is not a home: Constructing contexts for development. In R. Cohen & A. W. Siegel (Eds.), *Context and development* (pp. 305–316). Hillsdale, NJ: Erlbaum.

Sifneos, P. (1973). The prevalence of alexithymic characteristics in psychosomatic patients. *Psychotherapy and Psychosomatics, 22,* 255–262.

Silvestri, A. (1993). A quantitative theory of interaction: The formal aspects of the elementary-pragmatic model. In P. De Giacomo, *Finite systems and infinite interactions: The logic of human interaction and its application to psychotherapy* (pp. 371–397). Norfolk, CT: Bramble Books.

Silvestri, A., Lefons, A., De Giacomo, P., & Corfiati, L. (1988). Evaluation of interactional human behavior with age: A theoretical/experimental approach. *Cybernetics and Systems, 19,* 15–39.

Simpson, G. B., Lorsbach, T. C., & Whitehouse, D. (1983). Encoding and contextual components of word recognition in good and poor readers. *Journal of Experimental Child Psychology, 35,* 161–171.

Simpson, J., Rholes, W., & Nelligan, J. (1992). Support seeking and support giving within couples in an anxiety-provoking situation. *Journal of Personality and Social Psychology, 62,* 434–446.

Singer, I. (1987). *The nature of love: Vol. 3. The modern world.* Chicago: University of Chicago Press.

Skeen, P., Covi, R. B., & Robinson, B. E. (1985). Step-families: A review of the literature with suggestions for practitioners. *Journal of Counseling and Development, 64,* 121–125.

Skuse, D. (1987). The psychological consequences of being small. *Journal of Child Psychology, Psychiatry and Allied Disciplines, 28,* 641–650.

Smart, L. S., & Chibucos, T. R. (1990). Adolescent substance use and perceived family functioning. *Journal of Family Issues, 11,* 208–227.

Smith, H. C. (1968). *Personality development.* New York: McGraw-Hill.

Smith, P. K., Bowers, L., Binney, V., & Cowie, H. (1993). Relationships of children involved in bully/victim problems in school. In S. Duck (Ed.), *Learning about relationships* (pp. 184–204). Thousand Oaks, CA: Sage.

Snell, W. (1988, April). *The Relationship Awareness Scale: Measuring relationship consciousness, relationship-monitoring, and relationship anxiety.* Paper presented at the 34th Annual Meeting of Southwestern Psychological Association, Tulsa, OK.

Snyder, C. R., & Endelman, J. R. (1979). Effects of degree of interpersonal similarity on physical distance and self-reported attraction: A comparison of uniqueness and reinforcement theory predictions. *Journal of Personality, 47,* 492–505.

Snyder, C. R., & Fromkin, H. L. (1980). *Uniqueness: The human pursuit of difference.* New York: Plenum.

Soldz, S., Budman, S., Demby, A., & Merry, J. (1993). Diagnostic agreement between personality disorder examination and the MCMI-II. *Journal of Personality Assessment, 60,* 486–499.

Solomon, J., George, C., & De Jong, A. (1995). Children classified as controlling at age six: Evidence of disorganized representational strategies and aggression at home and at school. *Development and Psychopathology, 7,* 447–463.

Solomon, J., Zimberg, S., & Shollar, E. (Eds.). (1993). *Dual diagnosis, evaluation, treatment, training, and program development.* New York: Plenum.

Spanier, G. B. (1976). Measuring dyadic adjustment: New scales for assessing the quality of marriage and similar dyads. *Journal of Marriage and the Family, 38,* 15–28.

Sperling, M. B., & Berman, W. H. (Eds.). (1994). *Attachment in adults: Clinical and developmental perspectives.* New York: Guilford.

Sprecher, S. (1986). The relation between inequity and emotion in close relationships. *Social Psychology Quarterly, 49,* 309–321.

Srole, L., Langner, T. S., Michael, S. T., Opler, M. K., & Rennie, T. A. (1962). *Mental health in the metropolis: The midtown Manhattan study.* New York: McGraw-Hill.

Staub, E. (Ed.). (1980). *Personality: Basic aspects and current research.* Englewood Cliffs, NJ: Prentice-Hall.

Steadman, H. J. (Ed.). (undated). *Jail diversion for the mentally ill: Breaking through the barriers, effectively addressing the mental health needs of jail detainees.* Washington, DC: U. S. Department of Justice, National Institute of Corrections.

Steele, H., & Steele, M. (1994). Intergenerational patterns of attachment. In K. Bartholomew & D. Perlman (Eds.), *Attachment processes in adulthood* (pp. 93–120). London, UK: Kingsley.

Steere, D. A. (1982). *Bodily expressions in psychotherapy.* New York: Brunner/Mazel.

Sternberg, R. J. (1987). *The triangle of love: Intimacy, passion commitment.* New York: Basic Books.

Sternberg, R. J., & Beall, A. E. (1992). How can we know what love is? An epistemological analysis. In G. J. O. Fletcher & F. D. Fincham (Eds.), *Cognition in close relationships* (pp. 257–278). Hillsdale, NJ: Erlbaum.

Stevens, F. E., & L'Abate, L. (1989). Validity and reliability of a theory-derived measure of intimacy. *American Journal of Family Therapy, 17,* 359–368.

Stewart, C., & Zaenglein-Senger, M. M. (1982). The parent-adolescent power contest. *Social Casework, 63,* 457–464.

Stiles, W. B. (1994). Views of the chasm between psychotherapy research and practice. In P. F. Talley, H. H. Strupp, & S. F. Butler (Eds.), *Psychotherapy research and practice: Bridging the gap* (pp. 154–166). New York: Basic Books.

Stokols, D. (1978). Environmental psychology. *Annual Review of Psychology, 29,* 253–295.

Stokols, D. (1995). The paradox of environmental psychology. *American Psychologist, 50,* 821–837.

Stolorow, R. D. (1991). The intersubjective context of intrapsychic experience, with special reference to therapeutic impasse. In R. C. Curtis (Ed.), *The relational self: Theoretical convergences in psychoanalysis and social psychology* (pp. 17–33). New York: Guilford.

Stone, M. H. (1993). *Abnormalities of personality.* New York: Norton.

Stonewater, J. K. (1980). Strategies for problem solving. In R. E. Young (Ed.), *Fostering critical thinking* (pp. 33–57). San Francisco, CA: Jossey-Bass.

Stotland, E., & Canon, L. K. (1972). *Social psychology: A cognitive approach.* Philadelphia, PA: Saunders.

Stotland, E., & Dunn, R. E. (1963). Empathy, self-esteem, and birth order. *Journal of Abnormal and Social Psychology, 66,* 532–540.

Strack, S., & Lorr, M. (Eds.). (1994). *Differentiating normal and abnormal personality.* New York: Springer.

Stricker, G. (1992). The relationship of research to clinical practice. *American Psychologist, 47,* 543–549.

Stricker, G., & Trierweiler, S. J. (1995). The local clinical scientist: A bridge between science and practice. *American Psychologist, 50,* 995–1002.

Stroebe, M., & Stroebe, W. (1991). Does 'grief work' work? *Journal of Consulting and Clinical Psychology, 39,* 479–482.

Suls, J. M., & Miller, R. L. (Eds.). (1977). *Social comparison processes: Theoretical and empirical processes.* Washington, DC: Hemisphere.

Suls, J. M., & Wills, T. A. (Eds.). (1991). *Social comparison: Contemporary theory and research.* Hillsdale, NJ: Erlbaum.

Sundberg, N. D., Snowden, L. R., & Reynolds, W. M. (1978). Toward assessment of personal competence and incompetence in life situations. *Annual Review of Psychology, 29,* 179–221.

Surra, C. A. (1990). Research and theory on mate selection and premarital relationships in the 1980s. *Journal of Marriage and the Family, 52,* 844–865.

Surra, C. A., & Bohman, T. (1991). The development of close relationships: A cognitive perspective. In G. J. O. Fletcher & F. D. Fincham (Eds.), *Cognition in close relationships* (pp. 281–305). Hillsdale, NJ: Erlbaum.

Swanson, S. C., Templer, D. I., Thomas-Dobson, S., Cannon, G. W., Streiner, D. L., Reynolds, R. M., & Miller, H. R. (1995). Development of a three scale MMPI: The MMPI-TRI. *Journal of Clinical Psychology, 51,* 361–374.

Swift, C. F. (1988). Stopping the violence: Prevention strategies for families. In L. A. Bond & B. M. Wagner (Eds.), *Families in transition: Primary prevention programs that work* (pp. 252–285). Newbury Park, CA: Sage.

Swift, W. J., Andrews, D., & Barklage, N. E. (1986). The relationship between affective disorder and eating disorders: A review of the literature. *American Journal of Psychiatry, 143,* 290–299.

Szapocznik, J., Kurtines, W. M., Foote, F., Perez-Vidal, A., & Hervis, A. (1983). Conjoint versus one-person family therapy: Some evidence for the effectiveness of conducting family therapy through one person. *Journal of Consulting and Clinical Psychology, 51,* 889–899.

Tangney, J. P., & Fischer, K. W. (Eds.). (1994). *Self-conscious emotions: The psychology of shame, guilt, embarrassment, and pride.* New York: Guilford.

Taylor, I. A. (1960). Similarities in the structure of extreme social attitudes. *Psychological Monographs: General and Applied, 74* (Whole No. 489).

Taylor, S. E. (1991). Asymmetrical effects of positive and negative events: The mobilization-minimization hypothesis. *Psychological Bulletin, 110,* 67–85.

Taylor-Spence, J. (1963). Learning theory and personality. In J. M. Wepman & R. W. Heine (Eds.), *Concepts of personality* (pp. 3–30). Chicago: Aldine.

Teichman, M., Glaubman, H., & Garner, M. (1993). From early adolescence to middle-age adulthood: The perceived need for interpersonal resources in four developmental stages. In

U. G. Foa, J. Converse, Jr., K. J. Tornblom, & E. B. Foa (Eds.), *Resource theory: Explorations and applications* (pp. 157–165). San Diego, CA: Academic Press.

Tellegen, A. (1994). Foreword. In S. Strack & M. Lorrs (Eds.), *Differentiating normal from abnormal personality* (pp. ix–xi). New York: Springer.

Temoshok, R. (1995). On biobehavioral model of cancer stress and disease cure. *American Psychologist, 50,* 1104–1105.

Tharp, R. G. (1963). Psychological patterning in marriage. *Psychological Bulletin, 60,* 97–117.

Thase, M. E. (1994). The roles of psychosocial factors and psychotherapy in refractory depression: Missing pieces in the puzzle of treatment resistance? In W. A. Nolen, J. Zohar, S. P. Roose, & J. D. Amsterdam (Eds.), *Refractory depression: Current strategies and future directions* (pp. 83–95). Chichester, UK: Wiley.

Thompson, S. C. (1981). Will it hurt less if I can control it? A complex answer to a simple question. *Psychological Bulletin, 90,* 89–101.

Tice, D. M. (1995). The return of the interpersonal self. *Contemporary Psychology, 40,* 954–955.

Tiller, P. O. (1963). Isolation: Center and periphery. *Scandinavian Journal of Psychology, 4,* 90–96.

Toch, H., Adams, K., & Greene, R. (1987). Ethnicity, disruptiveness, and emotional disorder among prison inmates. *Criminal Justice and Behavior, 14,* 110–109.

Tomkins, S. S. (1980). Affect as amplification: Some modifications of the theory. In R. Plutchik & H. Kellerman (Eds.), *Emotion: Theory, research, and experience* (pp. 143–164). New York: Academic Press.

Torgenrud, J., & Storm, C. L. (1989). One-person family therapy? An analysis of family therapy schools. *American Journal of Family Therapy, 17,* 143–154.

Tornblom, K. J., & Nilsson, B. O. (1993). The effect of matching resources to source on their perceived importance and sufficiency. In U. G. Foa, J. Converse, Jr., K. J. Tornblom, & E. B. Foa (Eds.), *Resource theory: Explorations and applications* (pp. 81–96). San Diego, CA: Academic Press.

Tornblom, K. Y., Stern, P., Pirak, K., Pudas, A., & Tornlund, E. (1993). Type of resource and choice of comparison target. In U. G. Foa, J. Converse, Jr., Tornblom, K. Y., & Foa, E. B. (Eds.), *Resource theory: Explorations and applications* (pp. 197–218). San Diego, CA: Academic Press.

Turkat, I. D. (1990). *The personality disorders: A psychological approach to clinical management.* New York: Pergamon Press.

Tzeng, O. C. S. (Ed.). (1992). *Theories of love development, maintenance, and dissolution: Octagonal cycle and differential perspectives.* Westport, CT: Praeger.

Uehara, E. S. (1995). Reciprocity reconsidered: Gouldner's 'moral norm of reciprocity' and social support. *Journal of Social and Personal Relationships, 12,* 483–502.

Vaillant, G. E. (1977). *Adaptation to life.* Boston: Little, Brown.

Van den Brouchke, S., Vandereycken, W., & Vertommen, H. (1995). Marital intimacy: Conceptualization and assessment. *Clinical Psychology Review, 15,* 217–233.

Von Voorhis, P. (1988). A cross classification of five offender typologies: Issues of construct and predictive validity. *Criminal Justice and Behavior, 15,* 109–124.

Wachs, T. D., & Plomin, R. (1991). Overview of current models and research. In T. D. Wachs & R. Plomin (Eds.), *Conceptualization and measurement of organism-environment interaction* (pp. 1–8). Washington, DC: American Psychological Association.

Waites, E. A. (1993). *Trauma and survival.* New York: Norton.

Wakefield, J. C. (1989). Levels of explanation in personality theory. In D. M. Buss & N. Cantor (Eds.), *Emerging issues in personality psychology* (pp. 333–346). New York: Springer-Verlag.

Wakefield, J. C. (1992). The concept of mental disorder: On the boundary between biological facts and social values. *American Psychologist, 47,* 373–388.

Walfish, S., Massey, R. F., & Krone, A. M. (Eds.). (1989). Alcohol and the criminal justice system [Special Issue]. *Criminal Justice and Behavior, 16,* 267–386.

Walker, L. L. E. A. (1992). Foreword. In L. S. Brown & M. Ballou (Eds.), *Personality and psychopathology: Feminist reappaisals* (pp. vii–x). New York: Guilford.

Wallach, M. A. (1958). On psychological similarity. *Psychological Review, 65,* 103–116.

Walsh, A., Petee, T. A., & Beyer, J. A. (1987). Intellectual imbalance and delinquency: Comparing high verbal and high performance IQ delinquents. *Criminal Justice and Behavior, 14,* 370–379.

Walters, G. D., Mann, M. F., Miller, M. P., Hemphill, L. L., & Chlumsky, M. L. (1988). Emotional disorder among offenders: Inter- and intrasetting comparisons. *Criminal Justice and Behavior, 15,* 433–453.

Walters, R. P. (1984). Forgiving: An essential element in effective living. *Studies in Formative Spirituality, 5,* 365–374.

Watkins, J. T. (1983). Treatment of disorders of impulse control. In C. E. Walker (Ed.), *The handbook of clinical psychology: Theory, research and practice* (pp. 590–632). Homewood, IL: Dow Jones-Irwin.

Watkins, M. P., & Meredith, W. (1981). Spouse similarity in newlyweds with respect to specific cognitive abilities, socioeconomic status, and education. *Behavior Genetics, 11,* 1–21.

Watson, D., & Clark, L. A. (1991). Self-versus peer ratings of specific emotional traits: Evidence of convergent and discriminant validity. *Journal of Personality and Social Psychology, 60,* 927–940.

Watson, D., & Clark, L. A. (1993). Behavioral disinhibition versus constraint: A dispositional perspective. In D. M. Wegner & J. W. Pennebaker (Eds.), *Handbook of mental control* (pp. 506–527). Englewood Cliffs, NJ: Prentice-Hall.

Watson, D., Clark, L. A., & Tellegen, A. (1984). Cross-cultural convergence in the structure of mood: A Japanese replication and a comparison with U.S. findings. *Journal of Personality and Social Psychology, 47,* 127–144.

Watson, D., Clark, L. A., & Tellegen, A. (1988). Development and validation of brief measures of positive and negative affect: The PANAS scales. *Journal of Personality and Social Psychology, 54,* 1063–1070.

Watson, D., & Tellegen, A. (1985). Toward a consensual structure of mood. *Psychological Bulletin, 98,* 219–235.

Waxer, P. H. (1978). *Nonverbal aspects of psychotherapy.* New York: Praeger.

Wegner, D. M., & Pennebaker, J. W. (Eds.). (1993). *Handbook of mental control.* Englewood Cliffs, NJ: Prentice-Hall.

Weigert, E. (1973). Love and respect. In E. M. Curtin (Ed.), *Symposium on love* (pp. 211–228). New York: Behavioral Publications.

Weiner, B., & Handel, S. U. (1985). A cognition-emotion-action sequence: Anticipated emotional consequences of causal attribution and reported communication strategy. *Developmental Psychology, 21,* 102–107.

Weinstein, S. E. (1989). *Couple complementarity/similarity and the processing of non-verbal communication.* Unpublished doctoral dissertation. Georgia State University, Atlanta.

Weitz, S. (1974). *Nonverbal communication: Readings with commentary.* New York: Oxford University Press.

West, M. L., & Sheldon-Keller, A. E. (1994). *Patterns of relating: An adult attachment perspective.* New York: Guilford.

Wethington, E., Mcleod, J. D., & Kessler, R. C. (1987). The importance of life events for explaining sex differences in psychological stress. In R. C. Barnett, L. Biener, & G. K. Baruch (Eds.), *Gender and stress* (pp. 144–158). New York: Free Press.

Wheeler, L. (1970). *Interpersonal influence.* Boston: Allyn & Bacon.

Wheeler, L. (1974). Social comparison and selective affiliation. In T. L. Huston (Ed.), *Foundations of interpersonal attraction* (pp. 309–129). New York: Academic Press.

White, G. M. (1993). Emotions inside out: The anthropology of affect. In M. Lewis & J. M. Haviland (Eds.), *Handbook of emotions* (pp. 29–39). New York: Guilford.

White, J. M. (1991). *Dynamics of family development: A theoretical perspective.* New York: Guilford.

White, S., & Hatcher, C. (1984). Couple complementarity and similarity: A review of the literature. *The American Journal of Family Therapy, 12,* 15–25.

Wieman, J. M., & Harrison, R. P. (Eds.). (1983). *Nonverbal interaction.* Thousand Oaks, CA: Sage.

Wiggins, J. S., & Pincus, A. L. (1992). Personality: Structure and assessment. *Annual Review of Psychology, 43,* 473–504.

Willock, B. (1986). Narcissistic vulnerability in the hyperaggressive child: The disregarded (unloved, uncared-for) self. *Psychoanalytic Psychology, 3,* 59–80.

Wills, T. A. (1991). Social support and interpersonal relationships. In M. S. Clark (Ed.), *Prosocial behavior* (pp. 265–289). Newbury Park, CA: Sage.

Wilson, W. (1989). Brief resolution of the issue of similarity versus complementarity in mate selection using height preferences as a model. *Psychological Reports, 65,* 387–393.

Winch, R. F. (1955). The theory of complementary needs in mate selection: Final results on the test of the general hypothesis. *American Sociological Review, 20,* 552–555.

Winch, R. F. (1974). Complementary needs and related notions about voluntary mate selection. In R. F. Winch & G. B. Spanier (Eds.), *Selected studies in marriage and the family* (pp. 399–410). New York: Holt, Reinhart and Winston.

Witkin, H. A., Dyk, R. B., Faterson, H. F., Goodenough, D. R., & Karp, S. A. (1974). *Psychological differentiation.* Potomac, MD: Erlbaum.

Wood, J. V. (1989). Theory and research concerning social comparisons of personal attributes. *Psychological Bulletin, 106,* 231–248.

Wootton, B. (1978). *Social science and social pathology.* Westport, CT: Greenwood Press.

Worden, J. W. (1982). *Grief counseling and grief therapy: A handbook for the mental health practitioner.* New York: Springer.

Worthington, E. L. (1991). A primer on intake interviews for couples. *American Journal of Family Therapy, 19,* 344–380.

Wright, R. H. (1973). Love is neither necessary nor sufficient. In M. E. Curtin (Ed.), *Symposium on love* (pp. 89–94). New York: Behavioral Publications.

Wrightsman, L. S. (1992). *Assumptions about human nature.* London: Sage.

Wrightsman, L. S. (1994). *Adult personality development.* London: Sage.

Wyer, R. S., & Srull, T. K. (Eds.). (1993). *Perspectives on anger and emotion.* Hillsdale, NJ: Erlbaum.

Wynne, L. C., Ryckoff, I. M., Day, J., & Hirsch, S. L. (1981). Pseudomutuality in the family relations of schizophrenics. *Psychiatry, 21,* 297–318.

Yates, A. (1991). *Compulsive exercise and the eating disorders: Toward an integrated theory of activity.* New York: Brunner/Mazel.

Yochelson, S., & Samenow, S. (1977a). *The criminal personality: A profile for change* (Vol. 1). New York: Aronson.

Yochelson, S., & Samenow, S. (1977b). *The criminal personality: The process of change* (Vol. 2). New York: Aronson.

Zager, L. D. (1988). The MMPI-based criminal classification system: A review, present status, and future directions. *Criminal Justice and Behavior, 15,* 39–57.

Zanarini, M. C., Chauncey, C. L., Grady, T. A., & Gunderson, J. G. (1991). Outcome studies of borderline personality disorder. In S. M. Mirin, J. T. Gossett, & M. C. Grob (Eds.), *Psychiatric treatment: Advances in outcome research* (pp. 181–194). Washington, DC: American Psychiatric Press.

Zander, A., & Havelin, A. (1960). Social comparison and interpersonal attraction. *Human Relations, 13,* 21–32.

Zimbardo, P. G., & Formica, R. (1963). Emotional comparison and self-esteem as determinants of affiliation. *Journal of Personality, 31,* 141–162.

Zinbarg, R. E., Barlow, D. H., Brown, T. A., & Hertz, R. M. (1992). Cognitive-behavioral approaches to the nature and treatment of anxiety disorders. *Annual Review of Psychology, 43,* 235–267.

Zonderman, A. B., Vanderberg, S. G., Spuhler, K. P., & Fein, P. R. (1977). Assortative marriage and cognitive abilities. *Behavior Genetics, 7,* 261–271.

Author Index

Subject Index

Printed and bound by CPI Group (UK) Ltd, Croydon, CR0 4YY

18/09/2026

14964970-0001